NOVELS
for Students

Advisors

NOVELS
for Students

**Presenting Analysis, Context, and Criticism
on Commonly Studied Novels**

VOLUME 36

Sara Constantakis, Project Editor

Foreword by Anne Devereaux Jordan

GALE
CENGAGE Learning·

Detroit • New York • San Francisco • New Haven, Conn • Waterville, Maine • London

Novels for Students, Volume 36

Project Editor: Sara Constantakis

Rights Acquisition and Management: Leitha
    Etheridge-Sims, Jackie Jones, Tim Sisler

Composition: Evi Abou-El-Seoud

Manufacturing: Rhonda Dover

Imaging: John Watkins

Product Design: Pamela A. E. Galbreath, Jennifer
    Wahi

Content Conversion: Katrina Coach

Product Manager: Meggin Condino

For product information and technology assistance, contact us at
Gale Customer Support, 1-800-877-4253.
For permission to use material from this text or product,
submit all requests online at **www.cengage.com/permissions.**
Further permissions questions can be emailed to
permissionrequest@cengage.com

While every effort has been made to ensure the reliability of the information presented in this publication, Gale, a part of Cengage Learning, does not guarantee the accuracy of the data contained herein. Gale accepts no payment for listing; and inclusion in the publication of any organization, agency, institution, publication, service, or individual does not imply endorsement of the editors or publisher. Errors brought to the attention of the publisher and verified to the satisfaction of the publisher will be corrected in future editions.

Gale
27500 Drake Rd.
Farmington Hills, MI, 48331-3535

ISBN-13: 978-1-4144-6699-6
ISBN-10: 1-4144-6699-4

ISSN 1094-3552

This title is also available as an e-book.
ISBN-13: 978-1-4144-7365-9
ISBN-10: 1-4144-7365-6
Contact your Gale, a part of Cengage Learning sales representative for ordering information.

Printed in Mexico
1 2 3 4 5 6 7 15 14 13 12 11

Table of Contents

The Informed Dialogue: Interacting with Literature

When we pick up a book, we usually do so with the anticipation of pleasure. We hope that by entering the time and place of the novel and sharing the thoughts and actions of the characters, we will find enjoyment. Unfortunately, this is often not the case; we are disappointed. But we should ask, has the author failed us, or have we failed the author?

We establish a dialogue with the author, the book, and with ourselves when we read. Consciously and unconsciously, we ask questions: "Why did the author write this book?" "Why did the author choose that time, place, or character?" "How did the author achieve that effect?" "Why did the character act that way?" "Would I act in the same way?" The answers we receive depend upon how much information about literature in general and about that book specifically we ourselves bring to our reading.

Young children have limited life and literary experiences. Being young, children frequently do not know how to go about exploring a book, nor sometimes, even know the questions to ask of a book. The books they read help them answer questions, the author often coming right out and *telling* young readers the things they are learning or are expected to learn. The perennial classic, *The Little Engine That Could, tells* its readers that, among other things, it is good to help others and brings happiness:

"Hurray, hurray," cried the funny little clown and all the dolls and toys. "The good little boys and girls in the city will be happy because you helped us, kind, Little Blue Engine."

In picture books, messages are often blatant and simple, the dialogue between the author and reader one-sided. Young children are concerned with the end result of a book—the enjoyment gained, the lesson learned—rather than with how that result was obtained. As we grow older and read further, however, we question more. We come to expect that the world within the book will closely mirror the concerns of our world, and that the author will *show* these through the events, descriptions, and conversations within the story, rather than *telling* of them. We are now expected to do the interpreting, carry on our share of the dialogue with the book and author, and glean not only the author's message, but comprehend how that message and the overall affect of the book were achieved. Sometimes, however, we need help to do these things. *Novels for Students* provides that help.

A novel is made up of many parts interacting to create a coherent whole. In reading a novel, the more obvious features can be easily spotted—theme, characters, plot—but we may overlook the more subtle elements that greatly influence how the novel is perceived by the reader: viewpoint, mood and tone, symbolism, or the use of humor. By focusing on both the obvious and more subtle literary elements within a novel,

Novels for Students aids readers in both analyzing for message and in determining how and why that message is communicated. In the discussion on Harper Lee's *To Kill a Mockingbird* (Vol. 2), for example, the mockingbird as a symbol of innocence is dealt with, among other things, as is the importance of Lee's use of humor which "enlivens a serious plot, adds depth to the characterization, and creates a sense of familiarity and universality." The reader comes to understand the internal elements of each novel discussed—as well as the external influences that help shape it.

"The desire to write greatly," Harold Bloom of Yale University says, "is the desire to be elsewhere, in a time and place of one's own, in an originality that must compound with inheritance, with an anxiety of influence." A writer seeks to create a unique world within a story, but although it is unique, it is not disconnected from our own world. It speaks to us *because* of what the writer brings to the writing from our world: how he or she was raised and educated; his or her likes and dislikes; the events occurring in the real world at the time of the writing, and while the author was growing up. When we know what an author has brought to his or her work, we gain a greater insight into both the "originality" (the world of the book), and the things that "compound" it. This insight enables us to question that created world and find answers more readily. By informing ourselves, we are able to establish a more effective dialogue with both book and author.

Novels for Students, in addition to providing a plot summary and descriptive list of characters—to remind readers of what they have read—also explores the external influences that shaped each book. Each entry includes a discussion of the author's background, and the historical context in which the novel was written. It is vital to know, for instance, that when Ray Bradbury was writing *Fahrenheit 451* (Vol. 1), the threat of Nazi domination had recently ended in Europe, and the McCarthy hearings were taking place in Washington, D.C. This information goes far in answering the question, "Why did he write a story of oppressive government control and book burning?" Similarly, it is important to know that Harper Lee, author of

To Kill a Mockingbird, was born and raised in Monroeville, Alabama, and that her father was a lawyer. Readers can now see why she chose the south as a setting for her novel—it is the place with which she was most familiar—and start to comprehend her characters and their actions.

Novels for Students helps readers find the answers they seek when they establish a dialogue with a particular novel. It also aids in the posing of questions by providing the opinions and interpretations of various critics and reviewers, broadening that dialogue. Some reviewers of *To Kill A Mockingbird,* for example, "faulted the novel's climax as melodramatic." This statement leads readers to ask, "Is it, indeed, melodramatic?" "If not, why did some reviewers see it as such?" "If it is, why did Lee choose to make it melodramatic?" "Is melodrama ever justified?" By being spurred to ask these questions, readers not only learn more about the book and its writer, but about the nature of writing itself.

The literature included for discussion in *Novels for Students* has been chosen because it has something vital to say to us. *Of Mice and Men, Catch-22, The Joy Luck Club, My Antonia, A Separate Peace* and the other novels here speak of life and modern sensibility. In addition to their individual, specific messages of prejudice, power, love or hate, living and dying, however, they and all great literature also share a common intent. They force us to *think*—about life, literature, and about others, not just about ourselves. They pry us from the narrow confines of our minds and thrust us outward to confront the world of books and the larger, real world we all share. *Novels for Students* helps us in this confrontation by providing the means of enriching our conversation with literature and the world, by creating an *informed* dialogue, one that brings true pleasure to the personal act of reading.

Sources

Harold Bloom, *The Western Canon, The Books and School of the Ages,* Riverhead Books, 1994.

Watty Piper, *The Little Engine That Could,* Platt & Munk, 1930.

Anne Devereaux Jordan
Senior Editor, TALL (Teaching and Learning Literature)

Introduction

Purpose of the Book

The purpose of *Novels for Students* (*NfS*) is to provide readers with a guide to understanding, enjoying, and studying novels by giving them easy access to information about the work. Part of Gale's "For Students" Literature line, *NfS* is specifically designed to meet the curricular needs of high school and undergraduate college students and their teachers, as well as the interests of general readers and researchers considering specific novels. While each volume contains entries on "classic" novels frequently studied in classrooms, there are also entries containing hard-to-find information on contemporary novels, including works by multicultural, international, and women novelists. Entries profiling film versions of novels not only diversify the study of novels but support alternate learning styles, media literacy, and film studies curricula as well.

The information covered in each entry includes an introduction to the novel and the novel's author; a plot summary, to help readers unravel and understand the events in a novel; descriptions of important characters, including explanation of a given character's role in the novel as well as discussion about that character's relationship to other characters in the novel; analysis of important themes in the novel; and an explanation of important literary techniques and movements as they are demonstrated in the novel.

In addition to this material, which helps the readers analyze the novel itself, students are also provided with important information on the literary and historical background informing each work. This includes a historical context essay, a box comparing the time or place the novel was written to modern Western culture, a critical essay, and excerpts from critical essays on the novel. A unique feature of *NfS* is a specially commissioned critical essay on each novel, targeted toward the student reader.

The "literature to film" entries on novels vary slightly in form, providing background on film technique and comparison to the original, literary version of the work. These entries open with an introduction to the film, which leads directly into the plot summary. The summary highlights plot changes from the novel, key cinematic moments, and/or examples of key film techniques. As in standard entries, there are character profiles (noting omissions or additions, and identifying the actors), analysis of themes and how they are illustrated in the film, and an explanation of the cinematic style and structure of the film. A cultural context section notes any time period or setting differences from that of the original work, as well as cultural differences between the time in which the original work was written and the time in which the film adaptation was made. A film entry concludes with a critical overview and critical essays on the film.

To further help today's student in studying and enjoying each novel or film, information on media adaptations is provided (if available), as well as suggestions for works of fiction, nonfiction, or film on similar themes and topics. Classroom aids include ideas for research papers and lists of critical and reference sources that provide additional material on the novel. Film entries also highlight signature film techniques demonstrated, and suggest media literacy activities and prompts to use during or after viewing a film.

Selection Criteria

The titles for each volume of *NfS* are selected by surveying numerous sources on notable literary works and analyzing course curricula for various schools, school districts, and states. Some of the sources surveyed include: high school and undergraduate literature anthologies and textbooks; lists of award-winners, and recommended titles, including the Young Adult Library Services Association (YALSA) list of best books for young adults. Films are selected both for the literary importance of the original work and the merits of the adaptation (including official awards and widespread public recognition).

Input solicited from our expert advisory board—consisting of educators and librarians—guides us to maintain a mix of "classic" and contemporary literary works, a mix of challenging and engaging works (including genre titles that are commonly studied) appropriate for different age levels, and a mix of international, multicultural and women authors. These advisors also consult on each volume's entry list, advising on which titles are most studied, most appropriate, and meet the broadest interests across secondary (grades 7–12) curricula and undergraduate literature studies.

How Each Entry Is Organized

Each entry, or chapter, in *NfS* focuses on one novel. Each entry heading lists the full name of the novel, the author's name, and the date of the novel's publication. The following elements are contained in each entry:

Introduction: a brief overview of the novel which provides information about its first appearance, its literary standing, any controversies surrounding the work, and major conflicts or themes within the work. Film entries identify the original novel and provide understanding of the film's reception and reputation, along with that of the director.

Author Biography: in novel entries, this section includes basic facts about the author's life, and focuses on events and times in the author's life that inspired the novel in question.

Plot Summary: a factual description of the major events in the novel. Lengthy summaries are broken down with subheads. Plot summaries of films are used to uncover plot differences from the original novel, and to note the use of certain film angles or other techniques.

Characters: an alphabetical listing of major characters in the novel. Each character name is followed by a brief to an extensive description of the character's role in the novel, as well as discussion of the character's actions, relationships, and possible motivation. In film entries, omissions or changes to the cast of characters of the film adaptation are mentioned here, and the actors' names—and any awards they may have received—are also included.

Characters are listed alphabetically by last name. If a character is unnamed—for instance, the narrator in *Invisible Man*—the character is listed as "The Narrator" and alphabetized as "Narrator." If a character's first name is the only one given, the name will appear alphabetically by that name.

Variant names are also included for each character. Thus, the full name "Jean Louise Finch" would head the listing for the narrator of *To Kill a Mockingbird*, but listed in a separate cross-reference would be the nickname "Scout Finch."

Themes: a thorough overview of how the major topics, themes, and issues are addressed within the novel. Each theme discussed appears in a separate subhead. While the key themes often remain the same or similar when a novel is adapted into a film, film entries demonstrate how the themes are conveyed cinematically, along with any changes in the portrayal of the themes.

Style: this section addresses important style elements of the novel, such as setting, point of view, and narration; important literary devices used, such as imagery, foreshadowing, symbolism; and, if applicable, genres to which the work might have belonged, such as Gothicism or Romanticism. Literary terms are explained within the entry but can also be found in the Glossary. Film entries cover how the director conveyed the meaning, message, and mood of the work using film in comparison to the author's use of language, literary device, etc., in the original work.

Historical Context: in novel entries, this section outlines the social, political, and cultural climate in which the author lived and the novel was created. This section may include descriptions of related historical events, pertinent aspects of daily life in the culture, and the artistic and literary sensibilities of the time in which the work was written. If the novel is a historical work, information regarding the time in which the novel is set is also included. Each section is broken down with helpful subheads. Film entries contain a similar Cultural Context section because the film adaptation might explore an entirely different time period or culture than the original work, and may also be influenced by the traditions and views of a time period much different than that of the original author.

Critical Overview: this section provides background on the critical reputation of the novel or film, including bannings or any other public controversies surrounding the work. For older works, this section includes a history of how the novel or film was first received and how perceptions of it may have changed over the years; for more recent novels, direct quotes from early reviews may also be included.

Criticism: an essay commissioned by *NfS* which specifically deals with the novel or film and is written specifically for the student audience, as well as excerpts from previously published criticism on the work (if available).

Sources: an alphabetical list of critical material used in compiling the entry, with full bibliographical information.

Further Reading: an alphabetical list of other critical sources which may prove useful for the student. It includes full bibliographical information and a brief annotation.

Suggested Search Terms: a list of search terms and phrases to jumpstart students' further information seeking. Terms include not just titles and author names but also terms and topics related to the historical and literary context of the works.

In addition, each novel entry contains the following highlighted sections, set apart from the main text as sidebars:

Media Adaptations: if available, a list of audio-books and important film and television adaptations of the novel, including source information. The list also includes stage adaptations, musical adaptations, etc.

Topics for Further Study: a list of potential study questions or research topics dealing with the novel. This section includes questions related to other disciplines the student may be studying, such as American history, world history, science, math, government, business, geography, economics, psychology, etc.

Compare and Contrast: an "at-a-glance" comparison of the cultural and historical differences between the author's time and culture and late twentieth century or early twenty-first century Western culture. This box includes pertinent parallels between the major scientific, political, and cultural movements of the time or place the novel was written, the time or place the novel was set (if a historical work), and modern Western culture. Works written after the mid-1970s may not have this box.

What Do I Read Next?: a list of works that might give a reader points of entry into a classic work (e.g., YA or multicultural titles) and/or complement the featured novel or serve as a contrast to it. This includes works by the same author and others, works from various genres, YA works, and works from various cultures and eras.

The film entries provide sidebars more targeted to the study of film, including:

Film Technique: a listing and explanation of four to six key techniques used in the film, including shot styles, use of transitions, lighting, sound or music, etc.

Read, Watch, Write: media literacy prompts and/or suggestions for viewing log prompts.

What Do I See Next?: a list of films based on the same or similar works or of films similar in directing style, technique, etc.

Other Features

NfS includes "The Informed Dialogue: Interacting with Literature," a foreword by Anne Devereaux Jordan, Senior Editor for *Teaching and Learning Literature* (*TALL*), and a founder of the Children's Literature Association. This essay provides an enlightening look at how readers interact with literature and how *Novels for Students* can help teachers show students how to enrich their own reading experiences.

A Cumulative Author/Title Index lists the authors and titles covered in each volume of the *NfS* series.

A Cumulative Nationality/Ethnicity Index breaks down the authors and titles covered in each volume of the *NfS* series by nationality and ethnicity.

A Subject/Theme Index, specific to each volume, provides easy reference for users who may be studying a particular subject or theme rather than a single work. Significant subjects, from events to broad themes, are included.

Each entry may include illustrations, including photo of the author, stills from film adaptations, maps, and/or photos of key historical events, if available.

Citing Novels for Students

When writing papers, students who quote directly from any volume of *NfS* may use the following general forms. These examples are based on MLA style; teachers may request that students adhere to a different style, so the following examples may be adapted as needed.

When citing text from *NfS* that is not attributed to a particular author (i.e., the Themes, Style, Historical Context sections, etc.), the following format should be used in the bibliography section:

> "*Novels for Students*. Ed. Marie Rose Napierkowski. Vol. 4. Detroit: Gale, 1998. 234–35.

When quoting the specially commissioned essay from *NfS* (usually the first piece under the "Criticism" subhead), the following format should be used:

Miller, Tyrus. Critical Essay on "*Winesburg, Ohio.*" *Novels for Students*. Ed. Marie Rose Napierkowski. Vol. 4. Detroit: Gale, 1998. 335–39.

When quoting a journal or newspaper essay that is reprinted in a volume of *NfS*, the following form may be used:

> Malak, Amin. "Margaret Atwood's *The Handmaid's Tale* and the Dystopian Tradition." *Canadian Literature* 112 (Spring 1987): 9–16. Excerpted and reprinted in *Novels for Students*. Vol. 4. Ed. Marie Rose Napierkowski. Detroit: Gale, 1998. 133–36.

When quoting material reprinted from a book that appears in a volume of *NfS*, the following form may be used:

> Adams, Timothy Dow. "Richard Wright: 'Wearing the Mask.'" In *Telling Lies in Modern American Autobiography*. University of North Carolina Press, 1990. 69–83. Excerpted and reprinted in *Novels for Students*. Vol. 1. Ed. Diane Telgen. Detroit: Gale, 1997. 59–61.

We Welcome Your Suggestions

The editorial staff of *Novels for Students* welcomes your comments and ideas. Readers who wish to suggest novels to appear in future volumes, or who have other suggestions, are cordially invited to contact the editor. You may contact the editor via e-mail at: **ForStudentsEditors@cengage.com**. Or write to the editor at:

Editor, *Novels for Students*
Gale
27500 Drake Road
Farmington Hills, MI 48331-3535

Literary Chronology

1816: Charlotte Brontë is born on April 21 in Yorkshire, England.

1853: Charlotte Brontë's novel *Villette* is published.

1855: Charlotte Brontë dies due to complications from her pregnancy on March 31 in Haworth, England.

1860: Charlotte Perkins Gilman is born on July 3 in Hartford, Connecticut.

1866: H.G. Wells is born Herbert George Wells on September 21 in Bromley, Kent, England.

1881: Juan Ramón Jiménez is born on December 23 in Moguer, Andalusia, Spain.

1896: H.G. Wells's novel *The Island of Dr. Moreau* is published.

1898: Erich Maria Remarque is born on June 22 in Osnabrück, Germany.

1904: Graham Greene is born on October 2 in Berkhampsted, England.

1907: Jack Warner Schaefer is born on November 19 in Cleveland, Ohio.

1911: William Golding is born on September 19 in Cornwell, England.

1914: Juan Ramon Jimenez's novel *Platero y Yo* is published in Spanish; a longer version will be published in 1917, and the first English translation, *Platero and I, is published in 1957.*

1915: Charlotte Perkins Gilman's novel *Herland* is published in *Forerunner* magazine. It is published in book form in 1979.

1929: Erich Maria Remarque's novel *All Quiet on the Western Front* is published.

1929: Paule Marshall is born on April 9 in Brooklyn, New York.

1930: Director Lewis Milestone's film *All Quiet on the Western Front* is produced.

1930: Lewis Milestone is awarded the Academy Award for Best Director for *All Quiet on the Western Front.*

1933: Cormac McCarthy is born July 20 in Providence, Rhode Island.

1935: Charlotte Perkins Gilman commits suicide on August 17 in Pasadena, California.

1937: Thomas Pynchon is born on May 8 in Glen Cove, New York.

1946: H.G. Wells dies on August 13 in London, England.

1949: Jack Warner Schaefer's novel *Shane* is published.

1950: Graham Greene's novel *The Third Man* is published.

1951: Anita Diamant is born on June 27 in Newark, New Jersey.

1954: William Golding's novel *Lord of the Flies* is published.

1956: Juan Ramón Jiménez is awarded the Nobel Prize for literature.

1958: Juan Ramón Jiménez dies on May 29 in Puerto Rico.

1963: Director Peter Brook's film *Lord of the Flies* is produced.

1966: Thomas Pynchon's novel *The Crying of Lot 49* is published.

1968: Junot Díaz is born on December 31 in Santo Domingo, Dominican Republic.

1970: Erich Maria Remarque dies of heart failure on September 25 in Locarno, Switzerland.

1977: Jonathan Safran Foer is born on February 21 in Washington, DC.

1983: Paule Marshall's novel *Praisesong for the Widow* is published.

1983: William Golding is awarded the Nobel Prize for Literature.

1991: Graham Greene dies of a blood disease on April 3 in Vesey, Switzerland.

1991: Jack Warner Schaefer dies of heart failure on January 24 in Santa Fe, New Mexico.

1992: Cormac McCarthy's novel *All the Pretty Horses* is published.

1993: William Golding dies of heart failure on June 19 in Cornwall, England.

1997: Anita Diamant's novel *The Red Tent* is published.

2005: Jonathan Safran Foer's novel *Extremely Loud and Incredibly Close* is published.

2007: Cormac McCarthy is awarded the Pulitzer Prize for his novel *The Road*.

2007: Junot Díaz's novel *The Brief Wondrous Life of Oscar Wao* is published.

2008: Junot Díaz is awarded the Pulitzer Prize for Fiction for *The Brief Wondrous Life of Oscar Wao*.

Acknowledgments

The editors wish to thank the copyright holders of the excerpted criticism included in this volume and the permissions managers of many book and magazine publishing companies for assisting us in securing reproduction rights. We are also grateful to the staffs of the Detroit Public Library, the Library of Congress, the University of Detroit Mercy Library, Wayne State University Purdy/ Kresge Library Complex, and the University of Michigan Libraries for making their resources available to us. Following is a list of the copyright holders who have granted us permission to reproduce material in this volume of *NfS*. Every effort has been made to trace copyright, but if omissions have been made, please let us know.

COPYRIGHTED EXCERPTS IN *NfS*, VOLUME 36, WERE REPRODUCED FROM THE FOLLOWING PERIODICALS:

American Enterprise, May-June, 1998. Copyright © 1998 AMERICAN ENTERPRISE INSTITUTE. Reproduced by permission.—*ANQ*, v. 9, 1996, for "Passionate Intensity in Wells's 'The Island of Dr. Moreau' and "Yeats's 'The Second Coming': Constructing an Echo" by Alex MacDonald. Copyright © 1996 Taylor & Francis Ltd. Reprinted by permission of the publisher Taylor & Francis Ltd, http://www.informaworld.com.—*Brisbane Courier Mail*, Dec 8, 2007, for "A Storm of Exhilaration," by Cheryl Jorgensen. Reproduced by permission of the author.—*Christianity and Literature*, summer 2008.

Copyright © 2008 *Christianity and Literature*. Reproduced by permission.—*College Literature*, spring 1985. Copyright © 1985 by West Chester University. Reproduced by permission.—*College Literature*, spring 1998. Copyright © 1998 by West Chester University. Reproduced by permission.—*Commonweal*, Sept 25, 1992. Copyright © 1992 *Commonweal* Magazine. All rights reserved. Reproduced by permission.—*Explicator*, Mar. 1, 1989, for "Shaefer's 'Shane'" by Jean C. Phillip. Copyright © 1989 Taylor & Francis Ltd. Reprinted by permission of the publisher Taylor & Francis Ltd, http://www.informaworld.com.—*Explicator*, v. 59, summer 2001, for "Pynchon's 'The Crying of Lot 49'" by Matthew Eklund. Copyright © 2001 Taylor & Francis Ltd. Reprinted by permission of the publisher Taylor & Francis Ltd, http://www.informaworld.com.—*Explicator*, v. 66, spring 2008, for "Dreams as a Structural Framework in McCarthy's 'All the Pretty Horses'" by Chad Spellman. Copyright © 2008 Taylor & Francis Ltd. Reprinted by permission of the publisher Taylor & Francis Ltd, http://www.informaworld.com.—*Explicator*, v. 66, summer 2008, for "The Search for Utopia: Blood Imagery in McCarthy's 'All the Pretty Horses'" by Susan Lee. Copyright © 2008 Taylor & Francis Ltd. Reprinted by permission of the publisher Taylor & Francis Ltd, http://www.informaworld.com.—*Film Quarterly*, winter 1963-1964. Copyright © 1963-1964 University of California Press. Reproduced by permission.—*Globe and Mail* (Canada), June 13, 1992, for "A Wild Ride: 'All The Pretty Horses'" by Christopher Dewdney. Reproduced by permission of the author.—Harris-Fain, Darren "Review of 'The Island of Dr. Moreau: A Variorum Edition' by H. G. Wells" *Extrapolation*, v. 35, no. 1, Spring 1994. Copyright © 1994 by The Kent State University Press. All rights reserved. Reproduced by permission.—*Hispania*, Feb. 1, 1950. Copyright © 1950 *Hispania*. Reproduced by permission.—*Lion and the Unicorn*, winter 1980-1981. Copyright © 1980-1981 John Hopkins University Press. Reproduced by permission.—*Literature Film Quarterly*, v. 26, 1998. Copyright © 1998 *Literature Film Quarterly*. Reproduced by permission.—*London Guardian*, July 31, 1995. Copyright © 1995 Guardian News & Media Ltd. All rights reserved. Reproduced by permission.—*London Independent*, August 1, 1999. Copyright © 1999 Independent Print Limited. All rights reserved. Reproduced by permission.—*Los Angeles Times*, Sept. 9, 2007, for "A Love Supreme," by Susan Straight. Copyright © 2007 Susan Straight. Reproduced by permission of The Richard Parks Agency.—*National Catholic Reporter*, May 22, 1998. Copyright © 1998 The National Catholic Reporter Publishing Co. Reproduced by permission.—*New Criterion*, May 1, 2005, for "Kinderkampf: Review of 'Extremely Loud & Incredibly Close'" by Stefan Beck. Reproduced by permission of the author.—*New England Review*, v. 16, winter 1994, for "As Good as Money In the Bank: Cormac McCarthy's 'All the Pretty Horses'" by Allen G. Shepherd. Reproduced by permission of the author.—*New Republic,* August 17, 1963. Copyright © 1963 *The New Republic*. Reproduced by permission.—*New Statesman*, Feb 2, 2008 Copyright © 2008 *New Statesman*. Reproduced by permission.—*New Statesman*, Nov 10, 2003. Copyright © 2003 *New Statesman*. All rights reserved. Reproduced by permission.—*Newsweek*, Feb. 5, 2001. Copyright © 2001 Newsweek Inc. Reproduced by permission.—*off our backs*, Oct 1, 2007. Copyright © 2007 *off our backs*. Reproduced by permission.—*Philadelphia Inquirer*, September 12, 2007.

Copyright © 2007 *Philadelphia Inquirer*. Reproduced by permission.—Reprinted from *Commentary*, May, 2005, by permission; copyright © 2005 Commentary, Inc. Reproduced by permission.—*Spectator*, June 11, 2005. Copyright © 2005 The Spectator (1828) Ltd. All rights reserved. Reproduced by permission.—*Studies in American Fiction*, spring 1992. Copyright ©1992 *Studies in American Fiction*, Northeastern University. Reproduced by permission.—*Studies in the Novel*, spring 1997. Copyright © 1997 *Studies in the Novel*, University of North Texas. Reproduced by permission.—*Studies in the Novel*, winter 1996. Copyright © 1996 *Studies in the Novel*, University of North Texas. Reproduced by permission.—*The Crisis*, August-September, 1983 Copyright © 1983 Crisis Publishing Co., Inc. Gale/Cengage Learning wishes to thank the Crisis Publishing Co., Inc., the publisher of the magazine of the National Association for the Advancement of Coloured People, for the use of this material first published the August-September 1983 issue of *The Crisis*. Reproduced by permission.—*Toronto Star Syndicate*, Nov. 2, 2006. Copyright © 2006 by Toronto Star Syndicate. Reproduced by permission.—*Toronto Star Syndicate*, Oct. 24, 2008. Copyright © 2008 by Toronto Star Syndicate. Reproduced by permission.—*World Literature Today*, v. 82, March-April, 2008. Copyright © 2008 *World Literature Today*. Reproduced by permission.—*Writer*, April 1, 2001, for "Anita Diamant's 'Red Tent' Turns to Gold," by Jusith Rosen. Copyright © Judith Rosen. Reproduced by permission of the author.

COPYRIGHTED EXCERPTS IN *NfS*, VOLUME 36, WERE REPRODUCED FROM THE FOLLOWING BOOKS:

Doskow, Minna. From "Herland: Utopic in a Different Voice," in *Politics, Gender, and the Arts*, Susquehanna University Press, 1992. Copyright © 1992 Associated University Presses. Reproduced by permission.—From *Contemporary Popular Writers,* Global Rights and Permissions, a part of Cengage Learning Inc. Reproduced by permission. www.cengage.com/permissions.

Contributors

Bryan Aubrey: Aubrey holds a Ph.D. in English. Entry on *Praisesong for the Widow*. Original essay on *Praisesong for the Widow*.

Catherine Dominic: Dominic is a novelist and a freelance writer and editor. Entry on *Villette*. Original essay on *Villette*.

Diane Andrews Henningfeld: Henningfeld is an instructor in English and literature. Entry on *The Crying of Lot 49*. Original essay on *The Crying of Lot 49*.

Michael A. Holmes: Holmes is a writer and editor. Entries on *The Brief Wondrous Life of Oscar Wao* and *The Third Man*. Original essays on *The Brief Wondrous Life of Oscar Wao* and *The Third Man*.

Sheri Metzger Karmiol: Karmiol teaches literature and drama at the University of New Mexico, where she is a lecturer in the University Honors Program. Entry on *The Red Tent*. Original essay on *The Red Tent*.

David Kelly: Kelly is a college instructor of creative writing and literature. Entries on *All Quiet on the Western Front* and *Lord of the Flies*. Original essays on *All Quiet on the Western Front* and *Lord of the Flies*.

Michael O'Neal: O'Neal holds a Ph.D in English literature and linguistics. Entries on *Extremely Loud and Incredibly Close* and *Shane*. Original essays on *Extremely Loud and Incredibly Close* and *Shane*.

Laura Beth Pryor: Pryor is a freelance writer with twenty-five years of experience in professional writing, with an emphasis on fiction. Entry on *Platero and I*. Original essay on *Platero and I*.

Bradley A. Skeen: Skeen is a classicist. Entry on *The Island of Dr. Moreau*. Original essay on *The Island of Dr. Moreau*.

Leah Tieger: Tieger is a freelance writer and editor. Entry on *All the Pretty Horses*. Original essay on *All the Pretty Horses*.

Rebecca Valentine: Valentine is a writer with an extensive background in literary theory and analysis. Entry on *Herland*. Original essay on *Herland*.

All Quiet on the Western Front

1930

Lewis Milestone's film *All Quiet on the Western Front* was made early in the sound era of film, but viewers to this day are moved by its harrowing and honest depiction of war. The film shows the life of a young man, Paul Bäumer, who enrolls in the German army during World War I after he and his friends are stirred up in a patriotic fervor at their school. It follows the boys through the trials of war, showing the loss, misery, hunger, and disillusionment that they experience, one step at a time. Friends die and bullets and bombs constantly threaten their lives and the lives of those around them, but nobody outside of the army seems to understand, thinking that the fight is all about glory.

In 1930, the film won an Academy Award for outstanding production, and Milestone won for best director. It was also nominated for awards for best cinematography and best screenplay.

The novel by Erich Maria Remarque that the film *All Quiet on the Western Front* is based on has been considered a powerful and controversial piece of antiwar literature since its first publication. When the Nazis rose to power in Germany in the 1930s, Remarque's book was one of those that they burned, fearing that its depiction of war would discourage young recruits. American forces used the film for propaganda purposes as well: in a 1939 rerelease, Universal Studios inserted anti-Nazi news announcements into the film. However, these edited versions have not been available since

World War II. A 1997 restoration supervised by the Library of Congress has put the film together as Milestone originally intended it, in the form that left audiences stunned upon its first release.

PLOT SUMMARY

After the opening credits roll, *All Quiet on the Western Front* begins with a title card that quotes Remarque's brief introduction before his book's first chapter, changing "this book" to "this story" and ending with ellipses instead of a period. The first scene is of a man, Herr Meyer, talking to his wife as he polishes the handles of his front door. He opens the door just as uniformed troops are marching past, with citizens cheering them on. Himmelstoss, the postman, talks to him, smiling and laughing ingratiatingly, and says that he is off to the army soon.

In the classroom, Professor Kantorek lectures his students on their duty to their country and their responsibility to make Germany proud by going to fight in the war. They are the "iron men of Germany," he tells them. As he speaks, the boys have fantasies about how they will be received. One imagines that his mother will be shocked to see him in uniform but his father will be pleased. Another imagines himself surrounded by adoring girls. One hangs his head and sobs. At the end of the speech, they all jump to their feet and shout with enthusiasm. They pressure Behn to join them. In their enthusiasm, they march around the school room and sing, tossing around papers they will not need anymore.

The story resumes at the training facility, where the boys find themselves under the command of Himmelstoss, the former postman. They are surprised to find that he is not as friendly as he used to be. Because they do not show him the proper respect, Himmelstoss lectures them to forget everything they ever knew. He sends their platoon to do a series of grueling drills, forcing them to crawl through mud for hours at a time. He also requires them to sing and makes them work harder for not singing enthusiastically. (This event also appears in the book, but with another platoon, not Himmelstoss's.) When the troops receive word that they will leave for the front lines in the morning, they catch Himmelstoss in the night as he is stumbling back to his quarters drunk and give him a beating with the flats of their swords.

When Bäumer, Behn, Müller, Kropp, and Kemmerich arrive in the war zone, a bomb lands near them almost immediately. Behn, who was reluctant to enlist, freezes over the corpse of a dead man. In the house where they are to sleep, they meet the older soldiers. Tjaden acts gruff at first but warms to Paul's politeness. Kat Katczinsky, legendary for his ability to find food, steals a dead pig and returns with it, providing the younger troops something to eat in return for their supplies.

The troops are driven out into a war zone, where Katczinsky takes responsibility for them, telling them what to expect when the bombing begins. When the enemy begins firing on them they all run for cover. Behn, wounded, runs straight toward enemy fire. Kropp goes out to bring him back, but Behn is dead.

Soon the troops are sequestered in a house, unable to go out to acquire food and constantly rocked by enemy shell fire. Kemmerich loses his nerve after days of bombardment and runs out of the shelter, only to be hit by shrapnel almost immediately. He is taken off to the hospital, but the others remain in the shelter. When someone manages to bring in a loaf of bread, a swarm of rats attack, and the soldiers beat at them with their weapons.

The shelling stops. The troops all leave their bunker and line up in the trenches, prepared for battle, as thousands of enemy troops attack them. The film shows an extended battle scene with machine gun fire, whistling bombs, and hand-to-hand combat.

After the battle, the men of the Second Company go to have their dinner. The cook has been told to make food for a hundred and fifty men, but only eighty men return. Katczinsky insists that they should all be given whatever food the cook has prepared, double rations for each man. The commanding officer arrives and agrees. This scene, showing the hungry desperation of the men, who are momentarily happy that half of their comrades did not return, is the first scene in Remarque's book, though the film version adds the intercession of the commanding officer.

While at rest, the men have a philosophical discussion about how wars, and this one in particular, begin, and how they all think a war ought to be pursued. They then go to visit Kemmerich at the field hospital. He complains that his right foot hurts, and Müller blurts out the news that his right leg has been amputated,

FILM TECHNIQUE

Close-Ups

Because *All Quiet on the Western Front* is primarily about war, a broad visual subject with much going on, the director's use of close-up shots is very noticeable, as well as important to the storytelling. With a close-up shot of a character's face, the film is able to show what that character is thinking directly: viewers can read emotions on a face more clearly than they can interpret dialog or body language. This is used to very good effect in the early classroom scene, where the camera's tight focus on Professor Kantorek's face tells readers that his enthusiasm is beyond zeal, while the faces of the boys show that they are out of control with excitement. Another fine example occurs when the troops go on their first patrol, and Milestone's camera shows a close-up of each of the principal characters looking back over his shoulder. Their apprehension is vivid, and the same shot is used at the end, when they are all dead, to remind the audience of the innocence that showed clearly on their faces. The most significant close-up of the film shows Paul's hand going limp as he dies.

Wide Angle

The discussions among soldiers in this film are often shot with a medium angle, showing several people in the frame at a time. The battle scenes are effective partly because they are filmed at wide angle, taking in acres and acres of land at one time. Viewers can see bombs exploding in the foreground, soldiers advancing in the middle ground, and buildings burning in the background, all within the same frame. With a range of explosive sounds added, this copies the chaotic feeling of a war zone.

Framing

One notable technique that Milestone uses frequently throughout this film is framing action through a window or doorway. He introduces this technique very early, when Herr Meyer finishes polishing the handles of his front doors and opens the doors to show a parade going by outside; after a brief scene, the camera follows the marching soldiers and then pulls back to show that they are being viewed through the open windows of the classroom. The same technique is used in a number of places throughout the film, including when the training ground is entered through the opening doors on the gate, and when the volunteers arrive at the front by train, which is framed through the station's wide window. Throughout the film, soldiers are often seen walking by outside while characters converse inside.

Spatial Orientation

During the battle scenes in this film, the German army is usually seen attacking from right to left, while their opponents advance left-to-right. The battle could be filmed from any angle, but this visual consistency is an important tool for helping viewers keep the participants clear. When the German army runs from left to right, it is retreating, and viewers know that the film's main characters are in danger. Additionally, this would be geographically correct in the actual trench warfare setup.

Crosscutting

Filmmakers use crosscutting to show two different scenes that will affect each other, bouncing back and forth from one set of action to the other. This is often done so subtly that viewers do not notice it. One obvious use of crosscutting comes near the end, when the film cuts between Paul and Katczinsky's reunion, the plane above them, the discussion, the hand releasing the bomb on them, and so forth, preparing viewers for the coming bomb in a way that the characters cannot anticipate.

which is news to Kemmerich. Müller admires Kemmerich's boots and asks if he can have them. Paul lingers after the others have left. He prays to God to spare Kemmerich's life, but Kemmerich dies as Paul sits beside his bed. After watching him die, Paul runs back to the barracks, breathing the air and feeling hungry and glad to be alive.

Getty Images

Himmelstoss, the old postman, shows up at the front, and Paul and the others who followed his orders during their basic training mock him to his face. They laugh when he threatens to court-martial them. During the next attack, Himmelstoss loses his nerve when the shelling begins. He falls to the ground, crying, claiming to be wounded, and Paul drags him to his feet. Himmelstoss charges into battle and is killed by an exploding shell. The others wait out the bombing in a graveyard.

Paul curls up in a bomb crater as his troops race forward to attack, feeling a weakness of nerves like the one Himmelstoss felt before he foolishly charged forward. He stabs an attacker with his knife and stays hidden with the dying man, trying to comfort him, pinned down under machine gun fire until the next day. Paul begs the dead man for forgiveness. When the fighting is done, Paul crawls out of the crater.

Back with Katczinsky, Paul tries to explain what it was like to kill a man with his bare hands,

but Katczinsky tells him that feeling is normal for war. The camera cuts between their discussion and a marksman outside of their bunker, shooting down enemy soldiers.

The troops are happy in the next scene, singing as they march into a town. Drinking beer and eating sausage in a bar, they observe a poster showing a beautiful woman. The sight of her makes them want to bathe. While they are bathing in a river, several French women pass by on the other side. A sentry stops them from passing over to the French side of the river, but they arrange to meet the girls that night. At night, they leave Tjaden behind by having Katczinsky distract him with drinks. They swim over to the women's house, taking food provisions, and though the women are clearly only interested in the food they can provide, the soldiers spend the night.

Artillery fire disrupts their march the next morning. Paul and Kropp are both injured and end up in a hospital. Joseph Hammacher, a fellow patient with a head injury, tells them that patients who are taken away are sometimes taken to "the dying room," where they are left to die so that new patients can use their beds. When Paul is being taken away to be bandaged, he sees the orderlies take his clothes, thinks he is going to the dying room, and panics. Kropp is taken off to surgery and comes back worried that he has had his leg amputated. He is also worried about Paul until Paul is brought back.

Paul returns to his hometown on leave. He finds his family hungry and his mother sick in bed. He accompanies his father to a beer hall, where old men who do not have to fight in the war tell him how they think it should be waged, insisting that the army should keep pushing until they take Paris. At his old school, the schoolteacher, Professor Kantorek, brings Paul up before a group of schoolboys being lectured to join the army, but Paul has nothing to say about heroism. When he tells them that dying for one's country is wasteful, the boys turn on him, calling him a coward. Paul decides to return to the front, even though he still has four days of leave.

He returns to find that most of the people he knew in the Second Company are gone and that new, young recruits are in their place. Tjaden tells him that Katczinsky is out looking for food. Paul goes to meet him, and they have a happy reunion. A bomb lands near them, injuring Katczinsky's leg. Paul picks him up and carries him back to the base on his shoulders, but shrapnel from another bomb hits Katczinsky in the neck. Paul thinks that he is still alive when he reaches the hospital, disbelieving the bad news. He takes Katczinsky's pay book when it is offered to him.

In a trench, Paul sits, his face showing the desolation he feels. He smiles when he sees a butterfly land on a tin can just outside of the barricade. He reaches his hand out, and an enemy sniper fires, killing him. This scene is based on one that comes earlier in the novel, in which Paul watches two butterflies land on a human skull. It was filmed after the main shooting was completed and the actors were off doing other jobs. Legend has it that the hand shown onscreen is that of Lewis Milestone, the director.

After Paul's death, the film shows footage of the soldiers who went to war in the beginning of the film, superimposed over a shot of a military cemetery filled with acres of identical headstones. The screen then goes black.

CHARACTERS

Paul Bäumer

Paul is the main character of the movie and the first-person narrator of Remarque's novel. Paul is played by Lew Ayres, who went on to have a long, distinguished career in Hollywood. His career was interrupted when he was blacklisted during World War II because he refused to fight in combat, citing pacifist principles he had acquired while making this film.

In an early scene when the boys in Paul's classroom are lectured by their teacher about joining the war effort, Professor Kantorek singles Paul out as a boy who has aspirations to write. Later, when he comes home on leave, Paul stops to notice a frame of mounted butterflies on the wall of his bedroom, indicating a boyhood hobby that Remarque makes more of in the novel, one that plays a significant part in Paul's death. These are the few personal notes that the film gives Paul to set him apart from the other soldiers.

The film follows Paul's life, from the time when he and his friends are talked into military service by their professor to his death a few years later. In between, Paul experiences a number of events that are representative of military experience. The film shows him suffering humiliation throughout basic training and learning the unofficial ways of soldiering from an experienced elder. He stands by as a friend and former classmate dies, and he is forced to watch a man he has stabbed slowly die. He goes home on leave and finds himself unable to relate to the life he once lived, outraged at the civilians who have no idea of what life in the trenches is like. By the end of the film he finds himself so changed that he is more comfortable in the dangerous, hectic battle conditions than in his own home.

After the death of Katczinsky, Paul has little to live for, a fact that is conveyed by his expression of bleak hopelessness. He dies while reaching out toward a butterfly. It is a foolish thing for a soldier to do, but it recalls the boy that he was before he enlisted.

Mrs. Bäumer

Paul's mother, played by Beryl Mercer, is dying of cancer when he comes home on leave. He worries about her, but he cannot understand her. The battle zone represents constant danger and hunger for him, but Paul's mother, almost laughably, warns him to be careful of the duplicitous girls he might meet while in the army. Her concern reminds Paul of a time when his own view of the world was much simpler, causing him to wish he could stay in his mother's arms forever.

Behn

Behn is played by Walter Browne Rogers. He is the boy from Paul's class who does not want to join the war. After Professor Kantorek's speech to the class, however, the other boys pressure him to join. The first time they are under enemy fire, Behn is hit in the eyes. Blinded and terrified, he runs out onto the battlefield and is immediately killed.

Gérard Duval

Duval is the enemy soldier who jumps into the bomb crater where Paul is hiding, forcing Paul to stab him in the chest. He survives for almost a day, and his long death causes Paul to ponder the ramifications of killing a man. Eventually, Paul tries to do what he can to ease Duval's suffering. He talks to the man, promising to take care of his family, although they do not speak the same language. He gives him water from a puddle on the ground. After Duval's death, Paul looks through his pocket and finds a wallet where he finds the man's name and learns that he was a printer, and Paul sees a picture of the man's family.

Joseph Hammacher

Hammacher is a deranged patient who is in the Catholic hospital with Paul and Kropp. He tells them that patients who have their clothes taken away when they are removed from their beds are being taken to another room to die, causing Paul to become hysterical as he is wheeled out to have his bandages changed.

Himmelstoss

Himmelstoss is a postman when the film begins. When he is chided for failing to deliver mail on time, he laughs nervously. This brief scene prepares viewers for the strict commander he will be later on, when given a little power in the army. He forces the troops to crawl through mud when they do not show the respect he thinks he deserves. Eventually, they take revenge, jumping him as he is coming home in the dark and caning his backside with their swords. He comes back into their lives later, when they are at the front. When Himmelstoss shows cowardice, Paul physically forces him out of the trench to go and face enemy fire. In the film he is killed, but the book has him behaving honorably and helping a wounded soldier back to safety.

Professor Kantorek

Professor Kantorek is the instructor of Paul and the other schoolboys. He is played in the film by Arnold Lucy. Although he is a professor, he is more concerned with the war than he is with intellectual pursuits. He lectures the boys in his class about their responsibility to join the war and fight for their country, calling them the "iron men of Germany." As a result, they all march away from his classroom, singing. Later, they remember their old professor angrily, feeling that it is at least partially his fault that they are in the miserable environment of the war zone.

Home on leave, Paul passes by Kantorek's classroom just as his old teacher is giving a similar speech about joining the army to a new set of students. He insists that Paul talk to the boys about the glory of war, which is clearly a subject he knows nothing about himself.

In Remarque's novel, Kantorek ends up drafted into the army at a low position, and he is worked mercilessly by a commanding officer, a former student whom he bullied into enlisting.

Stanislaus "Kat" Katczinsky

Katczinsky is played by Louis Wolheim, who was set to become a major star because of this film but died the following year. Kat is famous among the soldiers for his ability to find and steal food when no one else, including the mess officials, can provide it. When he first appears in the story, he seems to be a gruff, angry man, but he soon warms to the new recruits in the Second Company. He becomes a friend and protector to Paul, a father figure to him and the others. He gives them advice on how to survive as soldiers, often contradicting the formal training they receive from the army and the patriotic notions taught to them as civilians. One of his first lessons, for instance, is to not venture out into the battle zone to save an injured comrade, a point about which he is adamant. When they are out in the field, Katczinsky tells the young men how to tell the differences between bombs, and when he cannot explain the differences, he simply tells them to follow his lead.

After his leave, when Paul returns to the unit as a veteran of several campaigns, he and Katczinsky are best friends. Their friendship is short-lived, however, as Katczinsky is almost immediately cut down by shrapnel. He looks forward to leaving the army, but he dies as Paul carries him back to the base.

Franz Kemmerich

Kemmerich, played by Ben Alexander, is one of the first to die. He comes from a well-to-do family and goes into the army with expensive boots and a valuable watch. In an early scene in the film, he and Müller discuss the boots, given to Kemmerich by his uncle. After Kemmerich suffers what seems to be a minor wound, his leg is amputated at the military hospital. When the other soldiers visit, they find out that he does not know about the amputation and try to hide it from him. When Kemmerich finds out, he sadly instructs Paul to give his boots to Müller. He dies later in the scene. Although the visit to Kemmerich's bedside occurs well into the film, it is in the first chapter of Remarque's novel, drawing attention to the pathos of war and to the greediness that occurs when supplies are scarce.

Albert Kropp

Albert, played by William Bakewell, is one of the boys who enlist into the army with Paul. He is Paul's closest friend among the boys, a partner in various exploits, and a sounding board for Paul's ideas. Albert is the one who begins the philosophical discussion about the cause of war, leading the others of the Second Company to suggest their own theories about the subject.

Müller

Müller is played by Russell Gleason. He is most notable as the man who admires Kemmerich's boots after Kemmerich finds out that his leg has been amputated, asking whether he can have them. Talking to Paul later, Müller expresses his deep sorrow for sounding crass. He explains that he would never have said anything if Kemmerich had a chance of ever using the boots again, but balanced against his sorrow is the joy he gets from having a decent pair of boots.

Tjaden

Tjaden is played by Slim Summerville, a familiar comic actor who performed in and directed hundreds of films from the 1910s through the 1940s. This film presents him as a peer of Katczinsky, another tired older recruit who has seen much and who helps show the younger men the ways of the enlisted man. In the novel, though, he is described as being the same age as Paul and the rest.

Because of his comic looks, Tjaden lightens every scene. He even has one scene that is explicitly played for broad laughs, as he stands behind his friend Katczinsky at a bar and deftly redirects every glass of beer that comes in Katczinsky's direction. He is on good terms with the younger men in the Second Company: when Paul gives him some food after returning from leave, Tjaden gives it to the new boys, even though he is starving himself.

THEMES

Idealism

To show that Professor Kantorek's speech to his students is effective in stirring their idealism about military service, Milestone shows viewers the fantasies that the boys have about life in uniform. One imagines his mother upset but his father enthused, and another daydreams about himself in uniform being celebrated in a parade, with a girl on each arm. These images show that the boys are naïve, but they are common examples of the ideals that make war seem appealing to young men.

Milestone's camera shows Kantorek's face in increasingly tighter close-ups as he becomes more worked up, making his speech look more and more like a crazed rant. The boys in his class, however, are moved by the teacher's words. They rise up out of their chairs and sing and march, showing their communal feeling. Professor Kantorek's speech makes each of them, even the reluctant Behn, feel that he is a part of something greater than himself. The final indicator of their idealism comes at the end of the scene, when they cross off the lesson on the chalkboard and throw their papers into the air. They have given up seeing themselves as students, an identity they held just moments earlier, and have completely accepted the idea that their lives will be better as soldiers.

Later in the film, Paul is sickened when he hears Kantorek giving almost the same speech to a new set of schoolboys. He regrets the idealism he felt when he was a student, and he warns the boys against it. They are so indoctrinated with the glory of war, however, that they cannot accept the word of someone who has actually been involved in the fighting. They call Paul a coward because his

READ, WATCH, WRITE

- Author Roald Dahl is best known for his imaginative books, such as *James and the Giant Peach* and *Charlie and the Chocolate Factory*. In the second volume of his autobiography, *Going Solo*, he writes about his adventures as a pilot in the Royal Air Force during World War II. Read Dahl's memoir and compare it with the treatment Remarque gave to his wartime experience. Explain the book's overall theme. List the scenes you think would have to be included in a *Going Solo* movie and how they fit with its theme.

- Some critics consider Ernst Jünger's 1923 novel *Storm of Steel* to be at least as effective as Remarque's novel, if not more so, in making the case against war. Read Jünger's novel and choose a key scene that you think would play well on film. Write a section of screenplay for a short segment of a proposed film of that novel. For further credit, gather a group of students and film the screenplay using iMovie or another video editing program and post it to YouTube.

- Read an account of civilians living in a war zone, such as *The Kite Runner* by Khaled Hosseini or *Zlata's Diary: A Child's Life in Wartime Sarajevo* by Zlata Filipovic. Compile a list of characteristics that you think are common to civilians during wartime. Write a short essay or Web log entry to summarize your findings.

- In the film, the soldiers have a discussion about how wars start, but at the end of their talk they are still unable to reach any agreement about the causes of war. Choose one soldier's position as it is explained in this film. Search print and Internet sources to put together a collection of clips from politicians and news pundits that support that soldier's theory. Use Wallwisher.com or LinoIt.com to create a bulletin board of clips for your classmates to view.

- When Paul is at home on leave he finds himself unable to connect with his former life. Interview one or two veterans who have been in combat, and based on their tips, prepare a kit of things you think will be essential items for soldiers returning to civilian life. Be prepared to explain the significance of each item in your kit.

- This film was produced in a matter of months. Investigate the budget of a war movie produced in the last few years and find out the costs associated with the film's special effects. Explain to your class whether or not you think such effects are necessary in a modern war movie, using scenes from *All Quiet on the Western Front* to illustrate your points.

- In this film, Kantorek, the school teacher, uses the phrase "*Dulce et decorum est pro patria mori.*" This Latin phrase, from the ancient Roman poet Horace, means "It is sweet and fitting to die for one's country" and was used in the title of one of the most famous poems from World War I. Read about the life of Wilfred Owen, author of the poem "Dulce et Decorum Est," and create a report comparing his life with Remarque's.

version of reality does not match the idealism that has been stirred up in their heads.

Heroism

With the constant sound of bombs and gunfire on the sound track, the film keeps viewers aware of the dangers of war. The soldiers are tested at every moment. Courage is not expected of them: after one of the first bombing attacks, Katczinsky, the grizzled veteran of numerous campaigns, tells a soldier who has soiled himself that it is nothing to be embarrassed about, that it has happened to every soldier.

The film presents courage as a detrimental quality that can lead soldiers into danger. When Behn is injured and, panicking, runs right into the field of fire, Kropp goes off to help his friend, but he is severely chastised for his heroism when he returns. He has risked his own life for nothing, as Behn is already dead. Katczinsky demands that he should never take such a risk again, that it is not worth it.

It is ironic, then, that Paul risks his life to carry Katczinsky back to the base after he is wounded. Kat's advice about not risking oneself still makes sense, even when it is his own life at stake. He is dead when they reach camp, so it turns out that Paul, like Kropp, has risked his life for a dead man after all.

Military Life

This film has become legendary since its premier in 1930 for the way that it presents the realities of military life during World War I. Some aspects of life in a combat zone were new to that war and would have been a revelation to veterans of earlier wars, as well as to people who had never been in a war zone, including the majority of Americans. The constant sounds of shells falling and exploding, for instance, were new with the advent of airplanes in battle. Machine guns became portable in that war, and the use of lung-destroying chlorine gas was a constant threat. The trench system, which linked miles and miles of tunnels and ditches, led to wet misery and waves of rats.

Other views of military life shown in this film are common to all wars. Some people of weak character, like the simpering postman Himmelstoss, manage to rise to superior rank over tougher, braver soldiers. The result of this is that the formalities drilled into recruits on the parade ground are often ignored in the heat of battle, as they are in the film when Himmelstoss is sent to the front.

The pressure of military life often leads to camaraderie among the men who face danger together. Katczinsky and Tjaden are shown to be brutal men who, in civilian life, would not be of the same social class as the young students who enlisted in the war with Paul, but they all learn to appreciate each other's personalities when they are in the same desperate circumstances. Their mutual disdain for their superiors helps promote their friendship.

This film also shows the ways that government promotes the idea that war is glorious. It suggests, though, that true soldiers feel glory to be nothing more than a myth.

Death

Paul's view of the world changes when he watches his friend Kemmerich die. He feels grief over the loss of his friend, but after observing death for the first time, he finds himself full of zest for life. On the way back to the barracks, he breaks into a run, pleased to be able to move and breathe. His close experience with death makes him appreciate life more.

He has a different revelation when he kills a man. After stabbing the French printer and watching him slowly die before his eyes over the course of a day, Paul finds himself on the brink of sanity. He talks to the dying man, promising to write to his family, to take care of his wife and parents. He is brought to tears over the death he has caused. The next day, however, he dismisses his intense feelings as having just been caused by the fact that he was trapped with the dying man. Katczinsky agrees that killing is nothing to be too upset about, pointing to a nearby sniper who is proud of the enemy deaths he is causing as they speak.

Because of the standards in Hollywood in the 1930s, the deaths in this film are not as graphic as they are in Remarque's novel, where severed body parts and gaping wounds are described in vivid detail. The film concentrates on how the characters respond to death without showing its viewers the horrors they have witnessed.

STYLE

Chronological Order

The film version of *All Quiet on the Western Front* presents most of the same scenes that are presented in Remarque's novel, and it retains much of the author's original dialogue, but it shifts the order in which scenes are presented. Viewers who have read the book will notice this immediately, when the film begins with the boys as students in Kantorek's classroom, being encouraged to go to war. Later, when the first scene of the book appears onscreen, viewers can see that little has been cut, but the order has been rearranged.

Written fiction is able to fade into and out of flashbacks more smoothly than a film can. In a film, viewers come to recognize characters from the way they are shown, instead of being told about them. The film is not able to move into a flashback by discussing a time similar to the one presently being shown, as fiction can. Film does

Getty Images

have techniques to indicate that a new scene happens at a different time, but readers have to figure out what time they have been taken to when they are there. To present this story in disjointed order and still make it clear to viewers, the film would have to take much more time establishing scenes and their relationship to each other, leaving less time onscreen for Remarque's original material. The screenwriters chose to present the story in chronological order in order to make the chaotic action as easy to follow as possible.

Point of View

Remarque's novel is told from the first-person point of view, with Paul Bäumer referring to himself as "I" throughout the book. It is difficult for film to present a story in the first person. There have been experiments with the camera standing in for the lead character, showing what his or her eyes would show, but these films have been rare and have had limited success.

The film does come close to a first-person point of view by having Paul present for all of the scenes. He may not be the subject of each scene, and the camera might draw back to show angles that he would not be able to see, particularly in the complex battle scenes. Still, viewers are left with no question that Paul is the film's main character.

Epic Film

When applied to poetry, the term "epic" usually refers to a story with a hero on a quest and the fantastic, mind-boggling feats that the hero accomplishes. The most commonly mentioned epics in literature are the Greek poet Homer's *Iliad* and *Odyssey*.

Film is a much younger medium, however, without the centuries of tradition that literature has. When applied to film, "epic" usually is a matter of quantity, not substance. Epic films usually follow many characters and show grand, sweeping, wide-angle scenes of action. *All Quiet on the Western Front*, like most films centered on a military unit, does indeed have a complex cluster of characters to follow, even though the center of the story is indisputably Paul Bäumer. The battle scenes are of epic proportion for a Hollywood production, involving thousands of extras in some scenes and dozens of sets, as well as a substantial investment in pyrotechnics to create simulated explosions. The grand scope of this film has led to *All Quiet on the Western Front* being included on the American Film Institute's list of top ten epic films of all time.

CULTURAL CONTEXT

Throughout this film, the soldiers feel confused about why they are there. Their confusion is justified, as World War I was one of the most complicated and convoluted wars the world had ever entered, in addition to being the most brutal. The war, also called the Great War, eventually earned the designation of World War because of its scope: it involved more countries across the globe than any previous war.

The immediate cause of the war was the assassination of Archduke Franz Ferdinand, heir to the throne of Austria-Hungary, on June 28, 1914. He was shot by a member of a Serbian extremist society. After three weeks of grieving for the fallen leader, the government issued a demand to Serbia to turn over anyone involved with the killing. Serbia, an independent nation, felt that its sovereignty was being violated and turned to Russia for support. Not really believing that Russia would become involved, Austria-Hungary obtained a similar promise for support from Germany, and it declared war against Serbia on July 28. Russia did in fact stand up for its treaty with Serbia and began mobilizing. Germany, in accordance with its treaty with Austria-Hungary, declared war against Russia on August 1. France, which had a treaty with Russia, declared war on Germany on August 3. Great Britain, which had an informal agreement to defend France, might have stayed out of the war, except that Germany attacked Belgium, a neutral country that Britain had agreed to defend, on August 4th. When Great Britain joined the war, its various colonies and dominions across the globe gave their support, including Australia, Canada, India, New Zealand, and the Union of South Africa. Japan entered the war on August 23, in accordance with its treaty with the British. Italy had treaties with Austria-Hungary and Germany but joined the battle against them in 1915. The United States declared itself neutral and stayed out of the war until 1917. At that point, though, the British intercepted a telegram from Germany to Mexico, proposing that Mexico fight the United States on Germany's behalf.

The Western front was a line of defense that stopped the Germans from advancing westward and the French from advancing eastward. For almost the entire war, from 1914 to 1918, opposing troops stayed frozen in a stand-off along a jagged line from Flanders, Belgium, along the Straits of Dover, in the north, cutting through eastern France, and down to Switzerland. Battles were fought along this line, but for most of the war it did not move. The Western front was so immobile that both sides lived in trenches dug for miles along it, a military development that helped soldiers hide from gunfire but also inhibited advancement on either side.

World War I marked a drastic change in the way that the world viewed war. Not only was it carried out across a wider scope than any war before, but it also introduced new fighting techniques, such as trench warfare. Airplanes, so common in warfare now, were first used in combat in this war. Submarines were used against war ships and civilian ships. Poisonous gases such mustard gas and chlorine gas were used; although they were not effective and were not used often, the deaths that they caused by attacking the lungs were so gruesome that soldiers who had survived such attacks were haunted by them. Flamethrowers were also used against troops.

After the armistice (a major, formal truce) in 1918, the world looked upon this war with horror. Even the hopeful description of it as "the war to end war" was now used with skepticism. The League of Nations, a precursor to the United Nations, was formed with the hope that such conflicts could be prevented in the future. By the end of the 1920s, when Remarque published his novel, the world was still shaken by what had happened. A generation of writers, dubbed the Lost Generation by Virginia Woolf, survived to tell of their experiences.

CRITICAL OVERVIEW

Remarque's novel *All Quiet on the Western Front* was such an international best seller, going through six printings in eight months when it was published in 1929, that a film version was considered inevitable. The film that was made was done with the best talent that Hollywood

Getty Images

had to offer. By the end of 1929, Carl Laemelle, the president of Universal Pictures, went to Berlin to meet with Remarque to secure the rights to the story. His son, Carl Laemelle, Jr., was assigned to produce the film, and the director chosen was Lewis Milestone, a Ukrainian immigrant who had served in World War I. Two of the film's writers, Maxwell Anderson and George Abbott, were celebrated playwrights. The result was a film that is considered one of the best war movies ever made.

Modris Eksteins, writing a historical overview of the film for *History Today* in 1955, calls attention to Sydney Carroll's review in the *Sunday Times* when the film was released. Carroll told his readers, "I hate it." Eksteins explains that Carroll was uncomfortable with the film and said, "It made me shudder. It brought the war back to me as nothing has ever done before since 1918." Carroll further explains that he admired the film, too, for the same realism that had disturbed him.

By the end of 1930, the film was recognized as a masterpiece in its own right. It was nominated for numerous Academy Awards, and it won the best picture and best director awards. It was also given *Photoplay Magazine*'s Gold Medal Award for the best picture of the year. The director, Milestone, and star, Ayres, both became overnight sensations.

As the Nazi party rose to power in Germany in the early 1930s, the film, like the novel, was banned from the country it was set in. A 1930 showing in Berlin was disrupted by Nazis who ran through the theater, set off stink bombs, and threw beer bottles. A 1939 rerelease took advantage of Americans' distrust of the Nazis to add a sentimental beginning and end and segments of anti-German propaganda, to which Milestone objected.

As the years passed, the film was still considered a unique achievement. It was ranked number fifty-four on the American Film Institute's *100*

Years . . . 100 Movies list in 1998 and number seven on the institute's 2008 list of ten best epic films. Reviewing the 1997 restoration done under the guidance of the Library of Congress, Clyde Jeavons, writing in the *Sunday Times*, calls it "an enduring masterpiece—perhaps the most effective war film ever made." Philip Kerr, in the *New Statesman*, notes its many powerful elements, advising that "this newly restored version should on no account be missed." He feels a personal connection to the film: "I will never forget the first time I saw *All Quiet on the Western Front* and, like many men and women of my postwar generation, I suspect that of all the anti-war pictures . . . it had the most profound influence on my subsequent and enduring pacifism."

CRITICISM

David Kelly

Kelly is a college instructor of creative writing and literature. In the following essay, he analyzes the final moments of All Quiet on the Western Front *and their part in making the film an antiwar statement with lasting power.*

Eighty years have passed since Paramount Studios released its adaptation of Erich Maria Remarque's *All Quiet on the Western Front*, but the film still stands as one of the fiercest and most moving indictments of war ever made, nearly as significant a piece of literature as the source novel itself. The film does show its age. Its expressive acting style can seem almost insulting to viewers who have been raised in a post-Method generation. However, adjusting for changing trends and expectations, the film still stands as one of the great antiwar statements of the twentieth century.

One reason for the movie's enduring power is the nature of the war that inspired it. The scope of World War I was enormous, of course; it spread across Europe into Africa and Asia, threatening North America. However, the ability of one war to encircle the globe was just an aftereffect of its modern industrial nature. More terrible and unforgettable than its range were the means of fighting, from air attacks above to trench warfare below. The basic premise of all wars is that soldiers are disposable, as replicable as parts in a machine, but World War I and the technologies that were developed for it pushed that premise to conclusions beyond the reach of the imagination. It

> THE FILM'S FIRST TWO HOURS ARE ABOUT BREAKING DOWN PAUL'S IDEALS, ONE BY ONE, BUT THE FINAL MOVEMENT IS NECESSARY TO SHOW PROSPECTIVE WARRIORS HOW A DISILLUSIONED MAN CAN STILL BE CRUSHED."

created a profound impact on a generation's philosophy about human existence.

It was the perverse fortune of Carl Laemelle, Jr., the film's producer, and Lewis Milestone, its director, that the horrors of this particular war were so very personal and graphic. The advent of air combat—which had earned the silent film *Wings* the first Academy Award for Best Production in 1928—also made for stunning effects in a film about ground troops, filling the sound track with the constant thunder of explosions and filling the screen with plumes of dirt flying up from the battlefield, as well as providing the story with the possibility that anything might explode at any time. The trench system that was so prevalent during World War I provided the filmmakers with a graphic way to illustrate the war's psychological constraints. War films had always shown troops running across open ground, but the soldier's tedium in his down-time and claustrophobia in battle are not very visual without the trenches. And then there was the gas. Before the use of color film to show blazing bright explosions in vibrant red and yellow, what else could serve for filmmakers as an image of death made manifest?

Still, war movies are almost always about the horrors of combat and the extremes of existing. *All Quiet on the Western Front* does a superb job of showing modern audiences the terrors of a war fought in a way that wars are not fought anymore, using filmmaking techniques that have been improved every year since it was made. What makes it still work as a powerful antiwar statement is the power of the storytelling on display. This is nowhere more apparent than in the film's final twelve minutes, crafted so carefully that they can stand up against any twelve minutes of any film, ever.

WHAT DO I SEE NEXT?

- A new version of *All Quiet on the Western Front* was made in 1979 for broadcast on television. Though not as critically acclaimed as the 1930 version, it does have an all-star cast of Richard Thomas, Ernest Borgnine, Ian Holm, and Patricia Neal, and was directed by legendary director Delbert Mann. It was released on DVD in 2002 by Lion's Gate.

- Michael Cimino's epic film *The Deer Hunter* tells a story similar to this one, about a group of friends who go off to fight in Vietnam and end up physically and emotionally wounded and unable to understand the world they fought for. The film won five Academy Awards, including best picture for 1978, and stars Robert De Niro, Christopher Walken, John Savage, and John Cazale. It was released on DVD by MCA/Universal Home Video in 1998.

- One of the most powerful antiwar movies ever made is one of the first films made by Stanley Kubrik, who later gained fame for his groundbreaking work in science fiction (*2001: A Space Odyssey*) and horror (*The Shining*). Kubrik's 1957 film *Paths of Glory*, starring Kirk Douglas, Ralph Meeker, and Adolph Menjeau, concerns a platoon of French soldiers in World War I who refuse to carry out an order that will lead them to certain death, and are prosecuted for it. It is available on DVD from MGM.

- Set at the same time as this film, Tsui Hark's 1986 film *Peking Opera Blues* mixes a number of genres, including action, political intrigue, romance, and even some comedy to give a sense of what life in China was like while Europe was embroiled in war. It is available in Cantonese with English subtitles from Image Entertainment.

- Director Robert Altman lampooned the absurdity of war with 1960s sensibilities in his 1970 release *M∗A∗S∗H*, a comedy about the operations of a Mobile Army Surgical Hospital during the Korean War of the early 1950s. Starring Eliot Gould and Donald Sutherland as the head surgeons, the film is much sharper and more critical than the long-running television series it inspired. Richard Hooker and Ring Lardner, Jr., wrote the adaptation of Hooker's novel. It is available on DVD from Twentieth Century Fox.

- The film *Jarhead*, based on the memoirs of U.S. Marine Anthony Swofford about his experiences in the Gulf War in 2003, depicts a sudden immersion into combat that mirrors the feeling of horror and futility depicted in *All Quiet on the Western Front*, but with modern sensibilities. It stars Jake Gyllenhaal, Peter Sarsgaard, and Jamie Foxx. The film was in theaters in 2005 and was released on DVD the following year by Universal, the same studio that produced *All Quiet on the Western Front*.

- Acclaimed director John Huston adapted Stephen Crane's classic Civil War novel *The Red Badge of Courage* to film in 1951, casting real war hero Audie Murphy and real war correspondent Bill Maudlin in the leads. The film is famous for having been changed by the studio that released it, to soften its antiwar focus. It is available on DVD from Warner Home Video.

- Producer Ian Stokell has announced that Daniel Radcliffe, who played Harry Potter in the popular series of films, and Bernard Hill will star in a remake of *All Quiet on the Western Front*, scheduled to be released in theaters in 2012.

The film follows the brutal war experience of Paul Bäumer up to that point, showing what have since become standards of the war film. It shows food shortages and the soldiers taking food from unarmed populations. It shows the bonding between men of equal rank and their disdain for those who have risen unfairly into positions of superiority. It shows the constant danger and the nerves of strong men that eventually fray. These are experiences familiar to every soldier.

In its last half, however, the film focuses more and more on Paul's experience. He kills a French soldier with his knife and is trapped with him while the man slowly dies, a situation that nearly drives Paul insane. He is injured and put in a hospital, expecting not to survive. He goes home on leave, and civilian life sickens him; the people at home, who think just as he once did, have no sense of life at the front. He has nowhere to turn but to the trenches once again, to a life he despises but at least understands.

When Paul returns to the front, director Milestone and his cinematographer, Arthur Edeson, briefly create a vision of purgatory—a war zone without war, thick with pathos and grief. The film's first two hours are about breaking down Paul's ideals, one by one, but the final movement is necessary to show prospective warriors how a disillusioned man can still be crushed.

This surreal experience starts with Paul walking through a ravaged town, looking for the address where he will find his company stationed. He is followed by a horse-drawn wagon, which is not particularly notable until Paul reaches his destination. Then he stops and stares at the wagon as it passes by, as if first noticing that the machinery-heavy war he left behind has been replaced with a more primitive environment.

At the door of the house, Paul scans the young faces of the new members of Second Company, finding them all unfamiliar. The boy at the door says he is sixteen years old, like the schoolboys who jeered Paul and called him a coward as he spoke at his old school. The boy expresses the optimism that relief troops are soon to be sent, a naïve hope to which Paul has no response. He is one of the old men of the war now.

Inside, he and a senior man of the company discuss with casual sadness those who have died since Paul went away. Their breath steams in the cold air as they talk, but they show no sign of noticing the cold. Paul suddenly panics about the fate of Kat. When he arrived at the war zone, Kat was his protector, a father figure. He goes out and finds Kat in a surreal landscape, a battlefield that is scarred with bomb craters and damaged trees but devoid of human life. They wave to each other across the distance, and when they do a lone plane, high in the air, lets loose a bomb. The two old soldiers dutifully drop and cover their heads, following the proper protocol almost without noticing, and then they continue their reunion.

In the scene, there are two men standing face-to-face. They are not centered, however, but stand on the right half of the screen. The space on the left side is dominated by a dead tree. As Paul describes his experiences away from the war, he speaks to Kat, once his mentor, as a peer. After all the deaths and charged emotions, the film comes down to one thing that people who have never seen a battlefield can understand: friendship. "You're all I've got left," Paul tells Kat, and the hardened old soldier replies, softly, "I missed you, Paul."

After an emotional exchange like that, Kat's death should come as no surprise, but Milestone films it in a way that properly makes it the most moving experience of the war. The warmth of their reunion is contrasted with the single, solo plane in the sky, as if it is carrying on a war against just these two. Kat apparently dies twice, actually. The first bomb to fall near them seems lethal, but he turns out to be all right except for a broken shin. Paul lifts him up on his shoulders and carries him, looking like a hero. The shrapnel from the second bomb makes such a small gash in Kat's neck that Paul does not notice it until Kat is pronounced dead at the hospital. The point being made by the film here is that death is absurd, coming from the smallest causes when it is least expected.

The real end of the film is Paul Bäumer's death, introduced by a shot of a field even emptier than the one where he found Kat. In the background is the mournful sound of a harmonica, and the trenches are half full of water. Paul has a bitter look on his face—he has nothing to live for anymore, but then he sees a butterfly. For a moment there is a chance that life might be worth something, and he smiles. The camera does not show his death, only his hand as he reaches out beyond the safety of his bunker, cross-cut with a sniper who looks like the man Paul killed earlier, taking aim. A shot rings out, and Paul's hand recoils almost immediately, then slowly drops.

The film follows Paul's death with two quick sequences. The first takes two clichés of the war movie—ghostly footage of those who have died and a cemetery filled with thousands and thousands of tombstones—and shows them simultaneously, with the moving footage of memory superimposed over the stationary field. As a reminder that war is horrible and young men die, it seems unnecessary, lacking the impact of the sudden death of the film's central character. Milestone follows it, however, with a very moving tribute. Before the words "The End" appear, the screen goes black for ten long seconds.

It is in that blackness that the filmmakers make their statement about the pointlessness and sorrow of war. After more than two hours of battle against the enemy, the army, and his peers at home, followed by twelve minutes of wandering in a strange, heartless landscape, there is nothing more to be said about the experience except darkness.

This is the art of filmmaking. It is not difficult to arouse viewers' interest with things exploding, or to stir their emotions with the deaths of characters they have gotten to know. It is difficult, however, to give viewers a moving experience that will stay with them. From decade to decade and culture to culture, *All Quiet on the Western Front* has constantly proven its relevance. Wars change and film technology changes, but a well-wrought story can last forever.

Source: David Kelly, Critical Essay on *All Quiet on the Western Front*, in *Novels for Students*, Gale, Cengage Learning, 2011.

Geoff Pevere

In the following excerpt, Pevere explains that All Quiet on the Western Front *reflected the anti-war sentiment of the period.*

The Academy Awards' third Best Picture began shooting on Armistice Day in 1929. The timing could not have been coincidental. Based on Erich Maria Remarque's searing autobiographical novel, *All Quiet on the Western Front* harrowingly depicted the experiences of a number of fresh-faced German soldiers who are destroyed, physically and spiritually, by their experiences in the killing trenches of World War I.

Although publishers had initially rejected Remarque's German-language novel as too bleak, it had become something of an international sensation by the time Universal chief Carl Laemmle secured the movie rights.

No expense was spared. At a cost of $1.2 million (U.S.), the hell of the European trenches was recreated in Los Angeles. Under the meticulous supervision of the 34-year-old Russian-born director Lewis Milestone (born Lev Milstein), real explosives were used to create the apocalyptically lunar landscape of the front, and the young cast—headed by the 21-year-old pacifist and big band banjo player Lew Ayres—was literally dragged through countless gallons of ready-made mud.

Even though sound was still in its infancy, and many theatres in North America remained unequipped for it, Milestone insisted the film convey not only the visual spectacle of war but the sound: the screaming of incoming mortars, the drone of bombers, the sound of the wounded crying in the night.

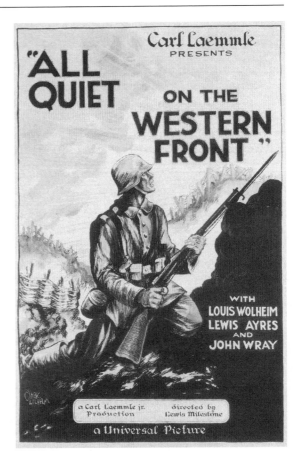

Getty Images

When the American Legion learned that the movie was intending to depict German soldiers in a sympathetic light, it threatened the production with pickets and boycotts, but nothing could be done to stop the momentum once the picture opened. For all its unflinching horror—which still carries a visceral charge more than 75 years later—*All Quiet on the Western Front* was both a popular and critical smash. Wrote one critic: "The League of Nations could make no better investment than to buy the master print, reproduce it in every nation to show every year until the word 'war' is taken out of the dictionary."

On Oscar night in 1930, held at the Coconut Grove in Los Angeles, *All Quiet on the Western Front* was declared Best Picture. Milestone took home the statuette for Best Director. Both were considered well earned.

It would be the first in a long line of liberal-minded anti-war movies to get Academy approval, and its influence was felt across the decades in such Best Pictures as *The Deer Hunter* and

Platoon. But if the movie reflected the popular sense of anti-war sentiment that coursed through the literature and movies of the period (much like Vietnam novels and films of the 1970s), that would change abruptly with Pearl Harbor.

When actor Ayres, a vegetarian and conscientious objector, announced his refusal to fight in World War II, studios refused to hire him and theatres declined to show his films. His career seemed over. But he redeemed himself by volunteering for non-combatant medical service and participating in three Pacific beachhead landings. In 1948, Ayres was presented with the ultimate gesture of industry rehabilitation: an Oscar nomination for his performance in *Johnny Belinda.*

Source: Geoff Pevere, "From the Trenches to the Highways," in *Toronto Star,* February 11, 2006, p. H2.

Philip Kerr

In the following review, Kerr contends that All Quiet on the Western Front *was ahead of its time in terms of camera work and dialogue.*

As Michael Hofmann makes clear in the introduction to his excellent new translation of Ernst Junger's book *Storm of Steel,* (. . .) Erich Maria Remarque's *All Quiet on the Western Front* was neither the first memoir of the First World War (it was published in 1929) nor the best. "Ernst Junger's book," wrote Andre Gide in 1942, "is without question the finest book on war that I know."

I wouldn't disagree with that. Even so, it's easy to see why Carl Laemmle, then head of Universal Pictures, should have chosen to purchase Remarque's book instead of Junger's. Of *Storm of Steel,* Hofmann writes: "It has no pacifist design. It makes no personal appeal. It is a notably unconstructed book. It does not set the author and his experience in any sort of context."

Remarque's book may lack the close detail and atmosphere of Junger's, but it did reflect the pacifism of the 1920s and, in T E Lawrence's phrase, "the distilled bitterness of the generation shot to pieces by the war." Remarque himself was not a Jew, as the Nazis claimed, but a Roman Catholic who, like Paul Baumer, the hero of the book, joined up with his German classmates and, fired by the romantic ideal of defending the Fatherland, went off to the front. Remarque was seriously injured at the Battle of Flanders in 1917, and he spent a year recovering in hospital while his remaining classmates were killed or maimed.

Having bought the book, Laemmle appointed Lewis Milestone to direct. While his version is easily the best, it isn't the only one; another version was made in 1979, starring Richard Thomas and Ernest Borgnine. It is the earlier version that has now been restored to its full glory.

The story is predictable enough. Paul (Lew Ayres) and his friends arrive at the front, the enlisted victims of an aging Prussian schoolmaster's classroom demagoguery. To the amused contempt of the old soldiers who have been there for a while, the new arrivals are full of enthusiasm for the war. The fatherly Kat (Louis Wolheim) takes Paul under his wing as he and his comrades face up to the bitter disillusionment of life and death on the front. None of these characters is particularly heroic. There are no great acts of valour performed by the men, and all that Kat, Paul and their comrades care about is a decent meal, a pretty face, home and survival. It is hard to believe a Hollywood-produced movie could ever end with all the protagonists dead, but that's what happens here, and reveals the final irony in the title. It is quiet on the western front because all of these men, young and old, are dead.

Milestone's camerawork was extremely innovative for its time, and the authenticity of the production is remarkable: the almost documentary-like action sequences provide as realistic a portrayal of the Great War as has ever existed on film. The editing is no less impressive and doubtless reflects Milestone's experience working as D W Griffiths's editor on *The Birth of a Nation.* But where the film really scores—and remember, this picture was one of the first "talkers"—is in the dialogue, in the scenes between Kat and Paul and, most famously, in the scene that takes place in a shell-hole between Paul and a French soldier he has mortally wounded—surely one of the most moving scenes in cinema history. Without wishing to take anything away from Milestone, I suspect that George Cukor, the film's line producer and dialogue coach, may have had a lot to do with the excellence of these particularly human scenes.

The film won the Best Picture Academy Award in 1930 and this newly restored version should on no account be missed. I will never forget the first time I saw *All Quiet on the Western Front* and, like many men and women of my postwar generation, I suspect that of all the anti-war pictures—*La Grande Illusion* (1937), *Paths of Glory* (1957), *Dr Strangelove* (1964), *Oh! What a Lovely War* (1969)—it had the most profound influence on my subsequent and enduring pacifism.

Tony Blair is only three years older than I am, and I find it almost incomprehensible that someone from a generation who came of age during the Vietnam war, who read the war poets and R C Sheriff's *Journey's End* at school, who listened to the songs of Joan Baez and John Lennon, who saw the war protesters on TV, and who must surely once have seen this marvellous film, could march this country into so many military conflicts.

If the film has one simple message, it is this: that all men are brothers. I suspect that the two million people who marched through London on 15 February 2003 felt exactly the same way.

Source: Philip Kerr, "Band of Brothers: Philip Kerr on the Re-release of the Great War Movie That Made Him a Pacifist," in *New Statesman*, Vol. 132, No. 4663, November 10, 2003, p. 44.

SOURCES

All Quiet on the Western Front (DVD), Universal Studios, 2007.

Carroll, Sydney, Review of *All Quiet on the Western Front*, quoted by Modris Eksteins in *History Today*, November 1995, p. 29.

De Groot, Gerald, "Origins," in *The First World War*, Palgrave, 2001, pp. 1–22.

Duffy, Michael, "The Causes of World War One," in *First World War.com*, August 22, 2009, http://www.firstworldwar.com/origins/causes.htm (accessed August 15, 2010).

Jeavons, Clyde, "*All Quiet on the Western Front*: End of the Talkie Straightjacket Brings Joy to Pacifists," in *Sunday Times* (London, England), February 9, 2003, p. 7.

Kerr, Philip, "Band of Brothers," in *New Statesman*, November 10, 2003, p. 44.

Remarque, Erich Maria, *All Quiet on the Western Front*, translated by A. W. Wheen, Little, Brown, 1993.

Storey, William Kelleher, "The Arts of War," in *The First World War: A Concise Global History*, Rowman & Littlefield, 2009, pp. 95–99.

FURTHER READING

Chambers, John Whiteclay II, "*All Quiet on the Western Front* (1930): The Antiwar Film and the Image of the First World War," in *Historic Journal of Film, Radio, and Television*, Vol. 13, No. 4, 1994, pp. 277–311.
    Chambers's scholarly essay concerns the significance of this film at the time when it was released.

Chapman, James, *War and Film*, Reaktion Press, 2008.
    Any survey of war movies has to include *All Quiet on the Western Front*, as Chapman does,

but his extensive knowledge of the field allows him to put this film solidly in perspective with others of the genre.

Gordon, Haim, "Heroism, Friendship, and History," in *Heroism and Friendship in the Novels of Erich Maria Remarque*, Peter Lang, 2003, pp. 125–37.
    Lang's book offers an interesting comparative study of Remarque's fiction, with this particular chapter focused on *All Quiet on the Western Front*.

Hilliard, Robert L., *Hollywood Speaks Out: Pictures That Dared to Protest Real World Issues*, Wiley-Blackwell, 2009.
    Hilliard includes a chapter about war films, but he also puts them in a wider perspective by covering other genres, such as poverty, racism, and homophobia.

Kelly, Andrew, *Filming "All Quiet on the Western Front,"* I.B. Tauris, 1998.
    Kelly provides a book-length examination of the complexities involved in creating one of the most powerful films in the history of cinema in just a few months.

Krimmer, Elisabeth, *The Representation of War in German Literature: From 1800 to the Present*, Cambridge University Press, 2010.
    Although the studio system of making movies gave this film a particularly American tone, Remarque's novel, considered groundbreaking at the time, fits into the wide scope of German war writings, as Krimmer explains in this book.

Millichap, Joseph, *Lewis Milestone*, Twayne Publishers, 1981.
    This book, part of Twayne's "Filmmakers" series, is one of the most complete surveys of the director's career available.

SUGGESTED SEARCH TERMS

Erich Maria Remarque

All Quiet on the Western Front

Lewis Milestone AND Erich Maria Remarque

Lewis Ayres AND All Quiet on the Western Front

Lew Ayres AND conscientious objector

Carl Laemelle AND All Quiet on the Western Front

Universal Studio AND war film

All Quiet on the Western Front AND antiwar

Erich Maria Remarque AND Hollywood

All Quiet on the Western Front AND cinematography

World War I AND cinema

Great War AND Germany AND pacifism

All the Pretty Horses

CORMAC McCARTHY
1992

Cormac McCarthy is considered one of the leading writers of the late twentieth and early twenty-first centuries. His novel *All the Pretty Horses*, published in 1992, was the work that secured that reputation. The novel was an instant best seller, popular with both critics and readers, and it was honored with a National Book Award and a National Book Critics Award. Beginning in 1949, the plot features sixteen-year-old John Grady Cole, a cowboy who travels with his best friend, Lacey Rawlins, from Texas to Mexico. Their travels lead them to murders, horse robberies, a forbidden and star-crossed love affair, and a stint in a Mexican prison, yet, for all of the masculine and action-packed adventure, *All the Pretty Horses* is a thoughtful and philosophical novel. Themes include the possibility of God's existence and the unnamed and unknown spiritual bond that exists between men, the land, their horses, and one another. *All the Pretty Horses* is a coming-of-age novel that traces John Grady's loss of innocence and idealism, a loss that is mirrored in Mexico's political history.

While it is mostly read as a stand-alone novel, *All the Pretty Horses* is the first volume in the "Border Trilogy," followed by *The Crossing* (1994) and *Cities of the Plain* (1998). The Vintage paperback edition of McCarthy's modern classic has remained in print since 1993.

Cormac McCarthy (WireImage)

AUTHOR BIOGRAPHY

McCarthy was born Charles McCarthy on July 20, 1933, in Providence, Rhode Island. He is the first son and third child (of six) born to Charles Joseph and Gladys Christina McCarthy. The McCarthy family moved to Knoxville, Tennessee, when McCarthy was four, and his father began working as a lawyer for the Tennessee Valley Authority. McCarthy studied liberal arts at the University of Tennessee from 1951 to 1952 and then enlisted in the U.S. Air Force in 1953. After a four-year tour (some sources say three years), he returned to the University of Tennessee, but he left without a degree in 1959. The early short stories he wrote as a student earned him an Ingram-Merrill Award for creative writing in 1960. The following year, McCarthy married the poet Lee Holleman, whom he met at the University of Tennessee. The couple had a son, Cullen, before divorcing a few years later.

In 1965, McCarthy published his first novel, *The Orchard Keeper*, and married Anne DeLisle in 1966 (some sources say 1967). The couple traveled throughout Europe before settling in Tennessee in 1967. In 1968, *Outer Dark*, McCarthy's second

novel, was published. His first two books received positive reviews, but his third novel, *Child of God* (1973), was met with mixed critiques. In 1976, McCarthy and DeLisle separated, divorcing a few years later. McCarthy moved to El Paso, Texas. His fourth book, *Suttree*, which McCarthy had been working on for nearly twenty years, was published in 1979. It was widely hailed as a masterpiece.

In 1985, McCarthy authored *Blood Meridian; or, The Evening Redness in the West*. The book was his first western, set in Texas and Mexico during the 1840s. It was overlooked by critics at first, but has since been referenced as a pivotal work in McCarthy's career. It was followed in 1992 by a second Western, *All the Pretty Horses*. The novel was McCarthy's first best seller and winner of a National Book Award and a National Book Critics Award. The book was the first installment in the "Border Trilogy," which includes *The Crossing* (1994) and *Cities of the Plain* (1998). Also in 1998, McCarthy married Jennifer Winkley, with whom he had a son, John.

McCarthy's tenth novel, *No Country for Old Men* (2005), fared well with both readers and critics. It was eclipsed, however, in 2006 by *The Road*, a best seller that was awarded the Pulitzer Prize in 2007. The popularization of McCarthy's work has risen after the release of three major film adaptations of his novels, *All the Pretty Horses*, *No Country for Old Men*, and *The Road*. As of 2010, McCarthy was writing and living in El Paso. He is considered one of America's greatest living writers.

PLOT SUMMARY

I

Told by an omniscient third-person narrator, *All the Pretty Horses* begins in San Angelo, Texas, in 1949 as John Grady Cole gazes at his grandfather's corpse. The ranch his grandfather founded in 1872 has now passed to his mother, and it is clear she intends to sell it. John loves the ranch and hopes to keep it. At the funeral, John sees his father, who stands apart from the other mourners.

John meets his father, who is staying at a hotel in town. They have dinner and speak to one another in clipped sentences. It is clear that John's mother and father are separated (and later John learns that they are divorced). This lessens John's chances of keeping the ranch in

MEDIA ADAPTATIONS

- In 2000, *All the Pretty Horses* was adapted as a film of the same title starring Matt Damon, Henry Thomas, and Penelope Cruz. The movie was released by Columbia Pictures.
- Several audio recordings of *All the Pretty Horses* exist, but the 2005 Random House edition features the entire "Border Trilogy" read by Brad Pitt.

the family. Later, John is on the ranch speaking with his best friend, Lacey Rawlins. When he goes back inside, he has a brief and uncomfortable exchange with his mother.

John's mother is an actress who has a habit of disappearing, a habit that began when John was only a baby. She leaves, and when she returns, John tries to lease the ranch from her. She refuses, saying the ranch is not profitable and that he is too young, only sixteen. By Christmas, John's mother is gone all the time. He informs the ranch hands of the impending sale. He leaves the next morning, hitchhiking to San Antonio, where it is snowing. John watches his mother perform in a play, but she does not know he is there. The next morning he goes to her hotel and sees her leave with a strange man. She does not see him, and he returns to San Angelo.

A few months later, John is riding with his father, who is frail and looking at the world as if he is seeing it for the first time. They go to eat in town at a cafe and John's father says that, although John's mother would often disappear, she always came back because of her son. He would like to see them reconcile.

John and Rawlins talk about leaving town. The ranch sale will be final in June. Rawlins debates going with his friend. John says he will leave regardless: "I'm already gone." Before dawn, John and Rawlins sneak away on their horses. Rawlins is surprised that no one is following them. They are headed to Mexico, and they travel through the desert, shooting game and stopping

now and then in small towns to refresh their supplies. Rawlins jokes that the folks back home have struck oil and become rich, but then he comments that he feels uneasy. Not long after, John says that a man has been following them. They decide to double back and wait for the man to pass by. When he does, they see he is a thirteen-year-old boy on a magnificent horse.

The boy denies following them and claims to be headed to Langtry. He says he is sixteen and that the horse is his, but John and Rawlins believe it is stolen. Because of the stolen horse, they are afraid that they will be arrested if they are seen with the boy. They leave him behind, but John knows that they have not "seen the last" of him. Near the Mexican border, they see a rider a mile away and recognize the boy's horse. The boy gives both John and Rawlins a bad feeling. They wait as the boy approaches, and Rawlins grabs his rifle. The boy assures him that no one will be looking for him in Mexico. He says his name is Jimmy Blevins. Rawlins thinks it is a fake name, taken from a radio broadcaster. John and Rawlins grudgingly allow him to join them, crossing the border together later that night.

John and Rawlins are headed to the big ranches in the south, and as they travel, Blevins reveals himself to be rash and impulsive. Blevins and Rawlins dislike one another and bicker constantly.

One day, when the boys are out of water, they buy liquor from some peasants. Blevins is so drunk he falls off his horse, but he sobers up quickly when he sees a storm coming. Blevins says nearly all the men in his family have been killed by lightning and that he has already been hit by it twice. Although it is impossible, he tries to outride the storm. John and Rawlins continue calmly into the rain. They find Blevins's horse by the side of the road, and then come across Blevins tucked under the roots of a tree wearing only his underwear. He is afraid that the metal in his overalls and boots will attract the lightning. He refuses to move.

John and Rawlins continue down the road and shelter under a tree. They go to find Blevins the next morning. His horse has run off, and his clothes have been washed away. John gives Blevins his spare shirt and sets the boy behind him on his horse. Low on supplies, they stop at a ramshackle camp and ask for food. They eat with twelve Mexicans who offer to buy Blevins, and the boys leave immediately. Blevins is determined to find his horse, and Rawlins knows no good will come of it. He says, "Somethin bad is goin to happen."

The next morning they see a man with Blevins's pistol, and further down the road they find his horse in an abandoned house. Rawlins knows that trying to steal back the horse will only lead to trouble. John agrees, but he cannot bring himself to abandon the boy. Blevins is impulsive and will likely get himself killed trying to retrieve his horse and gun. Rawlins would have left Blevins behind long ago if not for John. They make Blevins promise to forget about his gun, but they agree to get his horse.

Just before dawn, the boys attempt to steal back Blevins's horse. It is gone, and Blevins runs off. Finally, Blevins reappears, riding his horse with pistol shots ringing out behind him. Blevins's horse is the fastest, and he takes off to draw the men chasing them away from John and Rawlins. They plan to reunite later. John and Rawlins head into the wild, but they are soon out of food. The horses are also starving. John and Rawlins wonder how Blevins is doing, and Rawlins repeats John's earlier statement that they have not seen the last of him. The boys eventually find water and shoot a deer. Rawlins again wonders about Blevins and admits that he does not want him to come to harm.

John and Rawlins continue to make their way south, finally cresting the mountains to reveal a fertile valley and the ranches below. The next day, they happen upon cattle and *vaqueros* (the Spanish word for cowboys). John and Rawlins join them and help herd the cattle. On the way into the ranch, a beautiful girl on a black horse rides by. John is awestruck. He later learns that her name is Alejandra; she is the ranch owner's daughter.

That night John and Rawlins meet with the ranch manager. They are hired and sent to the bunkhouse. John says he would like to stay there for "about a hundred years."

II

The ranch is in a beautiful and fertile valley, and it is owned by Don Héctor Rocha y Villareal. His wife lives in Mexico City, and his daughter splits her time between their two homes. John and Rawlins have been on the ranch for a few days when the *vaqueros* bring in sixteen wild horses. John claims he can tame them in only four days, an astonishing feat. Given the area's wild horse population, this would mean huge ongoing profits

for the ranch. John does as he claims, and on the third day, he is out riding one of the newly broken horses. Alejandra rides by and nods in greeting. Another few days later, John and Rawlins are sent with a small group to capture more horses. Their cook, Luis, an ex-soldier, tells them stories about the war and about horses' souls. Three weeks later, the men have captured eighty horses and tamed most of them.

On the second day of May (the first time a specific date is given), John is invited to the ranch house to meet Don Héctor. The house is filled with finery, and John and Don Héctor discuss John's background and horse breeding. Don Héctor intends to breed a thoroughbred to some of the newly captured mares. John is offered a position as the horse master and moved into a private room in the barn. He often runs into Alejandra in the barn when she is taking her horse out or bringing it back in. While Luis, John, Rawlins, and the other men are out capturing horses, John and Rawlins talk about her.

John and Rawlins take some of the horses to market in town. They buy some new clothes and boots. That night, they go to a dance hall, where John has arranged to meet Alejandra. After they dance together, John and Alejandra buy lemonade and go for a walk. They tell one another about their lives.

During the third week of May, the thoroughbred arrives. When the horse is not being used to stud, John rides it out onto the land. At times, he sees Alejandra out riding or smells her perfume in the ranch house. He finally encounters her one morning while riding the stallion bareback. Alejandra switches her horse with his and John sneaks her horse back into the barn. He is afraid they will get into trouble if he is caught.

Alejandra's great aunt and godmother, Dueña Alfonsa, also lives in the ranch house. John has never seen her, but she invites him to play chess with her. He is well into the game before he notices that two fingers are missing from her left hand. She explains that she lost them in a shooting accident. They talk about chess and dreams. Dueña Alfonsa says she knows about his friendship with Alejandra, and she warns him of the damage it will do to the girl's reputation. She says John and Alejandra cannot be seen alone together.

Five nights later, John is asleep in his room when Alejandra knocks on his door. Alejandra is upset that they cannot be together. They go for a ride in the middle of the night, when no one can see them, and they do so almost every night after. One night, they go swimming and declare their love for one another. Soon Alejandra is sneaking into his bedroom and back into the ranch house before dawn. She does this for nine nights before returning to Mexico City.

Don Héctor invites John to play pool with him. The billiards table is in the ranch house's old chapel. As they play, Don Héctor tells John about his family's history. He says that Alejandra will likely be going to France to go to school.

John wants to ask Alejandra to marry him, but he learns she has returned to the ranch without coming to see him. When they are out in the mountains, John and Rawlins wonder if Don Héctor knows about John and Alejandra's affair. Three greyhounds appear at their fire and then disappear, as if they are ghosts. Rawlins wonders if the dogs belong to Don Héctor; he thinks the Don might be hunting him and John.

When John and Rawlins return to the ranch, the *vaqueros* seem to be avoiding them. The next morning they are arrested before dawn.

III

For three days, John and Rawlins ride their horses handcuffed, escorted by six rangers. They are not told the reason for their arrest. Rawlins does not speak to John until they reach La Encantada, the town where they recaptured Blevins's horse. Their horses are seized, and they are jailed. Blevins is in the cell. He admits he returned to the town to retrieve his pistol and killed a man in the process. John and Rawlins are taken separately to be interrogated by the captain, who does not believe their story. Three days later, John, Rawlins, and Blevins are loaded onto a truck with some guards, the captain, and a *charro* (a horseman; the word can also mean "bad man"). John later learns that the *charro* is the brother of the man Blevins killed. They believe they are being taken to the large prison in Saltillo. On the way, they stop at an abandoned estate. The charro, the captain, and some of the guards take Blevins into the woods. A while later John and Rawlins hear two shots. The men return without Blevins, carrying his empty handcuffs.

John and Rawlins are put back on the truck and taken to Saltillo. Their names are not on the prison's official roll call; there is no record of their existence. They spend the next few days fighting off other prisoners, and John loses two teeth in the process. Another two days pass and

they meet with the head prisoner, Emilio Pérez. He offers to help them buy their way out of prison, but the boys have no money.

Rawlins is later attacked by a man with a knife. He is wounded, but not fatally. John takes him to the guardhouse for treatment and then passes the next three days alone. He goes to Pérez to find out what happened to Rawlins, but Pérez only speaks of God, Americans, and evil. John then buys a knife in the prison yard. He is attacked by a boy in the dining hall and thinks he is going to die. He manages to kill the boy, but not without sustaining several knife wounds. He spends several days in the infirmary, and he thinks he will never see his father again. He thinks of Alejandra and "about horses and they were always the right thing to think about."

Eventually the prison's *commandante* brings John into his office, hands him an envelope of money, and tells him that Rawlins is waiting for him outside and that he is very lucky. A few minutes later, the boys are boarding a bus that takes them into the center of town. At a restaurant, John guesses that Dueña Alfonsa paid for their release. He intends to go back to the ranch to retrieve Alejandra, but Rawlins tells him not to. It is clear that Rawlins is no longer willing to put himself in harm's way for his friend.

They rent a hotel room, buy some new clothes, and purchase a bus ticket for Rawlins, who leaves the next morning. John spends the next week healing and exploring the city. He finds a surgeon to take out his stitches and then leaves town.

IV

John hitches rides on his way to the ranch. When he arrives, he goes to the ranch manager's house, where he is informed that Don Héctor and Alejandra are in Mexico City. He goes to the ranch house to see Dueña Alfonsa. She tells him about the Mexican Revolution and the family friends who fomented and ultimately fell victim to it. She speaks of God and blood and fate, of beliefs and ideals and their deadly cost. She confirms John's suspicion that she paid for his release but only with the condition that Alejandra agree never to see him again. John is still determined to see her, but the Dueña is confident that the girl will keep her promise. She even gives John money and a horse before sending him on his way.

John makes his way to a town and calls Alejandra, and she agrees to meet him in Zacatecas. He boards the horse Dueña Alfonsa gave him and stores his guns and bedroll before taking a train there. They declare their love for each other, and John asks her to marry him, but she refuses and says she must return home. They spend the night together in a hotel and then walk around the city the next day before she boards her train, crying as she leaves him. John goes to their hotel, checks out, goes to a bar, and gets very drunk. He wakes in a strange place and cannot remember much of the previous night. His luggage and most of his money are gone. He leaves Zacatecas to retrieve the horse and his bedroll. He buys supplies and rides north.

At a crossroads, John sees a sign for La Encantada and decides to get his own horse back. He returns to the jail, abducts the captain, and makes him lead the way to the horse. The captain takes John to the *charro*'s house, where they find Rawlins's horse. John holds both men at gunpoint, and they take him to another house where his and Blevins's horses are stabled. A gunfight ensues, and John is shot in the leg. He manages to escape with the horses and the captain without shooting anyone. John knows he is being pursued. In the wild, he releases the horse given to him by Dueña Alfonsa. That night, he cauterizes his wound. He and the captain keep riding throughout the night and the next day. On the second night, John handcuffs the captain to a saddle and goes to sleep. In the morning, John wakes to a group of men with guns. They are not his pursuers, but they release the captain and give John a blanket before going on their way.

John continues to the north. He wakes one morning and knows that his father is dead. When he finally crosses the border into the United States, he learns that it is Thanksgiving Day. He keeps to the borderlands, looking for the rightful owner of Blevins's horse. Eventually the horse is impounded, and John is brought before a judge. John recounts his adventures, and the judge returns the horse to him. That night, John visits the judge and talks of his guilt over killing the boy and of how and why he wanted to kill the captain. He also says he does not know what he would have done if the men in the woods had not freed the captain.

One morning in a cafe, John hears the Jimmy Blevins Gospel Hour on the radio. He learns the show is broadcast out of Del Rio, and he heads there to visit the Reverend Jimmy Blevins and see if the horse belongs to him. It does not. John never finds the rightful owner and heads back to San Angelo in March. He sees Rawlins, who tells him of his father's death. Rawlins also tells John that Abuela, the old ranch hand who raised John and John's mother, is dying. Rawlins asks John if he is going to stay, and he replies, "It aint my country."

John attends Abuela's funeral and thinks that the world does not care "for the living or the dead." He leaves town, and as he rides through the Texas desert, he passes Indians amidst the "bloodred" soil. He and his horse cast a shadow that "passed and paled into the darkening land, the world to come."

CHARACTERS

Abuela

Abuela, the ranch hand who helped raise John and John's mother, is dying when John returns to San Angelo. John attends her funeral before leaving town again. Her death is symbolic because *abuela* is the Spanish word for grandmother. Thus, *All the Pretty Horses* begins with the death of John's grandfather and ends with the death of his metaphorical grandmother.

Alejandra

Alejandra is the seventeen-year-old daughter of the ranch owner who employs John and Rawlins. She splits her time between the ranch and Mexico City, where she goes to school and where her mother lives. John is enamored with her from the first time he sees her. She is a member of the upper class and far removed from John's station in life. John notices an air of sadness in her when he first sees her and again in Zacatecas. This sadness may be due to the burden of her station and the rigid conduct required of her because of it. When John secretly arranges to meet Alejandra at the dance hall, he calls her "pretty," and she replies, "You must be careful what you say." Although Alejandra promises not to see him in order to secure his and Rawlins's release from prison, she agrees to meet him in Zacatecas. They spend the night together and Alejandra says she told her father about the affair and that he has stopped loving her, something she did not think possible. Although John asks Alejandra to marry him, she declines and leaves the next day.

Dueña Alfonsa

Dueña Alfonsa is Alejandra's great aunt and god-mother. When she was young, her closest friends began and gave their lives for the Mexican Revolution. She is a capable chess player who lost two of her fingers in a shooting accident when she was young. Dueña Alfonsa lives at the ranch house and invites John to play chess with her. She warns him that a woman's reputation is all that she has and instructs him to stay away from Alejandra.

After John and Rawlins are arrested, Dueña Alfonsa makes Alejandra promise never to see John again in exchange for payment for their release. When John leaves prison and returns to the ranch for Alejandra, she talks to him of God and fate, ideas, ideals, and the Mexican Revolution. Given that the story is told mostly through brief vignettes, this passage is remarkable because it is one of the longest in the entire novel.

Jimmy Blevins

Jimmy Blevins is the thirteen-year-old boy who follows John and Rawlins through the border-lands before being allowed to cross the border with them. He lies about his age and is evasive about his past. Both John and Rawlins believe that his horse is stolen. Jimmy Blevins is most likely a fake name, inspired by a popular radio host. The boy is rash and impulsive and is constantly bickering with Rawlins. He refuses to trade his horse for one not as likely to make people suspicious. He is also prideful, and he sleeps outside after embarrassing himself in front of a kind Mexican family that takes them in for the night.

Blevins's intense fear of being struck by lightning causes him to lose his horse and his clothes, and this leads John and Rawlins into trouble as they help him steal back his horse. Although John and Rawlins make him promise not to go back for his pistol, he does so and kills a man in the process, ultimately causing all three of them to be arrested. When Blevins knows he is about to die, he removes the money from his boot and hands it to John before being led into the woods. His boot lies abandoned in the grass.

Reverend Jimmy Blevins

The Reverend Jimmy Blevins broadcasts a radio gospel show, and Rawlins believes that Blevins's fake name was inspired by this. John travels to see the reverend to see whether Blevins's horse belongs to him.

Captain

The captain is the man who heads up the jail in El Encantada. He interrogates John and Rawlins but does not believe their story. He allows himself to be bribed by the *charro*, the brother of the man Blevins killed. There is no legal death penalty in Mexico, and so the Captain arranges to have Blevins killed in an abandoned estate on the way to the prison in Saltillo. When John returns to La Encantada for his, Rawlins's, and Blevins's horses, he takes the Captain hostage and forces him to ride with him for several days.

Charro

The *charro* is the brother of the man Jimmy Blevins killed, and he bribes the captain to allow him to take his revenge. However, it is not clear who actually shoots Blevins, as the Captain later tells John that the *charro* began to have second thoughts when it was time to kill the boy. Since the captain had already put himself at risk by making the illegal arrangements, he may have been the character who ultimately shot Blevins. Later, John abducts the *charro* at gunpoint, along with the captain, and he forces the *charro* to help retrieve the boys' confiscated horses.

John Grady Cole

John Grady Cole is the protagonist of *All the Pretty Horses*. He is sixteen years old when he decides to leave town with his best friend, Lacey Rawlins. John is a quiet boy and great horseman who loves living and working on his grandfather's ranch. He resents his mother for abandoning him as a child to pursue her acting career and for selling the ranch that has been his only home. He is quiet and thoughtful and very connected to the land. Although he is mostly referred to in the novel as John Grady, he is referred to as a boy whenever he is with his father. John and his father have a close but uneasy relationship. They speak in clipped sentences to one another, yet John awakes one day with the certainty that his father is dead (a feeling that later proves to be correct).

John is kind and refuses to abandon Blevins even though he knows that the boy will get him and Rawlins into trouble. He proves his loyalty again when he makes sure that Rawlins is okay with him moving out of the bunkhouse (he does this before he agrees to become the horse master). John is hopelessly in love with Alejandra and pursues her despite the danger of doing so. With both Blevins and Alejandra, John shows that he is a slave to his feelings even at the risk of personal harm (and harm to others, such as his friend Rawlins). When John and Rawlins are arrested, he calmly accepts his fate, and he and Rawlins are forced to stand helpless as Blevins is shot. He wants to kill the captain in the last chapter because he is angry for being made to feel so powerless.

John again follows his heart instead of his head when he returns to the ranch to retrieve Alejandra after being released from prison. The pain he experiences when she finally leaves him likely encourages him to act recklessly when abducting the captain and stealing back his, Blevins's, and Rawlins's horses. Still, he goes on a pilgrimage to find the rightful owner of Blevins's horse. Perhaps he is seeking absolution (forgiveness) by doing so. By the time Grady has completed his journey, he has killed a man and lost his lover, and his home is no longer his. San Angelo "aint my country," he says, and the novel ends with John riding his horse through the desert, an exile blindly riding into "the world to come."

John Grady Cole's Father
John Grady Cole's father is a poker player who has won and lost great amounts of money. He is divorced from John Grady's mother and is therefore unable to help John challenge his mother's inheritance of the ranch. While he is in town, he meets with his son several times. John loves his father, who stayed behind to raise him whenever his mother would disappear, sometimes for years on end. John's father says she would always return because of her son, and he would like to see them reconcile. John's father was a soldier, though it is not clear which war he fought in. He tells John that he would not have survived without John's mother. John's father leaves an early Christmas gift for his son, a fine saddle, in his hotel room. He does this to avoid any embarrassment.

John Grady Cole's Grandfather
Although John Grady Cole's grandfather is dead when the novel begins, he plays a pivotal role in the plot. John's grandfather leaves his ranch to John's mother, who intends to sell it. This precipitates John's journey to Mexico.

John Grady Cole's Mother
John Grady Cole's mother is an actress who mainly stays in San Antonio, although she once ran off to California. She abandoned her son periodically when he was a child, and she abandons him again when his grandfather dies. She does so literally and figuratively, the latter when she sells the ranch despite John's love for it. After his grandfather dies, John goes to San Antonio and watches his mother in a play, but he does not greet her. The next morning he goes to her hotel and sees her leave with a strange man. She does not see him, and he returns to San Angelo.

Judge
The judge listens to John's story after Blevins's horse has been impounded. In order to assess the truthfulness of the tale, he asks John to repeat some minor details and to show them his gunshot wound. Satisfied, the judge releases John and returns the horse to him. That night, John visits the judge and talks about his guilt over killing the boy in prison and about his conflicting feelings toward the captain. The judge listens and says that John is too hard on himself.

Luis
Luis is the cook and ex-soldier who accompanies John, Rawlins, and the *vaqueros* on their excursions into the mountains to capture wild horses. He tells the men stories about the wars and about horses. He says that horses share a common soul, while men possess no such commonality.

Emilio Pérez
Emilio Pérez is the head prisoner in Saltillo, and he offers to help buy John and Rawlins's freedom. Later, when John visits him to learn where Rawlins was taken after being attacked, Pérez speaks only of human nature and evil and Americans' perceptions of them.

Lacey Rawlins
Lacey Rawlins is John Grady Cole's best friend. Although Rawlins is older, John is clearly the leader. Rawlins is loyal to John, even when he knows that that loyalty will get him into trouble. He knows that they should leave Blevins behind, but he does not do so because John cannot bring himself to abandon the boy. He serves as the reliable sidekick but also as a sort of psychic, he feels uneasy before anything bad happens, and he is constantly warning John of the risks he is taking in sticking by Blevins and in pursuing Alejandra. Rawlins even knows when their time on the ranch is about to end.

Rawlins's loyalty reaches its limit, however, after he and John have been imprisoned. When the ordeal is over and John plans to return for Alejandra, Rawlins buys a bus ticket and returns home. They do not say goodbye to one another, they only say "take care." John is surprised when Rawlins sits where they cannot see one another through the window as the bus pulls away.

In addition to his role as trusty sidekick and foreteller of misfortune, Rawlins is something of a philosopher. He occasionally asks questions about the existence of God and his belief in Judgment Day, referring to John for the answers.

Don Héctor Rocha y Villareal

Don Héctor Rocha y Villareal is the owner of the ranch where John and Rawlins are hired. The ranch has been in his family almost 200 years, and he lives there, which is rare for a man of his class. He plays pool in the ranch house's old chapel, but he does not want a priest to come and deconsecrate it. He says that priests do not have the ability to banish God.

Don Héctor is Alejandra's father and suspects the affair she is having with John before he confirms it. He also suspects that John and Rawlins were the Americans responsible for stealing a horse in La Encantada. When he confirms both of his suspicions, he has John and Rawlins arrested.

THEMES

Existence of God

The existence of God is a prominent theme in *All the Pretty Horses*. It is first touched upon when Rawlins asks John whether or not he believes in Judgment Day. John does, but Rawlins is unsure. This question is striking since, for the most part, the men in the novel speak only of practicalities. Rawlins later asks John if he believes in heaven. Again, John does, and Rawlins is uncertain. These questions, so striking amidst the generally matter-of-fact dialogue, make it clear that Rawlins wonders about the existence of God, yet the novel's general meditations about the spirit of the land and animals around them (specifically the horses) seems to indicate that the novel itself can be seen as a meditative question about God's existence. The answer appears to arrive little more than half-way through the book, when the captain deposits John and Rawlins at the Saltillo prison. He says that "everybody knows that God is no here."

The matter would appear to be settled, but Pérez underlines the captain's assertion when he says that Americans believe too much in "good

TOPICS FOR FURTHER STUDY

- Read John Steinbeck's classic young-adult novel *Of Mice and Men*, which portrays two migrant farm workers, their friendship, and the hardships they endure together, much like *All the Pretty Horses*. In an essay, compare and contrast both novels and their themes.

- *All the Pretty Horses* presents a classic western novel with a post-modern twist. Do library and Internet research on the history and culture of the American West and present your findings to the class in a multimedia presentation or create a Web page on the topic. How has your research enhanced your understanding of the novel?

- One of the less prominent themes in *All the Pretty Horses* references women's rights, particularly in the passages in which Dueña Alfonsa is featured. Stage a class debate about women's rights. Be sure to discuss pertinent excerpts and quotes from the novel. Post a blog to your Web site or social networking site explaining which side of the debate you thought had the best insight into the women's rights movement. Ask your classmates to comment.

- John's travels through Mexico and Texas in *All the Pretty Horses* are extensive. To better understand the distances he traveled, visit a Web site like UMapper.com and create an interactive map of his journey. Attach links to various stops to provide visitors to the map with more information on the places he visited.

things and bad things" and that this "is the superstition of a godless people." The question of God also comes up several times in Dueña Alfonsa's long speech to John, but the most striking example links God and blood (a motif that appears throughout the novel). She states "nothing can be proven except that it be made to bleed. Virgins, bulls, men. Ultimately God himself." Later, when John abducts the captain, the very man who asserted "God is no here," he asks, "Are you no afraid of God?" John replies that he is not, that "he's even got a bone or two to pick with Him."

More positive and reverent portrayals of God are given by the people John briefly encounters while traveling. A man he eats with says grace, noting that without "the will of God...there is neither corn nor growing nor light nor air nor rain nor anything at all save only darkness." Later, as John heads back to the United States, he stops at a cafe and watches a wedding in the town square as he eats. Observing the young couple, the cafe owner comments, "It was good that God kept the truths of life from the young as they were starting out or else they'd have no heart to start at all." In another, albeit indirect, reference to God, John goes to see the Reverend Jimmy Blevins, who broadcasts the word of God into the homes of people from Texas to China. His voice, the reverend's wife comments, can even be heard on Mars.

Loss (Psychology)

Loss permeates the novel, both literally and figuratively. Loss first appears in the novel as death. *All the Pretty Horses* begins with the loss of John's grandfather, which precipitates the loss of the only home John has ever known. Over the course of the novel, John loses his father and his symbolic grandmother. His mother has been lost to him for some time. John experiences loss of love in his ill-fated affair with Alejandra. He loses his job and new home at the ranch because of it. John loses his freedom when he is jailed for his part in Blevins's crimes. More importantly, he loses his innocence when he is forced to kill a man in self-defense. Perhaps John loses his innocence before this, when he is helpless to act as Blevins is being led to his execution. Indeed, the entire novel can be read as a chronicle of John's lost innocence.

John also loses Rawlins's loyalty. Although Rawlins is at first willing to follow John into trouble despite his own misgivings, he is no longer able to do so after being imprisoned. Rawlins leaves John in Mexico, even going so far as to sit on the opposite side of the bus so they cannot see one another when the bus pulls away. Another notable loss is the loss of ideals, which both the Don and the Dueña mention on numerous occasions.

STYLE

Foreshadowing

Foreshadowing occurs when events are hinted at before they happen; it can be as vague as the uneasy feeling that Rawlins gets when they are headed to Mexico or as straightforward as Rawlins's assertion that "somethin bad is goin to happen." Rawlins also predicts that their time on the ranch is drawing to a close only days before they are arrested. In fact, he is the character through which most of the book's foreshadowing occurs. Largely, this is because he serves as the voice of logic and reason throughout. John follows his heart (helping Blevins and falling for Alejandra), even when his heart leads him into grave trouble. Through it all, Rawlins is there to warn him of the risks he is taking. John acknowledges that Rawlins is likely correct, but he proceeds anyhow. For the reader, this produces a sense of anticipation of, and anxiety for, the tragedies that surely await John and Rawlins.

Motif

While motif is generally a musical term for a series of repeating notes or bars that occur throughout a symphony (or even a song), it can also be used to describe a repeating series of symbols or metaphors in a work of literature. In either medium, motifs serve as a means of emphasis; with each repetition, the motif becomes more insistent, more significant. The most notable motifs in *All the Pretty Horses* pertain to horses and blood. Throughout the book, there is mention of the spirits and souls of horses. John feels it and thinks of it often, even dreaming of it. The souls of horses are also explained at length by Luis. Blood is another important motif, and it is seen in the "bloodred" soil, in the blood that is shed by the animals Rawlins and John kill for food, and in the blood they shed (and take) while in prison.

HISTORICAL CONTEXT

Cowboys

The origin of the cowboy can be traced back to medieval Spain. The cattle ranching techniques invented there were eventually adopted in Mexico and then in the American West, beginning in the sixteenth century with the Spanish colonization of Mexico, but because the land in Mexico and the southwestern United States is drier and sparser than that in Spain, cattle herding required greater areas of land. This in turn encouraged the use of horses. Cattle ranching in Mexico was undertaken by *vaqueros* and *charros* (cowboys and horse wranglers). Notably, the use of horses also relied on early Spanish colonizing influences; prehistoric

Matt Damon and Penelope Cruz portray John Grady and Alejandra in the 2000 film adaptation of the novel. *(© Photos 12 | Alamy)*

horses had become extinct on the North American continent, but their modern counterparts were successfully reintroduced by sixteenth-century settlers.

By the mid-1800s, cowboy culture and ranching techniques had spread along trading routes between Mexico and the Southwestern United States. By the late 1800s, railway systems required long cattle drives as herds were moved from isolated transfers to railway centers where cattle could be slaughtered, sold, and shipped throughout the country. The tradition was short lived, however, as the introduction of barbed wire and the shrinking area of undeveloped land on the plains made cattle drives nearly impossible by the 1940s. This time also marked an increased reliance on motorized transportation; the use of cattle trucks became an increasingly viable option to ranchers. Thus, by the time John and Rawlins undertake their journey to Mexico, the cowboy's relevance to the ranching industry was already in decline.

Mexican Revolution

The Mexican Revolution, which began in 1910, asserts a subtle influence on the events and atmosphere of *All the Pretty Horses*. It began after Porfirio Díaz had been in power for over thirty years. By the end of his rule, the gap between the wealthy and poor was immense, and injustice and nepotism prevailed. Francisco I. Madero (of whom Dueña Alfonsa speaks at length in the novel) led a group of young revolutionaries who wanted to establish Mexico as a democracy, and he was arrested in 1910. Madero managed to escape to the United States, where he declared himself the President of Mexico and promised to return land to the peasantry when he was officially instated in office. He appealed to the people to rise against their oppressors on November 20.

In the meantime, Madero enlisted Pascual Orozco and Francisco ("Pancho") Villa to his cause. They proved to be central figures to the revolution, winning the loyalty of the citizens of northern Mexico. Another important figure, Emiliano Zapata, led the rebellion of the people of Morelos in March 1911. Violent uprisings throughout the country soon followed, and Díaz's troops were vanquished by the end of September. Díaz resigned and escaped to France. In 1911, Madero

COMPARE
&
CONTRAST

- **1940s:** Horse ranching in Texas is losing ground to cattle ranching, and by 1946 it is represents only a subsidiary sector of the Texas ranching industry.

  Today: Cattle ranching remains a significant factor in the Texas ranching industry, particularly in central Texas.

- **1940s:** The death penalty in Mexico has been illegal since the passage of the Federal Penal Code of 1930. In the novel, the captain subverts this act by taking a bribe and allows Blevins to be shot without due process.

  Today: The death penalty in Mexico remains illegal, and it was abolished under all remaining state codes in 1975. However, the military death penalty, for crimes such as treason, is still enforceable.

- **1940s:** The transition from horses to cars as a means of transportation is already well underway. However, while motorized tractors have been common since the turn of the century, personal cars meant for transportation remain something of a luxury, especially in rural areas.

  Today: Horses are now considered a luxury item. They are nearly impossible to keep in urban centers and are increasingly expensive to maintain, even in rural areas.

was elected president, with José María Pino Suárez elected as vice president (the Dueña also mentions Suárez in her speech). Madero, sadly, proved to be a poor leader, and he and Suárez were deposed in 1913. They were both assassinated a week later.

CRITICAL OVERVIEW

Critical reaction to *All the Pretty Horses* was immediately positive. The book was a best seller that earned two prestigious awards, and it secured McCarthy's reputation as a major literary figure. In the *New York Times Book Review*, Madison Smartt Bell writes of "the extraordinary quality" of McCarthy's prose: "Difficult as it may sometimes be, it is also overwhelmingly seductive." She notes, "Powered by long, tumbling many-stranded sentences, his descriptive style is elaborate and elevated, but also used effectively to frame realistic dialogue, for which his ear is deadly accurate."

Irving Malin, in his 1992 *Commonweal* article, proffers additional praise, observing, "I assume that this brilliant novel will force readers to view McCarthy as an original stylist [and] one of the best contemporary writers." According to Malin, the novel "will, indeed, assume its place as an example of the great religious novels written by any American." Calling *All the Pretty Horses* a "grim and immensely powerful novel" in his 1993 *New Statesman & Society* review, Nick Kimberley comments that McCarthy "shows us what we take to be civilisation locked in mortal combat with all that is mean and bestial."

Critical opinion over the years has remained much the same, and in her 2010 *Southwestern American Literature* assessment, Petra Mundik points out, "McCarthy's descriptions of the otherworldly beauty of horses imbue the text with a numinous quality that hints at some wholly transcendent and absolute source of divinity."

CRITICISM

Leah Tieger

Tieger is a freelance writer and editor. In the following essay, she explores the religious nature and symbolism of All the Pretty Horses.

He loved watching the sunset over the horizon.
(James Laurie | Shutterstock.com)

All the Pretty Horses is highly religious in nature, filled with numerous references to God and the souls of men and horses. The spirit of the landscape through which John and Rawlins journey is also portrayed in a reverent, if not religious, light. While the novel is told mostly through brief vignettes and clipped dialogue, the passages pertaining to God, horses, and the landscape are longer in length and more poetic in language. Even the blood so often referenced in the story can be related to the book's religious themes and imagery. Christian theology, after all, is based on Christ's bloodshed as the defining act that redeems humanity. The Catholic practice of communion is also a blood ritual; Catholics believe that the wine imbibed during communion is transfigured into Christ's blood. McCarthy was raised as a Catholic and is familiar with these beliefs and practices. In the novel, the connection between God and blood is solidified when Dueña Alfonsa declares that "nothing can be proven except that it be made to bleed. Virgins, bulls, men. Ultimately God himself." Her comment can certainly be read as a reference to the crucifixion. When Christ bled, he proved God's existence to mankind.

One could even attempt to read *All the Pretty Horses* as a sort of post-modern bible story, with John acting as the Christ figure. John goes on a pilgrimage through the desert, as Christ does. He proves himself to be Christlike when he refuses to abandon Blevins despite the potential harm it may (and does) cause him and his friend. An example of John's Christian outlook can be seen when Blevins loses his hat in the road. Rawlins attempts to run over it with his horse, but John picks it up and carries it to Blevins. In addition, where Rawlins questions such theological constructs as Judgment Day, heaven, and hell (and in doing so ultimately questions God's existence), John proves himself to be a believer. John's travels through the desert with his doubting friend bear resemblance to the biblical story in which Jesus meditates in the desert and is tempted by the devil. Rawlins certainly tempts John to leave Blevins behind.

Following this line of reasoning, Rawlins can also be seen as a Judas figure (in the Bible, Judas is the disciple who betrays Christ). While Rawlins does not literally betray his friend, he does abandon him, first after he is knifed in prison and again when he leaves John in Mexico. The estrangement between John and Rawlins is undeniable (and surprising to John) when Rawlins sits where they cannot see one another as the bus drives away. Another possibility for the Judas figure is Alejandra. It is she who accepts the proverbial pieces of silver when she secures John's release from prison by agreeing never to see him again. By doing so, she betrays her own heart and the love that has grown between her and John. Alejandra proves herself to be a betrayer again when she breaks her initial promise and meets with John one last time.

In another religious interpretation, *All the Pretty Horses* represents the expulsion from the Garden of Eden. The novel is undeniably the story of John's loss of innocence. While he may start his journey as an idealistic boy who is happiest in the desert, surviving on wild game or riding his horse and ranching, he ends the novel as a man filled with "something cold and soulless." This interpretation is underscored by John's desire to stay on the ranch for "about a hundred years." He is expelled from it abruptly, just as Adam and Eve are banished from the Garden of Eden. Even the ranch's name bears a religious meaning, it is the *Hacienda de Nuestra Señora de la Purísima Concepción*, the House of Our Lady of the Purest Conception. Furthermore, in his loss of innocence, John is exiled not only from the ranch but also from San Angelo, which, by the novel's end, "aint my country." Still, all endings are accompanied by beginnings, and once John's expulsion is complete he is seen riding into "the world to come." This phrase echoes a line in the Lord's Prayer (perhaps the best-known Christian prayer), "thy kingdom come."

WHAT DO I READ NEXT?

- John Knowles's *A Separate Peace* is a classic young-adult novel that features two adolescent boys, best friends at a boarding school in New England. The novel, written in 1959, is set just before World War II begins. Much like *All the Pretty Horses*, *A Separate Peace* is a coming-of-age novel that plumbs the depths of the bonds between adolescent males.

- *Coming of Age Around the World: A Multicultural Anthology* (2007) is editor Faith Adiele's second coming-of-age anthology. The collection contains twenty-four stories from all over the world, many of which address the same themes of loss and adventure that are in *All the Pretty Horses*.

- In McCarthy's novel, John and Rawlins are minors who are unlawfully imprisoned. In the 1996 book *Hard Time*, editors Janet Bode and Stan Mack collect first-person narratives about teens who have also served time in prison and juvenile detention centers. This young-adult book presents a multicultural perspective of crime and the criminal justice system.

- Another nonfiction book that complements *All the Pretty Horses* is Geoffrey C. Ward's *The West: An Illustrated History*. The 2003 book, with contributions by Stephen Ives and Ken Burns, is a companion volume to the eponymous PBS documentary series. The book presents a history of the American West in the nineteenth and twentieth centuries.

- McCarthy's writing has often been compared to the work of William Faulkner. One of Faulkner's most accessible books is the novel *As I Lay Dying*, which was first printed in 1930. The plot follows the Bundren family as they take their matriarch's body to her birthplace to be buried.

- The second installment in McCarthy's "Border Trilogy" is *The Crossing* (1994). The novel portrays teenager Billy Parham, who travels from Texas to Mexico on a pilgrimage to release a wolf that he and his father have trapped.

- McCarthy's writing style has been described as being part of the southern gothic tradition. For more insight into this genre, read the 2009 anthology *Southern Gothic Shorts*, edited by Phillip J. Morledge.

Less biblical readings of the novel's religious nature can also be made. The many quotes about God portray either a paternalistic figure or a distant and unknowable entity that may or may not exist. The space between these two images, as Dueña Alfonsa claims, is likely something akin to the truth. Addressing the nature of belief, religious or otherwise, she asserts,

> In the end, we all come to be cured of our sentiments.... The world is quite ruthless in selecting between the dream and the reality, even where we will not. Between the wish and the thing the world lies waiting.

God, perhaps, is "the wish," the one that John believes in when he begins his journey. It is the belief behind his refusal to abandon Blevins, and it is this belief that consequently leads him to prison, where he kills a man in self-defense and finally begins to lose his faith. That loss is complete when Alejandra leaves him for the final time. In this way, John has been "cured" of his "sentiments."

Interestingly, while John believes in God, the people around him question God's existence. Rawlins doubts the concepts of Judgment Day and heaven and hell. The captain tells John that "God is no here." Pérez tells him that the American preoccupation with "good things and bad things...is the superstition of a godless people," but when John loses his faith and begins to doubt God (or at the very least has a "bone or two to pick with Him"), everyone and everything around

John Grady's dreams always included horses. *(Harry H. Marsh / Shutterstock.com)*

him espouses a belief in, and reverence for, God. A man who John stops to eat with reminds him that without "the will of God . . . there is neither corn nor growing nor light nor air nor rain nor anything at all save only darkness." In John's encounter with the Reverend Jimmy Blevins, the radio is a tool of God, one that allows his word to be heard all the way to China, and even on Mars.

Source: Leah Tieger, Critical Essay on *All the Pretty Horses*, in *Novels for Students*, Gale, Cengage Learning, 2011.

Susan Lee

In the following essay, Lee explains and provides examples of McCarthy's use of blood imagery throughout the novel.

In the first novel of his Border Trilogy, *All the Pretty Horses*, Cormac McCarthy describes a complicated landscape of verdant plains, lush forests, and deserted wastelands as his protagonist, John Grady Cole, travels through Texas and Mexico in search of identity. Cole's quest, however, emerges as a convoluted process; while the protagonist journeys to another land

to develop his imagined version of Utopia, the underlying inspiration for Cole is a return to the human emotions and internal desires displaced by the intrusion of modernity. In the novel, McCarthy equates the desire for utopia with inherent human features through the use of blood imagery, specifically in the appearance of "blood red" as an adjectival phrase rather than another addition to the author's extensive use of "blood" as a noun. The blood imagery in *All the Pretty Horses* emphasizes the integral life-sustaining features at the heart of the protagonist's desires while connecting Cole's quest, the landscape, and the necessities needed for survival in carefully chosen linguistic constructs.

From the novel's beginning, McCarthy's use of blood imagery when displaying Cole's longing for the simple life of breaking horses and living off of the land illuminates his protagonist's preoccupation with a previous form of existence. However, the possibility of living a life bound to the landscape appears bleak in Texas despite Cole's efforts to save the family's property and thus remain in his homeland. Instead, Cole finds himself surrounded by the growing

> **THE CONNECTION, THEN, BETWEEN McCARTHY'S USE OF 'BLOOD RED' AS AN ADJECTIVE AND ITS CLOSE PROXIMITY TO COLE'S QUEST AND HIS MEANS FOR IT, IS NOT AN ARBITRARY RELATION."**

presence of American industrialization. He thus turns to the Mexican frontier, hoping to discover the "openness" of undisturbed wilderness and welcoming inhabitants. Barcley Owens suggests that "Americans have consistently perpetuated two frontier myths, one that champions progress and Anglo-American might and one that champions the preservation of wilderness and its idealized natives." For Cole, the preservation of natural landscape in the United Slates pertains solely to a different age of American history, namely the nineteenth century, while Mexico remains untouched and wildly naturalistic in the present moment. Cole simultaneously avoids considering the violence of the nineteenth century's American West, portrayed rather graphically in McCarthy's *Blood Meridian*.

In his "return" to the frontier, Cole desires a world preserved from the effects of modernization. In place of his homeland, which is divided by barbed wire, fences, highways, and blacktop, McCarthy's protagonist imagines a terrain void of man-made separations; a place where he can investigate the interior disposition and life force of nature and man—the blood and heat of the living: "What he loved in horses was what he loved in men, the blood and the heat of the blood that ran them. All his reverence and all his fondness and all the leanings of his life were for the ardenthearted and they would always be so and never otherwise." Because of Cole's mythological views of landscape, he cannot encounter happiness in an industrialized territory that ignores the very life forces needed for its creation; he consequently opts to pursue "life" in another region.

McCarthy sparingly employs blood as a description throughout the novel. In the first instance, Cole conducts a preliminary "practice" journey before he actually recruits his friend Lacey Rawlins in an official border crossing. Cole rides his horse across former Comanche paths surrounded by the sun that "[. . .] sat blood red and elliptic under the reefs of bloodied cloud before him." The dramatic beauty of the landscape reaffirms Cole's idealistic expectations of what he will find once he abandons progress and industrialization in favor of natural terrain and maintained majesty.

On another occasion, after Cole and Rawlins encounter a young troubled boy with a dubious past, Jimmy Blevins, the two young men are faced with the decision of whether to abandon the boy and to prevent future skirmishes with the law. Cole, however, decides to support Blevins despite the apparent danger of doing so. Once again, the rising sun swelling "blood red along the horizon" coincides with a momentous occasion disguised as seemingly unimportant. Because of Cole's decision, Blevins causes, through association, the imprisonment of the protagonist and his friend in Saltillo, a Mexican jail. In the descriptions of the sun as blood red, Cole faces a decision about his future course of action, choosing each time the idealism of his frontier myth rather than the reality of such a powerful landscape.

As the boys proceed through a region that becomes progressively inhospitable and dangerous, they suffer possible starvation and the beginning stages of dehydration. Cole discovers a nopal fruit, native to the region, that "[. . .] stained their fingers blood red" as they eat. Simultaneously, on separating from Blevins, the two boys receive encouragement from the terrain as they not only encounter food but also the hacendado of La Purisima nearby. While David Holloway suggests that La Purisima's objective reality is the industrial breeding of horses for market, McCarthy indicates, from Cole's perspective, that the ranch and its surrounding landscape offer the protagonist the chance to pursue his interest in horses and, as a result, the opportunity to integrate himself into the naturalism of an "adopted" country's present condition. The landscape, though, merely displays what is in sight. Once Cole ingratiates himself into the industrialized reality of the ranch's "atmosphere," the untainted "purity" of the landscape disintegrates.

La Purisima's problematic nature results from its dualistic position between the traditional Mexican past of aristocratic custom and its necessity for progress and modernization. Although Cole briefly manages the rancher's horses, his relationship with Rocha's daughter and his consequent disregard for Mexican customs alert the young girl's aunt of possible familial disgrace. Much like the binary scenery of farmland and industry present in Texas, Mexico proves to be a frontier of deserted wilderness and a rising progressive state. Cole, driven by his high idealism, ignores the incongruent details of Mexican tradition and rising technological advancement.

At the novel's end, once Cole must confront the fallacy of his frontier myth, he finds little solace in the prospect of a return home. After his adventures in La Purisima, his unjust treatment in Saltillo, and his brief attempt at revenge with the Captain, Cole finds himself a man "without a country." Forced to make a decision, Cole opts to return once more to Mexico in hopes of discovering the central interior nature of man mirrored in an open landscape, all of which he neglected to encounter in his first journey. Cole notices the powerful landscape as he rides his horse toward Mexico: "There were few cattle in that country because it was barren country indeed yet he came at evening upon a solitary bull rolling in the dust against the bloodred sunset like an animal in sacrificial torment. The bloodred dust blew down out of the sun." Once again, the sunset colors the region blood red—so much so that the dust is converted as if directed by the sun's will.

Cole thus circles in action and practice as he begins a second journey that promises little, if not less, success than his first quest across the border. The blood and heat of man and animals propel him toward what he innately desires: to discover the integral features of the natural world and to live by them at the same time. The connection, then, between McCarthy's use of "blood red" as an adjective and its close proximity to Cole's quest and his means for it, is not an arbitrary relation. By emphasizing Cole's personal motivation through the blood of description, McCarthy parallels Cole's desires for the mythic frontier with the landscape that he truly encounters. Blood, as a result, becomes a life-sustaining force in body and spirit, yet it is as intangible for Cole as the purity of his Utopian visions.

Source: Susan Lee, "The Search for Utopia: Blood Imagery in McCarthy's *All the Pretty Horses*," in *Explicator*, Vol. 66, No. 4, Summer 2008, pp. 189–92.

Ched Spellman

In the following essay, Spellman discusses how dreams provide the profound narrative element in All the Pretty Horses.

In *All the Pretty Horses*, Cormac McCarthy weaves his novel about John Grady Cole's journey into Mexico and within himself together through a distinct structural framework. The entire narrative functions chiastically in a "there and back" structure. In this construct, dreams provide the textual seams that bind McCarthy's narrative. Cole's journey begins with a somber ending. After his grandfather's funeral, Cole senses he has "come to the end of something." An experienced reader of American literature will recognize that coming to the "end of something" often symbolizes coming simultaneously to the "beginning" of a profoundly new experience. In some of the short stories of Hemingway and Katherine Anne Porter, the end of something subtly signals transition and not simply termination. Accordingly, Cole has come to the end of his way of life in America, as well as the end of his family line. As he watches the warriors "ride on in that darkness they'd become...south across the plains to Mexico," his soul longs for freedom, renewal and escape. He recognizes that he has reached the conclusion of something and that he is "already gone." This ending is where Cole's dreams begin.

On the surface, dreams provide continuity between the novel's major plot elements. Cole dreams at every turn. As soon as Cole and Rawlins begin their adventure, it becomes apparent they are chasing their dreams. When Rawlins asks about the next town, as the two are heading down a darkened highway, Cole confesses that he would "make it Eldorado." Eldorado was the fabled city of gold that explorers of the New World endeavored in vain to discover in the sixteenth century. Eldorado promised wealth and adventure to anyone willing to set out in pursuit of this legendary city. In America, the concept of Eldorado was applied to the California Gold Rush as countless Americans journeyed westward to find their fortunes. Writers from Milton to Conrad have used Eldorado as a literary metaphor for an unattainable place of fulfillment, always just beyond reach. This is the experience of Edgar Allan Poe's gallant knight in "Eldorado," who sojourns his life away "in search of Eldorado," a place that lurks only in the shadows. Cole and Rawlins join Poe's gallant knight as they "ride, boldly ride" toward an imaginary place (Eldorado) that exists only in dreams. For them, Mexico is this place. As Daniel Alarcon observes, the boys must head south rather than west, because American industrialization "has placed too many obstacles in their path and erased the storybook Wild West." Cole and Rawlins seek

> THE 'THERE AND BACK' FEEL OF THE STORY IS NO ACCIDENT. VIEWED HOLISTICALLY, ALL OF COLE'S EXPERIENCES COALESCE INTO THE SEMBLANCE OF A MOST INTENSE DREAM SEQUENCE."

a country that still harbors circumstances able to quench their thirst for the wild. Cole intrinsically yearns for such a land where he can contemplate the "wilderness about him" and "the wilderness within" him.

Part of this longing for the wild is revealed by the dreams Cole often has as he slips into slumber each night. Although in different times and places, most of Cole's dreams share a single theme, namely, horses and the wild. Many times, as he falls asleep, Cole's "thoughts were of horses and of the open country and of horses. Horses still wild on the mesa who'd never seen a man afoot and who knew nothing of him or his life yet in whose souls he would come to reside forever." Cole continually parallels his soul and that of a horse. For Cole, horses represent the freedom for which he so desperately longs. He feels his soul and the souls of the horses will somehow become eternally intertwined. Cole also believes "the souls of horses mirror the souls of men," and for him, the horses reflect his hunger for freedom. He repeatedly dreams of horses in fields, and places himself among the young horses pounding the ground beneath them, running toward their destiny. Cole never relents from his conviction that horses "were always the right thing to think about." Indeed, his love for these animals proves "more reliable and less complicated than other dreams" (Owens 72). When he moves about in these dreams, he glides fearlessly and instinctively with "a resonance that was like a music." Cole views this intense connection as "the world itself" and something "which cannot be spoken but only praised." While in prison, Cole's soaring dreams supply the strength he needs to survive the drudgery and stagnant nature of his situation. They are for him an entrance into a reality higher than himself.

Aside from horses, love also affects his dreams. After hiring on to be a hand at a Mexican ranch, Cole gradually becomes smitten with his boss's daughter, Alejandra. As Cole watches Alejandra ride one day, he experiences an amalgamation of

his desires. He watches her gallop away until "the rain caught her up and shrouded her figure away in that wild summer landscape: real horse, real rider, real land and sky and yet a dream withal." Cole's love for Alejandra and his love for horses and the land combine to form the foundation of his dreams. Interestingly, rider and horse are swallowed up into the "summer landscape." This perhaps symbolizes the unattainable nature of a lasting relationship with Alejandra. Her love is real, but Alejandra represents only a transitory element of the fleeting reality that Cole has stumbled on in Mexico. Once again, he is dreaming of "Eldorado." Later in the novel, Alejandra reveals that she sees Cole in her dreams as well. As the two lovers part ways, Cole watches "her go as if he himself were in some dream." Alejandra proves to be an emotional Eldorado that eludes Cole's grasp and later haunts his memory. Even in love, Cole lives and moves about in a dream world.

Cole's dreams also carry vicious images of death and emptiness. While in prison he dreams of "the dead standing about in their bones," conveying a "terrible intelligence common to all but of which none would speak." His dreams continually reflect the reality in which he finds himself. After being released from this cell and while waiting to see the senorita at the hacienda, Cole attempts to think of "what sort of dream might bring him luck." He first thinks of memories of Alejandra, and then of his deceased friend, Blevins. He here recalls how his dreams again turn toward death. Haunted by Blevins' memory, Cole reflects that "He'd dreamt of him one night in Saltillo and Blevins came to sit beside him and they talked of what it was like to be dead." Cole thinks that if he dreams of him enough, Blevins would "go away forever and be dead among his kind." Significantly, for the first time, Cole then falls "asleep and [dreams] nothing at all." Later, he dreams again of horses, but contrary to before, they move "gravely . . . like horses come upon an antique site where some ordering of the world had failed." Something is happening to the nature of his dreams as they begin to convey an increasingly somber reality. Throughout, Cole's dreams are the constant factor in all his experiences.

Dreams also provide a more profound narrative element. In addition to using dreams as textual seams to tie his plot together, McCarthy also fashions his entire narrative in a dreamlike structure. The "there and back" feel of the story is no accident. Viewed holistically, all of Cole's experiences coalesce into the semblance of a most intense dream sequence. As he heads home, Cole begins to slowly and painfully "wake up" from his dreams, both the ones he has been having, and the one he is living. One morning, on his return to Texas, Cole experiences a sudden and defining moment. "When he woke he realized that he knew his father was dead." Following such a long and arduous struggle, Cole finally wakes up from the dream that he has been living in Mexico. The abrupt departure from this dream is painful for Cole. After he finally crosses back into Texas, Cole thinks "about his father who was dead in that country and he sat the horse naked in the falling rain and wept." He thus reenters his homeland as a seeming "apparition out of the vanished past."

McCarthy's introductory and concluding scenes further confirm this structural thesis. In the beginning, repressing the thought of his father's death and way of life, Cole journeys toward Eldorado, while at the end, he seemingly awakens empty-handed. At the beginning, after his father's funeral, Cole "turned south along the old war trail and he rode out to the crest of a low rise and dismounted and dropped the reins and walked out and stood like a man come to the end of something." While at the end, after Abuela's funeral, Cole "rose and turned and looked off toward the north where the lights of the city hung over the desert. Then he walked out and picked up the reins and mounted his horse and rode up and caught the Blevins horse by its halter." At the beginning of McCarthy's narrative, Cole comes to the "end of something," and at the end of the narrative, he comes to the beginning of something, namely, "the world to come." Cole's dreams and McCarthy's dreamlike narrative structure "have an odd durability for something not quite real," although they also show "very clearly how all ... life led only to this moment and all after led nowhere at all." In the final analysis, the effect of McCarthy's textual strategy is that both the reader and Cole experience the catharsis of entering and departing from an intense world of dreams.

Source: Ched Spellman, "Dreams as a Structural Framework in McCarthy's *All the Pretty Horses*," in *Explicator*, Vol. 66, No. 3, Spring 2008, pp. 166–70.

Allen Shepherd

In the following review, Shepherd examines how All the Pretty Horses *differs in accessibility and tone from McCarthy's previous works.*

Within a few weeks of its publication in May, 1992, Knopf was able to buy a page in the

> WHAT MAKES HIS WORK DISTINCTIVE AND POWERFUL IS NOT SO MUCH SUBJECT MATTER OR CHARACTER OR PLOT AS SETTING AND STYLE."

New York Times Book Review headed "Ovation for Cormac McCarthy's *All the Pretty Horses*." Quoted were people saying all sorts of ostensibly extravagant things about the novel, calling it "a genuine miracle in prose," a "true American original," an "absolutely marvelous novel," and identifying McCarthy as a "master," a "singular voice in American fiction" and a "talent equal to William Faulkner." As it happens, I tend to think they're about right. In fact, *All the Pretty Horses* is as fine and distinctive a novel as I've read (and re-read) in the last ten years. That it is identified as Volume One of *The Border Trilogy* is as good as money in the bank any time. Before I explain myself, a little information about McCarthy and his career, until recently hard to come by, might be in order.

Though he has long had distinguished admirers—Saul Bellow, Ralph Ellison, Robert Penn Warren—it has been only about five years since McCarthy vacated the title of Best Unknown Major American Novelist. No longer Knoxville's other writer (after James Agee), his entrance into the literary-academic mainstream has been signalized by such honors as his receipt of a MacArthur Fellowship and of both the National Book Award and the National Book Critics Circle Award for his best-selling sixth novel, *All the Pretty Horses*.

There are a number of likely explanations for McCarthy having subsisted since 1965 as a writer's writer and cult figure. He has been accounted, by common standards, a difficult writer, one who moreover remained practically anonymous, on the Pynchon model, wholly disinclined to assist in the promotion of his own work, all of which in Random House hardcover was out of print. In their original editions his first five novels sold probably no more than 15,000 copies. It seems likely as well that the very originality of his work, its uncategorizable quality, has deterred some prospective readers. And if for a presumably authoritative account of his subject matter we look into *The History of Southern Literature* we read, in part, that "Cormac McCarthy's fiction is filled with episodes of animalistic fornication, incest, murder and necrophilia"—a not wholly inaccurate but not altogether engaging description.

Typically in the novels antedating *All the Pretty Horses*, the characters are unreflective, almost without thoughts, their motives unclear, and the omniscient narrator generally offers minimal interpretive aid. Plots are episodic and anecdotal and, at least on first reading, may appear to include an unusual amount of unassimilated material. Chronology is often left uncharted. Here, for illustrative purposes, is a passage from *Blood Meridian* (1985), McCarthy's fifth novel, in which we meet a legion of "itinerant degenerates, bleeding westward like some heliotropic plague." As they pass in their half-page sentence we see that

> the trappings of their horses [are] fashioned out of human skin and their bridles woven up from human hair with human teeth and the riders wearing scapulars or necklaces of dried and blackened human ears and the horses raw-looking and wild in the eye and their teeth bared like feral dogs . . .

The prevailing mood is Gothic and nihilistic; the humor is chilling.

All the Pretty Horses is just as inimitably McCarthy's work as its predecessors, but differs substantially in accessibility and tone, which fact has led some recent essayists to dark imaginings about lost courage and abrogation of authorial values. These suspicions have been induced by McCarthy being on best seller lists and granting interviews and turning up as the subject of a university press book and—the final indignity—being studied at an academic conference. In fact, however, *All the Pretty Horses*, likable though it may be, much resembles McCarthy's first novel, *The Orchard Keeper* (1965), in that it memorializes, without a trace of sentimentality, a vanishing way of life.

All the Pretty Horses attends to a half-year of the adventures of John Grady Cole, a sixteen-year-old Texan from near the Pedernales (LBJ country), who, bereft of his patrimony, lights out for the Territory, riding south into Mexico with a friend, Lacey Rawlins, in 1950. They ride to be away, to seek adventure, to find a horse-cattle-cowboy culture, to enter the past. Shortly they acquire a hapless younger companion, Jimmy Blevins, and within months, as book jacket copy has it, one of these boys is dead and the other two aged beyond normal reckoning. Nonetheless *All the Pretty Horses*, as compared with its often apocalyptic predecessors, is an uncommonly sweet-tempered narrative, more likely to suggest Huck Finn and Tom Sawyer on horseback than *Easy Rider*.

McCarthy's trio are earnest, honest, funny, brave, and wonderfully likable, fixed in a natural hierarchy (Cole-Rawlins-Blevins), given to night-time speculation about the mysteries of religion, death, God, the afterlife, and women. Their discoveries extend from a version of paradise, Eve in residence, at the Hacienda de la Purisima, a huge ranch in mountainous Coahuila, where John Grady's uncommon talent for breaking, training, and understanding horses gains them employment, to a version of hell on earth, the prison at Saltillo, where, we're told, "every man was judged by a single standard and that was his readiness to kill." "I never knowed there was such a place as this," Rawlins says.

The novel is eminently readable, its narrative momentum effortlessly maintained, suspense durable, and the use of language sometimes almost overpowering. Though such descriptive phrases as "a man's novelist" and "macho mystique" have gained some critical currency, my own limited polling among women friends suggests that the novel's appeal is not so limited.

All the Pretty Horses presents some difficulties. A few are minor and mechanical; thus McCarthy omits apostrophes and quotation marks in dialogue. Absent identification, it is difficult sometimes to know who is speaking, and since some of the characters speak lines and lines of untranslated Spanish, *what* exactly they are saying may be mysterious. It takes a while as well to become accustomed to the various levels of thought and speech by which the characters, John Grady in particular, are represented.

As is often remarked, McCarthy is a highly original writer, unlikely to be mistaken for any other present-day practitioner. What makes his work distinctive and powerful is not so much subject matter or character or plot as setting and style. Sustaining the terror and grandeur with which he endows the physical world and the lyric reconstitution of the language which distinguishes his prose is an authorial self-possession which, like Melville's, can be wonderfully seductive and exciting. Here is a paragraph in McCarthy's high style, one which rises out of mundane, literal short-sentence statement through the figurative and, in the long last sentence, into the metaphysical empyrean.

They [John Grady and Rawlins] rode out along the fenceline and across the open pasture-land. The leather creaked in the morning cold. They pushed the horses into a lope. The lights fell away behind them. They rode out on the high prairie where they slowed the horses to a walk and the stars swarmed around them out of the blackness. They heard somewhere in that tenantless night a bell that tolled and ceased where no bell was and they rode out on the round dais of the earth which alone was dark and no light to it and which carried their figures and bore them up into the swarming stars so that they rode not under but among them and they rode at once jaunty and circumspect, like thieves newly loosed in that dark electric, like young thieves in a glowing orchard, loosely jacketed against the cold and ten thousand worlds for the choosing.

Balancing this vision of Keatsian promise is a later remark that "it was good that God kept the truths of life from the young as they were starting out or else they'd have no heart to start at all."

Since, as McCarthy observes, "the novel depends for its life on the novels that have been written," it isn't surprising to see his literary heritage reconceived, generally to good advantage, in *All the Pretty Horses.* McCarthy is in fact a very literary writer—Melville, Dostoievsky, and Faulkner principal among those he counts "good writers." The likes of James and Proust he disclaims interest in, since they "didn't deal with issues of life and death. To me, that's not literature." In *All the Pretty Horses* it is Faulkner and Hemingway whose presence is most noteworthy. As the three boys are recovering (stealing back) Blevins's horse, we read that

> All out bedlam had broken across the lot. Rawlins pulled his horse around and the horse stamped and trotted and he whacked it across the rump with the barrel of the gun. The horse squatted and dug in with its hind hooves and Blevins in his underwear atop the big bay horse and attended by a close retinue of howling dogs exploded into the road in a shower of debris from the rotted ocotillo fence he'd put the horse through.

It's only the nature of the fence, I suppose, that locates the scene in the Sierra de la Encantada rather than in a lot for Texas ponies in Yoknapatawpha County. The generally benign influence of the other Nobelist in question may be discerned in an account of John Grady and Rawlins, recently hired at the Hacienda de la Purisima, conversing with the resident vaqueros.

> They listened with great attention as John Grady answered their questions [about America] and

they nodded solemnly and they were careful of their demeanor that they not be thought to have opinions on what they heard for like most men skilled at their work they were scornful of any least suggestion of knowing anything not learned at first hand.

One thinks of Robert Jordan up in the mountains.

All the Pretty Horses is a classic western, a story of initiation and romance, mystery and adventure, and of the relation among free will, fate, and justice. Though the Western frontier spirit of boundless optimism has receded, there exists in its place a respect for and an enactment of the heroic virtues: fortitude, resolution, magnanimity. At novel's end there occurs an obligatory exchange between John Grady and Rawlins.

> "You could stay here at the house," says Rawlins. "I think I'm goin to move on," his friend answers.

I look forward to encountering John Grady again, out in "the Territory ahead of the rest...."

Source: Allen Shepherd, "As Good as Money in the Bank: Cormac McCarthy's *All the Pretty Horses,*" in *New England Review,* Vol. 16, No. 1, Winter 1994, pp. 176–79.

Irving Malin

In the following review, Malin discusses imagery, characterization, and the spiritual quest found in All the Pretty Horses.

Cormac McCarthy is one of our best—if least known—writers. In this, his fourth novel, he uses the archetypal journey to discuss important spiritual themes. He is primarily interested in the origins of evil; the search for redemption; the meaning of our brutal existence.

Although his latest novel deals with the relatively simple characters of three adolescents—Cole, Rawlins, Blevins—who light out for the unknown territory of Mexico to find their mixed fortunes—the year is 1949—he is less interested in their characterizations than in their spiritual recognitions. The plot involves various adventures, misfortunes, coincidences. It is, for the most part, merely an excuse to look for epistemological answers. On one level the novel resembles the traditional initiation we find in *Huckleberry Finn* or, for that matter, in Faulkner's *The Reivers.* (The novel seems particularly "American" because of its underlying structure; it is our kind of *adolescent picaresque.*) But on a second (and deeper) level it is an occult narrative of the ultimate meanings—if there are any—of these adventures. There are echoes of a religious quest, a trip to discover the Holy Grail.

McCarthy's imagery is, perhaps, more important than his characterization. (It is, of course, difficult to separate the two.) The imagery is one of hovering presences, secret omens, perverse signs. I quote at random: "it was like looking through something and seeing its heart." Another passage on the nature of earth-bound horses: "Lastly he said that he had seen the soul of horses and it was a terrible thing to see. He said that it could be seen under certain circumstances attending the death of a horse because the horse shares a common soul and its separate life only forms it out of all horses and makes it mortal. He said that if a person understood the soul of a horse then he would understand all horses that ever were." Cole leaves Mexico; his exit is described in poetic terms. "After a while he pulled his hat down over his eyes and stood and placed his hands outstretched on the roof of the cab and rode in that manner. As if he were some personage bearing news for the countryside. As if he were some newfound evangelical being conveyed down out of the mountains...." These examples are visionary, mystical, ghostly. They suggest that there is another world which somehow influences ours. They, indeed, offer a sense of *incarnation*.

McCarthy's language ranges from the laconic conversations of the three adolescents— even these conversations seem to hold ambiguous "presences"—to the almost biblical cadences of the following passage. "He thought that in the beauty of the world were hid a secret. He thought the world's pain and its beauty moved in a relationship of diverging equity and that in this headlong deficit the blood of multitudes might ultimately be exacted for the vision of a single flower."

I assume that this brilliant novel will force readers to view McCarthy as an original stylist, as one of the best contemporary writers. It will, indeed, assume its place as an example of the great religious novels written by any American. It will, without doubt, disturb us by its violent juxtapositions of beauty and blood, "prettiness" and terror.

Source: Irving Malin, "A Sense of Incarnation," in *Commonweal*, Vol. 119, No. 16, September 25, 1992, p. 29.

Christopher Dewdney

In the following review, Dewdney compares All the Pretty Horses *to another of McCarthy's novels,* Blood Meridian.

Cormac McCarthy is an American novelist who has inherited the southern gothic tradition of Carson McCullers and Flannery O'Conner. His first book, *The Orchard Keeper*, won the William Faulkner Foundation Award in 1965. Since then he has published four novels, not including *All The Pretty Horses*. Most of these novels are thematically dark, though *Blood Meridian*, published in 1985, outdid them all.

In *Blood Meridian*, a literary masterpiece, the young protagonist joins a group of bounty hunters who slake their blood-thirst in northern Mexico. This extraordinary novel is an anti-Western; its denizens are stupid, brutal, dirty people who enact scenes of fantastic cruelty and endurance under the impartial proscenium of a beautifully described landscape. Like *Blood Meridian*, *All The Pretty Horses* features a young protagonist on horseback who rides south into Mexico with his companions, but there the parallels stop.

All The Pretty Horses is as conventional as *Blood Meridian* was unconventional. Taking place somewhere in the mid-20th century (the only concrete indication of time is when a character in the novel remarks on Shirley Temple's divorce), the novel traces the journey of two young men in their mid-teens. They set off from Texas and cross the Rio Grande into Mexico illegally, where they eventually find work as cowboys on a large ranch. John Grady, the protagonist, falls in love with Alejandra, the rich hacendado's daughter, who because she is a member of an aristocratic Mexican family, is forbidden to see him. Grady and his friend Rawlins lose their jobs at the ranch and are incarcerated in a squalid, dangerous Mexican jail. Ultimately they are released but not until after close brushes with death.

Although the world depicted in *All The Pretty Horses* is one of irreducible masculinity, one of the strongest characters is Alejandra's grandmother. When she learns of the budding romance between her granddaughter and the gringo, John Grady, she delivers an impromptu monologue on fate that is one of the most compelling passages in the novel, including the following: "For me the world has always been more of a puppet show. Yet when one looks behind the curtains and traces the strings upwards he finds they terminate in the hands of other puppets, themselves with their own strings which trace upward in turn, and so on. In my own life I saw these strings whose origins were endless enact the deaths of great men in violence and madness. Enact the ruin of a nation. I will tell you how Mexico was."

Horses have figured largely in a number of McCarthy's previous novels—the three sinister riders in *Outer Dark*, the many horses of *Blood Meridian*. In *All The Pretty Horses*, however, they not only monopolize the title but they also occupy large sections of text. Cormac McCarthy's fascination with horses signifies his more general interest in things Western. This same passion impelled him to move from his native Tennessee to El Paso, Texas.

With publication of *All The Pretty Horses*, the first of a projected trilogy, McCarthy has made a remarkable departure from his earlier themes. He has abandoned the unremitting darkness which has been his trademark for the past 25 years. His basic concerns are still here, men and young men dealing with extreme conditions wherein their endurance is tested well beyond normal human capacities. But this novel dwells much more within the realm of normal human experience than any of his previous books excepting *Suttree*. It seems to me that this is a conscious strategy of Cormac McCarthy's—possibly to establish a larger audience for his work.

Like the rest of his novels, *All The Pretty Horses* has a restless momentum. This pacing easily sustains some very long passages. Also, like the rest of his novels, dialogue is not indicated by quotation marks. McCarthy's facility with language ensures that this absence is not the least bit confusing. Unlike his other novels, *All The Pretty Horses* does not use a vocabulary that requires an open dictionary while reading it. As well, it differs from his previous novels in being driven by a more tangible notion of plot. Given his lucid prose style and his ability to move a story there is no question that *All The Pretty Horses*, McCarthy's most mainstream book to date, will be successful.

Source: Christopher Dewdney, "A Wild Ride: *All the Pretty Horses*," in *Globe and Mail* (Toronto, Ontario, Canada), June 13, 1992.

SOURCES

Andersen, Elisabeth, *The Mythos of Cormac McCarthy*, VDM Verlag, 2008.

Arnold, Edward T., and Dianne C. Luce, eds., *Perspectives on Cormac McCarthy*, rev. ed., University Press of Mississippi, 1999.

Bell, Madison Smartt, "The Man Who Understood Horses," in *New York Times Book Review*, May 17, 1992.

Brenner, Anita, and George R. Leighton, *The Wind that Swept Mexico: The History of the Mexican Revolution of 1910–1942*, University of Texas Press, 1984.

Clayton, Lawrence, Jim Hoy, and Jerald Underwood, *Vaqueros, Cowboys, and Buckaroos: The Genesis and Life of the Mounted North American Herders*, University of Texas Press, 2001.

Combs, Susan, "Industry Profile: Ranching in Central Texas," in *Window on State Government*, http://www.window.state.tx.us/specialrpt/tif/central/indProfiles.php#39 (accessed July 24, 2010).

Consular, Gaceta, "The Mexican Revolution 1910," in *Mexconnect*, November 1996, http://www.mexconnect.com/articles/2824-the-mexican-revolution-1910 (accessed July 24, 2010).

Guerra, Elisa Speckman, "Justice Reform and Legal Opinion: The Mexican Criminal Codes of 1871, 1929, and 1931," in *Reforming the Administration of Justice in Mexico*, edited by Wayne A. Cornelius and David Shirk, University of Notre Dame Press, 2007, pp. 225–51.

Kimberley, Nick, Review of *All the Pretty Horses*, in *New Statesman & Society*, Vol. 6, No. 249, April 23, 1993, p. 34.

"The Lord's Prayer," in *The Lord's Prayer: A Survey Theological and Literary*, by Nicholas Ayo, Rowman & Littlefield, 2003, p. xvii.

Malin, Irving, Review of *All the Pretty Horses*, in *Commonweal*, Vol. 119, No. 16, September 25, 1992, p. 29.

McCarthy, Cormac, *All the Pretty Horses*, Vintage International, 1993.

McShane, Clay, and Joel A. Tarr, "Conclusion: The Decline of the Horse in the Twentieth Century," in *The Making of Urban America*, edited by Raymond A. Mohl, 2nd ed., SR Books, 1997, pp. 123–25.

Mundik, Petra, "Diverging Equity: The Nature of Existence in *All the Pretty Horses*," in *Southwestern American Literature*, Vol. 35, No. 2, Spring 2010, p. 9.

Priola, Marty, "Cormac McCarthy," in *Dictionary of Literary Biography*, Vol. 256, *Twentieth-Century American Western Writers, Third Series*, edited by Richard H. Cracroft, The Gale Group, 2002, pp. 162–73.

Richardson, T. C., and Harwood P. Hinton, "Ranching," in *The Handbook of Texas Online*, http://www.tshaonline.org/handbook/online/articles/RR/azr2.html (accessed July 24, 2010).

FURTHER READING

McCarthy, Cormac, *Cities of the Plain*, Knopf, 1998.
This novel concludes the "Border Trilogy," again featuring John Grady Cole. Bill Parham, who appeared in the trilogy's second installment, is also featured.

McCullers, Carson, *The Heart Is a Lonely Hunter*, 1940.
McCullers's novel is considered a definitive addition to the southern gothic tradition. Reprinted in 2000, the novel experienced a resurgence after being chosen as part of Oprah Winfrey's Book Club.

McLynn, Frank, *Villa and Zapata: A History of the Mexican Revolution*, Basic Books, 2002.
This volume provides an overview of the Mexican Revolution, which haunts the inhabitants of the ranch house in *All the Pretty Horses*.

Twain, Mark, *The Adventures of Huckleberry Finn*, Collector's Library, 2010.
Another author to whom McCarthy has been compared is Mark Twain. First published in 1884, *The Adventures of Huckleberry Finn* is a highly apt comparison with *All the Pretty Horses*, because it presents the friendship that grows between twelve-year-old Huck and the escaped slave Jim as they head down the Mississippi river on a raft.

SUGGESTED SEARCH TERMS

All the Pretty Horses

Cormac McCarthy

All the Pretty Horses AND Cormac McCarthy

All the Pretty Horses AND Border Trilogy

Cormac McCarthy AND southern gothic

All the Pretty Horses AND Mexican Revolution

Cormac McCarthy AND westerns

All the Pretty Horses AND coming-of-age novels

All the Pretty Horses AND Mexico

The Brief Wondrous Life of Oscar Wao

JUNOT DÍAZ

2007

The Brief Wondrous Life of Oscar Wao (2007), the first novel by the Dominican American author Junot Díaz, won the Pulitzer Prize for Fiction in 2008 and is one of the most acclaimed works of literature of the early twenty-first century. Díaz spent the first seven years of his life in humble circumstances in the Dominican Republic, then moved to New Jersey and underwent the sort of crash course in assimilation experienced by many immigrants. Always an avid reader, Díaz consumed comic books in his youth, moved on to fantasy and sci-fi novels and horror fiction by high school, and from there delved into serious literature. Following graduate school, he made his own mark on the literary world with *Drown* (1996), a short-story collection narrated by the streetwise Yunior, who tells of his experience growing up without a father, first in the Dominican Republic and then in New Jersey. In *The Brief Wondrous Life of Oscar Wao*, Yunior returns to tell the story of Oscar de Léon, a "fat sci-fi-reading nerd" whose solitary life is marked by romantic despair—and who may be weighed down by a curse wrought upon his family by the dictator Rafael Trujillo, who was crossed by Oscar's grandfather.

It should be noted that in relating the stories of Oscar, his sister, his mother, and his grandfather, the novel includes several extremely violent episodes, occasionally graphic discussions of sexual encounters, and brief mentions of drug use, and the narrator uses a contemporary vernacular,

Junot Díaz (Getty Images)

mixing Spanish with English, that features frequent profanity.

AUTHOR BIOGRAPHY

Díaz was born in Santo Domingo, Dominican Republic, on December 31, 1968, and raised in the Villa Juana neighborhood as the third of five children. His father, a military police officer who was usually stationed in the United States, raised his children under strict discipline and preached a strong work ethic; he also encouraged his boys to fight with neighbors in order to toughen up. For the first six years of his life, Díaz knew a city with few modern conveniences, with running water unreliable, electricity scarce, and the nearest television blocks away. His grandmother sometimes told fantastic folkloric stories about ancestors, dreams, and curses, and although he did not always believe in what she described, the stories were thrilling. When times became trying under Joaquín Balaguer and the nation's future

looked bleak, the family decided to move to Parlin, New Jersey, arriving in 1975.

Learning English was a challenging experience that spurred Díaz to delve into comics and literature, and he read tirelessly, drifting toward all kinds of science fiction. He was not a model student in high school, earning Fs in various subjects, behaving poorly, and getting in fights; although he was given a diploma from Cedar Ridge High School in 1987, he believes he did not actually gain the required credits. He first attended Kean College and then transferred to Rutgers University after a year, and meanwhile he worked, including at a steel mill and delivering pool tables. In college he planned to be a teacher but realized that he wanted to be a writer, and he was accepted to graduate school at Cornell University—a surprise, since his girlfriend at the time secretly applied on his behalf. He at first tried his hand at screenplays, but when he realized his professor was more interested in shark-attack cinema, he shifted to fiction.

Earning a master of fine arts degree in 1995, Díaz published his first work that year in *Story* magazine, and in 1996, he published his short-story collection *Drown*, widely considered a remarkable breakthrough effort. Living up to the subsequent expectations proved a formidable challenge. He worked on a novel about life in the United States following a devastating terrorist attack—but the events of September 11, 2001, rendered his idea obsolete. Fighting depression and doubts about his capability as a writer, he had a revelation while conversing with a friend in Mexico, whose Spanish inflection of the name Oscar Wilde as "Wao" left him with a vision of, as he told *Newsweek*, "this fat kid, can't get laid, loves *Star Trek*; his super-athletic, burning-with-rage-towards-her-mother-but-incredibly-forward-looking sister, and then this really [messed]-up mom. They just jumped into my head." The resulting novel, *The Brief Wondrous Life of Oscar Wao*, won the National Book Critics Circle Award, the Pulitzer Prize, and a host of other awards. As of 2010, Díaz held a professorship in creative writing at the Massachusetts Institute of Technology.

PLOT SUMMARY

The Brief Wondrous Life of Oscar Wao begins with a prologue in which the narrator, Yunior, introduces the reader to the idea of "*Fukú americanus*," or "the Curse and the Doom of the New World," which is deemed a legitimate supernatural force in Santo Domingo. There, many saw their lives overturned by the fukú disbursed by the Dominican dictator Rafael Leónidas Trujillo Molina—which wrought havoc on the family of John F. Kennedy, and on America, when the president oversaw Trujillo's assassination. (The narrator uses footnotes to provide the reader with the framework of Dominican history; Trujillo, who reigned for over thirty years, was one of the most notorious dictators of the twentieth century.) The tale of Oscar's life is a "fukú story."

I

ONE: GHETTONERD AT THE END OF THE WORLD, 1974–1987

The first chapter of part I of the novel covers Oscar's early years (which the reader later learns were set in Paterson, New Jersey). In the narrator's telling, Oscar is not a prototypically masculine Dominican, having no luck with girls—except for at the age of seven, when he has juvenile relationships with two, Maritza and Olga, at the same time. Under pressure from Maritza, Oscar coldly breaks up with Olga, but Maritza abandons him the following week in favor of some brute. From then through adolescence, Oscar only grows more overweight, awkward, and lonely.

In his all-boys high school, Don Bosco Tech, Oscar suffers constant ridicule over his weight and his appreciation for sci-fi and fantasy games, books, and movies. (The narrator peppers the text with references to comic books and fantasy literature, especially J. R. R. Tolkien's *The Lord of the Rings* trilogy.) Oscar's self-conscious nerdiness keeps him from relating well with girls, though he has aching crushes on many. His sister Lola counsels him to exercise to get in shape, but trying only leads him to despair. Meanwhile, Lola's friends taunt him with their burgeoning sexuality.

By senior year, even Oscar's "two nerdboys," Al and Miggs, find girlfriends, and Oscar realizes that his friends are embarrassed by him. He tries to revolutionize his image by cutting his hair and getting contact lenses. That summer he goes to stay with family in the Dominican Republic in Baní (an hour west of Santo Domingo) where he devotes himself to writing, which Nena Inca does not discourage. Upon his return, he forsakes Al and Miggs to stay focused on writing, despite his mother's ridicule.

The narration shifts back to the preceding fall, during Oscar's senior year, when, in the interest of getting into college, he takes an SAT class. There he meets an attractive full-figured girl named Ana who seems as quirky as himself. She dated twenty-four-year-old Manny when she was only thirteen. Oscar and Ana start chatting and spending time together, and one day Ana appears at Oscar's house, and they go on a date to a movie. On the ride home, she complains about a headache, and they talk very little. Nonetheless, Oscar is in love.

Ana and Oscar continue to see movies and hang out at the mall together, but the relationship turns out to be "one of those Let's-Be-Friends Vortexes," as Ana joyfully rejoins the abusive Manny when he returns from the army. Oscar's time with Ana turns sour as she talks only of her boyfriend, but Oscar is lovestruck—a problem that runs in the family. One night, he swipes his uncle's gun and stands waiting outside Manny's apartment building, but Manny does not appear. Eventually, he professes his love to Ana, to no avail. He graduates, to attend Rutgers New Brunswick in the fall. He is optimistic at first, but at college, he is shunned by white and ethnically diverse students alike. His only refuge is RU Gamers, the all-male gaming organization.

TWO: WILDWOOD, 1982–1985

The opening section of chapter two is written in the second person, as Lola projects onto the reader her experience, at the age of fourteen, of sharing her mother's discovery of a lump in her breast. Around then she becomes a punk, to which her mother, who was always oppressive and domineering in a characteristically Dominican way, fiercely objects. The mother habitually hit both Lola and Oscar. Throughout childhood, Lola had to be the family caretaker, doing all the housework and running errands while her mother worked. When she decides to turn punk, she has her friend Karen clip all her hair off. Her mother tries to force her to wear a wig, but Lola burns the wig, and that is when she first defies her mother's abusive hand, deflecting her aggression.

Despite her mother's cancer, Lola fights her endlessly. Her mother tries to tear up her punk belongings and clothes, but Lola finds safe places to keep them. Because of her mature appearance, she is able to gain entrance to and frequent a nightclub, and during her sophomore year she meets a nineteen-year-old named Aldo whom she begins dating. In September of her junior year, after a grand fight with her mother, she runs away to move in with Aldo in Wildwood, but Aldo and his aged father have a rocky relationship; the fridge is padlocked, and the cat litter has to be in Aldo's bedroom. Lola is soon bored and bitter; two days after Aldo makes a racist joke in front of his friends, she calls home, and Oscar answers. She asks him to steal money from their mother, and he agrees to bring it to her, but at the coffee shop where they meet, he is followed in by their mother, aunt, and uncle. Lola dashes past them out the door and down the street, leaving her mother sprawled on the pavement. At the sight of her mother crying helplessly, Lola returns, allowing her mother to leap up grinning and seize her; Lola was fooled.

Lola is then sent to Santo Domingo. At the time of her writing, she has been there six months and is attending a private academy, where she is a star on the track team. Her friend Rosío helps her shed her punk image and attend to her appearance like a "'real Dominican girl.'" Lola feels a mysterious visceral (intuitive or instinctive) sensation, the same feeling that led her to leave home in the first place, and she acts on it to consummate her relationship with Max, whose job is to shuttle film reels from cinema to cinema. However, the sensation lingers, until, looking over old family pictures, she sits bolt upright as her *abuela* (grandmother), La Inca, starts to tell her about her mother's father.

THREE: THE THREE HEARTBREAKS OF BELICIA CABRAL, 1955–1962

The narration is once again taken over by Yunior. He describes how Belicia Cabral, Lola and Oscar's mother, was raised in Baní from the age of nine by La Inca, a cousin of her father's; her early childhood is referred to as "Lost Years." La Inca runs a bakery, and Belicia duly helps La Inca work and keep house, and they attend church together. Beli is unsatisfied with her upstanding but routine life. Attending a prestigious school, El Redentor, from age thirteen, the very dark-skinned, coarse, and aggressive Beli has trouble fitting in and focusing on schoolwork. Instead gazing upon upper-class boys like Jack Pujols and dreaming of marrying, she lies about her school life to La Inca.

Beli makes a habit of colliding with Jack in the school's hallway, but she is ignored nonetheless—until she experiences abrupt physical development during the summer of her sophomore year, leaving her especially well endowed. At first dizzied by the attention she receives, Beli comes to understand the power her figure allows her to wield. Back at school, her grades somehow improve, and after reportedly breaking up with his girlfriend, Jack begins flirting with her.

Before long, Beli and Jack are having illicit relations in locations around school. After a month, a teacher is tipped off and catches them in the act—a major scandal, especially since Jack is actually engaged to his girlfriend. Jack is promptly shipped to military school, while Beli is expelled, to La Inca's dismay. Beli vows to lead her own life from then on. She gets a job waitressing at the Palacio Peking, a Chinese restaurant owned by the Then brothers, where she will work for a year and a half. She proves very responsible and is well appreciated by the owners and customers alike. She gives particular attention to two men, a white Fiat dealer and a revolutionary-minded student named Arquimedes, but remains in love with Jack. Not until invited out by a new waitress, Constantina, does Beli venture to a club called El Hollywood.

Belicia has a marvelous experience dancing at El Hollywood—until a well-heeled player, the Gangster, accosts her and sets off her temper. Then, back at home, Beli fights with La Inca, who threatens to kick her out. Unable to stop dwelling on the Gangster, Beli asks Constantina to take her back to El Hollywood, where she makes him dance with her. The narrator relates that the Gangster lived on the streets since the age of seven. He rose into the ranks of Trujillo's feared secret police and now operates a string of brothels. Cuba became a second home, but he was exiled from that home and left emotionally vulnerable after the Cuban Revolution—until he met Beli. He devotes much energy and money to courting her, promising her a house in Miami one day, and she appreciates sharing his social life. Her reputation suffers, and she is fired from her job. Meanwhile, her mysterious man, for whom she has no address, disappears for weeks at a time. He takes her on a romantic vacation to the tropical paradise of Samaná, but he is whisked away by a policeman who claims he was needed at "the Palacio," and she is left to find her own way back to Baní. There, La Inca realizes Beli is pregnant.

Beli lets gossip about her pregnancy spread; when she tells the Gangster, he tells her not to have the baby, but she does not really hear him. As it turns out, the Gangster is already married to Trujillo's sister, seventeen years his senior, known as La Fea—and she, too, soon learns of Beli's pregnancy. Beli is seized at a park by two thugs, called the "Elvises," who present her to La Fea, who informs her that the baby will be forcibly aborted. As Beli is being abducted, the Then brothers and their staff come to her rescue. She goes back home—only to be again seized by the thugs hours later. La Inca, helpless, devotes all of her energy to prayer. Beli is driven east, marched into the cane fields, and horrifically beaten. Barely conscious, she is visited by a mongoose with golden eyes that urges her to rise, and she manages to reach the road and get picked up by a traveling band.

La Inca fortunately has connections in the medical community, allowing Beli's life—though not that of her unborn child—to be saved. Although Trujillo was assassinated that very same night, La Inca's health is fading, and Beli remains in danger; La Inca decides to send Beli to New York. When the thugs return once more, La Inca brandishes a machete to turn them away, and she then hastens to arrange for Beli's departure. In a few weeks, after a last heartrending rendezvous with the Gangster, Beli boards a plane, still dreaming of him. As it turns out, the man sitting next to her will become the father of her two children.

FOUR: SENTIMENTAL EDUCATION, 1988–1992

The narrator, Yunior, at last reveals himself as a person in the lives of Lola and Oscar. Lola took care of the macho Yunior once when he was beaten by thugs. Though he typically developed temporary, shallow connections with women in college, he has true feelings for Lola. After Oscar nearly kills himself drinking alcohol, Yunior volunteers, since Lola will be away in Spain for the year, to room with Oscar and look after him, despite their vastly different personalities, interests, and lifestyles. After Yunior cheats on and is spurned by his girlfriend, he commits to helping Oscar get in shape and become more charismatic. Yunior's aggressive personal-trainer enthusiasm is effective at first, but eventually Oscar loses his motivation and gives up running, prompting a fight between them. Yunior, to whom Lola stops speaking, then leaves Oscar to fend for himself.

Through devoted flirtation, Oscar manages to strike up a relationship with a beautiful Puerto Rican goth named Jenni, whom Yunior also admires. Oscar is transformed by his loving interaction with Jenni, shaping up and gaining self-esteem, but then she strikes up a meaningful friendship with another boy, and Oscar is heartbroken. Oscar seems suicidal, so Yunior calls Lola, who counsels Oscar to move on. When Oscar walks in on Jenni and her new companion, he goes "berserk," trying to destroy her room until Yunior restrains him. By year's end, Yunior decides to room elsewhere the following year. On one of the last nights of the school year, Oscar gets extremely drunk and walks out on the train tracks on the bridge over Route 18. As a train approaches, he jumps, aiming for the road, but he lands on the shrubby median and survives, breaking his legs. Yunior visits Oscar and Lola in Paterson once over the summer, and Oscar visits Yunior once during the fall of his senior year (when Oscar is taking time off), but otherwise Yunior sees little of the siblings for a time. Yunior and Lola run into each other on the bus in December, however, and finally engage in a romantic relationship. With Oscar returning to college that spring, Yunior opts to be his roommate again.

II

In what reads like a letter from Lola to Yunior (written after the two of them break up and after Lola has become a mother), Lola relates how after fourteen months living in the Dominican Republic with La Inca, she was summoned back to New Jersey by her mother. Frustrated, she abandoned the track team as well as her boyfriend, Max. She also received money from a friend's father, a politician, in exchange for a physical relationship. Her mother flew down to join her, and she would have run away, but Max was killed in a traffic accident. She flew home with her mother, in tears.

FIVE: POOR ABELARD, 1944–1946

Yunior again picks up the narration, relating the tale of Belicia's father, Abelard, who was an upstanding doctor and businessman in La Vega before his third daughter was born. He hosts intellectual conversations in his parlor, wisely avoiding any political discussion during the reign of the tyrant Trujillo, and dutifully attends state functions. Once his eldest daughter, Jacquelyn, starts maturing into a beautiful young woman—making her vulnerable to advances by Trujillo—Abelard declines to bring his family to these functions, citing his wife's poor mental health. This is risky, since Trujillo might suspect Abelard's intentions and resort to kidnapping or worse. Abelard's wife, Socorro, declines to acknowledge that there is a problem, while his mistress, Lydia, suggests that Abelard ship Jacquelyn to Cuba. At one function, Trujillo asks about the daughters, and Abelard deflects the question by claiming that they are unattractive because they have facial hair. Fearing reprisal by Trujillo for his deception, Abelard worries constantly, and his health declines.

Time passes, business for Abelard is good, and he is publishing articles in professional journals, but then an invitation for a presidential event, to be held at a neighbor's house, explicitly requests the presence of his wife and daughter Jacquelyn. Unsure what to do, Abelard delays making any decisions drinks heavily; as the party nears, he tells his wife and daughter to prepare, but at the last minute he refuses to bring them. When Trujillo asks about their absence, Abelard has no explanation and is coldly dismissed. A month later, he goes drinking with friends and ends up arrested for slandering the president; the charges are spurious, but it makes no difference. He is taken away by the secret police and taken to Fortaleza San Luis, a notorious prison, to be labeled a Communist and homosexual and humiliated by the other prisoners. After a few days, he is tortured. Socorro visits to find her husband a broken man. As Yunior relates, an alternate version of Abelard's story holds that he was punished because he was in the process of publishing an exposé of the Trujillo regime's supernatural powers.

Abelard is sentenced to eighteen years in prison, and all of his business holdings are seized by the regime. After giving birth to Abelard's third daughter, Belicia, the distraught Socorro is run over by a truck and killed. A few years later, just after being accepted to medical school in France, Jacquelyn drowns in her godparents' pool. Several years after that, the second daughter, Astrid, is shot and killed while praying in church. Abelard will suffer in prison for fourteen years before dying. Belicia, with skin so dark no one in Abelard's family wants to raise her, is seized by distant relatives of Socorro, sold to strangers in the impoverished region of Azua, and treated like a slave. La Inca, mourning the death of her husband, fails to save either Jacquelyn or Astrid, so when she hears that Belicia has survived but is being treated horribly, she rescues her. Beli never speaks with her family about those first nine years of her life.

SIX: LAND OF THE LOST, 1992–1995

After graduating from college, Oscar moves back home and works as a substitute teacher, a demoralizing experience. He has no social life and starts despairing over his bleak future. After substituting for several years, he makes plans to visit Santo Domingo with his mom and sister in the summer, and he grows more optimistic. There, the tropical environs and beautiful women infuse him with energy, and he declines to return to America with his sister, instead staying for the summer. He then falls for an experienced older woman named Ybón.

Ybón is a neighbor who befriends Oscar, to his delight, eventually inviting him in for drinks. Her past work as a prostitute appalls his mother and La Inca, but even after he sees a car with a police license plate outside her house, Oscar spends as much time as possible with her, learning about her family and the difficulties of her profession. Oscar and Ybón do not yet have a physical relationship, but Ybón's boyfriend, the capitán, seems to be getting jealous, and Ybón suggests they spend less time together. Nonetheless, one night Oscar innocently lies in bed with her after she drunkenly disrobes and passes out, and two days later there is a bullet hole in the door of La Inca's house.

In August, Oscar is driving the intoxicated Ybón home when the police pull him over; Ybón stirs to kiss Oscar and then immediately passes out again when the police pull him from the car. When interrogated, Oscar hints at his impression that the capitán was Ybón's former boyfriend; the capitán punches him a couple of times and turns him over to his grunts, who drive him to the cane fields and beat him severely. Clives, the taxi driver who caters to Oscar's family, bravely follows the grunts' car. He finds help, drags Oscar from the field, and drives him to medical aid. His mother buys Oscar a ticket home. Ybón visits La Inca's house and tells Oscar she will marry the capitán. At home in Paterson, Oscar is a wreck.

III

In January, when Yunior and Lola are living separately in New York, Oscar comes to visit. Yunior lends him money, which Oscar claims is for a security deposit.

SEVEN: THE FINAL VOYAGE

Oscar flies back to Santo Domingo and waits with Clives outside Ybón's house; when she returns, she implores him to leave. For the next four weeks, he researches, writes, and seeks Ybón's company. After two weeks his mother arrives to insist he return to New Jersey, to no avail. Eventually the capitán sees Oscar at the club where Ybón works, the Riverside. Soon after, the capitán's two grunts car jack Clives's cab at a light, with Oscar inside. They again take him to the cane fields, where they execute him.

EIGHT: THE END OF THE STORY

Oscar's mother suffers a cancer relapse and dies a couple of years later. Lola and Yunior break up for good, and Lola moves to Miami, where she gets pregnant and becomes engaged to a man named Ruben. Yunior, who has cleaned up his act and is teaching writing at a community college, still sees Oscar in his dreams. Sometimes he runs into Lola and her daughter, Isis. Yunior imagines that one day, Isis will come to him looking for answers about her uncle's life and her family's past, perhaps to resolve everything.

The Final Letter

In a last package sent home from Santo Domingo, Oscar included novel manuscript chapters and a letter to Lola, telling of his investigations there and an ensuing package that would include his conclusions. That package never arrives. Oscar reports that he has at last lost his virginity by consummating his romance with Ybón, finding in their intimate companionship beauty beyond what he had ever imagined. (The closing lines are a counterpoint to the infamous dying words of Kurtz in Joseph Conrad's *Heart of Darkness*.)

CHARACTERS

Lydia Abenader

Abelard's mistress, Lydia is also his foremost confidante and urges him to send Jacquelyn away to Cuba to escape Trujillo's grasp.

Aldo

A nineteen-year-old who works the bumper cars on the boardwalk at Wildwood, New Jersey, Aldo meets Lola at a club and inspires her to run away and live with him and his bad-tempered father. He turns out to be the sort to tell a racist joke to make a point.

Alok

One of Oscar's two high school friends, Alok, called Al, is "one of those tall Indian prettyboys" whose interests lie in fantasy culture and role-playing games. Oscar grows resentful when Al gets a girlfriend senior year, and they drift apart.

Marco Antonio

Marco Antonio is a one-legged cook at the Palacio Peking.

Arquimedes

A student with revolutionary tendencies, Arquimedes modestly harbors hopes of a romance with Beli during her waitressing days.

Socorro Hernández Batista

Abelard Cabral's wife is a "famous beauty from the East" who escaped her impoverished childhood by catching Abelard's eye with her nursing expertise and folkloric knowledge. She refuses to acknowledge that Jacquelyn's beauty makes her a target for Trujillo. After Abelard's imprisonment, she steps in front of a speeding truck and is killed.

Indian Benny

Indian Benny is a forlorn waiter at the Palacio Peking.

Abelard Luis Cabral

A successful and wealthy doctor and businessman, Abelard wishes to give every advantage to his first two daughters (he dies before the third, Belicia, is born), duly bowing to the dictates of the Trujillo regime, but his meekness and hesitancy prove fatal flaws. When it becomes clear that Trujillo has his eye on Jacquelyn, rather than sending her away, Abelard lies to Trujillo about his daughter's appearance and Socorro's mental health—a lie that leads to the rapid decline of his own mental health. When Jacquelyn is explicitly invited to a party, he decides only at the last minute that she shall not attend, and he has no explanation when Trujillo inquires. He later makes a nervous drunken joke about bodies in his trunk, and the regime portrays it as slander and locks him away. As Yunior relates, Abelard was perhaps actually punished for writing a book about the supernatural powers of the Trujillo regime; of all his books and papers, not a trace remains to reveal the truth.

Astrid Cabral

Abelard's second daughter, Astrid is left with relatives after Abelard's imprisonment and several years later is shot while praying in church.

Hypatía Belicia Cabral

See Belicia de Léon

Jacquelyn Cabral

The strikingly beautiful and intelligent first daughter of Abelard, Jacquelyn comes to Trujillo's attention, and Abelard's refusal to bring her to a party, an attempt to keep her out of Trujillo's reach, leads to his imprisonment. A couple of years later, just after gaining acceptance to medical school in France, Jackie is found drowned in the shallow water of a drained pool.

The capitán

Ybón's officer boyfriend, called Fito but known as the capitán, a "tall, arrogant, acerbically handsome" man with a history of abuse of police power, grows jealous of her relationship with Oscar. When Oscar refuses to stay away from Ybón, the capitán orders his thugs to beat Oscar; when Oscar returns, the thugs execute him.

Karen Cepeda

A pale, black-wearing goth in Paterson, Karen inspires Lola to become a punk herself.

Maritza Chacón

Maritza breaks Oscar's heart in elementary school, dumping him in favor of a prepubescent military type; she proceeds as an adolescent to engage in serial relationships with abusive men.

Clives

Clives is the "evangelical taxista" who helps Oscar get Ybón home after her nights of heavy drinking and who rescues Oscar after his beating in the cane fields.

Constantina

When she gets hired at the Palacio Peking, the wayward Constantina convinces Beli to forget Jack Pujols and live life to the fullest—leading her to El Hollywood, a happening club, and the Gangster.

Dionisio

See The Gangster

Dorca

Dorca is the daughter of the woman who cleans for La Inca and thus one of the few girls with whom Beli speaks. For her amusement, Beli tells the impoverished Dorca wild lies about her school life.

Elvises

La Fea's thugs, with their "matching pompadours" (upswept hairstyles), are referred to as Elvis One and Elvis Two. After Beli escapes them at the park, they seize her at her house and take her to the cane fields to beat her.

La Fea

A sister of the tyrant Trujillo and a fierce businesswoman and feared personage in her own right, La Fea confronts Beli when she learns of her pregnancy and insists on an abortion. When Beli refuses, La Fea's thugs beat her senseless, causing her to miscarry.

Esteban El Gallo

A loyal Haitian servant to the Cabral family, Esteban helps Jacquelyn learn French. He is stabbed outside a cabaret after Abelard's imprisonment.

The Gangster

A street tough named Dionisio who married into the Trujillo family and joined their tyrannical empire, the Gangster senses the tides turning after the Cuban Revolution. Sparks fly when he and Beli first meet, and once she tracks him down afterward, he showers affection on her, in part to stabilize his sense of self. He never tells her where he lives, and when they do enjoy a romantic getaway, he skips out for urgent but unstated political reasons. He regrets Beli's pregnancy and, tragically, leaves the matter to his vindictive wife.

Gorilla Grod

Grod, named after a comic-book villain, is one of the capitán's thugs who beat and later murder Oscar.

Solomon Grundy

Grundy, named after a comic-book villain, is the other of the capitán's thugs who beat and later murder Oscar.

La Inca

A cousin of Abelard Cabral, La Inca or Nena Inca, whose given name is Myotís Altagracia Toribio Cabral, lost her husband, who drowned at a beach, when she was very young. She is so grief-stricken that she does nothing to help Abelard's daughters after his imprisonment. When she finds out Belicia is alive but being treated horrifically, she rescues her, resolving to never physically punish the girl. She tries to raise Beli to bring honor back to the family name through academic and professional achievement, but Beli rebels against La Inca's formulaic intentions. La Inca's monumental act of prayer is credited with saving Beli from dying at the hands of the Trujillo thugs. She remains the de Léon family's connection to Santo Domingo, living and working in nearby Baní and, when Oscar visits at the end, in the city itself, in Mirador Norté.

Isis

The beautiful daughter Lola has with Ruben is named Isis. Because she bears the name of the Egyptian goddess of motherhood, fertility, and magic, she is held up as a sign of renewal and, ideally, future redemption.

Belicia de Léon

While the modern reader may most easily relate to Oscar's trials and tribulations as a nerd and outcast, the suffering endured by his mother is of another order, from another world—that of a ruthless third-world dictatorship. By the time she is born, as Hypatía Belicia Cabral, her father is already in jail for having irked Trujillo, and her mother is later run over by a truck. She is whisked away by distant relatives to a hardscrabble corner of the island where she is treated like a slave, shuffled from one family to the next and obligated to work beyond exhaustion. For wishing to attend school, she has scalding oil splashed on her back by her father figure—and only then is she rescued by La Inca. Though she might have been ruined by those first nine years, she emerges, under La Inca's care, "with an expression and posture that shouted in bold, gothic letters: DEFIANT."

Belicia adopts but later defies La Inca's prim and proper routines, using her stunning looks to inspire a clandestine affair with Jack Pujols that ends with her expulsion from the prestigious El Redentor. She demonstrates her powerful work ethic at the Palacio Peking, where another waitress eventually convinces her to push aside her love for Jack and enjoy life. She immediately latches on to the idea of the Gangster, who at first irritates her immensely. Despite La Inca's misgivings and the ridicule of the neighbors, she

falls head over heels for the Gangster, who turns out to be married to a sister of Trujillo, La Fea. Belicia's vision of marriage and a home is what fuels her. Her pregnancy, however, leads La Fea to order her cruelly beaten, killing the unborn child. At last Belicia is sent to New York, and the unnamed man who sits next to her on the plane turns out to be her third and final love, the father of Oscar and Lola—who leaves her after only a few years for unstated reasons. As a mother, Belicia turns out to have substantial failings. She tries to rule Lola's life with an iron fist—a trait that Yunior informs the reader is common among Dominican mothers—but as an American daughter, Lola is only pushed toward rebellion of her own. Belicia tries to push Oscar out into the world, but by discouraging his writing, she only stifles him. Stricken with breast cancer, she is weakened by the time of Oscar's infatuation with Ybón, and she cannot overpower the force and motivation of her son's love to save his life. Her cancer kills her two years later.

Lola de Léon

As far as back as she can remember, Lola—short for Dolores—has been burdened with the responsibilities of managing the de Léon household: cleaning, running errands, and raising Oscar while their domineering mother works her various jobs. Even when Lola is raped by a neighbor at the age of eight, her mother only tells her to shut up and stop crying. Her conflicted relationship with her mother leads Lola to run away, joining Aldo in Wildwood—until, needing money, she calls Oscar, who betrays her by bringing their mother to collect her. Lola then experiences a rebirth in the Dominican Republic while staying with La Inca, with the help of her friend Rosío and boyfriend Max, but she is forced to return to Paterson, to end up attending the same college as her brother, Rutgers-New Brunswick. Until Oscar's demise, she serves as her little brother's caretaker, trying to help him shape up, interact with girls, and, later on, avoid killing himself. Lola also inspires Yunior to become an older brother to Oscar. She and Yunior join romantically, but they ultimately part ways. Lola ends up with a Cuban man named Ruben, and with him she has a daughter named Isis. Even Lola's sisterly love is not enough to keep Oscar from digging his own grave, so to speak, through his romantic love for Ybón.

Oscar de Léon

After he is dumped at the age of seven, Oscar's identity becomes wrapped up in his weight and appearance—and the shame his peers make him feel—as well as the alternate worlds he turns to as a means of escape, from cartoons to comics to video and board games and beyond. Through high school, he buries himself in nerd culture to avoid the constant affronts to his self-esteem, which leaves him unable to relate well with any of the steady stream of girls he has crushes on. As Yunior narrates, Oscar stumbles from one infatuation to the next, with every girl that enjoys his company perceiving him only as a friend. Given his extreme solitude—he has no girlfriend and experiences no requited love through adolescence —his self-destructive drinking and unbalanced habits, like courting disaster by taking long drives at night and nearly falling asleep at the wheel, are tragically realistic responses. When he finally has true love in his sights in the Dominican Republic, despite the imminent threat to his life, he will not be denied in his pursuit of Ybón. Indeed, he is blinded by his love—utterly failing to recognize the importance of the bullet hole in the door of La Inca's house. He and Ybón do unite for a weekend of enlightenment for Oscar; he at last understands what love is. To the end, he believes that he might be spared in light of the ferocity and truth of his passion—but he is executed by the capitán's goons nonetheless.

Lillian

Lillian, a stout woman, is another waitress at the Palacio Peking.

Manny

A recovering coke-addict and the older boyfriend of Ana Obregón, Manny foils Oscar's hopes of uniting with Ana when he gets out of the army and sweeps her back off her feet. He belittles and intimidates Oscar when they meet.

Marisol

Marisol is an intelligent friend of Lola's with whom Oscar is smitten as a youth.

Max

Max, who shuttles film reels between three theaters, becomes Lola's boyfriend when she is attending the academy in the Dominican Republic, and he speaks of moving to America. When Lola's mother insists that she return to Paterson, Lola breaks up with Max. While weaving through traffic, perhaps distracted by his broken heart, he gets crushed between two buses and dies.

Miggs

One of Oscar's two nerd friends in high school, the acne-riddled Miggs gets a girlfriend with Al's help, leaving Oscar feeling excluded. Both Al and Miggs end up dropping out of college and working at a video store.

Tío Carlos Moya

A sort of relative in the Dominican Republic, Carlos Moya is a former bakery employee and old fling of La Inca's.

Jenni Muñoz

Jenni is a Puerto Rican goth, dubbed "La Jablesse," whom Oscar falls for at college. She entertains him for awhile, but she moves on, and Oscar gets upset and trashes her room when he finds her hooking up with an arrogant punk.

Nataly

Nataly is a friend of Oscar's on the staff at Don Bosco Tech after his graduation from college. Oscar has a crush on her.

Ana Obregón

Ana is a girl whom Oscar meets in his high school SAT class. They go on a date but only become good friends, despite Oscar's puppy love for her. When Manny, her abusive old boyfriend, returns from the army, Oscar is pushed aside, with his confession of love only making Ana pity him all the more.

Pedro Pablo

Pedro is a cousin of the de Léon family who lives in the Dominican Republic.

Ybón Pimentel

An attractive thirty-six-year-old woman who has gone from touring Europe as a prostitute to entertaining a limited number of "boyfriends," Ybón befriends and bewitches Oscar, who treasures her company despite his family's objections over her profession. She teases him with moments of exhibitionism and romance, calling him "mi amor," but eventually advises him to back off out of consideration for her jealous Dominican cop boyfriend, the capitán. When Oscar, beaten senseless once, returns to pursue her, she at last relents and, with the capitán out of town, they head for a weekend at the beach at Barahona, where she gives Oscar a glimpse of the priceless beauty of true romance.

Olga Polanco

Oscar has a brief relationship with Olga as a seven-year-old but breaks up with her because she is Puerto Rican and homely. Like Oscar, she suffers the fate of a lonely life for being oversized.

Jack Pujols

The "handsomest (read: whitest)" boy at Beli's school, Jack is the man of her dreams. He ignores her until she develops a womanly figure and then has a clandestine relationship with her, promising marriage. When they get caught—and it turns out he is already engaged—he is sent to military school.

Marcus Applegate Román

A friend and neighbor to Abelard, Marcus recognizes that Abelard is putting himself at risk by deceiving Trujillo about his family. Marcus may be the "certain trusted neighbor" who was drinking with Abelard when he supposedly slandered Trujillo and later reaped a share of Abelard's redistributed holdings.

Rosío

Lola's best friend at school in the Dominican Republic, Rosío, a scholarship student and fellow track runner, brings Lola back to feminine norms of appearance.

Tía Rubelka

Living in the New Jersey area, Oscar's aunt Rubelka appears at various family events, such as when Lola is returned home after having run away. Rubelka, who has a family of her own, and Rudolfo may be relatives of Oscar's father.

Ruben

Ruben is the man Lola ultimately marries and lives with in Miami.

Tío Rudolfo

Living in Paterson at the de Léon residence when not in prison, Oscar's uncle Rudolfo is an expert at relating with girls—he has four children with three women—and is addicted to heroin.

Suriyan

Suriyan is Yunior's on-again, off-again girlfriend.

José Then

Co-owner of the Palacio Peking with his brother, José speaks better Spanish and is fiercely protective of the restaurant and rooms above. His family was killed years earlier by a warlord. He teaches Beli useful skills and rescues her from La Fea's thugs.

Juan Then

Gentle and somewhat naive, Juan Then succumbs to the provocative Beli's pleas for a job, hiring her as a waitress at the Peking Palacio.

Rafael Leónidas Trujillo Molina

The true-life dictator of the Dominican Republic for thirty years, Trujillo's tyrannical reign is portrayed as casting a fukú shadow over every Dominican in the book, especially the descendants of Abelard Cabral. Only briefly does Trujillo actually appear, at the parties held in his honor, inquiring about Abelard's wife and lovely daughter Jacquelyn. When Abelard fails to bring them, Trujillo scorns him, and within weeks—surely at Trujillo's behest—Abelard's life is destroyed.

Wei

A Chinese girl in Baní whose father is in league with Trujillo, Wei is discriminated against and, like the young Beli, is a social outcast.

Yunior

Yunior, the narrator, is a hypermasculine Dominican who moved to the United States and met first Lola and then Oscar at college. Yunior is frank about his antipathy toward the sorts of "weirdos and losers and freaks" who inhabit Demarest Hall, an artists' haven. Inspired by Lola—whom he admires but fears, since he knows that to be with her would mean meeting her high moral standards—he agrees to room with Oscar in the wake of Oscar's suicidal drinking. Yunior demonstrates sympathy at times and becomes Oscar's hardcore personal trainer, but when Oscar gives up, Yunior gives up on him. Yunior dates Lola for a time, but his habitual infidelity provokes her to leave him for good. Oscar clearly had a profound impact on Yunior, who has undertaken the task of memorializing Oscar's life and who has internalized the sense and importance of a wide variety of fantasy and science-fiction movies, television shows, books, comics, and games. He reveals that his "hope" and "dream" is that Lola's daughter might someday draw on all of Oscar's and Yunior's research and writing and "put an end to it"—to the fukú, the reader may presume.

Zoila

The dark-skinned Zoila cares for the infant Belicia for a short time after her mother's death.

THEMES

Fukú and Zafa

The central tenet and governing force of the novel is *fukú*, meaning "curse" or "doom," as explained in the prologue. Díaz traces the origins of the New World's *fukú americanus* to Christopher Columbus, who is generally hailed in modern North America as a heroic explorer but in this text is referred to only as "the Admiral," since "to say his name aloud or even to hear it is to invite calamity on the heads of you and yours." In the time frame of the book, this grand *fukú* is embodied by the tyrant Trujillo who, whether "the Curse's servant or its master," inflicted *fukú* on the families of the countless Dominicans who crossed him and even—somewhat supernaturally—on Americans, as a result of John F. Kennedy's approval of his assassination. The one force that opposes *fukú* is *zafa*, a "counterspell" that can be invoked when wishing to keep a spark of bad luck from flaring into fire.

Yunior expresses ambivalence about *fukú*, saying that whether he believes in it "is not really the point," since "no matter what you believe, *fukú* believes in you." He goes on to admit, "I have a *fukú* story too"—"one that's got its fingers around my throat." When Oscar blames the curse for his suicidal jump off the train track, Yunior claims, "I don't believe in that s—, Oscar. That's our parents' s—." However, Oscar asserts, "It's ours too," and the reader soon gathers that Yunior has indeed come to believe in the *fukú* that led to the demise of so many of the relatives of Abelard Cabral. When describing the fates of the Cabrals, he only hesitantly suggests *fukú*'s role: "Call it a whole lot of bad luck, outstanding karmic debt, or something else. (Fukú?)" Later in Oscar's story, Yunior invokes the concept more definitively; Oscar is described as despairing over his certain future in "bitter dork" purgatory, and the one-word paragraph explaining his fate is "Fukú."

An overarching question, then, is whether the *fukú* wrought upon Abelard's family can be countered or nullified. Upon noting Socorro's third pregnancy, realized just after Abelard's imprisonment, Yunior asks, "Zafa or Fukú? You tell me." He thus suggests that Belicia might be understood either as an agent extending Abelard's *fukú* into the future, or as an agent of *zafa* who will bring about the family's redemption. Since the *fukú* would have succeeded in erasing the entire Cabral clan if Belicia had died, her survival and procreation make her seem an agent of *zafa*—though she herself cannot escape the *fukú*. It is thus left to Oscar or Lola to bring about the needed *zafa*.

Oscar's fate, of course, is an early death, but a telling moment comes five years later, when Yunior dreams of a masked Oscar holding up a book with blank pages and smiling with his eyes. Whether Oscar speaks the word or whether it simply flares in Yunior's dreaming mind, the next line, a one-word paragraph, is "*Zafa*." At this point, Yunior is uncertain of what became of Oscar's final text—containing "the cure to what ails us," as he wrote Lola, which was supposed to be enclosed in a second package from the Dominican Republic that never arrived. Similarly, Oscar was uncertain of what became of "the Lost Final Book of Dr. Abelard Luis Cabral," which may have been "an exposé of the supernatural roots of the Trujillo regime." (Yunior calls the myth of this book the kind of tale "only a nerd could love," but in the prologue he admits, "These days I'm nerdy like that.") Oscar, too, dreamed, after his horrific beating, of a masked someone holding a book with blank pages—in this case "an old man," who must surely be Abelard. Thus, in both cases, with both lost texts, the dreamed person is revealing to the dreamer that, whether the book in question was written or not, at present the book does not exist; its pages are blank. In other words, in each case, the man dreamed about is telling the dreamer that the essential book in question still needs to be written. Just as Oscar burdened himself with the task of writing that book, Yunior assumes that responsibility upon Oscar's death—he reveals in the prologue that his book may be "a zafa of sorts" and so the very book that needs to be written turns out to be *The Brief Wondrous Life of Oscar Wao*.

Isolation

The three most significant protagonists in Díaz's novel—Oscar, Lola, and their mother, Belicia—are all social outcasts, and most of Oscar's companions and crushes are outcasts as well. The novel thus provides a comprehensive, sympathetic treatment of the many causes and consequences of social isolation. Belicia is shunned because of her exceptionally dark skin, her unfeminine belligerence, and her status as a scholarship student at an elite school.

TOPICS FOR FURTHER STUDY

- Think of a comic book series, work of fantasy or science fiction, or any sort of fictional universe with which you are familiar enough to readily allude to characters, style, and themes therein. Write a short story or fictional journal entry in which you narrate an event, whether a special occasion or a daily occurrence, while making frequent allusions to your favored fictional universe. Add footnotes that will provide readers with the meanings of your allusions.

- Read two stories from Díaz's short-story collection *Drown*, and write an essay discussing the narration by Yunior in these stories and in *The Brief Wondrous Life of Oscar Wao*, addressing the consistency of the voice, evidence of maturity over time, and any evolution in Yunior's perspective. Finally, analyze Díaz's decision to retain his established narrator for his debut novel.

- Create a Web site on the Dominican diaspora (people who settle far from their homeland), discussing historical patterns of immigration, characteristics of cities and regions that have become prominent enclaves for Dominican immigrants, and sociological aspects of Dominicans' integration into other cultures.

- Read *Before We Were Free*, a book for young adults by the Dominican American author Julia Alvarez, about a twelve-year-old named Anita (whose literary namesake is Anne Frank) who must go into hiding with her mother after her father is taken away by the secret police. Compare and contrast Anita with Belicia Cabral from *The Brief Wondrous Life of Oscar Wao*, considering the trials they must endure, the resilience they demonstrate, and the overall impact of their fathers' disappearances on their lives. Use Glogster or another online poster creator to show the results of your comparison.

- Write a paper on the effects of the advent and popularization of the Internet on beliefs in magic and the supernatural, analyzing the content of various relevant Web sites you find. Use *StumbleUpon* to help you discover and share great Web sites to determine whether belief in magic or the supernatural is confirmed, enhanced, distorted, or refuted in each case.

Lola clips off all her hair to self-identify as a punk outcast, largely to escape her mother's influence. Oscar is ridiculed for his weight and considered "a loser" because of his interest in fantasy and science fiction. As a voluntary outcast and runaway, Lola has some disheartening experiences but seems to make psychological gains, allowing her to resume a more socially acceptable persona at her Dominican academy (when she is beyond her mother's reach). Belicia and Oscar, on the other hand, both imagine that refuge from their isolation will come only in the form of love, yet both are so overwhelmed by their isolation that they become overly dependent on the idea of love, seeing it as their only hope for salvation, with tragic consequences for both. Belicia's infatuation with the pampered, egocentric Jack Pujols leads to her expulsion from school, while her affair with the Gangster leads to her horrific beating; in both cases, she is gripped by visions of a happy marriage. Similarly, Oscar's impossible vision of happiness with Ybón leads to his destruction. Both Belicia and Oscar, then, might have been spared much pain and suffering had they not been so desperate to escape their loneliness—had they not been outcasts.

Love

While Oscar and Belicia are in certain senses misguided by their obsessive loves, their experiences also highlight the transformative power of love. Belicia eventually realizes that what she had with Jack Pujols was not love, but the Gangster, whatever his moral failings, showers her with love that feels true. His "adoration was one of the greatest

Oscar spent much of his time on computer games. *(Patricia Malina / Shutterstock.com)*

gifts anybody had ever given her," and in a parenthetical line that Yunior presents as if quoting Belicia, she declares, "*For the first time I actually felt like I owned my skin, like it was me and I was it.*" She thus relates the palpable sense of self-assurance that can be inspired by mutual romantic love and devotion, especially when such a relationship is first experienced. This is just the sort of mutual love Oscar sought, without success, throughout his life. For a time in college, his affection for Jenni did inspire him with confidence and ambition, with Yunior noting "he was like I'd never seen him, love the transformer." He sharpened his appearance and resumed exercising, running as well as wielding a wooden sword on his dormitory's lawn in elaborate attack routines (a comical image, but Oscar would surely have benefited from the physical well-being and holistic sense of self fostered by education in the martial arts). When Oscar falls for Ybón, Yunior notes, "Love, for this kid, was a geas"—a binding oath, as in Gaelic mythology, or spell, as in the game *Dungeons and Dragons*—"something that could not be shaken or denied." Indeed, for many, the feeling of romantic love is not a choice

but a fate, compelling them to act and behave in ways they may not anticipate. Whether the consequences are positive or not, the enamored person, transformed by love, is drawn to a destiny as a new person with a more profound understanding of the possibilities of life.

STYLE

Dominican American Vernacular

The Brief Wondrous Life of Oscar Wao features a slang-laden bilingual lexicon, with Spanish words used frequently without italicization, which provokes various responses in readers. The occasional monocultural critic bristles at the absence of translations, but more typical is the response elicited by Michiko Kakutani, chief critic for the *New York Times*, who praises Díaz's vernacular as "a sort of streetwise brand of Spanglish that even the most monolingual reader can easily inhale: lots of flash words and razzle-dazzle talk, lots of body language on the sentences." While the reader may at first feel compelled to determine the meaning of every unknown word, to stop at each Spanish term would be to constantly disrupt the act of reading, and so the reader is forced to adapt by intuiting the sense of words without knowing their precise definitions—a strategy that immigrants, as well as children, must rely on every day, as Díaz has pointed out. Some of the Spanish words, like *guapa* ("beautiful") and *hijo* ("son"), become self-evident, while others are graphic terms and obscenities that, in being obscure, perhaps render the book slightly more palatable to conservative tastes. The significance of some passages, certainly, can only be understood if the meanings of the Spanish terms are known—for example, it is useful to know that *ciguapas* are mythical beautiful women who live underwater. Therefore those readers who speak Spanish or have a Spanish-English dictionary on hand will be privy to a more profound understanding of the narrative.

Díaz has confirmed in interviews that his use of Spanish without italicization or translation is a conscious choice made for aesthetic as well as political reasons. In a 2000 interview for *Callaloo*, he noted that, for his short-story collection *Drown*, he "sought coherence" with regard to which words appear in Spanish—and with his novel, the reader accordingly gets the sense that Yunior (who also narrated the stories in *Drown*) naturally uses Spanish whenever a concept seems better or more accurately expressed in Spanish. As for the politics, Díaz asserted, "Spanish is not a minority language. Not in this hemisphere, not in the United States, not in the world inside my head. So why treat it like one? Why 'other' it?" He acknowledges that his lexical choices can be characterized as violent, in that the English-language reader is forced to imbibe the Spanish without it being spoon-fed, so to speak, and so he likens this to the "violent enterprise" of being educated in English upon moving to America, which he experienced at age seven. He concludes,

> By forcing Spanish back onto English, forcing it to deal with the language it tried to exterminate in me, I've tried to represent a mirror-image of that violence on the page. Call it my revenge on English.

In exacting his revenge, Díaz is surely doing Americans (and others) a favor, firmly situating his readers in a multicultural twenty-first century in which to speak only a single language is inadequate to informed participation in the global community.

Science Fiction and Fantasy

The Brief Wondrous Life of Oscar Wao is drenched in the lingo, characters, powers, and ideas found in the vast array of popular fantasy and sci-fi entertainments classified as "Genres" by Yunior, including comic books, published by Marvel Comics (featuring the X-Men), and DC (with Darkseid); Japanese anime, especially the classic *Akira* (1988); old-school sci-fi films, like *Planet of the Apes* (1968); video and role-playing games, like *Dungeons and Dragons*; and fantasy literature. The most significant allusions may be to Tolkien's epic *The Lord of the Rings* novels, since Trujillo is deemed analogous to Sauron, the dark lord whose sinister eye has supernatural powers of perception; Trujillo is called "the Eye" several times.

Discussing the significance of his novel's genre motif for *Yale Literary Magazine*, Díaz observed that the "extreme narratives" present in works of fantasy actually align well with the extreme changes and circumstances experienced by an immigrant moving from the Third World to America. As a preadolescent learning English, he was not limited by his Spanish accent when reading to himself, and he found fantasy literature both accessible and fascinating. Comic books can be especially instructive in language acquisition, since the shared connotations of words and illustrations give the reader a better chance of decoding the text. Although the genres highlighted by Díaz have historically been given short shrift in the literary world, he affirmed in an interview for *World Literature Today* that "comic books, fantasy, and science fiction are like a very vibrant, alive, and very American language."

Magic and the Supernatural

The notion that supernatural phenomena are possible is central to this text, in that a persisting question is whether or not fukú is to blame for the fates suffered by the family of Abelard Cabral, including his grandson, Oscar. Yunior is ambiguous about his own belief in the supernatural, but as he remarks, "No matter what the truth, remember: Dominicans are Caribbean and therefore have an extraordinary tolerance for extreme phenomena." Furthermore, "In Santo Domingo a story is not a story unless it casts a supernatural shadow." Accordingly, several events in the novel he narrates verge on the magical. In their most trying moments, both Belicia, after her cane field beating, and Oscar, before drunkenly jumping from a bridge and after his own beating, have visions of a sort of golden-eyed mongoose that seems to seek to save them. Yunior notes in a footnote that the mongoose is "an enemy of kingly chariots, chains, and hierarchies"—and would thus be antithetical to Trujillo and his fukú—and "believed to be an ally of Man." Another magical moment occurs when Clives is led by heavenly singing to Oscar's beaten body, to be struck by a "tremendous wind" that was "like the blast an angel might lay down on takeoff," leaving behind the scent of cinnamon.

It would be a stretch, however, to pigeonhole Díaz's novel as a work of magical realism, the literary movement widely associated with Latin American authors such as Gabriel Garcia Marquez, whose novels feature profoundly improbable as well as impossible events. Díaz nods toward the distinction between magical realists of Marquez's generation and the globalized Latin American authors of his own generation when he notes in the prologue that the idea of zafa was "more popular in the old days, bigger, so to speak, in Macondo than in McOndo." Macondo is the town in which the Buendia family resides in Marquez's *One Hundred Years of Solitude*, where the fantastic is commonplace. The McOndo movement, sparked by the anthology *McOndo* (1996), edited by Alberto Fuguet and Sergio Gómez, is associated with Hispanic authors who have refused to kowtow to white critics' and publishers' expectations that any new work by a Latin American author should be magical realist. Much of Marquez's magic is associated not merely with the myth and mystery of traditional culture but also with the bizarre and seemingly magical technology that was suddenly introduced to Latin America by Western culture. The McOndo generation of authors, raised in a Latin America that has already been modernized and commodified, believe it would be specious to adapt the style of their forebears out of ethnic loyalty when their nations have evolved to the point where they necessarily see the world from an entirely different perspective.

Díaz, it seems, falls somewhere in the middle of the Macondo-versus-McOndo spectrum. He does not use magic as a trope to reflect the psychological nuances of traditional culture or colonial relationships, but he does not disavow its use, and the supernatural elements are essential to the plot of his novel. Indeed, if Yunior's novel can be understood as his fulfillment of Oscar's efforts to fulfill Abelard's legendary quest to write "an exposé of the supernatural

roots of the Trujillo regime," then *The Brief Wondrous Life of Oscar Wao* can be understood precisely as arguing "that it was possible that Trujillo was, if not in fact, then in principle, a creature from another world!" In a sense, then, the book amounts to an anecdotal argument for the existence of the supernatural and the irrational, as perpetuated by those who believe in the irrational as well as by those who profess not to. It is perhaps up to the reader to conclude whether something that is supernatural "in principle" is truly supernatural or not.

HISTORICAL CONTEXT

History of the Dominican Republic

In *The Brief Wondrous Life of Oscar Wao*, the stories of the protagonists are intertwined with the history of the Dominican Republic, with Díaz insinuating that a function of the novel is to demonstrate the effectively supernatural power of Trujillo's regime. As such, the author makes a point of ensuring the reader's familiarity with the essentials of modern Dominican history, especially the thirty-one-year period known as the Era of Trujillo—a designation used during his reign on all Dominican calendars, which counted the years beginning with his inauguration as president. Although much of the novel is set in New Jersey in the late twentieth century—an era not unfamiliar to modern readers of all ages by virtue of television and film—the lives of Oscar and Lola are portrayed as being in part determined by their family history, especially as scripted during the Trujillo era, and both make trips back to the Dominican Republic that prove essential to their psychic health. While Trujillo appears in person in the novel, and his pervasive influence on the nation is considered at length, Díaz avoided weighing the narrative down with historical details by using footnotes, which are informally written but concisely comprehensive. A summary of this period of Dominican history, then, would be little more than a reiteration of Yunior's impressionistic review in more conventionally academic terms.

A historical circumstance not mentioned by Díaz is the responsibility borne by the United States for the rise of Trujillo. In the opening years of the twentieth century, following the 1899 death of an earlier ruthless dictator, Ulises Heureaux, the Dominican Republic experienced

COMPARE
&
CONTRAST

- **1950s:** Though stepping down as president in 1952, Rafael Trujillo effectively remains the dictator in the Dominican Republic, overseeing a nation deluded by his propaganda, economically drained by his nepotistic monopolies, gripped by paranoia over his murderous secret police, and cut off from the international community.

  1980s: The elections of 1982 and 1986 are generally competitive, fair, and free; yet the government continues to be influenced by factors other than the results of the election.

  Today: President Leonel Fernández oversees a democratic Dominican Republic that struggles through a recession in the early 2000s caused by bank collapses and other factors, but tourism is a growing industry, and Dominicans living abroad send billions of dollars back to their homeland annually.

- **1950s:** With baseball having replaced soccer as the most popular sporting pastime during the American occupation, Dominican players first gain access to the American major leagues near the end of Trujillo's reign, with Ozzie Virgil, Sr., being the first to join the major leagues in 1956 and Felipe Alou joining in 1958, followed by his brothers, and eventually his son.

  1980s: Hundreds of Dominican baseball players are in the Major League Baseball system. Superstars include Rafael Ramirez, Tony Pena, Julio Franco, Andres Thomas, and Jose Rijo, among them.

  Today: More major league baseball players come from the Dominican Republic than any other nation outside the United States, with over two hundred Dominicans currently active, including the all-stars Albert Pujols and Miguel Tejada. Felipe Alou manages the Dominican national team.

- **1950s:** According to the 1950 census, the population of New Jersey is 93.3 percent white, 6.6 percent African American, and 0.1 percent Asian. Hispanic or Latino background is listed as N/A and calculated as part of the white population.

  1980s: As of the 1980 census, the population of New Jersey is 83.5 percent white, 12.6 percent African American, 1.5 percent Asian, and 0.1 percent Native American, while 6.7 percent claim Hispanic or Latino background as well.

  Today: As of 2005, the population of New Jersey is 76.6 percent white, 14.5 percent African American, 7.2 percent Asian, and 0.3 percent Native American, while 15.2 percent claim Hispanic or Latino background as well.

- **1950s:** The 1950s is considered to be "the Golden Age of Science Fiction Films," according to the *Filmsite* Web site. The interest in these films is a result of an interest in rocketry and space exploration, as advance by the cold war. Also of interest are films that portray alien invasions.

  1980s: Throughout the United States, science-fiction films become reliable mainstream entertainment with the enormous success of the *Star Wars* trilogy, though people who learn all the characters and memorize the lines from the movies are not likely to be considered "cool."

  Today: With Peter Jackson's *The Lord of the Rings* trilogy having dominated the box office and Academy Awards in the early 2000s, the *X-Men* films having become a hugely popular franchise, and James Cameron's three-dimensional film *Avatar* (2009) being the highest-grossing film of all time, fantasy, science-fiction, and superhero films can be said to dominate the minds and tastes of modern moviegoers.

Oscar was an avid reader of everything from science fiction to comic books. (liza1979 | Shutterstock.com)

rapid changes in its highest office—not an uncommon phenomenon in postcolonial Latin America—with four revolutions and five different presidents over six years. Owing to the established governmental habit of raising finances by simply printing more money, inflation was rampant, and the country verged on bankruptcy, frustrating creditors. To prevent European intervention to secure funds by force, the United States opportunistically assumed control of the Dominican Republic's customs receivership in 1905. President Theodore Roosevelt, the renowned Rough Rider who fought in Cuba during the Spanish-American War of 1898 and became known for his "Big Stick" diplomacy, was clear in declaring it "the duty of the United States to intervene in those wretched banana republics in order to protect and assure the economic investments and interests of the civilized nations." Through the Spanish-American War, the United States had gained jurisdiction over Puerto Rico and Cuba, and so economic and military control in the Caribbean were clear American priorities.

The political situation in the Dominican Republic remained unstable over the next decade, with increasing portions of the economy, especially the sugar-cane estates, falling under the control of foreign investors. In 1914, the United States tried to use its financial leverage to force the republic to accept a number of reforms that would grant significant government power to American politicos, but the Dominican Congress adamantly refused to accept the conditions, leading President Woodrow Wilson to authorize U.S. Marines to take control of the country in the spring of 1916. The congress was suspended, the supreme court's authority was nullified, and the succession of U.S.-appointed military governors—none of whom spoke any Spanish—were empowered to rule by decree. The Dominican Republic lost all autonomy, and to stifle public complaints, the military government censored local presses. Meanwhile, the populace was disarmed, which prevented the rise of any new military-backed dictators, and a new military force was installed in the form of the Guardia Nacional, which maintained order with zealous efficiency.

Over the ensuing eight years of occupation, improvements were made to infrastructure, including the road system, sanitation, communications, and education. However Dominicans remained fiercely opposed to the American presence and, despite being deprived of sophisticated weaponry, waged guerrilla campaigns against their occupiers, especially in the eastern region. It was this relentless resistance that finally spurred the American withdrawal in 1924, when a new Dominican constitution was enacted and a new president elected. The military force, however, remained disproportionately powerful, especially in light of the disarmament of the masses, and left in control of what was now the Policía Nacional Dominicana, which would evolve into the national army, was none other than Rafael Leónidas Trujillo. As the historian Howard Wiarda notes in *Dictatorship and Development: The Methods of Control in Trujillo's Dominican Republic*, Trujillo has thus been called "the bastard son of the occupation forces," and "it is for this reason that the United States is often held accountable by Dominicans for the entire Trujillo era."

CRITICAL OVERVIEW

As with his short-story collection *Drown* (1996), Díaz received wide acclaim upon the publication of *The Brief Wondrous Life of Oscar Wao*. Kakutani of the *New York Times* offered high praise, calling the work "an extraordinarily vibrant book that's fueled by adrenaline-powered prose," with "the slangy, kinetic energy of his prose proving to be a remarkably effective tool for capturing the absurdities of the human condition." The work stands out for its unified treatment of the national and the familial, as Díaz has "fashioned both a big picture window that opens out on the sorrows of Dominican history, and a small, intimate window that reveals one family's life and loves." Kakutani concludes that Díaz is "one of contemporary fiction's most distinctive and irresistible new voices."

In the *New Statesman*, Alice O'Keeffe notes how the "zinging, muscular Spanglish" draws on the "verbal riches" of "the precision of English, the rhythm and playfulness of Caribbean Spanish." She remarks, "This hybrid language works so well suddenly that it seems surprising it has taken so long for bilingual literature to emerge. How long can it be in our globalised world before it becomes the norm?" She calls the prose "consistently sharp and startling" and lauds "the raw energy of Diaz's storytelling," concluding that the book is a "gripping read." In the *Los Angeles Times*, Susan Straight calls the novel "panoramic and yet achingly personal," a tale "in which one family's dramas are entwined with a nation's,"

considering history not "as information but as dark-force destroyer." Recognizing Díaz's aesthetic intentions, she asserts that "it takes novelistic audacity for Díaz to make his narrator at first anonymous, unconcerned about whether his language is accessible, flawed and angry."

In a review for *Publishers Weekly*, Matthew Sharpe states that Díaz's "dark and exuberant first novel makes a compelling case for the multiperspectival view of a life, wherein an individual cannot be known or understood in isolation from the history of his family and his nation." He notes, "The book's pervasive sense of doom is offset by a rich and playful prose that embodies its theme of multiple nations, cultures and languages." He finds that the later chapters "lack the linguistic brio of the others," while "there are exposition-clogged passages that read like summaries," but "mostly this fierce funny, tragic book is just what a reader would have hoped for in a novel by Junot Díaz."

In *World Literature Today*, Jim Hannan speaks of Díaz's "potent style—sarcastic, cynical, terse, and, at just the right moments, sensitive." While there is freedom reflected in his "prose unburdened by sentimentality, unfettered by polite conventions," Díaz nonetheless "refuses to forget the heavy burden the past can place on the present," lending the novel profound historical depth and relevance.

CRITICISM

Michael Allen Holmes

Holmes is a writer and editor. In the following essay, he considers how the motifs of facelessness in The Brief Wondrous Life of Oscar Wao *and in the film* The Matrix *enhance the reader's impression of the supernatural forces associated with the Trujillo regime.*

The Brief Wondrous Life of Oscar Wao features such a multitude of allusions to fantastic and science-fictional elements of popular culture and literature, from "Chakobsa" to "Morlock" to "Gormenghast" and beyond, that the average reader will surely be unfamiliar with a wide variety of names and concepts. Referencing and research reveal that Díaz is not haphazard with his metaphors; the qualities and traits of the characters, forces, and worlds mentioned by Yunior invariably relate well with the people and circumstances under discussion. Still, the reader may wonder whether there are additional

WHAT DO I READ NEXT?

- Díaz's first publication, the short-story collection *Drown* (1996), narrated by Yunior, earned the author much acclaim—and pressure to follow up—and led to several fellowships.

- *In the Time of the Butterflies* (1994), an acclaimed work of historical fiction by the Dominican American author Julia Alvarez, treats the lives and deaths of the courageous Mirabal sisters, who are mentioned in Díaz's novel.

- Julia Alvarez has published a collection of autobiographical essays, addressing her personal life as well as her identity and work as an author, called *Something to Declare* (1998).

- Oscar Hijuelos, who was born in New York City to Cuban parents, won the 1990 Pulitzer Prize for *The Mambo Kings Play Songs of Love* (1989), about two Cuban musicians who emigrate to the United States.

- Díaz has declared that his favorite Caribbean author is Patrick Chamoiseau, of Martinique, whose novel *Texaco* (1992) is also a tale of multigenerational suffering.

- In *Ilustrado* (2010), the debut novel by Miguel Syjuco, a student seeks to solve the mystery of the death of a Filipino author living in exile in the United States, whose manuscript about corruption in his home country is missing.

- The title of Díaz's novel is a reference to "The Short Happy Life of Francis Macomber," by Ernest Hemingway—included in *The Complete Short Stories of Ernest Hemingway* (1987)—about a foolhardy man on safari in Africa.

- Díaz has asserted that a work of science-fiction literature that reflects his experience of immigration to America is *Time Machine* (1935), by H. G. Wells, about a Victorian-era gentleman who is astonished by what he finds when he travels forward to the year 802,701.

- *An Island Like You: Stories from the Barrio* (1999), a work of young-adult fiction by Judith Ortiz Cofer, tells of experiences of Puerto Rican teenagers living in New Jersey.

---

dimensions to any of the references—whether clues to the sense of the novel can be found in any of the works to which he alludes. One such source, *The Matrix* (1999), directed by Larry and Andy Wachowski, has on its own provoked much philosophical discussion, which would suggest that Díaz is mining the film's implications, perhaps to a greater extent than is evident on the surface. A symbolic motif in the novel that corresponds with a variant motif in *The Matrix* is that of facelessness.

The plot of *The Matrix* will be familiar to most of Díaz's readers. A hacker who goes by the name of Neo is identified by Morpheus and Trinity, two other notorious hackers, as worthy of learning the truth about the world he lives in, dubbed the Matrix. Morpheus presents him with a choice between two pills, a red and a blue: the red

will show him the truth about the Matrix, the blue will allow him to return to reality as he knows it. Neo chooses the red—and so begins a hallucinatory journey in which he discovers that the world he knows, the Matrix, is a computer-generated illusion. In the real world, which has been blackened and scarred by nuclear war, entire races of powerful and intelligent machines and computers are harvesting the electromagnetic energies of the planet's billions of human beings, who are unconscious and plugged into a vast cyber-biological network that situates their minds in the virtual reality of the Matrix. Some of these humans have escaped and, led by Morpheus and others, are seeking to find the One, a prophesied redeemer—possibly Neo—and thwart the machines. These revolutionaries have learned how to plug themselves into the Matrix and bend and break some of its rules, like gravity, to aid them in their quest.

REFERENCING AND RESEARCH REVEAL THAT DÍAZ IS NOT HAPHAZARD WITH HIS METAPHORS; THE QUALITIES AND TRAITS OF THE CHARACTERS, FORCES, AND WORLDS MENTIONED BY YUNIOR INVARIABLY RELATE WELL WITH THE PEOPLE AND CIRCUMSTANCES UNDER DISCUSSION."

Yunior alludes to *The Matrix* in only two related instances. In the film, when Neo has swallowed the red pill and is about to be shown the truth about the Matrix, Cypher remarks, "Buckle your seatbelt, Dorothy, 'cause Kansas is goin' bye-bye." This line of course alludes to L. Frank Baum's book *The Wonderful Wizard of Oz* (1900) or, more accurately, the film version *The Wizard of Oz* (1939). The film made revolutionary use of Technicolor to portray the fantasy land of Oz as having depth and beauty beyond that of the ordinary reality Dorothy knows in Kansas. Cypher's line, then, is ironic, since Dorothy leaves reality for fantasy, while Neo is leaving fantasy for reality. The Matrix—the illusory world Neo is leaving—is the more colorful and beautiful one, while reality turns out to be grim, dismal, and shaded almost exclusively in the blacks and grays of rocks, metal, and machines.

In the prologue of *The Brief Wondrous Life of Oscar Wao*, Yunior remarks, "One final note, Toto, before Kansas goes bye-bye." This phrasing echoes the line from *The Matrix* (although Yunior addresses "Toto," Dorothy's dog, perhaps as a play on words), and so, somewhat paradoxically, it can bear the connotations of both the original sense of *The Wizard of Oz* and the ironic sense of *The Matrix*. Díaz may be suggesting, then, that the world he is about to reveal to the reader is on the one hand like Oz, more magical, fantastical, and colorful than commonly understood reality, and on the other hand like reality outside the Matrix, the dark and dismal truth about how the world functions. Díaz revisits the same circumstances from *The Matrix* at the point in the novel when the balance of Oscar's psyche is tilting toward his fatal infatuation with Ybón; Yunior remarks to the reader, "This is your chance. If red pill, continue. If blue pill, return to the Matrix."

The Matrix is subtly referred to in two other instances, when Yunior makes reference to "the Real"—the term used by Morpheus to designate the real world, as opposed to the Matrix. When Oscar is being taken into the cane field the first time, he experiences something "worse than déjà vu" (another motif from the film—a glitch designating that the Matrix has been altered) and then a few words from Grod and Grundy "brought Oscar back to the Real." When Oscar finally wakes up several days later, just after dreaming about the old man holding a book with blank pages, "he broke through the plane of unconsciousness and into the universe of the Real." This wording evokes Morpheus's philosophical eloquence, as during his explanation of the truth about the Matrix to Neo. These allusions suggest that Oscar is figuring out the truth about the way the real world functions, as did his grandfather; just as the fukú is catching up with him, he is coming to understand how it works.

Although *The Matrix* is not directly referred to at any other point in the novel, readers may find that a certain motif is reminiscent of the film: that of facelessness. At various points in the novel, the protagonists are struck by the sight of a person who does not seem to have a face. The earliest instance occurs when Belicia, exhausted from long walking in the heat, is given a ride after being deserted by the Gangster in Samaná and sees a faceless man in a rocking chair—the first eerie sign that she is in mortal danger. The succeeding instances of facelessness perceived in reality happen in moments of extreme peril, such as when Belicia and Oscar are abducted and cruelly beaten. When Belicia is about to be kidnapped by La Fea's thugs, she sees a faceless third cop in their car. When Oscar is first abducted by Grod and Grundy, he, too, sees "a lone man sitting in his rocking chair," and he "could have sworn the dude had no face." When he is being beaten, "there were moments Oscar was sure that he was being beaten by three men, not two, that the faceless man from in front of the colmado was joining them." Later, when Grod and Grundy are on the verge of executing him, they speak with "their faces slowly disappearing in the gloom."

The instances of facelessness verge on the supernatural—but in each case, given the extreme physical or emotional strain of the circumstances, the character could surely be hallucinating. Whether considering the image as supernatural or as psychic distress, the reader gets the sense that the facelessness signifies a sort of inability to witness something: neither the people watching from the roadside nor the men who actually carry out the beatings will ever testify that this criminal abduction has taken place; to object to any action of the police is to defy the will of Trujillo himself, for which the sentence is certain death. Thus, as far as Oscar and Belicia are concerned, these people who appear faceless have seen nothing, none of what has taken place before them, and they will in turn say nothing. In negating their own identities by bowing to the will of Trujillo, in those moments, they are not exactly human; they are missing the part which by sight instinctively empathizes with those in need and by word communicates with others for the good of the community. In those moments, the identities of those silent, unseeing people are veritably erased; they become faceless.

The other instances of facelessness all occur in dreams, including one daydream. When Abelard's day of arrest nears, Socorro dreams "that the faceless man was standing over her husband's bed, and she could not scream, could not say anything, and then the next night she dreamed that he was standing over her children too." This, then, is a premonition that the faceless force that enables the erasure of people from existence is drawing toward her family. Indeed, one by one, her husband and first two daughters are erased from history, with the daughters killed and Abelard wasting away in prison. Interestingly, Díaz has Socorro's dream occur "not two days after the atomic bombs scarred Japan forever," which lends the impression that the faceless force of her dream is associated with, or even responsible for, the catastrophic use of atomic bombs by the United States to ensure the end of World War II. Belicia dreams, when she at last finds sanctuary with La Inca at nine years of age, "about the Burning, how her 'father's' face had turned blank at the moment he picked up the skillet." In that moment of astoundingly inhumane cruelty, the father was in a sense possessed by the faceless force.

Oscar is the one who has a daydreamed vision, when he is being transported by Grod and Grundy to his execution. Upon passing a bus stop, he imagines seeing his whole family, including his deceased grandparents, getting on a bus, "and who is driving the bus but the Mongoose, and who is the cobrador but the Man Without a Face, but it was nothing but a final fantasy, gone as soon as he blinked." The mongoose—described in a footnote as "one of the great unstable particles of the Universe and also one of its greatest travelers"—has been represented as a positive force, visiting Oscar's and Belicia's spirits in their times of greatest need, leading them back from the brink of death. However, here Oscar is being driven to his death, so the "unstable" mongoose is perhaps not a positive force but a random, neutral one—perhaps an embodiment of fate. Thus, where *cobrador* means "conductor" or ticket collector, the faceless man is ushering Oscar onto the bus and toward his fate.

Yunior mentions facelessness twice more. Five years after Oscar's death—before his writing of this text—Yunior has a curious dream in which Oscar is holding up a book with blank pages, perhaps representing the final sensational work of Oscar's that was lost to history, whether lost in the mail or never written at all. Yunior adds that, in a variation of the dream, after noting the blank pages, "I look up at him and he has no face and I wake up screaming." Yunior's dreams, then, can be understood as presenting him with alternate versions of the future. The version of the dream that ends with the word *zafa* signifies that he must accept the task that Oscar has implicitly bequeathed to him, the task of writing the exposé of the Trujillo regime originally conceived by his grandfather—the zafa, perhaps, to the family's fukú. If he does not accept this task, then even Oscar is fated to facelessness; he has been tracked down by the fukú and erased from history, and if all his research and writing were for naught, then his existence was meaningless. Yunior's final mention of facelessness occurs when he envisions Lola's daughter, Isis, one day having "a dream of the No Face Man," after which she will track Yunior down to look through all of Oscar's books, games, manuscripts, and papers. Yunior hopes that "she'll take all we've done and all we've learned and add her own insights and she'll put an end to it." The "it" in question must be the dreaded fukú, yet Yunior fears that, as declared in the comic panel circled by Oscar, "nothing ever ends"—including the supernatural force of fukú.

There is no facelessness per se in *The Matrix*—although there is a scene in which Agent Smith, who represents the Matrix's antiviral security program, tinkers with the Matrix to make Neo's mouth disappear, signifying how easily—and how supernaturally—the agents can control the existence of the humans who are plugged in. The manner in Díaz's novel whereby people around the protagonists suddenly appear faceless—as if they perhaps lost their faces only moments earlier—is reminiscent of the way the agents can suddenly inhabit the bodies of people plugged into the Matrix. When Neo is being chased, innocent bystanders suddenly change into agents bent on killing him. Indeed, Morpheus warns Neo that everyone is a potential enemy, because anyone can be suddenly inhabited by an agent. This is analogous to the sense in a dictatorship that, if you act, speak, or even think in opposition to the regime, any bystander could potentially report you to the authorities; indeed, it is often a serious crime simply to witness any so-called revolutionary act and fail to report it. Thus, in potentially serving as witnesses for the regime, people lose an aspect of their identity; if they see or hear something illegal, at that moment, one is not oneself but is an agent for others. While in real life this agency is figurative, in *The Matrix*, this agency is literal, as the innocent people become agents; the viewer is given a visceral sense of this possession in, at times, being shown the surreal transformation of the person's face into that of an agent.

The agents, of course, exist in bodily form but do not represent actual people or humanity; they are aspects of a computer program, designed to police activity within the Matrix. In operating with disregard for the rules of the Matrix, to those ordinary people within, they appear to be humans with supernatural powers. They thus function as a negative force that, if crossed, can bring about a person's doom in a supernatural way, disobeying the rules of reality with which the person is familiar. In Díaz's novel, the Dominicans who appear faceless can be understood as possessed by the spirit of the dictatorship—indeed, perhaps by Trujillo himself. As Lola notes, despairing in the wake of Oscar's death, "Ten million Trujillos is all we are." If Díaz had wanted to represent supernatural possession by Trujillo, he surely could have rendered the text in such a way that the victims see an image of Trujillo without realizing it is him; they would see only select features, and by the end of the novel, it might be apparent that the hallucinated faces were all that of Trujillo. Instead, Díaz represented this possession with facelessness, and he has made clear, in an interview with *Yale Literary Magazine*, that there is important significance to the motif:

> As a reader you have to put the book together in your head, but you could only do so by answering some important questions for yourself: why is Yunior telling THIS story? Who is the Man Without a Face? But I've said too much.

Yunior seems to be telling this story because he has taken up the cause originated by Abelard Cabral and adopted by his late friend Oscar: to argue

> that the tales the common people told about the president—that he was supernatural, that he was not human—may in some ways have been *true*. That it was possible that Trujillo was, if not in fact, then in principle, a creature from another world!

Indeed, Trujillo seems to have been effectively capable of the same supernatural possession practiced by the agents of the Matrix. In the moments witnessed by Belicia and Oscar and in the dreams of Socorro, Belicia, Oscar, and Yunior, both bystanders and aggressors are possessed by a faceless force that veritably erases their identity. Thus, where the agents are creations of a security program designed to ensure the doom of those who have crossed the delineated boundaries of the Matrix, the power at Trujillo's disposal, which ensures the doom of those who cross him, must be some similar force, supernatural in its operation. Yunior reveals just what this force is in the prologue: fukú, for which Trujillo was "a high priest." Yunior declares, "No one knows whether Trujillo was the Curse's servant or its master, its agent or its principal, but it was clear he and it had an understanding, that them two was *tight*." It would seem, then, that the faceless force that can possess the people of the Dominican Republic, embodied as the faceless man, is fukú itself. As an agent of fukú, or with fukú as his agent, Trujillo was, in principle if not in fact, an inhuman, supernatural force—a creature from another world—and in elucidating as much by telling the tragic, haunting tales of Oscar de Léon and his fukú-stricken kin, Yunior has succeeded in fulfilling Abelard and Oscar's legendary quest.

Source: Michael Allen Holmes, Critical Essay on *The Brief Wondrous Life of Oscar Wao*, in *Novels for Students*, Gale, Cengage Learning, 2011.

Susan Walker

In the following review, Walker claims that Díaz expands the boundaries of the novel form, while doing so in a second language.

The workers were taken into the sugar cane fields and beaten. *(Chris Hill / Shutterstock.com)*

Every once in a while an exciting new voice comes along in English-language fiction, to expand the boundaries of the novel.

Quite often that voice belongs to someone for whom English is a second language (think Joseph Conrad or Vladimir Nabokov or Salman Rushdie).

Such is the case with Junot Diaz, winner of this year's Pulitzer Prize for Fiction for his novel *The Brief Wondrous Life of Oscar Wao.*

Diaz's prose jives with an energy that marks him as a writer fuelled by a clash of cultures: "Our hero was not one of those Dominican cats everybody's always going on about—he wasn't no home-run hitter or a fly bachatero, not a playboy with a million hots on his jock."

Oscar Wao, in other words, is an unlikely hero. Born in New Jersey, raised by a single mom who is an immigrant from the Dominican Republic, he is a sci-fi and fantasy addict who wants to be a new Tolkien; an overweight nerd, forever in pursuit of unattainable women.

Diaz, on his cellphone from his home in New York City, admits there's a bit of himself in Oscar.

"I always had a great fascination with genre (writing): sci-fi, horror or fantasy." As a boy, he succumbed to "all sorts of normative adolescent pressure. I took all my childhood loves and pushed them into a deep, dark closet. Just to get a date, I sold my younger self right up the river. Oscar was the me that wasn't permitted to be, in some ways."

Unlike Oscar, Diaz was not born in the United States. As a Dominican child who arrived in New Jersey at the age of 6 without a word of English, he grew up with even bigger obstacles to overcome.

"Insecurity around a certain area tends to lead to hyper-achievement," he says, advancing a notion about his choice of a writing career.

The third of five children in a family where the father was permanently absent from the time he was 12 or 13, Diaz developed a huge love of reading. "Eventually that passion for reading led me to writing."

Like his alter ego, Yunior, the first-person narrator of the novel, Diaz attended Rutgers University, where he studied English. He completed an MFA at Cornell University in 1995. A year later, his first book, a collection of short stories entitled *Drown*, came out. In stories such as "How to Date a Browngirl, Blackgirl, Whitegirl, or Halfie," Diaz emerged as funny, irreverent, at once colloquially American and artfully Latino.

The author, not quite 40, worked 11 years on *The Brief Wondrous Life of Oscar Wao*. The many-layered novel contains a particularly vivid and personalized history of the Dominican Republic, laid out in long footnotes.

"My goal was to talk about the New World," he says, describing his native country as "Ground Zero of the Americas. It's the first place Europeans settled—the first iteration of that construct that would reach its apogee in (American society)."

Oscar clings stubbornly to his crazy, romantic ideals and never does find a circle he belongs in, ignoring all those who would save him from a tragic fate. In one way, Diaz can sympathize with him as the outsider.

"It's one of those weird things," he says. He may be an accomplished writer, a teacher of creative writing at MIT, but, he says, "there is always a one-second delay when I'm talking, to make sure I get everything correct. You never stop being an immigrant."

Source: Susan Walker, "Colloquially American, This Writer Is Artfully Latino: A Clash of Cultures Fuels the Work of Junot Diaz, a Native of 'Ground Zero of the Americas,'" in *Toronto Star*, October 24, 2008, p. E2.

Jim Hannan

In the following review, Hannan states that Díaz writes in prose unburdened by sentimentality, refusing to forget the heavy burden the past can have on the present.

In his first novel, Junot Diaz writes with the potent style—sarcastic, cynical, terse, and, at just the right moments, sensitive—that made *Drown* (1997), his first book of short stories, a success. *In The Brief Wondrous Life of Oscar Wao*, Diaz, who was born in the Dominican Republic and grew up in New Jersey, writes a novel of the Americas that follows the fate of one particular family of Dominicans as it transpires in the Caribbean and in Paterson, New Jersey. Throughout the novel Diaz explores history, violence (perpetrated by both the state and individuals), and diaspora while narrating a relentless obsession with sex (or, for poor Oscar Wao, the continual failure to have sex) and the often-stifling inadequacies of

love. What makes Oscar himself different, however, and continually victimized by the hypersexualized circumstances he inhabits, is that he has another, more troublesome, obsession. "Nothing compared to the amor he was carrying in his heart for Ana. The only thing that came close was how he felt about his books and everything he hoped to write." While Yunior, the tough-minded and serially unfaithful narrator, manages to combine his idea of Dominican masculinity with creative writing, Oscar, a fat, unattractive sci-fi addict with low self-esteem, suffers on account of his idiosyncratic and awkward personality. "You really want to know what being an X-man feels like? Just be a smart bookish boy of color in a contemporary U.S. ghetto. Like having bat wings growing out of your chest."

Much of Diaz's novel is a biting and justifiably angry portrait of the lamentable three decades, and continuing aftermath, of the Trujillo dictatorship in the Dominican Republic. In the first of several footnotes in the novel, Diaz brings his readers up to speed: "A portly, sadistic, pig-eyed mulatto who bleached his skin, Trujillo came to control nearly every aspect of the DR's political, cultural, social, and economic life through a potent (and familiar) mixture of violence, intimidation, massacre, rape, co-optation, and terror. He was a personae so outlandish, so perverse, so dreadful that not even a sci-fi writer would have made his ass up." Indeed, despite the sarcasm and grim humor that run throughout this novel, it is often a book of horrors. The sections on Trujillo's reign—his abuse of girls and women, and his ruthless imprisonment, torture, and murder of opponents (real and purported)—become increasingly chilling. The pages depicting the imprisonment and torture of Oscar's grandfather are at once impossible to stop reading and impossible to bear. When Oscar's mother, as a teenage girl, runs afoul of the Trujillo family, she is severely beaten. "All that can be said is that it was the end of language, the end of hope. It was the sort of beating that breaks people, breaks them utterly."

Throughout the novel, Junot Diaz writes in prose unburdened by sentimentality, unfettered by polite conventions, and unfazed by the seemingly unending number of "those very bad men that not even postmodernism can explain away." He refuses to forget the heavy burden the past can place on the present. Whether he writes about the dysfunctions of a whole society or the miserable failings of an individual, Diaz recognizes an unfortunate dimension of the human condition that his tough-guy narration cannot fully deny: "A heart like mine, which never got any affection growing up, is terrible above all things."

Source: Jim Hannan, Review of *The Brief Wondrous Life of Oscar Wao*, in *World Literature Today*, Vol. 82, No. 2, March/April 2008, pp. 65–66.

Alice O'Keeffe

In the following review, O'Keeffe states that The Brief Wondrous Life of Oscar Wao *is a sign that the Latin American diaspora is finding its literary voice.*

Oscar de Leon is not a typical swaggering Latino male. He can't dance, he throws like a girl, and he is obsessed with science fiction. (He relates to the idea of parallel universes: "You really wanna know what being an X-Man feels like? Just be a smart bookish boy of colour growing up in a contemporary US ghetto. Mama mia! Like having bat wings or a pair of tentacles growing out of your chest.") Most worrying of all, he has a chronic case of no-toto-itis (trans: he can't get laid). Is this just standard adolescent angst? Or is Oscar right to believe that his life has been blighted by a fuku, a curse that has hung over his family for generations?

Junot Diaz's immensely enjoyable novel explores the origins of Oscar's neuroses, tracing the de Leon family's journey back from present-day New York to the 1940s Dominican Republic. At the same time it tells the story of a diaspora from a small island with a brutal history—and examines how that history is played out in the lives of exiles and their children. Diaz, whose debut collection of short stories, *Drown*, was published in 1997, is a rare treat: a new author who has both something original to say and a fresh and idiosyncratic way of saying it.

The fuku that dogs Oscar is a legacy of his unfortunate grandfather Abelard, who got himself jailed by the Trujillo dictatorship (for readers with a less-than-extensive knowledge of Dominican history—and there may be a few—Diaz provides colourfully written footnotes on everything from the Trujillato to the "original JLo," the Dominican actress Maria Montez). The curse was passed on to his fiery, pig-headed daughter Beli, who unwisely became embroiled with the Gangster, a sinister Trujillo sidekick. When their

relationship ended, she escaped the island alive by the skin of her teeth.

Compared to the dramatic stories of their ancestors, Oscar and his sister, Lola, have things easy. Growing up in New Jersey, they suffer the usual teenage worries—fitting in, making friends, finding love—but both struggle in their different ways to reconcile themselves with their family's past. Unable to find a niche for himself in the macho Dominican community in the United States, Oscar finds himself irresistibly drawn back to the island, and to the same mistakes made by his mother and grandfather before him.

With its flights of surreal fantasy and its streetwise attitude, *Oscar Wao* belongs to a generation of Latin American-influenced writing that, to paraphrase Diaz, is "more McOndo than Macondo." A product of the lives of Latinos in the US, who are increasingly self-confident and culturally influential, it incorporates some of magical realism's magic, but none of its dewy-eyed nostalgia. It straddles two cultures and two languages: Diaz writes in zinging, muscular Spanglish, so a skinny waitress is a girl "whose cuerpo was all pipa and no culo"; Beli is "one of those Oya-souls, always turning, allergic to tranquilidad." He has an embarrassment of verbal riches to draw on: the precision of English, the rhythm and playfulness of Caribbean Spanish. This hybrid language works so well suddenly that it seems surprising it has taken so long for bilingual literature to emerge. How long can it be in our globalised world before it becomes the norm?

The prose is so consistently sharp and startling that it provides ample distraction from some of *Oscar Wao*'s weaker points. The novel works best when it focuses on the stories of Beli and Abelard, which have real narrative drive; the contemporary sections feel meandering by comparison. Diaz suffers from the common postmodern author's tendency to employ too many narrators. He creates a strong and convincing female voice in the chapters narrated by Lola (I loved some of her turns of phrase: "In the end, I just didn't have the ovaries"), but her interventions eventually only confuse the story. Yunior, who narrates the rest, is an inconsistent character who wobbles between being an objective authorial voice and an unreliable, self-satisfied ladies' man.

These are relatively minor flaws in a first novel, however, and they are more than compensated for by the raw energy of Diaz's storytelling. *The Brief Wondrous Life of Oscar Wao* is not only a gripping read, but also a sign that the Latin American diaspora is finding its literary voice.

Source: Alice O'Keeffe, "Spanglish Surrealism," in *New Statesman*, Vol. 137, No. 4885, February 25, 2008, p. 58.

Carlin Romano

In the following essay, Romano finds this novel to be stylistically inferior to Díaz's collection of stories in Drown.

Immigrant fiction became a main-lobby door to American literature more than a century ago, and Junot Díaz strode through it in 1996 with *Drown*, a taut, rapturously received collection of 10 interlinked episodes about a Dominican family in New Jersey and New York.

In the 11 years since, that one book has produced a tremendous payoff for Díaz, now 38: a Guggenheim and many other honors, a tenured teaching spot at MIT, a place among the literary princes of his generation.

It helped that *Drown* arrived when the publishing world, more than ever, welcomed fresh waves of up-from-the-streets ethnic literature, the natural follow-up to the Jewish, Irish and Italian varieties earlier on. Think of some writers working in America who have won acclaim in the last two decades—Amy Tan, Gish Jen, Jhumpa Lahiri, Ha Jin, Oscar Hijuelos, Gary Shteyngart, Uzodinma Iweala—and a belief that the ethnic (and usually immigrant novel) is passé looks passé itself.

Yet old-fashioned reservations, also raised in their time about novelists from previous "happening" ethnicities, persist.

For one thing, noblesse oblige often plays too big a role in critical responses. "Isn't it wonderful," exults the literary elite of established ethnic classes and the fading WASP establishment, that amid the bad news that so often accompanies new immigrant groups as they rise—poverty, drugs, crime—this one or that has produced a writer to give outsiders a peek at the humanity within?

It makes already-arrived literary commissars feel bold and edgy rather than what they are—bourgeois and patronizing.

Other awkward questions also frequently go unspoken. Isn't immigrant fiction often more a document than an imaginative creation, a not-so-artful reworking of the matter-of-fact life the

author grew up with? Aren't standards of wit, inventiveness, wordplay, incisive thinking, compelling storytelling that we apply to novels that don't come with green cards sometimes relaxed in appreciation of the author's taking us into ethnically new, if generically familiar, territory?

Junot Díaz's long-awaited first novel—Díaz confesses in the September issue of *Poets & Writers* to 11 difficult and at times depressing years trying to write the second book—reawakens such questions.

Alternately amusing and a mess, packed with both sweet, fun images and endless cliches of lower-class Spanish and non-Spanish street talk, an obvious reshaping for most of the book of Díaz's experiences growing up Dominican in central Jersey, *Brief Wondrous Life* [*The Brief Wondrous Life of Oscar Wao*] will receive thunderous praise this month, despite too many badly written passages and a hodgepodge of repetitive riffs on teenage sexuality, Caribbean exoticism, and "character is fate" (homeboy category).

Maybe that's because, if you stick with it to the end, it touches you.

Oscar Wao, like Díaz, comes to New Jersey from the Dominican Republic as a boy. Like Díaz growing up, Oscar's a big reader of comics (especially Marvel), sci-fi and fantasy fiction. Like Díaz, he imagines becoming the "Dominican Stephen King." Unlike Díaz, he's fat, dark-skinned and gross, rather than slim and attractive, unable to play the Dominican lady-killer.

Adolescence hit Oscar "especially hard, scrambling his face into nothing you could call cute, splotching his skin with zits, making him self-conscious; and his interest—in Genres!—which nobody had said boo about before, suddenly became synonymous with being a loser with a capital 'L.' Couldn't make friends for the life of him."

Brief Wondrous Life takes us A to Z through its title, dropping back along the way to explore the history of Oscar's family, including his bombshell mother, and the supposed fukú, or Dominican curse, that plagues the family.

For the first two-thirds of the book, Díaz annoys a reader not already 100 percent in his corner. He sprinkles sci-fi/comic book/fantasy references, and Spanish and Spanglish phrases, with abandon and no explanation, as if smugly unconcerned for any reader of the "universal" sort he's said he hopes to attract.

At the same time, Díaz indulges in oppressive, glibly written footnotes about Dominican history that, their usual vulgarity aside, might get him flunked out of a Dominican history course for incompleteness, if not inaccuracy.

The most confusing aspect of *Brief Wondrous Life* is the voice of its principal narrator, Yunior, unfaithful boyfriend of Oscar's beautiful sister, Lola. Even though it's Oscar who's the "ghetto nerd" and sci-fi-obsessed aspiring writer, Díaz likes to intersperse lame hip phrases between Yunior's sentences. We're constantly hit with "Bad move, cap'n," or "Shazam!" or "You get the picture" as if they're connectives reflective of Oscar.

Yunior's diction makes even less sense since he's also a street-talker. One moment he's offering phrases from a Victorian *How to Write English* guide ("He was totally and irrevocably in love with Ana") and the next he's going on about "Marilyn F-ing Monroe." When Yunior can't think of a noun, everything is really just "s-."

That cliched street jive is not remotely authentic given the places Díaz has been, and the one where Yunior (we learn late in the book) now operates. The result is that *Brief Wondrous Life* reads like Díaz's unformed freshman novel, and *Drown* the more polished second effort. Someone (perhaps himself) told Díaz to write onto the page the way he speaks, but for most of this book Yunior speaks in a digressive, all-over-the-place slang that doesn't ring true.

Then comes the surprise. Far from being unremittingly terrible, *Brief Wondrous Life* grows on you because Díaz slowly convinces us that Oscar, the sad sack Díaz might have become, is real and matters. He's not just a symbol, an odd Dominican boy who skews geekish rather than macho, but more of a real lover than all the guys who get the girls.

If you like multigenerational unpackings of families, Díaz's voyage eventually edifies, reminding us that every personality in a family (nasty mother, troubled sister) comes from somewhere that can be remembered, with a long, painful etiology of its own. He excavates what Yunior nicely calls at one point "a particularly Jersey malaise— the inextinguishable longing for elsewheres."

Almost as if a relief writer had been brought in from the non-bull bull pen, nearly all the showy, irritating prose tap-dancing falls away in the last quarter of *Brief Wondrous Life*, and Díaz, finally a true Watcher rather than a

> LOVE SURVIVES AS A STORY, WHICH HAPPENS SO OFTEN IN FICTION ABOUT THOSE IN DANGER FROM POVERTY, POLITICAL HORROR, SLAVERY, RACISM AND GENOCIDE."

Performer (sci-fi reference), expertly drives home Oscar's inescapable choice of wondrous over long and safe.

Brief Wondrous Life will not displace Julia Alvarez's *In the Time of the Butterflies* as the novel about Dominican life and history everyone should read. But a reader's initial sense that Díaz has nothing to tell us about immigrant life we haven't heard before, that his book feels more like the closing of a publishing contract than a decade-in-the-making revelation, also fades.

Somewhere along the way, Junot Díaz realized he was writing a love story and he stayed true to it. There is always room for one more of those.

Source: Carlin Romano, "*The Brief Wondrous Life of Oscar Wao*: It's Hard Going, But Stay with It," in *Philadelphia Inquirer*, September 7, 2007.

Susan Straight
In the following review, Straight considers the prominent theme of love in Diaz's novel, and declares that it engages readers on many levels.

Un maldito hombre. More dangerous than comic supervillains and monsters, devious and controlling, and in some cases, as with Rafael Trujillo, "the dictatingest dictator that ever lived," who wrecked the Dominican Republic for generations, stronger than prayer or God. *Un maldito hombre* is what Oscar Wao, the ghetto supernerd hero of Junot Díaz's much-awaited first novel, is not.

That is why his life is brief, and why it is wondrous.

Everyone will be talking about how 11 years have passed since *Drown*, Díaz's first book, and why it has taken so long for him to finish this one. But this summer, I saw my first panoramic painting in Switzerland. A circular work that takes up the top story of a museum, the panoramic is designed to illuminate and educate and move people; it took years to complete this painting, which is about the aftermath of one battle on the disputed French-Swiss border and includes thousands of human and animal subjects to draw the viewer in.

The Brief Wondrous Life of Oscar Wao is panoramic and yet achingly personal. It's impossible to categorize, which is a good thing. There's the epic novel, the domestic novel, the social novel, the historical novel and the "language" novel. People talk about the Great American Novel and the immigrant novel. Pretty reductive. Díaz's novel is a hell of a book. It doesn't care about categories. It's densely populated; it's obsessed with language. It's Dominican and American, not about immigration but diaspora, in which one family's dramas are entwined with a nation's, not about history as information but as dark-force destroyer.

Really, it's a love novel.

And it's narrated by a man who keeps rejecting love, not a member of Oscar's family but rather Yunior—yes, for those who've read *Drown*. I'm talking about Yunior, whose brother is gone and whose mother was raised in the D.R. Yunior is the last guy you'd expect to narrate this novel, which is why he might be perfect for the task.

So Yunior tells Oscar's story, ferociously and aggressively and with some guilt. And he doesn't care whether you, the reader, get lost. You'd better keep up, figure out the context and immerse yourself, which is the same thing I've always felt about those writers from the dominant culture who expect me to know terms and slang and references I might never have heard, considering where I grew up.

Oscar is a dark-skinned, overweight, obsessive consumer of books and comics, a writer who can't get a girl. In a swath of New Jersey that Yunior acknowledges is bursting with fine women, no girl will consider Oscar, except as pathetic confidant. After a series of rejections by his sister's friends, Yunior explains: "These were Oscar's furies, his personal pantheon, the girls he most dreamed about... who eventually found their way into his little stories. In his dreams he was either saving them from aliens or he was returning to the neighborhood, rich and famous—It's him! The Dominican Stephen King!—and then Marisol would appear, carrying one each of his books for him to sign.... Maritza he still watched from after, convinced that one day, when the nuclear bombs fell (or the plague broke out or the Tripods invaded)

and civilization was wiped out he would end up saving her from a pack of irradiated ghouls and together they'd set out across a ravaged America in search of a better tomorrow."

I told you, it's a love novel. When Oscar and Yunior room together at Rutgers, Yunior says, "Trying to talk sense to Oscar about girls was like trying to throw rocks at Unus the Untouchable. Dude was impenetrable. He'd hear me out and then shrug. Nothing else has any efficacy, I might as well be myself."

There you have it. Love equals sex, something no woman is willing to have with Oscar, and so begins his quest. Oscar comes by this naturally, not only because he's Dominican American but because he is the only son of Hypatia Belicia Cabral, who hijacks the book for long periods with Díaz's inimitable passion and style.

I haven't even brought up the fukú. This is the curse that suffuses the novel, precipitated by the arrival of an unnamed, yet easily identified, admiral who lands pale people on the shores of the D.R. The curse is, generations later, violently reinforced by Trujillo and his minions. It is specifically suffered by Belicia's father, who is not *un maldito hombre* but a weak and loving man, and then passed down to his daughter, who was born after his death.

O, Beli, for whom love also equals sex. She has the desire every girl has—a prince will come and save me from my life—only her prince is a 40-year-old married man known as the Gangster, *un maldito hombre* for sure, who doesn't save her at all. Pregnant, taken to a cane field where she is beaten savagely and left for dead, Beli saves herself with the help of her aunt, La Inca, who prays for her:

> All hope was gone, but then, True Believers, like the Hand of the Ancestors themselves, a miracle. Just as our girl was set to disappear across that event horizon, just as the cold of obliteration was stealing up her legs, she found in herself one last reservoir of strength.... Like Superman in [the graphic novel] *Dark Knight Returns*, who drained from an entire jungle the photonic energy he needed to survive Coldbringer, so did our Beli resolve out of her anger her own survival. In other words, her coraje saved her life.

Eventually Belicia flees to Paterson, N.J., where she is abandoned once more and raises her daughter, Lola, and her son, Oscar, with a deadly and unavoidable combination of anger and obsession—what other way would she know?

Lola has her own sections of the novel. Because she inherited her mother's ferocity and some of her looks, and has her own wide-ranging passions, she and Belicia fight. Lola is everything her mother is afraid of. "A punk chick. That's what I became. A Siouxsie and the Banshees-loving punk chick. The puertorican kids on the block couldn't stop laughing when they saw my hair, they called me Blacula.... But my mother was the worst. It's the last straw, she screamed. The. Last. Straw. But it always was with her."

Lola survives her battles, is sent to the D.R. to live with La Inca, and always, always tries both to save Oscar and not to love the promiscuous Yunior. She cannot accomplish the first but eventually achieves the second.

In the end, Oscar finds love, and has sex, with Ybon, mistress to *un maldito hombre*. Yet true to the characters he's created, Díaz doesn't let some artificial transformation take place in Oscar. He remains, lamentably, himself. He doesn't come to a grand realization that what he's previously had—platonic companionship—might be close to love. How could it, given what he's learned?

So yes, *The Brief Wondrous Life of Oscar Wao* is a love novel, but love does not conquer all. It does not save Oscar, or his mother, or rescue Lola, who rescues herself.

Yet love persists, weary and loyal and resigned at the end of the novel, in the friendship of Lola and Yunior. Love survives as a story, which happens so often in fiction about those in danger from poverty, political horror, slavery, racism and genocide.

Yunior? His dazzling wordplay is impressive. But by the end, it is his tenderness and loyalty and melancholy that breaks the heart. That is wondrous in itself. It takes novelistic audacity for Díaz to make his narrator at first anonymous, unconcerned about whether his language is accessible, flawed and angry at his upbringing (again, familiar to those who've read *Drown*).

Yunior cannot save himself either, for a long, long time. No victory at the end. Instead, he and Lola construct lives that are in their own ways triumphal, although washed with the regret of the left-behind and the not-quite. No all-encompassing heroic love for them.

Except that Yunior loved Oscar. And by the novel's close, he is ready to reveal that complicated history of love and violence and obsession, a history as recorded by Oscar Wao and by Yunior, the humble Watcher, the DarkZoner, the one who didn't dance but knows all the music by now.

Source: Susan Straight, "A Love Supreme," in *Los Angeles Times*, September 9, 2007, p. R1.

Cheryl Jorgensen

In the following review, Jorgensen states that though this book is not an easy read, it is incredibly rewarding.

Shaking with laughter and rage, *The Brief Wondrous Life of Oscar Wao* fleshes out the lives of whole families who have been mauled by history.

Set in Santo Domingo, capital of the Dominican Republic during the US-endorsed, bloody regime of Rafael Trujillo (aka El Jefe), the story moves to suburban Paterson, New Jersey, and to New York City and then back to its origins, though years after the dictator has been assassinated.

But the culture of violence and lawlessness, long before established on the beautiful island of Hispaniola, which is shared by two countries—Haiti and the DR—has not been erased and chief protagonist Oscar de Leon, who is following the tradition of the two generations of his family before him, is about to meet it head-on.

No muscle-bound machismo, Oscar is the antithesis of the stereotypical Dominican stud. The target of white-boy scorn in America, he also suffers every-colour-girl indifference there, and just about everywhere else.

He acquires his nickname at Halloween when he dresses as one of his alter-egos, Dr Who, but looks, in the opinion of the narrator at least, "like that fat homo Oscar Wilde."

Unfortunately, the literary reference is lost on another boy present who picks up "Oscar Wao" and this moniker becomes fixed.

Oscar is a nerd: he is a studious computer gamester into sci-fi, (or, as he himself calls it, "genre") which he reads and writes. He eats too much and doesn't like exercise.

But Oscar is lured by love into many undignified and desperate scenarios.

Perhaps, he considers, he is just another victim of the fuku, a curse which had destroyed (with the unstinting help of Trujillo) his grandparents.

It was the fuku, too, that blighted the life of his mother, the formidable Beli, and damaged the hopes of lovely Lola, his sister and champion.

The Brief Wondrous Life of Oscar Wao begins with a description of the fuku americanus which, according to author Junot Diaz in the probable persona of the story's narrator, was unleashed on the world at the arrival of Europeans on Hispaniola. The narrator emphasises that the people of his parents' time believed absolutely in this blight, which could distort your life unto death, soberly adding that its high-priest was dictator-for-life, Rafael Leonidas Trujillo Molina.

Diaz supplies his readers with many facts of El Jefe's regime in a series of lengthy footnotes.

These do not intrude on the story at all and certainly informed this reader. Never objective academic citations, they are furious, cynical finger-pointing diatribes against a monster, and they explain the pity and the sorrow and even the great big belly laughs which erupt during the story of Oscar's life.

We learn, for instance, something of the tension between the darker-skinned Haitians (though the narrator tends to address just about everybody on the island—and even in New York—as "nigger").

There was the time Trujillo ordered his soldiers to hack to death by machete some 20,000 Haitian cane cutters along with their wives and families, simply because the dictator did not want to pay them their wages, or have them camped too close to his border. So, against a backdrop of dark and desperate deeds where innocent but non-compliant Dominicans are taken into the cane fields of DR and beaten into a pulp, is the tragi-comedic plight of the fat boy trying to get laid. Perhaps it is the stupidity of Oscar's self-immolatory love quest that supplies the cure—if not the balm—to to the fuku dumped on the family de Leon.

This zafa, or counter-spell, is the power of love both to open wounds and to heal them. Though many of the events in the novel are horrific, we are left in a state of elation and wonder.

Oscar at the last emerges as hero triumphant, simply for being an unhopeful lover in a series of grim and loveless landscapes.

The Brief Wondrous Life of Oscar Wao is the first novel of Junot Diaz.

Eleven years ago, Diaz won accolades as the first Dominican-born man to be considered a major American author with his first published work, a collection of stories entitled *Drown*.

His novel is a compelling pastiche of engaging story with brutal politics, sprinkled liberally with street-wise Spanish and Spanglish, which is eminently decipherable and becomes a kind of incantation.

It may not be an easy read, for, in the best literary tradition, Oscar Wao demands an effort too, from his readers, but it is incredibly rewarding.

If asked to describe this book in a single word, I would not hesitate to call it simply an exhilaration.

Source: Cheryl Jorgensen, "A Storm of Exhilaration," in *Courier Mail* (Brisbane, Australia), December 8, 2007, p. 21.

SOURCES

Cambeira, Alan, *Quisqueya la Bella: The Dominican Republic in Historical and Cultural Perspective*, M. E. Sharpe, 1997, pp. 164–88.

Celayo, Armando, and David Shook, "In Darkness We Meet: A Conversation with Junot Díaz," in *World Literature Today*, Vol. 82, No. 2, March/April 2008, pp. 12–17.

Céspedes, Diógenes, and Silvio Torres-Saillant, "Fiction is the Poor Man's Cinema: An Interview with Junot Díaz," in *Callaloo*, Vol. 23, No. 3, Summer 2000, pp. 892–907.

Contreras, Jaime Perales, "Pulitzer for Díaz," in *Americas*, Vol. 61, No. 3, May/June 2009, pp. 4–5.

Danticat, Edwidge, "Junot Díaz," in *Bomb*, Vol. 101, Fall 2007, http://bombsite.com/issues/101/articles/2948 (accessed July 18, 2010).

Derby, Lauren, *The Dictator's Seduction: Politics and the Popular Imagination in the Era of Trujillo*, Duke University Press, 2009, pp. 1–12.

Díaz, Junot, *The Brief Wondrous Life of Oscar Wao*, Riverhead Books, 2007.

Dirks, Tim, "Science Fiction Films: Part 2," in *Filmsite*, http://www.filmsite.org/sci-fifilms2.html (accessed November 21, 2010).

"Dominican Republic," in *CIA: World Factbook*, https://www.cia.gov/library/publications/the-world-factbook/geos/dr.html (accessed July 19, 2010).

"Dominican Republic—Government and Politics," in *Mongabay.com*, http://www.mongabay.com/reference/country_studies/dominican-republic/GOVERNMENT.html (accessed November 21, 2010).

Ellison, Jesse, "I'm Nobody or I'm a Nation," Interview with Junot Díaz, in *Newsweek*, April 3, 2008.

Gibson, Campbell, and Kay Jung, "Historical Census Statistics on Population Totals By Race, 1790 to 1990, and By Hispanic Origin, 1970 to 1990, For the United States, Regions, Divisions, and States," in *U.S. Census Bureau*, http://www.census.gov/population/www/documentation/twps0056/tab45.pdf (accessed November 21, 2010).

Gross, Terry, "'Wondrous Life' Explores Multinationality," in *Fresh Air*, October 18, 2007, http://www.npr.org/templates/story/story.php?storyId=15400391 (accessed July 12, 2010).

Hannan, Jim, Review of *The Brief Wondrous Life of Oscar Wao*, in *World Literature Today*, Vol. 82, No. 2, March/April 2008, pp. 65–66.

Kakutani, Michiko, "Travails of an Outcast," Review of *The Brief Wondrous Life of Oscar Wao*, in *New York Times*, September 4, 2007.

Lantigua, Juleyka, Interview with Junot Díaz, in *Progressive*, Vol. 70, No. 9, September 2007, pp. 33–38.

"Major League Baseball Players Born in Dominican Republic," in *Baseball Almanac*, http://www.baseball-almanac.com/players/birthplace.php?loc=Dominican%20Republic (accessed July 20, 2010).

"New Jersey: Quick Facts from the U.S. Census Bureau," in *Infoplease*, http://www.infoplease.com/us/census/data/new-jersey/ (accessed July 20, 2010).

O'Keeffe, Alice, "Spanglish Surrealism," Review of *The Brief Wondrous Life of Oscar Wao*, in *New Statesman*, Vol. 137, No. 4885, February 25, 2008, p. 58.

Romano, Carlin, Review of *The Brief Wondrous Life of Oscar Wao*, in *Philadelphia Inquirer*, September 7, 2007.

Sharpe, Matthew, Review of *The Brief Wondrous Life of Oscar Wao*, in *Publishers Weekly*, Vol. 254, No. 25, June 18, 2007, p. 31.

Stetler, Carrie, "A Decade of Writer's Block Over, Díaz Publishes His Novel," in *Newhouse News Service*, August 29, 2007.

Straight, Susan, "A Love Supreme," Review of *The Brief Wondrous Life of Oscar Wao*, in *Los Angeles Times*, September 9, 2007, p. R1.

Wachowski, Larry, and Andy Wachowski, *The Matrix*, Warner Bros., 1999.

Wiarda, Howard J., *Dictatorship and Development: The Methods of Control in Trujillo's Dominican Republic*, University of Florida Press, 1968, pp. 1–24, 174–86.

"Yale Literary Magazine Interviews Junot Díaz," in *Yale Literary Magazine*, Vol. 20, No. 1, Spring 2008, pp. 26–34.

FURTHER READING

Brown, Isabel Zakrzewski, *Culture and Customs of the Dominican Republic*, Greenwood Press, 1999.
    In this readable academic volume, Brown gives an overview of Dominican history and considers religion, social customs, and the arts in the nation.

Cabrera Infante, Guillermo, *Three Trapped Tigers*, translated by Donald Gardner and Suzanne Jill Levine, Harper & Row, 1971.
    This experimental, allusive work, originally titled *Tres Tristes Tigres* (which would be literally translated as "Three Sad Tigers"), has earned comparisons with the work of the monumental Irish author James Joyce.

García Márquez, Gabriel, *Love in the Time of Cholera*, A. A. Knopf, 1997.
    In this novel, published in Spanish as *El Amor en los Tiempos del Cólera* (1985), the renowned magical realist García Márquez tells of a hopeless romantic whose love for one woman, who marries another, endures through all the decades of his life.

Vargas Llosa, Mario, *The Feast of the Goat*, translated by Edith Grossman, Farrar, Straus, and Giroux, 2001.
    In *The Brief Wondrous Life of Oscar Wao*, Díaz makes passing mention of Vargas Llosa, a historically renowned and prolific Peruvian author who, in this novel, originally published in Spanish as *La Fiesta del Chivo* (2000), deals with the assassination of Trujillo and the historical echoes of his dictatorship.

SUGGESTED SEARCH TERMS

Junot Díaz

The Brief Wondrous Life of Oscar Wao

Junot Díaz AND Drown

Junot Díaz AND Pulitzer Prize

Dominican Republic AND literature

Dominican literature and Junot Díaz

Dominican American AND literature

Junot Díaz AND New Jersey

Junot Díaz AND Dominican Republic

The Crying of Lot 49

THOMAS PYNCHON
1966

Since the early 1960s, critics and scholars have recognized Thomas Pynchon as one of the most important writers of his generation. *The Crying of Lot 49*, published in 1966, is Pynchon's second novel. Scarcely longer than a novella, *The Crying of Lot 49* is the story of Mrs. Oedipa Maas, a young housewife who returns home from a Tupperware party one day to find that she has been made the executrix of the estate of her former lover, the immensely wealthy real estate mogul Pierce Inverarity. In her journey to fulfill her duties, Oedipa discovers not only an ancient postal service operated by Thurn and Taxis but also a secret underground organization called the Tristero, dating from the thirteenth century, that opposes all official forms of communication. She begins to see signs of the Tristero everywhere. The novel is thick with clues that lead Oedipa ever deeper into a wide-scale conspiracy, or an immense hoax, or her own paranoia. Neither she nor the reader can be sure.

Tony Tanner, in his book-length study of Pynchon, writes, "*The Crying of Lot 49* is one of the most deceptive—as well as one of the most brilliant [books]—to have appeared since [World War II]." The book has been called a quest story, a social satire, an exploration of the sacred and profane, detective fiction, and a conspiracy theory thriller. Decidedly not realistic, *The Crying of Lot 49* is dense with allusions from history and popular culture, making it a work that requires close study. At the same time, it is an

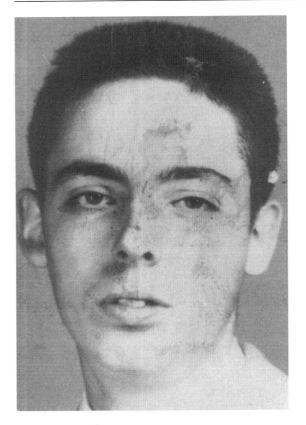

Thomas Pynchon (© *Bettmann* / *Corbis*)

extraordinarily funny book, often looping out into surreal scenes of chaos.

Readers should be aware that there are sexual references and scenes as well as drug and alcohol used throughout the book, and the novel may not be suitable for younger readers for a variety of reasons. For adults and more mature readers, however, *The Crying of Lot 49* offers a rich and ultimately rewarding reading experience.

AUTHOR BIOGRAPHY

Pynchon was born on May 8, 1937, the son of Thomas Ruggles Pynchon Sr. and Katherine Frances Bennett Pynchon, in Glen Cove, New York. His father was a surveyor and highway engineer, and also a town supervisor for Oyster Bay, New York. Pynchon grew up in the East Norwich-Oyster Bay area. He graduated from Oyster Bay High School when he was sixteen,

having won the distinction of having the highest grade in English in his class, according to Bernard Duyfhuizen and John M. Krafft in the *Dictionary of Literary Biography*.

In 1953, Pynchon began studies at Cornell University in the field of engineering physics, though he later changed his major to English. At the end of his second year of college, he enlisted in the U.S. Navy, serving for two years. He returned to Cornell and graduated in 1959. During his final years at Cornell, he became close friends with classmate Richard Fariña, the author of *Been Down So Long It Looks Like Up to Me*. He also published his first short story, "The Small Rain," in the *Cornell Writer* in March of 1959.

Over the next few years, he published many other short stories in magazines and literary journals. Most of these had been composed during his final two years at Cornell. "Entropy," published in 1960 in *Kenyon Review*, in particular, has attracted much critical attention, and the themes of this story echo throughout *The Crying of Lot 49*.

In 1960, Pynchon took a job with Boeing Corporation in Seattle writing about missiles. During this time, he wrote his first novel, *V.*, was published in 1963. The novel won the William Faulkner Foundation Award for the year's best first novel.

In December 1965, Pynchon published portions of *The Crying of Lot 49* as "The World (this One), the Flesh (Mrs. Oedipa Maas), and the Testament of Pierce Inverarity" in *Esquire*. The novel appeared shortly afterward, published in 1966. Duyfhuizen and Krafft assert that, although the novel is quite short, "Its appearance helped solidify [Pynchon's] reputation as a major American novelist."

Pynchon's next major work was *Gravity's Rainbow*, published in 1973. This book was critically acclaimed and made him one of the most important American writers of his generation. The novel shared a 1974 National Book Award with Isaac Bashevis Singer's short-story collection, *A Crown of Feathers and Other Stories*. Although Pynchon accepted the award, he did not attend the ceremony. In addition, *Gravity's Rainbow* was nominated for a Pulitzer Prize before being rejected by the Pulitzer advisory board. Pynchon dedicated the book to his friend Fariña, who had died in 1966, just two days after his own novel, *Been Down So Long It Looks Up to Me*, was published.

In the following years, Pynchon became even more reclusive and private; very little information is available about his life. However, in 1984, a collection of his early short stories, *Slow Learner*, was published and he did provide a few autobiographical notes. In 1988, Pynchon was awarded a John D. and Catherine T. MacArthur Fellowship. In 1990, his novel *Vineland* was published to excellent reviews. Pynchon's later work includes *Mason and Dixon* (1997), *Against the Day* (2006), and *Inherent Vice* (2009).

MEDIA ADAPTATIONS

- An unabridged audio version of *The Crying of Lot 49*, narrated by George Wilson, was produced by Recorded Books in 2007.

PLOT SUMMARY

Chapter 1

The plot of *The Crying of Lot 49* has an unlikely start and becomes increasingly chaotic throughout the book. The first two sentences provide an effective plot overview:

> One summer afternoon, Mrs. Oedipa Maas came home from a Tupperware party whose hostess had put perhaps too much kirsch in the fondue to find that she, Oedipa, had been named executor, or she supposed executrix, of the estate of one Pierce Inverarity, a California real estate mogul who had once lost two million dollars in his spare time but still had assets numerous and tangled enough to make the job of sorting it all out more than honorary.

Some years earlier, before her marriage to Wendell "Mucho" Maas, Inverarity had been Oedipa's lover. She had not heard from him except for a strange middle-of-the-night telephone call a year earlier, and she is confounded as to why Inverarity has named her to sort out his will.

Oedipa's husband, Mucho, formerly a used car salesman and presently a disk jockey, tells her that he cannot help her with the task. Oedipa resorts to a visit with Roseman, their lawyer. She is exhausted, having been awakened in the night by a phone call from her psychiatrist, Dr. Hilarius. Roseman is preoccupied with the television show *Perry Mason*, a popular 1960s legal drama.

The chapter ends with Oedipa recalling a trip to Mexico with Pierce where they saw a painting by artist Remedios Varo of girls held prisoner in the top room of a tower, where they embroidered tapestry. The image mirrors Oedipa's image of herself as a Rapunzel-like figure, waiting to be released from her own tower.

Chapter 2

In the second chapter, Oedipa travels from her home in Kinneret-Among-the-Pines to San Narciso, a city to the south where Inverarity's books and records are located. As she looks down on the city from a hill, she suddenly thinks that the city looks like the circuit board in a transistor radio. She feels that the image has a "hieroglyphic sense of concealed meaning, of an intent to communicate." Viewing the city, Oedipa experiences a religious moment.

Resuming her drive, she passes the Galatronics Division of Yoyodyne, Inc., an aerospace corporation owned in part by Inverarity. Ultimately, she arrives at the Echo Courts motel, where she takes a room. She also meets the manager, a teenager named Miles who speaks with an English accent and is dressed like one of the Beatles. He is a member of a music group called the Paranoids.

Later, Metzger, an attorney who is Oedipa's co-executor, shows up at her room and asks to come in. They begin drinking the wine he has brought and watching a movie on television that stars Metzger as a child who was known as Baby Igor. The reels, however, are all mixed up, and the sequence of the movie is out of order. Metzger reveals information about Inverarity's business ventures. One of these is a filter process for cigarettes that uses bone charcoal.

Metzger challenges Oedipa to a game of Strip Botticelli. Botticelli is a game in which participants are able to ask yes or no questions about a topic or person in order to guess the identity of the subject or person. In Metzger's version, Oedipa must take off one piece of clothing for every answer he gives regarding the movie. In a comic scene, Oedipa goes into the bathroom and puts on every article of clothing and jewelry she has.

Chapter 3

The chapter opens with a foreshadowing of the curious events to come, including a description of Inverarity's stamp collection and the Tristero. The narrative next turns to a letter Oedipa receives from Mucho. She does not open it but examines the outside, noting that there is a blurb stating, "Report all obscene mail to your Potsmaster." Oedipa finds the misspelling curious.

Later that evening, she and Metzger go to The Scope, a bar near the Yoyodyne plant. They meet Mike Fallopian, a member of the Peter Pinguid Society, a right-wing organization dedicated to the memory of a Confederate navy commander. Their discussion is interrupted by a mail call by a young man with a Yoyodyne badge.

Oedipa goes to the restroom and notices a message asking for a reply through the WASTE system. She does not know what this means, and she sees a symbol beneath the message that looks like a muted horn. She is consumed by curiosity.

When she returns to the table, Fallopian tells her that they were not intended to see the mail delivery. His group is opposed to using the government postal service and is surreptitiously using a private mail delivery system.

The narrative resumes with Metzger and Oedipa waiting for letters to help settle Inverarity's estate. While waiting, they decide to go with the Paranoids, a rock group modeled on the Beatles, and their girlfriends in tow to spend the day at Fangoso Lagoon, also one of Inverarity's projects. The Paranoids decide to steal a boat. Suddenly, Manny Di Presso, a friend of Metzger's shows up. Di Presso is an actor who is also a lawyer, just as Metzger is a lawyer who was a child actor. Di Presso is being chased by one of his clients, and the whole group takes off in the boat.

Di Presso tells Metzger that he is going to sue the Inverarity estate on behalf of a Mafioso who claims that Inverarity never paid him for human bones he supplied for cigarette charcoal. Di Presso relates the story of a group of American troops stranded on the shores of Lago di Pietà who all died there. The Germans threw the bodies in the lake, where they sank. The Mafioso later excavated the bones and sold them to Inverarity.

One of the girls with the Paranoids says that the plight of the American soldiers was very similar to a Jacobean revenge tragedy they had seen the previous week called *The Courier's Tragedy* by Richard Wharfinger.

The next day, Oedipa and Metzger go to see the play. The plot is both bloody and convoluted. One important historical detail of the play is its representation of the Thurn and Taxis family, who "at that time held a postal monopoly throughout most of the Holy Roman Empire." There comes a point in the fourth act, however, where "things really get peculiar, and a gentle chill, an ambiguity, begins to creep in among the words.... Certain things, it is made clear, will not be spoken aloud; certain events will not be shown onstage." Finally, there is a massacre of a group of armed troops by three figures in black. The bones of the troops are thrown into the lake, then later dug up and made into charcoal.

Most importantly, in this act, the name Trystero (or Tristero) is mentioned as a chilling threat. After the play is over, Oedipa goes to speak with the director, Randolph Driblette. She asks if she can borrow the script from the play, and is given, instead of the original, a dittoed copy. She asks for the original and Driblette tells her to go to Zapf's Used Book Store and ask for the anthology *Jacobean Revenge Tragedy*, edited by Professor Emory Bortz.

Driblette warns Oedipa that she could spend the rest of her life trying to figure out who and what the Tristero are, who the assassins were, following clues, and trying to make sense of it. But it would be for naught, since she would "never touch the truth." He offers to fall in love with her and let her know everything he knows.

Chapter 4

Oedipa next goes to the Yoyodyne stockholders meeting, where she hears a speech by the company's president, Clayton "Bloody" Chiklitz. She then promptly gets lost taking a tour of the plant. She discovers Stanley Koteks, who is scribbling the figure of the muted horn on a tablet. Oedipa wants to find out more. Koteks describes for her an invention called the Nefastis Machine, invented by John Nefastis at Berkeley. Using a thought experiment devised by the Scottish scientist James Clerk Maxwell, Nefastis invented a box with a tiny demon in it that would sort fast-moving molecules from slow ones. The box worked through telepathy.

Oedipa is intrigued and wants to find Nefastis. She takes a chance and uses the word WASTE to Koteks, who suddenly distrusts her and says that it is W.A.S.T.E, an acronym. He wants to know where she heard it before. She confesses to having seen it on the wall in the restroom at The Scope.

Oedipa leaves and turns next to Mike Fallopian for more information. Oedipa is beginning to realize that there has been a pattern to the strange events and that the pattern has to do with mail delivery. She recalls a historical marker at the Fangoso Lagoon that commemorated the murder of a dozen Wells Fargo men, at the side of the lake by black-uniformed assassins.

She tries to phone Driblette to ask what he knows about it, but Driblette does not answer. So Oedipa decides to visit Zapf's Used Book Store. She purchases the anthology containing *The Courier's Tragedy*. Across from the line containing the world "Tristero," she finds a note that says it is a variant from the original. She discovers that the original text of the play is available in another book, published in Berkeley.

The next day, Oedipa goes to Vesperhaven House, a home for senior citizens that was built by Inverarity. There she meets a Mr. Thoth, who has been dreaming of his grandfather, who was a Pony Express rider. He says that there were men dressed as Indians all in black who attacked his grandfather. Mr. Thoth has a ring that his grandfather cut off the finger of one of the attackers. On the ring is the muted horn symbol.

Oedipa goes to find Fallopian again for more information, but he has little to tell her. She next runs into Genghis Cohen, a philatelist, or stamp collector. He has been retained by Metzger to evaluate Inverarity's stamp collection. Cohen has found some irregularities in several stamps including the post horn symbol, but without the mute, appearing on a Pony Express stamp. Cohen relates to her more of the Thurn and Taxis history and reveals that the post horn is the Thurn and Taxis symbol, a part of their coat of arms. Oedipa realizes that the black-costumed assassins were out to mute Thurn and Taxis. When Oedipa tells him all that she has discovered, Cohen grows nervous and ends the conversation.

Chapter 5

Oedipa decides to drive to Berkeley to research Richard Wharfinger and see inventor John Nefastis. She goes to the Lectern Press to find a copy of *Plays of Ford, Webster, Tourneur and Wharfinger*. When she examines the book, she discovers that the line including the reference to Trystero has been changed. She also finds that there is yet another edition of the book.

She locates the inventor Nefastis, who explains his machine and sets up a test of Oedipa's sensitivity. Oedipa tries to move the pistons in the machine by communicating silently with the demon while focusing on a picture of James Clerk Maxwell, but meets with no success. She begins to cry. Nefastis tells her not to worry, and then tells her they will have sex while the news is on the television. Oedipa is horrified, and runs away.

Oedipa begins to doubt her own sanity. She decides that she will drift at random around San Francisco to see if the post horn or other clues show up without her looking for them. Over the course of the night, she ends up in a gay bar, where she finds the post horn pin on the lapel of a tall man. She asks him what it means. He tells her it is the symbol of the Inamorati Anonymous, a self-help group for people in love. The post horn has been the group's symbol since its founding by a Yoyodyne executive. The IA uses the WASTE system to send their messages to each other.

Oedipa is nearing despair. All of the men in her life have deserted or betrayed her. She spends the rest of the night walking through the streets of San Francisco, seeing the symbol everywhere. It is a dark night of the soul. She finds a group of children in a jump-rope game using words like Thurn and Taxis and Tristero.

Oedipa wanders on through the night until, in the morning, she encounters an old sailor with the muted post horn symbol tattooed on the back of his hand. He asks her to post a letter to his wife through the WASTE system. It is clear the man has delirium tremens, or DTs, a reaction to years of alcohol abuse. She searches for the place where the sailor has told her to mail the letter and waits until she finds someone who comes to pick up the letters; then she follows him. He leads her to the home of John Nefastis, the point from which she started twenty-four hours earlier.

She returns to her hotel and winds up in a party of deaf-mutes, each of whom is dancing to whatever music he or she finds in his or her own mind. The next day, she drives back to Kinneret. She is frightened that she might be psychotic.

When she arrives at Dr. Hilarius's clinic, she discovers that he is shooting at people. She learns that he is a Nazi war criminal who worked on experimentally induced insanity at the Buchenwald death camp. Oedipa talks him down, and the police take him away in a straitjacket. Outside, reporting from a KCUF mobile unit, is Mucho Maas, Oedipa's husband. He has been recruited by Hilarius to participate in a study of LSD, a study that Oedipa has steadfastly refused to join. Mucho seems to be insane.

Chapter 6

Oedipa drives back to San Narciso, only to find that Metzger has run off with the girlfriend of one of the Paranoids. She decides to see Professor Bortz to ask him questions about Richard Wharfinger. When she drives by Zapf's Used Books on the way, she discovers that it has been burned down. She finds Bortz drunk with three of his students.

She asks him about the lines concerning Trystero in *The Courier's Tragedy*. He looks at her book and says that it is a corrupt text. He also tells her that Randy Driblette has committed suicide by walking into the ocean two nights earlier. Oedipa thinks to herself,

> They are stripping from me... they are stripping away, one by one, my men. My shrink, pursued by Israelis, has gone mad; my husband, on LSD, gropes like a child.... I was hoping forever, for love; my one extra-marital fella has eloped with a depraved 15-year old; my best guide back to the Trystero has taken a Brody.

Oedipa next discovers that the line concerning Trystero that she heard in the play was only performed the night she was there. Bortz invites her in to look at pornographic pictures, from a pornographic version of *The Courier's Tragedy*, written by a sect of Puritans known as the Scurvhamites. He offers her a look at a book detailing yet another attack by a lake by black-cloaked assassins, now known as the Trystero. A long history of Thurn and Taxis ensues, along with the rise of the Trystero. By the end of the saga, it appears that the group has been behind all sorts of plots, including the entire French Revolution.

Over the next days, Oedipa continues her research, speaking with Bortz and Cohen at length. She also attends Driblette's funeral. She is devastated by his death, wondering if it has anything to do with Trystero. She tries to communicate with him, but cannot.

A few days later, Cohen shows her an envelope he has just received in the U.S. mail. The stamp is an old American one, but it has the muted post horn. The motto on the stamp reads, "We Await Silent Tristero's Empire." Oedipa finally knows what WASTE stands for.

Oedipa feels the world closing in on her; she thinks, "Every access route to the Tristero could be traced also back to the Inverarity estate." She offers herself these explanations: she is in a dream, she has stumbled on a huge conspiracy, she is hallucinating, Inverarity has planned and executed the plot against her, or she is a "nut case." She simply does not know.

Finally, the arrangements are complete to auction off Inverarity's stamp collection. Cohen tells Oedipa, however, that in addition to bidders who will be present, there will also be a book bidder, who will send his bid by mail. Cohen believes the bidder is from Tristero.

In the final scene, Oedipa is at the auction house. Cohen tells her that the stamps are lot 49, and that auctioneers "cry" a sale. Oedipa walks into the auction room and sees men dressed in black mohair with "pale, cruel faces." The door is locked, the auctioneer clears his throat, and "Oedipa settle[s] back, to await the crying of lot 49."

CHARACTERS

Emory Bortz

Emory Bortz is a Wharfinger scholar who has written a preface to a collection of plays, including *The Courier's Tragedy*. Oedipa finds him to try to learn more about the Tristero.

Clayton "Bloody" Chiklitz

Chiklitz is the president of Yoyodyne Corporation, one of Inverarity's investments. He first appears in Pynchon's earlier novel, *V*. His nickname is a pun, derived from a common expression in the 1950s and 1960s. Chiclets gum comes in a box of small, white, candy-coated rectangles resembling teeth. "Do you want a mouthful of bloody Chiclets?" would be the equivalent of asking someone if he or she wants a punch in the mouth.

Genghis Cohen

Genghis Cohen is a philatelist, or stamp expert, hired by Metzger to evaluate Inverarity's stamp collection. He offers Oedipa information about the Tristero and the Thurn and Taxis private mail system. In addition, he finds irregularities in the stamps that suggest that Inverarity was deeply involved in the Tristero. His name is a pun on the name of the ancient Mogul warrior Genghis Khan.

Demon

A tiny artificial intelligence, the Demon sorts air molecules in James Clerk Maxwell's box.

Manny Di Presso

Manny Di Presso is a friend of Metzger's. Manny is both an actor and a lawyer. His name is an obvious pun on manic-depressive, the term used for bipolar disease in the 1960s.

Randolph Driblette

Randolph Driblette is the director and producer of the play *The Courier's Tragedy*. He has inserted a line about the Trystero into the text of the play, attracting Oedipa's interest. When Oedipa visits him to try to find answers, he tells her the she can fall in love with him, record his dreams, ask questions, and look for clues, but never find the truth. He commits suicide when the play closes.

Mike Fallopian

Mike Fallopian is a leader in the Peter Pinguid society who hangs out at The Scope nightclub. Oedipa meets him there, and finds out about the medieval Thurn and Taxis private mail system from him. Fallopian's politics are ultra-conservative. His last name is a pun on the small tubes in a woman's body through which eggs descend.

Baby Igor

See Metzger

Dr. Hilarius

Dr. Hilarius is Oedipa's psychiatrist. He experiments with LSD and continually tries to talk Oedipa into joining his study of the drug. Later in the novel, it is revealed that he was a Nazi and that he experimented on prisoners in the Buchenwald concentration camp. By the end of the book, he is quite mad. His name can be interpreted as a pun on the word hilarious, since he is loud and funny.

Pierce Inverarity

Pierce Inverarity is an immensely wealthy California real estate mogul who owns part or all of nearly every business in San Narciso. He was

formerly Oedipa Maas's lover. He added a codicil to his will shortly before his death naming Oedipa the executrix of his estate. He serves the role of trickster in the novel, and it is not certain if he is behind all of the conspiracy and the complicated plotting that Oedipa uncovers. His name is also of interest to scholars who associate it with such concepts as variety, rarity, and veracity.

Stanley Koteks

Stanley Koteks is an engineer at Yoyodyne. When Oedipa attends the stockholders' meeting, she gets lost and runs into Koteks. She notices that he is scribbling the muted post horn symbol, so she tries to get information from him. He describes for her John Nefastis and his Nefastis machine. Koteks's name is a pun on the brand name of a feminine hygiene product.

Mucho Maas

Mucho Maas is a radio disk jockey for station KCUF. He was a used car salesman until he lost all faith in car lots. He hates his job except for the fact that he is able come in contact with and seduce young girls. He is married to Oedipa Maas. In Spanish, his name means literally "Too Much," though it also carries with it the connotation of machismo, or macho, meaning aggressively masculine. Given his penchant for young girls, the name seems to fit.

Oedipa Maas

Oedipa Maas is a housewife who discovers one afternoon that she has been named executrix of the very complicated and large estate of her former lover, Pierce Inverarity. Oedipa is twenty-eight years old and is married to Mucho Maas, a radio disk jockey. Her life seems to be mundane and perhaps even boring; in the opening sentence, she has just come home from a Tupperware party. However, once she decides to act as the executrix of the estate, her life becomes increasingly complex. The novel is in many ways a story of Oedipa's growth and coming of age as she stumbles into the mystery of the Tristero and a huge plot involving mail delivery.

Critics have made much of Oedipa's name. In the first place, it recalls the Freudian Oedipus complex, in which a young man falls in love with his mother and wants to kill his father. Since Oedipa is a woman, it is a little difficult to make the leap to thinking of her in a Freudian sense. The other possible interpretation of her name is rooted in the original Oedipus from Greek mythology. Before Oedipus was born, the oracle at Delphi predicted that he would marry his mother and kill his father. Horror-struck by the prediction, his father gives him to a servant to take him out and abandon him on the mountain. The servant is unable to do so, and instead, Oedipus is adopted by a childless couple. One day, he discovers that he has been adopted, and so goes out in quest of his true parentage. Through an odd set of circumstances, he ends up killing a man he meets along the road, who, unbeknownst to Oedipus, is his real father. Then he journeys on to Thebes, where he encounters the Sphinx, who challenges everyone traveling to the city to solve a riddle. If the traveler cannot provide the correct answer, he is killed by the Sphinx. Oedipus solves the riddle successfully, the Sphinx kills itself, and the people of Thebes are set free. Gratefully, they make Oedipus the king and offer him the queen in marriage. Little does Oedipus know that his queen, Jocasta, is his mother.

Like Oedipus, Oedipa Maas seeks to find the truth, but always finds it hidden. It is her quest to solve the riddle of the Tristero.

Wendell Maas
See Mucho Maas

Metzger
Metzger is a lawyer who handles Inverarity's estate. He is a co-executor with Oedipa. Very handsome, he succeeds in seducing Oedipa on their first meeting. As a child, he was an actor known as Baby Igor. The name Metzger means "butcher" in German.

Miles
Miles is the manager of the Echo Courts motel. A sixteen-year-old dropout, he is also a member of a band called the Paranoids. He and his mates copy the Beatles in nearly every way, including adopting English accents and phrases.

John Nefastis
John Nefastis is a scientist who has devised a machine that takes literally James Clerk Maxwell's thought experiment involving a Demon who can sort fast-moving molecules from slower ones. He welcomes Oedipa to his office and invites her to test her sensitivity by trying to communicate with the Demon. She is unsuccessful, and Nefastis tries to seduce her. Nefastis's

name can be linked to the English word "nefarious," meaning evil.

The Paranoids
The Paranoids are a rock group modeled on the Beatles. Led by Miles, the other members of the group are Serge, Dean, and Leonard. The members are interchangeable; their biggest contribution to the book is their singing at opportune moments. Pynchon includes the lyrics to their songs in the text. They are usually accompanied by four young women, and they are usually stoned on marijuana.

Roseman
Roseman is Oedipa's lawyer in Kinneret. He watches the television show *Perry Mason* obsessively and is writing a book about the show. He advises Oedipa to take on the rule of executrix of Inverarity's estate.

Richard Wharfinger
Wharfinger is not technically a character in the book, although he figures prominently. He is the seventeenth-century author of the play *The Courier's Tragedy*, which mirrors many of the other events in the book. In addition, the textual corruptions to his play are important clues for Oedipa.

THEMES

Entropy
Pynchon began his undergraduate studies in physics before switching to an English major; however, his love of science and the challenging ideas he found in the study of science remained with him, as is obvious from the thematic concerns of his short stories and *The Crying of Lot 49*. An understanding of entropy, in particular, is important in reading the novel. Entropy can be defined as the measure of disorder or randomness in any closed system. It has applications in both thermodynamics (the branch of science that studies the relationship between heat and other forms of energy) and information systems.

The first law of thermodynamics states that the energy of the universe is constant. That is, energy cannot be lost nor created, although it can be converted from one form to another. The total amount of energy in the universe is therefore constant. Thus, the energy in sunlight can be converted through photosynthesis to chemical

TOPICS FOR FURTHER STUDY

- Read Frank Portman's young-adult novel *King Dork*, the story of fourteen-year old Tom Henderson, a boy whose detective father has died under mysterious circumstances. He looks for clues in a box of books he finds in the basement. Write an essay comparing and contrasting Tom's search with that of Oedipa.

- Read either "The Garden of Forking Paths" or "Death and the Compass," two short stories by the Argentine writer Jorge Luis Borges. Prepare a large poster board or digital poster detailing the clues the main character finds and showing how he responds to the clues. Illustrate the poster board with pictures, maps, drawings, and text. Present it to your class or post it on your Web site.

- Choose one of Pynchon's references in *The Crying of Lot 49* and create a hypertext essay using software such as Storyspace and linking ideas, illustrations, artwork, or music. For example, James Clerk Maxwell, the nineteenth-century Scottish scientist, plays an important role in the book and could be the basis of your hypertext. Other possibilities include entropy, Remedios Varo, the Beatles, and Greek mythology. When your hypertext is completed, compare yours with those of other members of your class to see if there are places where you could link your essay to theirs. Post your essays online as a Web site.

- Compose music, using Garageband or other computer software, with three classmates to go along with the Paranoids' lyrics. Present a concert in which you perform the Paranoids' songs.

- In *The Crying of Lot 49*, Pynchon uses the concept of entropy as one of his most important themes. Take an idea from mathematics or physics, such as Heisenberg's Uncertainty Principle, or the Pythagorean theorem and use it as a starting point for a creative short story. Present your short story to your class, and explain how you incorporated your scientific or mathematical idea.

- Many of the historical events in *The Crying of Lot 49* have a basis in reality. Others do not. Sort through the events mentioned in the text, such as the Pony Express and the Thurn and Taxis postal systems and identify which are real and which are not. Write an essay exploring the uses of historical and fictional elements in the same story.

- Research the work of Mexican artist Remedios Varo, finding examples of her paintings and learning something about her background. In addition, read the fairy tale "Rapunzel." Why do you think Pynchon connected Varo and Rapunzel in *The Crying of Lot 49*? Write an essay explaining your answer.

---

energy, providing food. The energy in plant foods is converted to kinetic energy in walking and movement when people eat plants. Scientists describe this as the conservation of energy.

The second law of thermodynamics states that in any closed system not in equilibrium, entropy will increase until equilibrium is reached. That is, an ordered system will become increasingly disordered until it cannot be more disordered. One way to illustrate this is through the example of an ice cube in a mug of hot water.

Initially, the ice cube and the hot water are two distinct, organized entities. However, with the passage of time, the ice cube will melt, and the cold molecules will disperse among the hot molecules in a random fashion. The ice cube will become warmer and disappear, while the hot liquid will become cooler as a result of the dispersal of the cold molecules. At equilibrium, maximum entropy is reached. It is no longer possible to organize and separate the hot molecules from the cold ones, since the entire liquid is

The bar had only electronic music. (afaizal | Shutterstock.com)

all the same temperature. Another important feature of entropy illustrated by this example is that entropy always increases and cannot go backwards. That is, the cold molecules cannot reform themselves into an ice cube once the cube has melted.

By metaphor, entropy functions as a part of information theory. Information entropy is the measure of randomness in a communication. A simple example is the childhood game of Telephone. In this game, a person will quickly whisper a message to the person next to him or her, who will then pass it along to the next person, and so on until the last person hears the message. This person reveals what the message is that he or she heard. Generally, there is little relationship between the original message and the one

revealed at the end of the game. Rather, the message has been distorted and garbled. Thus, although the information, that is, the sounds and letters of a message, remains, entropy has destroyed the coherence and logic of the original message. The resulting message is random and chaotic and does not convey the intended meaning. Again, entropy works in one direction: information will become increasingly disordered until it is little more than static rather than a conveyance of meaning.

Oedipa's world is a closed system. The novel begins with Oedipa in a seemingly well-ordered life. She is married, attends Tupperware parties, and sees her psychiatrist regularly. The insertion of Pierce Inverarity's codicil to his will, naming her executrix, into her otherwise ordered existence puts in motion a series of events and begins a flow of information that Oedipa struggles to make sense of. It is ultimately impossible for her to find any meaning at all in the growing randomness and incoherence of the information streaming toward her. Entropy increases as she finds herself unable to sort meaningful communication from noise.

Paranoia

Paranoia is an important theme for Pynchon. Throughout *The Crying of Lot 49*, Pynchon does not hide this thematic concern, going so far as to name the young rock group "The Paranoids." In addition, Oedipa frequently questions her own sanity, wondering if she is the victim of paranoia.

The word "paranoia" comes from ancient Greek, and for the Greeks, it meant roughly the equivalent of insanity. According to the *Encyclopedia Britannica*, "Toward the end of the 19th century, [paranoia] came to mean a delusional psychosis, in which delusions develop slowly into a complex, intricate, and logically elaborated system."

As Oedipa tries to make sense of her increasingly chaotic world, she must decide whether all of the signs and coincidences she experiences concerning the Tristero are markers of real conspiracy, or if her own paranoia is imposing a pattern on random events. As she reflects that "every access route to the Tristero could be traced also back to the Inverarity estate," she is forced to conclude that she is either dreaming the whole thing, or that she has stumbled into a vast conspiracy, or that she is hallucinating, or that Inverarity is playing a joke on her, or, finally, that she is mentally ill with paranoia. Indeed, she hopes that she is only suffering from paranoia rather than any of the alternatives.

Perhaps the most frightening alternative of all, however, is that the events are entirely random, pointing to an absurd and meaningless universe that is "exitless." Pynchon's use of this term calls to mind the existential philosopher Jean Paul Sartre, who denied any ultimate meaning to life. For Oedipa, paranoid delusions are preferable to the abyss of such a world.

STYLE

Postmodernism

According to Rachel Adams, in "The Ends of America, the Ends of Postmodernism," Pynchon has been discussed in literally hundreds of articles, and his writing is generally considered to be a prime example of literary postmodernism. She argues that

> the formal and thematic concerns expressed by his work—a preoccupation with paranoia and conspiracy, radical skepticism about foundational truth and authority of all kinds, deft mixing of genres, distrust of received historical knowledge, and confrontations with the sublime and apocalyptic—have come to define the study and teaching of postmodern fiction.

Adams's articulation of postmodern fiction provides a useful lens through which to view *The Crying of Lot 49*. In the first place, conspiracy and paranoia echo throughout the novel. The Tristero is a large secret society. Once Oedipa starts noticing clues concerning the Tristero, however, she sees an ever greater number of signs of their existence. The ordering of random clues into a pattern is a common theme in both conspiracy theory and paranoia.

Pynchon also calls into question the notion of foundational truth. As much as Oedipa wants to have a revelatory experience that will somehow connect all the disparate pieces of information, the word is never spoken. When Pynchon uses "Word" with the initial capital letter, he is referring to the creator God, as in John 1:1 in the Christian Bible: "In the beginning was the Word, and the Word was with God and the Word was God." Through words, the organizing force of the universe calls all into being. This, however, is the code that Pynchon rejects in the novel. Even at the end of the book, the words have not coalesced into a coherent message, though Oedipa continues to hope, as evidenced by her attendance at the crying of lot 49.

Third, Pynchon mixes a wide variety of genres in the novel. On the one hand, he uses the conventions of the detective story; on the other, the novel is a coming-of-age story about a young woman. Indeed, a reader needs more than two hands on which to count the various genres. The book is a parody of conspiracy theory thrillers as well as a statement of the religious sublime—and an undercutting of that sublime. A quest story, a historical novel, a cultural critique of the 1960s, a pastiche of popular culture—each of these generic forms flash through the pages.

Fourth, Pynchon plays games with history throughout the text. Some of his historical details have reality outside the pages of the novel. Others are pure fiction, existing nowhere but on the pages of the novel itself. In this characteristic, Pynchon's writing is reminiscent of that of Jorge Luis Borges in short stories such as "Tlön, Uqbar, Orbis Tertius" and "The Garden of Forking Paths." In both Borges and Pynchon, the introduction of historical facts decenters and destabilizes the reader and the text. What is true? What can be traced back to reality? And what is fiction? The resulting uncertainty problematizes the whole historical narrative and leads the reader to consider how history itself is a kind of fiction.

Finally, Pynchon provides numerous examples of Oedipa's confrontation with the sublime, a concept that had its roots in the eighteenth-century writings of Edmund Burke, who associated the sublime with awe-inspiring beauty. When Oedipa first looks down on San Narciso from the hill above the city, she is overcome with a feeling of vastness, of a plan and organization she cannot comprehend because it is so overwhelming. Pynchon uses religious language throughout the book to convey feelings of the sublime.

Allusions

A literary allusion is a reference to a person, place, or thing from history, popular culture, or fiction. When a writer inserts an allusion into a text, he or she also inserts all of the corollary meanings of the allusion from its original source. For example, if a young woman in a modern romance novel snuggles her little dog and whispers in its ear, "There's no place like home," readers immediately identify the woman with Dorothy from *The Wizard of Oz*, who travels on a fantastic adventure to fully realize how much she appreciates and loves her family. Thus, the author of the modern romance does not have to explain any of this; the reader intuitively knows it, through his or her appreciation of the allusion.

In *The Crying of Lot 49*, Pynchon alludes to many people, places, objects, and literary works. For example, he calls his play within a play a Jacobean revenge tragedy. Readers familiar with the genre will know immediately that *The Courier's Revenge* will be a tale of intrigue, conspiracy, lies, Machiavellian maneuvering, horrible torture, and gruesome death scenes. As a result, Pynchon is able to parody the genre effectively. Because he can assume that his audience will know the conventions of the revenge tragedy, he can hyperbolize them, rendering the play comic at the same time it is tragic.

HISTORICAL CONTEXT

The Cold War

During World War II, the United States and Great Britain allied themselves with the Soviet Union in order to defeat the Germans. However, after the war, the alliance grew increasingly problematic. The Americans held sway in the countries of Western Europe, chiefly through the large amount of aid provided through the Marshall Plan and the Truman Doctrine. In Eastern Europe, however, the Soviets quickly established dominance and began installing Soviet-style communist governments in the countries they had liberated from the Germans.

The cold war lasted from 1947 until 1991, with periods of rapprochement followed by long periods of heightened tension between the United States and the Soviet Union. One particular troubling period occurred around the time that Pynchon was in college, served in the navy, and began writing.

Until 1949, the Americans had been the only atomic power on Earth; however, in that year the Soviets exploded their first atomic warhead. This marked the start of an arms race. By 1958, both the United States and the Soviet Union had begun a large buildup of nuclear weapons and developed intercontinental ballistic missiles to deliver nuclear warheads to each other's major cities.

Thus, the early 1960s were a time of high anxiety in the United States. In elementary schools, children hid under their desks in air raid drills, and citizens built fallout shelters in their basements. In 1962, in a show of military and political brinksmanship, the Soviets secretly began constructing missiles in Cuba that could mount a nuclear attack on the United States. When the United States discovered the missiles through spy plane photography, they demanded that the missiles be removed and prepared to engage in military conflict. For several very tense days, it appeared that the world could be thrown into a nuclear holocaust; each of the nations had more than enough nuclear weapons to annihilate the planet. However, an agreement was reached, leading eventually to the Nuclear Test Ban Treaty of 1963.

Nevertheless, both sides continued to distrust each other and to build up huge arsenals of weapons. The fear of infiltration by Soviet agents circulated through the country, and covert operations around the world were stepped up.

COMPARE & CONTRAST

- **1960s:** British bands such as the Beatles, Gerry and the Pacemakers, the Troggs, Freddy and the Dreamers, Manfred Mann, and the Dave Clark Five take the United States by storm in the so-called British Invasion.

  Today: Bands included in the British Invasion are largely forgotten by the younger generations, except for the Beatles, whose music continues to enjoy great popularity.

  1960s: The cold war is a time of fear and anxiety for Americans, who worry that the world will end in a nuclear explosion.

  Today: Terrorist plots concern government officials and citizens who attempt to decode hidden messages and identify cell groups such as those of Al Qaeda.

  1960s: The theories of Sigmund Freud underpin virtually all psychiatric care and psychotherapy.

  Today: Although Freud remains an interesting philosophical and literary figure, his theories are no longer considered vital to psychotherapy.

  1960s: Fictional detectives such as Joe Mannix and Peter Gunn track down clues in weekly television dramas.

  Today: Investigators such as the *C.S.I.* teams use computers, science, and laboratory skills to solve crimes on weekly television shows.

The Vietnam War

The American involvement in the war in Vietnam began with small-scale backing of the French colonial forces after the end of World War II. However, by the time the French were defeated at the Battle of Dien Bien Phu in 1954, the United States was shouldering some 80 percent of the French military budget for the conflict, according to Howard Zinn in *A People's History of the United States*. After the French pulled out, the United States began sending military advisors and finally troops to enter the fray on the side of the South Vietnamese against the communist (or nationalist, depending on one's perspective) North Vietnamese and Viet Cong troops under the leadership of Ho Chi Minh.

By 1966, the year *The Crying of Lot 49* was published, the war was a decidedly American war, according to Marilyn B. Young in her book *The Vietnam Wars: 1945–1990*. As more and more American troops were drafted and deployed to Vietnam, resentment against the war, particularly among young people, grew. Indeed, opposition to the Vietnam War became a key characteristic of the 1960s counterculture. Pynchon's novel carries with it traces of the divisive atmosphere in the United States. As Paul Maltby argues in *Dissident Postmodernists: Barthelme, Coover, Pynchon*,

> While the term "Tristero" denotes groups which cannot simply be identified with ... countercultural radicals, one can see how, for a politically conscious author of the mid-1960s, the alternative communications network might also serve as a symbol of mass alienation from the official culture.

CRITICAL OVERVIEW

Although *The Crying of Lot 49* won the Richard and Hilda Rosenthal Award of the National Institute of Arts and Letters upon its publication, initial reviews were mixed. The novel was much shorter than its predecessor *V.*, and many reviewers in 1966 found it lacking in depth and characterization. In an otherwise favorable review, Richard Poirier, in the *New York Times*, takes issue with the strength of Oedipa's character, for example, preferring the assemblage of characters found in *V.* He writes, "In *The Crying of Lot 49* ... the role given to Oedipa makes it impossible to divorce from her limitations the large rhetoric about

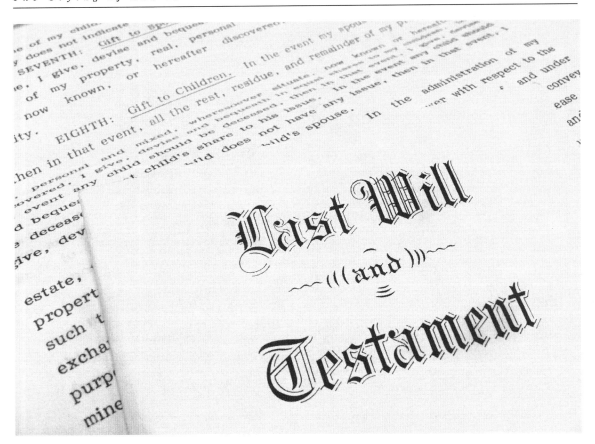

She was named executor of her former boyfriend's estate. *(Lane V. Erickson | Shutterstock.com)*

America at the end of the novel. This is unfortunate simply because Oedipa has not been given character enough to bear the weight of this rhetoric."

A 1966 contributor to *Time* calls the novel "a metaphysical thriller in the form of a pornographic comic strip" and concludes, "Why was it written? What is the meaning of the gibberish literature that is currently being published as fast as it can be gibbered?" Ironically, in 2005, *Time* included *The Crying of Lot 49* in its list of the 100 best English-language novels from 1923 to the present. Richard Lacayo, one of *Time*'s literary critics, cites its "slapstick paranoia and heartbreaking metaphysical soliloquies."

In spite of the early mixed reviews, critical acclaim for *The Crying of Lot 49*, along with Pynchon's reputation as a major American writer, has grown steadily. There are a plethora of critical articles studying the novel from a wide variety of perspectives. Edward Mendelson, for example, in his article "The Sacred, the Profane

and *The Crying of Lot 49*" argues that all characters and events in the novel can be sorted into two categories: the sacred and the profane. He writes, "The manifestations of the Trystero . . . and all that accompanies it, are always associated in the book with the language of the sacred and the patterns of religious experience; the foils to the Trystero are always associated with sacrality gone wrong."

Another writer interested in religious themes in the novel is Robert E. Kohn, who, in his essay "Seven Buddhist Themes in Pynchon's *The Crying of Lot 40*," argues that the novel "can be better understood (or at least some of its ambiguity resolved) in the context of Tibetan Buddhism." Kohn asserts further, "When *The Crying of Lot 49* is contrasted with the writing of many of Pynchon's postmodern contemporaries, his spirituality stands out. He is an author who can infuse the ordinary with the sacred."

In a radically different reading, Mark D. Hawthorne addresses questions of gender and homosexuality in his essay, "'Hi! My Name Is Arnold Snaub!': Homosexuality in *The Crying of Lot 49*." Hawthorne observes,

> On the one hand, Pynchon treats the hidden gay-world as an undesirable, almost unthinkable, underside of San Francisco, carrying the mark of the pariah; on the other hand, he makes it a necessary component of a distorted and distorting heterosexuality. Through her encounter with this homosexual underworld and its symbolic value system, Oedipa learns what it means to be a heterosexual woman capable of standing on her own in a world dominated by (supposedly) straight men.

A number of critics focus on Oedipa's journey as a kind of parody of a mythological quest. David Cowart, for example, in his book *Thomas Pynchon: The Art of Allusion*, likens Pynchon to Cervantes, who also undertook such a parody in *Don Quixote*. He argues that the theme of the quest is central to Pynchon's work, stating, "The quest, however circular, would seem to be the single indispensable ingredient in Pynchon's book."

Indeed, at times, it seems as if there are as many different critical approaches as there are readers of Pynchon's text. Some scholars look at the connection between science and literature in Pynchon's work and focus their attention on his treatment of Maxwell's Demon in *The Crying of Lot 49*. Others read the book as a detective story. Still others see it as a novel about politics or communication. Finally, many critics read in the pages of *The Crying of Lot 49* a statement on the culture and milieu of 1960s America.

That the book has elicited so many critical responses, and so many critical approaches, is evidence of the depth and allusiveness of the novel. Just as Oedipa searches for meaning among the many clues Pynchon strews in her path, readers and critics, too, find signs leading to more signs in their quest to better understand this rich and compelling work.

CRITICISM

Diane Andrews Henningfeld

Henningfeld is a professor emerita at Adrian College. She writes widely for educational publishers on literature. In the following essay, she traces the development of the detective story, beginning with Poe and concluding with an examination of The Crying of Lot 49 *and* The X-Files *as examples of postmodern detective stories.*

WHAT DO I READ NEXT?

- *The Giver* (1993), by Lois Lowry, is a young-adult novel about a young man in the near future who must figure out what is really going on in the society in which he lives.

- "Entropy" is a short story by Pynchon, written in 1960 and first published in the *Kenyon Review*, that has some themes in common with *The Crying of Lot 49*. The story was later collected in the volume *Slow Learner and Other Stories*, published in 1984.

- *Labyrinths: Selected Stories and Other Writings*, originally published in English in 1962, with a new edition published in 2007, is a collection by Argentine writer Jorge Luis Borges that includes many uncanny and interesting stories, including several examples of detective fiction.

- J. Kerry Grant's *A Companion to The Crying of Lot 49*, 2nd edition, published in 2008, offers an excellent introduction and a complete commentary on each section of the novel. It is an essential resource for anyone studying the book.

- *The Beekeeper's Apprentice* (2008), by Laurie R. King, is a young-adult novel featuring an aging Sherlock Holmes teaching a young woman everything she needs to know about detection. A good coming-of-age story, it also demonstrates the major features of the detective novel.

- *Borges and the Eternal Orangutans* (2005), by Luís Fernando Veríssimo and translated from the Portuguese by Margaret Jill Costa, is a delightful exploration of the detective novel featuring conspiracies, paranoia, and Jorge Luis Borges. Veríssimo is a well-known Brazilian writer who spent much of his young life in the United States.

Question: what do Auguste Dupin, Sherlock Holmes, Oedipa Maas, and Fox Mulder have in common? Answer: all are detectives of a sort, caught in a puzzle not of their own making, looking

IN SUM, THOUGH THE TRUTH MAY BE OUT THERE, MULDER AND OEDIPA FIND, AT THE END OF THE DAY, NOT TRUTH BUT A SURPLUS OF INFORMATIONAL BITS."

for answers. They all believe that, with enough clues and enough inductive observation and deductive reasoning, they will find the truth. However, as the traditions of detective fiction travel across time, there are subtle and not-so-subtle variations and subversions. Whereas Edgar Allan Poe's Dupin and Arthur Conan Doyle's Sherlock Holmes could always be depended on to offer the one, and only one, true explanation for a crime, Thomas Pynchon's Oedipa and Chris Carter's Mulder are postmodern detectives: they uncover clues that always and only lead not to the truth but to ever more clues. The truth may be out there, but what does it mean if no one finds it?

In his famous 1841 short story "Murders in the Rue Morgue," Poe introduced his amateur private investigator, C. Auguste Dupin. Dupin is a reclusive philosopher and logician, someone who is both perceptive and able to read the clues. In later stories such as "The Mystery of Marie Rogêt" and "The Purloined Letter," Dupin returns to help the police solve crimes through his own amazing powers of deduction. In these stories, Poe stresses the importance of reading: Dupin uses newspapers, books, and other texts as the basis for his encyclopedic knowledge. This knowledge, in turn, allows him to accurately "read" clues. In detective fiction as created by Poe, the emphasis is on analysis, not just on the mystery. Thus, the reader is invited to analyze the clues along with the detective. Poe is generally regarded by literary scholars as the father of detective fiction, and Dupin serves as a prototype for many later fictional detectives.

In 1887, Sir Arthur Conan Doyle created Sherlock Holmes in the short novel *A Study in Scarlet*. Holmes is, like Dupin, an eccentric, brilliant man. He uses scientific reasoning to solve crimes, and is able to deduce facts from minute details. One of the most enduring fictional characters in all literature, Holmes has

made appearances in many other novels, such Laurie R. King's *The Beekeeper's Apprentice* (1994); television shows such as *Star Trek: The Next Generation* (played by Data, the android); and movies such as *Sherlock Holmes* (2009). Indeed, it is possible to see traces of Holmes in other fictional characters, such as forensic scientist Gil Grissom in the television show *C.S.I.* Through encyclopedic knowledge, careful observation, scientific gathering of evidence, and brilliant deduction, detectives are able to identify the perpetrators of crimes and solve mysteries. Not only is the truth out there for these detectives, they have the ability to access it.

By the twentieth century, the conventions of the detective genre were well established and easily recognized by readers. These include conventional characters such as a seeker of truth, usually the detective; a series of witnesses or informants, who have information to pass on to the detective; allies, who help the detective solve the mystery; and antagonists, who attempt to thwart the detective. In addition, the plot of detective fiction usually follows a conventional, recognizable structure. A mysterious crime is committed. A detective is called in to examine the scene. He or she gathers clues and then begins to locate witnesses and experts who can fill in gaps in his or knowledge. Often there is a revelation when the detective suddenly discovers something that helps establish a pattern. The detective formulates a series of hypothetical solutions to the mystery, based on the evidence at hand. Generally, these hypotheses turn out to be disproved as the detective gathers more information. Often, the detective is in danger from criminals or others who do not want the crime solved. The detective faces obstacles and problems as he or she moves closer to the truth. Ultimately, all of the facts of the crime are known, and the detective is able to connect all the dots, leading to the true solution to the mystery.

Indeed, these conventions were so well established by the twentieth century that Argentine writer Jorge Luis Borges could adopt and adapt the conventions in strange, new ways. A great fan of Poe, Conan Doyle, and English mystery writer G. K. Chesterton, Borges wrote a series of stories, notably "Death and the Compass," that turned the genre on its head.

For readers of "Death and the Compass," the story violates many expectations. Generations of detective stories have led readers to believe that the detective will find out the truth and prevail over the villain. In this case, the detective ultimately learns the truth, but it is far too late for him to do anything about it. Although the detective has pieced together convincing clues into a strong, coherent hypothesis, he is simply wrong. Though the hypothesis is brilliant and elegant, the detective loses his life because he has misread the motive for the crime. Borges succeeds in turning the conventions of the detective story on their heads and giving birth to a new framework for the genre.

Frank Palmieri, in an article for *English Language History*, argues that "the scientist working within the framework of a new model actually sees a different world, for observed data are shaped by the questions the paradigm formulates and the criteria it sets for acceptable answers." While Palmieri is writing about scientists, he could just as easily be writing about the postmodern detective, who finds herself or himself in a different world, one that may or may not yield ultimate truth. Thus, Pynchon's departure from the established conventions of detective fiction is mediated by the strange new world of the 1960s, a world of paranoia, distrust of authority, a world of new media and new technologies. Oedipa's journey is one that takes her from the old paradigm of Dupin and Holmes and thrusts her into the postmodern world of Borges and Pynchon. As she attempts to gather information under the old paradigm, meaning continually slips away from her.

As soon as the reader opens the book and sees the name "Oedipa," he or she knows that this is not business as usual. At first glance, the reader might think that Pynchon is alluding to the Freudian concept of the Oedipus complex and that Pierce Inverarity could stand in for Oedipa's absent father. However, it becomes clear (and there are few clear things in this novel) that Oedipa is a latter-day detective, and her name, according to Edward Mendelson in his chapter "The Sacred, the Profane and *The Crying of Lot 49*," "refers back to the Sophoclean Oedipus who begins his search for the solution of a problem (a problem, like Oedipa's, involving a dead man.)"

Philosopher Roland Barthes, in *S/Z*, formulates what he calls a hermeneutic code. A hermeneutic code functions as plot elements that raise questions in the reader's mind. The push to find the answers to the plot-related questions is what moves the narrative forward. As Maltby contends,

"It should be evident that the genre which preeminently exploits the hermeneutic code is the detective novel in which an enigma is, after tantalizing deferrals, resolved." As an example of detective fiction, readers might expect *The Crying of Lot 49* to follow this pattern.

Such is not the case. Tanner, early in his analysis of *The Crying of Lot 49*, recognizes the fundamental difference between this novel and the earlier articulations of detective fiction. He writes that, although the novel appears on the surface to be in the tradition of the Californian detective story, "in fact it works in a reverse direction. With a detective story you start with a mystery and move towards a final clarification, all the apparently disparate, suggestive bits of evidence finally being bound together in one illuminating pattern." In *The Crying of Lot 49*, however, according to Tanner, "the more we *think* we know, the less we *know* we know."

Oedipa's ability to gather information is keen; she follows the detective's instincts in gathering clues and by talking to various witnesses and experts. She finds both allies and antagonists. She appears to be growing in knowledge. Nonetheless, although she finds pieces of information that relate to other pieces of information, and although the web she constructs seem to point to some larger truth, she is never able to resolve the enigma. In the final scene, she waits for the representative of the Tristero to arrive for *The Crying of Lot 49*, but the book closes before the auction begins.

It is no surprise, therefore, to find some critics connecting Pynchon's work with a popular 1990s–2000s television program, *The X-Files*. Like Oedipa, the two FBI agents assigned to investigate the enigmatic cases that make up *The X-Files*, Scully and Mulder, only and always accumulate more information that seems to point to the truth but never arrives at it.

Palmieri, in a fascinating article titled "Other than Postmodern?—Foucault, Pynchon, Hybridity, Ethics," attempts to argue that, while *The Crying of Lot 49* is an example of "high postmodernism dominant in the sixties, seventies, and eighties," *The X-Files* is something different, a product of "late postmodernism." He contends that "*The X-Files*…insists on the accessibility of a single, unqualified truth. The prospect of learning the hidden truth motivates first Mulder and later Scully in their efforts to uncover the government conspiracy." What Palmieri fails to acknowledge is

Pierce had been an avid stamp collector. (Flavia
Morlachetti / Shutterstock.com)

that, while Mulder and Scully may insist on the
possibility of finding the truth, viewers never find
it. Like Oedipa sitting in the auction room, believing that soon all of the clues she has gathered will
finally make sense, viewers are left sitting in their
family rooms at the last episode, waiting for a
conclusion that never comes. More than one
viewer must have asked, "Where is Miss Marple
when we need her?"

Palmieri further argues that, in *The X-Files*,
unlike in *The Crying of Lot 49*, "paranoid visions
are unrelieved by black humor, and hybrids
invariably constitute threats." While it is true
that there are moments of high drama and suspense in *The X-Files*, it is also true that in episodes such as "The Post-Modern Prometheus,"
originator Chris Carter is winking at the audience, with the same kind of satiric, parodic gesture Pynchon embeds in *The Crying of Lot 49*.
Just because Mulder and Scully are often
humorless does not mean that the program is
without humor; likewise, though Oedipa may
be caught in existential angst and a serious
attempt to find the truth, her situation is ultimately absurd.

In sum, though the truth may be out there,
Mulder and Oedipa find, at the end of the day, not
truth but a surplus of informational bits. Like
Maxwell's Demon, they try to sort the meaningful
bits from the nonsense bits, to establish an ordered
system. Try as they may, however, entropy prevails. The increase in information leads to an
increase in disorganization, not to an increase of
knowledge. Their situation as postmodern detectives in a skewed, self-referential, fictional world
prevents them from ever reading anything but
scraps of text, and leads them finally, to paranoia,
not truth.

Source: Diane Andrews Henningfeld, Critical Essay on
The Crying of Lot 49, in *Novels for Students*, Gale, Cengage Learning, 2011.

Matthew Eklund

*In the following essay, Eklund considers the
importance of musical signifiers in* The Crying
of Lot 49.

For Oedipa Maas in Thomas Pynchon's
novel *The Crying of Lot 49*, the world of the
sign is one that she would transcend to know
the meaning behind the post horn and the reality
of the Tristero. Such knowledge, though, must
remain uncertain because she can only "recognize
signals like that, as the epileptic is said to—an
odor, color, pure piercing grace note announcing
his seizure." Indeed, Pynchon's metaphor of the
epileptic attack is appropriate for a world where
only signals or signifiers remain "but never the
central truth itself," no remnant of the signified
that may have existed before the onset of the
seizure. It is within the context of this epileptic
world where Oedipa must search for the meaning
behind the "clues, announcements, imitations"
that define her reality. The post horn and the
organizations associated with it are the dominant
signifiers in the novel, but another that is often in
the background but important nevertheless is the
representation of music. Music in *The Crying of
Lot 49* is always in some way artificial, with the
effect that real music—natural sounds produced
by true musicians—has been replaced by musical
signifiers that exist outside the original music that
they signify. The musical signifiers include the
Paranoids, Baby Igor's song, the Scope's "music
policy," the Yoyodyne songfest, and finally,
Muzak.

The first example of how musical signifiers
have replaced their original is the teenage band
that Oedipa meets early in the novel. This band is

obviously an imitation of another—the lead singer, Miles, has a "Beatle haircut," and Oedipa asks, "Why do you sing with an English accent?" Of course, the band's manager says they "should sing like that," so they "watch English movies a lot, for the accent." The Paranoids, then, are simply an image; their music is a representation of another band's music, perhaps the Beatles or possibly "Sick Dick and the Volkswagens," another English group whose song Oedipa hears Mucho, her husband, whistling. The fact is that nobody can tell what band the Paranoids stand for, only that they and their music are an image.

The meaning of musical signifiers sinks deeper into uncertainty when in Oedipa's motel room, Metzger hears Baby Igor's song on television. The song is part of Metzger's childhood movie, *Cashiered*, and the song itself is attached to an image on television, so it is not surprising that the narcissistic Metzger sings along. If Metzger's youthful image is what prompts him to sing, then the signifier, Baby Igor's song, is dictating the meaning of the signified, the real musical sounds coming from Metzger's vocal chords. And because Metzger does not exist outside his own youthful image on television, the musical signifier must lose any certain meaning.

Later Oedipa encounters the music scene in the Scope bar. "A sudden chorus of whoops and yibbles burst from a kind of jukebox," and Oedipa finds out that the Scope is "the only bar in the area [. . . with] a strictly electronic music policy." Whether "whoops and yibbles" can be considered music is anyone's guess, but in this case it is how the music is produced that suggests that electronic or artificial sounds render the existence of real musicians uncertain. The bartender informs Oedipa and Metzger that in the live jam sessions held in the Scope "they put it on the tape live." If electronic music was ever meant to signify the natural sounds of real music, then that possibility is blurred even more when musicians only appear live in order to encapsulate their music in yet another imitation, the tape. Therefore, the sound is removed from its source, and the original shrinks only further into the background.

Even traditional or sentimental music does not retain the meaning of its original sound, as in the Yoyodyne stockholders' meeting, where they hold a company songfest. A song that would in another setting have great emotional importance, "the tune of Cornell's alma mater," is

butchered into a corporate hymn that contains none of the music's original meaning. The same goes for "the tune of 'Aura Lee,'" which in its original form would have had sentimental meaning, but in the world of mixed musical signifiers it can also be associated with a lifeless corporate entity.

The final but perhaps most telling of the musical signifiers is Muzak, which is music designed to imitate other well-known tunes. At the beginning of the novel, when Oedipa is at the market in Kinneret-Among-The-Pines, she hears "the Fort Wayne Settecento Ensemble's variorum recording of the Vivaldi Kazoo Concerto, Boyd Beaver, soloist." The Muzak is supposed to be a representation of a Vivaldi concerto, and the link between the signifier and the signified seems clear enough. But also at the end of the novel, when Oedipa confronts Mucho at his radio station, Mucho suddenly begins talking about a passage of violin music, and "it dawned on her that he was talking about the Muzak." She does not notice it at first because it had "been seeping in, in its subliminal, unidentifiable way." The sad truth behind this statement is that Muzak, even if it is designed to have sounds corresponding to a popular tune, has nothing to do with its original because the reality of Muzak is that it is not meant to be consciously heard or identified. Therefore, the signified original is inconsequential to the existence and pervasiveness of the signifier. Furthermore, if real music is meant to be heard and is meant to make us feel, then Muzak can only have the effect of making us feel nothing by taking the original's place. Indeed, the excess of musical signifiers in *The Crying of Lot 49* can only further distance Oedipa from the "epileptic Word."

Source: Matthew Eklund, "Pynchon's *The Crying of Lot 49*," in *Explicator*, Vol. 59, No. 4, Summer 2001, pp. 216–18.

Mark D. Hawthorne

In the following excerpt, Hawthorne analyzes the symbolic significance of the labyrinth in the novel, using sources from ancient mythology and modern psychology.

From the maze of Minos to the knots that fascinated the Renaissance to Borges's metaphors for the interaction of text and reader, the labyrinth has captured the Western imagination. Its architecture may be so complex that it defies analysis and thus appears aimless, but to the insider, the architect or whoever knows the plan, a labyrinth is

> **WHILE FIRST USING IT TO DESCRIBE ESCAPE FROM A CONFINING MIDDLE-CLASS MARRIAGE, PYNCHON SLOWLY TURNED THE LABYRINTH INTO A METAPHOR FOR THE QUEST FOR EVASIVE SELF-AWARENESS."**

never formless. To the outsider or the person trapped in it, it may seem as formless as a garbage dump, the canals of Venice, or the crisscrossing of forest paths; escape from it may seem impossible or, if finally possible, very difficult, achieved only by a few initiates. To traverse it may require either the most astute intellect, actively noting each turn and remembering each passage, or it may require complete unthinking acquiescence, a Zen-like blending of the self into the maze until it is fully internalized within the wanderer. The labyrinth may contain a center or secret room, the discovery of which brings joy, or it may conceal a hidden chamber inhabited by evil so devastating that the world is saved only because the evil cannot escape. Mythically, it may be the chapel that hides the Holy Grail from profane or unworthy eyes; psychologically, it may be a buried secret that haunts consciousness but is hidden by layers of sublimation, distortion, or self-deception. The encounter in the center of the labyrinth is either an encounter with "evil," or, at least, a desired, secret "self," a Minos's, a family's, a culture's shadow that it would deny or forget or a revelation of divinity so awesome that the wanderer, like Parsifal, can never return to ordinary life.

Hermann Kern (1982) and Penelope Doob (1990) distinguish between unicursal and multicursal labyrinths: in the former, the wanderer is confused by an "inherent disorientation" caused, and fully controlled, by the maze architect who knows the single pathway to the center; in the latter, the wanderer repeatedly chooses which path to take and by choosing correctly transcends his confusion. We can apply this distinction to the different labyrinths we find in Pynchon. The labyrinths crossed by Dennis in "Low-Lands," the boys in "The Secret Integration," and Profane in *V.* are unicursal: if they merely survive through their confusion, they will find the pre-ordained center

determined by the maze-maker. However, Stencil's search for V. and later Oedipa's search for the Tristero are more like the multicursal labyrinth in that the maze-wanderer takes on responsibility for repeated choices (see Doob 1990, 56–57). One problem with the verbal multicursal labyrinth is that, while the outcome depends on the moral or psychological nature of the wanderer, the reader follows the wanderer's pathway as a linear progression; the reader, unlike the wanderer, cannot determine progress or make choices to alter the outcome. Nonetheless, as in the "Wandering Rocks" episode of Joyce's *Ulysses*, where individual episodes are read chronologically but perceived spatially by means of the heterotropic interpolations (Schwarz 1987, 62–63), the reader follows Stencil in chronologically determined patterns while understanding that he freely chooses his path as a result of accidental discoveries and his obsession to fit all the clues into a pattern that may finally merely reflect his own obsessive desire to find meaning and/or purpose.

By focusing on Thomas Pynchon's references to and uses of labyrinths, we can isolate a major, often neglected, problem with his early writing: in our critical attempts to valorize Pynchon's writings, we frequently read early works through the filters of later achievements. But this problematizing of the early works creates a view of Pynchon quite unlike that which he presents of himself in his introduction to *Slow Learner* (1984) and consequently fails to read the early works in their own light. In that introduction, Pynchon, who may well write disingenuously, constructs a portrait of himself as an apprentice, literally the "slow learner," who has "stolen" from other writers (we may say, following Kristeva and Bloom, that he "parodied" others, building his works on misreadings), and that he sometimes tended to focus too much on theme rather than on character. We have read some of these works—especially "Entropy" and "Under the Rose"—as if he already had the postmodernism of *V.* and *Gravity's Rainbow* under his belt. Thus we have given them more weight than they probably deserve. In contrast, when we read the early stories as Pynchon's apprenticeship, what we find is a writer facing the complexities of the 1960s and trying to discover his own voice without being absorbed either in the "postures and props" of the Beats (1984, 9) or the high culture intertextuality of T. S. Eliot (1984, 15), a writer trying out the forms and techniques of modernism but finding them inadequate. Looking at his use of the labyrinth metaphor can help us evaluate these early stories more accurately as remarkable achievements of a young writer who is still trying to find his unique voice.

. . . In both stories, labyrinths describe externalized physicality, spatial arrangements that remain separate from the characters' inner modality, although they provocatively suggest a concretion in or against which the characters act. This objectification of the metaphor limits it insofar as the textual object insists on being simply a textual object. Functioning as structural devices, these labyrinths are spatial constructs like the modernistic and decipherable maze of Joyce's "Wandering Rocks." Although we may read the labyrinth as possessing meaning outside itself, Pynchon, like Joyce, does not problematize its spatiality.

. . . While Profane seems to reach the center of unicursal labyrinths, Stencil wanders through a multicursal labyrinth without finding a hidden room that gives him an answer either benevolent or malicious. If the unicursal labyrinth suggests an architect, a designer who built the maze itself and thus determines the character's movements, Stencil's and Oedipa's multicursal labyrinths suggest that there is no plan and offer no rest from wandering. Instead, as Werner Senn points out about other modern verbal labyrinths, they draw attention to the text itself, alerting the reader to its discontinuity (1987, 229). As theme, the labyrinth underlies "the finely wrought ambiguity" of Pynchon's account of Oedipa's education, her movement toward awareness and a sense of inner fulfillment. In other words, the labyrinth functions subtextually in *The Crying of Lot 49*. It shapes the paper chase both through Pierce's estate and through the gathering of tidbits to discover the identity of the Tristero, and, at the same time, the text itself is a multicursal labyrinth that thwarts our readerly desire to find a hidden room that contains traditional certitude.

One revealing sentence acts as a syntactic complement of the novel as a textual multicursal labyrinth; in this sentence Pynchon makes the word "labyrinth" a description of confused, uncentered reasoning:

Out of some murky train of reasoning, which may have included the observed fact that American tourists, beginning then to be plentiful, would pay good dollars for almost anything; and stories about Forest Lawn and the American cult of the dead; possibly some dim hope that Senator McCarthy, and others of his

persuasion, in those days having achieved a certain ascendancy over the rich cretini from across the sea, would somehow refocus attention on the fallen of WW II, especially ones whose corpses had never been found; out of some such labyrinth of assumed motives, Tony Jaguar decided he could surely unload his harvest of bones on some American someplace, through his contacts in the "family," known in these days as Cosa Nostra.

(Pynchon 1984)

As the modifiers of the object of the preposition "out of" cause the sentence to meander through a complexity of interrelated ideas, the grammatical apposition of "train of reasoning" and "labyrinth" may also describe the novel as a whole; that is, by meandering through a "murky" chain of associations, Oedipa may slowly discover a truth about herself, not necessarily about the outside world.

A related use of the word "labyrinth" further suggests that the text itself may be a labyrinth that will thwart our expectations. Almost at the end of her quest when she sits on Driblette's grave, Oedipa tries to figure why he had inserted the two mysterious lines into *The Courier's Tragedy*:

Changing the script had no clearer motive than his suicide. There was the same whimsy to both. Perhaps—she felt briefly penetrated, as if the bright winged thing had actually made it to the sanctuary of her heart—perhaps, springing from the same slick labyrinth, adding those two lines had even, in a way never to be explained, served him as a rehearsal for his night's walk away into that vast sink of the primal blood the Pacific. She waited for the winged brightness to announce its safe arrival. But there was silence.

(Pynchon 1984)

Here "labyrinth" signifies a sexual passage that can bring life, understanding, and hope while simultaneously moving toward death. The association of sex and death suggests the distance that Oedipa has matured since her "Barbie doll" affair with Metzger. This labyrinth seems to lead to its hidden room—"the sanctuary of her heart"—a place that she has dared neither to expose to others nor to confront for herself. Only after "the winged brightness" does not enter safely, does she begin to confront the possibility of total aloneness. To Oedipa, who is the Reader in a text, and to us, as readers of the text, the possibility that the text lacks signification outside itself turns the text inside out, the absolute alienation that paradoxically renders usual speech (such as surrounded Profane) silent and gives silence (such as haunted Stencil) a voice.

Unlike earlier uses of the labyrinth, Pynchon here joins the description of outer physicality and an account of Oedipa's inner thoughts. Oedipa's entrance into a spatial, physical labyrinth occurred in San Narciso, a locale that seems, at the same time, to be a pun on the words "San Francisco" and "narcissism," in the motel called Echo Courts, where the face of the billboard nymph seems to resemble her own (1984). As she drove into the town, she saw the labyrinth from the outside: "She looked down a slope...onto a vast sprawl of houses which had grown up together, like a well-tended crop, from the dull brown earth; and she thought of the time she'd opened a transistor radio to replace a battery and seen her first printed circuit" (1984). If in and out are conflated, her inability to break the semiotic code of the circuit integrates the two different types of labyrinths. Thus she plunges into the maze as Profane had entered into the sewers and, at the same time, as Stencil had "stepped" into his maze in 1945 when he read the Florentine entry in his father's journals (1984). Her Stencil-like search for signification begins, not in the tower of romance or on the couch of seduction, but in the privacy of the women's toilet at The Scope: unlike the other graffiti, the muted horn symbol so fascinates her that she copies it into her memo book and asks Mike Fallopian what it means, only to be told "You weren't supposed to see that," a dismissal that increases her curiosity (1984) and awakens her desire to find answers.

Perhaps stemming from his enjoyment of spy novels and the novels of intrigue (1984), the conundrum evolves into Pynchon's most sophisticated metafictional use of the labyrinth. Through solving, or at least attempting to solve, the conundrum, the character, like Stencil, solemnly undertakes a quest toward fulfillment and, in undertaking the quest, moves further and further from the ordinary world. In classical form, the knight overcomes each trial to earn a vision of the Holy Grail or traverses the Labyrinth to kill the Minotaur and thus free the maiden. This form Pynchon fully internalizes. If his character were to be successful—and the maze were a road of trials—that character's reward would be to enter a hidden chamber that would contain a truth closed to others who continue within the normative world. But in *Lot 49* Pynchon parodies this classical form: he changes the

quester's usual gender and thus leaves the traditional reward of the maiden's hand out of the story.

As Stencil's quest cannot end with certainty, Oedipa's quest abruptly ends when she enters the auction room, apparently the hidden room of her search. While the quester remains serious, having little or no sense of the ridiculous, the reader increasingly suspects that Pynchon has created a maze to befuddle, confuse, and finally poke fun at the reader him/herself, a maze that we traverse hoping to find a solution, only to discover in the end that all we can do is traverse the maze again and again. Thus the last words of the novel, rather than solving the mystery, force us back to the title page as if the reader, not Oedipa, were somehow the butt of a joke and needed to traverse the maze again, perhaps with greater attention or perception, perhaps finding some overlooked clue. In this respect, the novel becomes its own hidden room, giving voice to the silence that it itself creates, a silence that we cannot translate past the context in which we hear the voice of the silence.

Pynchon seems to indicate Oedipa's plunge into voiced silence—"a paranoia more protective than psychotic" (Schaub 1981a)—by her name. Easily an allusion to the Freudian Oedipa (1) Complex, a reading supported during the madness of Dr. Hilarius, the lack of any references to parents, as Edward Mendelson has pointed out (1978b), seems to make this reading untenable. Like her namesake, Oedipa tries to use reason and logic to sift through evidence to find hidden truth. As a female quester (see Cowart 1980), she searches for evasive truth in a world of confused and misleading signs. In this sense, the name can allude to her "bound feet," her "rational" unwillingness to leave the relative safety of her tedious marriage, and the relative comfort of reacting to responsibility within socially "accepted" modes. Unwilling to experiment with mind-altering drugs, she dislikes not being able to control events around her. Later, she relies entirely on intuition; finally, she moves from "noisy" rationality that poses more questions and few answers to a Zen-like silence that accepts without asking questions or seeking answers; she internalizes the reason Dennis Flange refused to tell sea stories:

> ...as long as you are passive you can remain aware of the truth's extent but the minute you become active you are somehow, if not violating a convention outright, at least screwing up the perspective of things, much as anyone

observing subatomic particles changes the works, data and odds, by the act of observing.

(Pynchon 1984)

For Oedipa, the multicursal labyrinth is this passive silence that spurs her to action and thus infolds upon itself so that inner mental state and external physicality flow endlessly and imperceptibly into each other. Until silent, she relied on the power of words, as if to name were to understand. She refused to face the possibility that the entire Tristero plot might be "all a hoax, maybe something Inverarity set up before he died," discounting this possibility "like the thought that someday she would have to die" (Pynchon 1984). At the beginning both she and the reader limit identity to traditional, seemingly concrete, sureties, but outside a gay bar, she dons an ID badge, announcing to her and others that she is Arnold Snarb, who is "looking for a good time" (1984). Concealed under another's name and appearing to be in drag (1984), she confesses, "I really think I am going out of my head" (1984). The next day, she goes to Dr. Hilarius because she wants him to tell her that she is "some kind of nut" (1984), but Hilarius, who has built his practice by perverting words, has reverted to the identity he had tried to conceal. Immediately afterwards, Mucho again confuses her identity by calling her Mrs. Edna Mosh in his news cut for KCUF (1984).

With each alias, she moves further from the reliability of tags and from the logically verifiable. Professor Bortz, who cannot talk of history, knows only words: he orders her, "Pick some words" (Pynchon 1984), and later argues that the artist either does not exist or is anonymous because only the play has a clear identity (1984). But he cannot talk about the play without talking about the history of the text, the circumstances under which it evolved through different editions, and its references to historical events. Bortz, like Hilarius though not sinister, cannot help Oedipa because he is as hopelessly enmeshed in delusion as Mucho is in LSD fantasies. Oedipa's attempt to find articulated answers through "established" or normative authorities causes silence—greater confusion and disorder—blurring the lines between reality and fantasy and seeming to muddle all experience (Mangel 1976). Oedipa's final silent passivity enables her to transfigure mere words, just as earlier she had been moved to tears when looking at Remedios Varo's "Bordando el Manto Terrestre" in Mexico City (1984). She becomes the voice of silence by infolding words so that we hear the same voice repeating the same words each time we read her text and turn to the beginning to complete the ending.

Though Pynchon himself may act as the paranoiac in creating plots where there are none (Sanders 1976). Oedipa realizes the artistic horror of the reader who might lose identity trying to make the plots rational. Joseph W. Slade has suggested that *Lot 49* may take its shape from the critical reaction to the shapelessness of *V.* (1974). If so, we can, perhaps, read Oedipa's search for the Tristero as a comment on the reader's struggle with *V.*, both involving a distance between the rational mind that attempts to structure confusion and the mind of the artist who has created a self-reflexive text out of nothing.

As she advances through this maze of (mis)-information, Oedipa increasingly relies upon intuition. On the one hand, the reader who concentrates on the impenetrability of the maze will find with Robert Merrill that Pynchon's vision in *Lot 49* "is darker than we have yet acknowledged" (1977); on the other, a reader who concentrates on Oedipa may well agree with Carole Holdsworth that the novel is "Pynchon's most positive novel" (1983). One by one, Oedipa loses each of the men whom she had used to protect herself—lover, husband, analyst, and the men who might help her resolve her search; in each case, the removal comes with a revelation of the man's identity. Her childish husband has become addicted to LSD, moving hopelessly through infantile fantasies; her lover has run off with a girl young enough to be his child; her Freudian analyst has been captured as a war criminal by the Israelis; the egoistic director of the play has committed suicide, thus revealing that he has no clear grasp of his own self. She may have escaped the confines that imprisoned her and have learned that Pierce's "legacy was America" (1984). If Pynchon denies the reader a definite answer by excluding the reader from the inner room, just as Angel had excluded Profane from the hidden room that held the raped Fina, he also gives the reader a definite answer by forcing us to retrace the very words that will finally deny themselves and make us again repeat our efforts.

In "Low-Lands" and "The Secret Integration," Pynchon simplistically described labyrinths as either architectural or natural constructs, places of twisting, winding passages through which characters move from one location to another. In *V.* he contrasted this sort of architectural maze (for example, the New York sewer system) with a controlling image of the labyrinth as process (Stencil's search for *V.*). Here the image suggested narrative discourse itself, wherein the text may explore the character's thinking while it metafictionally describes the making of that character, but Pynchon inscribed the image in a text that posits differing images of the labyrinth and thus conflates the maze wanderer in the text and the reader of the text in such a manner that the possibility of finding hidden rooms—if they, indeed, exist—confuses us. Thus while the text, like a Moebius strip, turns endlessly in on itself, we are left with the uncertainty of trying to locate resolutions or clarity where such resolutions themselves become deceptive, leaving us, like Benny in Malta, "run[ning] through the absolute night" because we "haven't learned a goddamn thing" from our experience. Finally in *The Crying of Lot 49* Pynchon fully transforms the labyrinth into a metaphorical process that describes the fragile human condition and the forces of disruption, evil, irrationality, or disorder that threaten to upset it. By ironically contrasting Oedipa's desire to find the truth about Tristero, her version of Stencil's search for *V.*, and the possibility that there is no answer, he built what Werner Senn described as a "confusing, discontinuous and multicursal maze...where...the way itself, not the goal (centre, exit) to be reached, provides the focus of interest" (1987).

Thus the metaphor of the labyrinth, used rather simply as a physical description in "Low-Lands," becomes fully sophisticated only in *The Crying of Lot 49*. From a unicursal architectural setting, in which characters move in clearly manipulated directions, to the multicursal verbal icon that metafictionally calls attention to itself, the labyrinth in Pynchon's fiction of the 1960s moves from the externality of a complex physical world to the internality of a discontinuous, confused, and confusing creating mind. While first using it to describe escape from a confining middle-class marriage, Pynchon slowly turned the labyrinth into a metaphor for the quest for evasive self-awareness. Though the unicursal labyrinth and its hidden room later appear in *Gravity's Rainbow* in such striking paragraphs as the description of Pointsman and the first Forty-One Lectures, *Gravity's Rainbow*, like *Lot 49*, uses the multicursal labyrinth as structure (Seed 1988). While Pynchon used the labyrinth with more control and greater subtlety in this later novel, he had already shaped

it in the 1960s from a description of characters' physical settings to an image describing the novel itself.

Source: Mark D. Hawthorne, "Pynchon's Early Labyrinths," in *College Literature*, Vol. 25, No. 2, Spring 1998, pp. 78–93.

D. Quentin Miller

In the following essay, Miller contends that all of Pynchon's novels are governed by paranoia and the law of entropy.

Like a Cheshire Cat, Thomas Pynchon has somehow managed to maintain invisibility in the contemporary literary scene, leaving his substantial body of fans only a mocking grin and four exquisitely wrought novels. In the literary world, where invasive interviewers and book-length biographers lurk in every shadow, Pynchon has raised privacy to an art form, allowing nothing of himself to be scrutinized except a grainy high-school yearbook photo and his fiction.

The details of Pynchon's life might not matter as much if readers did not cry out for some sort of clue to understanding the mysteries and secrets of the extraordinary mind behind his fiction. His massive masterpiece, *Gravity's Rainbow* (1973), is considered by many to be the most arresting and mystifying novel written in the latter half of the 20th century. Rich and complex in texture and style, *Gravity's Rainbow* explores the psychology of a world gone mad with information. From the famous first sentence—"A screaming comes across the sky"—the reader is taken on a chaotic journey beginning in London besieged by German V-2 rockets, then into "the zone," an unreal post-war landscape in which everything, including the character we had thought was the protagonist, literally and irrevocably falls apart. The intellectual layers of the novel run deep, but something prevents us from penetrating the ever-expanding surface, informed as it is by cinematic flourishes and surreal fantasies. We come away from the book unsure of what we just experienced, but certain enough that paranoia is the pervasive condition of the contemporary world, and that we are all at the mercy of some manipulative System. The anti-establishment overtones of this most cryptic of novels might explain why it has captured the imagination of the baby-boomer generation despite its complexity.

Less dedicated readers can find the same theme of paranoia in *V.* (1963) and *The Crying of Lot 49* (1966), novels which showcase Pynchon's celebrated style to considerably shorter and easier degrees than does *Gravity's Rainbow*. Pynchon's playfulness is evident from even a quick glimpse at these novels; readers delight in his tendency to move his self-consciously fictional characters with names like Oedipa Maas and Benny Profane through absurd scenarios, such as shooting alligators in the New York sewer system. These hapless ciphers bumble across their changing landscapes on a perpetual quest for something that will inevitably mutate before it can be discovered. Pynchon's narrators break gleefully into hilarious song lyrics and limericks, or they address the reader directly just as things have begun to become somewhat understandable. "You want cause-and-effect?" the narrator of *Gravity's Rainbow* asks us, and we know full well that he's not going to give it to us. There is nothing conventionally logical about these works. We must give in to the whims and humorous caprices of a storyteller whose imagination is more entertaining than realism could ever hope to be.

These three novels set up high expectations for Pynchon's reading public, who waited breathlessly for 17 years for *Vineland* (1990). In the meantime, Pynchon released *Slow Learner* (1984), a collection of his early stories published in the late 1950s and early 1960s. The significant contribution in this collection is the title essay in which Pynchon talks about himself as a young writer. Acknowledging such influences as Jack Kerouac, Saul Bellow, and the surrealist art movement, Pynchon comes closest to revealing an official statement about his work. He also seems to communicate the weariness he feels after completing *Gravity's Rainbow*, leaving the public to speculate whether he would ever write anything again. Despite the excessive wait, *Vineland* does not hold a candle to *Gravity's Rainbow* in terms of scope or sheer virtuosity, and reviews of it communicate disappointment. Still, it is an entertaining romp through disillusioned post-1960s America in classic Pynchon style, focusing on a logging community in California rather than war-torn Europe.

Besides paranoia, Pynchon's novels are all governed by the law of entropy (the idea that all systems eventually lose their energy). This condition is an apt metaphor for his own writing career, which is evidently ending with a whimper rather than a bang. Rumor has it that Pynchon is now done with writing for good, but with such an erratic past, who could hope to predict his

future? Perhaps he's waiting to fire another devastating masterpiece in our direction. The chief delight in anticipating such an event is like reading Pynchon in general; we finally have no definite idea what he is up to.

Source: D. Quentin Miller, "Thomas Pynchon: Overview," in *Contemporary Popular Writers*, edited by Dave Mote, St. James Press, 1997.

SOURCES

Adams, Rachel, "The Ends of America, the Ends of Post-modernism," in *Twentieth Century Literature*, Vol. 53, No. 3, Fall 2007, pp. 248–72.

Barthes, Roland, *S/Z*, Hill and Wang, 1974, pp. 17–19.

Cowart, David, *Thomas Pynchon: The Art of Illusion*, Southern Illinois University Press, 1980, p.127.

Duyfhuizen, Bernard, and John M. Krafft, "Thomas Pynchon," in *Dictionary of Literary Biography*, Vol. 173, *American Novelists Since World War II, Fifth Series*, edited by James R. Giles and Wanda H. Giles, Gale Research, 1996, pp. 177–201.

Hawthorne, Mark D., "'Hi! My Name Is Arnold Snaub!': Homosexuality in *The Crying of Lot 49*," in *Pynchon Notes*, Vol. 44–45, Spring/Fall 1999, p. 65.

John 1:1, *The Oxford Annotated Bible*, Revised Standard Edition, 1962, p. 1284.

Kohn, Robert E., "Seven Buddhist Themes in Pynchon's *The Crying of Lot 49*, in *Religion and Literature*, Vol. 35, No.1, Spring 2003, pp. 73, 91.

Lacayo, Richard, "All TIME 100 Novels: *The Crying of Lot 49* (1966)," in *Time*, October 16, 2005, http://www.time.com/time/specials/packages/article/0,28804,1951793_1951939_1952272,00.html (accessed July 1, 2010).

Maltby, Paul, *Dissident Postmodernists: Barthelme, Coover, Pynchon*, University of Pennsylvania Press, 1991, pp. 138, 147.

Mendelson, Edward, "The Sacred, the Profane and *The Crying of Lot 49*," in *Individual and Community: Variations on a Theme in American Fiction*, edited by Kenneth H. Baldwin and David K. Kirby, Duke University Press, 1975, p. 182.

Palmieri, Frank, "Neither Literally Nor As Metaphor: Pynchon's *The Crying of Lot 49* and the Structure of Scientific Revolutions," in *English Language History*, Vol. 54, No. 4, Winter 1987, p. 979.

———, "Other than Postmodern?—Foucault, Pynchon, Hybridity, Ethics," in *Postmodern Culture*, Vol. 12, No. 1, September 2001.

"Paranoia," in *Encyclopedia Britannica*, 2010, http://www.britannica.com/EBchecked/topic/443095/paranoia (accessed July 1, 2010).

Poirer, Richard, Review of *The Crying of Lot 49*, in *New York Times*, May 1, 1966, p. 42.

Pynchon, Thomas, *The Crying of Lot 49*, Harper Perennial, 1965.

Review of *The Crying of Lot 49*, in *Time*, May 6, 1966, www.time.com/time/magazine/article/0,9171,901889-2,00.html (accessed July 1, 2010).

Tanner, Tony, *Thomas Pynchon*, Contemporary Writers Series, Methuen, 1982, pp. 56–73.

Young, Marilyn B., *The Vietnam Wars: 1945–1990*, Harper Collins, 1991, pp. 172–92.

Zinn, Howard, *A People's History of the United States*, Harper Collins, 2003, p. 471.

A collection of essays by scholars on *The Crying of Lot 49*, the book features a particularly useful essay by Debra A. Castillo on Pynchon and Borges, as well as an excellent introduction.

Wilson, David L., and Zack Bowen, *Science and Literature: Bridging the Two Cultures*, University Press of Florida, 2001.

This book offers an easily understood and well-expressed chapter, "Preparing for Pynchon: Thermodynamics, Maxwell's Demon, Information, and Meaning," that explores the scientific background of the novel and another chapter, "Thomas Pynchon's *The Crying of Lot 49*," that interprets the novel in light of the scientific background.

FURTHER READING

Bertens, Johannes Willem, and Joseph Natoli, *Postmodernism: The Key Figures*, Blackwell Publishers, 2002.

This book is an excellent reference on all the major figures of postmodernism, situating Thomas Pynchon among Roland Barthes, Jorge Luis Borges, John Fowles, and other important writers.

Hilfer, Anthony Channell, *American Fiction since 1940*, Longman, 1992.

This book offers readings of many important writers of the twentieth century, including Pynchon, and focuses attention on the metafictional qualities of Pynchon's writing.

O'Donnell, Patrick, ed., *New Essays on The Crying of Lot 49*, Cambridge University Press, 1991.

SUGGESTED SEARCH TERMS

Thomas Pynchon

The Crying of Lot 49

paranoia

entropy

detective fiction AND The Crying of Lot 49

postmodernism

science AND literature

metafiction

20th-century American literature

Thomas Pynchon AND Maxwell's Demon

Thomas Pynchon AND Jorge Luis Borges

Extremely Loud & Incredibly Close

JONATHAN SAFRAN FOER

2005

Jonathan Safran Foer's complex and idiosyncratic second novel, *Extremely Loud & Incredibly Close*, was published in 2005 to widespread critical acclaim. The novel tells the story of Oskar Schell, a nine-year-old boy who lost his father in the terrorist attack on New York City's World Trade Center on September 11, 2001. Throughout the novel, Oskar searches for a lock that fits a mysterious key that belonged to his father. As he wanders about the boroughs of New York City, he encounters a wide assortment of people such as a 103-year-old war reporter and a tour guide who never leaves the Empire State Building. Always at the center of the novel is Oskar, a precocious, troubled child who loves French, plays the tambourine, performs the works of Shakespeare, makes jewelry, and in particular, dreams up inventions that would keep people safe, because he is a pacifist. The novel is unique not only for its protagonist and the story he tells but as a piece of writing. Foer makes extensive use of what is called "visual writing." This refers to narratives that consist not only of normal text but also illustrations, odd typographical effects, pages with only a single word or a few words, lists, struck-out words, and unconventional arrangement of the text on the page. At one point, the typeface of a letter written by Oskar's grandfather becomes smaller and smaller because the grandfather fears he is running out of space; eventually, the typeface becomes so small and cramped that the

Jonathan Safran Foer (© *Kathy deWitt | Alamy*)

text is illegible and the page is almost black. The novel concludes with a fifteen-page flip-art section that, if flipped backwards, depicts an image of a person jumping from the World Trade Center as it burned on the day of the terrorist attack; flipped forward, though, it depicts a human figure rising to the top of the building.

AUTHOR BIOGRAPHY

Foer was born on February 21, 1977, in Washington, DC, to a tight-knit Jewish family. His father, Albert, was a lawyer; his mother, Esther Safran, was born in Poland and headed her own public relations firm. Writing seems to have been in the Foer family blood, for one of Jonathan's brothers was the editor of *New Republic*, and his other brother became a freelance journalist. Foer reports that one of the most significant events of his childhood occurred when he was injured in a classroom chemical accident at the age of eight that resulted in a three-year period during which he suffered a kind of nervous breakdown.

Foer attended the Georgetown Day School, then enrolled at Princeton University in 1995. There he took a writing course taught by prominent American author Joyce Carol Oates, who showed interest in his writing. She supervised his senior thesis, which examined the life of his grandfather, who survived the World War II Holocaust

in Europe. After graduating from Princeton with a degree in philosophy in 1999, Foer traveled to Ukraine to expand his thesis. He also edited *A Convergence of Birds: Original Fiction and Poetry Inspired by the Work of Joseph Cornell*, to which he contributed a short story. During this time his thesis grew, and in 2002, it was published as a novel titled *Everything Is Illuminated*. He published his second novel, *Extremely Loud & Incredibly Close*, in 2005. That year, he also wrote a libretto for *Seven Attempted Escapes from Silence*, an opera that premiered at the Berlin State Opera in Germany. In 2009, Foer published his first nonfiction book, *Eating Animals*, which explores his shifting views about vegetarianism over the years. Additionally, Foer has published short stories and commentary in a variety of publications. In 2008, he was a visiting professor at Yale University, where he taught fiction. As of 2010, Foer was on the faculty of New York University in the Graduate Creative Writing program and was married to novelist Nicole Krauss, with whom he has two children.

PLOT SUMMARY

What The?
The first chapter introduces Oskar Schell and makes reference to his father and his mother, who is now in a relationship with a man named Ron, whom Oskar sees as his nemesis. The reader begins to get a sense of Oskar's mind as he thinks about a number of "what ifs," such as inventions he dreams up. He remembers riding in a limousine in order to purchase a coffin, then later riding in a limousine to dig up the empty coffin. Oskar's mother allows him to read any book he wants. His favorite book, which is far above his reading level, is *A Brief History of Time* by real-life astrophysicist Stephen Hawking. Oskar remembers details about his father, such as his love of Beatles' tunes. Reference is made to messages Oskar's father left on the answering machine at home. The times of the messages hint that they were left on the morning of the September 11, 2001, terrorist attacks on New York City. The messages infer that Oskar lost his father on that day.

Why I'm Not Where You Are: 5/21/63
Extremely Loud & Incredibly Close includes numerous letters, many of which were never

MEDIA ADAPTATIONS

- In 2005, Recorded Books released an unabridged audiobook version of *Extremely Loud & Incredibly Close*. The audiobook is on CD; running time is about nine hours.

mailed. The second chapter consists of a letter that Thomas Schell Sr., Oskar's grandfather, writes to his unborn son, Oskar's father, Thomas Schell Jr. The senior Thomas is an immigrant who develops aphasia, or the inability to speak. He often uses intricate hand gestures to communicate. The letter tells how he came to have a relationship with Anna, the sister of Oskar's grandmother, back in Germany.

Googolplex

Oskar's mother wears a bracelet Oskar made of colored beads; the beads encode his father's last telephone message. Oskar examines things in his father's closet, where he finds a mysterious key in a blue vase. He goes to a locksmith to get some ideas about what kind of lock the key might fit. The key has the word *Black* written on it, so for the next several months, Oskar spends weekends trying to contact all the people in the New York phone book with the surname Black. Oskar replaces the phone that contains the messages from his father. He keeps the original phone under his bed and listens to the messages when he wants to hear the sound of his father's voice.

Grandma Schmidt, who appears to be growing senile, lives in a building across the street. She claims to have a renter whom no one has seen; her family concludes that the renter is a figment of her imagination. Grandma Schmidt is the sister of Anna and eventually married Thomas Schell Sr. in America. Thomas, though, abandoned her when Thomas junior was born. Oskar uses binoculars to read notes that she writes. Oskar and his grandmother talk about trivial things, but Oskar asks her why his grandfather left, although his mother has forbidden

him to ask his grandmother about that matter. Oskar puts the mysterious key on a string with his apartment key.

My Feelings

The core of this chapter is a letter that Grandma wrote on September 12, 2003. The letter appears in parts throughout the novel. The reader learns that, in 1921, Grandma asked her father to write a letter for her to a prisoner in a Turkish labor camp; this letter is the only remembrance of her father she has. Grandma, like Oskar, wrote letters to many people. She collects letters from others, including an imprisoned murderer, and tries to find connections among them. She tells how she met Thomas Schell Sr., and married him in America. Thomas, who wanted to be a sculptor, also wanted to marry Grandma's sister, Anna, who was killed in the firebombing of Dresden, Germany, in World War II.

The Only Animal

Oskar embarks on his quest to visit all of the people in New York City named Black. The first one he meets claims not to have known Thomas. He then meets Abby Black, a beautiful but unsmiling woman who, Oskar senses, does not tell him the whole truth. Oskar visits his grandmother, who appears to have been crying. Whenever Grandma calls his name, Oskar responds, "I'm OK." He wonders about his grandparents' broken marriage. A few months after the death of his father, Oskar accompanies his mother to a storage locker where some of his father's things were kept, but Oskar cannot bear to throw anything away.

Why I'm Not Where You Are: 5/21/63

This chapter resumes the letter that Oskar's grandfather writes to his son, Oskar's father. The letter discusses the many rules that governed his marriage with Oskar's grandmother. Each of them had a "nothing place" where they could get privacy, and their apartment was divided into Somethings and Nothings. Thomas senior continues to think of Anna and remembers a time when the two of them literally ran into one another. At the same time, Oskar's grandmother is writing the story of her life, but when she hands a stack of paper to Thomas, he sees only blank pages; he declares the writing to be wonderful. Thomas thinks about the first time he and Anna made love. He tells his wife that she should keep her memoir a secret. He worries that he is running out of space to tell his son everything he wants to. The reader learns that, one morning, he went out for a walk and never returned. His letter, though, indicates that he loves his son.

Heavy Boots—Heavier Boots

Oskar takes part in performances of Shakespeare's *Hamlet* that are adapted for children with attention deficit disorder. Many of the Blacks he has encountered attend the performances, along with Oskar's grandmother. Jimmy Snyder mimics the grandmother, and while Oskar laughs, he fantasizes about beating Jimmy. One member of the audience is Abe Black. Abe introduces Oskar to Ada Black, who likes Oskar but is of no help in solving Oskar's mystery. He also meets the elderly A. R. Black, who lives in Oskar's building and who tells Oskar stories about his life. A. R. Black is deaf and a widower, and he has not left his apartment for twenty-four years, but Oskar concludes that Mr. Black can help him with his quest. That night, Oskar has a confrontation with his mother when he demands to know where she was on the day Oskar's father died. He tells her that, if he could have chosen, he would have picked her to die that day, though he realizes the cruelty of what he has said and tries to take it back.

My Feelings

This chapter resumes the letter Oskar's grandmother is writing. It jumps between past and present as Grandma discusses her marriage with her husband, her pregnancy with Oskar's father, and the departure of Oskar's grandfather. When Grandma reflects on her childhood, it becomes clear that she lost her family in the firebombing of Dresden, Germany, during World War II.

Happiness, Happiness

Oskar plays for his classmates an interview with Mr. Tomoyasu, who survived the atomic bombing of Hiroshima at the end of World War II. The next day, Oskar and A. R. Black take the subway to meet Agnes Black, who had been a waitress in a restaurant at the World Trade Center, leading Oskar to wonder whether she might have served Oskar's father on the day of the terrorist attack. Oskar goes on to visit several more Blacks. He gets responses from people he has written letters to, including naturalist Jane Goodall and scientist Stephen Hawking. He visits his psychiatrist, Dr. Fein, and wants to lash out at him. He listens to one of the recorded messages his father left on the phone on the day of the terrorist attack.

Why I'm Not Where You Are: 4/12/78

This chapter consists of a letter Thomas Schell Sr. wrote to his son, Oskar's father, who was fifteen years old at the time. The letter was never mailed. It contains a vivid description of the firebombing of Dresden and Thomas senior's futile search for his loved ones, including Anna and his parents. He describes the carnage of the bombing and his task of killing all the carnivores in the Dresden zoo. On the night of the bombing, he learns that Anna is pregnant. He is injured and is taken to a hospital.

The Sixth Borough

In this chapter, the reader learns the fantasy story that Oskar's father told him on the last night of his life. The core of the story is that New York City used to have a sixth borough. (New York City consists of five boroughs: Manhattan, the Bronx, Staten Island, Brooklyn, and Queens.) The sixth borough has a large hole in its center and moves about the planet, finally settling in Antarctica.

My Feelings

This chapter focuses on Grandma's reactions to the events of September 11, 2001. She watches news broadcasts on the television showing the World Trade Center towers burning, then collapsing. Oskar's father, who owns a jewelry business, does not work at the World Trade Center but is attending a meeting there that morning. Oskar's mother calls and, for the first time, tells Oskar's grandmother that she loves her. Oskar knows that something is wrong, but his mother and grandmother try to hide it from him. Grandma reflects on how Oskar has given meaning to her life. The ride to the cemetery to bury an empty coffin is described. Grandma receives a letter that says simply, "I'm sorry." The handwriting is that of Thomas Schell Sr., who apparently has returned.

Alive and Alone

Oskar's quest has gone on for six months. A. R. Black, who has been helping him, announces that he is through with the quest. Oskar searches Grandma's apartment, where he finds hundreds of letters. The renter emerges, and it turns out that the renter is Thomas senior, although Oskar does not know this. Pretending that the renter is Grandma, he talks about his quest, including meeting Ruth Black, who lives on the eighty-sixth floor of the Empire State Building. Ruth gave him a tour and discussed facts about the building and its history that are eerily similar to the events of 9/11. Oskar plays for Thomas the phone messages, his father's final words.

Why I'm Not Where You Are: 9/11/03
This chapter is essentially narrated by the grandfather, who fills his diary with his version of the events of 9/11: how he learned about 9/11 and came to New York to search for his son. The reader learns that he has been following Oskar and A. R. Black around. He has an awkward relationship with Grandma, his estranged wife, who refuses to include him in the life of her son and of Oskar. Grandpa writes asides to his son in his diary, and as he worries about running out of space, the words in his diary are overwritten and cramped until they are illegible.

A Simple Solution to an Impossible Problem
The title of the chapter is taken from a letter Oskar receives from Stephen Hawking that is included at the end of the chapter. The chapter is filled with revelations. Oskar listens to a message from Abby Black, who confesses that she has not been entirely honest with Oskar. She tells him that her ex-husband, William Black, has information. Oskar visits William and learns that the mysterious key has nothing to do with Oskar's father; it is a key to a safe deposit box and wound up in a blue vase that William sold to Oskar's father as an anniversary gift. Oskar listens to a final phone message from his father, one that he could not bear to listen to before. The message consists of one minute and twenty-seven seconds of Thomas asking, "Is anyone there?"

My Feelings
This chapter concludes Grandma's reflections. She describes how Grandpa tries to leave her again after he helped Oskar dig up his father's grave. The chapter is, in essence, a dream sequence, with Grandma's dreams running in reverse. In this way, her mistakes can be erased.

Beautiful and True
The novel concludes with the story of Oskar's limousine ride to the cemetery and the digging up of his father's grave. The coffin, of course, is empty. He dreams that the events of 9/11 happen in reverse so that they did not happen. He forges a new relationship with his mother and even comes to accept Ron, whom Oskar's mom met at a support group for people who have lost loved ones. By running events in reverse, Oskar

feels safe. The book concludes with fifteen pages of flip art that depict one of the people who jumped from the World Trade Center towers, but rather than falling, the person is rising.

CHARACTERS

A. R. Black
Mr. Black, Oskar's upstairs neighbor, becomes Oskar's sidekick. He says that he is 103 years old. He is partially blind and deaf and a widower. He says that he was a journalist and covered both world wars. Every day he drives a nail into a bed that he made out of a tree that his wife tripped over during their courtship. He keeps a catalog of everyone he has ever interviewed or written about. Mr. Black is a recluse, but in accompanying Oskar on his quest, he engages with the world again and helps Oskar overcome some of his fears. By withdrawing from Oskar, he allows Oskar to abandon his futile quest and forge a relationship with his grandfather.

Abby and William Black
Abby, age forty-eight, is the second of the Blacks Oskar meets. She is a beautiful but unsmiling woman, and Oskar wishes that he could invent something that would make her like him. She denies knowing Oskar's father, but Oskar senses that she is not telling him the whole truth. Only later does the reader learn that Abby contacted Oskar's mother to alert her to her son's quest. Later, too, the reader learns that Oskar's mother contacted all the Blacks herself to ensure her son's safety. Abby suggests that Oskar contact her ex-husband, William, who has been trying to find the person to whom he sold a blue vase just before 9/11. The vase contained the key to a safe deposit box that contained William's father's papers.

Abe Black
Oskar meets Abe Black at the amusement park at Coney Island. Abe claims to know nothing of Oskar's father, but he takes Oskar for a ride on the Cyclone.

Ada Black
Ada Black owns two paintings by Picasso. She knows nothing about the key. She and Oskar debate the ethics of having wealth. Ada knows Oskar's name, but he cannot remember telling her his name, foreshadowing the revelation that

Oskar's mother knew of his quest and contacted all the people named Black to ensure her son's safety.

Ruth Black

Ruth Black is a recluse who cannot bear to leave her apartment in the Empire State Building. She shares her extensive knowledge of the building and its history with Oskar.

Dr. Fein

Dr. Fein is Oskar's psychiatrist. Oskar sees him only because he will not receive his allowance if he does not. He is a source of annoyance to Oskar, for he condescends to the boy and tries to be his buddy. Oskar fantasizes about giving Dr. Fein a beating. During one of their sessions, Oskar wants to respond to the doctor with an obscenity, but instead merely shrugs his shoulders.

Simon Goldberg

The disheveled Simon is part of the novel's World War II backdrop. He was introduced as one of the great minds of the world to the elder Thomas Schell when he was trying to find Anna. Anna's father tries to protect Goldberg, a Jew, but Goldberg is later held in a Nazi concentration camp.

Stephen Hawking

Hawking does not appear directly in the novel. He is a real-life astrophysicist and the author of Oskar's favorite book, *A Brief History of Time*. Oskar writes letters to Hawking, who lives in Cambridge, England. Hawking's movements are limited because he uses a wheelchair as a result of amyotrophic lateral sclerosis. Hawking sends back form letters, but late in the novel sends an actual letter to Oskar inviting him to Cambridge. He says that being an astrophysicist is boring and that he wishes he could be a poet.

Mom

Oskar's mother, a lawyer, was married to his father for twelve years when she was widowed by the terrorist attacks of September 11. That morning, she received a phone call from her husband saying that he had safely escaped the World Trade Center, but she senses the truth. She insists on having a funeral for her husband and burying an empty coffin. She is extremely protective of her son and forces him to see a psychiatrist, though she seems to ignore evidence that Oskar is physically hurting himself. Early on, she learns about

Oskar's quest to find the lock that fits the key by interviewing all the people named Black in New York City. She recruits A. R. Black, who lives upstairs, to accompany Oskar on his quest, thus uncharacteristically giving Oskar permission to travel about the city on weekends. Through Mr. Black, she knows everything Oskar is doing. At a support group for bereaved people, she meets Ron; Ron's frequent presence in the home troubles Oskar.

Ron

Oskar's mother has some sort of relationship with Ron. Oskar is convinced that the two are having a sexual relationship, but this is unclear. Oskar's mother met Ron at a support group for grieving people who have lost family members. Oskar dislikes Ron, but by the end of the novel he accepts that his mother should have a relationship with Ron if she wants to.

Oskar Schell

Oskar, age nine, is the main narrator of the novel. He is precocious but troubled. He carries a business card that identifies him as, among other things, an inventor, jewelry designer, amateur entomologist, Francophile, vegan, origamist, pacifist, percussionist, amateur astronomer, computer consultant, and amateur archaeologist. His favorite book is *A Brief History of Time* by astrophysicist Stephen Hawking, though the book is too complex for him to understand. He lives on the fifth floor of a New York City apartment building with his mother; his paternal grandmother lives in a building across the street. He is a bit of a computer "nerd" whose psychological problems were worsened when his father died in the terrorist attacks of September 11, 2001. He imagines inventions that will make people safer in a frightening world.

While going through his dead father's things, he discovers a key in a blue vase. Written on the key is the word *Black*, so Oskar embarks on a quest to find the lock the key fits by contacting all the people named Black in the New York City phone book. During this quest, he is accompanied by a neighbor, A. R. Black, who lives upstairs in his building. The quest goes on for months until Oskar learns from William Black that the key has nothing to do with Oskar's father; it is a key to a safe deposit box containing papers left behind by William's father, but it was in a vase that William had sold to Oskar's father, who bought it as an anniversary present. Having solved the mystery of the key, Oskar undertakes a project to dig up his father's empty coffin. Helping him is his long-lost grandfather, who has been living with Oskar's grandmother as a renter. Oskar finally confesses that, on the day of his father's death, he was too scared to answer the phone and take his father's final phone call before the World Trade Center collapsed.

Thomas Schell Jr.

Thomas Schell Jr., Oskar's father, was born in 1963 after his own father abandoned his mother, "Grandma" in the novel. He studied law in California, but he earned his living in New York as the owner of a jewelry store. He received a letter from his father in Germany and traveled there to find him in Dresden, though neither man would admit to recognizing the other. He died when the World Trade Center collapsed during the terrorist attacks of September 11, 2001. During the event, he called home several times, leaving messages on the phone. To calm his wife, he called her and told her, falsely, that he had escaped from the building. He was a good father to Oskar, sparking his son's intellectual curiosity. Just before his death, he purchased a blue vase from William Black at an estate sale; the vase was to be an anniversary present for his wife. The vase contains the key that prompts Oskar's quest.

Thomas Schell Sr.

The elder Thomas Schell, Oskar's paternal grandfather, is one of the novel's narrators. A native of Dresden, Germany, he wanted to be a sculptor in his youth, but he loses his family and his pregnant lover, Anna Schmidt, in the Allied firebombing of the city near the end of World War II. Later, he suffers from aphasia and cannot speak. In New York City, he meets Anna's sister, "Grandma," and agrees to marry her, but the marriage is haunted by his memories of Anna. One of the rules of the marriage is that Grandma is not to become pregnant; Schell does not want to bring another person into a difficult world. When she breaks the rule, he slips away and returns to Dresden. Later, he learns that his son died in the terrorist attacks, so he returns to New York and moves in with Grandma as a presumed renter. He makes good on his promise never to reveal his identity to Oskar, though he meets with Oskar and helps the boy in digging up his father's empty coffin. He has written unmailed letters to his son over the years, but he buries them. He tries to flee to Germany again, but Grandma follows

him to the airport and persuades him to live with her there.

Anna Schmidt

Anna Schmidt, Grandma's sister, died in the firebombing of Dresden, Germany, during World War II. Thomas Schell Sr. was in love with her. Although she does not appear directly "onstage," her memory haunts his marriage with Grandma.

Grandma Schmidt

Grandma Schmidt, Oskar's paternal grandmother living under her maiden name in a building across the street from Oskar, is one of the narrators of the novel. She is depicted as somewhat senile, but she has been one of Oskar's primary caregivers and his confidant after the death of his father. She knits mittens and scarves for him, and she gives him his grandfather's old camera and a subscription to *National Geographic*. She lives with a mysterious renter no one has ever seen, though in time the reader learns that the renter is her husband. Grandma wishes that she could have lived her life differently. She survived the firebombing of Dresden near the end of World War II, but her parents and her sister Anna died in the attack. Years later, she encounters Thomas Schell Sr. in New York City, proposes to him, and promises not to become pregnant. Later, she decides that she needs a child and becomes pregnant with Thomas junior, Oskar's father. At the prompting of her husband, she tries to write her life story, but the pages of her supposed narrative are blank. She collects the empty envelopes from letters Thomas writes to his son but cannot send. Near the end of the novel, she writes Oskar a letter that explains her life.

Jimmy Snyder

Jimmy is one of Oskar's classmates. He plays the role of Hamlet in performances of the play. A bully, he threatens to beat Oskar up if Oskar will not admit that his mother is a whore. Oskar fantasizes about beating Jimmy up on the night of the final performance of the play.

Gerald Thompson

Thompson drives for the Sunshine Limousine company. He takes Oskar and his family to the funeral of Oskar's father. Later, he drives Oskar and his grandfather to the cemetery to dig up the father's grave.

Tomoyasu

Mr. Tomoyasu is a survivor of the atomic bombing of Hiroshima, Japan, that ended World War II in the Pacific. Oskar plays a tape for his classmates on which Tomoyasu describes the horrors of the bombing and his search for his daughter, ending with her dying in his arms.

THEMES

Death

Death pervades *Extremely Loud & Incredibly Close*. Central to the novel is the death of Oskar's father in the terrorist attacks of September 11, 2001. Oskar was close to his father, and the novel becomes a quest to understand why and how his father died. As backdrops for the events of 2001, the novel also refers extensively to two other events that led to widespread death. One was the firebombing of Dresden, Germany, late in World War II. During the Allied attack on the city, Thomas Schell Sr. lost his family and his girlfriend, Anna Schmidt, as well as their unborn baby. Thomas searched frantically for Anna in the rubble, just as people searched frantically for their loved ones in the wake of the terrorist attacks on the United States. Additionally, the atomic bombing of Hiroshima, Japan, is introduced through a tape that Oskar plays for his class. On the tape, Mr. Tomoyasu, a survivor of the bombing, describes the horror of that day and his own search for his daughter. Oskar, already a psychologically troubled child, contends with phobias, all of them worsened by the events of September 11. He dreams up inventions that he believes would keep people safe. At the end of the novel, the flip art pages that show a person ascending rather than falling from the World Trade Center towers represent Oskar's need to find safety in a world filled with war, death, and destruction.

Love

Extremely Loud & Incredibly Close depicts a number of relationships based on some form of love, but all of these relationships are tempered by a sense of tragedy and loss. Clearly, Oskar loves his now dead father, and the narrative makes clear that the father, Thomas Schell Jr., loved his son. Oskar's love for his father motivates many of his actions throughout the book, particularly his need to discover for himself the truth about his father's death. It is clear, too, that Oskar's mother loves her son, although that love is sometimes expressed by overprotectiveness. Oskar sometimes seems to resent his mother, particularly because of her relationship with Ron (who himself has experienced the tragedy of losing loved ones), but in the end, he forges a new, closer bond with her.

The novel also deals with complex love relationships from the previous generation. Thomas Schell Sr. fell in love with Anna Schmidt, who became pregnant. Like Oskar, Thomas experienced tremendous loss when Anna, as well as his parents, were killed in the firebombing of Dresden. Continuing this theme, Mr. Tomoyasu loved his daughter and searched for her through the ruins of Hiroshima, much as Oskar searches New York City for the lock that fits the key he has found. Eventually, he found his daughter, but she died in his arms. The love relationship between Grandma, Anna's sister, and Thomas senior is more complex and in fact is not much of a love relationship at all. Nevertheless, Thomas junior is a product of that relationship, and when Thomas learns that his son has died, he travels to New York City from Germany, moves in with his estranged wife, and tries to establish a relationship with Oskar, his grandson. While generations come and go and war leads to destruction and loss, love survives and is a source of optimism.

Memory

Extremely Loud & Incredibly Close is filled with various forms of remembrances. Chief among these are letters that people write to record their lives for others. Much of the novel is taken up, for example, with Grandma's narrative of her life in the form of a letter. Oskar's grandfather keeps a daybook, or diary. The key that comes into Oskar's possession belongs to William Black and fits a safety deposit box that contains William's father's papers. The tape that Oskar plays for his classmates is a memorial of Mr. Tomoyasu's experiences as a survivor of the atomic bombing of Hiroshima. When Oskar and his mother go through Thomas Schell's things, Oskar cannot bear to throw any of them out. Grandma preserves letters from her father. A. R. Black is a former war correspondent who preserves a catalog of everyone he has ever interviewed or written about. Oskar makes a beaded bracelet for his mother that encodes a phone message from his father on the day he died. After his father's death, Oskar writes letters to famous people, including Stephen Hawking, in an effort to establish a link with them, and he hums Beatles' tunes as a way of remembering his father. He preserves the telephone answering machine that contains his father's messages on 9/11. These are just some examples of

TOPICS FOR FURTHER STUDY

- Conduct an Internet examination of hypertext writing. This is writing, including fiction and poetry, which contains hyperlinks that allow the reader to, in effect, create his or her own story by following links. Often, these narratives contain tables, illustrations, and other forms of visual writing. These links are nodes that allow the narrative to branch off in different directions. Locate a story that contains hyperlinks, then prepare a demonstration to your class showing how hypertext writing works. Explain how a passage in *Extremely Loud & Incredibly Close* might be converted into a hypertext novel.

- Research the events surrounding the terrorist attacks of September 11, 2001. In particular, focus on the psychological effects that the attacks had on the nation as a whole and how those attacks altered or affected American culture. Write a brief report discussing your findings.

- Oskar is a pacifist, and what he learns about war and terror confirms him in his pacifism. Imagine a debate between Oskar and someone who willingly fought in World War II, perhaps a soldier such as General George Patton, an outspoken and tough leader of American troops in Europe. What arguments would each make? Prepare your debate as a script

and, with the help of a classmate, "perform" it for your class.

- Develop a family tree for your family. Locate all the information you can about your grandparents and perhaps great-grandparents— and, if possible, any ancestors before that. Were any of them immigrants? Did any of them fight in World War II? Were any of them affected by the Allied bombing of Germany, the atomic bombing of Japan, or a similar catastrophic event? Prepare a multimedia representation of your family tree on your Web page and share on your blog any compelling stories surrounding your ancestors.

- *Extremely Loud & Incredibly Close* is, in part, an epistolary novel, or novel in letters (epistles). This type of narrative is told through primary sources, predominantly letters, although diary entries, newspaper articles, and in recent years, e-mails, blog, and social networking posts are also used. Locate another epistolary novel. Possibilities include Bram Stoker's *Dracula*, Alice Walker's *The Color Purple*, and specifically for young adults, *The Perks of Being a Wallflower* by Stephen Chbosky. Write a brief report on how the use of the epistolary technique is similar to or different from its use in *Extremely Loud & Incredibly Close*.

mementoes, particularly written documents, that preserve memories and forge links between people, generations, and events.

STYLE

Point of View

Three points of view are adopted in *Extremely Loud & Incredibly Close*. The chief narrator is Oskar, who narrates events in the first person. Secondary narrators include his grandmother, who narrates her experiences in the form of a letter,

and his grandfather, who records his experiences in a daybook, or diary. The use of multiple perspectives allows Foer to interweave multiple plot lines and to give the experiences of the characters greater immediacy. Rather than summarizing and interpreting the viewpoints of the characters, allowing them to tell their own stories allows the reader to see interconnections and to form a coherent interpretation of the significance of events.

Visual Writing

A chief characteristic of *Extremely Loud & Incredibly Close* is its use of what is called visual writing. This is a type of writing that relies not only on

He searched for every person named "Black." *(Michal Mrozek | Shutterstock.com)*

traditional text but on illustrations, photos, unorthodox page layout, colors, and other more visual elements. Thus, the novel contains a picture of the key, doors and doorknobs, tortoises, the back of a boy's head, a flock of birds, and other pictures. Some pages contain only a single brief sentence, even a single word. In some places words are crossed out. One passage contains proofreader's marks. Oskar's business card is reproduced. The most notable example of visual writing is the flip art section that concludes the book by depicting a jumper from the World Trade Center ascending to safety rather than falling. Critics are sharply divided in their views about the usefulness of these devices. Whatever the reader's reaction to them, they create within the covers of the book a kind of multimedia experience that enriches the reader's understanding of Oskar and his quest.

HISTORICAL CONTEXT

September 11, 2001

The chief event that forms the historical context for *Extremely Loud & Incredibly Close* is the terrorist attacks on the United States on September 11, 2001. At about 8:30 that morning, nineteen Islamic terrorists, working in teams, hijacked four commercial jetliners that had just departed from Boston, Washington, DC, and Newark, New Jersey. All of the planes were bound for California, so each carried a large amount of fuel. At 8:46, the hijackers deliberately flew one of the planes into the North Tower of the World Trade Center in New York City. Just after 9:00 a.m., a second plane crashed into the South Tower. By then, much of the nation was watching events unfold on television. Then at 9:37 a.m. a third plane crashed into the west side of the Pentagon building in Arlington, Virginia. A fourth airliner reversed course over Ohio and appeared to have been heading toward the nation's capital before passengers, having learned of what was happening through cell phone conversations, wrested control of the plane from the hijackers and crashed the plane into a field near Shanksville, Pennsylvania. Its target remains unknown, but was likely the White House or the Capitol Building. In New York City, the planes' burning jet fuel weakened the structure of the Trade Center towers. The South Tower collapsed at 9:58 a.m., the North Tower at 10:28 a.m. Lower Manhattan was turned into a dust-choked war zone as the authorities scrambled to handle the crisis.

In all, nearly 3,000 people died as a result of the attacks, including the passengers and crews of the jetliners and over a hundred people on the ground at the Pentagon. Most of the casualties, though, were employees trapped in the World Trade Center. Some, facing a fiery death, chose to leap from the towers—a horrifying sight depicted in reverse in the flip art pages at the end of *Extremely Loud & Incredibly Close*. The terrorist attacks of 2001 became a defining moment in modern American history and would influence U.S. policy, both domestically and internationally, for years to come.

Dresden Firebombing

Reference is made in *Extremely Loud & Incredibly Close* to the firebombing of Dresden, Germany, during World War II. From February 13 to February 15, 1945, England's Royal Air Force and the U.S. Army Air Force (the U.S. Air Force did not exist as a separate military branch at the time) dropped some 3,900 tons of explosives on the city of Dresden. Much of the city center was destroyed, and estimates of casualties range from 18,000 to 40,000, most of them civilians. The bombing campaign was justified on the basis that Dresden was a major communications, railroad, and industrial center in support of the Nazi war effort. The bombing took place in the context of the Nazis' refusal to surrender as the war turned against Germany. The belief among the Allies was that a campaign of strategic bombing would weaken not only Germany's war-making capability but also its will to continue the war. Ultimately, Germany would surrender on May 7, 1945. In later years, though, many observers argued that the bombing was disproportionate and that it targeted civilians rather than, for example, industrial facilities. Historians and others continue to debate the morality of the bombing of Dresden, with some suggesting that it was at best unjustifiable, at worst a war crime.

Atomic Bombing of Japan

Although Nazi Germany surrendered in May 1945, ending World War II in Europe, the war against Japan continued in the Pacific. In February and March of that year, thousands of Allied and Japanese troops were killed in the battle for the island of Iwo Jima. Then from April to June, tens of thousands were killed in the battle for Okinawa. As the Allies closed in on the Japanese mainland, Japan

Oskar cannot find the lock to match the key.
(Dewitt | Shutterstock.com)

refused to surrender. War planners believed that it would be necessary for Allied troops to invade the Japanese mainland, a campaign that could have led to the deaths not only of an enormous number of troops on both sides but of hundreds of thousands of civilians, who were being armed for a fight to the death. Accordingly, President Harry Truman authorized the use of the newly developed atomic bomb on the cities of Hiroshima and Nagasaki. On August 6, 1945, the first wartime use of an atomic weapon occurred when the United States dropped an atomic bomb on Hiroshima, leveling the city and killing an estimated 80,000 people, with another 100,000 seriously injured. Three days later, on August 9, a second atomic bomb, the last ever used in war, was dropped on Nagasaki, killing some 40,000 people. Finally, faced with the savage destructiveness of the bomb, Japan surrendered on August 14, ending World War II. In *Extremely Loud & Incredibly Close*, Oskar plays for his classmates a tape in which Mr. Tomoyasu, a Hiroshima survivor, describes the horrors of the bombing and his search for his daughter.

CRITICAL OVERVIEW

The reaction of critics to *Extremely Loud & Incredibly Close* was sharply divided. Many critics were exuberant in their praise. Writing in *Spectator*, Olivia Glazebrook finds the character of Oskar "beautifully realized," and states that "from the very first page [the novel] is a hugely involving read; the voice of Oskar Schell is utterly engaging." She concludes that "this book is a heartbreaker: tragic, funny, intensely moving." In *Library Journal*, Rebecca Miller says that Foer's "excellent second novel vibrates with the details of a current tragedy but successfully explores the universal questions that trauma brings on its floodtide." In *Booklist*, John Green calls the book "arrestingly beautiful," while in *O, The Oprah Magazine*, Pam Houston writes that the book is "a funny, wise, deeply compassionate novel that will renew readers' faith that the right book at the right time still has the power to change the world." Finally, Tom Bissell in the *New Leader* states that the novel is "empathetic writing of a high order" and that Foer has succeeded in "the hard work of diligently imagining one's way into another life." He concludes, however, that although it is a "good novel," it is "not nearly good enough."

Numerous critics, though, excoriated the novel. Writing in the *National Review*, Ross G. Douthat concludes that the novel is too "pleased with its bag of tricks, its crushing banalities, its sound and fury signifying zilch." In *New Statesman*, Benjamin Markovits allows that the book has "moments of genuine charm" but concludes that it is "relentlessly gimmicky" and that "at its heart, the novel has little to offer but the obvious and sentimental." In the *Atlantic*, B. R. Myers refers to Oskar as a "secondary sitcom character" and levels a common criticism about the book's style and structure: "After a while the gimmickry starts to remind one of a clown frantically yanking toys out of his sack: a fatal image." In the *New York Times*, Michiko Kakutani, like Markovits, concedes that the book "contains moments of shattering emotion and stunning virtuosity that attest to Mr. Foer's myriad gifts as a writer," but she also states that "the novel as a whole feels simultaneously contrived and improvisatory, schematic and haphazard." Later, Kakutani describes portions of the novel as "precious and forced" and refers disparagingly to its "razzle-dazzle narrative techniques." Perhaps the most severe critic of the book is Harry Siegel. Writing in the *New York Press*, Siegel's review is titled "Extremely Cloying

and Incredibly False." He calls the author a "fraud and a hack." He says that "the plot is a series of contrivances" and that the author "pillages other authors' techniques, stripping them of their context and using them merely for show." Additionally, he refers to the novel's "fortune-cookie syllogisms," "pointless illustrations," and "typographical tricks."

CRITICISM

Michael J. O'Neal

O'Neal holds a Ph.D. in English literature and linguistics. In the following essay, he discusses Extremely Loud & Incredibly Close *as an example of a postmodern novel and analyzes why some critics responded to the novel so harshly.*

Literary critics nearly always uses terms to classify works of literature. These terms are not meant to pigeonhole a work and suggest that it is somehow the same as every other member of its class. Rather, these terms are a shorthand device used to refer to a cluster of characteristics that a reader might expect to find in a work that seems to belong to a particular class, in much the same way television watchers and moviegoers rely on such terms as "drama," "comedy," or "adventure" in deciding whether to watch a particular show or film. A great novel embodies some of these characteristics but does so in an original way, one that transcends the strictures of the classification.

In discussions of fiction (and poetry), some of these terms include realism, modernism, and postmodernism. These terms refer to movements or styles that characterize the fiction of the twentieth century and beyond, though hints of some of these movements can be found in earlier literature. They indicate that, since the nineteenth century, novelists have experimented with the form and style of their works. During the eighteenth and nineteenth centuries, when fictional narration became a dominant form of English literature in the hands of such authors as Henry Fielding, Jane Austen, Charles Dickens, and George Eliot, novelists, in a sense, were finding their way with such elements of narration as plot, structure, point of view, and language. The works of these and many other novelists are today regarded as conventional, with straightforward, chronological storylines, an authorial point of

WHAT DO I READ NEXT?

- Laurence Sterne's *The Life and Opinions of Tristram Shandy, Gentleman*, originally published over a ten-year period beginning in 1759, has many characteristics in common with *Extremely Loud & Incredibly Close*. Although it purports to be a fictional biography of the title character, it wanders, is filled with digressions, and makes use of some of the techniques of visual writing.

- Günter Grass's novel *The Tin Drum* (1959) tells the story of Oskar Matzerath, who now lives in a mental hospital but lived in Danzig, Poland, before and after the Nazi era in Germany. His life story is absurd and incredible, but readers will find many similarities between Grass's Oskar and the Oskar Schell of *Extremely Loud & Incredibly Close*.

- Nicole Krauss's novel *The History of Love* (2005) narrates the story of a Polish war refugee, Leo Gursky, who, six decades earlier, has written a book with the same title but lost it. At the same time, he lost the woman he loved, Alma. But the book still exists and will tie him to another woman named Alma. The novel, written by Foer's wife, weaves together multiple plots to examine how loss affects the characters.

- Readers who enjoy Foer's novels have also enjoyed Arundhati Roy's Booker Prize-winning novel *The God of Small Things* (1997), which tells the story of young twins living in India. Although the plot and themes of the novel differ from those of Foer's novels, Roy employs similar literary techniques, including dazzling language, word play, multiple story lines, and shifts in time.

- Alan Bradley is the author of a novel suitable for young adults, *The Sweetness at the Bottom of the Pie* (2009), which is narrated by a precocious eleven-year-old girl with a passion for chemistry, especially poisons. She uses her wit and keen sense of observation to solve a murder mystery in which her distant father is implicated.

- *A Heartbreaking Work of Staggering Genius* (2000) by Dave Eggers is a blend of memoir and fiction as it narrates the lives of a family of children who lost both parents to cancer. The book employs unconventional storytelling devices in much the same way as *Extremely Loud & Incredibly Close*.

view (except in the case of first-person narratives), and language that is consistently recognizable to readers. The movement in the late nineteenth century and into the twentieth was toward greater realism, referring primarily to the rejection of idealized, almost fairy tale images of characters in favor of close observation of their motives, inner lives, and the social context of their lives.

So-called modern novels—those written roughly in the first half of the twentieth century—tried to build on the realist movement of the nineteenth century. The modern novel, as practiced by writers such as James Joyce and William Faulkner, experimented with form and structure. Narrative voices, whether the authors' or those of a first-person narrators, were often no longer regarded as reliable, forcing the reader to recognize their limitations and determine whether the narrative voice is to be trusted. Linguistic techniques such as stream-of-consciousness tried to recreate directly the inner workings of a character's mind; one thinks of the final chapter of Joyce's *Ulysses*, consisting of page after page of a character's thoughts rendered without punctuation. Storylines were often no longer chronological but relied on flashbacks and similar techniques in an effort to examine reality in different, unconventional ways. Language often became more inventive, again with a view to seeing reality in new ways and indeed creating a new reality.

He hears the message from his father, at the top of one of the Twin Towers. (*Moyseeva Irina / Shutterstock.com*)

At some point around the middle of the twentieth century, some novelists began to see fiction in terms of what many critics came to call postmodernism. Like most such terms, this one is difficult to define precisely, but as used by most critics, it refers to a fundamental reaction against an ordered vision of the world and to the belief that the form and meaning of texts is fluid and, in many cases, unknowable. Some critics have regarded *Extremely Loud & Incredibly Close* as embodying many of the characteristics of the postmodern novel. Indeed, even a casual reading of the novel makes clear that Foer employs numerous unconventional techniques: multiple narrators, odd typographical effects, discontinuities in the storyline, quirky language (such as Oskar's continual reference to "heavy boots," his term for depression), visuals (including photos, Oskar's business card, and most notably, the flip art at the novel's end), and the like. The fundamental question a reader (and critic) has to ask is why Foer uses these techniques.

The question has no easy answer. But a start would be to say that by using them, he induces the reader to look not at reality but at *Oskar's* reality

in a new and different way. Oskar's reality is confused and troubled. He suffers from phobias and other psychological problems. He is trying to make sense out of the chaos surrounding not only his father's death but also the strange and troubled history of his parents and grandparents. The multiple storylines, conveyed through multiple narrators, allow him to see connections between events, specifically the terrorist attacks of 9/11, the firebombing of Dresden, and the atomic bombing of Japan at the end of World War II. To describe Oskar's reality, which the nineteenth-century novelist would likely have tried to do, is almost impossible. The reader can only experience that reality by entering into the strange, jumbled, disjointed world in which he lives and moves, particularly considering that he is a child who is in many ways incapable of fully grasping the reality around him. Ultimately, the reader is called on to form a coherent, intellectually satisfying understanding of that reality. The author's job is to provide the raw materials, not the finished product.

This, perhaps, explains why so many critics found the novel a failure (though to be sure, many others described the novel as a tour de force and praised it highly). The problem with "unconventional" narration is that the unconventional features in themselves can quickly become conventional, the kind of features that draw attention to themselves and seem to announce to readers, "This is a new kind of novel." The fundamental problem is that the techniques Foer employs, to some critics at least, serve little purpose but instead seem to be ends in themselves. Thus, a reader might ask, "Would this work be any worse for elimination of the photos?" "Would it be worse without the flip art section?" "Would it be diminished if the red proofreader's marks were eliminated from the chapter titled 'Why I'm Not Where You Are: 4/12/78?'" "What about the two and a half pages that consist of nothing but row after row of digits, each separated from the next by a comma, or the cramped and ultimately illegible typography of the chapter titled 'Why I'm Not Where You Are: 9/11/03,' or the pages with single brief sentences, such as the one that says simply 'I'm sorry,' followed by a page with a photo of a doorknob?" In the final analysis, each reader has to decide whether these techniques are mere "gimmicks" or representations of new ways of experiencing reality. Each reader has to decide whether they are genuinely new, or whether they are a tired recycling of techniques other authors have tried in the past. Most importantly, each reader has to decide whether the novel's unorthodox form and structure lead to new insights: about character, about 9/11; about war and violence; about links between historical events and generations; about death, love, and memory; about uncertain and shifting relationships with other people; and about the very nature of fictional worlds and how readers construct meaning from them. Ultimately, each reader will find one set of commentators dead wrong in their assessment of this novel.

Source: Michael J. O'Neal, Critical Essay on *Extremely Loud & Incredibly Close*, in *Novels for Students*, Gale, Cengage Learning, 2011.

Stefan Beck

In the following review, Beck questions Foer's choice of hiding behind a child while addressing the tragic topic of 9/11.

The plot of *Extremely Loud and Incredibly Close* hinges on a mysterious key. Fitting: it's a roman a clef in several ways. Look at Oskar Schell, age nine, the book's precocious, insufferable Montessori casualty of a narrator. Wordsworth wrote that the child is father to the man,

but in this case, "father" doesn't cut it: the child is indistinguishable from the man. Harry Siegel, who wrote a vicious review of *Incredibly Close* for the *New York Press*, noted that Oskar "writes letters to Stephen Hawking and other luminaries" and that Foer "wrote letters to Susan Sontag when he was nine." That's not all: upon finishing his first novel, Foer wrote to Sontag, John Barth, Joyce Carol Oates, David Foster Wallace, Zadie Smith, John Updike, and other "luminaries" to request "the next sheet of paper that he or she would have written on."

Blank page: emptiness, potential, magic. Heavy. Oates is very fond of Foer; a *New York Press* list of the "50 Most Loathsome New Yorkers" japed that she invented him in a Princeton laboratory. Updike penned an avuncular review of *Incredibly Close* for the *New Yorker*. Wallace, the postmodern godfather of droll, is present in spirit on every page of Foer's new book. (Trace the lineage: Wallace gave us *A Supposedly Fun Thing I'll Never Do Again*; his disciple Eggers, *A Heartbreaking Work of Staggering Genius*; now Foer drops *Extremely Loud and Incredibly Close* and chapter headings like "A Simple Solution to an Impossible Problem." If brevity is the soul of wit, these guys have all the wit of a telephone directory.) The confidence man Foer appealed to their vanity, and they fell hard. Yet the biggest loser hero is Foer himself.

Foer's homunculus, Oskar, is likeable only to Foer and his ilk. Oskar pretends to childlike innocence, but children learn at an early age how to manipulate, and this kid is all cocktail-party-pleasing, scratch-behind-my-ears calculation. Had we a real Oskar, we'd shut him up, Kaspar Hanser-style, in some damp and cobwebbed oubliette—that is, if we couldn't just send him the way of Little Nell.

Oh, but Oskar's father died in the World Trade Center. This is a 9/11 book, and that's a neon sign: Do be KIND, this is IMPORTANT. The McGuffin, the mysterious key, is found by Oskar among his father's belongings. He wonders what lock it fits, i.e., Where are my existential answers? The key is in an envelope marked Black, so Oskar's quest is to visit—in the real world, we'd say harass—everyone in New York City named Black. Here he is with one Abby Black:

> 'Since you're an epidemiologist,' I said, 'did you know that seventy percent of household dust is actually composed of human epidermal matter?' 'No,' she said, 'I didn't.' 'I'm an

"FOER, LIKE THE AUTHOR OF THE NORTH KOREA PIECE, FAILS TO UNDERSTAND TRAGEDY—IT WASN'T INVENTED OR PERFECTED ON 9/11, AND THOSE WHO HAVE EXPERIENCED IT, SAY, OVER A SPAN OF DECADES DO NOT SEE IT AS AN OCCASION FOR CUTE WORKSHOP PROJECTS OR SNARKY MEDIA-CULTURE COMMENTARY."

amateur epidemiologist.' 'There aren't many of those.' 'Yeah. And I conducted a pretty fascinating experiment once where I told [the maid] Feliz to save all the dust from our apartment for a year in a garbage bag for me. Then I weighed it. . . . That doesn't actually prove anything, but it's weird.'

Uh oh—somebody's been cribbing from himself! Foer's essay about blank pages, entitled (I kid you not) "emptiness: the joy and terror of the blank page, empty and infinite, source of anxiety and inspiration for all writers, including this one," says: "I've read that 90 percent of household dust is actually composed of human epidermal matter. So I like to think of the page as holding the face that once looked over it. . . ."

Do you, really? I guarantee that Foer's lone similarity to less pretentious writers is that he used a computer to write *Incredibly Close*. He deploys plenty of typographical gimmickry that only a modern word processor could make possible—for instance, a chapter in which the kerning gradually becomes so tight that the text is illegible. But I doubt the monitor on his blueberry iMac accrued much epidermal matter in the half hour it apparently took him to spit out this nonsense. And if it did, so what? The words are the words, regardless of the care or (highly dubious) pain that went into them. An honest reader could care less about process.

Everyone cringed when he learned that Foer's sophomore effort was to be a 9/11 novel. Foer countered by asking, "Why do people wonder what's 'OK' to make art about, as if creating art out of tragedy weren't an inherently good thing? . . . Too many people hate art." Nothing is inherently good, and people, often despite themselves, hate bad art, not art qua art. It's all in the execution. Foer, setting out to examine and memorialize tragedy, was faced with a

choice: will I be an adult, or will I retreat into childish fantasy? He made the wrong choice.

That's this roman's real clef—not the answer to "Who is Foer?" but to "Why can't his generation answer—or even ask—the questions that ought to matter to it?"

A young author who debuts in August has written a book as a letter to Osama bin Laden, along the lines of "I know you're upset with the West, but if you could just understand how much I loved my husband and son, you'd back off." Not likely. A Dave Eggers clone, some registered member of the Long Title Club, wrote a piece for Eggers's *McSweeney*'s magazine called "Translated Thoughts and Questions that are Running Through a North Korean Refugee's Mind When He is Awarded Political Asylum in the United States, Settles Down, Turns on the Television, and the First Thing He Sees is a Fancy Feast Cat Food Commercial":

> This commercial brings back memories of a difficult childhood in Pyongyang, when my pet cat, Mr. Finicky Timbers, ran away and tried to cross the demilitarized zone, unsuccessfully, making it through the razor wire but then . . . the land mine.

> And the international community is worried about North Korea's development of weapons of mass destruction?

> In America, cats eat choice cuts of chicken out of handcrafted Tiffany goblets.

Yawn. It's heartbreaking folly, a staggering failure of imagination—the same mentality that birthed Foer's book, which is stuffed to the gills with embarrassing bromides about pacifism and the futility of war. Oskar's business card, one of the book's many groan-making illustrations, notes that he is a Francophile and pacifist, among other things that would make you send your kid straight to football camp.

The story of Oskar's quest is intercut with the story of his grandfather's traumatic survival of Dresden's firebombing. (He elects not to speak, but writes frantically on notecards.) The pitiable Grandpa goes to America, marries, and impregnates his wife; then he leaves her, because he doesn't know how to live, or love, or something. Later, he comes back. He spies on his wife, and his grandson Oskar. Eventually he and Oskar, who doesn't know his elderly friend's true identity, dig up Oskar's dad's (empty) grave and stuff it with letters Grandpa has written to his now-dead son. For a man dumbstruck, Grandpa is an incredibly prolific writer.

Foer, like the author of the North Korea piece, fails to understand tragedy—it wasn't invented or perfected on 9/11, and those who have experienced it, say, over a span of decades do not see it as an occasion for cute workshop projects or snarky media-culture commentary. And they do not, as so many of our writers have done, take comfort in wishes and daydreams. Foer's book, you may have read, concludes with a flipbook in which a man who has jumped from the Trade Center actually rises toward the sky.

> When I flipped through them, it looked like the man was floating up through the sky.
>
> And if I'd had more pictures, he would've flown through a window, back into the building, and the smoke would've poured into a hole that the plane was about to come out of....
>
> We would have been safe.

Fin[e]. While you're at it, imagine there's no countries. But it did happen, and Foer's book does nothing to address why or why not. It only pushes us deeper into the sheltering bosom of self-pity and, inevitably, cowardice. For Foer himself, one suspects, it harkens back to his childhood, when he was a special little Sontag-idolizing wunderkind and not one of a thousand MFA brats grasping after another fix of senseless praise. It rather gives up the game when, at one point, Oskar scolds someone for making him feel "unspecial."

Gerald Seymour, a British author of spy novels and "thrillers," wrote a book, *The Unknown Soldier*, about an al Qaeda terrorist—not sympathetic or relativistic, but accurate, as he guessed it—but don't expect it to receive the notice *Incredibly Close* has. It deals with the problems (to put it lightly) of terrorism and evil, but doesn't stir any of Foer's shallow pools of aphoristic wisdom; it doesn't hide behind a child. We can cock our ears to the mouths of babes, or we can, like Saint Paul, become men and put away childish things. The former may be pleasant—it might even sell—but our survival depends upon the latter. If Foer is one of the unacknowledged legislators of our age, its time to whip out the veto.

Source: Stefan Beck, "Kinderkampf," in *New Criterion*, Vol. 23, No. 10, June 2005, pp. 92–95.

Olivia Glazebrook

In the following review, Glazebrook describes how Foer uses the young boy protagonist to draw us into the aftermath of tragedy.

'I used to be an atheist,' says ten-year-old Oskar Schell, 'which means I didn't believe in things that couldn't be observed . . . It's not that I believe in things that can't be observed now, because I don't. It's that I believe things are extremely complicated.'

On 11 September 2001, Oskar is sent home from school when the World Trade Center is attacked. He is not anxious for his parents, since neither of them works near the Twin Towers. But when he gets home, he plays the messages on the answering machine, and discovers that his father is trapped at the top of one of the burning towers. Minutes later, the tower collapses.

Oskar is a brainy, precocious, charming, confident boy whose father has been his god. For all his brilliance, he can find nothing to help him out of the misery into which he has been pitched. 'I'll wear heavy boots for the rest of my life,' he says. With his mother locked in a grief of her own, Oskar battles to untangle his turbulent feelings. Loss is complicated by fear, resentment, guilt and anger. He is confounded. And then he finds, in his father's closet, a key he has never seen before. Seizing on this key as a mysterious 'clue,' he sets out on a quest to find its lock—'finding the lock was my ultimate raison d'etre—the raison that was the master over all other raisons.'

But Oskar is not the only victim in his family. His grandparents—his father's parents—survived the Dresden fire-bombing, his grandfather so profoundly affected that he eventually lost the power of speech. Their history is also told, through a series of letters which punctuate the book. Oskar's grandmother writes letters to him (which go unsent), and Oskar's grandfather has written (but also not sent) letters to his son, whom he has never known. 'I am so afraid of losing something that I love,' he writes, 'that I refuse to love anything,' and so he abandons his pregnant wife in New York, and Oskar's father grows up without a father.

So this is a book about loss, and about individual suffering amid (and following) cataclysmic events. From the very first page it is a hugely involving read; the voice of Oskar Schell is utterly engaging. His character is so beautifully realised, one would go with him anywhere. His grandparents' letters are almost an unwelcome intrusion in Oskar's narrative, but they do broaden the reach of the book beyond the complex miseries of its hero. Safran Foer is describing a suffering that spreads across continents and generations.

> BOTH THE SEARCH AND ITS POSSIBLE MEANING ARE NEATLY SYMBOLIZED BY A MYSTERIOUS KEY, IN AN ENVELOPE LABELED 'BLACK,' THAT OSKAR FINDS AMONG HIS FATHER'S POSSESSIONS."

The book has whimsical elements—illustrations, photographs, the account of the Dresden bombing 'corrected' in red pen—which I could do without (I suppose they are a trademark of the author's, since *Everything is Illuminated* was studded with similar gimmicks) but, all told, this book is a heartbreaker: tragic, funny, intensely moving.

Source: Olivia Glazebrook, "Wearing Heavy Boots Lightly," in *Spectator*, Vol. 298, No. 9227, June 11, 2005, p. 40.

Sam Munson

In the following review, Munson declares that, unlike authors of many novels about tragedy, in Extremely Loud & Incredibly Close, *Foer adapted his writing to the condition of radical uncertainty without the condition of defeat.*

Writing a novel about catastrophic events that are still inescapably present in our collective imagination makes strenuous demands—demands that have hindered or defeated even writers of great intelligence and ability. But in the case of 9/11, and in spite of the dangers, American and European novelists have found the challenge irresistible. Heidi Julavits opened the floodgates last year with *The Effect of Living Backwards*. Joyce Carol Oates contributed a short story, "The Mutants," included in her latest collection, *I Am No One You Know*. Frederic Beigbeder's French bestseller *Windows on the World* appeared in March in English; Nick McDonell's *The Third Brother* will be out in September. And that is only a small sampling.

Even in this decidedly mixed company, Ian McEwan and Jonathan Safran Foer make the strangest of bedfellows. McEwan is British; Foer, American. McEwan is the author of a series of intelligent, highly regarded novels, most recently *Amsterdam* (1998) and *Atonement* (2001); Foer made his debut in 2002 with the bestseller *Everything Is Illuminated*. Formally McEwan is a traditionalist, and an unapologetic realist, as deeply interested in the voluminous physical data of life as he is in its large, stony questions. Foer is an experimenter and a comic surrealist, playful and endlessly loquacious.

Despite the differences between them, 9/11 is a natural subject for each. Death, murder, crime, abandonment, and social breakdown are persistent themes in McEwan's work; Foer's career-opening novel is about the Holocaust. That they have both turned their attention to September 11, 2001, and that their books have appeared more or less simultaneously, gives readers an opportunity to observe two sharply distinguished, even opposed, writerly temperaments placed at the service of a common end.

McEwan's *Saturday* narrates a day in the life of Henry Perowne, a successful neurosurgeon. The Saturday in question—February 15, 2003—falls a little more than a month before the beginning of the American-led campaign in Iraq. The day opens with Perowne standing naked, in the early morning, before his bedroom window, watching a cargo plane with one engine on fire descending to its uncertain fate over London. As his weekly day of rest progresses, the peculiar story of this plane and its pilots plays itself out in the background, depressing him, elating him, and disillusioning him by turns.

Perowne putters about his house waiting for the early television news to come on; watches an exuberant crowd of protesters gathering in the square on which he lives; retrieves his Mercedes from the garage; plays a round of squash with his anaesthetist; visits his senile mother, and prepares dinner for his family—prosecutes, in short, the unremarkable, absorbing weekend routine of an affluent Westerner. But the sense of unease the plane has brought into his sunny life turns out to be justified.

As Perowne wends his way through the protest march to his squash game, a deranged, twitchy thug named Baxter sideswipes his car. Held down by one of Baxter's flunkies, Perowne avoids a beating by diagnosing the gang leader's twitch as a symptom of a neurological disorder, Huntington's chorea. Hours later, however, Baxter reappears at Perowne's house as he is serving the dinner he has prepared, holding his wife at knifepoint and threatening his newly pregnant daughter with rape. With the help of his daughter and his son, Perowne subdues Baxter, who then ends up in the emergency room under his care. Perowne spares his life, and the novel ends with the neurosurgeon gratefully surrendering to sleep in his wife's arms.

The disruption of the established movements of life, often by means of violence, is a preoccupying theme of earlier novels by McEwan—in particular, *The Cement Garden* (1978), *Enduring Love* (1997), and *Atonement*. Rather than enervating him or making him facile, the subject appears to put him at his ease. In *Saturday* the prose is as supple and as replete as Henry Perowne's own minutely observed responses to his life's rich, menacing, and incomprehensible tapestry. His first confrontation with Baxter, a moment of isolation and terror, forms a piece of that fabric:

> The men have stopped to look at something in the road. The short fellow in the black suit touches with the tip of his shoe the BMW's shorn-off wing mirror.... They stare down at it together and then, at a remark from the short man, they turn their faces toward Perowne simultaneously, with abrupt curiosity, like deer disturbed in a forest. For the first time it occurs to him that he might be in some kind of danger.... There, behind him on Gower Street, the march proper has begun. Thousands packed in a single dense column are making for Piccadilly.... From their faces, hands, and clothes they emanate the rich color, almost like warmth, peculiar to compacted humanity. For dramatic effect, they're walking in silence to the funereal beat of marching drums.

The highly textured but low-pitched prose, with its accretion of detail and its insistent use of the present tense, allows the submerged uncertainty of life after 9/11 to emerge not as an occasion for rhetorical or stylistic fireworks but as one of the many tonal strains, albeit an intense one, pervading a man's daily experience. Perowne's ambivalence about the state of the world—he shifts between cautious support for the Iraq war and anxiety about it, tempered in each case by a groundnote of despairing detachment—does not impair his everyday moral compass. One of the last scenes of the book has him sitting by Baxter's bedside, contemplating "precisely what should be done." McEwan leaves open here the possibility of a quiet, undetectable murder; only as the book ends are we given to understand in a deliberate anticlimax that the question Perowne has been trying to answer for himself is whether he should press charges.

In no way does Perowne serve as a stand-in for the author, although there are a few autobiographical flourishes: like his protagonist, McEwan lives in a large private house on a busy square, and Rosie Perowne bears a suspicious resemblance to McEwan's wife, Annalena McAfee. But Perowne himself is devoid of all writerly sentiment: he does not think in vivid or elaborated figures of speech, and his closest involvement with literature comes only by way of his daughter Daisy, a poet; in the confrontation with Baxter, it emerges that he does not even know who Matthew Arnold is. A master of his own difficult art, Perowne is an exceptionally alert, receptive, and meditative man; but he is not a mouthpiece for his creator. By thus absenting himself, as it were, from his protagonist, McEwan has paradoxically permitted this novel's conflicted vision of life in the aftermath of 9/11 to step forth in its own colors. In that respect among others, *Saturday* stands in stark contrast to Jonathan Safran Foer's *Extremely Loud & Incredibly Close*.

Foer has a natural gift for choosing subjects of great import and then pitching his distinctive voice sharply enough to be heard above their historical din. This may be in part what accounts for his coronation as the voice of his generation (a laurel that admittedly gets bestowed afresh every three to five years). His first novel, *Everything Is Illuminated*, concerned a young man named Jonathan Safran Foer in search of the unknown woman who saved his grandfather's life during the Holocaust. *Extremely Loud & Incredibly Close* concerns an even younger protagonist, the nine-year-old Oskar Schell, a New Yorker of German-American ancestry (the allusion to Günter Grass's Oskar in *The Tin Drum* is anything but accidental), who is in search of the meaning of his father's death in the terrorist attack on the World Trade Center.

Both the search and its possible meaning are neatly symbolized by a mysterious key, in an envelope labeled "Black," that Oskar finds among his father's possessions. Key in hand, he wanders determinedly through the five boroughs of the city, searching out everyone named Black in the hope of revelation. In the process he meets a whole cast of characters: Abby Black, the beautiful scientist; Ada Black, the socialite; A.R. Black, the quirky old man who ends each of his sentences with an exclamation point (and these are just the As).

In the course of his wanderings, Oskar also comes face to face with the fact of his own isolation from his peers, of his mother's budding friendship with the widowered Ron, and of his crushing guilt at having failed to pick up his father's final phone calls, recorded on the morning of 9/11 on an answering machine that Oskar has kept hidden in a closet. By the novel's end, Oskar discovers that the key has an entirely different meaning from the one he had so fervently hoped to find; presumably, he must now look elsewhere for a way of coming to terms with his life.

The plot, however, is only half the story. As he did in *Everything Is Illuminated*, Foer makes use of a variety of formal devices in *Extremely Loud & Incredibly Close*, two of them prominent by their familiarity. Like Alex Perchov in the earlier novel, Oskar speaks in a chirpy, whimsical dialect—"heavy boots" is his clever, private idiom for depression, "dip-shiitake" his clever, public bowdlerization of "dipshit." And Foer again tells a story about the brutality of World War II. In *Everything Is Illuminated*, this story centered on the destruction of a shtetl in the Ukraine; in *Extremely Loud*, it centers on the firebombing of Dresden as experienced by Oskar's traumatized grandfather, Thomas Schell.

Oskar is, in principle at least, an ideal subject—a precocious, winsome, obsessively curious boy, a constant dreamer-up of improbable inventions, from a detachable pocket to a shirt made of birdseed to various other instruments of concealment and escape. One of his most elaborate technological fantasies is of a

> device that knew everyone you knew....So when an ambulance went down the street, a big sign on the roof could flash DON'T WORRY! DON'T WORRY! if the sick person's device didn't detect the device of someone he knew nearby. And if the device did detect the device of someone he knew, the ambulance could flash the name of the person in the ambulance, and either IT'S NOTHING MAJOR! IT'S NOTHING MAJOR! or, if it was something major, IT'S MAJOR! IT'S MAJOR! And maybe you could rate the people you knew by how much you loved them....

And so on and, garrulously, on. All this is Foer's way of showing us, or belaboring us with, Oskar's great pain, fear, and susceptibility. The trouble is that, despite the long stretches of time a reader spends listening to Oskar's hyperactive narration, his habitual and unstoppable overstatement prevents one from ever coming to know the inner character of his pain and fear and susceptibility. The same is true of his grandfather, whose recital of his climactic, painful reunion with Oskar becomes, literally, less and less legible as it goes on, the spaces between the letters decreasing to the point of near-total blackness. We are meant to understand, obviously, that an impenetrable darkness descended on Thomas's life after the firebombing of Dresden, that this darkness persists just as strongly in the present, and that it has been revived at the sight of Oskar's own suffering—an understanding that presumably excuses Jonathan Safran Foer from conveying the actual experience of this darkness by means of language or, in a sense, from writing about it at all.

Oskar himself has been invested by Foer with little other than an intense desire for our attention. Perhaps for that reason, in those moments when he finally has our ear, he appears an utterly empty vessel. This would be a serious flaw in any novel so dependent on the voice of a single character. In a novel about a recent, world-altering tragedy, the failure is particularly egregious. There is little in Foer's book that we are not meant to grasp as a signpost, but what these ubiquitous and stagey signals direct us to remains unclear. In striving to come to terms with evil, *Extremely Loud* falls back on that most convenient of crutches, a child's suffering; in the process, it reduces the attack on the Twin Towers—an event filled with black intent—to a mere symbol, a conceptual shorthand.

Admittedly, few works of literature have succeeded in drawing lasting meaning, whole or fragmentary, from modernity's string of catastrophes: Ford Madox Ford's *Parade's End*, Robert Musil's *The Man Without Qualities*, Thomas Mann's *Doktor Faustus*, the poems of Paul Celan, Aleksandr Solzhenitsyn's *The Gulag Archipelago*, a handful of others. A recent book that can be added to this list, and one relevant to Foer's enterprise, is W.G. Sebald's *Austerlitz* (English translation, 2001). A dense, hypnotic novel, it is dominated by Jacques Austerlitz's focused but circuitous account of his childhood, youth, and manhood, his obsessive researches into his own history and that of his century, and his slow-won but inexorable conclusion that every supreme human effort casts a long and prominently visible shadow—the shadow, in Sebald's phrase, of its own destruction.

Extremely Loud & Incredibly Close owes a large, unacknowledged debt to *Austerlitz*—from the coincidence of subject, to Thomas Schell's recursive, comma-peppered narrative style, to the polymath protagonist, to the black-and-white photographs that appear in its pages. But the two books are on such vastly different levels that comparison becomes ridiculous. Where *Austerlitz* proceeds from a profound knowledge of history and its depredations, *Extremely Loud* is little more than a collection of information gathered from history's grab-bag. And where *Austerlitz* leaves the reader with a shattering climactic scene—a family of ghostly dark-haired musicians at a third-rate circus near the Austerlitz train station in Paris, their wild, Eastern notes an emblem both of life's possibilities and its awful potential for extinction—*Extremely Loud* ends with a flipbook. In it, a series of doctored photos shows a man, in the midst of falling from one of the towers, reversing his course and ascending to an unseen heaven. Foer evidently considers this piece of bathos a worthy final meditation on history and time.

Sebald's title, *Austerlitz*, refers to Napoleon's brilliant victory in a major battle that took place in the fall of 1805. Bound up with this is another reference, namely, to the moment in *War and Peace* when Tolstoy first hints at his book's true theme, which is the powerlessness of the individual before the massed forces of history:

> Just as, in a clock, the result of the complicated motion of innumerable wheels and pulleys is merely a slow and regular movement of the hands which show the time, so the result of all the complicated human activities of 160,000 Russians and French—all their passions, desires, remorse, humiliations, sufferings, outbursts of pride, fear, and enthusiasm—was only the loss of the battle of Austerlitz, the so-called battle of the three emperors—that is to say, a slow movement of the hand on the dial of human history.

Tolstoy's terrible "only" looms large throughout the novels of W.G. Sebald. It tints Ian McEwan's latest novel as well. *Extremely Loud & Incredibly Close* remains completely untouched by it. It may be the case that tragedy defeats us, particularly tragedy on a historical scale. But the best writers can, somehow, adapt themselves to the condition of radical uncertainty. Others, like Foer, baselessly confident, fond of the obvious, imposing on their readers' good will, simply pretend it away, and impoverish not only their novels but us.

Source: Sam Munson, "In the Aftermath," in *Commentary*, Vol. 119, No. 5, May 2005, pp. 80–85.

SOURCES

Bissell, Tom, "Whimsy in the Face of Terror," in *New Leader*, March/April 2005, p. 28.

Douthat, Ross G., "After Tragedy," in *National Review* June 20, 2005, p. 48.

Foer, Jonathan Safran, *Extremely Loud & Incredibly Close*, Houghton Mifflin, 2005.

Glazebrook, Olivia, "Wearing Heavy Boots Lightly," in *Spectator*, June 11, 2005, p. 40.

Green, John, Review of *Extremely Loud and Incredibly Close*, in *Booklist*, February 1, 2005, p. 917.

Houston, Pam, "Boy, Interrupted: Jonathan Safran Foer Follows His Smash Debut, *Everything Is Illuminated*, with a Witty, Heartbreaking Tour de Force," in *O, The Oprah Magazine*, April 2005, p. 158.

Kakutani, Michiko, "A Boy's Epic Quest, Borough by Borough," in *New York Times*, March 22, 2005.

Markovits, Benjamin, "The Horrors of History: A Novel of Post-9/11 Is Let Down by Its Obsessive Whimsy," in *New Statesman*, June 6, 2005, p. 50.

Miller, Rebecca, Review of *Extremely Loud and Incredibly Close* in *Library Journal*, March 1, 2005, p. 78.

Myers, B. R., "A Bag of Tired Tricks: Blank Pages? Photos of Mating Tortoises? The Death Throes of the Postmodern Novel," in *Atlantic*, May 2005, pp. 115–16.

Siegel, Harry, "Extremely Cloying and Incredibly False," in *New York Press*, April 20, 2005.

FURTHER READING

Colón, Ernie, and Sid Jacobson, *The 9/11 Report: A Graphic Adaptation*, Hill & Wang, 2006.

> In the wake of the terrorist attack of September 11, 2001, the government created the 9/11 Commission, which examined the events in detail. This book takes the comprehensive but dry government report and makes it more accessible to readers with graphics and text.

O'Neal, Michael, *President Truman and the Atomic Bomb*, Greenhaven Press, 1990.

> This volume, written for young adults, examines the decision to use the atomic bomb against Japan, particularly the issue of whether use of the bomb was necessary to end the war and whether its use actually saved lives.

Raines, Howell, *Portraits: 9/11/01: The Collected "Portraits of Grief" from the New York Times*, introduction by Janny Scott, New York Times, 2003.

> In the days after the terrorist attacks of September 11, 2001, the *New York Times* daily

published photos and biographies of those killed in the attacks. This book collects those pieces, which many readers saw as giving a human face to the wrenching events of that day.

Vonnegut, Kurt, *Slaughterhouse-Five*, Dell, 1969.
This novel is a semiautobiographical account of the firebombing of Dresden, Germany, which the author witnessed as a prisoner of war, held in a slaughterhouse; many critics regard it as Vonnegut's greatest novel. Using many of the techniques of contemporary fiction, it tells the story of Billy Pilgrim, blending satire, historical fiction, science fiction, and discontinuous narrative to reconstruct the protagonist's frame of mind.

SUGGESTED SEARCH TERMS

9/11 AND terrorist attacks

atomic bombing Japan

Dresden firebombing

epistolary novel

Extremely Loud & Incredibly Close

Jonathan Safran Foer

September 11, 2001 AND terrorist attacks

visual writing

Foer AND 9/11

Foer AND visual writing

Herland

CHARLOTTE PERKINS GILMAN

1915

Originally published as a series of chapters in the magazine *Forerunner* in 1915, Charlotte Perkins Gilman's *Herland* was rediscovered in 1979 and published for the first time in novel format. It is widely available today as both a stand-alone novel and in collections of her works. As feminist utopian literature, the novel challenges early twentieth-century values and norms and boldly suggests that women as a collective population have the power to transform society into a cohesive unit of peace-seeking, cooperative people.

The first of her three utopian novels, *Herland* introduces three male protagonists, each symbolic of commonly held viewpoints of women during the Victorian age. Although Van, Jeff, and Terry make the journey through the book together, each has a unique experience dependent upon his attitude and willingness to let go of gender stereotypes and attitudes.

The novel was not written as mere entertainment but as a vehicle for social change. That said, Gilman infused elements common to popular fiction of the day—adventure, romance, even a bit of suspense—to draw readers into the perfection of the all-female society discovered on the eve of World War I.

Herself a victim of the era's beliefs that women belonged in the domestic sphere and that to stray beyond it was not only inappropriate but dangerous for this "weaker sex," Gilman's personal experiences with postpartum

Charlotte Perkins Gilman

depression and near insanity led her to embrace the philosophy behind socialist feminism, which posits that true freedom is possible only when the social and political forces that oppress women are conquered. This was a highly controversial viewpoint during the early twentieth century, and it made Gilman a somewhat scandalous public figure. *Herland* was ahead of its time not because it explored the idea of utopia, or the perfect world, but because that perfect world was possible only through the destruction of the existing patriarchal society.

AUTHOR BIOGRAPHY

Gilman was born Charlotte Anna Perkins on July 3, 1860, in Hartford, Connecticut. Her father was related to the abolitionist Harriet Beecher Stowe. Soon after Charlotte was born, her father abandoned her, her brother, and their mother. Living in constant poverty, Gilman's childhood was a transient, unhappy existence. The family moved nineteen times in eighteen years.

Gilman supported her family on income earned as a teacher, governess, and greeting card designer. In 1884, she married Charles Walter Stetson, and their only child, Katharine Beecher, was born a year later. Shortly after the baby's birth, Gilman experienced intense depression, with symptoms so severe she sought professional help from S. Weir Mitchell, a famous Philadelphia neurologist whose specialty was women's nervous disorders. Weir recommended his infamous "rest cure," which demanded she keep her child with her at all times, focus only on domestic activities, and refrain from ever writing again. Reading—and any other intellectual activity—was severely limited. As a result of the doctor's orders, Gilman nearly went insane.

Recognizing what was happening, she chose instead to ignore Mitchell's orders and instead ran away to California, leaving behind both Charles and Katharine. There her health improved. Eventually divorcing her husband, Gilman brought Katharine to California to live with her, and it was during this time of struggling to make ends meet that she took up writing again. In 1892, Gilman published the piece for which she is most famous, the short story "The Yellow Wallpaper." The story was autobiographical and chronicled her experience with Dr. Mitchell and his "rest cure." The story continues to be one of the most-often anthologized short stories in the country.

Throughout the 1890s, Gilman published her work and edited that of others. As a contributing editor to the periodical *American Fabian*, Gilman crossed paths with the writer Edward Bellamy, whose novel *Looking Backward* featured a futuristic utopian society based on the concept of socialism. He called this concept nationalism, and his novel led directly to the formation of nationalist clubs across the country. Gilman, already a dedicated member of the feminist movement, embraced the ideas of the nationalist movement as well and, like many of her peers, found much overlapping in the philosophies and end goals of the two schools of thought.

Gilman supplemented her writing income with money earned through public speaking and lecturing. Her audiences included labor unions and women's suffrage organizations, church groups, and Nationalist clubs. Her speeches on the importance of rights for women and the benefits of cooperation over competition brought her public attention but also criticism, as did the fact that she relinquished custody of her daughter to her former husband and his new wife, who happened to have been one of Gilman's good friends.

At a time when society almost unilaterally judged that a child should live with its mother, this was a bold move. Gilman was publicly ridiculed for abandoning her daughter.

In 1898, she published the influential book *Women and Economics.* Translated into seven languages, the feminist treatise earned her international fame and recognition. She continued publishing books related to women, children, and social norms into the early twentieth century. In 1900, she married George Houghton Gilman, a first cousin. The couple moved to Connecticut and lived what appeared to all a happy existence until George's sudden death in 1934. At that time, Gilman returned to Pasadena, California, where she would live until the end of her life.

In November 1909, Gilman began publishing her own literary magazine, called the *Forerunner.* The monthly publication was written entirely by Gilman herself, and it was published through December 1916. It was in this magazine that the story that would eventually be published as the novel *Herland* appeared as a series. In addition to fourteen articles and essays, Gilman serialized two books each year, so that the entire seven-year run of *The Forerunner* was equal in length to twenty-eight books.

In 1932, Gilman was diagnosed with inoperable cancer. She completed the writing of her autobiography in 1935 and, after bidding her daughter and loved ones farewell, committed suicide on August 17 by inhaling chloroform. The note she left indicated that she preferred death by chloroform to death by cancer. She was seventy-five years old.

Gilman's reputation declined during the years immediately preceding her death, due in large part to the fact that she espoused two controversial belief systems: feminism and socialism. She was, however, named the sixth most influential woman of the twentieth century in a poll conducted by the Siena Research Institute in 1993. In 1994, she was inducted into the National Women's Hall of Fame. Over the course of her lifetime, she wrote more than two hundred works of literature.

PLOT SUMMARY

Chapter 1: A Not Unnatural Enterprise

Sociologist Vandyck Jennings explains that he lost his notes and other supporting documents from his discovery of Herland but vows to do his

MEDIA ADAPTATIONS

- *Herland* was recorded as an audiobook by Babblebooks in 2008.
- LibriVox made *Herland* available as a podcast in 2007.

best to describe the experience—both physically and emotionally—in as accurate and detailed a way as possible.

Van introduces his two companions, Terry O. Nicholson and Jeff Margrave. The men have been friends for years and share varying degrees of interest in science. Wealthy Terry is considered a ladies' man who travels around the globe seeking adventure. Jeff is a medical doctor with a romantic streak, an idealist. The three are members of a scientific expedition on a mission to chart tributaries along a river in an undisclosed region of North America.

The men overhear others in the party talking about "a strange and terrible Woman Land" as they travel further upstream. The land is rumored to be populated solely by women and girls, and the explorers admit their fear and wonderment. The guide shows the men a river consisting of red and blue water, and further inspection reveals a tattered scarlet cloth in the water. The fabric's pattern is too detailed to be made by savage tribes, and the trio takes it as a sign that the people living in that Woman Land must be civilized.

Although skeptical, the men are excited at the possibility of such a hidden female civilization and decide they would like to try to find it. Terry funds the adventure, and they use his yacht as well as his motorboat and bi-plane. Each man, as he prepares to set out on this expedition, imagines what such a society would be like. Van believes they will find a primitive population in which there actually are men but they are forced to live apart from the women. Jeff imagines a peaceful coexistence among the women, much like what one finds in a convent.

Terry insists the women will be jealous of one another and in constant competition, for he believes women are incapable of cooperation with other women.

The trio reaches the foot of a cliff, and the men board the bi-plane loaded with supplies and guns. A fly-over shows them that there is indeed a society on the cliff, safely protected. The outside is rimmed with well-cultivated forests while the center is dotted with pink and white houses and parks. Noticing the architecture and tended forests, Van refuses to believe only women live there, saying, "But they look—why, this is a *civilized* country!" and protesting, "There must be men." Terry answers, "Of course there are men," and suggests that they go find them. Women emerge from the buildings at the sound of the plane, and the men land and disembark onto this land have nicknamed Herland.

Chapter 2: Rash Advances

Van, Jeff, and Terry walk fifteen miles to the village, ready to draw their guns and fight if they meet the men they are certain built the village. As they draw nearer to the village, they notice that everything in their natural surroundings has a purpose. All of the trees grow fruit or can be used as timber; none are merely ornamental. From a tree in the middle of the glade, the men hear giggling and notice three young women, all with short hair and plain clothing. Though they do not recognize the women's language, they notice it lacks the intonation and sounds of savage language and decide it is civilized. Terry uses hand gestures to introduce everyone, and one of the women, Ellador, introduces the others: Celis and Alima. Ellador signals to the men that they should leave, but instead Terry tries to tempt the women with a shiny necklace. He is tricked by Alima, who grabs the necklace, and all three women escape as the men chase them.

As the men follow the women into town, they notice and admire the quality of construction of the main road. When the buildings come into view, they are impressed at how they blend into their surroundings. The city was carefully planned, and Jeff remarks on the lack of noise and pollution.

At the center of town, the women of Herland are waiting for the intruders. Van notices that the women appear neither young nor old, but each is physically fit and seemingly in good health. The men recognize the confidence of the women, who

show no fear whatsoever. Six women—two to a man—escort the trio to a gray building that sticks out among the pink and white structures in town. At the entrance, it becomes clear the men are expected to go inside. They hesitate, fearful they will be imprisoned. Terry pulls his gun but is disarmed immediately. Van and Jeff reluctantly try to fight the women, but they are easily overtaken and subdued with anesthesia.

Chapter 3: A Peculiar Imprisonment

When the men awaken, they find themselves in a clean, comfortable room, their belongings neatly collected in the bathroom. They realize their weapons, razors, and clothes have been confiscated. They have been provided with alternative clothing, which is simple but efficient and comfortable.

In an adjoining room, the men are greeted by eighteen older women whom Terry nicknames the Colonels. Fifteen guards stand at the ready, and there is one host for each man, seated at a table filled with food and books. The men realize these hosts are actually tutors, brought to teach them the local language. They eat and finish a lesson before retiring to their room, where they discuss the situation. Even though the trio has encountered only women, they still cannot believe women designed, planned, and built the town, and they wonder where the men might live.

Escape is on their minds, and together they decide that it is best not to try to escape through the windows, which lead to a cliff. Instead they agree to keep an eye out for a more practical and safer opportunity.

Van, Jeff, and Terry are all surprised that not one of the women has reacted to their maleness but that they have instead treated the men merely as their peers. Terry expresses dissatisfaction with the Colonels and wishes he had caught one of the three younger women they first met up with at the entrance to Herland. The men agree that the women look unfeminine with their short hair, but Jeff and Van both begin to enjoy themselves.

As time progresses, Terry becomes more vocal about his dislike of Herland and its inhabitants. He has no patience for the lack of competition in the society and finds the women dull. Jeff and Van, conversely, begin to appreciate their hosts more and more, and they derive enjoyment from their lessons. Van's tutor is Somel, Jeff's is Zava, and Terry's is Moadine. As Terry's frustration and anger grow, he manages to talk Jeff and Van into attempting a nighttime escape over the cliff.

Chapter 4: Our Venture

The men travel throughout the night in the direction of their bi-plane. By dawn's light, they find the plane but are dismayed to discover it has been covered by a tarp that has been sewn shut. Without knives, they cannot cut the tarp. At that point, they hear again the laughter of Elladore, Celis, and Alima, and they explain their dire situation in hopes that the young women will assist them in their escape. Although the women give them food, they refuse to help them escape, and when the men finish their meal, they realize that the Colonels have surrounded the bi-plane.

Fearing some form of punishment, the men are leery as the women drive them back across the country and even stop to feed them lunch. To their surprise, there is no punishment awaiting them, only their rooms. Van expresses his bewilderment at the lack of punishment, but even more so at what he perceives to be his captors' amusement. He says, "Of course we looked for punishment—a closer imprisonment, solitary confinement maybe—but nothing of the kind happened. They treated us as truants only, and as if they quite understood our truancy."

The men feel like naughty little boys, foolish at their escapade. They realize the women had been watching them all along and knew exactly what they were doing. Their tutors explain to them that they are imprisoned because of the violence to which they so quickly resorted upon entering Herland. The men promise they have no desire to hurt the women, so they are allowed to live in the fortress without guards but also still without their razors and guns.

When Terry asks if there are men in Herland, Somel tells him the society has been without males for two thousand years and that the women have learned to reproduce without men. She then provides a full history of Herland and explains that they keep cats and birds but not larger animals because they are inefficient and take up too much space. Somel professes to believe that male animals are, by and large, useless except for mating. A discussion of farms and meat industry practices leaves Somel feeling ill, and she leaves the men.

Chapter 5: A Unique History

The sociologist in Van is impressed with the women's ability to breed cats that do not meow or attack birds. As the women question the men about the world beyond Herland, Van and his friends become uncomfortable with a line of questioning that seeks logic and reason in the way things are done in American society. When the women's attempts to truly understand the outside world corner the men, Vandyck explains, "We found ourselves up against some admissions we did not want to make."

The tutors continue educating the explorers about the history of Herland. Thousands of years ago, the society included men and women, and it was ruled by a king. War decimated the population, and the survivors were forced off the coastline and sought safety at the top of the cliff. Theirs was a society of polygamy and slaveholders. One day, a volcano erupted without warning and abruptly sealed off the passage to the ocean and buried alive the army that dwelled at the foot of the cliff. The few men still living were slaves, and in the chaos of the volcano's aftermath, they rebelled and killed their masters and the old women.

As these slaves attempted to possess the society's young women, the would-be victims retaliated and killed every last one of the men. Fearing they were doomed in their isolation, the women nevertheless turned their energies toward caring for one another and learning to grow crops and perform other valuable work. Years passed, and out of nowhere, a baby was born. Unable to find a man who could have fathered the child, the women labeled the baby girl a gift from God and built a temple in honor of Maaia, the goddess of motherhood. Over the course of the next few years, the young mother gave birth to four more girls.

Each of the babies grew up to be women who possessed the power of creation and childbirth, and each had five female babies of her own. Called the Mothers of the Future, these babies took the places of the older women as they died, and soon Herland was a society filled with several generations of women who lived through cooperation. The culture rejuvenated itself, all because of one woman's ability to multiply and give birth. The women of Herland came to value motherhood above all else.

Terry is shocked at the story and, as a man who made his wealth in a capitalist society, cannot fathom how cooperation trumps competition when it comes to building a successful, thriving community. The women are astonished that Terry believes people will not work without incentive because everything they do is for the good of their children.

With pride, Terry informs the women that in America, men do the work. Eventually he admits that some women work—poor women. When asked how many poor women there are, Jeff explains that there are seven or eight million.

Chapter 6: *Comparisons Are Odious*

When asked what poverty is, Van explains Darwin's theory of survival of the fittest and applies it to economic theory. The conversation continues until the men grow so uncomfortable that they begin to lose sight of the logical reasons for the existence of poverty.

Terry, ever the frustrated bachelor, asks Moadine what the women plan for the men. She explains that they just want to learn from and teach the men, but that they must stay imprisoned for their own safety because some of the younger women might not react kindly to them.

Motherhood is the cornerstone of Herland's culture. It is honored and respected above all else. In comparing it with motherhood as it is practiced in America, Van writes, "Mother-love with them was not a brute passion, a mere 'instinct,' a wholly personal feeling; it was—a religion." In this simple sentence, he is recognizing that individuality and personal desire has little room in Herland society, where collective thought and action lead to a comfortable, happy, fulfilling life for everyone.

Mothering is done communally in Herland after the first year or two, and only women deemed fit are allowed to mother. Most women are allowed to have just one child, but those judged exceptionally fit may have more. Called Over Mothers, these women are considered near royalty.

The education system in Herland is developed out of the study of psychology. Once the men have learned this and demonstrate an understanding of the importance of motherhood and children in this unique society, they are freed from their confinement and allowed into Herland.

Chapter 7: *Our Growing Modesty*

Somel, Zava, and Moadine accompany the trio on a tour of their country. While Van and Jeff have, by this time, come to respect and admire the women, Terry has not been able to let go of the need to dominate them. Because of this, he has fallen in Jeff and Van's esteem, and they now see him as arrogant and brash.

When the men learn that no one in Herland has a last name, they ask why children are not given surnames and wonder if it is because the women are not proud of their children. Moadine negates that idea and answers with her quiet logic, "Because the finished product is not a private one."

There are two main roles in Herland: the critic and the inventor. Critics have mastered critical thinking and are trained in a specialized field. Their job is to notice shortcomings. Inventors respond to the criticism by suggesting improvements. As they listen to the logic behind this system, Jeff and Van begin to realize and understand the superiority of this all-female society.

Herland's food supply is maintained by a carefully contemplated strategy in which crop cultivation has been deemed inefficient while food-bearing trees offer the highest yield. Terry does not understand how acquired traits can be passed down genetically, although that is clearly exactly what has happened in Herland.

Van recognizes the perfection of Herland society, even as he struggles with the idea that many girls are forbidden to have children, and even those girls allowed to breed are not considered fit to raise their children. Somel explains that this poses no problem because mothers willingly allow their children to be raised by those women known to be wiser and more suited to the task.

Chapter 8: *The Girls of Herland*

The men are asked to lecture the young girls of Herland on the history of the outside world. While Van turns out to be a popular teacher, Terry's students find his overbearing demeanor offensive. Jeff is more popular than Terry, but not by much.

Van discovers that the women view the three men as a chance to reestablish Herland as a society of men and women. Careful to choose partners for the men wisely, the elder women pick Celis, Alima, and Ellador to be the mates of Jeff, Terry, and Van, respectively.

Jeff is attracted to Celis, but his tendency to look at her as something near perfection makes it difficult for her to relate to him. Terry continually tries to overpower Alima, and theirs is a stormy relationship. Van and Ellador become friends first and eventually enter into a romantic relationship. All three men have difficulty bonding with their mates to a certain extent because gender roles have been erased over the past two thousand years. As the women have no understanding of the words "marriage," "family," and "home," it is difficult for the men to establish relationships with them on a level they all understand.

Chapter 9: Our Relations and Theirs

Terry begins to complain about Herland because it is too perfect. He is bored with its lack of vices, but Jeff is at ease and enjoys the way everyone gets along. Van continues his studies in an attempt to understand the underlying philosophy of Herland's society.

He finds that, basically, the girls are raised to believe in the safety of the world. There is no good versus evil, and the education system is developed with the promotion of two qualities: individual will and critical thinking. Vandyck is impressed with this system and admits it works better than what is used in the United States.

Chapter 10: Their Religions and Our Marriages

The women of Herland believe that all of life is service to God. When Van explains to Ellador that Christianity includes belief in the devil, eternal damnation, and purgatory, she is horrified and wonders how a society can cling to such outdated ideas without ever considering better ones. Van eventually regards Herland's religion as the most practical and beautiful he has ever encountered. The three couples marry.

Chapter 11: Our Difficulties

Marriage for everyone turns out to be a challenge because the men assumed their wives would forsake their own opinions on matters in deference to their husbands. The men also believed they would live with their wives, but this does not happen because in Herland, everyone lives together in communal buildings.

Van wants to express his love for Ellador sexually, but she cannot understand why he would want to do that unless the purpose is to create a child. Although this view frustrates Van, he comes to understand sex as a form of self-indulgence. Terry wishes to use sex to dominate Alima, and when he tries to rape her, he is banished from Herland forever.

Chapter 12: Expelled

Van decides to accompany Terry back to the States because it is unsafe for Terry to pilot the plane solo. Ellador, eager to see the outer world, agrees to join her husband on the trip. Jeff and his pregnant wife remain in Herland.

Terry and Van want to bring other men back to Herland, but they are refused. The women believe it would be unsafe to open their society to a world of poverty, disease, and violence. Van understands and agrees, but Terry refuses until he is told he would live out the remainder of his life as a prisoner in Herland. He, Van, and Ellador leave Herland and head to the United States.

CHARACTERS

Alima

Alima is one of the three main female characters in the novel, yet she is not particularly well developed. She is intelligent, and the reader knows that she works, but her job is never revealed. By pairing her with Terry, Gilman intimates that Alima is somehow inferior to Ellador and Celis. In the end of the story, however, Alima rejects Terry, thus conquering and mastering him.

Celis

Like Alima and Ellador, Celis is one of the first three women the men encounter when they arrive in Herland. She is described by Gilman as a woman who belongs to the impractical class, that is, teachers and artists. By doing so, Gilman has categorized Celis and made her flawed in that she chooses to love the romantic Jeff, who cannot help but idealize women. Again, her actual job is never described, and though Gilman has drawn her as a resourceful woman, the reader never sees evidence of that quality in her words or behavior. Celis is the first woman to enter the New Motherhood, however, and by that she earns the admiration of all of Herland.

The Colonels

The Colonels are the eighteen older women who act as leaders of Herland. They teach the visiting men and try to learn from them.

Ellador

Ellador is the major female character in *Herland*. She, along with Alima and Celis, is one of the first women of Herland to meet the men. At that point, Gilman establishes Ellador as the leader of the three women by having her make introductions and speak for the group. Ellador eventually becomes Vandyck's wife.

Ellador is arguably the most well-developed character of the three women. Gilman gives her qualities that challenge the Victorian ideal of a woman. She is both beautiful and athletic, strong yet still womanly. She is smart and curious, unafraid to show her strengths. Altogether, this portrait of a woman is almost diametrically opposed to what society during Gilman's lifetime considered the perfect woman. Ellador is equal to a man in every way—physically, mentally, and spiritually.

As Vandyck gets to know Ellador more fully, he appreciates her strength and traits as virtues rather than eccentricities. From her he learns what it truly means to love a female not only as a woman, but as another human being. She refuses to fit herself into the gender role Van wants to impose upon her, and by standing up to him, she opens the door for his understanding of marriage as something more than sexual relations and domestic service.

As Van struggles to accept his wife's rejection of his sexual advances, it becomes clear that Ellador has taken on the role of the traditional male, in which she views sex only in its physical aspect, advocating sex only as a means to reproduce. Van, conversely, argues in favor of it on an emotional basis. His perspective is more representative of the traditional female point of view.

Vandyck Jennings

Vandyck (Van) is the narrator of the story, and Gilman wisely made him a sociologist. As such, he is looked at by the reader as a logical man, a scientist. He is someone who studies cultures and people and comes to conclusions based on evidence and reason. Therefore, he is the ideal person to help lead readers into an acceptance of the socialist-feminist ideology that Gilman promotes.

Van initially refuses to believe—cannot believe, perhaps—that women were responsible for and able to create a civilized society. In his line of work, the only societies led by women have been primitive, and the women have been mothers and caretakers, not teachers and builders and engineers and leaders. Because Van is better educated and more critical than Jeff or Terry, his opinion and ultimate conversion are more important than theirs. By the final chapter, Van is converted into the socialist-feminist philosophy.

Jeff Margrave

A medical doctor, Jeff Margrave is idealistic and romantic. Although his intentions are always good, his insistence on putting women on a pedestal frustrates women who want to be considered equal, not idealized. During those early years of feminism in which Gilman lived, men like Jeff seemed, on the surface, to support the feminist philosophy, but the reality was far different. This sort of worship put added pressure on women to be perfect, and when they failed, they were judged harshly.

Jeff, like Terry, views women as inferior to men. The difference is in how he responds to that perception. Whereas Terry wants to dominate, Jeff's gentility leads him to see women as objects in need of protection, and he treats them in a chivalrous manner. While some degree of chivalry can be flattering and even welcomed by some women, Gilman uses Jeff's character to illustrate the idea that equality is preferable to chivalry. Jeff, like Van, but not as quickly or for the same reasons, eventually recognizes the utopian Herland society as superior to the American culture he knows and chooses to remain there for life. Jeff's acceptance of Herland is based more on emotion than on logic or ethics. He never seems to truly grasp that women are equal to men, but Gilman honors his evolution anyway by allowing him to be the first father to reproduce in Herland in two thousand years.

Moadine

Moadine is Terry's tutor, and she earns the respect of both Jeff and Vandyck as they witness the patient, wise way in which she works with the challenging Terry. Terry, on the other hand, takes an immediate dislike to his tutor and dismisses her as unworthy of his time because he does not feel she is pretty enough for him to spend time with. For Terry, only the young and beautiful deserve attention; a woman's mind never figures into the equation because he simply refuses to acknowledge she might have anything to contribute.

Moadine is a smart woman, but she treats Terry with an air of contempt that is not encouraged or promoted in Herland. So subtle is she in her contempt that Terry himself never recognizes it for what it is. Although raised to show respect, Moadine cannot respect her student, and so she considers him inferior.

Terry Nicholson

Terry is a wealthy, intelligent man who is successful with women. His hobbies include mechanics and electricity, two traditionally male fields. In early twentieth-century America, he was a member of society's upper class, perceived as a real man, complete with all the material things money can buy and an adventurous spirit. Through the lens of his era, Terry was the best sort of male specimen. Jeff and Van view their friend as just that when the story opens, but as their journey unfolds and their minds are opened to new possibilities and norms, they begin to see Terry differently. What were once virtues are now limitations, and unlike his friends, he does not function well when his beliefs are challenged.

Terry is never able to view women as equal to men, and his failure leads to his banishment. Gilman did not give Terry any redeeming qualities but created him as a way to clearly depict the shortcomings of the typical chauvinist perspective. It is easy to dislike Terry, and that is the role for which he was created.

Somel

Somel is responsible for tutoring Vandyck, and it is through her that he truly learns the value of women not as they compare to men, but in their own inherent right. Somel is largely responsible for converting Vandyck.

Zava

Zava tutors Jeff and is one of the elders of Herland. It is because of her that Jeff learns to leave behind the outdated idea that only young women have something to offer. The astute reader cannot help but recognize that while Terry continues to loathe his tutor throughout the novel, Jeff's personal growth and open mind allows him to respect his teacher and recognize her value.

THEMES

Cooperation

The success of Herland's society is built entirely on the concept of cooperation. It is the root of every system in this utopian society: from child rearing to education and daily existence. This theme is underscored by the way in which all choices and actions are made based on the impact on the greater good of Herland. Individualism and self-identity are sacrificed for the overall collective health and well-being of society as a whole. For example, particular individual women are allowed to give birth, but they are not necessarily the same individuals who actually raise the children. The children of Herland do not belong to anyone; they are raised to embrace being a part of the whole community. Toward that end, no one in Herland even has a last name because that would symbolize belonging and individuality.

Cooperation as a theme in the novel is also stressed by the fact that the culture Gilman has created does not even have words for concepts that, though they signify a connection with someone else, also somehow separate larger groups into smaller groups. Ideas like "family" and "marriage" do not exist in Herland's utopia because everyone cooperates to live together as one big group.

Education is based on cooperation as well, with surprising results. While it would seem logical that the emphasis on cooperation leads to a loss of one's sense of self, that does not happen in Herland. Instead, as girls are educated to participate in and contribute to the societal system as a whole, they discover and nurture their unique individual talents and skills. In this way, cooperation trumps competition. There simply is no need of competition in utopia.

Gender Roles

Gilman weaves this theme throughout the novel in both obvious and subtle ways. The most obvious way in which she explores this theme is in the relationships formed between the three male characters and their mates.

Each male character represents a different degree of stereotype in Western society. Terry is the least likable character and the one who most often offends the women of Herland—and eventually, his own friends—with his attitude toward women. He views them as inferior, put on earth to serve men by making themselves physically appealing and sexually available. Terry's character is so extensively stereotypical of men of the early twentieth century that he is almost a caricature, or a joke.

Jeff is more moderate. Through him, Gilman gives readers an everyman for whom there exists hope of enlightenment and personal growth. Jeff is a romantic who idolizes women, but as the story progresses, he opens his mind to the idea that women are men's equals. In doing so, he finds greater personal happiness and chooses, in the end, not to return to the life and society he knows. For Jeff, Herland holds greater potential for fulfillment.

TOPICS FOR FURTHER STUDY

- Research the social norms and values of early twentieth-century America. What specific values and norms does Gilman critique in her novel? Using a computer software program, create a presentation on those criticisms and explain what they are and how they reflect Gilman's personal beliefs.

- Some critics believe Gilman's attitude that men are useless except for procreation is as detrimental to equality as traditional patriarchal views of women are. Do you agree or disagree? Write an analysis and use specific evidence from the text of *Herland* to support your argument.

- Read *33 Things Every Girl Should Know About Women's History: From Suffragettes to Skirt Lengths to the E.R.A.*, by Tonya Bolden. Choose three topics covered in that book that Gilman also includes in *Herland*. Write a paper discussing how Gilman incorporates those three feminist issues or topics in her novel.

- Draw on what Gilman describes about the educational system in Herland. Imagine you are a teacher there, and prepare a lesson plan for an English class. Keep in mind the focus and goals of Herland's educational system, and provide a detailed explanation—including possible outcomes—of the lesson plans.

- Imagine a Hisland. Rewrite the first chapter of the novel using role reversal, that is, you are a woman who stumbles upon an all-male society. What are the differences? Similarities? How do the men behave, what values do they hold, and how do they respond to the appearance of a woman? Post your chapter to your Web page and invite comments from your teacher and classmates.

- Using any artistic medium, create a visual picture of what Herland looks like to you. Consider the passages of the novel that describe the society as well as the women in it. Your picture can be a scene from the novel or one out of your imagination.

- Read Margaret Atwood's novel of a dystopia (the opposite of utopia), *The Handmaid's Tale*. Compare and contrast the descriptions and behaviors of women in both societies. Develop a side-by-side list and use passages and evidence from the novels to bolster your claims. Use Inspiration (or Kidspiration), prepare a presentation, and deliver it to the class.

- Imagine that you have been commissioned to design a promotional poster for *Herland: The Movie*. Using Glogster or other online poster creater, create that poster, and print it. Remember to include all pertinent information as well as a teaser to make viewers want to see the film.

- Consider the ending of *Herland*. Is there another way the novel could have concluded? Rewrite the final chapter, including the fate of Van, Jeff, and Terry. Be sure to fully develop this revised ending, keeping in mind that while the original end leads naturally into the possibility of a sequel, your ending does not have to.

Vandyck is the most evolved of the three men even at the beginning of the story. As a sociologist, he has studied various cultures and is able to apply scientific theory and objective observation to Herland and its residents in a way Jeff and Terry cannot. Van is always the quickest to break through his gender-determined role and attitude because he does not follow the strict mold of American male to begin with. At the end of the book, his reward is the chance to take his new wife back to his world, forever or simply to visit, the reader cannot be sure.

All the women of Herland break with traditional gender roles except for the fact that they give birth and raise children. However, even in those pursuits, they act with a sense of confidence and direction typically lacking in the Western society in which Gilman lived. Pride in their individual achievements does not exist, and yet all of the women of Herland are personally fulfilled and content. It is the absence of gender identity that allows for this.

Motherhood

Motherhood is treated as sacred in *Herland*. Everything the women do, all of the rules and systems and beliefs, are directed so as to be in service of motherhood. That they can create life without sex—a miracle—establishes mothering as a near religion in that utopian society. Motherhood is an honor in Herland.

Consequently, children are given the highest priority in society, and Gilman compares that value to the real society in which she lived, where the value of children was given lip service but was not truly an inherent or integral part of civilized culture. She makes this point by having Somel react viscerally to Van's mention of abortion. Somel's disbelief shows the reader that Gilman believes the views of Herland's society regarding this topic are just and right.

Tradition

Traditional values, specifically, the rejection of them, is another major theme in the novel. It is played out in the relations between Terry, Jeff, and Van and all the women, but also in the way in which Herland's society is developed. Men are not valued at all, not for their physical strength, intelligence, or ability to lead. By creating a culture in which men are wholly absent, Gilman makes a strong social commentary by rejecting those values American society holds highest.

There is nothing traditional whatsoever about Herland. There, females are held in the highest esteem. Cooperation is valued over competition, the collective over the individual. Peace overrules conflict, the dichotomy of good and evil does not exist. Tradition itself is given little weight in utopia. When Jeff explains to the women that America's society is based on traditions dating back thousands of years, Moadine expresses surprise and acknowledges that most laws are fewer than twenty years old and that none have been in place for a hundred years because they are constantly being evaluated and reassessed based on changing circumstances. In Herland, the present is given more emphasis than the past.

He read to study their history and learn their language. *(vgstudio / Shutterstock.com)*

STYLE

Feminist Utopia

The word utopia means *ideal world*. Writers have long explored the idea of utopia and its opposite, dystopia (nightmare world). More than one thousand utopian works were published in the twentieth century alone.

Gilman's *Herland* belongs in a subgenre of utopian literature called feminist utopia. Political in nature, the feminist utopia seeks to call readers to action, most often in a way that allows the work to be categorized as science fiction for its futuristic settings. Gilman broke that mold when she set her novel in 1915, the same year in which she first published it serially.

Feminist utopias perceive men and male systems as the primary cause of social, cultural, and political problems. Gilman depicted this in *Herland* by portraying Terry, Van, and Jeff as inherently violent. The social and cultural conflicts become obvious in the men's relationships with the Celis, Ellador, and Alima. Because the men cannot initially consider the women their equals, conflict arises, and for Terry, who never can overcome his view of women as second-class citizens, that limited perspective leads directly to his banishment, but not before he resorts to violence when he tries to force Alima to have sex with him.

Feminist utopias have been explored in literature throughout history, but when *Herland* was rediscovered and published for the first time in novel format in 1979, it joined a general surge of such works that were being published in America in the mid-1970s. Among the most recognized titles from that time are Marge Piercy's *Woman on the Edge of Time* (1976) and Ursula K. Le Guin's *The Dispossessed: An Ambiguous Utopia* (1974).

Symbolism

Gilman uses symbolism throughout the novel. The most obvious symbols are the three male protagonists, each one representing a common social attitude toward women prevalent during the time Gilman lived.

Van embraces the early-twentieth-century view that women are inherently inferior to men, but his scientific, fact-based background makes him the man most likely to evolve into having an enlightened, more egalitarian view of women. Terry is the opposite of Van. His wealth and intelligence elevate him to an elite social status, and he is viewed by Van and Jeff as a man's man. By the end of the novel, Terry's attitude that women exist to please and service him is revealed for the arrogance it is: "Terry's idea seemed to be that pretty women were just so much game and homely ones not worth considering." Terry cannot survive in an enlightened society, and he is banished. Jeff is a combination of the other two men. An idealist, he believes in chivalry as well as romance, in which it is a man's job to court and protect women, whom he views as something akin to saints. Though not as offensive as Terry's viewpoint, Jeff's is one that was quite common in early twentieth-century America, and one feminists wished to reform so that women would be seen as men's equals in every way.

Other symbolism in the novel includes the carefully cultivated forestland. Jeff observes that every single tree is useful in that it produces something of value and is not merely ornamental. In addition, the entire forest is well-tended. "'Talk of civilization,'" he cried softly in restrained enthusiasm. 'I never saw a forest so petted, even in Germany. Look, there's not a dead bough—the vines are trained—actually!'" The forestland symbolizes the women's ability to create a kinship with their environment rather than a domination of it. When the women learn the details of the meat industry's practices, they are sickened and disgusted at the subjugation of the animals. It stands in sharp contrast with the relationships they foster with nature in Herland.

The clothing of Herland is symbolic of the value of usefulness versus ornamentation in this all-female society. At first put off by the simplicity and androgyny of the garments, Van and Jeff eventually come to favor the clothing. Van even misses it when he leaves Herland, a feeling symbolic of also regretting leaving behind the simple, comfortable, harmonious lifestyle of the society.

First-Person Narrative

Gilman made Van the narrator of the story and in doing so, gave the reader the viewpoint of someone directly involved in the unfolding of the tale. She counterbalanced any bias or faulty memory he may have had by making him a sociologist, someone who favors facts and statistics over inference and influence.

Choosing to write in first person gives the tone of *Herland* one similar to that of a travelogue or diary. Here and there, Van injects his own personal opinions, giving the story flavor and insight the reader otherwise would not get. The first-person narrative makes the discovery of Herland and its inhabitants a much more vivid experience because of the involvement of the narrator. Told from a different perspective, it may have read more like a report.

HISTORICAL CONTEXT

Social Darwinism and Feminism

Social Darwinism is an ethical theory that flourished in the late nineteenth century and continued to hold favor with Victorian America throughout the early decades of the twentieth century. Social Darwinism holds that the strongest or most fit members of a society should thrive, while the weak should be allowed to perish. This elitist view was formed primarily by philosopher Herbert Spencer, who took Charles

COMPARE
&
CONTRAST

- **1910s:** Marriage is legally considered a contract of ownership, and wives are treated as property, with limited rights. Husbands can force their wives to do almost anything, and the law is on their side.

  Today: Marriage is a contract stipulating the legal protection of the union of two people of equal stature and rights. Women are no longer considered property but are legally recognized as individuals possessing the same rights as men. Marriage does not automatically give husbands the right to treat their wives in whatever way they deem fit.

- **1910s:** Gender roles are clear: men pursue intellectual and business activities, while women remain relegated to the domestic sphere. Even reading is considered an intellectual pursuit, unless it is a religious or domestic text. The popular concept of women of this era is known as the Angel in the House, whereby the woman is passive and meek, completely supportive of and submissive to her husband. For women who long for something more, who wish to engage in activities that require thought—such as writing, politics, or anything beyond household work and raising children—the Angel in the House is a repressive ideal.

  Today: Although they still typically earn lower wages for performing the same duties and holding the same responsibilities, women are no longer considered second-class citizens, intellectually inferior to men. They hold high-ranking positions in business as well as the military and have great impact on the arts and humanities. Women, technically speaking, have the choice to stay home and raise children, enter the work force, or both. Any of these choices is socially acceptable.

- **1910s:** America becomes involved in World War I in 1917, and the event is foremost in everyone's mind. Prior to that, the country is operating on a policy of international neutrality. America is prospering in what is known historically as the Progressive Era, but citizens are concerned about the toll the war will take on families.

  Today: America's military is involved in Afghanistan, where hostilities began in 2001. American troops are also engaged in the fighting in Iraq since 2003. Thousands of American lives have been lost, and the country is divided on the moral and political value of continued participation in the violence overseas.

Darwin's scientific theory and adapted it to fit his own agenda.

In that adaptation, Spencer endorsed the claim that the wealthy and powerful were better suited to the economic conditions and social progress of the era, and so it was only "natural" that they survive at the expense of the weak. He presented social Darwin as not only natural but also moral.

Gilman took the concept of Social Darwinism and applied it to feminist thought. Believing humans could determine their own destinies and thereby promote social change, Gilman promoted the idea that repressed groups of people—women,

in particular—could collectively choose to be the guiding force in reorganizing a more equitable society.

Industrial Revolution and Socialism

As the nineteenth century came to a close, America experienced an Industrial Revolution in which it transformed from an agrarian society to an industrial society. Between 1860 and 1900 alone, the number of workers in manufacturing quadrupled to six million. It was a time of robber barons—those men whose fortunes were made by exploiting the needy and poor, mostly semi-skilled immigrants whose desperate circumstances

Much of the land was covered in fruit trees. *(Ioana Drutu | Shutterstock.com)*

forced them to accept whatever menial work they could find, however low the wages.

Labeled the Gilded Age for its pretentious displays of wealth, the last decade of the nineteenth century widened the gap between the wealthy and the poor. Millions of people were living in unsanitary tenement homes, whereas those who employed them had more money than they could spend.

While the rise of industrialism was a positive direction in terms of capitalism and the ability of the individual to make good, it clearly divided America into the haves and have-nots, and soon those who struggled merely to survive found themselves wondering how they could better their situations. To this end, labor unions began organizing; promising that collectively with a united front, workers could fight unfair employers and unsafe working conditions. In tandem with the formation of labor unions was the concept of socialism, an economic and political policy that depends on cooperation over competition. Socialism is diametrically opposed to capitalism, the foundation of America's economy.

Gilman espoused socialism and took it one step further, thereby becoming an adherent to socialist feminism, a branch of feminism arguing that liberation for women in both the public and private sectors can be achieved only through socialism. This viewpoint made Gilman a woman ahead of her time, as did her belief in the idea that a peaceful collective strategy would be more powerful than the classic socialist view of revolution. She weaves this belief throughout *Herland*, where women are autonomous and grow up in an environment that nurtures female development not as a substandard alternative but as the only choice.

CRITICAL OVERVIEW

Herland is the second of Gilman's three utopian novels and by far the most well known of the trio. It is generally considered one of the first authentic feminist utopian novels in America and received more critical acclaim when it was first published in novel form in 1979 than it did when it was published serially in 1915. The reason for this could be that the feminist movement was in full swing in the late 1970s and was only just in its infant stages in the mid-1910s. The American reading audience was more open to feminist literature in the 1970s because the idea of equality for women had saturated the culture, media, and society in general. In the early twentieth century, the idea of feminism was considered radical, and people were only just beginning to grasp its meaning and potential influence.

A self-proclaimed humanist—one who believes it is the duty of all to promote human welfare—Gilman believed that what was most important about men and women were the commonalities they shared, not the differences, yet the subordination of women prohibited them from growing and developing in an environment that would allow them independence. She sought to portray a society—a utopia—in which those limitations were nonexistent so that the world might share her vision of a strong collective culture in which everyone shared the same goals. The result of that desire is *Herland*.

During her lifetime, Gilman was known more for her nonfiction work and analysis of political and economic theory and thought. *Herland* was not extensively reviewed in 1915, perhaps because Gilman's literary magazine in which the utopian story was published (*Forerunner*) did not reach a wide audience. The story has been categorized as science fiction because it derives its plot, themes, and setting from fact but creates a situation that does not, in reality, exist.

More modern critics consider *Herland* as a reflection of its author's personal beliefs. Although it is clear Gilman has a story to tell, her more important goal is to depict a utopia that her readers can actually envision as reality. According to Ann J. Lane, Gilman's biographer and the author of the introduction to the 1979 edition of *Herland*, Gilman's work "was an effort to devise and to carry out a strategy for change." In other words, she used this second utopian novel as a catalyst for social and cultural change, a goal for which she also wrote her now-classic economic treatise, *Women and Economics: The Economic Relation Between Men and Women as a Factor in Social Evolution*. For Gilman, the story was secondary; the message was her primary concern, but she knew that in order for anyone to hear the message, it would have to be cloaked in an entertaining plot.

Storytelling is, for Gilman, a tool. In her critical essay "Herland Revisited: Narratives of Motherhood, Domesticity, and Physical Emancipation in Charlotte Perkins Gilman's Feminist Utopia," critic Anna Lathrop compares *Herland* to Gilman's highly acclaimed short story, "The Yellow Wallpaper." "In both . . . through the fiction of storytelling, one may see the interconnections between private life experiences and public discourse. Storytelling reveals the powers that establish reality."

Herland has been singled out among utopian novels for its use of subtle humor. Rather than beat her readers over the head with her message, Gilman chooses instead to let her characters' gentle wisdom deliver their messages of irony as they contemplate a society in which men purposely wage war and create disharmony. Feminist author Marge Piercy praises the book in a review for *Powells*, writing that "*Herland* is utopia with a smile, a gentle, witty version of what women can be."

CRITICISM

Rebecca Valentine

Valentine is a writer with an extensive background in literary analysis and theory. In the following essay, she suggests that Gilman takes her socialist-feminist theory in Herland *too far and is guilty of favoring women over men.*

In her introduction to Charlotte Perkins Gilman's novel *Herland*, Ann J. Lane explores the influences on Gilman that helped shape her personal belief system and philosophy. It becomes clear that Gilman's feminist perspective was extensively informed by her own experience with men as well as her lack of control over her own psychological well-being. While Gilman espoused a blend of socialism and feminism as key to the liberation of women, the attitudes and beliefs evident in *Herland* indicate not a desire for equality between the sexes but more of a turning of the tables.

Having lived in the Victorian age, with its unyielding social norms, repressive gender roles, and ingrained attitude of women as property, Gilman's experience as a woman and a mother was difficult at best. When she fell into what we understand today as postpartum depression, the world-renowned Dr. S. Weir Mitchell prescribed his infamous rest cure, and she lost access to the only creative outlet she had: writing. Insanity nipped at her heels. Eventually, she left her husband, who later married his ex-wife's best friend,

WHAT DO I READ NEXT?

- *With Her in Ourland* is Gilman's sequel to *Herland*. Published serially in 1916, this novel significantly changes the utopian vision presented in *Herland*.

- Carol Smith-Rosenberg's 1986 essay collection *Disorderly Conduct: Visions of Gender in Victorian America* explores ways in which women—and even some men—broke with Victorian-era conventions. She examines the transitions in male-female relations and how they were affected by industrialization and the resulting shift in class, family structure, and social customs.

- *Women: Images & Realities, a Multicultural Anthology* (2006) is a best-selling anthology written by Amy Kesselman, Lily D. McNair, and Nancy Schniedewind. The volume interprets the meaning and nature of feminism from a multidisciplinary and multicultural perspective through essays, poetry, short stories, and academic analyses. The writing touches on numerous issues pertaining to women and is used as a text in many women's studies courses.

- *Colonize This! Young Women of Color on Today's Feminism* (2002) is a collection of essays compiled by editors Daisy Hernandez and S. Bushra Rehman. Each provides a different perspective on the contributor's attitude toward feminism as it has been influenced by her personal experiences within her culture. With a focus on cultural identity as it relates to family and feminism, these essays provide readers with insight into a more radical feminism than commonly found in mainstream America.

- Cherie Turner's *Everything You Need to Know About the Riot Grrrl Movement: The Feminism of a New Generation* (2001) is written for the young-adult reader. It explores an often-overlooked segment of feminism, one in which younger women are encouraged to express their outrage and raise a fuss. Originating in the 1970s, today's "Riot Grrrl" attitude is expressed in music and literature. Turner's contribution provides a valuable exploration of this relatively young branch of a centuries-old movement.

- *2060: A Love Story in a Utopian Future* (2007) is Janette Rainwater's vision of a new world order. For fifty years, women have struggled to find a cure for the virus that wiped out the male population. Experimental groups of boy babies begin to emerge, creating a society in which critical thinking and interdependence are the norm. This treatment of the question of survival revolves around themes of gender equity and multiculturalism.

- *The Mommy Myth: The Idealization of Motherhood and How It Has Undermined All Women* (2005), written by Susan Douglas and Meredith Michaels, critiques modern society's attitudes toward and expectations of mothers and illustrate why the standards promoted are impossible to achieve. The authors explore the idea that media and culture have interfered in motherhood to the point that women have been pitted against each other, thereby weakening the fabric of sisterhood that is crucial to happy moms and happy children.

- Robert Axelrod's *The Evolution of Cooperation: Revised Edition* (2005) is considered a classic, the psychologic research of which provides an understanding of why cooperation among humans not only works but is valuable. Based on scientific and mathematical principles, the research supports the idea that cooperation is the best survival strategy.

and the two raised Gilman's only daughter. The author's life was scandalous because it bucked every Victorian norm possible. The stress and constant ridicule must have taken a remarkable toll on Gilman and left her with a deep-seated anger.

> THE WOMEN OF HERLAND DO NOT END THE
> BOOK ON EQUAL FOOTING WITH MEN BUT RATHER AS
> THEIR SUPERIORS IN EVERY WAY, AND GILMAN
> CLEARLY PORTRAYS MEN AS HAVING NO VALUE OR
> PURPOSE IN SOCIETY."

In this way and without doubt, Gilman was oppressed. Retaliation against one's oppressor is a common response of victims of persecution, and judging by the treatment given the three men in Gilman's feminist utopia, she had not a desire for the sexes to live together harmoniously but to reverse the traditional role and create a society in which women dominated men. That scenario was Gilman's own personal concept of utopia. The women of Herland do not end the book on equal footing with men but rather as their superiors in every way, and Gilman clearly portrays men as having no value or purpose in society.

Gilman clearly believed society could and should be consciously shaped and that this molding was dependent upon women because men traditionally had an affinity for violence, a natural tendency that was in direct opposition to her idea of a socialist society or one based on collective thought and goals. Gilman sets up Herland to be the dichotomy of the Victorian age in which she herself lived. In Herland, women are valued for their intelligence and critical thinking skills, whereas in Gilman's reality, these two assets were considered appropriate only if they belonged to men. In chapter 2, readers first come to understand Terry as the symbol for typical male chauvinist attitudes of the era. He objectifies women and perceives them as valuable only in how they can serve him. The idea that women have inherent value never enters his mind.

In that same chapter, Gilman neglects to explore the idea of traditional gender roles as having any value of their own. For Gilman and countless other women of her time, those concepts commonly upheld as desirable—marriage, child rearing, home-making, even sex—seemed to enhance only the male quality of life at the expense of their own happiness and fulfillment. Early feminists considered these traditional

aspects of life to be repressive, and so the idea of achieving equal rights developed into an inverse relationship with any facet of life perceived to be male-dominated.

When the men are imprisoned in chapter 3 of the novel, much is made of the fact that their captors make no attempt to humiliate or physically harm them. This implies that male captors would automatically take advantage of the situation and beat their prisoners, simply because they are men and have the power to do so. Likewise, in chapter 4 when the trio tries to escape their prison, they are recaptured and treated as nothing more than naughty little boys. By allowing her female protagonists to hold this condescending attitude, Gilman completely ignores the very basic human desire/need for freedom. In that way, her utopian society is no better than the Victorian one in which she lives and struggles because one sex is still dominant.

Chapter 6 is the very middle of the book, and it argues that socialism and feminist domination are superior to any other social system. As the men talk with their tutors and learn more about the foundation and history of Herland society, it becomes clear that Gilman wants the reader to view the women the way Van eventually does, as somehow better, stronger, smarter, more ethical, logical, and wiser than the men. The women of Herland surpass the men in their degrees of courage and honor, their willingness to "go without a certain range of personal joy" for the good of the entire society. Ironically, however, when the men attempt to exhibit those same qualities in the manner in which they have been socialized, they are looked down upon as primitive. Is this not simply a turning of the tables? Especially during the Victorian age, women who acted out in anger or displayed characteristics traditionally considered masculine were viewed as hysterical. This sort of reverse discrimination is not progress; it is not equality. It is simply more discrimination.

Feminism in the 1970s was in a transitional phase. The movement was trying to figure out what and who it wanted to be in terms of goals. For many women struggling with the issue of gender equality and social liberation, marriage and motherhood were seen as obstacles to overcome. The National Center for Health Statistics indicates that the divorce rate in America rose nearly 40 percent between 1970 and 1975. It was a decade of change for women, and for some of the more extreme feminists, there was no way to

They flew over the new land in the biplane they assembled. *(George Lamson / Shutterstock.com)*

reconcile obtaining equality with living along-side men. It was not a matter of finding a common path. It was an either/or situation. Gilman's Herland utopia supports this idea.

In chapter 8, Gilman supports another facet of the early, more radical feminist sects. By developing female characters who wear their hair short and dress in plain clothing, she created an androgynous (asexual) society in which physical attraction and beauty were nonexistent. In the earlier years of the feminist movement, it was a common notion that to promote gender equality, femininity must be destroyed because it created sexual tension and attraction. The problem with this view, feminists quickly realized, was that women could not be held accountable for the phenomenon of lust, and twenty-first century feminists, for the most part, do not promote androgyny. In this way, Gilman's text is outdated, but it is an accurate depiction of her own personal beliefs.

Chapter 11 includes a degree of obvious autobiographical bias on Gilman's part in the way she presents and considers sex. Van and the other two men urge their new wives to engage in

sexual relations with them not as an act of pro-creation but as a fulfilling act of mutual love that would develop and encourage an even deeper bond. While the suggestion seems wholly logical to the men, the idea of sex for pleasure and a more profound intimacy is ludicrous to the women of Herland.

Gilman lived in an era when wives were considered property, owned by their husbands, who could do with them what they wished. Sexual relations were a husband's right, regardless of how the wife felt or what she desired, so perhaps it is not surprising that Gilman presents sex as a black-and-white issue. One thing becomes clear: sex is to be endured by the women, not initiated or enjoyed. Its sole purpose is to conceive and reproduce. When Van suggests otherwise, Ellador is quick to object. Given that Ellador is Gilman's most perfect feminist character, it is safe to assume that Ellador's ideas mimic those of Gilman. In her utopia, sexless unions would be the norm. This is another instance where male desires are seen as obstacles to be overcome. Again, there is no integration between the sexes, only domination.

Finally, the novel culminates with Terry's banishment from Herland in chapter 12. For Gilman, it is a role reversal of the Garden of Eden. The man has sinned by succumbing to temptation and must pay for that sin. Terry, symbolic of the stereotypical Victorian male, is exiled from civilization. Only the two men who have adapted and adopted the dominant gender's attitudes and values are allowed to remain, and Van—the most evolved (read: feminist) of the men, is rewarded with his freedom.

What Gilman crafted in *Herland* was indeed a feminist utopia, but it was not one based on gender equality. Instead, her perfect world was little more than reverse discrimination as she herself objectified the women and persecuted the men.

Source: Rebecca Valentine, Critical Essay on *Herland*, in *Novels for Students*, Gale, Cengage Learning, 2011.

Gary Scharnhorst

In the following essay, Scharnhorst challenges the interpretation of Carol Farley Kessler regarding Gilman's utopian impulse in her writings.

Since the republication of her story "The Yellow Wall-paper" by the Feminist Press in 1973, Charlotte Perkins Gilman has been resurrected from the footnote. Few American writers attract more attention than Gilman nowadays, a canonization epitomized by the recent founding of an academic Gilman Society, the publication by the University Press of Virginia of a two-volume edition of her diaries, and the publication by Bucknell University Press of the letters she wrote her future husband during their courtship. Carol Farley Kessler's *Charlotte Perkins Gilman* is a timely addition to this spate of scholarship, and Kessler's insistence on the centrality of the utopian impulse in Gilman's writings is a commendable (though not particularly original) insight. However, like Gilman's autobiography, which conceals as much as it reveals, Kessler's thesis-ridden study often skates uncritically on the surface of Gilman's career.

The narrative thread Kessler presumes to trace is appealing in its simplicity: Gilman escaped from a patriarchal marriage to the artist Charles Walter Stetson by divorce in 1894, healed her wounded psyche during her subsequent engagement and marriage to Houghton Gilman, and was thus "empowered" to envision a feminist utopia in the first years of this century, adding stroke to stroke especially in the stories she wrote for the *Forerunner* between 1909 and 1916. By this chain of logic,

> GILMAN'S STORIES SHOULD BE READ, IT SEEMS, NOT BECAUSE THEY ARE INTRINSICALLY PLEASING, BUT BECAUSE THEY ARE SOMEHOW USEFUL—NOT BECAUSE THEY ARE GOOD, BUT BECAUSE, LIKE COD LIVER OIL, THEY ARE GOOD FOR YOU."

"the climax of her utopian fiction" was *Herland*, a romance serialized in the magazine and thereafter lost until it was reprinted in 1979. According to Kessler, Charlotte Gilman's almost-daily letters to Houghton Gilman between 1897 and 1900, with their painstaking self-analysis, enabled her to establish "a liberating, empowering relationship, a central part of the context for creating Herland" in 1915. Her second husband "compensate[d] for her mother's unavoidable lacks," and "it may have been his behavior that provided Gilman with a model for *Herland*'s Over-Mothers."

Bosh. Such a taut plot line, embellished with a bit of armchair psychiatry, erases the loops and whorls from Gilman's life. Her utopian writing was not, as Kessler suggests, all "published from 1904 to 1921" (p. 44). In fact, Gilman began her public career in 1890 as a foot-soldier in the Nationalist army inspired by Edward Bellamy's utopian romance *Looking Backward* (1888), and she was an active Nationalist lecturer and writer for over three years. Yet Kessler scarcely mentions Bellamy or Nationalism save for one brief paragraph on page 23. (In contrast, Kessler devotes pages 90 through 93 to Gilman's two-month stay at Hull House in 1895. Obviously, Jane Addams ranks higher than Bellamy in the feminist pantheon.) Inexplicably, Kessler insists upon "the fit between Gilman's living and her utopian writing." The preponderance of evidence, I believe, points in the opposite direction. Even Kessler admits later that Gilman's autobiography, largely completed by 1925 and published posthumously in 1935, "is a monument to the public persona of Charlotte Perkins Gilman, very much a social construction authored by herself," and that in it "she occasionally adjusts information that would reduce her stature as a model." Would but Kessler had read Gilman's utopian romances from the same critical perspective.

In plumbing her "progress toward utopia," Kessler tends to minimize or ignore the discrepancies among Gilman's theoretical posturings, the events in her life, and ideas or behavior often attributed to her. Kessler begins such a project by 1) readily acknowledging Gilman's xenophobia and racism; 2) conceding that, her profession of Fabian socialism notwithstanding, Gilman did not endorse cooperative ventures "such as bartering services"; 3) allowing that Gilman occasionally confused such essentialist notions as "sex instinct" with "learned gender socialization"; and 4) recognizing that Gilman harbored a "restricted view of sexuality and possibilities for a nonvirginal woman." In fact, Gilman was horrified by the modest sexual freedoms of the 1920s and the cult of Freud that, she thought, only enhanced the potential for the sexual exploitation of women. In fact, while Gilman claimed in her autobiography that she and her new husband moved into a "home without a kitchen" in New York soon after their marriage, her diary reveals that they rented a standard apartment and simply boarded at a local restaurant. As Dolores Hayden concluded in the *Radical History Review* in 1979, moreover, Gilman's ideal of the "kitchenless home" was little more than a "belated and conservative" response to "the consequences of industrialization and urbanization" upon the middle class. That is, far from a radical or utopian proposal, Gilman's idee fixe was basically a petit-bourgeois solution to the "servant problem."

Such glaring gaps between what Gilman actually wrote and how she has been appropriated inform a reading, too, of her best-known utopian romance. Though Kessler claims that "to read *Herland* is to experience echoes of Gilman's living," I suspect few other novels in print today enjoy so inflated a reputation—and for such dubious reasons. As Kathleen Lant explains in "The Rape of the Text: Charlotte Gilman's Violation of Herland" (*Tulsa Studies in Women's Literature*, Fall 1990)—an essay conspicuously absent from Kessler's bibliography and nowhere cited in her book—even as Herlanders "deconstruct the patriarchal ideology of marriage, sex, motherhood, love and education, Gilman herself reconstructs that ideology in the shape of her novel," particularly "by centering the narrative on the issue of Terry and Alima's uncertain sexual union and by generating suspense through exploiting the potential violence of that union." Rather than a radical alternative to the pulp fiction of the period, *Herland* is "in many ways the archetypal story of war and adventure." Put another way, it is a feminist fantasy much as Harold Bell Wright's *When a Man's a Man* or the final chapters of Owen Wister's *The Virginian* are masculinist fantasies.

No responsible critic would recommend Wright or Wister as exemplary types who incarnated their readers' struggles, of course, though Kessler evidently regards Gilman in precisely these terms. She was "a real-life model of one courageous woman's conflicted effort to actualize possibilities for women," according to Kessler, and "analysis of her life" may "enable us who follow to avoid her pitfalls and create in our lives more joy than she knew." "Dive now into the imaginative legacy of Charlotte Perkins Gilman: experience her utopian ways," Kessler urges the reader. Gilman's stories should be read, it seems, not because they are intrinsically pleasing, but because they are somehow useful—not because they are good, but because, like cod liver oil, they are good for you. Such an argument is reminiscent of Gilman's own defense of her writing, which she sometimes compared to a toolbox. But beware: Gilman's didacticism is wearisome even in small doses. Mary Austin averred in *Earth Horizon* (1932) that "Everything [Gilman] wrote was in the same key," and the "worst of it" was that "she couldn't write." Years before, Austin had discontinued her subscription to the *Forerunner* "with its terrible sameness, its narrow scope." Kessler doesn't mention Austin in her book, either.

A final point: as it stands, Kessler's study proves the worth of rigorous editing if only by negative example; that is, a more active editor might have chastened its occasionally sophomoric prose. For example, Kessler refers to "the birth of Gilman in July 1860 and, fourteen months later, her brother Thomas Adie Perkins on 9 May 1859." Four pages later, she cites a passage from Gilman's diary ostensibly describing Charles Stetson ("an original: eccentric because unconventional"); in fact, the passage appears in Stetson's diary, published in 1985 by Temple University Press, and it refers to Gilman. At many points, Kessler's writing is startlingly infelicitous, as in this strained statement: "That literary realism was in fashion during her historical moment offered her a serendipitous coincidence." Elsewhere, the prose is opaque or virtually incoherent; e.g., "Because my aim in this chapter is to demonstrate how in her utopian fiction she actualized the recommendations of her polemical writing, I shall consider first her nonfictional exposition, then the fictional actualization of that exposition." Kessler concedes that Houghton Gilman nurtured Charlotte Gilman, but by a type of formulaic logic that will unsettle few of her readers' assumptions, she describes that nurture as a form of mother-love and adds that he "could provide what rarely mother or daughter in a 'man-made world' has the capacity [to] offer." The inconsistencies and incongruities of Gilman's career justifiably inspire discussion and debate. However, rather than cutting through the confusion, Kessler's study, I fear, only adds to it.

Source: Gary Scharnhorst, "Charlotte Perkins Gilman: Her Progress toward Utopia with Selected Writings," in *Studies in the Novel*, Vol. 28, No. 4, Winter 1996, pp. 594–96.

Thomas Galt Peyser

In the following excerpt, Peyser argues against prevailing interpretations of Herland, *claiming that "the imagination of utopia depends on the pre-existence of a utopian imagination."*

According to the prevailing view of Charlotte Perkins Gilman's *Herland*, the utopian novel suited the aims of a radical feminism by subverting the confinements of a realism dedicated to the representation of, and thus acquiescence to, a patriarchal order. Summing up this position, Susan Gubar argues that "women abused by the probable refuse it by imagining the possible in a revolutionary rejection of patriarchal culture"; "feminism imagines an alternative reality that is truly fantastic." Along these lines, *Herland* is seen as a sanctuary for the imagination, a place the reader can visit in order to gain a vantage point outside the prevailing culture. As Christopher Wilson puts it, "*Herland* is conceived as a mythological Archimedian standing point." *Herland* itself may therefore be less of a prescriptive model than a prelude to a critique, a machine for dismantling popular prejudices with an eye to some future reconstruction. Critics who take this position underscore the importance of Gilman's humor, seeing it as a key to her method of pointing out the antinomies and irrationality of everyday patriarchal life. According to Gilman's latest biographer, "*Herland* is an example of Gilman's playful best." The utopian novel complements *Women and Economics*, Gilman's serious critique of things as they are, with a shattering laughter that disregards and uproots the signposts of a patriarchal thought allegedly grounded in the bedrock of nature.

Such readings rely too heavily on the assumption that a refusal to portray the existent amounts to a rejection of social order, overlooking the

> HERLAND, HOWEVER, SUGGESTS QUITE EMPHATICALLY THAT THERE CAN BE NO DISCREPANCY BETWEEN INDIVIDUAL AND COLLECTIVE NEEDS."

possibility that even a vociferously adversarial ideal can underwrite dominant ideology. This in fact was particularly likely in Gilman's America, where the espousal of radical causes had become a therapeutic diversion for many members of the middle class. Another problem lies in imagining the preconditions for Gilman's, or anyone's, arrival at an allegedly Archimedean point of view from which to offer a critique of society. According to Gubar, an abusive reality (what she calls "the probable") prompts women to imagine a revolutionary possible. But this image is presumed to come from a space already outside domination, an already liberated ground of play not subject to the strictures on thought imposed by patriarchal culture. In other words, the imagination of utopia depends on the pre-existence of a utopian imagination, a realm of interior freedom sequestered from the necessitarian dictates of the patriarchs.

... Like most utopias, *Herland* has a fairly rudimentary plot. Three male explorers, an anthropologist, a doctor, and a rich adventurer, hear of a land somewhere in South America inhabited entirely by women, a land from which no man has ever returned. With the help of a native guide they find the country, which is perched on a plateau accessible only by airplane. Landing in Herland, the explorers encounter a large number of native women, who when provoked anaesthetize and imprison them. Once the men have learned the language and what is expected of them as guests, they are released from prison, though they are not allowed to leave the country, and are gradually introduced, along with Gilman's readers, to the history and culture of the Herlanders. Descended from a European expedition whose men were all killed in war with the natives, the Herlanders were saved from extinction by a miraculous instance of parthenogenesis, a power that became endemic to the race. The three men duly fall in love with three Herlanders, are married, and subsequently frustrated by their wives' total lack of interest in, and prohibition against, sex. When the most misogynistic of the men attempts unsuccessfully to rape his wife, the men are expelled. Accompanying them is Van's wife, who intends to explore the United States and report back to Herland on the desirability of establishing a connection to the outside, male-dominated world.

The challenge to critics who want to preserve *Herland* as an open-ended instance of negating, literary play lies in a sentence like this one of Van's: "we had quite easily come to accept the Herland life as normal, because it was normal." Gubar's strategy is instructive. Comparing *Herland* to another tale of male exploration, H. Rider Haggard's *She*, Gubar attempts to demonstrate "the misogyny implicit in the imperialist romance," a romance Haggard blatantly provides, and which the male trio in *Herland* attempts to enact in the paradise they discover. Gubar's analysis of Haggard and of Gilman's male characters is convincing. What she does not take into account are the very preconditions of the existence of Herland itself: it is, after all, a settlement of white, European women in the middle of the South American jungle. As Van notes, "there is no doubt in my mind that these people were of Aryan stock, and were once in contact with the best civilization of the old world," presumably because their culture does not resemble the implicitly inferior ones surrounding it. Even though they were "somewhat darker than our northern races because of their constant exposure to sun and air," Van assures his readers, "they were 'white.'" By these quotation marks Gilman indicates that whiteness expresses something other and deeper than pigmentation. This whiteness that persists even when it disappears echoes the logic of the Louisiana State Legislature and United States Supreme Court's 1896 decision to define Homer Plessy as black, even though this could not be determined by the color of his skin. Gilman's metaphysical racial categorizations, however, also participate in an international theme: the essentializing of races that underwrote the imperialist ventures of European powers. It seems more than chance that in Gilman's tale it takes representatives of one such power to uncover the secrets of utopia. The "savages" who first tell the explorers of a "strange and terrible Women Land" can say only that it is "a Big Country, Big Houses, Plenty People." Their inability to master English grammar is a correlative of their inability to know or understand the transplanted European culture near which they have always lived, even though a new arrival like Van, a sociologist, has little trouble understanding them, making out "quite a few legends and folk myths of these scattered tribes"—tribes so scattered that he plainly believes he understands them better than they do themselves. The European will to knowledge is ultimately what makes the discovery of Herland possible in the first place: the three young men had been lured to South America by the "chance to join a big scientific expedition." Herland remained unknown until the imperialist projects of the nineteenth century and the discourse that validated them designated the Southern Hemisphere as an object of study and destination for tourists, suggesting that for Gilman, as for most of her era, it took whites to know "whites," and vice-versa.

In a way, such exposition is extraneous: Gilman's acceptance of racist attitudes is well-documented. What it does show is that if Gilman does not think there should be a single definition of what constitutes the female, she does seem to think there is a single definition of what constitutes the best civilization. *Herland*, however, suggests quite emphatically that there can be no discrepancy between individual and collective needs. When the men escape their prison, they are confronted with a large group of Herlanders, who "evidently relied on numbers, not so much as a drilled force but as a multitude actuated by a common impulse." Just how this unanimity is achieved without acquiescence to some notion of what a person should be is hard to imagine.

For Gilman, collective action that overrides any individual objections, or rather collective action that arises spontaneously from rigorously like-minded citizens, has an unquestioned value. Even writing in the utopian mode, however, she cannot imagine such community coming into being spontaneously. Among the more dangerous imports brought by the men is their knowledge of ecclesiastical history, and when Van reports to Ellador, his wife-to-be, that some have held to the damnation of unbaptized infants, we learn that Herland is presided over by a priestly caste: "Every smallest village had its temple, and in those gracious retreats sat wise and noble women . . . always ready to give comfort, light, or help, to any applicant." Thrown into despair by Van's statements, Ellador runs "blinded and almost screaming" to one such counsellor, who tells her, "Why, you blessed child . . . you've got the wrong idea altogether. You do not have to think that there ever was such a God—for there wasn't.... Nor even that this hideous false idea was believed by anybody." "You see," Elladar explains, "we are not accustomed to horrible ideas.... We haven't any.... As soon as our religion grew to any height at all we left them out." At one point Van describes the mothers of Herland as "Conscious Makers of People." Even utopia requires an institutional structure to insure that that consciousness is the right kind.

Gilman clearly favors reliance on authority to independence of thought, and, indeed, values conformity for its own sake, even in matters of no social concern whatever. In *Women and Economics*, for example, she provides a rather chilling account of the common kitchens she wanted to establish, and which in fact were attempted in several communities, in order to relieve women of the chores of cooking. Cooking, for Gilman, "is a matter of law, not the harmless play of fancy." The new kitchens would therefore be law-abiding. "This will not, of course, prevent some persons' having peculiar tastes; but these will know that they are peculiar, and so will their neighbors." In matters as diverse as diet and theology, Gilman hopes for a self so thoroughly saturated with the beliefs of its community that there is really no longer any point in maintaining the distinction between public and private. The erasure of the boundary between the me and the not-me is in effect the political version of the narrator's conflation of self and other in "The Yellow Wallpaper": both depict a self that can survive its own liquidation, whether it becomes lost in the idiosyncrasies of a private pathology or absorbed into the unquestioned beliefs of the collective.

History, of course, is one of the great enemies to any continued state of equilibrium, but here Gilman solves that problem by putting Herland on the other side of historical change. "The untroubled peace, the unmeasured plenty, the steady health, the large good will and smooth management which ordered everything, left nothing to overcome." The unperturbable mental universe of the Herlanders, in allowing for nothing to be overcome, seems to preclude, for example, the possibility of self-definition: by virtue of being born in the one posthistorical community on earth, the one place where nature and culture are no longer opposed, a Herlander also inherits a social formation beyond the influence

not only of the individual will, but of any force we might recognize as an incitement to dialectical progression. It is difficult to arrive at the vision of a posthistorical world without finding Nietzsche's last man at the end of the road. Setting up a proleptic defense against such objections, Gilman has Van argue the foolishness of "that common notion of ours—that if life was smooth and happy, people would not enjoy it." The whole point of Nietzsche's critique, however, is that people would love a smooth and happy life, and that it could only be produced by such an absorption of the individual by the community as Gilman depicts.

Pointing out the Platonic cast of Gilman's thought may suggest that hers is the essential version of essentialism; this is not the case. As we have seen in her reaction to the rising culture of consumption, Gilman's escape from history takes a particular historical form. The disposition of Herland's houses "among the green groves and gardens like a broken rosary of pink coral" may give the impression of an absolute standard of beauty, but that standard is firmly grounded in the concerns of an America dislocated from the alleged security of village life. The resemblance of Herland to a well-ordered, extraordinarily clean, extraordinarily picturesque country town signals a nostalgia for a rather dehistoricized version of the American past.

In trying to describe Herland, Van comes up with another familiar institution that can act as a reference point. "As we neared the center of the town the houses stood thicker... grouped among parks and open squares, something as college buildings stand in their quiet greens." Just at this moment the explorers run up against the massed Herlanders, much as thirteen years later Virginia Woolf was to be intercepted by an officious beadle for attempting to cross an Oxbridge green. This incident, which Woolf used to open *A Room of One's Own*, is useful in understanding Gilman's depiction of the cultural space occupied by Herland. Here is Woolf's famous description:

> Strolling through those colleges past those ancient halls the roughness of the present seemed smoothed away; the body seemed contained in a miraculous glass cabinet through which no sound could penetrate, and the mind, freed from any contact with facts (unless one trespassed on the turf again), was at liberty to settle down upon whatever meditation was in harmony with the moment.

For Woolf the university provides a sense, though her parenthetical remark shows it to be only a sense, of detachment from the social pressures that always threaten attempts at thought. The quiet of the campus serves to make it a privileged site of contemplation, a place where one can at least enjoy the illusion of independence, and therefore a vantage point for critical thought, even thought against the society that makes such refuges possible. *A Room of One's Own* is, of course, a perfect example of such an attack upon dominant ideology. The whole point of a university is thus to be "outside" the society in which it finds itself, and this seems to be the ground of Gilman's comparison.

Herland, however, is an outside that no longer defines itself in relation to an inside; the miraculous glass cabinet is no longer the illusion of a moment, but a permanent condition. Coincidentally, the sense of display in Woolf's metaphor actually applies to the arrangement of Herland. When they enter the town the men call out, "'It's like an exposition'.... 'It's too pretty to be true.'" In addition to resembling a broken rosary, Herland is thus related to the White City of staff at the Columbian Exposition of 1893. A pretty town that looks like an exposition, however, that seems to be modelled on a simulation of a town, sounds more like a symptom of a growing taste for kitsch than like a utopian *novum* beckoning society onward. Matei Calinescu has argued that kitsch objects "are intended to look both genuine and skillfully fake.... Such a fakeness calls the viewer's attention to certain agreeable qualities of proficiency, imitative skill, versatility and cuteness." Kitsch provides ersatz experience for those whose sense of the real seems to have slipped away, for those who, like Gilman, felt that their culture had become completely unmoored from just grounds in nature. If Herland is an attempt to reestablish that ground, it still cannot help but express one of the pervasive conditions it seeks to correct: the sense of vicariousness with which one experienced one's own culture. Thus when one of the explorers presents jewels to the Herlanders, the recipients "discussed not ownership, but which museum to put them in." Instantaneous assumption into the museum, a characteristic of our own times, paradoxically makes of the museum not so much a special kind of space as merely an image of what the rest of the culture has

become. Woolf's miraculous glass case in a sense encloses all of Herland, and this museumification of reality simultaneously expresses a longing for a natural culture immune from history, and the idea that such a culture must always exist in an antiseptic place behind plate glass.

Ultimately, of course, *Herland* most powerfully and most consistently expresses a nostalgia for the natural place of women as mothers, or rather for a society in which a woman's place as producer of children, instead of consumer of goods, will be judged natural. For the Herlanders, motherhood is clearly the fulfillment of their being, an honor allowed only the most revered among them, and the culminating instance of all the highest aspirations of civilization. By comparison, the men in *Herland* belong to a culture in which vocation seems a rather arbitrary choice. What is perhaps most dangerous about the men, therefore, is that their biology is so little a determinant of their lives. Their nature, as it were, is exiguous, has little content.

To return to some of the earlier terms of Gilman's argument, mothers represent "the deep, steady, main stream of life," and men "the active variant"; mothers are essential, men are "adjuncts." Strikingly, Veblen sets up much the same opposition between the two principal modes of civilization. For him, "predatory emulation . . . is but a special development of the instinct of workmanship, a variant." When we keep in mind that Gilman presents the mothers of Herland as "Conscious Makers of People" and the men as makers of nothing, we begin to see a complex of attitudes on Gilman's part whereby men are to women as variant to essential, predation to production, and convention to nature. We see here that, contrary to many recent estimations, Gilman's recourse to the utopian mode did not allow her to create a purely negating, playful deconstruction of patriarchal thought. At best she inverted that thought, a striking innovation that might, in fact, awaken readers to the problems of any discourse that attempts to ground essential human being in any biological or racial group whatever. This awakening, however, comes only from reading Gilman against the grain; there is no indication that *Herland* is meant to be an ironic vision.

It is interesting to recall that Gilman's first publication, in 1890, was a satirical poem that appeared in the *Nationalist*, one of the leading publications espousing the utopian aspirations of Edward Bellamy. Just as Bellamy's adversarial stance succeeded only in universalizing the conditions of consumer culture by turning the world into a department store, Gilman could imagine "humanism" only as another version of the sexism rampant in her society, and in ours. In both cases, the problem with utopia is not that it represents an impossible noplace, but that, all unconsciously, it represents a place we already know very well. Masking from itself, and from its readers, its ground in the dominant culture, utopia can act as an obstacle, instead of an incitement, to a genuine criticism.

Source: Thomas Galt Peyser, "Reproducing Utopia: Charlotte Perkins Gilman and *Herland*," in *Studies in American Fiction*, Vol. 20, No. 1, Spring 1992, pp. 1–16.

Minna Doskow

In the following excerpt, Doskow examines Gilman's approach to the notion of utopia in Herland.

From earliest times, humanity has longed for a perfect world, one in sharp contrast to whatever its particular surrounding reality happened to be. Such utopian longings are still prevalent, still written about in our literature, and still, as always, unrealized. Expressed in the story of the Garden of Eden or a lost golden age, in classic works such as Plato's *Republic* or More's *Utopia*, in nineteenth-century socialist visions or twentieth-century behaviorist ones, man's longing for the ideal has been seen through many eyes and taken many shapes. Yet, it has always been man's view; "man" used in the generic sense, of course, but unavoidably expressing the male perspective and carrying with it limitation in the sexual sense as well. Nowhere is this limitation more apparent than in the contrasting vision of Charlotte Perkins Gilman's feminist utopia, *Herland*. The differences in her approach and angle of vision underscore the lacunae in and one-sided development of the utopian literary tradition. These differences, moreover, correspond closely to what Carol Gilligan describes as a historically female approach to self-definition and moral decision-making in her book, *In a Different Voice*. Gilligan's analysis thus

> RECOGNIZING GILMAN'S DIVERGENT APPROACH, THE PARTICULAR KEY SHE PLAYS IN, WE SUDDENLY BECOME AWARE OF ITS ABSENCE ELSEWHERE IN THE UTOPIAN CHORUS REVERBERATING ACROSS THE AGES."

suggests a gender-based rationale underlying Gilman's approach.

Written in 1915 and serialized by Gilman in her magazine, the *Forerunner*, *Herland* was not published in book form until 1979. It has been, for the most part, ignored by histories of utopian literature. Yet Gilman's book deserves the attention of modern readers. Engrossing, satiric, and cogent, the book, like other literary works in the utopian genre, establishes a standard by which to judge contemporary society. For the present reader, however, it does more than that, because it not only aims its criticism at the position of American women in 1915, it also satirizes our contemporary views and practices. Seen within the context of the Utopian literary corpus, it provides, in addition, a striking contrast in approach and perspective to male-authored utopias.

Most male-authored utopian literature concentrates on political, economic, social, or religious structures as the foundation of the utopian state and assumes that these institutions shape the relationships and feelings of the respective inhabitants. Gilman reverses the procedure. She founds her utopia on a basic human relationship—motherhood—and an emotion—the love that accompanies it, and assumes that these shape appropriate and equitable institutions. Instead of concentrating on *how* the society functions, on particular social structures and their operation, as the male utopian authors do, Gilman focuses on *why* the society functions as it does, because of the motivations, feelings, and relationships of the utopian inhabitants. In this respect, as several critics have pointed out, Gilman sets the pattern for much contemporary feminist utopian science fiction writing. Gilman thus reverses the normal figure and ground of utopian literature. Male authors trust to institutions to shape consciousness in appropriate utopian ways. They hardly mention the interpersonal relationships of the inhabitants or analyze the nature or basis of those relationships. Gilman, on the other hand, directs attention inward to consciousness and assumes its outward reflection in suitable institutions and events. The particular forms that the outward reflections should take are left vague with hardly a passing reference to political, economic, or legal institutions, much less full descriptions.

If we look for political structures in *Herland*, we find that the entire book yields but a single sentence devoted to that topic, and even there the reference is tangential, lodged within a discussion of proper names. We are told that sometimes a woman's name is lengthened to reflect her particular individual merit. "Such as our present Land Mother—what you call president or king, I believe." This passing reference furnishes us with all the political information the novel grants. Even the tantalizing promise: "You shall meet her," is never kept. Nor is she mentioned again. We never learn how she is chosen, what her responsibilities are, what powers she has, or whether she has assistants or auxiliaries.

Although the Land Mother appears to be *Herland*'s philosopher queen, she differs greatly in her role and treatment from Plato's philosopher king in the *Republic*. Plato's figure is the apex and culmination of the entire hierarchical structure of the *Republic*. He is the crux of the vision and the person whom the entire elaborate and fully delineated structure relies upon and leads up to, whose wisdom controls the state and keeps all elements in balance there as the faculty of reason does within the individual soul. All the elements (or classes) of the state (or soul), their nature, characteristic functions, hierarchical relationships, and subordination to the philosopher king are described at length. In contrast, any description of hierarchical structure as a whole, or its particularities in form and content at any level, is completely absent from *Herland*. Instead, there is that single passing reference to a "president or king," an intentional ambiguity between two different types of rulers. So casual is Gilman's interest that she devotes only a single fourteen-word sentence in a 146-page book to political rule, and even then does not distinguish between the two very different types of rulers.

Hierarchies are absent from all spheres of life in *Herland*, not only the political. Instead, a relationship—sisterhood—is substituted. Competition as a motive for action is also absent and replaced by caring or love. "They had had no kings," Gilman tells us, "and no priests, and no aristocracies. They were sisters, and as they grew, they grew together—not by competition, but by united action." An egalitarian basis of existence is substituted for a hierarchical one in all spheres of life, and the organic metaphor of growth merges with it to depict nurture rather than struggle. Gilman is concerned with the relationship of sisterhood, growing out of common descent, that leads in her utopia not to sibling rivalry but to cooperation and "united action." She does not describe how the non-hierarchical society functions, but simply why it does—because of sisterhood—and leaves the picture of the resulting institutions to the reader's own imagination.

If we next examine economics, we find the same lack of attention to structure, hierarchical or otherwise. The reader can gather from indirect references that there is some kind of communal economy in operation, that there are centralized eating facilities, and that the entire population works at various specialized occupations for which they are somehow trained according to their particular abilities. We know that Herland has foresters, educators, carpenters, masons, and part-time priestesses (that is, wise elders who are summoned for consultation and comfort occasionally, but who do some other unnamed work most of the time). But how all this is organized, how houses get built, roads paved, clothing produced, crops raised, what systems of production and distribution are employed, how labor is assigned or carried out remain a mystery for the reader. On this topic, too, Gilman grants us a passing reference in a single sentence: "I see I have said little about the economics of the place; it should have come before, but I'll go on about the drama now." So much for economics.

Even the little Gilman claims to have said about economics in the first ninety-eight pages of her book is incidental and disconnected. Glimpses of economic institutes or structures emerge from the plot, from what the three male adventurers encounter as they eat their meals, are clothed, housed, educated, and meet the natives. No overarching system is described, however, and no general plan laid out. Only unconnected particularities and individual instances are mentioned. This is in sharp contrast to the systems of production, labor credits, and centralized warehouses for distribution of goods described at length by Edward Bellamy in *Looking Backward*. Or, to cite a pre-industrial vision, it is in equally sharp contrast to Sir Thomas More's description of the economic organization of Utopia, its agriculture, trades, and labor system, as well as its political and social structures. Even B. F. Skinner, whose main concern in *Walden II* is behaviorist conditioning pays more attention to economics than Gilman. Indeed, it is difficult to think of a male-authored utopia in which the description of economic structures gets as little attention as in *Herland*.

...The extension of motherhood and accompanying sisterhood into social organization has multiple consequences. Connected by bonds of affection and kinship, the inhabitants of Herland develop their peaceful, nonhierarchical and noncompetitive society. To reiterate, "They were sisters, and as they grew they grew together—not by competition but by united action." The organic concept of growth, rather than struggle for survival, is used here, as it is throughout the book. Gilman's organicism runs counter to the social Darwinism popular in her day and articulated earlier by Van, the male social scientist in the novel. Indeed, the incredulity of a skeptical male American adventurer whose capitalistic background makes him unable to envision work or progress without the motivating force of competition is faced head on and answered with the all-purpose relationship of motherhood. "Do you mean," he is challenged, "that with you no mother would work for her children without the stimulus of competition?" Even he is forced to admit the possibility of other motivations. Once admitted as a possibility within the context of family relationships, motherly love in a society that resembles an extended family may then be generalized to encompass national motivation as well.

The extension of the family to the state harkens back to an older morality evident in myth and folklore based on family ties rather than political allegiances. We see this older morality in conflict with and being superseded by the newer one in ancient Greek tragedy. When Agamemnon chooses to sacrifice his own daughter, Iphigenia, to advance political ends and pursue the war in Troy, we see the clear choice made. Or again, in the *Oresteia* when the tribunal is established at the end of the trilogy and the Furies are transformed into the Eumenides, included but subsumed under the *polis*, the shift from family allegiances and blood ties to abstract allegiances, principle, and political ties is completed. Gilman goes back to the earlier tradition, but rather than seeing family allegiances at war with political ones, she extends them to include the political, the exact reverse of Athena's action at the end of the *Oresteia* when she includes the Eumenides within the Athenian state.

In Herland not only politics but religion, too, grows out of the basic relationship of motherhood: "Their great Mother Spirit was to them what their own motherhood was—only magnified beyond human limits." A projection of their own motherhood, their god is an active, in-dwelling spirit of love within each person who works for good and is evident in their love of one another. As Ellador explains, "You see, we recognize in our human motherhood, a great tender limitless uplifting force—patience and wisdom and all subtlety of delicate method. We credit God—our idea of God—with all that and more." They thus recognize no independent and external deity separate from their own indwelling spirit, which gains its necessary outward expression in their actions and institutions. Their religion is thereby woven into the fabric of their entire society, their personal development, and their relationships. Here we see the enactment of "God is mother-love" on a national scale.

Certainly Gilman presents an idealized version of motherhood. But in a utopian work such as hers, this is no problem. Utopian literature is, after all, a workshop for human ideals to be cast in whatever mold most pleases a particular author's imagination. What seems to please Gilman is an idealized love expressed as glorious motherhood and sisterhood. She relies on inner states and relationships to reflect themselves outward in institutions and form the utopian world, rather than the usual utopian mode of relying on various institutions to shape character.

This unusual reversal of figure and ground appears strange to the reader of utopian literature and may even, at first glance, seem misguided or soft-headed. But in dealing with utopian literature, hard-headedness is not a necessary quality, nor one that comes immediately to mind when analyzing the genre. We are still in the land of nowhere, albeit perhaps in a good place as well. With Gilman there has simply been a shift in the foundation of goodness from abstract principles, hierarchies, and formalized structures to feelings and relationships.

This attention to feelings and connections as motivating moral forces shaping decision-making is described as a typically feminine way of defining the self and structuring moral action by Carol Gilligan in her book *In a Different Voice*. Writing sixty-seven years after Gilman's book and concerned with a different subject, Gilligan nevertheless systematically analyzes and describes those qualities forming the basis of Gilman's ideal state and distinguishing her literary utopia from those of her male predecessors or successors in the genre.

Gilligan distinguishes between historically male and female modes of personality development and moral decision-making, noting that masculinity is traditionally defined through separation and individuation while femininity is defined through connection and attachment or relationship. Following Piaget (1932) and Lever (1976), she further characterizes male development as based on abstract principles, rules, and various formal structures and female development as having a "greater orientation toward relationships and interdependence [implying]...a more contextual mode of judgment and a different moral understanding." This difference between male individuation and measurement against an abstract ideal and female connection and measurement through activities of care also describes the basic difference in approach between the male-authored utopias I have mentioned and Gilman's *Herland*. It is the difference between the emphasis on abstract systems expressed in formalized political, economic, social, and legal structures, and the emphasis on caring and connection between mother and child, or sister and sister. As a female-created and female-inhabited utopia, *Herland* reflects remarkably closely the principles of the psychology of women described by Gilligan and suggests a gender-based utopian literary distinction that demands further study.

The underlying logic of each gender-based approach is further characterized by Gilligan as follows: "Thus the logic underlying an ethic of care is a psychological logic of relationships, which contrasts with the formal logic of fairness that informs the justice approach." Again, Gilligan's analysis is suggestive in illuminating the contrast between Gilman's and the male-authored utopias mentioned above. Taking as part of any working definition of literary utopias the fact that they are written in an attempt to create a just state, if only on paper, we can recognize the male emphasis on equitable structures as a reflection of the formal logic of fairness, while we recognize Gilman's emphasis on connections as a reflection of the psychological logic of relationships.

If, as Gilligan's studies seem to indicate, the moral imperative for women is by and large the ethic of care, then it is logical that their emphasis will be on connections between self and other, the central operating principle in Gilman's utopia. Because all are descended from the Ur Mother and are related to each other, the connections are structural and inevitable. The ethic of care thus prevails, and the society necessarily produces the appropriate institutions to embody that ethic.

On the other hand, if the moral imperative for men is by and large the ethic of fairness, then it is logical that the emphasis will be on separation, individual rights, codes of abstract principles, and institutions to ensure fairness. Again, this is reflected in the attention to laws and structures that prevail in the male-authored utopias.

A glance at the informing myths of two utopias, Gilman's and Plato's, is illustrative in this context. There is a sharp contrast between the historical-mythic tale of a common ancestor that molds Herlandian society and the myth, or noble lie, of class distinctions in spite of a single earth mother that Plato uses to explain the hierarchical order of his republic. Descent from a single mother stresses connection in Gilman but is overshadowed by distinctive, separate, and hierarchical descent from gold, silver, or iron that stresses individuation in Plato. Each carries the logic of its own truth into the nature of the society that it undergirds. Each illustrates the distinctive vision of its author.

Gilligan notes two recurrent gender-based images—the web and the hierarchy—in the texts of women's and men's responses, thoughts, and fantasies that she analyzes. These images describe the two kinds of utopias I have been discussing as well. The nonhierarchical society of Herland is perpetuated by the interconnected web of relationships among its inhabitants. The utopias of Plato, More, and Bellamy, on the other hand, depend on various hierarchical structures for their establishment and continued existence.

Although Gilligan calls for an androgynous balance between separation and connection in individual development, utopian authors are under no such compulsion to find balance and may be allowed their one-sided imaginative reaching after an ideal. It is, nevertheless, significant that in doing so they are far from haphazard in their choices and reflect the particular gender-specific psychological mode of imagination that Gilligan systematically analyzes.

In the context of utopian literature, therefore, it is crucial to pay particular attention to Gilman's contrasting utopian approach. Rather than criticizing her for certain omissions, we need to seek her out for the different notes she sounds in the chorus of utopian literature and the particular harmony she provides. Recognizing Gilman's divergent approach, the particular key she plays in, we suddenly become aware of its absence elsewhere in the utopian chorus reverberating across the ages. With Gilman, the distaff side is sounded, and we are presented with a utopia that is truly "in a different voice."

Source: Minna Doskow, "*Herland*: Utopic in a Different Voice," in *Politics, Gender, and the Arts*, edited by Ronald Dotterer and Susan Bowers, Susquehanna University Press, 1992, pp. 52–63.

SOURCES

"About Charlotte Perkins Gilman," in *Charlotte Perkins Gilman Society*, http://sites.google.com/site/gilmansociety/about-charlotte-perkins-gilman (accessed on August 9, 2010).

"Divorce Rates," in *Divorce Reform*, http://www.divorcereform.org/rates.html (accessed on August 9, 2010).

Gilman, Charlotte Perkins, *Herland*, Pantheon Books, 1979.

Kessler, Carol Farley, Review of *Herland*, in *Utopian Studies*, Vol. 11, No. 2, Spring 2000, p. 259.

Lane, Ann J., "Introduction," in *Herland*, Pantheon Books, 1979, p. x.

Lathrop, Anna, "Herland Revisited: Narratives of Motherhood, Domesticity, and Physical Emancipation in Charlotte Perkins Gilman's Feminist Utopia," in *Vitae Scholasticae*, January 1, 2006, pp. 47–64.

McVeigh, Andrea, "Charlotte Perkins Gilman's Utopian Novels: Moving the Mountain, Herland and With Her in Ourland," in *Utopian Studies*, Vol. 10, No. 2, Spring 1999, p. 231.

Piercy, Marge, Review of *Herland*, in *Powells Books*, http://www.powells.com/biblio/17-9780394736655-0 (accessed August 9, 2010).

FURTHER READING

Freedman, Estelle, *No Turning Back: The History of Feminism and the Future of Women*, Ballantine Books, 2003.

Stanford historian Freedman provides an expansive, highly readable history of feminism from its inception into the twenty-first century. She examines issues from within the movement related to race, politics, economics, and explores why the ideas that launched the movement are still valid today.

Gilman, Charlotte Perkins, *The Living of Charlotte Perkins Gilman: An Autobiography*, University of Wisconsin Press, 1991.

Originally published in 1935, this autobiography reveals a woman whose views on birth control, women's rights, marriage, and sex education were vastly ahead of her time.

———, *Women and Economics*, Dover Publications, 1997. Gilman's social-science masterpiece was originally published in 1898 and has since become a classic of feminist theory. In it, she explores the history of women's economic dependence on men and its lasting negative effects.

Plante, Ellen M., *Women at Home in Victorian America: A Social History*, Facts on File, 1997.

Plante provides a practical overview of the social and cultural values and norms imposed upon women in Victorian America. Topics range from what to expect in marriage (safety, if you marry within your class), how to dress (uncomfortably), the multifaceted housecleaning experience (it took days of planning), to keeping a comfortable home and raising children. This is not a scholarly treatment of the era but a more lighthearted exploration of a society not so long gone.

Sargent, Lyman, *The Utopia Reader*, NYU Press, 1999. Sargent brings together a collection of utopian texts and provides a detailed introduction to the field of utopian literature. This book provides excerpts from some of the most famous utopian literature, including Aldous Huxley's *Brave New World*. Altogether, Sargent offers a strong overview of the images and roles of utopia in literature from classics through contemporary works.

Wollstonecraft, Mary, *A Vindication of the Rights of Woman*, Dover Publications, 1996.

British writer and activist Wollstonecraft is a feminist icon whose famous treatise on women's rights argues that women should cultivate power not through their sexuality or physical allure but through intelligence and independence. Originally published in 1792 to high praise despite its unconventional perspective, this lengthy essay is written in a tone that is at once rational and sensible.

SUGGESTED SEARCH TERMS

Herland

Charlotte Perkins Gilman AND utopia

Charlotte Perkins Gilman AND feminism

Charlotte Perkins Gilman AND socialism

feminist AND utopia

socialist feminism

utopian literature

Herland AND socialism

Victorian age AND women

The Island of Dr. Moreau

H. G. WELLS

1896

H. G. Wells and Jules Verne are known as the fathers of science fiction. They helped create the new themes of the genre that carried the Victorian myth of progress into the future. Like the works Wells called his scientific romances, such as *The Time Machine*, *The War of the Worlds*, and *The Invisible Man*, *The Island of Dr. Moreau* explores the nature of man in light of the science of evolution, relatively new in public consciousness in 1896. Evolution is still at the forefront of the sciences with recent developments in genetics. The field is more controversial than ever as a magnet for calls to reject science by religious fundamentalists, especially by some in America and the Islamic world.

In the novel, Wells draws on ancient myths of animal-human chimeras to create a Swiftian satire about the competing roles of science and religion in society. *The Island of Dr. Moreau* is often imagined in popular culture to be a prediction of genetic engineering, something Wells could hardly have foreseen based on the science of his day. However, what the human imagination conceives, it is usually also eventually able to carry out, though genetic engineering changes living creatures in a way different than the particulars imagined by Wells.

AUTHOR BIOGRAPHY

Wells was born on September 21, 1866, in England, to parents who were in domestic service but

H. G. Wells

who had also managed to open a not very successful retail shop. In addition Wells's father played professional cricket, which was also not very lucrative. They intended for Wells to become a draper. However, by reading in the libraries of his mother's employers, Wells educated himself. A primary influence on Wells was his early reading of Plato's *Republic*, which left him with an abiding interest in ideal states and utopias. In his own writing, he often combined that ideal with the Victorian concept of progress.

Due to his self-education, Wells was able to find work as a teacher and attend University College London. There he studied biology under Thomas Huxley, a colleague of Charles Darwin, the most vociferous proponent of the theory of natural selection, commonly known as evolution. In the early 1890s, Wells was incapacitated by tuberculosis and had to resign from teaching (though after a few years the disease became dormant). Wells had actively published in student journals and now began to attempt to earn a living from writing. He had immediate and spectacular success.

Able to support himself and his family as an essayist, Wells found his true métier as a novelist

in 1894, when he serialized *The Time Machine*. In this best seller, Wells explored his ideas about evolution, eugenics, class warfare, and socialism in a fantastic futuristic setting. He followed with a number of similar novels, including 1896's *The Island of Dr. Moreau*, which introduced into the mix the newly controversial topic of animal vivisection, and his famous story of space invasion, *The War of the Worlds*, in 1898.

In the first decade of the twentieth century, however, Wells transitioned to a middle period of more realistic novels, such as *Kipps* in 1905, which drew on his experience as a draper's apprentice to explore issues of class. In 1909, his *Ann Veronica* espoused early feminist ideas.

Wells's novels tend to be didactic, a tendency he indulged in book-length essays like *Anticipations* (1901), in which he plainly imagines how technology will have transformed life by the year 2000, and *The Outline of History* (1920), perhaps the most popular of his books during his own lifetime. In old age, he returned to fantastic and utopian themes, most importantly in his novel (1933) and film script (1936) for *Things to Come*. The story depicts a utopian future fulfilling Wells's dream of a single world government, paradoxically made possible by a devastating world war that completely destroys traditional society. Wells continued writing until his eightieth year, when he declined rapidly, dying on August 13, 1946.

PLOT SUMMARY

Introduction

The Island of Dr. Moreau begins with an introduction, supposedly written around 1895 by Charles Edward Prendick, who states that the following novel is actually the memoirs of his late uncle Edward. The events described took place in 1887 and 1888, when Edward Prendick's family in England believed him to be lost at sea. Considered mad whenever he tried to speak of what happened during that time, Prendick left a memoir among his papers, found by his nephew. The adventure he had took place on an island near the Galapagos Islands in the South Pacific. Charles Edward believes the only logical island for the setting of his uncle's tale is Noble's Isle (a reference to the noble savage of Jean Jacques Rousseau). Though sailors of the HMS *Scorpion*, visiting in 1891, found nothing unusual,

MEDIA ADAPTATIONS

- *L'Ile d'Epouvante*, released in English as *The Island of Terror*, was the first film adaptation of *The Island of Dr. Moreau*. It was made in France in 1913 and directed by Joë Hamman. Like most films of that era, it appears to be lost.

- *The Island of Dr. Moreau* was adapted in 1932 by Paramount Pictures in the United States as *The Island of Lost Souls*, directed by Erle C. Kenton. Charles Laughton plays Moreau, while Bela Lugosi makes a notable early performance as the Sayer of the Law.

- The 1959 Hollywood film *Terror is a Man*, directed by Gerry de Leon and released by Lynn-Romero Productions, is a very loose adaptation of *The Island of Dr. Moreau*.

- *The Twilight People*, directed by Eddie Romero in 1972 and produced in the Philippines by Four Associates, is another loose adaptation.

- Joel Stone's experimental play, *Horrors of Dr. Moreau*, was produced in New York in 1972.

- Director Don Taylor's 1977 film *The Island of Dr. Moreau*, produced by American International Pictures and starring Michael York, is one of the best-known adaptations of Wells's novel. This film was further adapted as a comic book written by Doug Monech and drawn by Larry Hama, published by the Marvel Comics Group, also in 1977.

- The most recent film adaptation is director John Frakenheimer's 1996 *The Island of Dr. Moreau*, starring Marlon Brando and produced by New Line Cinema.

the nephew is willing to vouch for the truth of the story's beginning.

Chapter 1: In the Dingey of the Lady Vain

Edward Prendick begins his first-person narrative recalling how the ship he was traveling on, the *Lady Vain*, has sunk. He is cast adrift in a dingy with two of the crew, but no food or water. After eight days, they agree that one of the three ought to be killed so the others can sustain themselves through cannibalism. One of the sailors is chosen to be the victim by lot. He is unwilling to make the sacrifice, however, and fights another sailor. Both fall overboard into the sea. As Prendick becomes increasingly delirious, he is spotted and rescued by a passing schooner.

Chapter 2: The Man Who Was Going Nowhere

Prendick wakes in a bed in a ship's cabin where he is being tended by a doctor named Montgomery. The doctor is eager for news of London and apparently pleased to find out that Prendick, like himself, has been trained in biology. He seems to have fled from London because of some disgrace he is unwilling to talk about. He tells Prendick that the ship is going on to Hawaii, but only after stopping at the island where Montgomery himself lives.

Chapter 3: The Strange Face

After a few days of recovery, Prendick and Montgomery go up on deck, where a puma and a llama are in a cage, and a brace of hunting hounds are on tethers. The men encounter Montgomery's servant, M'Ling, whom Prendick describes as a black man and the ugliest person he has ever met. There is something about his appearance and mannerisms Prendick seems to recognize but cannot quite put his finger on. Because of his ugliness, M'Ling is hated by the crew of the ship. The drunken Captain Davies physically assaults M'Ling, and Montgomery seems ready to provoke a fight with the captain over the effrontery, but Prendick is able to intervene and keep the peace.

Chapter 4: At the Schooner's Rail

Prendick and the doctor smoke cigars at the ship's rail, observing the volcanic island where Montgomery lives, which is just visible in the distance. Prendick thanks him for saving his life. Montgomery again speaks of the life he had loved in London as a medical student but, he now reveals, he had to abandon because "eleven years ago—I lost my head for ten minutes on a foggy night." This is all the reader learns of Montgomery's secret past.

Chapter 5: The Man Who Had Nowhere to Go

Once they reach the island, Doctor Moreau, as yet unnamed, comes aboard to collect Montgomery and his animal cargo. Prendick expects to go on to Hawaii on the schooner. But Davies, wounded over his earlier intervention to prevent a fight with Montgomery, forcibly puts Prendick ashore too, though Moreau and Montgomery are reluctant to receive him.

Chapter 6: The Evil-Looking Boatmen

Prendick is towed to the island in the dingy from the *Lady Vain* by a ship that belongs to Moreau, which is crewed by more men whom Prendick is at a loss to characterize. He comments on their ugliness, and mentions how strange their movements and the proportions of their bodies are. Moreau welcomes Prendick, explaining to him they might not see another ship for a year. He questions him about his education and takes some interest in the fact that Prendick has studied biology with Thomas Huxley (the same education Wells had). He explains that the island is essentially a biological research station. Moreau and Montgomery busy themselves in releasing several dozen rabbits that are among the animals left by the ship. They wish the rabbits to become feral and breed a population of game animals.

Chapter 7: The Locked Door

Prendick is given a room in the compound occupied by Moreau and Montgomery. Moreau tells him that his work is secret and he can hardly share it with a stranger, whatever his scientific training, until he is better known. Hence Prendick is locked out of the laboratory. When Prendick overhears the name Moreau for the first time, he remembers a scandal from some years previous in which an undercover journalist got himself hired by Moreau as an assistant. The man exposed Moreau's practice of vivisection, causing a public scandal that drove Moreau, a prominent scientist, out of the country. Prendick begins to wonder about the connection between the notorious vivisectionist and the deformed and hideous men who inhabit the island.

Chapter 8: The Crying of the Puma

Over lunch, Prendick challenges Montgomery with the fact that M'Ling has pointed, furry ears. Montgomery disingenuously pretends surprise. Moreau is absent and, from the terrible screaming of the puma left by the ship, Prendick

deduces that Moreau is vivisecting it. Tormented by its terrible cries, "as if all the pain in the world had found a voice," Prendick walks outside to get away from it.

Chapter 9: The Thing in the Forest

Walking away from the compound, Prendick comes upon a stream where he observes one of the characteristically deformed men of the island getting down on all fours to drink water like an animal. When the man notices he's been observed, he gives Prendick a guilty look, then runs off. Prendick next finds the body of a rabbit with its head torn off. He then secretly observes three of the inhabitants singing and dancing. He realizes for the first time the odd thing that he could never pin down. Though they are undeniably human in appearance, however grotesque, the familiar thing about them is that they are reminiscent of animals—in this case, pigs.

Prendick realizes that it is dusk and decides it would be better not to remain in the forest with these creatures, whatever they are, after dark. He returns to the compound but is followed, then chased, by the same Thing (as he calls it) that he saw drinking. Finally he uses his handkerchief as a sling to knock it unconscious with a rock.

Chapter 10: The Crying of the Man

When Prendick returns and meets Montgomery, he demands to know if he was chased by a man or an animal. Montgomery suggests it was a phantom of Prendick's own fear. He gives Prendick a sleeping draught that Prendick, exhausted, is glad to take. The next morning, Prendick wakes to Montgomery rushing through the locked door to the laboratory. He is in such a hurry that he leaves the door unlocked. When Prendick hears screams that do not come from a puma but a person, he goes through the door, and sees Moreau vivisecting what appears to be a human being. The physically large and powerful Moreau throws him out and locks the door. Prendick hears him arguing with Montgomery about what they ought to do with him.

Chapter 11: The Hunting of the Man

Prendick deduces from what he has seen that Moreau is not only vivisecting human beings, but that he has devised some method to turn men into beasts. When he opens his outside door just as Montgomery seems about to lock him in, Prendick becomes convinced that Moreau intends to torture and experiment on him and makes a run for it into the jungle surrounding the compound. Chased by Montgomery, who has a pistol and is tracking him with a dog, Prendick meets one of the island's inhabitants (whom he calls Beast People). The creature is part human, part ape. Prendick persuades the Beast Person to take him to the village where the creatures made by Moreau live.

Chapter 12: The Sayers of the Law
Prendick finds that the Beast People worship Moreau and consider him a law-giver. He is forced by the Sayer of the Law to repeat a litany of Moreau's laws against animalistic behavior and then a liturgy of praise for Moreau as creator. Finally Moreau and Montgomery arrive with guns and dogs and order the Beast People to capture Prendick. He manages to elude them and leads them on another wild chase through the jungle. Prendick is trying to reach the sea, where he hopes to drown himself rather than submit to the torture he fears at the hands of Moreau.

Chapter 13: The Parley
Once Moreau has Prendick cornered in the ocean, Prendick starts to shout out, talking to the Beast People directly, that Moreau has been turning men into animals and that he doesn't understand why they don't take revenge when they could very easily kill their tormenters. Moreau manages to shout him down and explains to him (in very broken school boy Latin so the Beast People will not understand), *"Hi non sunt homines; sunt animalia qui nos habemus*—vivisected." The Beast People are not men turned into animals as Prendick believes, but rather animals Moreau has turned into human beings. Montgomery and Moreau convince Prendick that he is in no danger, partially through reason, but mainly by a show of good faith, giving him their guns.

Chapter 14: Doctor Moreau Explains
Back at the compound, Moreau explains to Prendick what he has been doing to his animal subjects. Wells's technique in this section is to move from known premises step-by-step toward the fantastic. (Moreau's technique seems far more fantastic today to the extent science has discovered how much more complex living beings are than was imagined in the 1890s.) Moreau begins by reminding Prendick that reconstructive surgery (such as making a new nose for an accident victim) is possible, as are other surgical modifications. While other scientists feared to go far in this direction because of

ethical concerns, Moreau proceeded dispassionately and discovered nearly unlimited potential for such techniques. He is able to take any animal and reshape its skeleton and muscles to human form, and is also able to change the very nature of its organs (including the brain).

Grafting and transfusions between species play an important part in Moreau's work. He is able to create a human consciousness in his transformed animals through techniques like hypnosis. But eventually, Moreau always fails, because as soon as he done, the subjects start to revert back to their animal nature. Prendick objects that the pain the animals suffer through vivisection does not seem worth its outcome. Moreau replies that pain is a useless evolutionary vestige that humanity must overcome. He claims that the religion practiced by the Beast People is their own invention based on evangelizing they experienced from human servants he kept on the island years ago.

Chapter 15: Concerning the Beast Folk
Montgomery introduces Prendick to the Beast People. The most intelligent of them was originally a gorilla. Others were made from pigs. Many are hybrids, like the Fox-bear woman and Montgomery's servant M'ling, who is a Bear-dog. The crew of Moreau's boat were originally bulls, and there is even a Rhinoceros-mare. The most dangerous are the Leopard-man (the one that stalked Prendick through the forest) and the Hyena-swine. Some of them are able to breed, and if they bear live young they are wholly animal, but Moreau immediately goes to work vivisecting them. There are about seventy remaining Beast People of about 120 Moreau created during his eleven years on the island.

Chapter 16: How the Beast Folk Taste Blood
While walking in the forest, Prendick and Montgomery encounter the partially eaten body of a rabbit. This alarms Montgomery and alarms Moreau more when they tell him. It means one of the Beast People is breaking the law. They rush to the village to investigate. When Moreau asks which of the Beast People has broken the law against eating flesh, the Leopard-man attacks Moreau and runs off into the forest. The three men and the Beast People give chase and Prendick and the Hyena-swine happen to find the fugitive. Rather than allow Moreau to torture the creature through more vivisection, Prendick shoots and kills it. But at almost the same instant

he fires, the Hyena-swine attacks its throat. This causes Prendick to believe that the Hyena-swine was the rabbit killer all along.

Chapter 17: A Catastrophe

Eight or more weeks later, when Prendick is taking the air outside the compound, he hears the puma scream as usual under Moreau's vivisection. Suddenly, the partially humanized puma, swathed in bandages, comes rushing past him, knocking him down and breaking his arm. Moreau follows, and Montgomery follows, stopping long enough to examine Prendick's arm. Left alone all day, Prendick occasionally hears gunshots from the jungle. In the afternoon, Montgomery returns, explaining that he never found Moreau but had to shoot several of the Beast People when they attacked him, a thing that has never happened before.

Chapter 18: The Finding of Moreau

After Montgomery attends to Prendick's arm, they set out again to search for Moreau. They find a group of Beast People who have evidently seen his corpse. Thinking quickly, and fearful that their animal natures might lead them to attack if they are no longer controlled by fear of Moreau, Prendick assures them that Moreau is not dead but has left his body to go into the sky where he can watch them better, and that someday he will return. They indeed find Moreau's body and that of the puma who apparently killed him. The puma herself, although she has a gunshot wound, has been partially eaten. They take Moreau's body back to the compound and lock themselves in for the night. They euthanize the animals Moreau had in various states of vivisection.

Chapter 19: Montgomery's Bank Holiday

In Britain, a bank holiday is similar to a federal holiday in the United states. It is used in chapter 19 to mean an unrestrained celebration. Drunk, Montgomery becomes agitated when Prendick suggests they have to somehow get back to the mainland. Since Montgomery is evidently wanted for a crime in England, he does not feel that he can return to civilization. He decides to go to the Beast People and get them drunk. The next day, Prendick is planning to set out in Moreau's boat when he hears a terrible commotion coming from the beach. Prendick finds that Montgomery and the Sayer of the Law have killed each other. M'Ling is also dead. Montgomery had the Beast People destroy the boat and turn the wood into a bonfire, determined that if he could not go back to the world, then Prendick would not go either. Prendick finds that in his rush to get to the beach, he knocked over a kerosene lamp, burning down the compound.

Chapter 20: Alone with the Beast People

At dawn Prendick, still by the dead bodies on the beach, is approached by three Beast People. He has the presence of mind to forestall any attack by overawing them, cracking his whip and acting like Moreau. He gives them orders to dump the bodies in the ocean. When the Hyena-swine comes, Prendick immediately tries to kill him, but misses his pistol shot and is too exhausted to give chase when the creature runs into the jungle. Prendick goes off by himself to consider what to do, but to little purpose, and then goes to the Beast People's village. At last he succumbs to sleep.

Chapter 21: The Reversion of the Beast Folk

Prendick gains a loyal companion in a Beast-man who had originally been a Saint-Bernard. Prendick is able to convince most of the Beast-People to continue their worship of Moreau, which he considers a means of protecting himself through the Law's prohibition of murder. He instructs the Saint-Bernard-man to kill the Hyena-swine on sight. Not very adept at carpentry, Prendick builds a raft over many months of labor. During this time the Beast People all revert with increasing rapidity to their animal natures, losing the power of speech, the ability to walk upright, and other human characteristics. The Saint-Bernard-man finally fights the Hyena-swine and is killed, but Prendick is able to shoot the Hyena-swine, the most dangerous of Moreau's creatures. Shortly thereafter, a small ship drifts ashore on the island, containing two dead bodies. One of them, Prendick suggests, may be Captain Davies of the *Ipecacuanha*. Prendick sees how lucky he is to escape before the reverting Beast People inevitably kill him.

Chapter 22: The Man Alone

Prendick is eventually rescued and returned to England. He finds it impossible to fit back into human society. He cannot shake the feeling that all the people he sees on the streets of London are really Beast People on the verge of degenerating into animals. Prendick tells his story to the captain of the ship that rescued him, who can't believe it, considering it delirium produced by the castaway's ordeal. Prendick eventually finds some help by talking to a psychiatrist who knew Moreau years before. Prendick finally retires to a country house and devotes himself to studying the unchanging perfection of the stars.

Note
In this brief epilogue, Wells creates himself as a character and assures the reader that, however fantastic they seem, the technical details of vivisection presented in the story are true.

CHARACTERS

Captain John Davies
Davies is the owner and captain of the *Ipecacuanha*, the ship that rescues Prendick from the life-boat. He is also transporting animal specimens to Moreau's island. He is an alcoholic who has lost his master's license. While he is incompetent and difficult, Moreau or Montgomery no doubt chose him because he would be in no position to call for official inquiries regarding anything he might accidentally find out about Moreau's research.

Fox-bear
The Fox-bear is a female of the Beast People.

Hyena-swine
The Hyena-swine is the most dangerous of Moreau's Beast People. Although it is feral, in the sense of returning to its animal habits before any of its fellows, it is made from a pig, an animal that has many startling similarities to human beings. The pig is often used to characterize the worst human traits, especially in Wells's day; to call someone "Swine!" was a deadly insult, however old-fashioned it might seem today. This disposition is combined with the hyena, arguably a more violent and effective predator than a lion or tiger. The Hyena-swine is so dangerous, perhaps, not because it is the least human of the Beast People but because it is the most human in its rejection of authority and rebellion against conformity. In any case, after Moreau's death, Prendick's chief concern, save only escape from the island, is to hunt down and kill the Hyena-swine. He views it as an existential threat in a way that none of the other Beast People, even those made from predators such as wolves, are.

Leopard-Man
The Leopard-man is another dangerous Beast Person. He stalks Prendick, and one of the chief causes of Moreau's difficulties in managing the Beast People is the necessity of controlling the Leopard-man's feral instincts. Nevertheless, many of the transgressions of the Law the Leopard-man is accused of may actually have been performed by the Hyena-swine.

M'Ling
M'Ling is Montgomery's servant who accompanied him on the voyage from the mainland with the new specimens. He was originally a bear grafted with elements of a dog. Montgomery treats him exactly the same way people treat dogs, playing with him, petting him, and talking soothing gibberish to him. But when Montgomery is drunk, he abuses M'Ling horribly, beating him and frightening him with fire crackers. Like a dog, M'Ling remains affectionate and obedient anyway. When Montgomery is eventually attacked by the Beast People, M'Ling fights and dies trying to protect him.

Montgomery
Montgomery is a physician who works as Moreau's assistant. He also tends to Prendick after he is rescued from the life-boat and is the first person Prendick sees on regaining consciousness. He is "a youngish man with flaxen hair, a bristly straw-coloured moustache and a dropping nether lip." He studied biology at University College London and thus shares some of the same background as Wells. Montgomery shows his violent and uncontrolled temper on the voyage to the island. He works with Moreau because a terrible disgrace he committed, which is never explained, has driven him from civilization. Despite Prendick's gratitude to Montgomery for saving his life more than once, the two men are never able to form a friendship. Montgomery is an alcoholic, and his reaction to Moreau's death is to become drunk and then to introduce the Beast People to alcohol. He is killed during this celebration by the Sayer of the Law, perhaps because his lawlessness was more than the overwhelmed creature could take.

Doctor Moreau
The name Moreau is French, and by a pun, it can be interpreted as a combination of the French words for *death* and *water*. This interpretation gains importance given that in Wells's earlier novel, *The Time Machine*, Wells's name for the

more bestial of the two species of human beings the Time Traveler finds in the future, "Morlock," could have the same meaning (*lock* or *loch* is a dialectical word for lake). The name thus equates death and, using water as a symbol, life. In both cases, the goals of the name bearer are futile. The name Moreau may also be meant to recall Gustave Moreau, the leading French painter of Wells's era, whose most famous painting is *Oedipus and the Sphinx* (1874), rendering a monster with the head of a beautiful woman and the body of a lion.

When Prendick first sees Moreau, he describes the doctor as "a massive white-haired man in dirty-blue flannels." When Prendick hears the name Moreau, he recalls him as "a prominent and masterful physiologist, well-known in scientific circles for his extraordinary imagination and his brutal directness in discussion," a description that could apply equally to Wells's teacher Huxley.

Moreau is on a quest. His first purpose is primarily scientific. He explains to Prendick, "You see, I went on with this research just the way that it led me. That is the only way I ever heard of true research going. I asked a question, devised some method of obtaining an answer, and got—a fresh question." But, Moreau is also insane: although he claims to have happened upon the human form as the target of his operations by chance and does not think that evolution leads upward from the beast to the human as a teleological goal, he departs from science entirely when he claims to know that evolution is leading in the direction of eliminating pain, and moreover claims to be doing the work of evolution by way of justifying the pain inflicted on his animal subjects. Moreau imagines that he, an ordinary human being, is acting on an equal footing with natural law. He is no longer aware of his own mortality.

Charles Edward Prendick

The author of the introduction, Charles Edward Prendick is the nephew of Edward Prendick and the supposed editor and publisher of his uncle's memoirs.

Edward Prendick

Prendick is the main character and narrator of *The Island of Dr. Moreau*. He is a young man of independent means who takes up the study of natural history (as biological science was then

called). He takes a voyage in the South Seas to study relatively untouched and unexplored natural environments as Darwin did, and indeed as his (and Wells's) teacher Huxley had done. However, his motives are not noble but comic: he was bored and rich and had nothing better to do. Taken by chance to Moreau's Noble's Isle, he is confronted with new and nearly unimaginable circumstances. His character is designed by Wells to be one whose inner life will not distract the reader from the dramatic thread of the narrative, though at the same time he does undergo realistic transformations of character.

If Moreau is the anti-hero of the novel, it would nevertheless be difficult to call Prendick the hero. He constantly adapts himself to his circumstances and, by a series of lucky chances, survives, fulfilling the evolutionary process. But Prendick fails as a scientist. Given the chance to use inductive reasoning to predict what Moreau is doing in his experiments, he reasons in too constrained and pedestrian a manner and guesses wrongly that Moreau is turning human beings into animals. This leads to a gothic horror story conjured up out of Prendick's imagination that the reader, following Prendick, must follow. But Moreau makes up for Prendick's defective reasoning and explains to both Prendick and the reader that really, since Moreau is turning beasts into human beings, Prendick is rather experiencing a satiric horror story of a more nearly theological character, like *Frankenstein*.

Puma

The Puma is first introduced as a caged animal on the deck of the *Ipecacuanha* on its way to Moreau's island. It escapes while still being vivisected, presumably still fully animal in its intellect. It kills Moreau, who succeeded in shooting it during the death struggle. It is also attacked, and perhaps finally killed, by the Hyena-swine.

Rhinoceros-mare

The Rhinoceros-mare is a female of the Beast People.

Saint-Bernard-man

One of Moreau's Beast Men had originally been a Saint-Bernard dog. He retains even more doglike characteristics than M'Ling. After Moreau's death, when all of the other animals begin to reject the dominance hierarchy that Moreau established over them, the Saint-Bernard-man is anxious merely to find a new master and happily accepts Prendick in that role. As the Beast People revert to their animal nature, the Saint-Bernard's loyalty to Prendick does not wane, and on Prendick's orders, he fights, and is eventually killed by, the Hyena-swine.

Sayer of the Law

The Sayer of the Law is the head of the Beast People and leads them in the litany of the Law handed down to them by Moreau. His hands are misshapen like hooves and he is covered in gray hair. Prendick thinks he may have originally been a kind of deer. He does little throughout the novel but constantly repeat the Law. Finally, however, perhaps because he feels a special depth of betrayal when Moreau's death signals the Law's falsity, he turns on his human master Montgomery during a drunken, lawless celebration, kills the man, and is fatally shot himself in the struggle.

THEMES

Evolution (Biology)

On the first page of *The Island of Dr. Moreau*, Wells establishes the groundwork for the evolutionary context for his novel. Moreau's Noble's Isle is located near the Galapagos Islands, where Darwin famously did his field work. There, Darwin noticed the special adaptations of the islands' finches, tortoises, and other animals to very specific biological niches. Moreover, Prendick, before his shipwreck, set out to study natural history (as evolutionary biology was then called). His interrupted voyage is modeled on Darwin's famous cruise on the HMS *Beagle*, as well as on the similar research expedition undertaken by Darwin's follower Thomas Huxley to New Guinea and Australia on the HMS *Rattlesnake* (perhaps the model for the HMS *Scorpion* Wells has survey Noble's Isle).

Wells studied biology with Thomas Huxley, who, after Darwin, was the leading proponent of evolutionary science in Victorian Britain. It is not a surprise, then, that one of the things *The Island of Dr. Moreau* encompasses is an intimate conversation on the subject with Huxley's "Prolegomena" to *Evolution and Ethics* from 1893. In this essay, Huxley makes a case that human beings, since the beginning of civilization, have been removed from the natural selection that drives evolutionary adaptation. Evolution is essentially the changing of species over time to better fit their environment. The change comes from the selection of variations within a population of those individuals best fitted to their circumstance: they will have more successful offspring and pass on more genetic information to the next generation. But human beings, according to Huxley, are no longer subject to predation—living solely off of hunting prey—and in general not to starvation, so everyone has an equal chance to pass on their genetic inheritance. Individual fitness is no longer an issue. When human beings do react to environmental pressures—for example, famine—it is not by the change of the genetic make-up of populations but by concerted social action. It is society, not individuals, that evolves now. In short, the bodies of human beings are not like other organisms living in a state of nature subject to evolutionary pressure but like the inhabitants of a garden carefully protected from competition and evolutionary pressure.

Modern scientists would no doubt hasten to add many caveats to the margins of Huxley's analysis, such as genetic resistances to disease as a selective force, however sound the general point is. Competition for the basic necessities of life no longer exists among human beings, and competition within the society that guarantees access to those resources is instead to fulfill desires, to avoid pain, and to experience pleasure at an individual level.

Moreau, in contrast, has a distorted view of evolution. He believes that human beings are evolving in a specific pre-determined direction, namely to lose the ability to feel pain, and more generally to replace feeling of all kinds with reason. This may somehow be the larger background of his experiments. But, of course, evolution shapes organisms to their immediate circumstances, and does not aim for any specific teleological goal to attain in the future. But Moreau's confusion is deeper, because what he is doing is the opposite of evolution, as Huxley explains it:

> The tendency of the cosmic process [evolution] is to bring about the adjustment of the forms of plant life to the current conditions; the tendency of the horticultural process is the adjustment of the conditions to the needs of the forms of plant life which the gardener desires to raise.

Moreau is playing the role of the gardener by shaping his Beast People to his own ends, not those of nature to which evolution had already shaped them. The monstrosity of Moreau consists in his imagining himself playing an even grander role than that of the gardener in Huxley's scheme. As a thought experiment, Huxley imagines human

TOPICS FOR FURTHER STUDY

- It is a common motif of steampunk literature—speculative fiction that uses steam-era technology in science-fictional ways—to depict Dr. Moreau using biological warfare against the Martians that invade the earth in Wells's *The War of The Worlds*. In both Alan Moore's comic book *The League of Extraordinary Gentlemen* and in the young-adult novel *The Martian War* by Kevin J. Anderson (writing under the pseudonym Gabriel Mesta), Moreau does so at the behest of the British government. But what if Moreau were left to his own devices during the chaos created by the Martian invasion? What if he had to turn for help to whoever was nearest at hand, say the population of another South Seas island? What if Moreau had to use the aid of the multi-cultural utopia described in the novel *The Island* by Aldous Huxley (grandson of Wells's teacher Thomas Huxley)? Read at least one of these sources and write a short story about Moreau's confrontation with a different culture in a time of crisis. Points to consider include how Moreau's philosophy might be changed by his contact with the islanders, or how Moreau would be viewed by another culture.

- Use the Internet to research the historical introduction of rabbits into island environments, especially Australia. Create a multimedia presentation suggesting how Moreau's introduction of rabbits onto Noble's Isle might have affected the ecology there.

- Wells used the concepts of evolution and creation in a very complex way to illustrate his beliefs about religion. This topic was already controversial in 1860 when Thomas Huxley debated against Archbishop Wilberforce. How is evolution used in such debates today? Both YouTube and TedTalks have video records of hundreds of debates between scientists and church and political leaders on this topic. Use clips from these debates to illustrate a class presentation on the topic.

- The boundary between the human and non-human is a main theme of many novels of the late 1800s, including not only *The Island of Dr. Moreau* but also *Dr. Jekyll and Mr. Hyde* by Robert Louis Stevenson, *The Great God Pan* by Arthur Machen, and *Dracula* by Bram Stoker. Write a paper comparing the various approaches taken and conclusions reached by some of these books regarding human and nonhuman interaction.

beings, instead of being freed from selection by culture, instead subject to the same kind of selection that the gardener makes, killing weeds and uprooting plants whose flowers fail to please him: "Let us now imagine that some administrative authority, as far superior in power and intelligence to men, as men are to their cattle, is set over [human society]." Moreau imagines himself to be exactly such an authority, in that he is reshaping not merely human society but nature itself through his operations.

Racism

Racism was pervasive in the nineteenth century in a way that can hardly be imagined today. Even the most progressive proponents of the abolition of slavery and of the equality of rights for all human beings, such as Abraham Lincoln and Thomas Huxley, did not think that what they called different races of men were equal in intellect and other areas of life. The superiority that Western European countries and the United States enjoyed in the system of colonization was taken as proof that the men of those cultures were also superior. In fact, however, modern biological science does not acknowledge the existence of race as a scientific category, since there has been no significant isolation of human groups since the last common ancestor of all human beings, known as mitochondrial Eve, about 70,000

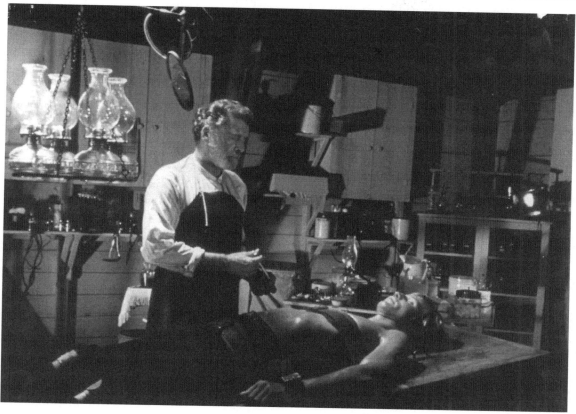

A scene from the film adaptation of the novel, starring Burt Lancaster and Michael York
(© Photos 12 / Alamy)

years ago. The equality of achievement among human beings from all parts of the world makes the falsity of distinctions based on arbitrary racial categories obvious.

Wells did not depart from the common racist attitudes of his day, and racism is clear in *The Island of Dr. Moreau*. One of the things that makes Prendick nervous about the Beast People when he first encounters them is that he is unable to fit them into his pre-conceived racial categories. Moreau is equally enmeshed in racism when he describes his first successful experiment: "Then I took a gorilla I had; and upon that, working with infinite care and mastering difficulty after difficulty, I made my first man. . . . I thought him a fair specimen of the negroid type when I had finished him." The statement implies that black Africans are closer to being animals than other human beings.

But Wells's pre-conceived notions prevent him from taking mere facts into account. The

Beast People have their own racism, no doubt imposed on them by Moreau's hypnotic indoctrination. They judge each other by how closely their hands approximate a human hand, so the Ape-man thinks himself superior to his fellows. This embraces the core racist fantasy: that there is an ideal human type and each human individual is to be measured against that as being closer to the human or the animal. But biological science makes it plain that there is not an ideal type of any organism, and that fitness of a species consists in the widest possible diversity.

STYLE

Science Fiction
Science fiction did not exist as a genre in Wells's day, nor, indeedd did the phrase. He called his fantastic stories scientific romances. Wells is often paired with his older contemporary, French

novelist Jules Verne, as the fathers, or precursors, of science fiction. While Verne was interested in describing emergent technology, Wells's premises are usually utterly fantastic. Jorge Luis Borges summed up the difference between them precisely when, in his obituary of Wells (translated in Parrinder's collection of Wells Criticism) he has Verne apocryphally exclaim of Wells, "*Il invente!*" ("He's making it up!").

More seriously, Wells was concerned with how science could be applied to reshape human society. *The Time Machine* and *The War of the Worlds* show what might happen if society were not reformed on scientific lines. Most of his other novels show science in charge, no matter how fantastic the means of it getting there. *In the Days of the Comet*, the means is a gas that makes everyone in the world think rationally, while in *Things to Come*, scientists rebuild the world after a devastating war destroys civilization. *The Island of Dr. Moreau* fits into this category with its message favoring eugenics, the practice of improving human or animal stock through selective breeding.

Wells's utopian and dystopian themes were taken up by the next generation of British novelists, such as Aldous Huxley in *Brave New World* and George Orwell in *1984*, and by more recent authors, notably Margaret Atwood. Though in his later life, Wells discounted his early scientific romances in favor of more purely sociological projects, there is no doubt his popularity and lasting fame are based on these very works.

The Education Act of 1870, a reaction to the fear that Britain might lose its scientific and industrial supremacy to a rising Germany just victorious in the Franco-Prussian War, provided for extensive scholarship funds to educate young men of the lower classes in science. This not only was the source of Wells's own education but also provided a large scientifically literate readership for Wells's new Scientific Romances.

Documentary Novel

The Island of Dr. Moreau is a novel and therefore wholly fictitious, but Wells strains every nerve to make his narrative voices suggest otherwise to the reader. The main text of the novel is narrated by Charles Prendick. It is written completely in the form of a memoir rather than a novel. This form gives the reader an expectation of truthfulness on the part of the narrator. The expectation is supported by an introduction supposedly written by Prendick's nephew, attesting to the genuineness of the main text as a manuscript written by his uncle and left to him for publication. The nephew even describes his research into ships's registries, travel schedules, and other records to verify the story as far as humanly possible. In short, Wells gives his fiction verisimilitude by casting it precisely in the form of genres that are ordinarily accepted as true.

Wells is not trying to trick his readers by any means, but the form allows the reader an added excitement by allowing him to pretend that the work is true. This relates to what the romantic poet Samuel Taylor Coleridge called the willing suspension of disbelief: that when a fantastic narrative is brought before the reader, the author must beguile the reader's objections to keep him from thinking about how patently false it is. Throughout the twentieth century, critics held this suspension to be a vital element of the science fiction genre, which necessarily deals in fantastic subject matter. In later times, the original concept was somewhat misunderstood, with critics acting as if it meant the reader had to give up skepticism.

Wells returns to lending fictional credibility to his narrative in his final Note, where he apparently speaks in his own voice to assure the reader that he has already published many of the substantive ideas of the novel in non-fiction, didactic essays. He states, "There can be no denying that, whatever amount of credibility attaches to the detail of this story, the manufacture of monsters—and perhaps even of quasi-human monsters—is within the possibilities of vivisection." Wells reassures the reader of the truth of what he full well knows not to be the truth: the very essence of fiction.

The use of fictitious documentary forms to create verisimilitude was a specialty of popular novelists of the 1880s and 1890s, though it has since fallen out of favor. Compare the elaborate efforts of Conan Doyle to place Watson the memoirist as a screen between his fictions of Sherlock Holmes and the reader. Bram Stoker's *Dracula* (1897) is also composed of letters, transcripts of meetings, and other documentary forms. If Wells can be said to have a particular model in mind for *The Island of Dr. Moreau*, it is Swift's *Gulliver's Travels*, another pseudo-memoir.

Although Wells and his generation were not aware of it, this use of non-fiction forms to provide verisimilitude for fiction harkens back to the birth of the novel as the romances of the Roman Empire. Roman aristocrats were trained at a university level in rhetoric, and most of their advanced course work consisted in producing sample documents: administrative letters, political speeches, trial summations, and so forth. Since these were merely for the sake of perfecting the form, students were free to invent any substantive details they wished. In other words, they wrote fictive versions of real documentary forms. The art of purposefully writing fictions and finally the novel perhaps grew directly out of this work.

HISTORICAL CONTEXT

Vivisection

As modern surgical techniques were developed throughout the nineteenth century, it became possible to examine the functioning of living systems, rather than merely studying anatomy through dissection of dead specimens. This practice led to important and continuing advances in medical science, with life-saving results for millions of human beings. Such operations are called vivisection, meaning surgery on living specimens. Criticism of vivisection was immediately offered on the grounds that some animals that are vivisected are ultimately killed or otherwise suffer harm. Organized opposition to vivisection formed around groups like the Theosophical Society, which opposed the practice in accord with ancient Pythagorean and Vedic religious teachings relating to reincarnation.

The popular press was anxious to promote views opposing vivisection since the dramatic portrayal of animal experiments as acts of cruelty performed by sadistic men (despite the fact that the scientists who work with animals are generally more concerned about their welfare than anyone, for practical as much as ethical reasons) were sensationalistic and sold newspapers. Even the reputation of the fictional Doctor Moreau fell to such a newspaper campaign. Wells himself fully exploited, in *The Island of Doctor Moreau*, the sensationalism associated with vivisection in 1890s England.

But despite Wells's constant use of the term "vivisection," Moreau's techniques not only have nothing to do with real vivisection but they are not even physically possible. It is clear from their constant screams that Moreau's subjects are conscious during his operations. But any animal undergoing surgery has to be anesthetized; otherwise it would not be possible to restrain them securely enough to prevent their movements, making surgery impossible. Any animal (or for that matter a human being) undergoing major surgery without anesthetic would die of shock very quickly, as Wells very well knew.

Eugenics

Like many intellectuals of his generation, Wells embraced the originally American pseudoscience of eugenics. This is the belief that positive steps should be taken to improve the genetic characteristics of human beings. Wells feared that, since evolutionary pressures for the most part do not operate on human beings, they would be subject to evolutionary degeneration, with nothing to weed out any newly appearing bad traits. This is clearly the message of his novel *The Time Machine*, which depicts a future in which the Homo sapiens species has split into two species, both of them barely sentient. One is incapable of defending itself and the other is cannibalistic. Wells stated his views plainly in the *American Journal of Sociology* in 1904:

> I believe that now and always the conscious selection of the best for reproduction will be impossible: that to propose it is to display a fundamental misunderstanding of what individuality implies. The way of nature has always been to slay the hindmost, and there is still no other way, unless we can prevent those who would become the hindmost being born. It is in the sterilization of failures, and not in the selection of successes for breeding, that the possibility of an improvement of the human stock lies.

With the events of the Holocaust still in the future, it must have been difficult for Wells to imagine the enormity of what he was proposing. He may well have believed that he was following the dictates of his teacher Huxley. But Huxley's famous "Prolegomena" is essentially an argument against eugenics, for Huxley there says, "There is no hope that mere human beings will ever possess enough intelligence to select the fittest." This might seem to agree with Wells's statement. But Huxley goes on to observe that selecting the fit and the unfit is exactly the same process, and that either is equally impossible.

It was also evident to Huxley that no program of eugenics could possibly be put into practice without the disastrous, society-destroying, consequences that would be realized in the

COMPARE
&
CONTRAST

- **1890s:** Vivisection, a relatively new phenomenon in medical science, is a controversial issue exploited by the press.

  Today: Vivisection, and more generally experimentation on living animals, despite a proven track record of contribution to life-saving research, is still highly controversial.

- **1890s:** Evolution, already firmly established as the basis of biology, is highly controversial in Britain because of perceived conflicts with religion.

  Today: Religious opposition to biological science is led by fundamentalists among the Islamic immigrant community in Britain.

- **1890s:** Racism is pervasive and easily accepted in society.

  Today: Racial discrimination is outlawed in Britain, a world leader in multicultural education.

- **1890s:** Essential transformation of animal physiology is essentially fantasy.

  Today: Developments in genetic science have made the manipulation of living organisms commonplace (for example, cloning of animals), though there seems to be little reason to bridge animal to human forms in the way Moreau attempted.

Holocaust: "I do not see how such selection could be practiced without a serious weakening, it may be the destruction, of the bonds which hold society together." Huxley also demonstrates conclusively that the criticism, made both then and now, that evolutionary science somehow leads to eugenics, is false. The fantasies of the eugenicist are the opposite of evolutionary science. Their actions do not conform to natural selection, as they think, but rather are like the action of a gardener, pulling out native plants to protect their favored species that are too maladapted to their environment to survive on their own. Eugenics could in no sense "improve" the genetic character of a species (a concept that has no meaning in biological science), but would rather serve to decrease its diversity and therefore its ability to adapt to changes in environment, making it less fit from an evolutionary viewpoint.

Huxley's disproof of eugenics notwithstanding, Wells wove eugenic themes into *The Island of Dr. Moreau* as well as *The Time Machine*. The Beast People Moreau creates constantly undergo reversion to their animal condition unless Moreau works on them to keep them human. This is a symbolic expression of Wells's irrational fear that humanity will revert to an animal condition if

natural selection is not replaced by some kind of artificial eugenic selection. The veil of symbolism lifts when Prendick returns to London and says, "I could not persuade myself that the men and women I met ... would [not] presently begin to revert, to show first this bestial mark and then that."

CRITICAL OVERVIEW

Coming soon after the best-selling success of *The Time Machine*, *The Island of Dr. Moreau* was widely reviewed in the British press. Many of the reviews are collected in Patrick Parrinder's anthology *H. G. Wells: The Critical Heritage*. Critics generally reacted to the title as a sensational exploitation of vivisection. This is well expressed in a review from the *Speaker* of April 18, 1896, that was included in *H. G. Wells: The Critical Heritage*:

> Mr. Wells ... has talent, and he employs it here for a purpose which is absolutely degrading. It is no excuse that he should have made his book one that sends a thrill of horror though the mind of the reader. After all, even among writers of fiction, talents are accompanied by responsibilities—a fact which Mr. Wells seems to have forgotten.

The island looked so innocent. *(CAN BALCIOGLU | Shutterstock.com)*

Another complaint was that a literal understanding of Moreau's technique was physically impossible. Wells (in an essay reprinted in appendix 6 in the edition of the novel edited by Robert M. Philmus titled *The Island of Doctor Moreau: A Variorum Text* went to some lengths to defend this. He cites current scientific papers that seem to suggest inter-species transplantation and grafting are possible. But any such hints were never confirmed. The rejection response by the immune system, which was hardly even suspected in 1896, makes any such transplantation impossible.

Literary scholars have largely rejected these early lines of criticism and found some interesting new lines of interpretation. Peter Kemp, for instance, in *H. G. Wells and the Culminating Ape*, doubts the hopefulness many scholars find in Prendick's final turn to astronomy on account of this, too, leading to disaster and bloodshed in *The War of the Worlds* with its invasion of the earth by Martians. Steven McLean, in his *Early*

Fictions of H. G. Wells, makes something out of a stray remark of Wells's that part of the inspiration for *The Island of Dr. Moreau* was Oscar Wilde's trial for sodomy (then a crime in England) in the spring of 1895. In that case, Moreau's recreation of his animals into men through pain stands for the gratuitous punishment the state inflicted on Wilde in order to correct him into something society arrogantly regarded as superior to his own nature.

Something should also be said about the text of the novel itself. Unusual for a modern, widely published novel, two different critical editions of the text of *The Island of Dr. Moreau* were published in the 1990s. The Philmus edition is based on the first American publication of *The Island of Dr. Moreau* by Stone and Kimball in May of 1896. The text edited by Leon Stover, on the other hand, is based on a British edition that Heinemann published in April of 1896. The American edition is not in any sense a simple reprint of the British.

Rather, both seem to have been based on a largely finished typescript (not now extant) that Wells supplied to the publisher. Each then had different handwritten annotations, or different changes agreed with the publisher through correspondence. Wells could have decided the matter when the text was reprinted in the so-called Atlantic edition of his early novels in 1924. But by then Wells held his early scientific romances in some disdain and evidently allowed a friend, novelist Dorothy Richardson, to oversee the extensive changes in that text. Most mass market reprints of *The Island of Dr. Moreau* are based on this later text, but this discussion uses Philmus's edition.

CRITICISM

Bradley A. Skeen

Skeen is a classicist. In the following essay, he explores The Island of Dr. Moreau *as a Swiftian satire.*

The Island of Dr. Moreau has generally been treated in film and received in popular culture as a horror story. That is in line with the way Wells began to write it, judging from his handwritten first draft (transcribed as appendix 1 in the Philmus edition). But it is not a very persuasive reading of the finished novel. The text grew into something quite different as Wells developed it. Although Wells took pains to make his fictions seem to proceed with meticulous scientific accuracy, their true character is wholly other, as most critics of Wells have discovered. As Jorge Luis Borges summed up in his obituary of Wells (translated in Patrick Parrinder's *H. G. Wells: The Critical Heritage*), Wells is "an heir to the concise style of Swift and Edgar Allan Poe." Wells's works are not only fantastic but are satires. Wells holds his world up to a distorting mirror and shows his reader a grotesque version of reality. The reader may well laugh as if in the funhouse, but will also have to do the mental work of matching the distorted images to reality. It is in this sense that the Beast People are, as described by the narrator, "grotesque caricatures of humanity," and still more pointedly, "horrible caricatures of my Maker's image." It is Wells the satirist's hope that in seeing what realities are thus caricatured, the reader will see those realities in a new way.

WELLS EXAMINED CHRISTIANITY IN THE FUNHOUSE MIRROR AND SHOWED HIS READERS A DISTORTION OF THE FAITH THAT REVEALED HIS CRITICISMS OF IT."

Swiftian is, indeed, the adjective most commonly used by critics to describe *The Island of Dr. Moreau*. Its reader must be reminded of the last chapter of *Gulliver's Travels*, in which Gulliver encounters Yahoos, human beings living in the condition of beasts, and Houyhnhnms, horses who are far more civilized than human beings. Gulliver, once he returns to England, cannot abide to live in the society of creatures he perceives as Yahoos and so retires to the seclusion of the country, in many ways the same experience Prendick has in Wells's novel. Swift's mirror reveals that civilized people are not quite as civilized as they seem.

Wells's own opinion of *The Island of Dr. Moreau* varied wildly. Sometimes he offered it as his favorite among his works, and at other times dismissed it as a comic trifle, something not worth bothering with. Certainly he does not mention it in his *Experiment in Autobiography* from 1934. By then he looked down on his scientific romances. But if Wells's novel is an allegory, he offers a key to more deeply understanding its meaning in his introduction to the 1924 Atlantic edition, in which he describes *The Island of Dr. Moreau* as youthful blasphemy. An initial review of the book in the *Guardian* of June 3, 1896 (reprinted in Parrinder's critical anthology), takes up this theme and claims that Wells's "object seems to be to parody the work of the Creator of the human race, and cast contempt upon the dealings of God with His creatures." Wells's own beliefs oscillated between deism and atheism, and certainly he considered religion, especially his native Christianity, as a regressive force in society. That he would write such a work is hardly surprising.

Wells examined Christianity in the funhouse mirror and showed his readers a distortion of the faith that revealed his criticisms of it. Moreau acts the part of the misshapen god. He is the creator of the Beast People, a kind of

WHAT DO I READ NEXT?

- *The League of Extraordinary Gentlemen* is a comic book series begun in 1999 by writer Alan Moore and illustrator Kevin O'Neil. It takes place in Edwardian London and features characters, including Doctor Moreau and Edward Prendick, from several novels and stories of that era written by H. G. Wells, Arthur Conan Doyle, Jules Verne, Bram Stoker, H. Rider Haggard, and other writers.

- Richard Consta's *H. G. Wells*, revised in 1985 for Twayne's English Authors Series, provides a general introduction to Wells and his writing.

- *Fruits Basket*, a young-adult manga series by Natsuki Takaya serialized in Japan from 1999 through 2006 and published in U.S. editions from 2004 to 2009, deals with a curse that turns members of a prominent family into animals of the Chinese zodiac. The cursed characters are human most of the time, but often view themselves as monsters.

- Joseph D. Andrioano's *Immortal Monster* (1999) discusses *The Island of Dr. Moreau* in connection with its film adaptations and in the genre of fictional monsters.

- Part of the power of the concept of *The Island of Dr. Moreau* comes from its updated treatment of the boundary that exists between animal and human. This idea is a prominent feature of world mythology in the concept of half-human, half-animal creatures, such as a faun, and of beings such as werewolves that can change between the two states. Rosemary Guiley's 2004 *The Encyclopedia of Vampires, Werewolves, and Other Monsters*, published for young adults, surveys world mythology and folklore for such monstrous crossovers of the human-animal boundary.

- Edwin Black's popular 2004 history of the eugenics movement, *War against the Weak: Eugenics and America's Campaign to Create a Master Race*, shows how the eugenics movement and the Holocaust arose from pseudo-scientific misunderstandings of biological science.

- Of Wells's own works, his 1895 novel, *The Time Machine*, most closely approaches *The Island of Dr. Moreau*'s theme of human degeneration.

---

intelligent designer who is not satisfied with evolution and takes matters into his own hands. He changes the animals from the shape into which they had been fashioned by natural selection and reshapes them toward an arbitrarily chosen form, his own. He thus acts out the book of Genesis: "And God said, Let us make man in our image, after our likeness." The Beast People are given a set of laws that satirize the form and language of the Ten Commandments and the Mosaic Law:

> Not to go on all-fours; *that* is the Law. Are we not Men?
> Not to suck up Drink; *that* is the Law. Are we not Men?
> Not to eat Flesh or Fish; *that* is the Law. Are we not Men?

> Not to claw Bark of Trees; *that* is the Law. Are we not Men?
> Not to chase other Men; *that* is the Law. Are we not Men?

Just as the Ten Commandments enshrine moral laws that are common to all societies, whether or not they follow one of the Abrahamic faiths, such as to not murder and steal, Moreau's Law defines the things that men do by nature, that would require no legal injunction, except among animals who are not men.

Nor can there be any question that the Beast People imagine Moreau to be God when they give him all of God's cosmic attributes: "*His* is the lightning flash . . . *His* is the deep, salt sea . . . *His* are the stars in the sky." Moreau is also the master of the House of Pain, his surgical laboratory, where he corrects the Beast People's failed humanity through vivisection. These failures come about when the beasts' natural animal instincts reassert themselves, as expressed in their liturgical formula: "For every one the want is bad." Sooner or later, a Beast-man will want to taste blood or claw a tree, natural impulses the Law denies as forbidden. In other words, desire leads to sin. Prendick sees that Moreau is wantonly cruel in punishing the Beast People for being what they are, and that the failure is Moreau's, since as he admits, he has never yet got his work in making Beast People right and they always revert. There is something pathetic in the Ape-man's gratitude for his punishment: "I am burnt, branded in the hand. He is great. He is good."

Wells hopes that his reader will start to think about Christian doctrines like original sin in the same light. Similarly, Prendick points out about the Beast People that "during these earlier days of my stay they broke the Law only furtively and after dark; in the daylight there was a general atmosphere of respect for its multifarious prohibitions." Any reader of *Dr. Jekyll and Mr. Hyde* or *The Picture of Dorian Gray* would recognize this as a criticism of the hypocritical actions of carousal and prostitution that were a prominent feature of British aristocratic life in the 1890s, despite high society's pious Christian façade.

The Beast People are largely kept in control by their fear of Moreau and his House of Pain. When they discover that he has died, they undergo a crisis of faith and begin to think that it may be possible to disregard the Law. This threatens the safety of Prendick and Montgomery, but the former is quick to supply them with new doctrines to continue the religious control of their behavior:

> "Children of the Law . . . he is *not* dead! . . . He has changed his shape; he has changed his body . . . For a time you will not see him. He is—there," I pointed upward, "where he can watch you. You cannot see him, but he can see you. Fear the Law!"

No reader can help but realize that Prendick is lying, and again Wells's intention is to make the reader think about his own religious beliefs: to what extent are they mere tools of social control?

One of the Beast People, the Saint-Bernard-man, supplies the final religious element, the apocalyptic return of God and the destruction of the Beast People. The Saint-Bernard-man tells Prendick that the other Beast People no longer believe that Moreau exists or that Prendick is a divine being, but he, the dog, is faithful to the truth. The other animals do not believe, but faithlessly pretend they will keep the Law (from a Christian viewpoint, these would be secularists like Wells himself). One day, the Saint-Bernard-man believes, Prendick will reveal his hidden divinity and then kill all of the faithless. This prospect fills the Saint-Bernard-man with joy. Prendick has no choice but to go along with this to at least keep the Saint-Bernard-man's loyalty as a bodyguard against the other Beast People. If the reader is shocked by the bloodthirstiness of the Saint-Bernard-man's fantasies, Wells hopes, he might find himself thinking about the similarities to Christian apocalyptic expectations.

The basic idea about religions that Wells offers is that, for all their utility as a means of social control, they are inherently false, even immoral. It was a conclusion Wells reached for himself when he was twelve years old in a dream he recounted in his autobiography:

> But one night I had a dream of Hell so preposterous that it blasted that undesirable resort out of my mind forever. In an old number of *Chambers Journal* I had read of the punishment of breaking a man on the wheel. The horror of it got into my dreams and there was Our Father in a particularly malignant phase, busy basting a poor broken sinner rotating slowly over a fire built under the wheel. I saw no Devil in the vision; my mind in its simplicity went straight to the responsible fountain head. That dream pursued me into the day. Never had I hated God so intensely.

Once Wells came to believe that god the creator was ultimately responsible for human suffering and supernatural punishment, the whole system no longer made sense to him: God was punishing his imperfectly made creatures for their imperfections that He himself had made. The figure of Moreau the creator, the giver of the Law, and master of the House of Pain, was a way of explaining this unsettling realization to an audience little prepared to hear it.

Wells suggests in *The Island of Dr. Moreau* that, while human civilization could not exist without some kind of social control, the control exercised by religion rests on a false foundation: "An animal may be ferocious and cunning enough, but

Some of the island people resembled wild hogs. *(Eduard Kyslynskyy / Shutterstock.com)*

it takes a real man to tell a lie." Wells's teacher Thomas Huxley stated that while human bodies are no longer shaped by natural selection, human society is capable of growth and change. This may have suggested to Wells that a new social arrangement not deceptive to the masses was ready to emerge. Indeed, much of Wells's later career was devoted to trying to imagine that order. Remarkably, because Wells preceded him in publication by decades but is rarely credited with the fact, the psychoanalyst Sigmund Freud came to precisely the same conclusion in his 1927 *The Future of an Illusion.*

For Freud, religion as a social control was breaking down as the sciences, including the philological sciences, showed errors in sacred texts. Like Wells, Freud was highly conscious of class and noted that the greater mass of the laboring classes in Christian Europe and America did not fully enjoy the fruits of civilization. They thus had little reason to protect it if the regulating forces of religious belief were removed. In his view the upper classes were in the same position as Prendick, protected from revolution by religion and having little recourse but physical violence if religions should fail: "Thus either the dangerous masses must be held down most severely and

kept most carefully away from any chance of intellectual awakening, or else the relationship between civilization and religion must undergo a fundamental revision. " Wells had faith that a classless restructuring of society, so that the great mass of men did fully enjoy the benefits of civilization, was the answer to the problem. *The Island of Dr. Moreau* shows that for Wells, religion was a relic of the past, an organ of human culture becoming vestigial.

Source: Bradley Skeen, Critical Essay on *The Island of Dr. Moreau,* in *Novels for Students,* Gale, Cengage Learning, 2011.

Alex MacDonald

In the following essay, MacDonald details the symbolic depiction of cultural disorder in Yeats's poem "The Second Coming" and Wells's The Island of Dr. Moreau.

The words "passionate intensity" seem to belong to Yeats because of his publication in 1919 of these famous lines:

The best lack all conviction, while the worst
Are full of passionate intensity.

(Yeats)

However, twenty-three years earlier, in 1896, the expression appeared in *The Island of Doctor Moreau* by H. G. Wells. Edward Prendick lands on an island where the notorious vivisectionist, Doctor Moreau, conducts experiments upon animals. After many frightening experiences, Prendick throws open a door and sees "something bound painfully upon a framework, scarred, red and bandaged." Moreau appears and lifts Prendick as though he were a little child. Prendick says: "I fell at full length upon the floor, and the door slammed and shut out the passionate intensity of his face." How to explain the echo of Wells's novel in Yeats's poem is an interesting question, but, as always in such cases, the significance of the echo is not its mere existence but what it means, or what we think it means.

A case for conscious borrowing by Yeats would have to be based upon direct evidence of some kind. Although Yeats and Wells seem to have been very casually acquainted (Pritchett 348), I have not found evidence that Yeats owned a copy of Wells's novel, that he read it, or that he knew of the passage from some other source. That does not mean, of course, that Yeats did not know the novel.

The case for unconscious influence is based on the familiar idea of defense mechanisms. M. H. Abrams summarizes Harold Bloom's suggestion that a later author is in the ambivalent position of son to father. The influence occurs, but the writer "unconsciously safeguards his own sense of autonomy and priority by reading a parent-poem 'defensively,' in such a way as to distort it beyond his own conscious recognition." This is a sensible explanation of the common phenomenon of forgetting or transforming influences, and perhaps it applies to Yeats in this case.

In support of the view that there was at least an unconscious influence are many similarities between the novel and the poem, including the animal and animal-human imagery, the sense of blind historical forces working, as Prendick says, like a "vast pitiless mechanism," and the coming of anarchy. Eventually Moreau's poor creatures escape confinement, falcons who cannot hear their falconer, and go "rushing about mad." They kill Moreau, their creator, a god who gave them their "law"—fixed ideas to counter their natural instincts. Their reversion to bestiality suggests Yeats's rough beast and the disorder it heralds. Prendick, lacking "all conviction," reproaches

himself for not taking control of the island and for letting his courage "ebb away in solitary thought." His final retreat to an isolated house is an attempt to escape from the realization that the civilized world is really not civilized at all. There is so much in both works that suggests the existential crisis of the early twentieth century, such overlap in ideas and atmosphere, that the argument for influence can seem compelling.

However, work by scholars on other possible sources, and on Yeats's process of composition, tends to dilute the case for influence. T. R. Henn suggests that Yeats was echoing lines from Shelley's *Prometheus Unbound*: "The good want power, but to weep barren tears, / The powerful goodness want," a suggestion supported by A. Norman Jeffares. Geoffrey Thurley relates the lines to the anticipation of an age of disorder in Wordsworth's *Prelude X*. A number of possible influences, for the passage if not for the particular expression, has the effect of reducing the apparent significance of any one influence.

Accounts of the process of composition of "The Second Coming" weaken the case for influence in a different way, by suggesting how Yeats may have arrived at the expression independently. Yeats first used the word "intensity," crossed it out, then settled upon "passionate intensity." From the second section of the poem he discarded some lines that used the word "intensity" in a less interesting way: "Scarce have the words been spoken / and a new intensity rent as it were cloth / Before the dark was cut as with a knife" (Stallworthy 22). This suggests that Yeats developed some lines of what Ezra Pound called work of "second intensity" and refined them toward their final expression independent of any outside influences. However, the possibility that Yeats was influenced by Wells is certainly not disproved by these other possibilities, no more than it is proved by similarities in the two texts.

If Yeats did not read Wells's novel and if the expression was not transmitted via other works, then this was not a case of influence but of coincidence. There are only so many ways to express ideas, and for two writers to hit upon the same words to express a similar theme is not all that surprising. However, Graham Hough seemed to recognize the interestingness of this particular echo when he wrote an imaginary dialogue between the rationalist and the mythologist after the deaths of Wells and Yeats:

W. ... if Homo Sapiens is such a fool that he cannot realise even now what is before him, he is not worth pity. Those who see will not or cannot act: those who act are the blind and the greedy, the intriguers and the thugs.

Y. The best lack all conviction while the worst are full of passionate intensity.

W. Who said that?

Y. I, years ago.

W. You were right.

I do not know whether Hough consciously had Moreau in mind, whether the expression "passionate intensity" in both sources might have connected the two works in his subconscious mind and prompted the idea for this imaginary dialogue, or whether this is simply another coincidence.

Computer scanning of texts would undoubtedly reveal that such echoes, or coincidences, are much more common than might be thought from the isolated examples we happen to notice. Another example is Thoreau's famous statement that "the mass of men lead lives of quiet desperation," in a passage in *Walden* (1854) in which prison is mentioned. This is echoed by some words of Pip's in *Great Expectations* (1860–61): "'I wonder who's put into prison ships, and why they're put there?' said [Pip] in a general way, and with quiet desperation." In this case, the expression is attributed in the quotations dictionaries to Thoreau, probably because he used it first and because the context in *Walden* is broader and closer to the epigrammatic.

The repetition of "passionate intensity" could be, therefore, a conscious echo, an unconscious echo, a drawing by all concerned upon some archetypal "passionate intensity" in the "Spiritus Mundi," or a coincidence that I happened to recognize, or to construct, because it resonated with something in my own psyche. Whatever the explanation for the echo, it draws our attention to one of the critical moral problems of this century. Both the novel and the poem use the expression to define those who are evil or who lack moral convictions to prevent them from doing evil. Specifically, Moreau is the "mad scientist" who misuses the Promethean fire and whose fanatical curiosity leads him to commit atrocities. His character exemplifies the destructive power of human intelligence without values and ideals. Both works can now be understood as foreshadowing the rise of fascism, which promised order

at the cost of humanity. The sphinx-like beast of Yeats's poem evokes fear of a new world of savagery, regression, and disorder, and it threatens the vision, as does Moreau, of a utopia of abundance based on the wise application of human intelligence to solving problems. This positive vision, the mirror-image of the negative vision of the poem, is suggested in Yeats's long note to the poem, in which the word "intensity" is used in the positive context of the "Beatific Vision" (*Variorum Edition* 824). Both works imply the contrary to their bleak visions, that the "passionate intensity" for good, by appropriate means, is what is needed, rather than complicity or apathetic despair.

Source: Alex MacDonald, "'Passionate Intensity' in Wells's *The Island of Dr. Moreau* and Yeats's 'The Second Coming': Constructing an Echo," in *ANQ*, Vol. 9, No. 4, Fall 1996, pp. 40–43.

Darren Harris-Fain

In the following review, Harris-Fain focuses on the comprehensive notes and appendices included in The Island of Dr. Moreau: A Variorum Edition.

At present, science fiction scholarship is a tenuous field at best, often misunderstood and unsupported by colleagues who, for all the recent challenges to the literary canon, fail to see any value in the endeavor. It is encouraging, then, to look at the work of scholars like Robert M. Philmus, work that has enriched our understanding and appreciation of a literature we love and that lends credibility to the study of science fiction. In particular, Philmus's variorum edition of *The Island of Doctor Moreau* is a shining example of the quality of work that can and should be done in the field.

The significance of this book, according to Philmus and his publisher, is that it is the first variorum edition of any work by H. G. Wells or, for that matter, any work of SF. It's doubtful that, say, *Slan* or *The Skylark of Space* merits this kind of treatment, but the absence of previous scholarship of this sort for Wells is both striking and deplorable, an indication of the relative neglect Wells has undeservedly received.

Philmus's claim for the book as the first of its kind in this area is a bit of a slam at the edition of *The Time Machine* that appeared in 1987, although he graciously thanks its editor in the acknowledgments, among others. There is a difference between the two books, however; this is altogether a different kind of beast. As a variorum edition, Philmus's book provides a text of Wells's powerful, resonant novel that represents the most authoritative version scholarship could possibly produce. Through a scrupulously detailed history of the novel's inception and publication, Philmus's introduction fully describes the differences in Wells's manuscripts and the corrections he made in the various proofs and published editions. An authoritative text of *Moreau* [*The Island of Doctor Moreau*], he argues, would logically entail a variorum edition due to the complexity of the novel's story and the competing claims to authority of its different versions. The result here is a painstakingly reconstructed text, with variants and rationales for editorial decisions described in copious but relatively unobtrusive footnotes. The authority of this particular text is by no means absolute, as Philmus explains, but this is as close as we are ever likely to get, and scholars will have to reckon with it in making interpretive claims about *Moreau*.

Were this the extent of Philmus's contribution, it would be enough to commend the book. Fortunately, there's more. In addition to its skillful recounting of the stages of Wells's novel, the introduction provides much of interest beyond the editorial work that, as such work should, lays the foundation for literary criticism. These include compelling links between certain facts of Wells's life (especially his illnesses) and his early fiction; a good overview of scholarship on Wells; an excellent examination of possible influences, intellectual and literary, on *Moreau*; and several insightful interpretations of the novel's themes. While the minutiae concerning textual variants and the accompanying apparatus may be somewhat dry for all but the most assiduous of Wells scholars, such passages demonstrate that well-reasoned and well-researched textual editing can establish the basis for persuasive criticism.

Nor is everything pertaining to the textual development of *Moreau* entirely isolated *ipso facto* from interpretive matters, for, as Philmus points out in the introduction, an analysis of alternations [sic] in "matters of content . . . point[s] to meaningful aspects of the text that might otherwise escape our attention." For instance, Wells's observations on colonialism, his linking of alcohol use and bestiality, and constructions of gender in this work are all highlighted by examining original manuscripts and revisions he made at various points in the text's development. Additionally, by studying Wells at work one can see that, while he worked quickly,

he also revised extensively, at least in his early scientific romances.

Added to all of this helpful material are endnotes annotating the more obscure references in *Moreau* and eight appendices, including a transcription of the first manuscript (one of whose more interesting features is the existence of a Mrs. Moreau and son!) and other manuscript data. A transcription of a draft of a scientific essay by Wells bearing on the composition of *Moreau* differing from its publication in the *Fortnightly Review* is here as well. Of interest also is the appendix listing works, "*Moreau*'s Literary 'Children,'" influenced by Wells's novel, many of them quite obscure.

Philmus is to be praised for bringing together so much work in such a compact and accessible volume. His previous contributions to SF scholarship in general, and Wellsian scholarship in particular, are substantial, as seen in his many writings on Wells and SF included in the selected bibliography on *Moreau* that ends the book. Recently retired but still active with *Science-Fiction Studies*, Philmus here delivers a fitting capstone to his career, though of course one hopes it is by no means his last offering to the field. As with his earlier scholarship, he has provided a valuable contribution to an area of study that needs intelligent work. In SF there is a hard enough time keeping books in print, let alone being able to establish dependable texts for them. For this reason, the University of Georgia Press is also to be commended for publishing such a book in such a professional and attractive format. If they were to follow with a paperback version that would increase the book's availability to students and its use as a classroom text, this would certainly be the best of all possible worlds.

Source: Darren Harris-Fain, "Review of *The Island of Dr. Moreau: A Variorum Edition* by H. G. Wells," edited by Robert M. Philmus, in *Extrapolation*, Vol. 35, No. 1, Spring 1994, pp. 80–82.

Spectator

In the following excerpted review, an assumption is made by critics that The Island of Dr. Moreau *served some didactic purpose such as promoting antivivisectionism.*

The ingenious author of *The Time Machine* has found in [*The Island of Dr. Moreau*] a subject exactly suited to his rather peculiar type of imagination. When he tried to conceive the idea of making a man of the nineteenth century *travel* in time, so that he was at the same moment both contemporary with and far removed from the people of a prehistoric age, he conceived an idea which was really quite too self-contradictory to be worked out with any sort of coherence. But in this little book he has worked out a notion much less intrinsically incoherent, and though impossible, yet not so impossible as to be quite inconceivable. In other words, the impossibility is of a less unworkable order, though it is also much more gruesome. He has taken a few of the leading methods of the modern surgery and exaggerated them in the hands of an accomplished vivisector into a new physiological calculus that enables its professor to transmute various animals into the semblance of man.... It should be explained that the accomplished vivisector described has found a small island in the Pacific far out of the track of ordinary mariners where he can practise his gruesome manipulations of living organisms without fear of being disturbed.... Of course, the real value for literary purposes of this ghastly conception depends on the power of the author to make his readers realise the half-way stages between the brute and the rational creature, with which he has to deal. And we must admit that Mr. Wells succeeds in this little story in giving a most fearful vividness to his picture of half-created monsters endowed with a little speech, a little human curiosity, a little sense of shame, and an overgrown dread of the pain and terror which the scientific dabbler in creative processes had inflicted. There is nothing in Swift's grim conceptions of animalised man and rationalised animals more powerfully conceived than Mr. Wells's description of these deformed and malformed creations of Dr. Moreau, repeating the litany in which they abase themselves before the physiological demigod by whom they have been endowed with their new powers of speech, their new servility to a human master, and their profound dread of that "house of pain" in which they have been made and fashioned into half-baked men. The hero of the story, who has been thrown into Dr. Moreau's grisly society, comes suddenly on the huts of these spoiled animals who have been fashioned into a bad imitation of men, and hears them proclaim their new law in the following creed:...

> 'Not to go on all-Fours; *that* is the Law. Are we not Men?' 'Not to suck up Drink; *that* is the Law. Are we not Men?' 'Not to eat Flesh nor Fish; *that* is the Law. Are we not Men?' 'Not to

> claw Bark of Trees; *that* is the Law. Are we not Men,?' 'Not to chase other Men; *that* is the Law. Are we not Men?'...

> '*His* is the House of Pain. *His* is the Hand that makes. *His* is the Hand that wounds. *His* is the Hand that heals.'...

Our readers may gain from this passage some faint idea of the power with which this grim conception of the mauling and maiming of brutes into bad imitations of human beings has been worked out by Mr. Wells. It is, of course, a very ingenious caricature of what has been done in certain exceptional efforts of human surgery,—a caricature inspired by the fanaticism of a foul ambition to remake God's creatures by confusing and transfusing and remoulding human and animal organs so as to extinguish so far as possible the chasm which divides man from brute. Mr. Wells has had the prudence, too, not to dwell on the impossibilities of his subject too long. He gives us a very slight, though a very powerful and ghastly, picture, and may, we hope, have done more to render vivisection unpopular, and that contempt for animal pain, which enthusiastic physiologists seem to feel, hideous, than all the efforts of the societies which have been organised for that wholesome and beneficent end. Dr. Moreau is a figure to make an impression on the imagination, and his tragic death under the attack of the puma which he has been torturing so long, has a kind of poetic justice in it which satisfies the mind of the reader. Again, the picture of the rapid reversion to the brute, of the victims which Dr. Moreau had so painfully fashioned, so soon as the terrors of his "house of pain" are withdrawn, is very impressively painted. Altogether, though we do not recommend *The Island of Dr. Moreau* to readers of sensitive nerves, as it might well haunt them only too powerfully, we believe that Mr. Wells has almost rivalled Swift in the power of his very gruesome, but very salutary as well as impressive, conception.

Source: "A Review of *The Island of Dr. Moreau*," in *Spectator*, Vol. 76, No. 3537, April 11, 1896, pp. 519–20.

SOURCES

Aldiss, Brian, and David Wingrove, *Trillion Year Spree: The History of Science Fiction*, V. Gollancz, 1986.

Freud, Sigmund, *The Future of an Illusion*, translated by James Strachey, W. W. Norton, 1961.

Galton, Francis, "Eugenics: Its Definition, Scope, and Aims," in *American Journal of Sociology*, Vol. 10, July/May 1904–1905, pp. 10–11.

Guerrini, Anita, *Experimenting with Humans and Animals from Galen to Animal Rights*, Johns Hopkins University Press, 2003.

Holzberg, Niklas, *The Ancient Novel: An Introduction*, translated by Christine Jackson-Hollzberg, Routledge, 1995.

Huxley, Thomas H., *Evolution and Ethics and Other Essays*, D. Appleton, 1920, pp. 1–45, http://books.google.com/books?id=CbzZAAAAMAAJ&source=gbs_navlinks_s (accessed June 30, 2010).

Kemp, Peter, *H. G. Wells and the Culminating Ape: Biological Imperatives and Imaginative Observations*, Macmillan, 1992, pp. 19–23, 201–203.

McLean, Steven, *The Early Fictions of H. G. Wells: Fantasies of Science*, Palgrave MacMillan, 2009, pp. 41–61.

Parrinder, Patrick, ed., *H. G. Wells: The Critical Heritage*, Routledge and Kegan Paul, 1972, pp. 43–56, 330–32.

Reed, John R., "The Vanity of Law in *The Island of Dr. Moreau*," in *H. G. Wells under Revision: Proceedings of the International H. G. Wells Symposium, London, 1986*, edited by Patrick Parrinder and Christopher Rolfe, Susquehanna University Press, 1990, pp. 132–43.

Rupke, Nicolaas, A., *Vivisection in Historical Perspective*, Welcome Institute, 1990.

Smith, David C., *H. G. Wells: Desperately Mortal, A Biography*, Yale University Press, 1986.

Stover, Leon, "Applied Natural History: Wells vs. Huxley," in *H. G. Wells under Revision: Proceedings of the International H. G. Wells Symposium, London, 1986*, edited by Patrick Parrinder and Christopher Rolfe, Susquehanna University Press, 1990, pp. 125–33.

Swift, Jonathan, *Gulliver's Travels*, Oxford University Press, 1919.

Wells, H. G., *Experiment in Autobiography: Discoveries and Conclusions of a Very Ordinary Brain (Since 1866)*, MacMillan, 1934.

———, *The Island of Doctor Moreau: A Variorum Text*, edited by Robert M. Philmus, University of Georgia Press, 1993.

———, *The Island of Dr. Moreau: A Critical Text of the 1896 London First Edition, with an Introduction and Appendices*, edited by Leon Stover, McFarlane, 1996.

———, *Works, Vol II: The Island of Dr. Moreau, The Sleeper Wakes*, Charles Scribner, 1924.

Williamson, Jack, *H. G. Wells: Critic of Progress*, Mirage, 1973, pp.74–82.

FURTHER READING

Draper, Michael, *Modern Novelists: H. G. Wells*, St. Martin's Press, 1988.
> Draper provides a biographical and literary survey of Wells's work.

Hammond, J. R., *H. G. Wells: Interviews and Recollections*, Barnes & Noble, 1980.
> Hammond collects press interviews and brief autobiographical published articles with or by Wells.

Kevles, Daniel J., *In the Name of Eugenics: Genetics and the Uses of Human Heredity*, Harvard University Press, 1995.
> Kevles chronicles the standard history of the eugenics movement.

Suvin, Darko, and Robert M. Philmus, eds., *H. G. Wells and Modern Science Fiction*, Bucknell University Press, 1977.
> This anthology contains scholarly articles analyzing Wells from a variety of perspectives. Several touch on *The Island of Dr. Moreau* in relation to traditional folklore and fantasy literature, rather than science fiction.

SUGGESTED SEARCH TERMS

H. G. Wells

The Island of Dr. Moreau

science fiction

H. G. Wells AND science fiction

H. G. Wells AND Aldous Huxley

scientific romance

Wells AND Evolution

Wells AND eugenics

Moreau AND Gustave

genetic engineering

Lord of the Flies

1963

The 1963 film of *Lord of the Flies*, based on Nobel-prize winning author William Golding's first novel, is considered a modern film classic. Golding's novel was not a commercial success upon its publication in 1954, going out of publication after selling just a few thousand copies. By the end of the decade, though, it was being assigned often as required reading in schools. Still, it might have been forgotten if it had not been brought to the attention of renowned stage director Peter Brook, at that time primarily known for his work in theater and as a director of television plays. Brook filmed a cast of unknown actors in jungles in and near Puerto Rico, taking two years to edit down the sixty hours of film he had shot into a coherent narrative. The resulting film was nominated for the Golden Palm award at the Cannes Film Festival when it was released by Janus Films in 1963, and it has been considered an important film and one of the great film adaptations of a novel since its release.

Though he did not shoot with a formal script and therefore does not use all of Golding's precise dialogue, Brook did structure the final film to follow the novel's story closely. It tells the story of a group of schoolboys who, in the process of being evacuated from London during a mythical war, end up stranded on a deserted island in the Pacific Ocean. Social order is formed but then abandoned as fear, hunger, and a propensity toward tribalism cause the

boys to turn against each other. The change in the boys over the course of the film is shocking and yet understandable. Brook, like Golding, questions whether savage behaviors are traits taught by some cultures or are inherent in human nature, revealing themselves in children who have not learned to keep their brutal appetites in check.

PLOT SUMMARY

The opening credits of *Lord of the Flies* roll over a series of still photographs, establishing background information that Golding never spells out explicitly in his novel. Under the soothing sounds of a school master lecturing and choirboys singing, photos show what life at a British public school would be like. The music turns more ominous as missiles are shown, introducing the coming war. Planes flying into smoky skies and one falling to earth after a flash of lightning indicate how the boys all came to be stranded on a remote island in the Pacific ocean, a fact that Golding's novel conveys by stating that they were being evacuated from an unspecified war.

The story begins with Ralph, in his school uniform, wandering alone through the forest. He is met by a boy with glasses who does not give his name but only says that he does not want to be called by the name they called him at school, which is Piggy. On the beach, they come across a conch shell, and Piggy, having seen one like it before, tells Ralph how to blow it to make a trumpeting sound. As Ralph blows it, children come out of the forest in response.

A regiment of disciplined children in heavy black cloaks comes marching up the beach. They are a choir, led by Jack, who eventually gives them permission to remove their capes and stand at ease. In introducing each other, Jack refers to the boy with glasses as "Fatty," and Ralph volunteers that his name is actually Piggy, to the delight of the other boys. After a brief discussion, the boys decide that they ought to elect a leader. Jack nominates himself, but the majority votes for Ralph. Ralph takes Jack and Simon with him to explore the island, leaving Piggy behind to learn each of the boys' names.

Ralph, Jack, and Simon find a boulder perched at the edge of a cliff and work together to push it over, establishing their curiosity about the powers of destruction. Later in their trip, they come close to a piglet in the woods. Jack takes out his knife and holds it to the pig's throat, but finds himself unable to stab it. As Simon examines a flower with curiosity, Jack slashes menacingly at the flower, frustrated with his own humanity.

In a meeting, Ralph and Piggy explain the importance of keeping a fire going at the top of the mountain, so that a plane passing by might see its smoke. One of the unnamed little children, speaking through Piggy, tells the crowd that he has seen a "snake-thing" or "beastie" that comes from the water. The children laugh, but they are wary.

At the top of the mountain, they realize that they do not have the capacity to make fire, but then they take Piggy's glasses and use them as a prism, concentrating the sunlight onto a leaf that bursts into flame. Jack volunteers his choir members, who designate themselves as the island's hunters, to tend the fire.

Soon, Jack and the other boys find a pig and take off hunting it. While they are caught up in the excitement of the chase, they let the fire burn out. Down on the beach, Piggy hears a plane overhead and tells Ralph, who is swimming. They race to the top of the mountain. A confrontation takes place between Jack, who defends his actions because he caught a pig, and Ralph, who is enraged that a chance to be rescued was lost because of the spent signal fire. Piggy shouts at the hunters, and Jack, unwilling to fight against the island leader, walks over to him and slaps him. Piggy's glasses fall on a rock, and one lens shatters.

At a meeting, Percival Wemys Madison, one of the younger boys, tells the others about a beast he saw coming out of the ocean. The boys are uneasy. Jack says that his "warriors" will fight the beast. Simon suggests that the beast might be the boys themselves. Ralph wonders out loud if it might be a ghost, and most of the boys vote their belief that ghosts exist. Piggy adamantly states that he does not believe that ghosts exist, which enrages Jack. He leads the boys off on a hunt.

Later, on the hill, Sam and Eric wake to find that they have let the fire go out. They look over a ridge and see something that terrifies them and sends them running back to the base near the beach, explaining the terrible thing they saw. A

FILM TECHNIQUE

Black-and-White Film

The fact that this film was made on a tight, independent budget might account for the fact that it was filmed on black-and-white stock. In 1963, color film had been in common usage for more than twenty years. Audiences were used to major studio releases in color, and so *Lord of the Flies* would not have been a success if its black-and-white visuals were not appropriate. Brook and his crew used the hues of black, white, and gray to emphasize particular elements, creating stark contrasts sometimes, such as when the black-clad choir members walk up along the white beach, or the stark contrast between the naval uniforms and the tanned boys, or when the white body paint stands out during the bonfire ritual. In scenes shot in bright sunlight, the shadows of the trees across the characters' faces are more pronounced when color is absent.

Dubbing

Because this film was shot in tropical outdoor locations rather than in a studio, the sound of the wind and ocean made it impossible for the cameras to pick up the dialogue the boys spoke as the cameras rolled. After each day's filming, they went back to a studio and read their lines into a microphone, and more than a year of editing was required to synchronize voices with actions. The only scene with direct sound is the one in which Piggy tells the younger boys about Camberley, which was filmed in a studio. Often, audiences cannot see characters' faces when they talk, though their words sound as if they are speaking directly toward the audience. This explains some of the feeling of tribal community created in the film, as voices come from unexpected directions, disorienting the viewer,

similar to the way Ralph is disoriented by sounds in the film's chaotic final scenes.

Low Angle

This film is often shot from a low angle, with the camera closer to the ground than to the actors' faces. Often, a low angle has the effect of making the character seem larger and therefore more imposing. In the low-angle shots, however, Brook often leaves ample room for the sky or trees in the background behind his actors' heads. The resulting images achieve the opposite of the usual effect, emphasizing the boys' smallness in comparison to the natural world surrounding them.

Close-Up

The phrase "lord of the flies" is not used in this film. The novel, but not the film, contains a scene in which the pig's head talks to Simon, identifying itself. Instead, Brook conveys what Simon comes to understand from it by filming the decaying head with a close-up shot. As they watch flies land on the pig and hear the exaggerated sound of the flies' buzzing, viewers can imagine a message being conveyed from the pig's head toward the camera.

Long Shot

The boys are often filmed as a group, in a long shot, with the camera situated far away in order to capture them together. The long shots treat the boys as what they are: a group and, later, a tribe. There are only a few stand-out characters: Ralph, Piggy, Jack, Simon, Roger, and the twins. These characters are given independent scenes with one or two or three actors talking, but the way that Brook uses long shots creates a single united personality out of a group of ten or twenty characters.

---

hunting party goes out, leaving Piggy behind with the young children. Left alone with the young children, Piggy bores them with a story about how the place where he lives, Camberley,

was given its name. The hunters come across the thing that Sam and Eric saw and, still not recognizing it as a dead parachutist, they run, terrified. At the meeting when they return to camp,

© *Photos 12 / Alamy*

Jack brands Ralph as a coward. He leaves alone, inviting the others to join him.

Roger is the first boy to join Jack. They paint their bodies and faces with berries. In the following scenes, they are joined by more and more boys, and they become more and more elaborately painted. When they do capture a pig, Jack commands the boys to put its head on a stick that is sharpened at both ends, as an appeasement to the beast.

Simon wanders across the pig head, which is covered with flies. In Golding's novel, the head talks to Simon, announcing itself as the Lord of the Flies. In the film, though, the eerie sound of flies buzzing is used to convey the misery in Simon's mind.

Jack and his hunters attack Ralph's band on the beach to steal fire from them. They have a nighttime feast with the pig they caught and offer meat to Ralph and his people if they will join them. The feast becomes more frantic and

primal, with chants about killing the beast, dancing, and screaming. Simon, who has looked at the dead parachutist on the mountain, arrives to tell them that it is nothing to fear, but as he comes out of the darkened jungle the overexcited boys identify him as the beast. They attack and kill him, leaving his body to float off in the surf.

The next morning, Ralph talks about the death of Simon, but Piggy tries to stop him from saying that the boy was murdered. They realize that no one has stayed with them to tend the signal fire except Sam and Eric. They agree that there is going to be real trouble on the island soon.

In his fort, Jack has a boy whipped. He promises the other boys a feast the next day; when someone asks how they can start a fire, he leads them in the night to steal Piggy's glasses.

Blind without his glasses, Piggy has Ralph and Sam and Eric lead him to Jack's camp, where the boys are all painted like savages and armed with spears. He cannot climb up to them, but Ralph does, angering Jack by calling him a common thief. While they fight with each other, Piggy asks the boys who are jeering him if it is better to be savages, or to be sensible like Ralph. Roger, up at the top of the hill, pushes a lever wedged under a boulder. It rolls down the hill and crushes Piggy to death. Ralph runs away in fear.

Later, Ralph climbs the hill and finds Sam and Eric with painted faces—they have been incorporated into the tribe. They quietly tell him to run and hide, saying that Jack has ordered them to capture him and has said that the boys should sharpen a stick on both ends for when they catch him. The implication is that his head will be removed and put on the sharpened stake, the way the pig's head was. When some-one comes, Ralph flees and hides in a thicket.

Ralph wakes up the next morning to the sounds of boys, led by Sam and Eric, whispering outside the thicket. When someone reaches in, he pokes with his own pointed weapon, which they take as a sign that he is dangerous. The fire begun to smoke him out of the thicket grows. As he runs, he hears the boys beating drums and chanting about killing the pig, and the smoke around him thickens.

By the time Ralph reaches the beach, the entire island behind him appears to be on fire, and the chanting is deafening. He falls to his knees, crawling in the tattered remains of his clothes, and is suddenly stopped when he comes across a pair of white shoes. All sound stops. The camera pans slowly up the front of a naval officer standing calmly in the sand. He turns to look at other white-clad naval officers as the other boys run out of the jungle and put their weapons down. Unlike the scene in the book, no words are spoken between Ralph and the naval officer. As the sailors stand by their landing ship, discussing the sight of boys painted like savages and an island engulfed in flames, tears roll down Ralph's cheeks.

CHARACTERS

Jack

Jack is played by Tom Chapin. The novel gives Jack's last name as Merridew, though that name is not used in the film. Jack enters the story as the leader of a choir, directing them in a regimented

march and giving them orders. He quickly finds himself embarrassed when a vote is taken to choose a leader and the majority of boys choose Ralph. Throughout the film, Jack's actions, such as leading the hunt and calling the boys to follow what he self-consciously calls his tribe, often seem motivated by his struggle to bolster his self-esteem. This insecurity can be seen in several of his actions, such as when he slashes his knife close to Simon's face just after realizing that he does not have the nerve to stab a peaceful pig and when he leaves to form a new tribe after being frightened by the dead paratrooper he thought was the beast.

When the boys desert Ralph to follow Jack, the power goes to his head. At first, he issues orders and leads hunts, showing that they will be better fed and safer for following him. As time goes on, however, he adopts a regal bearing, treating the other boys as if they are there for his amusement. He makes rules about appeasing the beast and orders boys who displease him to be flogged. He eventually orders the death of Ralph, who was once his friend, to put an end to any potential for competition for leadership.

Percival Wemys Madison

Played by Kent Fletcher, Percival Wemys Madison is one of the few younger boys to have a speaking role. In the beginning of the film, when Piggy asks him his name, he responds with a memorized speech, reciting his full name and address. Later, when he is given the conch shell and allowed to talk to the entire assembled meeting, he gives his full name and address but is unable to come up with his phone number. He is embarrassed until the older boys encourage him, and then he whispers into Jack's ear about a beast that comes up out of the sea. Although his story echoes the one about a snake-like beast that was told earlier, it has a chilling effect. At the end of the story, when the naval officer appears, Percival Wemys Madison approaches him, but he finds himself unable to remember even his name.

The Naval Officer

At the end of the film, Ralph, being pursued by the other boys through the smoke of the burning forest, falls at the feet of a naval officer in a crisp white uniform. In Golding's novel, he engages in some dialogue with Ralph, but the film allows the look on his face to convey his assessment of the situation. After Ralph backs away from him,

Percival Wemys Madison steps forward and touches the officer's leg but is unable to say his own name: the naval officer stares, sympathetically, but after remaining patient for a few minutes, he turns away to issue orders to the other sailors in his landing party.

Piggy

Piggy is the most mature character in the film, and this trait earns him the scorn of the other boys. Hugh Edwards plays this role. Piggy is prevented from being as physically active as the other boys by his poor eyesight and his asthma. He often recalls the ways his aunt, who raised him, forbade him to participate in physical activities. His physical limitations make him view the world as an adult would. He frequently wishes that there were adults around and longs for the security of social order.

Piggy's adult viewpoint is one of the things that give the island what little social order it has. He cannot blow the conch shell himself, but he tells the athletic Ralph how to do it. The other boys make fun of him, particularly after Ralph reveals that his name is Piggy, but he continues to arrange rules about holding the conch to speak and keeping the fire going. Though Ralph is the elected leader, Piggy is the power behind the power.

Piggy's downfall comes gradually. After Jack strikes him, one of the lenses of his glasses breaks, leaving him half blind. Later, the boys from Jack's tribes steal the other lens, leaving him entirely unable to see. Although he is disabled, his sense of justice remains strong: he has the other boys lead him to Jack's fort and shouts up to the boys he cannot see about the rightness of returning his broken glasses to him. Despite his earnestness, the boys do not take him seriously. Roger releases a giant stone down on Piggy, who is crushed to death.

Ralph

Ralph is the film's protagonist. He is the first character to appear on screen, and the action up to the last scene revolves around him. He is played by James Aubrey.

Early in the story, Ralph is elected the leader of the island by the other boys, who are drawn to him although they have just met him. He struggles with the task of leadership throughout the rest of the film. Ralph tries to keeps the boys focused on the possibility of rescue, which he knows will happen only if the signal fire is seen, but they are constantly distracted by more interesting pursuits, such as hunting and swimming, or are simply inclined to sleep in the midday heat. The more Ralph tries to impress on the boys the importance of behaving sensibly, the more they see him as an oppressor, and they drift away from him. At one point, when Piggy tells him to blow the conch to gather the boys together, Ralph balks, realizing that they might ignore his call and, if they do, then his power as leader will evaporate.

Although Ralph is shown as a sympathetic figure, he does have his dark side. Early in the film he betrays Piggy, telling the boys the nickname that Piggy specifically asked him not to tell them. After he sees that he has hurt Piggy, he shows remorse, and he does rely on Piggy's advice throughout the rest of the film, but that initial betrayal shows that Ralph cannot be entirely trusted to behave honorably. His relationship with Piggy is based on the values they hold in common, not on friendship. In the end, however, he realizes that Piggy was a true friend, a revelation that is not shown in the movie but is stated in the last line of the novel.

Ralph's relationship with Jack is closer to a friendship. They seem to enjoy similar pursuits. As Jack becomes more powerful, though, he becomes a threat to Ralph, and eventually has the boys trying to kill him.

When he runs into an adult on the island, Ralph's tears indicate that he realizes the larger ramifications of what has gone on: his life is safe at last, but the boys' behavior has serious implications about human nature.

Roger

Roger is the most aggressive of the boys. He is played in the film by Roger Elwin. When Jack leaves the group to strike out on his own, Roger is the first one to join him. The film shows them experimenting with face paints, in an early foray into savagery. Roger becomes Jack's closest assistant, overseeing the boys who eventually join his tribe. In the end, after Simon has been killed by all of the boys in a murderous frenzy, Roger is solely and directly responsible for killing Piggy, pushing the lever that sends a boulder down, crushing him.

Sam and Eric

Sam and Eric are twin brothers who are always together. They are on duty to watch the signal fire and both fall asleep; when they awaken, they find the parachutist's body, which they do not recognize as that of a human, and they run to the other boys with a tale of having seen the beast. As the boys shift their allegiances toward Jack and the savage tribe he is starting, Sam and Eric are the only ones, except for Piggy, to stay with Ralph. Jack orders them taken prisoner during the meeting in which Piggy is killed. Later, they have been incorporated into his tribe, and they are painted with war paint and standing guard at his fort. They still have enough loyalty to Ralph to secretly tell him about Jack's plans and to give him food, but later, during the fire, Ralph hears one of them leading the others to his hiding place.

In the novel, Golding presents the twins as being so closely bound that they are often referred by one combined name, Samneric. The two actors who play them share one line in the film credits, as "the Surtees Twins."

Simon

Simon, played by Tom Gamin, is the one truly gentle soul in the group. He approaches the island's strange environment with curiosity, staring into the petals of a flower and watching a salamander as it skitters across his shirt. To calm the rising temperaments of the group, Simon often volunteers for things. He fetches Piggy's glasses for him when Jack knocks them off and gives Piggy his own portion of meat when Jack refuses to give him any. When the boys are in the forest hunting the beast and no one wants to return to camp with a message for Piggy, Simon volunteers, because he does not fear the beast. During a discussion about the beast from the ocean, Simon wisely conjectures that the beast may exist, but that it might be a part of the boys themselves. For this insight, he is mocked.

In the novel, Golding explains Simon's disconnection from reality by letting readers know that he is prone to epileptic seizures. There is no such explanation in the film, though. When Simon comes out of the forest, having seen the thing they call the beast and observed that it is just a dead man, he is unable to call out to stop them before they all, in their savage fury, attack him and kill him with their primitive weapons.

THEMES

Authority

The conch shell as a symbol of authority is emphasized more strongly in Golding's novel than it is in the film *Lord of the Flies*. The novel refers to the need to have the conch in hand when speaking several times, practically every time there is a communal meeting. Still, the film lets viewers know of this object's symbolic power in several subtle ways. When the boys are first drawn to the beach by the sound of the conch, Jack asks to see the man who is calling them, and he is disappointed to find that the conch is being blown by a boy. Soon after that, the assembled boys vote for Ralph to be their leader, presumably because he holds the shell that called them together. The film does not stress the importance of holding the conch when speaking to the assembly, but it does show that the speakers in the early scene always have the conch in hand.

Jack eventually challenges Ralph's right to rule the island community by raising questions about Ralph's authority. He points out that he and his hunters provided meat for the boys and that Ralph was frightened when they went to find the beast. He belittles Ralph's concerns by linking him to Piggy, whom the rest of the boys routinely mock. Finding himself with his authority diminished, Ralph is afraid to blow the conch to call the boys back to him; he knows that the power of the conch exists only because of mutual consent. If the other boys choose to ignore it, he will have no chance of controlling them. The conch is destroyed by the boulder that rolls down on Piggy. Its destruction is emphasized in the novel but only implied in the film. At that point, Ralph, the elected leader, becomes marked for death. Jack becomes leader of the boys, ruling with violence and cruelty. He plays on their fears while emphasizing that he can protect them, proving his worth with superstitious tricks such as leaving a pig's head as a present for the feared beast. He has a boy publicly whipped and derided, though the film does not explain why.

Fear

The boys are not intimidated by the challenge of providing for themselves on this island. They eat, rest, and play in relative comfort. They find themselves able to create shelters and catch animals, when they set their minds to it. However, although they are not frightened by the challenges of living, they are still frightened by

READ, WATCH, WRITE

- Watch the 1951 film *The Browning Version*, released on DVD in 1995 by Criterion, to form an opinion about the sort of school background the children in this film might have experienced. Write a brief story in which the main character of that film, pedantic schoolteacher Andrew Crocker-Harris, arrives on the island to take control of the boys. Try to follow the film's sense of social dynamics as you show how Crocker-Harris is accepted or rejected into the island's society.

- Jack has his body painted like a British flag early in this film, but by the end he has a headpiece that makes him look like a bird. Look at the film again carefully and identify at least four other designs of body paint on characters. Search the Internet for corresponding pictures that can be used to identify the designs you have found, and use Glogster to create an explanatory poster for the symbols.

- Conduct a trial in your classroom regarding the death of Simon, with one side arguing the case that social circumstances can drive even the most reasonable person to violent acts and the other side arguing that murder is murder under any circumstances. Have most of the class take the part of the jury, and have each student explain which was the more persuasive case, and why.

- The director of this film, Peter Brook, is mostly known as a stage director, particularly for his work with the Royal Shakespeare Company. Read Shakespeare's play *A Midsummer Night's Dream*, which was one of Brook's most notable successes. Film a scene from that play in the style of *Lord of the Flies*, editing and refining it using iMovie or another video editing program. Post your film to YouTube or your Web page and ask your fellow students to review it.

- When Piggy is left behind with the younger boys, he tells them the story behind the name of his hometown, Camberley, which they listen to with very little interest. What sort of lesson should Piggy have given the young boys to help them adapt better to life on the island? Prepare this lesson and teach it to your classmates.

- Choose a television series about teens or young adults and write an explanation about how their social grouping reflects the society formed in this film. Relate particular characters to characters in the film. Who is the show's Jack? Who is Ralph, Simon, or Piggy? Explain these parallels or similar ones in your essay.

---

the products of their imaginations. The most frightening figures are suggested by the youngest children, who have their words spoken to the assembled group by older boys. The first one, fearful of a "snake-thing" or "beastie," whispers into Piggy's ear, and later another boy, probably influenced by the earlier story, tells Jack about a beast that comes from the ocean at night. Brook shows viewers that the boys take the second story quite seriously by having the camera pan slowly across their stunned faces. The discussion that follows about whether ghosts might explain

the presence they fear shows how the older boys, such as Jack and Ralph, are trying to make sense out of their own superstitions. Piggy, the rationalist, openly refuses to believe in ghosts, while Simon, with his customary depth of understanding, says that what they think is a beast might something be within themselves. Tom Gaman's performance as Simon is so quirky and introspective, though, that it is easy to see why the other boys do not pay much attention to him.

The boys' fears of the beast seems confirmed when they come across the dead parachutist.

When Sam and Eric see it, the film does not show what they see. When Ralph, Jack, and Roger find the body, it is filmed from an angle that emphasizes the opaque helmet and the parachute strings, making it difficult for viewers to tell what it is the boys see. It is only when Simon looks at it that the film clearly shows it to be the form of a dead man, confirming Simon's claim that the beast the boys fear is a projection of something inside themselves.

Primitivism

One of the key points made by both the novel and the film *Lord of the Flies* is the process by which young men, freed of the bonds of society, move back toward their primitive instincts. This point is dramatized in the story's actions, but the graphic aspect of film also allows Brook to emphasize it visually. The boys' appearance changes from the beginning to the end of this film: their hair grows longer and their skin darkens. They wear fewer and fewer clothes, since the clothes stand as symbols of culture. This process

is especially notable in Piggy, whose asthma and weak eyes prevent him from fully casting off the trappings of society. His glasses are broken as the social order begins to fall apart, and they are completely taken away when the primitive instinct becomes dominant. One of the film's most powerful images comes on the morning after the ritualistic killing of Simon, when the film shows a close-up of Piggy adjusting his socks, as if to reaffirm his place as a civilized person. This camera shot is echoed later with the shot of the naval officer's long white socks, bringing an end to the primitive rule of the island.

As the boys become more primitive in the film, their body painting expands. Brook first shows paint used when Roger joins Jack in rejecting the island's established civilization. As more boys join Jack's tribe, they are identified as crossovers by their body paint, as happens to Sam and Eric between the time that Jack orders them taken prisoner and when Ralph later encounters them.

STYLE

Cinéma Verité

Cinéma verité is a documentary style that was popularized in France in the 1950s and 1960s, around the time this film was made. The name means "truthful film." It is a style meant to capture the feel of real life on film by showing ordinary people interacting with the filmmakers who are filming them, often in a confrontational way. Though the camera is never acknowledged in *Lord of the Flies*, as it would be in a cinéma verité documentary, Brook uses several techniques that give his film a documentary feeling. The use of untrained actors, for instance, helps to give readers the feeling that they are observing reality: the boys in this film, particularly Hugh Edwards as Piggy, talk in a way that seems natural to boys of their age. Brook often films his actors from a distance and then adds dialogue later, so that viewers see a large group, often dwarfed by the jungle or beach surrounding them, but they also hear their words from up close. This conflict of perspective gives the film a documentary's feeling of observation while retaining the intimacy of a narrative story.

Soundtrack

Brook uses the film's music in several ways, to highlight the contrast between the boys' descent into primitivism with their backgrounds at formal British public schools. Over the still photographs that accompany the main titles, the film plays the droning voice of a headmaster to symbolize the boys' customary routines and the taps of a snare drum to symbolize the movement toward war. When Jack and his choir march up the beach in their first scene, wearing formal capes and caps, they sing a regimented, disciplined Kyrie Eleison, part of the Latin mass. Brook augments their singing, however, with trumpets and drums that are not present on the island, to suggest the regal tradition that the boys are following. The trumpet version of the song repeats throughout the film, as does the choir's song. As the boys shed their culture, though, the beauty of their vocal harmony devolves into the brutality of their "kill the pig" chant. In the last scene, as Ralph tries to outrun the savage boys and the fire, the soundtrack adds the sound of tribal drums. Although some of the boys bang sticks on logs in earlier scenes, it is unlikely that they could have learned to play rhythms as complex and fast as these, indicating that Brook

added the drumming to the soundtrack for a primitive effect. The chants, fire and drumming grow louder and louder and then stop abruptly when Ralph comes across the naval officer, as if these sounds were all just in his head.

CULTURAL CONTEXT

World War II

Between 1939, when Britain declared war on Germany, and 1954, when *Lord of the Flies* was first published, the citizens of England suffered tremendously. While the British army was fighting in Germany, France, and North Africa during World War II, the citizens at home were being bombed relentlessly by the German air force, the Luftwaffe, in the Battle of Britain in 1940. The suffering continued even after the end of the bombings. The end of the war in 1945 saw the Allied Forces, which included Great Britain, victorious, but the strength of the British Empire was severely diminished, and most of it was lost to independence movements.

During World War II, Great Britain was in constant danger of attack. Even before the formal declaration of war, the government arranged to distribute tens of millions of gas masks to its citizens, in case Germany and its Axis powers were to attack British cities with chemical weapons. Throughout the war, life in larger towns of Britain, as well in those along the coast, was continuously affected by the possibility of invasion. Blackout orders required streetlights to be turned off and heavy curtains to block out windows during times of air raid threat, to make it harder for Axis planes to locate towns. Still, the war had tremendous effects on the country. As Kristin Olsen points out in *Understanding "Lord of the Flies,"* 458,000 homes were destroyed by German bombs during the war, and 60,000 people were killed.

In cities that were deemed targets by the German army, great numbers of citizens were evacuated. The main focus of the evacuations was the children, although women and disabled citizens were also removed to safer areas. These evacuations usually entailed moving to quieter parts of the British Isles, but sometimes people were moved to different countries. Evacuation schemes were written up before the war began, so that civil administrators were prepared to move vulnerable members of the population

© *Moviestore collection Ltd / Alamy*

when the need arose. The greatest of these evacuations, one of the largest evacuations of a population in modern history, was the relocation of 3.5 million people during Operation Pied Piper, which the British government instituted in preparation for the Battle of Britain in September of 1939. Evacuations continued throughout the war. The Children's Overseas Reception Board was organized in 1940 to arrange the evacuation of children to British Dominions, primarily Canada, plus South Africa, Australia, and New Zealand, but the board was closed after most of the children on the evacuation ship *City of Benares*, sailing out of Liverpool for Canada, died after the ship was sunk by a Nazi submarine in September of that year.

The Cold War

Although Golding's novel of the evacuation of British schoolboys was based on events in World War II history, neither the novel nor the film takes place during any particular war. The battle that the boys are fleeing from is a fictitious one. At one point in the novel, Ralph thinks of the world beyond the island and considers the possibility that "we might get taken by the Reds." After World War II, a great rivalry sprang up between the countries of the West, most notably the United States and Great Britain, and the satellite nations of the Soviet Union, which was newly empowered by annexation of several countries that had previously been occupied by Germany. The Communist powers that ruled the Soviet Union were referred to as "Reds." The ensuing competition was dubbed a cold war because it consisted of political posturing, arms build-ups, and negotiations but no real fighting. It lasted until the dissolution of the Soviet Union in 1991.

During the cold war, the western powers and the Soviet Union never came into direct conflict. They did give their support to combatants, most notably when the Soviets and the Communist government of China gave weapons and training to North Korea while the countries of the United Nations gave similar support to South Korea during the Korean conflict, from 1950 to 1953. Although the cold war opponents helped different sides in smaller conflicts across the globe, history shows no record of any evacuation of British schoolchildren under threat of Communist aggressors, which is the situation described in the novel. The film *Lord of the Flies* shows nuclear warheads in the still photographs under the opening credits; because nuclear bombs have never been used in a war against Great Britain, these photos establish that this film takes place in an imaginary, but quite possible, world of the future.

CRITICAL OVERVIEW

Peter Brook's adaptation of *Lord of the Flies* was not widely considered a success when it was released. Many critics found problems with the way Brooks brought the material to the screen. A reviewer in *Time*, for instance, calls the film "flawed in many ways," noting that the cast, though authentically British, sounded "like schoolboys putting on a play for old boys' day." The *Time* reviewer concludes by noting, "In reducing the novel to a gristly, occasionally shocking adventure story, the producers have chosen not to risk failure. And so they have failed." Stanley Kauffmann, writing in the *New Republic*, dubs Brook's method of filming real boys in a real situation a failure: "Scenes sag heavily because cues are not picked up, lines are emitted rather than spoken. As a result, characters are not defined, drama is not joined, terror is a long time in coming and is mild when it arrives." Bosley Crowther notes in the *New York Times* that Golding's novel "is as stirring and shocking a story as has been published in a long time. But, alas, the picture made from it by writer-director Peter Brook is a curiously flat and fragmentary visualization of the original." Crowther calls the film "loosely and jerkily constructed" and faults its "strangely perfunctory, almost listless flow of narrative in most of its scenes."

Although the film was not well received by mainstream reviewers, it was recognized in some areas as an artistic achievement. Brook was nominated for the Palme d'Or (Golden Palm), the highest prize available, at the Cannes Film Festival. Several generations of schoolchildren came to know the film in classrooms, viewing it while studying Golding's novel. Over the years, Brook's film has become a standard of the American educational curriculum.

Later reviewers have given more appreciation to the film's achievements and less attention to its shortcomings. Part of this is due to the poor critical reception of the 1990 adaptation of the book, directed by Henry Hook: the new version left many critics to look back at Brook's movie with admiration. Another element that helped cement the film's reputation was its 2000 DVD release as part of the prestigious Criterion Films Collection's "Essential Art House Films" series. The extras included with that release, particularly the audio commentary track by Brook and others, gave viewers insight into just how much Brook's filming method had succeeded. As Keith Phipps notes in his review of the Criterion DVD for the *Onion A. V. Club* Web site, the commentary track may be fascinating, but "the edginess of the shoot is clear without it . . . the verité approach and the actors' naturalistic performances only grow more effective as the movie progresses and the boys' society regresses toward a chilling climax."

CRITICISM

David Kelly

Kelly is a college instructor of creative writing and literature. In the following essay, he considers a claim against the moral view of Golding's novel and explains how the film version of Lord of the Flies *presents a more balanced view.*

William Golding's novel *Lord of the Flies* is considered a modern classic, but it was never the subject of universal adulation. One line of criticism tended to fault the book for its cynical view of human nature. Golding was steeped in the idea that humans are inherently evil, according to this line of thought, and worse, he spread cynicism while pretending to be an open-minded humanist. A clear statement of this comes from critic R. C. Townsend, who discussed the book in the mid-1960s in an essay called "*Lord of the Flies*: Fool's Gold," which was later reprinted, in a shortened form, as "The Unwarranted Popularity of *Lord of the Flies*." Townsend's point is that the book, regardless of all else, is based on a flawed

WHAT DO I SEE NEXT?

- The film *The Naked Prey*, released in 1966, has similarities to the final scenes of this film. Directed by and starring Cornell Wilde, it shows a mid-1960s vision of savages and civilization with the story of a man on safari in South Africa who ends up being pursued through the veldt, left to survive by his wits. Lauded for its innovative filming and condemned for its racist views, this film was released in a Criterion Collection edition in 2008.

- Francis Ford Coppola's film *Apocalypse Now*, based on the novella *Heart of Darkness* by Joseph Conrad, features a classic performance by Marlon Brando as a member of the U.S. military who, after living in the jungle of Vietnam for years, becomes a charismatic leader to a tribe of people who follow his commands, as the boys in this film follow Jack. This film won several major awards upon its release by Paramount in 1979, and it is available on Paramount Home Video.

- *Lord of the Flies* was remade in 1990, starring Balthazar Getty, Chris Furrh, and Danuel Pipoly. Critics and filmmakers found the remake to be inferior to the original, mostly for ways in which director Harry Hook took liberties with Golding's original story. It was released on MGM Home Video in 2001.

- Golding's trilogy *To the Ends of the Earth*, consisting of the novels *Rites of Passage*, *Close Quarters*, and *Fire down Below*, was adapted into a miniseries for the BBC in 2005. The series, starring Benedict Cumberbatch as a nineteenth-century British aristocrat who takes a sea voyage to Australia, was directed by David Attwood. It is available on DVD from Timeless Media Group.

- Acclaimed French director Francois Truffaut is responsible for the 1970 film *The Wild Child*, a film based on the true story of a boy, about eleven years old, who was found in the wilderness in the south of France in 1798, having had no human contact up to that point in his life. Starring Jean-Pierre Cargol and Truffaut himself, it was released on DVD by MGM Video in 2001.

- There have been several films made of John Knowles's classic 1959 novel *A Separate Peace*, about British school boys during World War II. The most recent version, produced by Showtime and directed by Peter Yates, has received much more critical acclaim than its 1972 predecessor. Yates's film was released on DVD by Paramount in 2005.

premise, that human nature is unavoidably drawn toward evil. He quotes Golding's line about "the infinite cynicism of adult life," which is what Simon sees in the dead eyes of the impaled pig head, and quotes again from the part when tears roll down Ralph's face because he realizes "the end of innocence, the darkness of man's heart." The book leans toward redemption at points, according to Townsend, but the defeat of hope is just more evidence of its true despair. In his view, the book enjoys a widespread popularity that a dismal message like this just does not deserve.

Townsend wrote his essay with full knowledge of Peter Brook's adaptation of the book, which he mentions briefly and dismissively. While talking about the way the book was frequently, even then, adopted for high school and college curricula, he casually notes that "a film has been made of it," as a way to introduce what he calls a "cozy" ad in the *New Yorker* that touted its academic popularity. It might have been better for Townsend, though, to actually pay attention to Brook's film. This is a book that lends itself to visualization—it has been adapted

> **THIS IS NOT A WORK THAT THINKS THAT EVIL WILL ALWAYS RULE, AND IT IS NOT A WORK THAT TOSSES IN A COMFORTABLE ENDING LIGHTLY."**

to two movies and has been presented on the stage in countless productions—but Brook took care to film it in a particular way. His method might have cured some of Townsend's concerns that the evil in the novel outshines its sense of human virtue.

The film derived its story from the novel with few changes, none of them substantial enough to be thought of as a contradiction to what Golding wrote. Putting Golding's words into the mouths of actors, though, gives the boys a coating of objective reality that was missing from them when they were made from words on a page. Brook cast the movie with amateurs and, in doing so, was forced to consider a number of additional elements, such as how British they sounded and whether they were available to go to Puerto Rico for three months of filming. The boys' loss of focus, which was such an element in their descent into savagery in the book, was real for the actors. Given a choice between hitting cues and reciting dialogue or running around on the beach with spears, these children clearly preferred the latter. It is one thing to tell readers about a group of boys who cast off the trappings of civilization but another thing to follow those boys step by step as they loosen up. Golding did not have to force his perspective about the boys' descent into savagery. It is thoroughly believable on film, no matter how it is presented.

The film also gives readers more control of the message with its chosen visual style. Shooting it in black and white blends the story with the still photographs of the introduction. Though the photos are of real items and events from the 1940s and 1950s, their graininess, as well as the vague, echoing voices on the soundtrack, marks them as hallucinations from some far-away, imaginary time. It depicts the speculative future in which Golding set the book, but his prose does little to establish the imaginary feel of the outside world. The black and white film makes it all appear as a dream.

The absence of any actual Lord of the Flies in the film is one place where Brook clearly softened the book's moralistic tone. Golding has the impaled pig head identify itself as the Lord of the Flies to Simon. The phrase refers to Beelzebub, one of the most prominent fallen angels in hell. In the book, the reality of this event is muted by Simon's epilepsy, giving readers the leeway to interpret it as having never really happened at all. Brook takes this effect one step further by eliminating the talking pig head altogether. The interaction between Simon and the pig's head is wordless, told visually with close-ups. The boy knows that there is something horrible going on, but he is not told that it is a manifestation of the devil. In this case, it is as if Brook agreed with Townsend that the novel's case for humanity's inevitable attraction to evil is overstated, and he therefore decided to let a decaying head and buzzing flies signify the horrors of the island without comment.

Readers might be wondering how critics can make the case that either the book or the film is trying to promote the idea of inherent evil, given the fact that both end with the triumphant appearance of the Royal British Navy—the most regimented, civilized organization short of the public school system that spawned these boys. This ending does not represent a triumph of order to Townsend because he just does not accept the novel's ending. As a reader, he appreciates the way the novel backs away from its own reality: Golding reduces his characters to savages, but the book does not leave them that way, which makes for a much more comforting ending. As a critic, Townsend seems to actually admire Golding for willingly changing course in the last few pages of his book in order to make his story more accessible to readers. Ethically, though, Townsend finds the move dishonest. The transparency of this happy ending means, to Townsend, that it does not really count. For him, the inevitable descent toward savagery still stands as the novel's message.

Though Townsend dismisses this ending, he really has no right to do so. The final scene might be a fantasy, but it is there, and as such, it makes a statement. This ending might say that all humans would be murderous savages, given the chance, which is the interpretation he puts on it, but it could also be read as a message that savagery is just an anomaly that may grow in the right circumstances but will easily wither away when faced by grown-ups.

© *Lebrecht Music and Arts Photo Library | Alamy*

Since he was working with Golding's book, it is no surprise that Townsend would interpret it as having the more fatalistic message. Golding does society no favor when he lets the naval officer on the beach talk. The officer's speech is balanced, but there is good reason to believe that he is clueless about what he is witnessing, dismissing a struggle for life as a child's game. He might bring the island perspective that it has been missing, but it is not unreasonable for Townsend to read him as someone who does not recognize evil when it stands in front of him.

This interpretation cannot be drawn from the film, though. There is no question that the naval officer represents a clean, benevolent authority, with the power to quash savage instincts without even thinking. The naval officer is so imposing that his sudden appearance stops jungle drums and raging fires. Instead of giving him dialogue, drawing attention to what he does not know, Brook has his camera pan up the naval officer's uniform. This is civilization, and it is triumphant. This is not a work that thinks that evil will always rule, and it is not a work that tosses in a comfortable ending lightly.

The film version does add one touch, though, that leans toward the fatalistic interpretation of *Lord of the Flies*. In the final scene, Brook lets his camera linger for a moment on two yeomen in the naval landing craft. They are baby-faced lads decked out in sailor suits that look like something their mothers might have dressed them in; they are not much older than the rioting savages who have just burned down the island. They stare at Jack and his tribe with the same ambivalence that all of the boys on the island have gone through at one time or another. It is a look that says that stripping down, painting one's body, and chasing a prey with a spear would be fun, if they were not navy men; they regret that it cannot be. If Townsend had analyzed the film version, he might have found this to be an honest way of implying that evil is bound to creep into any soul. Instead, he examined the novel and determined that Golding forced a bleak view that was not warranted.

The passage of time does affect a work's legitimacy. When Townsend wrote about the novel, he might have been inclined to think that a work that was suddenly being assigned in schools all over the country was merely a fad, lacking in the intellectual or moral substance that would qualify it as a true classic. Now, more than a half century later, *Lord of the Flies* is still assigned and discussed, and it is still worthy of the critical questions it raises. It has proven itself thought-provoking. Its moral center has proven to be more than a delusion.

Source: David Kelly, Critical Essay on *Lord of the Flies*, in *Novels for Students*, Gale, Cengage Learning, 2011.

Maeve Walsh

In the following review, Walsh discusses the problems associated with the adaptation of The Lord of the Flies.

On 31 July 1964, a low-budget, black-and-white film adaptation of *Lord of the Flies* was released in London. William Golding's debut novel, an allegorical tale about a group of schoolboys who descend into savagery on a desert island, had met with a series of rejections before its publication in 1954. (One reader at Faber had marked the first draft "Rubbish and dull. Pointless" before it was rescued and championed by a colleague.) The final version was respectfully received in Britain, but it found enormous success in the US, mainly thanks to cult-making student fans. The novel went on to be translated into 28 languages. It won a permanent place on exam syllabuses, and launched a long and Nobel-lauded career for Golding.

Peter Brook's film, however, was another story. The *Times* made the "unkind but also unavoidable judgement" that it was "the sort of adaptation which sets one wondering whether the original was all that good." But like the original, it too had made a tortuous trip from personal conception to public consumption. Brook had made his name as an innovative young theatre director during the late 1940s, and became the RSC's first co-director in 1962. *Lord of the Flies*, his third film, had initially involved mainstream producer Sam Spiegel. When Spiegel pulled out, the plans were scaled down and funds raised from numerous small investors.

An island off Puerto Rico was chosen as the location, and 30 non-actors between the ages of nine and 13 were recruited and paid in pocket money. The film was shot over three months in 1961, with Brook encouraging his "real" boys to experience the anarchic freedom of their fictional counterparts, and then to improvise within the original plot. He finished with 60 hours of footage.

Edited down to 90 minutes, the film then ran into further problems. Despite being presented at Cannes in 1963—where, according to the *Telegraph*, a French critic had implied that "their boys wouldn't behave like this, putting the whole thing down to a failure of the prefect system"—it didn't find British distributors for another year. On release, it was given an X certificate: "this terrifying tale of schoolboy evacuees would either frighten the under-16s to death—or give them ideas!" said the *Sunday Mirror*.

British reviewers were well aware of the film's history. The *Guardian's* Richard Roud wrestled with his critical conscience in print: "A director of talent who has made an ambitious film ought to be given special consideration even if the film, by ordinary standards is not successful." The *FT* conceded that it was "impossible to be less than sympathetic," but admitted that it wasn't a "really good film." The *Times* said Golding's novel was "almost unfilmable," while the *Telegraph* thought Brook had "reproduced nearly all of its qualities."

Many other critics also felt that Brook had risen to a difficult challenge. He had "wrenched a barbaric power out of the weird locations and kept a model fidelity to (the) novel" (*Standard*) and "checked" the "natural warmth of the film" throughout: "Hugging the kids in this film would be like embracing a heavily mined porcupine" (*Observer*). The film was "a shocker with serious intent" (*Sunday Telegraph*), "a startling piece of junior Grand Guignol" (*Mail*), and "often repellent but harshly fascinating" (*Mirror*). The *Sunday Express* urged "every student of humanity" to see it.

Inevitably, critics were divided in their responses to the "natural" actors: "unconvincing" (*Guardian*); "variable" (*Standard*); "they simply behave normally—and the result is vital and horrific" (*Mirror*). "However suitable the boys chosen look, only one of them, James Aubrey as Ralph, shows any sign of acting at all," said the *Times*.

In 1996, the BBC and Brook brought the "boys" back to the island to see how their intense experience had affected their lives. Brook claimed that each was chosen because "he was clearly a type that corresponded to his role in the story. Now one sees that life works on each person's type within the limits of a type—but the type doesn't change." Conveniently, Aubrey had become an actor while Piggy (Hugh Edwards) managed pet-food factories.

Another film about social breakdown in paradise is currently in production. Following its reviews, reprints of Alex Garland's *The Beach* could have had a delete-as-applicable blurb on the covers: "a backpackers'/hippies'/druggies' *Lord of the Flies*," or "*Lord of the Flies* meets *Lonely Planet*/ *Apocalypse Now*/ *The Magus*." But the comparison stops with the film. "Real" travellers plucked from Thai beach-huts were never going to be a casting option on the big-budget *Beach*.

Source: Maeve Walsh, "It Was 35 Years Ago Today; *Lord of the Flies* Hits the Big Screen," in *London Independent*, August 1, 1999, Features p. 3.

Richard Roud

In the following review, Roud criticizes Brook's decision to use ordinary boys instead of actors in the 1963 film Lord of the Flies.

Where is a film critic's first duty: to his readers or to the cinema as an art and industry? Many people would reply that, as a journalist, his only duty is to his readers, to the man who has put down his fourpence and thus purchased the right to the newspaperman's prime consideration. There is however, another—perhaps nobler—view that the critic's main responsibility is the furtherance of the art which he is writing about.

This week the problem has been posed in its most acute form with Peter Brook's *Lord of the Flies*. I greatly admire Mr Brook's achievement in the theatre. It is common knowledge that his desire to film William Golding's novel was achieved only after years of struggle. And it has taken over a year for the film to reach London after its Cannes premiere. One desperately wants Mr Brook to make more films and, God knows, the British cinema needs men like him.

And yet, on the simplest of levels, *Lord of the Flies* is a failure: one just does not believe it. Golding's novel about a group of boys marooned on an island and their gradual reversion to savagery is—or seemed at the time—an extremely powerful allegory. But allegory is the hardest of form for the cinema to achieve. Mr Brook has chosen a realistic approach, using ordinary boys—non-actors. This would seem to be the way to do it but it has not worked out that way. With the exception of Ralph and Piggy, the boys are unconvincing and as a result, the symbolic action of the piece is seen all to clearly as just

that. In a laudable attempt to avoid the beautiful image trap, Mr Brook has deliberately foregone studies of sun, shadow and palm fronds, but the baby seems to have gone out with the bath water; visually the film is undistinguished.

Of course, there are moments: Piggy's tale of how Cambridgetown came to be called Camberley; the first appearance of the choir boys in their black robes advancing along the sand; and best of all the final scene of Ralph's rescue: in his eyes, the Fall of Man made plain.

Source: Richard Roud, "Past Notes: A Flawed Film That Fails," in *London Guardian*, July 31, 1995, p. T2.

Jackson Burgess

In the following review, Burgess applauds Brook's ability to preserve Golding's plot in detail while emphasizing two crucial points at which the film changes the emphasis of the story.

Lord of the Flies is a rough English equivalent of the Hebrew "Beelzebub," and in his remarkable novel of that title William Golding set out to verify the existence of the Fiend and to show just where he lives in us all. The novel's translation to film, by Peter Brook, is a brilliant and disturbing picture in which Golding's grim parable of human depravity undergoes a subtle secularization.

Brook's screenplay preserves Golding's simple plot in detail: a planeload of English school-boys is marooned on an hospitable but remote Pacific Island. Under the leadership of Ralph, a decent and intelligent boy guided by a strong sense of fair play, they take care of the smallest boys, build huts, and maintain a signal fire. There are wild pigs on the island, and some of the older boys, led by a moody and egotistical lad named Jack, organize as hunters. Their success in killing a pig excites and elates them and Jack manipulates their excitement and the younger boys' terror of supposed "beasts" on the island against Ralph, whom he gradually supplants. When Ralph refuses to join Jack's bloodthirsty and squalid band of savages—they have let the fire go out and live only for hunting, dancing, feasting, and sadistic terror—he is hunted like an animal. Ralph is saved, however, by a landing party from a British warship, drawn to the island by the smoke of the brush-fires lit to drive Ralph out of hiding.

There are two crucial points at which the film changes the emphasis of this story. The first is the beginning: Brook has superimposed the titles on blurry halftone stills suggesting a nuclear war, an evacuation of children from Britain (to Australia?), and a crash. This plus his treatment of "*The Beast*" of the island, is almost enough to make war the villain of the film . . . that is, to deal with collective rather than individual depravity. The second important alteration occurs at the very end of the film. Golding has a trick, practiced in all four of his novels that I've read, of committing a book to one, narrow point of view, then violently shifting to another point of view, radically opposed to the first, for the final chapter. The loss of this ironic shift, which is simply impossible in a film, seems to me pure gain in *Lord of the Flies*. Nonetheless, it contributes to the "sociological" tendency I mentioned, and makes the rescue seem simply a Providential happy ending, while in the novel the rescue served to extend the parable of the boys' ordeal to all the rest of mankind, and was not at all reassuring. In the film, Ralph ceases to be a decent man defeated by human selfishness and brutality, and becomes the last Social Democrat, flying before the Stalinist liquidators. Perhaps those are the only terms in which we can read a parable these days, but the pell-mell pace of the film (which is horrendously exciting) and Brook's insistence in the script upon the issues of fair play and "rules" both increase this feeling, while the film's principal attempt to deal in terms of personal morality, the portrayal of a saintly boy named Simon, who is Jack's first victim, is sentimentally vague. (Simon was a weakness in the novel, too.)

Still, as an adventure story with Orwellian political overtones, this is a first-rate film. Brook has handled his young actors (all amateurs, by report) splendidly. They were allowed to improvise most of their lines—as well as their make-up and many of their props. The result is a little strange, but effective: the dialogue (there isn't much) has a slow, stilted, self-consciousness which perfectly embodies the groping moral and social improvisation to which the boys are reduced. I think, too, that a child's idea of how grownups talk is the way children talk, while a grownup's idea of how children talk is the way that nobody ever talked. It is this groping, awkward speech that creates the film's most touching moment. All the older boys go off to hunt, leaving the fat, near-sighted "intellectual," named Piggy, to care for the smallest boys. To entertain them, Piggy tells the story of how his home town got its name of "Camburly." Pedantically, self-consciously, blinking and scratching, Piggy talks—the shot juxtaposed with shots of Jack's howling tribe on the trail of a pig. So dignified and poignant is the scene that I couldn't help feeling that any species represented by Piggy telling the story of Camburly cannot finally be brought low by its Jacks.

The photography is black and white, with some fine low-key work, and throughout the film the camera exploits the landscape of the boys' island to the limit, with wide long shots and slow pans. The reliance, particularly in the early scenes, on long and medium-long shots, gives the visuals a certain old-fashioned feeling, but that's not inappropriate to a parable, and the shots work, creating a perspective in which the boys' frailty and helplessness contrasts frighteningly with their hopes and their uncertain courage.

The score is straightforward and effective, developing the Kyrie which we first hear as the marching-song of Jack's choir-boys into a sinister, thumping march and finally into a wild war-chant.

It's impossible to write of this film, finally, without comment on its propositions about human nature. While Brook has altered the emphasis, I think he shares Golding's much-discussed views on "natural depravity," and the film conveys them with disturbing effectiveness. I find two dubious assumptions, however, underpinning both the novel and the film: that the essential nature of man is peculiarly visible in the behavior of children, and that brutality (that is, brutishness) equals sin. If children are naturally brutal (and the film shows us that they are, and shows us convincingly) then man is naturally sinful. But what makes man most human is precisely his experience of having grown up, and mindless brutality is less a sin than a failure to have grown up into the realm of good and evil.

Source: Jackson Burgess, Review of *The Lord of the Flies*, in *Film Quarterly*, Vol. 17, No. 2, Winter 1963–1964, pp. 31–32.

Stanley Kauffman

In the following excerpt, Kauffman criticizes Brook's choices regarding characters and plot development in the 1963 film version of Lord of the Flies.

In his film of *Lord of the Flies*, Peter Brook has chosen to look out of the corner of his eye at William Golding's straightforward allegory. It seems to have been made obliquely, in a kind of hurried, snatched, newsreel way, then patched together later into the best continuous film possible. For this tale of English schoolboy castaways, Brook took his boys to a Caribbean island and, in effect, turned them loose, photographing them when they were seemingly unaware. (Yet the best shot is one that is carefully staged: the entrance of the marching choristers along the edge of the sea.) Brook's approach has been tempered neo-realism: put "real" boys in the "real" situation, let them feel it themselves, don't turn them into actors. Well, he hasn't. Scenes sag heavily because cues are not picked up, lines are emitted rather than spoken. As a result, characters are not defined, drama is not joined, terror is a long time in coming and is mild when it arrives. The chi-chi cinema décor—arty shots of tree-tops, quivering leaves, light on the water—does not indemnify.

In this free-swinging method, some swipes are bound to hit. Some of the savagery towards the end is on the Golding standard. Piggy (Hugh Edwards) tells a story about Cámberly—supposedly impromptu—that is funny. James Aubrey, as Ralph, has some good boyishly manly moments. But the core of the book's meaning is lost. The title is only literal; we hear the buzz from the beginning. The key scene between Simon and the pig's head—given voice in the novel through Simon's imagination—is reduced to a series of silent close-ups. The scene is thus made meaningless.

Two additional egregious errors. The producers and director went to great pains to find a location and use a technique which, they hoped, would avert artificiality. Then they recorded the dialogue in such a way that the ear is constantly reminded of a studio; and they smeared on music, by Raymond Leppard, which—in the phoniest Hollywood tradition—predicts what is to come and attempts to raise audience temperature when the scene on screen is tepid.

Source: Stanley Kauffman, "Gold, Gilding, Gilt," in *New Republic*, August 17, 1963, pp. 27–28.

SOURCES

"Cold War," in *Encyclopaedia Britannica*, http://search.eb.com/eb/article-284222 (accessed August 17, 2010).

Crowther, Bosley, Review of *Lord of the Flies*, in *New York Times*, August 20, 1963, http://movies.nytimes.com/movie/review?res=9F0DE3D71731E33ABC4851DFBE6683886 79EDE (accessed July 16, 2010).

Golding, William, *Lord of the Flies*, Coward-McCann, 1962.

Kauffmann, Stanley, "Gold, Golding, Gilt," in *New Republic*, August 17, 1963, pp. 27–28.

Lord of the Flies (DVD), Criterion Collection, 2008.

Olsen, Kristin, *Understanding "Lord of the Flies,"* Greenwood Press, 2000, p. 178.

Phipps, Keith, Review of *Lord of the Flies*, in *Onion A. V. Club*, March 29, 2002, http://www.avclub.com/articles/lord-of-the-flies-dvd,19891 (accessed July 16, 2010).

Review of *Lord of the Flies*, in *Time*, August 23, 1963, http://www.time.com/time/magazine/article/0,9171,8751 44,00.html (accessed July 16, 2010).

Speller, Katherine, "Cinema Vérité: Defining the Moment," in *Sense of Cinema*, December 2000, http://archive.sensesofcinema.com/contents/00/11/verite.html (accessed August 16, 2010).

Townsend, R. C., "The Unwarranted Popularity of *Lord of the Flies*," in *Readings on Lord of the Flies*, Greenhaven Press, 1997, pp. 147–52.

FURTHER READING

Boyd, S. J., "The Nature of the Beast: *Lord of the Flies*," in *Bloom's Modern Critical Interpretation: Lord of the Flies—New Edition*, edited by Harold Bloom, Infobase Publishing, 2008, pp. 37–44.

Boyd is one of the most widely published critics on Golding's works. In this essay, he explores one of the central and most obvious allegories in the Golding canon.

Brook, Peter, *The Shifting Point: Theatre, Film, Opera 1946–1987*, Theatre Communications Group, 1994.

The film's director talks about his stage productions at length in this memoir, but he also explains the erratic process of bringing *Lord of the Flies* to film.

Carey, John, *William Golding: The Man Who Wrote "Lord of the Flies": A Life*, Free Press, 2010.

Among the revelations of this recent biography is the resentment Golding felt for having his reputation forever associated with his first published novel, which he considered somewhat of a joke while writing it.

Golding, William, "Nobel Lecture 1983," in *Critical Essays on William Golding*, edited by James R. Baker, G. K. Hall, 1988, pp. 149–57.

Three decades after the appearance of *Lord of the Flies*, his first published novel, Golding was awarded the highest honor in literature. In his acceptance speech he outlined the view of the world that made his works important in their time.

Reilly, Patrick, "Caliban's Freedom," in *Lord of the Flies: Fathers and Sons*, Twayne Masterwork Studies No. 106, Twayne Publishers. 1992, pp. 56–91.

Reilly draws a literary comparison from the deserted island of Shakespeare's *The Tempest* to the island on which the boys find their freedom in Golding's novel.

Winter, Jessica, *The Rough Guide to American Independent Film*, Rough Guides, 2006.

Although this film is just one of hundreds covered here—most of them recent—this book is valuable for helping readers put Brook and his production style into the context of the artistry of the early 1960s.

SUGGESTED SEARCH TERMS

Lord of the Flies

Lord of the Flies AND film

Lord of the Flies AND 1960s

Peter Brook

Piggy AND Ralph AND Jack

Lord of the Flies AND challenged

Lord of the Flies AND editing

Tom Hollyman AND Lord of the Flies

Peter Brook AND film

Lord of the Flies AND cinéma verité

William Golding AND film

Lord of the Flies AND 1990 film

Platero and I

JUAN RAMÓN JIMÉNEZ
1917

Platero and I by Juan Ramón Jiménez, is a collection of vignettes, or prose poems, that describe the relationship between the narrator and Platero, his donkey. A much shorter version of the work was first published in 1914, but the longer, definitive version was released in 1917. This longer version is available in English (translated from Spanish by Antonio T. de Nicolás) from iUniverse.com publishers. Both English, Spanish, and dual-language editions are readily available in hardcover and paperback.

Jiménez is known primarily as a poet, and the short pieces have a lyrical, poetic quality. There is no conventional story line; the vignettes convey a series of impressions of Platero, the narrator's emotions, and the natural beauty of Moguer, his rural hometown. The book, though not well known in the United States, is a well-loved classic in Spanish-speaking countries.

Jiménez's lyrical descriptions of nature, poetic metaphors, and philosophical musings elevate the simple story of a man and his donkey beyond a mere book for children to a moving and beautiful portrait of friendship.

AUTHOR BIOGRAPHY

Jiménez was born in Moguer, a small town in the Andalusian region of southern Spain, on December 24, 1881. His father, Victor Jiménez, was a

Juan Ramón Jiménez

successful vintner, and so Juan Ramón had a privileged childhood. The youngest of four children, he was a sensitive child who had a love of nature. At the age of eleven, Jiménez was sent to a Jesuit secondary school in Puerto de Santa Maria; at fifteen, he finished his studies and returned home to Moguer.

Jiménez was a talented artist, and after his secondary education he went to Seville to study painting. In addition to painting, he also began writing poetry, and early success getting his poems published in newspapers and magazines convinced him to choose poetry over painting. Two of his greatest literary influences were the celebrated Nicaraguan poet Rubén Darío and Spanish poet Gustavo Adolfo Bécquer. When Darío read some of Jiménez's poetry, he was very impressed; he invited Jiménez to join him and some other modernist poets in Madrid. While in Madrid, Jiménez wrote his first two published volumes of poetry, *Almas de violeta* (Violet Souls) and *Ninfeas* (Water Lilies). Though his work showed promise, these early poems were marred by excessive sentimentality and melancholy.

Shortly after Jiménez returned home from Madrid, his father died; Jiménez was so affected by his father's death that he fell ill and spent the next several years recuperating. During his recovery, he published several more volumes of poetry, using the time in the sanatorium to study and perfect his work.

In 1905, Jiménez returned home to Moguer, where he would spend the next six years in seclusion, writing numerous volumes of poetry. In 1912, he moved to Madrid, where he met his future wife, Zenobia Camprubi Aymar. Zenobia's bright and cheerful disposition tempered Jiménez's tendency toward brooding and melancholy, bringing a new balance and maturity to his work. In 1914, the first version of *Platero and I*—Jiménez's first prose work—was published (the longer version was released in 1917). The story of a man and his donkey, which painted an affectionate portrait of Jiménez's hometown of Moguer, became an enduring Spanish classic.

Zenobia had American relatives and had been educated in the United States. In 1916, Jiménez traveled to New York to marry her. Later that year, Jiménez published a volume of poetry, *Diario de un poeta recien casado* (*Diary of a Newly Married Poet*), later re-released as *Diario de poeta y mar* (*Diary of the Poet and the Sea*). Poems in this volume include Jiménez's impressions of his sea voyage to New York, as well as love poems written about Zenobia. The volume was well received by critics, many of whom thought it was his finest poetic work to date.

After their marriage, Jiménez and his wife returned to Madrid, where they would live until 1936. Jiménez continued to write acclaimed volumes of poetry and was by now a very famous and influential literary figure in Spain. In 1936, the Spanish Civil War prompted Jiménez and Zenobia to leave Spain, first visiting Zenobia's relatives in the United States, then living briefly in Puerto Rico and Cuba. In 1939, he began lecturing at a series of American universities, beginning at the University of Miami in Florida.

In 1956, Jiménez was awarded the Nobel Prize in literature. The award, however, brought little pleasure to Jiménez, because his wife Zenobia was very ill, and she died just two days after they received the news of his achievement. Devastated, Jiménez never wrote again; he died two years later, in 1958, in San Juan, Puerto Rico.

PLOT SUMMARY

Platero and I is not a traditional, plot-driven novel, but rather a collection of vignettes, short pieces that paint a picture of Moguer, a small Spanish town, and describe the relationship between the narrator and his donkey, Platero. Some vignettes describe present-day adventures of the narrator and Platero, and others tell tales of the narrator's past, with Platero as the audience. Most are less than a page long. They are divided into two sections: "The Elegy," which constitutes the majority of the book, and "Afterthoughts of the Poet."

The Elegy

The book begins with the vignette "Platero," in which Jiménez describes the donkey Platero and illustrates the fond relationship between him and the narrator. After this opening vignette, the pieces vary greatly in focus and subject matter. Many of the pieces are devoted to lyrical description of nature and its beauty. For instance, Jiménez devotes an entire vignette to pomegranates: "Now, Platero," he writes, "the tight-knit center, all health, whole with thin veils, the exquisite treasure of edible amethysts, juicy and firm like the heart of some princess." In "Scarlet Landscape," he describes a brilliant sunset, "all dressed in purple, wounded by its own crystals, which make it bleed all over." In "Autumn," he writes that the trees with yellow leaves are "like soft bonfires of clear gold."

Many other pieces are devoted to animals, both Platero and others. In the vignette "Swallows," the narrator is concerned that an early warm spell has fooled the sparrows into believing winter is over, and he fears they have come to Moguer too soon; "They will die of cold, Platero!" he exclaims to his donkey. In "Sparrows," the narrator is envious of the sparrows' freedom from the expectations and institutions of human society. In "The Gelding," Platero and the narrator watch Darbón, the veterinarian, castrate a young horse, and in "The Mangy Dog," a guard impulsively shoots a sickly dog that has followed Diana, the narrator's dog, home; afterward the guard feels remorse for his actions.

The narrator also tells Platero of animals he knew as a child; in "Almirante," he tells of a horse he once had, who was sold away, and in "Lord," he describes his childhood dog, who was bitten by a rabid dog and had to be taken away.

MEDIA ADAPTATIONS

- Italian composer Mario Castelnuovo-Tedesco composed guitar pieces to accompany a narrator reading a selection of the vignettes from *Platero and I*. The readings are available on CD (1995) on the Summit classical record label, featuring Frank Koonce as guitarist and Don Doyle as the narrator.

- Pianist Sandrine Erdely-Sayo has written and performed several piano compositions inspired by *Platero and I*, though the pieces are not accompanied by a narrator. The 2010 CD features fifteen pieces, each inspired by a different vignette from the book, and it is available on the Arabesque Recordings label. It is also available as an MP3 download.

In these pieces, the narrator reveals his tender affection for all the animals in his life, and his highly emotional nature.

Many of the vignettes feature children; the narrator spends far more time with children and animals than with other adults. (It is not specified if any of these children belong to the narrator; Jiménez himself had no children of his own, but he did have nieces and nephews.) Some pieces illustrate the joy of childhood, as the children play with Platero and the narrator. For instance, in "The Crown of Parsley," the children race against each other to win the prize of a book that the narrator has recently received; Platero joins the race, and when he wins, the narrator fashions a crown for him from parsley leaves. In "The Forgotten Grapes," some little girls playing joyously in the country find one last cluster of grapes left from the harvest. The narrator divides the grapes between them, throwing the last to Platero.

Some of the pieces illustrate the poverty of Moguer's children. In "Games at Dusk," the children pretend to be wealthy royalty and brag of their fathers' possessions, which the narrator knows to be few; in "Bread," poor children go from door to door, begging for a bit of bread; in "Christmas," poor children gather around an outdoor fire on Christmas Eve to warm their chilled hands. These poor children, the narrator says, "have no Nativity crib."

Life in rural Andalusia can be harsh, and the narrator tells of two children who pass away. In "The Half-Wit Child," Jiménez writes of a handicapped child who dies, and the narrator imagines him seated in a chair in heaven, surrounded by roses. In "The Consumptive" and "The Little Girl," he tells of a girl who is very fond of Platero, who dies of tuberculosis.

The day-to-day life of Moguer is the subject of several pieces; in "Bread," "Wine," and "The Grape Harvest," Jiménez describes the daily delivery of bread, the harvesting of crops, and the business of winemaking.

Throughout this section, which makes up the majority of the book, the narrator confesses his deepest thoughts and fears to Platero, who is clearly his closest friend and confidant. Their relationship is poignant and moving; in the vignette "Friendship," the narrator says, "He well understands that I love him, and he bears me no grudge. He is so much like me that I have come to believe he dreams my own dreams."

Though the book has no conventional plot, there is a climax: the death of Platero. In "The Death," the narrator finds Platero lying in the straw, unable to stand; he calls Darbón, but nothing can be done to save him. In the three vignettes that follow—"Nostalgia," "The Sawhorse," and "Melancholy"—the grieving narrator struggles to come to terms with the event.

Afterthoughts of the Poet

This section, which is much briefer than the first, was written later, after the original version of the book had been released; in the second vignette, "The Cardboard Platero," Jiménez writes,

> Platero, when a year ago a bit of this book . . . left here for the world of men, a friend of yours and mine gave me as a present this Platero made of cardboard.

In "Obstinacy," he regrets that he did not let Platero have his own way more often, and in the last vignette of the book, "The Best Friend," he writes, "I continue preferring you, Platero, through all my days (I told you so many times!) to any other male friend."

CHARACTERS

Almirante

Almirante was a horse owned by the narrator's family in his youth, who was sold to a wealthy wine maker and taken away. The event left the narrator distraught; he says, "I do not know for how many days my heart was sick. They had to call the doctor and they gave me bromide and ether."

Blanca

The narrator often spends time with children, and Blanca, "tender, white and pink as a peach blossom," is mentioned in several different vignettes. Whether she is the narrator's own child, a niece, or another relation, is not clear.

Darbón

Darbón is Platero's veterinarian, a huge man ("large as a piebald ox") with no teeth. Despite his imposing bulk, he is "tender like a child with Platero," a quality that endears him to the narrator. Darbón's daughter died in childhood; at the end of the vignette devoted to his description, he looks toward the cemetery and says sadly, "My little girl, my poor little girl."

Diana

Diana is a dog that the narrator describes as "the beautiful white bitch that resembles the crescent moon." Though it is not clear if the dog belongs to the narrator or not, she appears in several different vignettes.

Don José

Though the priest Don José is not a major character, he is significant because he personifies the hypocrisy of religion the narrator disdains. Don José hurls stones at children who trespass in his orchard, as well as at birds, washerwomen, and even flowers. He uses profane language and has little regard for nature, seeing in it only "examples of disorder, hardness, frigidity, violence, decay." However, "When time to pray comes, all turns around." Then the priest becomes pious and reverent, puts on his vestments, and rides to the village, "like Jesus going to his death."

The Half-Wit Child

The narrator tells of a mentally disabled child who sits on his porch and watches the world go by. Sadly, the child dies from an unnamed illness, and the narrator imagines him in heaven.

The Little Girl

One piece is devoted to a little girl who is very fond of Platero. When the girl falls ill, the narrator can hear her calling for Platero in the delirium of fever. When she dies, the narrator is deeply affected and mentions her in a later vignette along with Lord and Almirante.

Lord

Lord was a fox terrier the narrator owned in his youth, who died after being bitten by a mad dog. The narrator was clearly deeply affected by the dog's passing, as evidenced by this passage:

> The look he left behind when they were taking him away down the little street still pierces my heart as it did then, Platero; in the same way that the light of a dead star, forever alive, survives its own nothingness through the exalted intensity of its painful trail.

Narrator

The narrator, the owner of Platero, identifies himself in one vignette as Juan Ramón Jiménez. A solitary man who prefers the company of animals to people, he feels a deep connection to nature and its beauty. The reader gets the sense that the narrator has experienced tragedy in his life; at the opening of the vignette "The Crazy Man," Jiménez writes, "Dressed in mourning, with my Nazarene beard and my narrow, black hat, I must cut a strange figure riding Platero's gray softness." Whom he is mourning, the narrator does not specify. Throughout the book, he laments the death of his dog Lord; Almirante, a horse from his childhood; and a little girl who was kind to Platero.

The narrator seems estranged from society and disdains its rituals, conventions, and religion. In the vignette "Sparrows," he says:

> Everyone has gone to church. The sparrows, Platero and I have stayed in the garden. . . . Blessed birds with no holidays! Within the free monotony of their condition, their truth, the bells mean nothing to them, except, perhaps, a vague joy. Happy, with no fateful obligations, without those heavens and those hells that bring ecstasy or fright to the poor slave people, without any morals but their own, nor any God but the blue sky, they are my brothers, my sweet brothers.

The narrator spends little time with other adults, but he sometimes enjoys the company of children, especially those who are kind to Platero. However, his allegiance is always to

nature and animals; in "Freedom," some children set a trap to catch birds, and the narrator, hearing the birds singing, laments, "Poor, innocent concert, so close to such evil hearts!"

Platero

Platero is a gray donkey who belongs to the narrator. The word "platero" in Spanish is used to describe someone who deals in silver and gold, and it is also commonly used to describe donkeys that are silvery gray in color. Platero is the narrator's closest friend and confidant, and the narrator idealizes him, attributing to him human qualities. When Platero gets a thorn in his foot, the narrator says, "But man, what is the matter?" as though speaking to a person. In another vignette, the narrator says of Platero, "He is so much like me that I have come to believe he dreams my own dreams." In another scene, when the village is having a carnival, the narrator says, "Like me he wants nothing to do with carnivals. . . . We are no good at this sort of thing."

While the narrator sees Platero as very much like him, he also feels that Platero is superior, lacking the human vices that plague the narrator. In "The Best Friend," the narrator says, "How superior you are to me and to everyone, Platero!"

Sarito

Sarito is a young black man who used to be the servant of the narrator's girlfriend. He left to become a bullfighter, without success, and when the narrator encounters him, he is penniless.

THEMES

Andalusian Culture

Many of the short pieces that make up *Platero and I* give the reader a glimpse into the daily life of Moguer, a town in the Andalusian region of Spain. In one piece, the narrator says, "Moguer's soul is bread." In a later piece, he changes his mind and says, "No. Moguer is like a reed of heavy and clear crystal which awaits the whole year, under the round blue sky, its wine of gold." Frequent mention is made of the town's wine-making heritage, of donkeys laden with grapes returning from the harvest, of grapes being crushed into wine by men's feet. Moguer is "a

TOPICS FOR FURTHER STUDY

- One of the difficulties of studying literature from other cultures is inconsistency in translation. Find two different translations of *Platero and I* (for example, there is a translation by Antonio T. de Nicolás, and another by Eloise Roach). Choose one vignette and highlight the differences in translation between the two. Which translation do you prefer? Write an essay that explains why you prefer one over the other.

- In *Platero and I*, Jiménez paints an affectionate portrait of his hometown of Moguer. Research Andalusia and Moguer online. Use GoogleMaps and GoogleEarth to create a map of Spain and indicate the location of the Andalusian region and Moguer, and set up links to all the facts you can find about the town. Present your map to the class on your Web page.

- Write a short vignette, like those in the book, dedicated to a pet you have owned or known. Base the vignette on a specific experience you had with your pet (going to the vet, taking a walk) rather than writing general feelings ("He was a great dog."). Find a photo or draw a picture of your pet to include with your vignette.

- Read the young-adult novel *Tell the Moon to Come Out* by Joan Lingard or *Lost in Spain* by John Wilson, both of which concern the Spanish Civil War. What kind of effect do you think the war and the subsequent dictatorship of Francisco Franco had on artists and writers? Write a short report on the book and what you learned about the Spanish Civil War. Compare your findings to those of other students in your class by creating a Wikispace that all students can add information to. Does your information agree, or did other students come away from the book with different ideas about this war?

---

fountain of wine which, like blood, rushes again and again to any of its wounds."

The narrator also mentions various festivals, parades, and gatherings, such as the bullfights, and the Fair of the Rocío. He prefers to stay away from these events, however, watching them from afar with Platero, or just enjoying the solitude: "How beautiful the countryside is on these holidays when everyone abandons it!"

Bereavement

More than once in the book it is mentioned that the narrator is "dressed in mourning." Jiménez leaves the question of who is being mourned open to interpretation. A feeling of melancholy pervades Jiménez's writing, despite the light-hearted tone he often uses when describing Platero's antics, and the obvious joy he derives from the miracles of nature. The narrator mourns many loved ones throughout the book, most of

them animals and children. In a foreshadowing of Platero's death, he promises Platero early in the book that when he dies, he will not go to the boneyard where unloved animals are taken but will be buried "at the foot of the great round pine tree in the orchard at La Piña, which you like so much." The narrator also mourns the land of his childhood; in the vignette "The River," he says, "Look Platero, what they have done to the river with those mines, those bad hearts and bad politics." In another, he reminisces about how the grape harvest used to be plentiful, requiring twenty wine presses, and now one press is all that is needed.

The main portion of the book is "The Elegy"; elegy is a term usually used to describe a poem that laments the departed. Some versions of the book are subtitled "An Andalusian Elegy," implying that Jiménez is mourning not just Platero and his other loved ones, but a whole

The bakers sell fresh bread from baskets in the streets. (*Sony Ho | Shutterstock.com*)

way of life, a simpler, slower way of life that he enjoyed in Moguer. Jiménez wrote *Platero and I* after spending six years in Moguer. He moved to Madrid in 1912, and though he visited family in Moguer over the years, he never lived there again.

Friendship

The friendship of Platero and the narrator is the centerpiece of the book. Through his "conversations" with the donkey, the narrator expresses himself fully, discussing his love and awe for nature and speaking of his feelings unselfconsciously. With Platero, the narrator is not confined by his culture's concept of masculinity. In the last piece of the book ("The Best Friend"), he says, "Together we listen to distant birds, smell the roses . . . roll on the grass; everything people say in the back room of the pharmacy is not the proper thing for men to do." He also points out that Platero, as well as horses, dogs, and bulls ("by their strength at the top of the *macho* scale"), all like the same "delicate" things that he does and are not ashamed. Only with Platero

can the narrator be himself, without reserve. This freedom of expression is especially critical for the narrator, a poet. (He identifies himself as Jiménez in the book).

Hypocrisy

While the narrator is a deeply spiritual man who speaks frequently of God and heaven, he is skeptical of the institutions of organized religion. Jiménez, in his own life, was estranged from the Catholic church, and according to Jiménez's biographer Donald F. Fogelquist, he saw the church as "an unnecessary intermediary between him and Christ." The narrator, likewise, says that he has always had "an instinctive horror of apologists, as well as the church, the Guardia Civil, bullfighters and accordions." He prefers the activities of nature to those of the church: "And when the people (poor people!) go to church on Sundays, closing their doors, the sparrows, in a joyful example of love without rituals, appear suddenly, with their fresh and youthful uproar."

Nowhere is this hypocrisy more evident than in the portrait of the priest Don José, an angry man who pelts birds and children with stones and swears viciously while off duty and then becomes pious and reverent when it is time to pray. The narrator once again expresses his preference of nature to organized religion, and animals to people, when he tells the reader, "The one who is really always an angel is his donkey, a true lady."

Nature

Jiménez evokes the beauty of his Andalusian home in lavish descriptions of nature; sunsets, flowers, streams and pools, trees, and animals are all described with reverence and affection. The narrator's communion with nature is, in effect, his religion. This is amply illustrated in this passage from the piece "Spring":

> I go out to the orchard and sing praises to God of the blue day. Free concert of beaks, fresh and endless! The swallow, capricious, curls its song down the well; the bluebird whistles over the fallen orange; firebright, the oriole chatters from oak to oak; the nightingale laughs long and softly from the top of the eucalyptus; and in the great pine tree the sparrows argue passionately.

Shunning the society of other men, the narrator turns to nature for company and solace, and so it is not surprising that his best friend is Platero, a donkey. He describes the sparrows as his "brothers," and when a branch of his favorite pine tree must be cut off following a hurricane, the narrator says, "I felt as if they had snapped one of my own limbs; and, at times when a pain catches me unexpectedly, I believe the pine tree of La Corona hurts with me."

Poverty

Though the narrator's home is one of great natural beauty, Jiménez reminds us that, in Moguer, beauty and poverty live side-by-side. In one scene, some children, in a game of pretend, boast of their fathers' riches: "'My father has a silver watch,'" says one. "'And mine a horse,'" brags another. "'And mine a shotgun,'" says a third. Jiménez follows their boasts with the sobering reality: "A watch that will rise at dawn. A shotgun that will not kill hunger. A horse that will ride towards poverty." Similarly, when the village "bread man" comes with fragrant, fresh-baked loaves, and "the whole town opens its mouth," Jiménez reminds us once again

that not all can share in the event; the poor children, whose families cannot afford the bread, knock on doors and cry, "'Please, one little bit of bread!'" And when the village children excitedly gather about "the man with the peep-show," waiting with their coins, those without money look at the man "with a humble and flattering plea."

STYLE

Prose Poetry

The majority of Jiménez's work is poetry, and though *Platero and I* is written in prose, the lyrical language and striking metaphors Jiménez uses give the work the feel of poetry. This style of writing is often called prose poetry. Since the book is written in short pieces unconnected by any conventional story line, it feels more like a collection of poems than a novel.

Jiménez elevates descriptions of mundane scenes and everyday events with lyrical imagery, as in this description of Platero in his stable:

> When, at noon, I go to see Platero, a transparent ray from the overhead sun lights up a great patch of gold on the soft silver of his back. Beneath his belly, on the dark floor, vaguely green that touches everything with an emerald glow, the old roof sheds clear coins of fire.

In the same scene, he also describes the sunlight as "the iridescent treasure of the zenith." Such metaphors make the vignettes of *Platero and I* feel more like poetry than ordinary prose.

Symbolism

Of the many symbols Jiménez uses in *Platero and I*, two recur frequently: roses and butterflies. Jiménez often applies the rose as a symbol for perfection and beauty, both in this book and in much of his poetry as well. In one vignette, he compares Platero's eyes to roses: "Your eyes, Platero, which you do not see, and which you meekly raise to the sky, are two beautiful roses." In another vignette that describes a particularly beautiful spring morning, he writes, "We seem to be in a large honeycomb of light, as if we were in the bosom of an immense, warm, burning rose." When a little boy of his acquaintance dies, the narrator imagines him in heaven, "by the side of exquisite roses"; likewise, after Platero's death, he describes him in heaven "happy in your meadow of eternal roses."

Jiménez uses butterflies to symbolize the soul, the source of imagination and inspiration. In the second vignette of the book, a "dark man" stops the narrator to check Platero"s saddlebags. He asks the narrator, "'Carrying anything?'" The narrator replies, "'See for yourself . . . white butterflies. . . .'" When the man checks the bags, he sees nothing; "And so the imagination's heavenly food passes, free and innocent, paying no tribute to the tax collectors." Platero and the narrator, Jiménez tells the reader, are carrying nothing but their souls. In "The Old Cemetery," just before the narrator lists for Platero the names of friends and loved ones buried there, he says, "Platero, look at those two white butterflies." After Platero's death, the narrator visits his grave and asks aloud, "'Platero, tell me: do you still remember me?' And as if answering my question, a light white butterfly I had not seen before, was insistently flying, like a soul, from lily to lily."

Use of Color

Jiménez uses color abundantly in his descriptions. He employs language to paint his scenes in the mind of the reader, as in this description of a garden park in the city:

> the strolling coach passes, decked with tiny mauve flags and a little green canopy; the boat cart of the nut vendor, all covered red and gold, with the rigging full of peanuts and its smoky chimney; the little girl selling balloons, with her gigantic flying cluster, blue, green and red.

Through the use of color, Jiménez makes Moguer seem like an almost enchanted land, bathed in gold (golds and yellows are the most frequently used colors). He often employs precious metals and stones in his color descriptions, heightening this impression of enchantment. Pomegranates are "edible amethysts," the autumn sky is "a wide sword of clean gold," spots of sunshine are "coins of fire," and a thorn in Platero's foot is an "emerald dagger."

HISTORICAL CONTEXT

Spanish Government

Platero and I was first published in 1914; a longer version, which is the edition analyzed in this essay, was released in 1917. Jiménez wrote the book after spending six years in his hometown of Moguer. During the years that Jiménez spent in Moguer, there was much political upheaval in

Spain. Rapid economic industrialization in the early 1900s led to increasing labor unrest and strikes, which often led to violence. Strikes by impoverished workers in Andalusia were often brutally suppressed. In July 1909, when the government called up military reserves to serve in Morocco, a general strike was called in sympathy with the military men, many of whom had settled down and had families after their term of active service. Police lost control of the striking mobs, and violence ensued; hundreds were killed and injured.

The government of Spain during this time was determined by an alternating party system; one party would rule, and then the other would take over. King Alfonso XIII, however, had the power to remove and appoint leaders as he saw fit. After the "Tragic Week" in July, as the strike riots became known, he removed the conservative leader Antonio Maura and appointed the liberal Segismundo Moret, who then yielded to a younger liberal, Jose Canalejas. Canalejas lowered taxes on the poor and championed many reforms to help labor. However, Canalejas took a strong stand when labor strikes became violent, sometimes using the military to establish order. In 1912, he was assassinated by an anarchist.

Because *Platero and I* has such a narrow focus (mainly, the relationship between the narrator and Platero), most of these issues do not affect the narrative. However, Jiménez sometimes mentions the Guardia Civil (Civil Guard), the Spanish military police force. In one vignette, "The Fable," the narrator says he has an "instinctive horror of apologists, as well as the church, the Guardia Civil, bullfighters and accordions." In another, he says, "I was born here, Platero, in this large house now headquarters for the Guardia Civil." And when the townspeople are firing guns at the effigy of Judas, the narrator says, "Only that Judas today, Platero, is the politician, or the teacher, or the lawyer, or the tax collector, or the mayor." The reader can see the effects of the country's political unrest: figures of authority are viewed with suspicion and distrust, and the house of the narrator"s once prosperous family has become a base for the military police.

Between the first publication of *Platero and I* in 1914 and the second in 1917, much of Europe became embroiled in World War I; Spain, not obligated by any alliances, remained neutral. This neutrality allowed Spain to profit economically by exporting to Allied powers and selling goods to

COMPARE & CONTRAST

- **1914:** Agriculture, such as the vineyards Jiménez writes of, constitutes the majority of Spain's economy.

  Today: Agriculture accounts for less than 4 percent of Spain's gross domestic product (GDP). Services such as hospitality, retail trade, information, education, and government make up the majority of Spain's GDP.

- **1914:** The government of Spain is a constitutional monarchy, a government ruled by a monarch whose powers are limited by a written constitution. King Alfonso XIII is the reigning monarch.

  Today: Spain is once again a constitutional monarchy and is ruled by Juan Carlos I (the grandson of Alfonso XIII) and an elected government presided over by Prime Minister José Luis Rodríguez Zapatero. However, it has only been a constitutional monarchy since 1978; from 1939 to 1975, Spain was a dictatorship ruled by the oppressive dictator Francisco Franco.

- **1914:** The main business in Moguer is winemaking, and grapes are the main crop grown in this rural town.

  Today: Over the years, the dominance of the winemaking business in Moguer gradually dwindled, and now strawberries are the chief cash crop of the area; however, thanks to more modern methods, winemaking is making a comeback in the region.

- **1914:** The period from 1914 to 1920 is sometimes known as the "Golden Age of Bullfighting," in part because of the rivalry between two expert matadors, Juan Belmonte and Joselito, who are competing during this time. Jiménez, an animal lover, does not enjoy the bullfights, though it is a favorite spectacle in the Andalusian region.

  Today: Bullfighting is still a popular attraction for tourists in Andalusia and other parts of Spain, despite the vehement opposition of animal rights groups all over the world.

markets that the combatants were no longer able to supply. Greater prosperity did not translate to greater peace, however; distrust of politicians was still high, and in the elections of 1916, less than half of Spanish citizens voted.

Spain's Literary Renaissance

At the turn of the century, Spain was undergoing an intellectual renaissance. The Generation of '98, a group of writers, philosophers, and other intellectuals, began a discussion of Spanish culture and government, prompted by Spain's defeat in the Spanish-American War. The writers of this generation felt that Spanish poetry of the past was verbose and pompous, and they were looking to inject a new vitality into Spanish literature. This movement was known as modernism, and two of its key figures were the poets Miguel de Unamuno and Rubén Darío. Darío

was an inspiration and mentor to Jiménez, and the two poets remained good friends until Darío's death in 1916.

By the time Jiménez wrote *Platero and I*, he was already a well-regarded poet in Spain. In 1910, though he was only twenty-eight, he was elected to membership in the Royal Spanish Academy, Spain's greatest literary honor. He turned down the membership, however; according to biographer Fogelquist, he considered the Academy a "casino for the aged and aging."

CRITICAL OVERVIEW

In an essay on Jiménez's work, Howard T. Young calls *Platero and I* a "masterpiece" and claims that "*Platero y yo* must be, after *Don*

They were from a little mountain village called Moguer. *(anweber | Shutterstock.com)*

Quixote, the most widely read book in the Hispanic world." Though Jiménez is known primarily as a poet, ironically, this book of prose is his best-known work. For many years, it was considered a children's book; in many Spanish-speaking countries, *Platero and I* is regularly taught in primary schools. In a prologue to the book, however, Jiménez states emphatically, "I have never written nor will I ever write anything for children, because I believe that the child can read the books that grownups read, with some few exceptions that come to everyone's mind."

Most of the English-speaking world knew little of Jiménez's work until 1956, when he was awarded the Nobel Prize in Literature. As reviewer Dudley Fitts writes in the *New York Times Book Review* in 1957, "When Juan Ramón Jiménez was awarded the Nobel Prize for literature last year, there must have been a good deal of scurrying about in public libraries and editorial back rooms to find out exactly who he was." In Fitts's review of *Platero and I,* he describes the vignettes as "exquisite little prose pieces," but qualifies his praise, saying that the work does not fully represent Jiménez's later, more mature work.

More effusive praise comes from Edwin Honig of the *Saturday Review of Literature,* who claims the book is "a good deal more than the children's classic it has been called for forty years," and says, "the kind of realism, love, and

restraint that characterizes the poet's vision has the quality of [William] Blake's songs of innocence and experience."

While reviews of *Platero and I* are largely positive, Jiménez's work has had its detractors. In a harsh review of the collection *Three Hundred Poems, 1903–1953,* reviewer John Frederick Nims of the *New York Times Book Review* comments that Spanish poet Luis Cernuda characterized Jiménez as "self-obsessed, contemptuous of humanity, essentially brainless," and then adds, "Nothing in my own reading of Jiménez leads me to disagree very strongly with this."

Many critics agree that Jiménez's very early work is flawed, and that his writing matures and improves significantly with the passing years. His first two volumes of poetry, according to biographer Fogelquist, are marred by "exaggerated sentimentality," and many of the poems are "contrived, morbid, wordy, superficial." Young concurs, calling them "vulgarly sentimental and pointlessly prolific." Jiménez must have agreed with these assessments, because later in life, according to Young, "He set about systematically trying to destroy all copies of *Ninfeas* and *Almas de violeta* he could get his hands on."

In later works, Jiménez tempers his tendency toward melancholy and morbidity. Many consider the book *Diary of a Newly Married Poet* a milestone in his career, and Jiménez himself considered it his finest work. Some credit his wife Zenobia as a positive influence; her cheerful disposition served to counter his gloomy outlook and help Jiménez produce more balanced work.

Whatever the limitations of his earliest works, they are easily compensated for by the huge volume of work Jiménez produced in the rest of his career. Jiménez is recognized as a landmark figure in Spanish culture; Fogelquist calls him "a universal poet, whose work was clearly one of the enduring values of Spanish literature."

CRITICISM

Laura Beth Pryor

Pryor is a freelance writer with twenty-five years of experience in professional writing, with an emphasis on fiction. In the following essay, she examines the character of Platero in Platero and I *as a projection of the author's imagination.*

WHAT DO I READ NEXT?

- Jiménez left Spain in 1936 to escape the Spanish Civil War, which lasted from 1936 to 1939. Joan Lingard's 2003 young-adult novel, *Tell the Moon to Come Out*, relates the story of Nick, a young Scottish man whose father went to Spain to fight in the war and never returned. Nick goes to Spain to try and find him and meets Isabel, the daughter of a brutal sergeant in the Civil Guard.

- The 1957 volume *The Selected Writings of Juan Ramón Jiménez*, translated by H. R. Hays and edited by Eugenio Florit, organizes a selection of Jiménez's poetry from the earliest times of his career until he stopped writing in 1956. It also includes a selection of vignettes from *Platero and I* and profiles of other writers and artists written by Jiménez.

- The nineteenth-century poet Gustavo Adolfo Bécquer was an enormous influence on Jiménez. The book *Rhymes and Legends (Selection)/Rimas y Leyendas (seleccion): A Dual Language Book* (2006) includes both the original Spanish version and the English translation of Bécquer's two most famous works: *Rimas*, a collection of melancholy poetry, and *Leyendas*, six tales featuring the supernatural.

- Robert Louis Stevenson's 1879 travel memoir, *Travels with a Donkey in the Cevennes*, tells of Stevenson's twelve-day hike through the Cevennes, a mountain region in France, accompanied by an irascible donkey named Modestine. By the end of the journey, Stevenson's exasperation with the donkey has turned to affection. The book includes Stevenson's reflections on the history of the area; a Protestant rebellion took place in the Cevennes in 1702.

- The Spanish-American War of 1898 had a significant effect on Spain's culture and political status as a nation. Albert Marrin's 1991 history of the war, *The Spanish-American War*, takes a closer look at America's motives for going to war and how American involvement in this war led to later conflicts with other nations.

- Like Jiménez, poet and playwright Federico García Lorca was a native of Andalusia. Though he was killed by Franco's soldiers at the beginning of the Spanish Civil War when he was only thirty-eight, he is one of Spain's most revered poets. The 1973 collection (re-released in 1997) *Lorca & Jiménez: Selected Poems*, edited and translated by Robert Bly, includes both the original Spanish version of the poems and the English translations, as well as a preface by Bly.

- Ernest Hemingway's 1940 novel, *For Whom the Bell Tolls*, based on his own experiences in Spain during the Spanish Civil War, tells the story of Robert Jordan, a young American fighting against Franco's forces. The story is set in the Andalusian town of Ronda (famous as the birthplace of bullfighting).

- Like *Platero and I*, Anton Ferreira's 2002 children's novel, *Zulu Dog*, tells of the strong relationship between a person and his pet. Young Vusi is a poor black boy living in postapartheid South Africa who finds a stray, three-legged dog he names Gillette. Vusi and Gillette become friends with Shirley, the daughter of a wealthy white farmer, but Shirley's father does not approve.

Jiménez knew well the difficulties of being a sensitive man of letters in a society that treasured the image of the macho male. Like many artists, he resented having his experience of life restricted by roles or stereotypes to which others expected him to conform. In *Platero and I*, he laments to his donkey, Platero, that he is the only male friend with whom he can "listen to distant birds, smell the roses, drink from the fountain, remain silent, eat oranges, smile, look at the clouds, roll on the grass; everything people say in the back room of the pharmacy is not the proper thing for men to do." Likewise, Jiménez was uncomfortable with the strict dogma of the Catholic church, and in *Platero and I*, he prefers to stay home with his beloved donkey and commune with nature on holy days, rather than accompany the rest of the town to church. He envies the sparrows, "without any morals but their own, nor any God but the blue sky." In the character of Platero, Jiménez creates a being endowed with the best of human qualities, without the restrictions to which Jiménez, a man of Spanish society, is subjected. Platero is complete, an individual allowed to encompass the full range of experience and expression. He is macho, he is feminine, he is strong, he is weak, he is fearful, he is brave. No donkey code of conduct forces him to limit his emotions or actions to one end of the spectrum.

In the first piece of the book, "Platero," Jiménez immediately introduces this idea; he writes of Platero, "He is tender and cuddly, as a little boy, as a little girl . . . but inside he is strong and dry as a stone." Here on page one, Platero has already embraced a host of opposites: tender and strong, cuddly and stonelike, boy and girl. In the vignette "The Fair of the Rocío," Platero is at first described as something of a ladies' man: "I took him, handsome and elegant, so that he could bray sweet nothings to the girls along the Calle de la Fuente." Later in the same piece, the narrator says, "Platero then bent his front legs and knelt gently, like a woman—one of his little tricks!—soft, humble and willing." Here Platero is able to embrace both male and female qualities, without risking censure from the people "in the back room of the pharmacy." It is only the narrator who is restricted by societal expectations, as when he encounters a young black man, whom he knows and likes. Some nearby field workers look upon the man "with ill-concealed disdain," and the narrator says, "Sarito, not daring to caress me, was petting Platero." Here a simple gesture of affection must be redirected from the narrator to Platero to conform to the expectations and prejudices of society.

Platero is able to encompass not only both male and female but also both human and animal characteristics. In many instances, Platero behaves as one would expect a donkey to behave: he brays loudly, eats flowers, and carries heavy loads for the narrator. Yet, Jiménez often endows Platero with human traits and emotions as well. When the narrator stretches out beneath a tree and begins to read poetry, Platero joins him, "attracted, no doubt, by Orpheus' lyre." In another piece, Jiménez calls Platero "patient and thoughtful, melancholic and lovable, the Marcus Aurelius of the fields." He is the ideal confidant and friend; as the narrator tells Platero, "I can always tell you everything in my joy and in my pain, Platero, and everything is all right with you. While you, on the other hand, being so good, never interrupt me for anything." Platero is credited with an understanding of interpersonal relationships superior to that of any of the narrator's human friends. The narrator calls Platero his best male friend, adding that "woman is different, incomparable, now you understand that about this there is no need to talk."

The reader could assume that the narrator is simply exaggerating the capabilities of his pet out of affection, as pet owners are wont to do. However, Jiménez provides us with clues that what he is doing is not just exaggerating but creating an alter ego, a gray furry Jiménez that represents the author's ideal self. In several scenes, the narrator and Platero become mirrors of each other, or even merge into one being. In "The Last Siesta," Platero looks at the narrator with sleepy eyes, and "staring at his tired eyes, my eyes become tired again." In another vignette, the narrator is reading a book, Platero is eating, and their actions reflect each other: "From time to time, Platero stops eating and looks at me. . . . I, from time to time, stop reading and look at Platero." Even the wording is parallel, with "from time to time" repeated for both the narrator and Platero. It is as though Jiménez is looking into a silvery, furry mirror. In "Return," Jiménez and Platero become one; riding in the dark, the narrator says, "I suddenly thought of Platero, who, though walking under me, I had forgotten as if he were my own body." In "Friendship," the narrator claims, "He is so much like me that I have come to believe he dreams my own dreams." And in "The Garden," when a guard refuses to let Platero enter a public park, saying, "'The donkey cannot get in, sir,'" the narrator replies, "'The donkey? What donkey?'" Jiménez tells the reader he has forgotten

The old man rode his little donkey, Platero, everywhere. *(Aleksandar Todorovia / Shutterstock.com)*

Platero's "animal shape." Here, only his form is animal; in spirit he is entirely human.

Platero is not, however, a mere clone of the narrator; in "The Best Friend," the narrator says, "How superior you are to me and to everyone, Platero!" For the narrator, Platero represents who he could be, in an ideal world, free of the constraints of gender, religion, prejudice, or politics. Free, too, of the all too human failings that Jiménez laments near the end of the book: "my evil deeds, my cynicisms, my impertinences." Jiménez projects only his best qualities onto the little burro; even in the most stereotypical quality of the donkey, obstinacy, the narrator claims to be more flawed than his beloved Platero: "I, a stubborn donkey, too, but devilish donkey, envious donkey, unjust donkey."

Even after Platero's death, the narrator continues to talk to him, much as he did before; he says, "Nothing has happened. You are alive and I with you." Because the idealized Platero was a product of the narrator's imagination, he lives on, now in the form of this book, which "carries on its back of paper my soul." Jiménez draws a parallel between his relationship with Platero and his relationship with his writing. Both represent a safe, cherished outlet for the thoughts and emotions Jiménez does not dare express aloud; like Platero, the pen and page do not judge or censure, but listen patiently to the tales Jiménez tells them.

Source: Laura Beth Pryor, Critical Essay on *Platero and I*, in *Novels for Students*, Gale, Cengage Learning, 2011.

Leonard S. Marcus
In the following excerpt, Marcus challenges Jiménez's belief that he never wrote a children's book.

Like the *Alices* and *Huckleberry Finn*, to recall two companion anomalies not otherwise often associated with it (much less with each other), Juan Ramón Jiménez's full-hearted prose poem meditation *Platero and I* stands among the very few acknowledged masterpieces both of children's literature and of literature as a whole. In the poet's native Spain, where school children read it, university students reread it and scholars continue to discuss its merits, *Platero* is a national classic, perhaps second only to *Don Quixote* in the popular estimate. It has, since its

> IN *PLATERO AND I* CHILDHOOD REPRESENTS A SPIRITUAL STATE OF GRACE, A CONDITION, HOWEVER, MODIFIED AT TIMES IF NOT UTTERLY REVERSED BY CONTRADICTORY TENDENCIES IN HUMAN NATURE AND BY SOCIAL INFLUENCES—POVERTY AND OTHERS—THAT CAN LEAD TO EARLY DISILLUSIONMENT."

publication more than sixty years ago, also circulated in hundreds of editions throughout the Spanish speaking world. Nor has interest in the book remained limited to readers, young or old, of Hispanic culture, *Platero* has been translated into French, German, Italian (three versions), Portuguese, Norwegian, Swedish, Dutch, Basque and Hebrew—many though by no means all of these editions intended mainly for the young. When two English language renderings appeared in the mid-fifties (as a consequence of Jiménez's winning the Nobel Prize for Literature for 1956), they shared the curious cultural distinction of being favorably reviewed for adults in such serious-minded popular magazines as the *New Republic* and the *New Yorker* while also turning up on the New York Public Library's annual list of recommended "juveniles"—an auspicious enough North American welcome, which was to be followed in 1978 by still another English language translation. All the stranger, then, that as far as one can tell, *Platero and I* is hardly known among English speaking readers today, except to poets and other devoted toilers-in-literature, to high school and college students of Spanish who attempt it in the original as those learning French tackle *The Little Prince*, and (probably least of all) to older children.

Jiménez (1881–1958) had not, by his own account, written *Platero* as a children's book but as the second of a three-part poetic work, *Ballads of Spring*. In 1913 the Spanish publisher La Lectura, having heard about the project, invited him—a poet by then greatly admired in his own country—to submit portions of the manuscript to the house's Biblioteca Juventud (Youth Library), to which he agreed. An abridged *Platero* appeared at Christmas the following year; the full text was first brought out by Calleja in 1917.

A variety of circumstances, in addition to the publication of La Lectura's "short" *Platero*, may also have contributed to the book's becoming widely known—and in some instances dismissed by critics—as *children's* reading. At the time Jiménez was finishing it, he had just met his future wife, Zenobia Camprubi Aymar, who did herself take a serious interest in children's literature. Together they translated Rabindranath Tagore's vignettes about childhood, *The Crescent Moon*; throughout their life together the couple were known for their love of the young. Several years after *Platero* appeared, Jiménez also published Spanish renderings of some of Blake's *Songs of Experience*, including "The Tyger"—and so on. Yet Jiménez himself insisted, in comments that reveal his fierce respect for the young, "I have never written anything for children"—this, in a prologue reprinted in some editions of the book—"because I believe that the child can read what the man reads, with certain exceptions that come to everyone's mind. . . ."

There are of course other substantive reasons relating directly to *Platero's* contents that account both for the warm response many children have given it and—what is not necessarily the same thing—for the conviction of many adults that the book is for children only; we will come to these matters presently.

. . . In *Platero and I* childhood represents a spiritual state of grace, a condition, however, modified at times if not utterly reversed by contradictory tendencies in human nature and by social influences—poverty and others—that can lead to early disillusionment.

In his warm embrace of childhood—as touchingly immediate as Dickens'—Jiménez is entirely at ease among the young: they joke with him as he takes part in their games and outings. He acts in an endearing though dignified, fatherly or perhaps grandfatherly way—there is none of the tension that usually exists between parents and their own young—nor does one suspect that he wishes to turn back the clock on his own past. There is scarcely a hint of regression in his special regard for children but rather an identification-in-parallel of the poet's situation with certain aspects of the child's: the intense and playful awareness of the sensory world and the struggle to find within it one's own terms of expression, one's identity; the sense of being a marginal figure in society.

Platero is, as books of lasting interest to children are likely to be, subversive of adult authority. Readers quickly seal a conspiratorial pact with the poet, whose shrewdest and bitterest satires concern teachers, priests, unfeeling doctors and heartless nuns, Limpiani the school master who "makes each child share his lunch with him ... and so eats thirteen halves himself ...."; the Curate Don José in whose orchard at the end of each day the rocks lie "in a different place, having been hurled in furious hostility against birds and washerwomen, children and flowers."

Jiménez in these passages throws a few stones of his own of course in championing the defenseless things of the world. But it is not in any case primarily as a protector that he seeks out children's company. Once, he says, there was a girl who in high-spirited, coquettish fun would dress up as a ghost to scare her friends and who during one such escapade was struck dead by lightning. The story as related has no moral—there is no hint that the girl's mischievous conduct was the cause of her death. Rather its aspects of phantasmagoria and the macabre are what fascinate Jiménez. Like a mystery play the story deepens rather than dissolves one's sense of the ineffable strangeness of life. The girl, on the night of her death, had in a sense, dressed for the occasion; a child's spirit-game had metamorphosed into ghostly reality.

The child for Jiménez, then, is a figure of candor and spiritual change. As contemporary psychology begins increasingly to view adulthood as an experience of ongoing inner developments it may be that the emphasis on the child in *Platero*, and in the literary tradition that begins with Thomas Traherne, William Blake, and William Wordsworth will someday seem gratuitous, as in fact in certain instances—Jiménez's reference to "the magic sun of my childhood" and others—it already does.

But in *Platero* an attentive psychological realism asserts itself repeatedly to give the lie to mere nostalgia and wishful thinking about the young. The poet reconstructs from memory features of a child's mental world, the limited powers of generalization, for one, which yield a disjointed—though truthful in its way—perception of experience. A certain tree across the street from his boyhood home appeared to him then as "two myrtle trees, which I never saw as one: one that I could see from my balcony, top rife with wind or sun; the other, the one that I saw in Don José's yards, from the trunk up ...."

He remembers the importance of one's name in the formation of a child's identity, as when from a traveling salesman in stationery supplies the poet had as a boy once ordered an ink pad and rubber stamp with which to print his name.

> At last ... [the salesman] brought it.... When I touched a spring, the stamp appeared, brand new, shining bright.
>
> Was anything left unmarked in my house? What was not mine? ... The following day with what gladsome haste I carried everything to school, everything—books, smock, hat, shoes, hands, marked with the legend: JUAN RAMÓN JIMÉNEZ MOGUER.

Thus the self takes title to its world. The novelist Richard Hughes describes a similar incident in a middle-class British colonial girl's growing-up: "There was hardly an article of ship's use ... but she had marked it as her property: and what she had marked ... no one might touch—if she could prevent it. To parody Hobbes, she claimed as her own whatever she had mixed her imagination with." So too Jiménez's anecdote is a kind of parody and still more a parable of the art of the poet to whom a pear tree "displays its triple crown of leaves, pears, and sparrows"; the crickets' song at dusk, low at first, "changes tone, learns a little from itself, rises ... "; and twilight yields a "contagious enchantment which holds the town as if nailed on the cross of a long sad thought." With such artifice the poet, too, puts his signature or stamp on reality.

Yet Jiménez strikes no easy identification between children and poets, being himself too much the artist-as-perfectionist to accept that bit of Romantic soothsaying. And even in moments of ardent sympathy for children's suffering he views matters dispassionately, considering the child's condition first from one perspective, then from another. A certain idiot boy is to him "one of those wretched children to whom the power of speech and the gift of beauty never come; gay in himself, sad to look upon; all in all to his mother, nothing to others." Jiménez likewise records the callousness and brutal disregard for life that children, as much as their elders, are capable of. He dotingly compares Platero to a child and children to his benign four-legged companion—without condescension toward either party—but he also describes the sense of mastery children sometimes seek in the mistreatment of a defenseless animal.

The poet recalls having enjoyed that peculiar satisfaction himself and relates the story of a childhood friend who once fired a shot at a turtle to test the hardness of its protective shell: "The lead pellets ricocheted and killed a poor white pigeon that was drinking water under the pear tree," a child's playful cruelty compounded, alas, by unintended consequences. The poet renders the incident with directness and a vivid delicacy—the passage encompasses a miniature portrait-as-elegy of the hapless small bird—and one also recognizes in this story an affinity with Blake's "The Tyger," that lyric meditation on the absolute connectedness of innocence and annihilation as factors in the world.

Like Blake in his *Songs of Experience* Jiménez calls attention to social conditions that intrude on some children's lives leaving them prey to neglect of various kinds. He describes the street games of a group of poor children who play at being beggars, a brutal irony that he lets speak for itself; he reports the fact tersely. Shifting games, the children pretend to be princes and princesses. The poet's anger again becomes clear from what goes *un*said: the children's imagining that they can change their lot on a moment's whim contrasts with the less generous social realities they are apparently innocent of, and which may never give them any such chance. They boast about their kingly fortunes:

> "My father has a silver watch."
> "And mine has a horse."
> "And mine, a shotgun."

Fantasies the poet transforms into a definitive commentary on their plight: "A watch that will rise at dawn, a gun that will not kill hunger, a horse that will lead to poverty. . . . Sing, dream, children of the poor! Soon, at the first blush of youth, Spring will frighten you like a beggar in winter's guise." At which moment the poet abruptly withdraws:

> Let us go, Platero.
>
> How beautiful the country is on these holidays when everyone forsakes it!

. . . Children's literature is, as the social critic John Berger has observed, virtually the last literary preserve of the animal world. Yet Berger and others have been too hasty in deciding that animal characters in children's books generally amount to little more than lifeless "human puppets"—further evidence of the trivialization, or in Berger's terms, the "marginalization" of the rest of nature by industrial man. Certain memorable children's books—*Make Way for Ducklings*, *Charlotte's Web* and others—have expressed an opposite and one might also say a culturally subversive point of view merely by treating human respect for nature as an underlying matter of concern, as an important question.

Yet one rarely feels about Jiménez that he is teaching us a lesson. He ridicules fable writers for insisting on their moral, "that dry appendage, that bit of ashes, that fallen feather of an ending," praising only La Fontaine for having found in his verses the "real voice" of animals. (Jiménez deftly addresses these comments not to us but to Platero as though to an expert witness.) Even more so than in the poetry of that other literary close observer of nature, Marianne Moore (who translated La Fontaine), ethical and spiritual insights in *Platero* most often arise out of ordinary experiences intensely seen, felt and pondered with (for the most part) the simple language and clear-headed wit of a peasant story teller. Jiménez issues his reports as though merely telling what befell him the other day: alone or with Platero, the poet of solitude harnesses the precarious breach between self and world to the imagination's ends.

Source: Leonard S. Marcus, "The Beast of Burden and the Joyful Man of Words: Juan Ramón Jiménez's *Platero and I*," in *Lion and the Unicorn*, Vol. 4, No. 2, Winter 1980–1981, pp. 56–74.

Walter T. Pattison

In the following essay, Pattison declares that Jiménez's attitude toward reality is fundamental to understanding him.

Juan Ramón Jiménez has never written a long-deliberated poem with an analytical catalogue of his poetic ideas and attitudes. His failure to do so reveals much of his concept of the nature of poetry. It is an interplay between the poet's soul and reality, a flash of comprehension, a moment of ecstatic oneness with some natural beauty, a wave of emotion disclosing the essence of some thing. Poems are, by the very nature of poetry, momentarily-caught butterflies: Each poem is a glimpse into the realm of the poet, not a Baedeker.

Since Juan Ramón Jiménez writes for "la inmensa minoría," he feels that his readers can make their way through his kingdom without a guide. Yet the fleeting, fragmentary nature of his individual works makes desirable some kind of a chart of his realm of gold. If each poem is a glimpse, what is the total vision? Only after many readings and much meditation and feeling do we get a mountain-top view over the whole area.

As we assemble the fragments, we find that Juan Ramón's attitude toward reality is fundamental to our understanding him. His reality is immensely rich in facets. Most of it—the real, or inner meanings of things—remains hidden to the eyes of the average mortal, but stands partly revealed to the eyes of the poet:

Riqueza de la noche,
¡Cuántos secretos arrancados
de tí, cuántos por arrancarte!

Even a single part of reality—here, night—is infinite in aspects, and consequently never completely comprehensible. But secret after secret can be won by the poet through his delicate emotional perception, his catching of the subtle feeling of the thing. The essence of the poetic gift is this capacity of infinitely shaded emotion; in fact the infinite phases of a thing are partly the multifold aspects of that reality and partly the multifold emotional reactions which the thing can provoke.

Feeling, emotion, is the prime way of approaching the incomprehensible: "Donde la inteligencia fracasa, empieza el sentimiento." Our intelligence can tell us the chemical composition of a thing but only our emotion can tell us what the thing means to us. Scientific truth is inferior to human (or poetic) truth.

The same physical thing can be the origin of many different emotions; hence it can be many "different" things. The emotional reactions vary in the individual with the lighting effects (sunlight, moonlight, twilight, various kinds of cloudy days), the season of the year (compare the brook in winter to the same in summer), with

the point of view (compare the mountain seen from its base with the same mountain seen from its peak), and the background of recent emotions (think of home as we enter it after a wedding and then after a funeral).

Juan Ramón is well aware of divergent emotional reactions from the same thing. As he looks at a quiet valley with its village and river sleeping in the moonlight, he exclaims:

. . . Todo
lo que era alegre al sol, sueña
no sé qué amores llorosos.

Elsewhere he notes the immense difference between the lighthouse sending forth its beam at night and the sad brick tower it becomes in daytime. Again he compares the dock at twilight (when it seems to reach almost to the sunset) to the dock at night (when it seems, or is, a tiny toy).

Given the infinite variety in both reality and poetic reaction to it, it is obvious that the poet must limit himself to a part of the whole. In a general way the realities Juan Ramón Jiménez prefers are, in order of descending importance, nature, man-made things, humanity, and individuals. But each one of these categories must be limited further, for within the class the realities Juan Ramón Jiménez prefers frequently correspond to his favorite emotion—an elegaic, sweet sadness. Nature as seen through his eyes is one of gardens and parklands, usually lighted by the sunset, the moon, or the stars, where fountains and beds of flowers give a rather domestic effect, and where the strains of a Beethoven sonata come tearfully from a distant piano. Most prominent in the category of things are household objects, which Juan Ramón loves in the manner of Francis Jammes:

¡Qué quietas están las cosas,
y qué bien se está con ellas!
Por todas partes, sus manos
con nuestras manos se encuentran.
¡Cuántas discretas caricias,
qué respeto por la idea;
cómo miran estasiadas,
el ensueño que uno sueña!

The love of humanity is the feeling of emotional unity with the nameless, shadowy inhabitants of the poet's world.

¡Cómo no somos únicos!
¡Cómo nos entrañamos, uno en otro, siempre,
con la sangre mezclada
del sentimiento! ¡Cómo ríe uno, cómo llora
con los otros!

Juan Ramón is naturally most interested in the more gifted, more poetic element of humanity:

... ¡Luminosos roces
de otras manos que buscan sus tesoros!

The vagueness which characterizes humanity is also typical of the few individuals appearing in Juan Ramón's poems. The bodiless spirit of the person and the poet's emotional reaction to it are the all-important things. A woman momentarily glimpsed, whose image and impression the memory cannot quite bring into sharp focus; another woman whose spirit captures the quintessence of springtime, such are the women in Juan Ramón's lyrics. Most of them are not only individuals but symbols of the highest beauty of nature. Men, except as decorative figures—the shepherd, the ox-driver—are practically never found. The one ever present individual is the poet himself.

Although these favorite elements of reality can never be thoroughly understood, the poet's love for them can lead to an ecstatic oneness with nature, a mystic exaltation in which comprehension or knowledge is superseded. When the poet is thinking of the immense plenitude of the night, he cries:

¡Oh, goce inenarrable,
hundir la mano en tus entrañas,
remover tus estrellas!

Or he speaks to the solitary wild flower enjoying

... el encanto bendito
de tu soledad única, estasìada y divina

when, at the twilight hour, the flower (or the poet projecting his feelings into the flower) reads the innermost secrets of nature. In a third case, on a hot, passionate night

... el mundo
se viene, en un olvido májico, a flor de alma;
se cojen libélulas con las manos caídas;

that is, the things of the world, reality, rise to the spiritual level, where the poet's soul can feel its unity with them, and where he can without raising a hand catch the most elusive ideas (*libélulas*).

Along with this mystic ecstasy goes a loss of usual sense perceptions and an unawareness of the flesh.

... Está preso el corazón
en este sueño inefable
que le echa su red; ve sólo
luces altas, alas de ánjeles

Sólo le queda esperar
a los luceros; la carne
se le hace incienso y penumbra ...

It must surely have occurred to anyone reading the above paragraphs that Juan Ramón's attitude parallels that of Christian mystics point for point. The one great difference is that the poet substitutes an infinite, incomprehensible reality for an infinite, incomprehensible God. Not that Juan Ramón's reality is devoid of God, for the contemplation of nature's beauties is frequently fused with an awareness of the divine presence:

Nadie.—Un pájaro.—Dios.

The difference lies rather in emphasis; for Juan Ramón's thoughts are oriented toward things of this world while the mystic usually disdains terrestial things to concentrate all his intensity on the Creator alone. As the poet says: "Los estados de la contemplación de lo inefable son panteísmo, misticismo (no me refiero precisamente a lo relijioso), amor, es decir, comunicación, hallazgo, entrada en la naturaleza y el espíritu, en la realidad visible y la invisible, en el doble todo. ..."

Juan Ramón clearly acknowledges his kinship with the Christian mystics but proclaims that a poet may be a lay mystic, a mystic without God:

... en España, país hondamente realista y falsamente relijioso en conjunto, católico más que cristiano, eclesiástico que espiritual, país de raíces y pies más que de alas, la verdadera poesía, la única lírica escrita posible, la iniciaron, con el sentir del pueblo, los escasos y estraños místicos, cuyo paisaje era la peña adusta y el cielo maravilloso. ... Por eso la mejor lírica española ha sido y es fatalmente mística, con Dios o sin él, ya que el poeta, vuelvo a decirlo de otro modo, es un místico sin Dios necesario.

Juan Ramón's first great contribution to the modern concept of poetry is precisely the idea of the poet as a mystic of nature. The idea was already implicit in Bécquer, but Juan Ramón gave it its complete development and modern emphasis. In this century most Spanish poets have followed his lead.

But Juan Ramón goes on to even more radical concepts and attitudes in which he leaves the mystics behind and joins hands with the exponents of the subconscious mind. The mystics lead the way, for they are soul searchers, analysers of subtle emotions, craftsmen who seek to express the ineffable. But Juan Ramón's probing of emotional recesses takes him even further than the mystics. "¡Qué gusto analizar lo inconciente propio; y qué sorpresas de lo inconciente a la conciencia!"

Poetry, we have said (for Juan Ramón), is an interplay between the poet's soul and reality. The sense impression received from reality provokes an emotion, which emotion then goes forth from the poet to become part of the original object. A sunset seen with the eyes may arouse a vague, elegiac, sweet sadness, which mood, working outward, becomes the "meaning" of the sunset. But sometimes the poet's subconscious reactions carry him above and beyond this normal process. The sense impression may stir all sorts of subconscious associations so that the emotion which goes forth from the poet toward the object is greater than the emotion inherent in it. The poet is a creator (through his wealth of subconscious "associations"), and his contribution to the poem (or poetic ecstasy, which results in the poem) is at times even greater than the contribution of reality. Juan Ramón, viewing a golden sunset, exclaims:

> Al ver este oro entre el pinar sombrío,
> me he acordado de mí tan dulcemente,
> que era más dulce el pensamiento mío
> que toda la dulzura del poniente.
> ¡Oh dulzura de oro! ¡Campo verde,
> corazón con esquilas, humo en calma!
> No hay en la vida nada que recuerde
> estos dulces ocasos de mi alma.

The ecstasy of the poet differs from that of the mystic in the much greater active participation of the poet's soul. The mystic is absorbed in God, but the poet's soul is never so fused with reality that it loses its identity. Indeed it can remain superior to the reality, the more important element in the poetic fusion.

By this process, words—the notation of things—can take on a large emotional content above and beyond their dictionary meanings. By this I do not mean the onomatopoetic or suggestive value in the sound of the word itself, although Juan Ramón is well aware of these values. Such connotations could suggest themselves to anyone hearing the word. But when words carry with them extra "higher meanings" in addition to their usual meaning, we know it is because of a series of subconscious relationships in the poet's innermost mind. Examples are

mujer, "woman; the highest form of natural beauty;" *pájaro*, "bird; music, song, poetry;" *rosa*, "rose; perfection;" *estrellas*, "stars; lofty, poetic thoughts;" *agua*, "water; purity;" *pino*, "pine; enduring strength;" *mariposa*, "butterfly; illusion, fleeting thought." These words are not symbols (that is, one word substituted for another); they still retain their original values besides the poet's additions.

These delicate emotional reactions to things (or subtle subconscious associations) are, we repeat, the gift which distinguishes a poet from an ordinary man. But the poet's task, his daily torment, is to try to put his reactions, his truths, his *sueño inefable*, into words. No man can claim the title of poet unless he can catch the fugitive emotion in words. Juan Ramón expresses this thought in his criticism of a poet who failed in the poet's task:

> Encuentra la rosa, el diamante, el oro, pero no la palabra representativa y transmutadora; no suple el sujeto o el objeto con su palabra; traslada sujeto y objeto, no sustancia ni esencia. Sujeto y objeto están allí y no están; porque no están entendidos.

The poet must find the words which express not just the exterior appearance of the thing but its inner meaning, the emotional content which the poet's soul pours into it:

> . . . Que mi palabra sea
> la cosa misma,
> creada por mi alma nuevamente.

Or as he says to another poet,

> Creemos los nombres.

Every poem of Juan Ramón Jiménez gives evidence of his skill at noting down the emotional-realistic aspect of things. Although I intended to cite examples here I renounce the idea since examples would imply that this type of notation was not universally present in Juan Ramón's works.

The poet, utilizing his poetic gift and struggling with his poetic task, catches and transmits fleeting beauty to less artistic souls.

> Que por mí vayan todos
> los que no las conocen, a las cosas;
> que por mí vayan todos
> los que ya las olvidan, a las cosas;
> que por mí vayan todos
> los mismos que las aman, a las cosas . . .

Each thing of beauty is unique and can never be long-enduring; the uniqueness of each emotional reaction results in the uniqueness of beauty; the shifting and changing of its emotional element makes it impossible for beauty to endure any length of time. Often the poet has not time fully to note its appearance:

> Mariposa de luz,
> la belleza se va cuando yo llego
> a su rosa.
> Corro, ciego, tras ella . . .
> La medio cojo aquí y allá . . .
> ¡Sólo queda en mi mano
> la forma de su huida!

But since he can at least partially note down beauty—unique and fleeting though it may be—not only for his contemporaries but also for people in ages to come, the poet imparts immortality to that beauty. What he catches remains for posterity; what he fails to catch is lost forever.

> Belleza que yo he visto,
> ¡no te borres ya nunca!
> Porque seas eterna,
> ¡yo quiero ser eterno!

The poet is central in his universe, like a great tree trunk, supporting the sky and its stars. His universe, his reality and his reactions to it, will end with his death:

> Sé bien que cuando el hacha
> de la muerte me tale
> se vendrá abajo el cielo.

The universe is *his* universe because he has felt, loved, understood the things which make it up. He has given things a poetic, human meaning by apprehending the subtle emotional bonds which bind him and them together. He is a part of everything that he has loved:

> ¡Qué inmensa desgarradura
> la de mi vida en el todo,
> para estar, con todo yo,
> en cada cosa;
> para no dejar de estar,
> con todo yo, en cada cosa!

So in this mystical experience, this interplay between reality and the poet's soul, there is a divine spirit not only in infinite, incomprehensible reality, but also in the poet himself. He creates his universe; he gives names and meanings to its things. He catches and gives immortality to its beauties. And when he is gone, much beauty he has not had time to express will perish with him.

Source: Walter T. Pattison, "Juan Ramón Jiménez, Mystic of Nature," in *Hispania*, Vol. 33, No. 1, February 1950, pp. 18–22.

SOURCES

Bentley, Logan, "What the Horns Couldn't Do," in *SI Vault*, April 23, 1962, http://sportsillustrated.cnn.com/vault/article/magazine/MAG1073716/index.htm (accessed July 15, 2010).

Fitts, Dudley, Review of *Platero and I*, in *New York Times Book Review*, August 11, 1957, pp. 7, 16.

Fogelquist, Donald F., *Juan Ramón Jiménez*, Twayne Publishers, 1976.

"Gastronomy—The Wines of Huelva," in *andalucia.com*, http://www.andalucia.com/gastronomy/huelvawines.htm (accessed July 15, 2010).

Honig, Edwin, Review of *Platero and I*, in *Saturday Review of Literature*, December 7, 1957, p. 50.

Jiménez, Juan Ramón, *Platero and I*, translated by Antonio T. de Nicolás, iUniverse.com, 2000.

Nims, John Frederick, Review of *Three Hundred Poems, 1903–1953*, in *New York Times Book Review*, May 5, 1963, pp. 4, 28.

Pierson, Peter, *The History of Spain*, The Greenwood Histories of the Modern Nations Series, Greenwood Press, 1999, pp. 1–16, 117–34.

Young, Howard T., "Juan Ramón Jiménez," in *Columbia Essays on Modern Writers*, No. 28, Columbia University Press, 1967.

FURTHER READING

Chandler, Richard E., and Kessel Schwartz, *A New History of Spanish Literature*, rev. ed., Louisiana State University Press, 1991.

   This helpful reference volume groups information on Spanish authors by genre, rather than by time period, making it easier to trace the development of a particular form of literature (such as poetry or fiction) over time. A thorough index allows readers to find information easily. The volume was originally published in 1961, but it was updated in 1991 to include the many authors that emerged after the end of Franco's oppressive regime in 1975.

Jiménez, Juan Ramón, and Antonio T. de Nicolás, *Time and Space: A Poetic Autobiography*, iUniverse.com, 2000.

   This volume is not a traditional autobiography but a collection of writings by Jiménez. It includes the complete text of Jiménez's long poem "Space," which author Octavio Paz called "the greatest poem in this century," and a selection of prose writings by Jiménez that give insights into his artistic preferences and personality.

Johnson, Roberta, *Crossfire: Philosophy and the Novel in Spain, 1900–1934*, University Press of Kentucky, 2009.

In this study, Johnson examines the interaction between philosophy and fiction in the Spanish literature of this period. The writers featured include Jiménez, as well as many of the writers of the "Generation of '98," including Miguel de Unamuno and Ramón Pérez de Ayala.

Williams, Mark R., *The Story of Spain: The Dramatic History of Europe's Most Fascinating Country*, Golden Era Books, 2009.

Telling the story of Spain from prehistoric to modern times in just 352 pages, this book is an excellent and entertaining overview of Spanish history. Maps, illustrations, color photos, and lists of historic destinations to visit are also included to further the reader's understanding of both historic and modern Spain.

SUGGESTED SEARCH TERMS

Platero and I

Juan Ramón Jiménez

Juan Ramón Jiménez AND nature

Juan Ramón Jiménez AND Moguer

Juan Ramón Jiménez AND Platero

Platero and I AND children's literature

Platero and I AND Andalusia

Juan Ramón Jiménez AND Nobel Prize

Juan Ramón Jiménez AND Spanish literature

Juan Ramón Jiménez AND poetry

Praisesong for the Widow

PAULE MARSHALL

1983

Praisesong for the Widow is a novel by twentieth-century African American writer Paule Marshall. Her third novel, it was first published in 1983. The origin of the novel lay in the early 1960s. After submitting a summary of the novel she wanted to write, Marshall was awarded a Guggenheim fellowship in 1961, which enabled her to travel to Grenada, where some of the novel would be set, and do her research. In 1962, Marshall lived for nearly a year in Grenada, an island in the eastern Caribbean.

In her memoir, *Triangular Road*, she describes how she conceived the novel at the time: "It would be set in the present, the characters would be modern-day folk of various races and backgrounds, yet their lives, their situations, their relationships, their thinking and politics would reflect the past four-hundred years history of the hemisphere and its continuing impact on them." The result was *Praisesong for the Widow*, which tells the story of Avey Johnson, a middle-class African American woman who rediscovers her racial and cultural heritage while visiting Grenada and the nearby island of Carriacou. The novel is notable because it connects the experience of African Americans to their ancestral past in Africa and also to people of African descent in the Caribbean. In its portrayal of a woman throwing off a false identity and discovering her authentic self, it also has universal appeal.

Paule Marshall (*AP Images*)

AUTHOR BIOGRAPHY

Marshall was born on April 9, 1929, in Brooklyn, New York. Her parents were Samuel and Ada Burke, who were second-generation immigrants from Barbados, in the West Indies. As a child Marshall developed a love of reading. At first she read the great English novelists such as Charles Dickens and Henry Fielding, but later she discovered the work of African American poet Paul Lawrence Dunbar, which fueled her own desire to become a writer. At first she wrote poetry, but she later devoted her talents to fiction.

In 1950, Marshall graduated from Brooklyn College. She worked as a librarian in the New York Public library and then, from 1953 to 1956, as a writer for the small African American magazine *Our World* in New York City. She married Kenneth E. Marshall in 1957 and began to pursue her own creative writing ambitions. Her first novel, *Browngirl, Brownstones*, about the development of a black woman within a black cultural environment, was published in 1959. In 1961 Marshall received a Guggenheim fellowship and also published the collection of four short stories, *Soul Clap Hands and Sing*, which won the

Rosenthal Award for the National Institute of Arts and Letters. Eight years later, her second novel, *The Chosen Place, the Timeless People*, was published. The novel explores, among other themes, a woman's quest for reconciliation with her African ancestry.

Marshall was divorced in the late 1960s, and she married Nourry Menard in 1970. In 1983, she published her third novel, *Praisesong for the Widow*, which was well received by reviewers and won the American Book Award in 1984.

Marshall's later work includes the novels *Daughters* (1991) and *The Fisher King* (2000), *Reena, and Other Stories* (1983), and *Triangular Road: A Memoir* (2009). As of 2010, Marshall is a professor of English at New York University, where she holds the distinguished chair in creative writing. She has also taught creative writing at Columbia University, University of Iowa, and University of California, Berkeley, and has won many awards, including the Don Passos Prize for Literature.

PLOT SUMMARY

Part I: Runagate

CHAPTER 1

When *Praisesong for the Widow* begins, the protagonist, a sixty-four-old African American woman named Avey Johnson, is hastily packing a suitcase in secret. It is just before dawn, and Avey is in a cabin on a cruise ship in the Caribbean with two of her friends. But she has suddenly decided that she must leave the cruise at the next port of call, later that day, and return home.

CHAPTER 2

When one of her companions, Thomasina Moore, a woman in her seventies, discovers that Avey has abruptly decided to return home, she is furious. She summons Clarice, the third of the travelers, who is six years younger than Avey. However, despite the anger and bewilderment of her two friends, Avey offers no explanation to why she is leaving.

CHAPTER 3

This and the next chapter flash back to several days earlier. Avey dreams of her great-aunt Cuney. Before she tells of the dream, Avey recalls the walks she used to take as a child with her great-aunt on Tatem Island in the summer. The island was off Beaufort on the South Carolina tidewater. They would walk through woods, past some houses, through an abandoned rice field, and into a forest. They arrived at a river and a place called the Landing, where African slaves were first brought when they arrived on ships. Great-aunt Cuney used to tell little Avey about how the first slaves took a good look around them, decided they did not want to be there, and walked back to the edge of river. Then, still in their chains, they walked on the water, past the ship that had brought them there, singing as they went, on their way home. In the dream, Great-aunt Cuney beckons to the adult Avey to take their familiar walk, but Avey does not want to. The old woman grabs her and tries to pull her along. Avey resists, and a tug-of-war ensues, followed by a fistfight.

CHAPTER 4

Avey recalls the dinner they had on the cruise ship the day after her disturbing dream. She did not want to eat the delicious dessert, a parfait, because of indigestion. She felt the same discomfort in the morning. She decided to spend the morning alone on the upper decks, but found it hard to escape the noisy presence of the other passengers. Eventually she went to the ship's library, where she remained until dinnertime.

CHAPTER 5

By late morning the next day, Avey has left the cruise ship and is on the island of Grenada, waiting in the dock area for a taxi. Crowds of people pass her, and she later finds out they are people from the tiny island of Carriacou who live and work in Grenada and are returning home for a few days. They are all friendly to her but she keeps her distance. Eventually a taxi arrives.

CHAPTER 6

The young taxi driver takes Avey to a luxury hotel and talks to her about the people from Carriacou and his own life. She books a room and makes a plane reservation for the following day. However, she feels uneasy again and wonders if she has made the right decision.

Part II: Sleeper's Wake
CHAPTER 1

Avey hears her late husband's voice reproaching her for wasting money by abandoning the

cruise. This leads to a long flashback about Avey's married life with Jerome (Jay) Johnson. They started out poor, living in an apartment in Brooklyn. Avey is pregnant with her third child. Jay works hard in a shipping room of a department store, and Avey falsely believes he is having an affair with another woman. It is a source of continual tension between them.

CHAPTER 2

One Tuesday night, the simmering tension between Jay and Avey comes to a head. When he comes home, she berates him, and he yells back. Sis, the eldest daughter, hears the commotion and is upset by it. Avey threatens to leave her husband. Angry, he is to the point of leaving the apartment, but he thinks better of it and embraces his wife.

CHAPTER 3

Jay works several jobs in order to get ahead. He takes a correspondence course in accounting but cannot find a job. He then enrolls in Long Island University, studies hard, and after four years gets his degree and is also certified as an accountant. Avey gives birth to Marion and raises all three children while also working at the Motor Vehicle Department. Gradually, Jay builds up his own accountancy practice and is successful.

CHAPTER 4

Becoming more prosperous, Jay and Avey buy a house in North White Plains. She recalls how they danced together in the living room, and spent lazy Sundays listening to music on the radio. Jay entertained her and the daughters by singing and reciting poetry. However, over the years, as Jay spent more time studying and working, a distance grew up between them. At the time of his death from a stroke, ten years after they moved to North White Plains, Avey does not feel close to him anymore.

CHAPTER 5

In her hotel room in Grenada, Avey finally starts to grieve for her dead husband. She empathizes with his life struggle. However, she also realizes that in seeking material success, they had over the years alienated themselves from their own race and from their cultural heritage. She becomes angry about this, as if she collaborated in somehow losing her own soul. She is still angry as she goes to bed and falls asleep.

Part III: Lavé Tête

CHAPTER 1

Avey awakes in the morning in the hotel, has breakfast, and then walks for miles on the deserted beach, taking careful note of everything she sees. She gets tired and is nearly overcome by the heat, but as exhaustion sets in she manages to reach one of the thatch-covered shelters on the beach.

CHAPTER 2

It turns out that Avey has stumbled into a bar, known on the island as a rum shop. A grumpy old man tells her the place is closed but allows her to stay for a few minutes. Then he gets talkative and tells her all about his family history. He comes from the small island, Carriacou, and he tells her of the excursion that takes place every year when the islanders visit their families and perform ceremonies that honor their ancestors. Avey is confused by all the details. When he asks her what "nation" she belongs to—referring to the African tribe from which she is descended— she does not know what he is talking about and tells him she is a tourist from New York. Then she tells him why she has left the cruise, and he listens sympathetically.

CHAPTER 3

The man gives her rum and coconut water, and she feels soothed by it. He talks about the dances that take place during the excursion to Carriacou and asks her if she knows any of them. Then he sings and dances himself, and after a while invites her to come to the excursion with him. He says she can stay at his daughter's house. Reluctant at first, Avey finally agrees to go.

CHAPTER 4

Avey waits at the wharf to get in one of the schooners that are going to Carriacou. While she is waiting she realizes that the busy, colorful scene reminds her of a regular event in her early childhood, when the family took a boat ride up the Hudson River. This was arranged by the neighborhood social club, and Avey now remembers how she felt part so much a part of the community during those trips. Back in the present, she boards the crowded schooner, accompanied by the man, whose name is Lebert Joseph. The other passengers look after her, and she feels comfortable and calm.

CHAPTER 5

Avey remembers the sermons given by the Reverend Morrissey in the Baptist Church that she and her family used to attend when she was a child. The preacher energetically denounced sin and told the congregation to invoke the power of God to work changes in their lives. She does not enjoy the sermon; the emphasis on the wrath of God made her feel nauseous.

CHAPTER 6

On the schooner, Avey is violently seasick. Two female passengers offer her compassionate assistance. They take her to a bunk in a deck-house and allow her to lie down. By dusk the schooner approaches port, and Avey starts to feel slightly better but she still feels ill.

Part IV: The Beg Pardon

CHAPTER 1

At noon the next day Avey is at the house of Lebert Joseph's daughter, Rosalie Parvay. Preparations have been made for the celebration to honor the ancestors. Avey has slept for a long time, and lies in bed, awake and still recovering. Rosalie bathes her with the help of Milda, a maid. The bath brings back memories of Avey's childhood. Rosalie massages her with oil and then provides food. Lebert Joseph arrives and asks her if she will go to the Big Drum Nation Dance that night, and she agrees.

CHAPTER 2

In the evening, Rosalie, Milda, and Avey climb a hill and reach the backyard of an old house where the festival is to take place. Lebert Joseph joins them. There are about thirty people there, mostly elderly. There is singing, drumming, and dancing, and the people from the different "nations" (the African tribes from which the Carriacou people are descended) dance in their own distinctive way. Avey listens and watches for several hours. Young people arrive and the dancing and drumming become more vigorous. Lebert Joseph dances and appears to be in charge of the proceedings. Eventually Avey joins in. She is reminded of her childhood and feels connected to everyone present.

CHAPTER 3

The following morning Avey bids Lebert Joseph and Rosalie a fond farewell. She leaves the island by plane and resolves to tell everyone back home about her experiences. She decides to live part of the time in Tatem, where she spent some of the memorable years of her childhood, and have her two grandsons visit her each summer.

CHARACTERS

Annawilda

Annawilda is Avey Johnson's daughter. As a child she was demanding and unmanageable, but she grew up to become a doctor. She plays no direct part in the narrative.

Clarice

Clarice is one of Avey's companions on the cruise. She is six years younger than Avey, and they work together at the State Motor Vehicle Department, where Clarice is a Grade Five clerk. She is a serious, anxious woman who looks older than she is. She has had many troubles in life, including a difficult marriage that ended in divorce, nursing her mother through a long illness, and the fact that her son, an outstanding student, chose to drop out of college.

Great-aunt Cuney

Great-aunt Cuney was Avey's strong-willed, independent relative who had a big influence on her childhood. When Avey was young, Great-aunt Cuney would take her for walks on Tatem Island and tell her stories at the Landing, where the slaves were first brought to that part of South Carolina. Avey's dream about her great-aunt, where she battles the old woman, helps to produce the restlessness inside her that causes her to abandon the cruise.

Avey Johnson

Avey Johnson is a sixty-four-year-old African American woman and the novel's protagonist. She is a widow with three children. Her husband, Jay, has been dead for several years when Avey takes her cruise of the Caribbean. She works as a supervisor in the State Motor Vehicle Department in Brooklyn, and the cruise is part of her vacation.

Avey grew up in Harlem but also spent summers in South Carolina with her great-aunt Cuney, who told her stories and legends about the arrival of the first African slaves in the state. Avey married fairly young and only attended a year of college, while her husband was serving in the U.S. Army during World

War II. For a while she was a union organizer at her place of work. However, when she started having children it appears that she lost interest in these wider social concerns. Her marriage quickly became strained due to her unreasonable jealousy; she thought that her husband must be having an affair because he worked long hours. She was also frustrated with the limitations of her life, living in an upstairs apartment in a run-down neighborhood, raising children. She and her husband grew further apart over the years, but he was financially successful, and Avey, up to the point when the novel begins, has enjoyed the comfortable life that money brings. The cruise she is on is the second she has taken.

However, despite her material comfort, Avey is an alienated woman who has forgotten her racial heritage and the feelings she once had as a child of being connected to everyone in her community. Within three days of starting the cruise she realizes that she does not fit into her environment, although at the time she cannot conceptualize this and is confused by her feelings of unease. In the events of the following few days, she undergoes a profound change, rediscovering her more authentic self in the company of the people of Carriacou. This is not without some resistance on her part, but she manages to overcome her adverse judgments and her initial incomprehension regarding the islanders. She learns to appreciate their kind nature and the singing and dancing that go on at their community celebration. She realizes that the islanders possess the values that, over the years, she has lost touch with. At the end of the novel, she is quite different from the rather self-centered woman who set off on the cruise with six suitcases full of dresses, evening gowns, hats, and so forth. She has rediscovered a sense of community and a simpler, more fulfilling way to live.

Jerome ("Jay") Johnson

Jerome Johnson was Avey Johnson's husband. When the novel begins, he has been dead for several years. Avey used to call him Jay when they were young, but as they grew apart over the years she thought of him more formally as Jerome. As a young man, Jay is intelligent and hard-working. He has a job in the shipping department in a department store in downtown Brooklyn and actually does the work of two men, allowing his Irish boss to have an easy time while taking all the credit. Jay is eager to get ahead in life and to escape the impoverished area in Harlem where he and Avey live when they are first married. With that aim in mind, he studies accountancy and business by correspondence courses, but because white employers discriminate, he cannot find employment. Determined to succeed, he attends university and becomes a certified public accountant. He tries for a year to find suitable employment but is still unable to break through the barrier of racism. He decides instead to start out on his own and build up an accounting business, seeking out local clients. Gradually he becomes successful, but he tends to scorn other black people who have not been able to do as well as he has. He thinks they are lazy and too occupied with superficial pleasures, like the dance halls in Harlem.

At home, when he is young, Jay is lively and charming, a good dancer, keeps Avey entertained. He is "open, witty, playful" and affectionate. However, early on the marriage is spoiled by Avey's jealousy. She thinks, without cause, that he must be having an affair. They quarrel frequently, and over the years become less intimate with each other. Material success changes Jay, and Avey hears in his voice an "unsparing, puritanical tone." He dies of a stroke while still relatively young (in his fifties), leaving Avey financially comfortable. She does not mourn his death.

Lebert Joseph

Lebert Joseph is an old man who befriends Avey. He is from Carriacou but lives for the most part in Grenada, where he keeps a rum shop on the beach. His daughter is Rosalie Parvay. Avey stumbles into Lebert's shop when she is exhausted from walking on the beach. At first she does not know what to make of him, finding him odd and possibly senile, since she does not understand his talk about the customs of the people from Carriacou. She notices that he walks with a limp because one leg is shorter than the other, and she thinks he must be nearly ninety years old. When Lebert hears Avey's story, he insists that she accompany him to the celebration on Carriacou. He is very kind and considerate toward her, although he deceives her by telling her that the sea crossing will be easy, when he knows very well it will be rough. Avey forgives him for the deception, even though the crossing makes her sick. Despite his age and physical handicap, Lebert is strong and agile, and at the festival he sings and dances. He is the most senior figure there, respected by everyone, and he acts as the perfect host. When he dances he seems to shed his years: "Out of his stooped and winnowed body had come the illusion of height, femininity and power. Even his foreshortened left leg had appeared to straighten itself out and grow longer as he danced."

Marion

Marion is Avey's youngest daughter. When Avey was pregnant with her, she tried without success to end the pregnancy. As a child, Marion was quiet and well-behaved, although as an adult she is fiercer. She was married and divorced by the age of twenty-eight. Unlike her mother, Marion took an interest in the civil rights movement in the 1960s, and at the end of the story, Avey feels that Marion is the one who will most understand the story of her excursion to Carriacou.

Milda

Milda is the maid who works at Rosalie's house on Carriacou. She is a quiet young woman of about twenty who assists in bathing Avey and accompanies Avey and Rosalie to the festival.

Thomasina Moore

Thomasina Moore is an African American woman in her early seventies who is a friend of Avey Johnson. She accompanies Avey on the cruise, and she is furious when Avey abruptly decides to leave. She thinks Avey has lost her mind. Unlike Avey, Thomasina Moore fits in perfectly with the well-off, mostly white people on the cruise. At dinner, for example, "her face under a hairstyle that rivaled any to be seen in the room, blend[ed] easily with the other faces at the tables."

Reverend Morrissey

During the sea crossing, Avey remembers Reverend Morrissey, a pastor from her childhood church. In Avey's memory, the preacher gives a sermon that makes her feel sick to her stomach, much like the sea voyage she is experiencing.

Rosalie Parvay

Rosalie Parvay is Lebert Joseph's daughter. She is in her fifties and is a widow. Her five children have all gone to live in Canada, and she lives alone in a big bungalow on the island of Carriacou. She tries to persuade her father to come and live with her but he refuses. Rosalie is very kind to Avey when Avey arrives at her house, sick from the sea crossing. She bathes and massages Avey tactfully, efficiently, and tenderly.

Sis

Sis is Avey's eldest daughter. She is married to a systems programmer and has two sons. She lives in Los Angeles.

Taxi Driver

The taxi driver is a young man who picks Avey Johnson up at the wharf on Grenada after she has left the cruise ship. He drives her to the hotel and tells her about the annual excursion made by the Carriacou people who live in Grenada.

THEMES

Alienation

During her first few days on the cruise ship, Avey Johnson discovers, to her alarm and in a way that she does not understand, that she has suddenly become alienated from the kind of life she has been living for many years. Thanks to the financial success of her late husband, she is well off and can afford to take luxury cruises of the Caribbean with her two friends. She is a well-dressed, middle-class African American woman with little knowledge or interest in her African cultural heritage or in African American issues. Even many years earlier, in the 1960s, she expressed no interest in the civil rights movement. However, on the cruise ship, she becomes restless after dreaming of her great-aunt Cuney, who used to tell her stories about the arrival of the first slaves in South Carolina. Next she is unable to eat the peach parfait at the dinner in the luxurious Versailles Room on the ship, and she feels a vague sense of indigestion.

What Avey is really reacting against is the kind of person she has become, indulging in pointless luxury. As her daughter Marion put it when Avey was planning her first cruise: "Why go on some meaningless cruise with a bunch of white folks anyway. . . ? What's that supposed to be about?" Avey no longer fits in

this environment. She looks into a mirror and does not at first recognize herself, dressed as she is "in beige crepe de Chine and pearls," and she cannot stand being anywhere near the other passengers. There are fifteen hundred people on board for the cruise, but she feels isolated and disoriented, unable to integrate herself into this floating community of mostly white, elderly people.

Cultural Identity

At the beginning of the novel, Avey Johnson does not identify with her own race or culture. She has adopted her late husband's scorn of fellow African Americans who do not adapt well to the dominant white culture. While she was on the previous cruise she had only contempt for the black tour guide who went off to dance in a carnival parade with the locals. Her friend Thomasina Moore, who married a white man, is openly disparaging of economically deprived black people and even uses the most offensive of derogatory terms to describe them. Avey's journey in the novel is to rediscover her sense of community with other black people and her entire racial heritage. She must overcome her prejudices and restore an understanding of who she really is, underneath all the trappings of her middle-class life in the United States.

The vehicles for this transformation are the people from Carriacou. When she first encounters them as she waits for a taxi at the wharf, she does not understand their natural friendliness toward her and is irritated by it. But after she has checked in at the hotel on Grenada, she is drawn to walk on the deserted part of the beach, not the part where all the luxury hotels are. It is as if something other than Western civilization is calling her. This turns out to be a significant decision, since it is in the old rum shop on the beach where she first meets Lebert Joseph. As with the other island folk, she is initially baffled by and wary of Joseph. In time, she learns to respect him and is intrigued by his ability to sing and dance despite his old age.

From this point on, all her encounters with the simple island people are positive. These people are not individualistic; the meaning of their lives is bound up in their sense of community and the rituals with which they celebrate their connection to each other and to their shared history. They all remember what

TOPICS FOR FURTHER STUDY

- Read *The Chosen Place, the Timeless People* (1969), another novel by Marshall that deals with issues of African American ancestry. Like *Praisesong for the Widow*, it is set on a Caribbean island, and it features an African American woman, Harriet, who tries to understand the local culture. Write an essay in which you compare and contrast these two novels. What themes do they have in common?

- Consult *African American Women Writers* (Wiley, 1999) by Brenda Wilkinson, a book for young adults that contains biographies of the lives of twenty-three African American women writers, including Marshall. Write an entry in your blog in which you discuss in your own words why Marshall decided to become a writer. What are the main themes of her work as a whole, and why did she choose these themes? How does her life connect with her work? Invite your classmates to view your entry and comment on it.

- In *Praisesong for the Widow*, Avey comes to honor and value her heritage as an African American. In the United States today, there are millions of immigrants whose origins lie in cultures very different from the dominant American culture. With two or more classmates, investigate the issue of cultural integrity and assimilation. Should immigrants to the United States, whether they are first-, second-, or third-generation immigrants, retain ties to their cultural heritage? Or should they simply identify themselves as Americans? How are your views related to the traditional idea of the United States as a "melting pot"? What is meant by this phrase? Create a Web page or Wikispace with information about the immigration assimilation issue. Describe what value there is in retaining an awareness of one's cultural heritage and what drawbacks that awareness might cause. Add links to interviews, stories, and news articles that would help people understand the issue.

- Using the Internet, research the Ring Shout. What is the Ring Shout? Who practiced it in former times and who does so now? Write an essay in which you begin by noting the way the Ring Shout is used in *Praisesong for the Widow* and then discuss your research findings. You can start your research at http://www.ringshout.org. Show the class a video of the Ring Shout or perform it with a group of classmates, stopping at various points in the dance to explain the symbolism.

"nation" they came from in Africa, the memory having been preserved across the generations. They are also unfailingly kind to and accepting of strangers. When Avey is violently seasick on the schooner that takes her to Carriacou, two old women, never named, treat her very gently, holding her and whispering soothing words into her ear. Later, when she is on the island and Rosalie Parvay bathes and massages her, Avey at first tenses up and is unresponsive to the woman's gentle touch, but she eventually relaxes and comes to accept and value the basic goodness and kindness Rosalie shows to a stranger. When she attends the celebration on the island, she joins in the dance and realizes that she has rediscovered something that she has not known properly since her childhood. She once again feels connected to her own personal history and to the collective racial history of black people. This gives her a sense of hope and purpose. As she feels at one with the other elderly people who are dancing in the yard, "their brightness as they entered her spoke of possibilities and becoming."

Avery is tormented by her grief and bad dreams. (Cheryl Casey / Shutterstock.com)

STYLE

Symbolism

A symbol is a word or phrase that stands for something else as well as its literal meaning. There are several symbols in the novel. The cruise ship, named the *Bianca Pride*, is a symbol of the luxury and materialism provided by Western technology. It represents the best that an advanced Western nation can produce. When Avey first sees it she is awed by "all that dazzling white steel" and the fact that the ship's turbines "produced enough heat and light to run a city the size of Albany!" (Albany is the capital city of New York State.) When she first toured the ship with a group, they were shown the ship's computer and "stood awestruck and reverent before the console with its array of keyboards, switches and closed-circuit television screens." The ship's efficient technology, and the luxurious lifestyles of those who can afford to take cruises on it, stand in complete contrast to the simple life of the Carriacou islanders that Avey later

comes to embrace. The ship is therefore a symbol of everything she rejects. The name itself, *Bianca Pride*, is significant, since *bianca* is the Italian word for white. In rejecting "white pride" she is affirming pride in her own African American identity and heritage. She rejects materialism for more enduring human values.

The fur stole that she and her great-aunt fight over in Avey's dream is another symbol. In the dream, Avey is dressed up in an elegant suit, about to go to a luncheon. She is wearing a hat and gloves, and carrying a fur stole. When the two women start to struggle—the aunt pulling her toward where they used to walk together and Avey resisting—the stole falls to the ground. This infuriates Avey and she starts hitting her aunt. The stole is a symbol of that affluent, middle-class life that Avey identifies with and is trying to cling to, although the aunt is pulling her in a different direction. The stole represents the old lifestyle that she must leave behind if she is to grow. The fact that the stole falls to the ground is a sign that the time for change has come.

COMPARE
&
CONTRAST

- **1980s:** The United States and six other Caribbean nations invade Grenada in 1983. They oust the leftist military government that has just seized power.

  Today: Grenada is a parliamentary democracy with an estimated 2010 population of 107,818 citizens, 75 percent of whom are of African descent. The Grenadian economy depends a lot on tourism.

- **1980s:** In the United States, the African American middle class is strengthened as a result of the civil rights movement of the 1960s and the institution of affirmative action programs that favor historically disadvantaged groups.

  Today: African Americans are hit more severely by the economic recession of 2008 and 2009 than whites. The African American middle class has ceased to grow and is losing ground. A majority of the children of

  African American middle-class parents earn less than their parents did, and almost half of that majority are in the lowest income levels.

- **1980s:** The term African American comes into wide use to describe American citizens of African descent. It replaces the terms black and Afro-American that were current in the 1970s. The term African American becomes popular because it is preferred by many black people and contains an easily recognizable link to their history and origins, thus encouraging cultural pride.

  Today: The term African American refers to any of three racial groups in the United States: black people born in the United States; black immigrants with recent roots in sub-Saharan Africa; and black immigrants with recent roots in the Caribbean, including Haiti.

Myth

Introducing a mythic element into a novel can deepen and reinforce its themes. In this novel, the story that Great-aunt Cuney tells the young Avey has a mythic dimension. She tells the girl that when the first slaves arrived in Tatem, South Carolina, at the place known simply as the Landing, they took one look around them and knew everything that would happen if they stayed. These "pure-born Africans" were gifted with special powers and "can tell you 'bout things happened long before they was born and things to come long after they's dead." When they saw the situation they turned around and walked back over the water, past the ship that had brought them there, singing as they made their way home. The introduction of a myth that contains a miraculous element acts as a positive counterpoint to the long history of suffering that was the slaves' lot. When Avey resolves, at the end of the novel, to tell the same

story to her grandchildren, the myth infuses both history and the present-day alike with inspiration and hope.

HISTORICAL CONTEXT

Grenada and Carriacou

Much of *Praisesong for the Widow* is set on the Caribbean islands of Grenada and Carriacou, located in the eastern Caribbean, about one hundred miles north of Venezuela. Carriacou is a tiny island just seven miles long, located twenty miles north of Grenada. On these two islands, Avey Johnson comes to a fuller understanding and appreciation of her racial heritage, including slavery. Slavery was introduced to Grenada in the seventeenth century, when French colonists imported slaves from Africa to work in the sugar plantations. The French also colonized

Carriacou. Both islands passed into British hands in 1762, during the Seven Years' War between England and France (1756–1763). This was a period when the Western powers continued to colonize much of the rest of the world, including the Caribbean islands. In the Treaty of Paris that ended that war, signed in 1763, Britain retained most of the Caribbean islands it had captured. In addition to Grenada, these were Dominica, Saint Vincent, and Tobago. Britain handed Martinique and St. Lucia back to France.

The Caribbean islands continued to be at the mercy of the great powers and became spoils of war once again during the American War of Independence. At the Treaty of Versailles in 1783, Britain gave up Tobago to France, and also returned St. Lucia, which it had taken from the French during the war. The French returned Grenada (which they had recaptured in 1779), St. Vincent, and Dominica to Britain. The Treaty of Versailles was one of the treaties that, in the novel, Avey Johnson's daughter was referring to when she said to her mother after hearing about the luxurious Versailles Room on the cruise ship, "Do you know how many treaties were signed there . . . divvying up India, the West Indies, the world?" (The Versailles Room thus becomes a symbol of the oppression of many people by the colonizing Western powers, although at that point in the novel, the comment made by her daughter makes no impression on Avey.)

The British authorities banned slavery on Grenada in 1834, and Britain retained control of the island until granting it independence in 1974. Grenada thus became the smallest independent nation in the Western hemisphere.

In 1962, Paule Marshall lived in Grenada for nearly a year, during which she conducted her research for *Praisesong for the Widow*. In her 2009 memoir, *Triangular Road*, she described Grenada almost as a paradise, "a small but gloriously variegated volcanic beauty of cratered mountains, shapely green hills, waterfalls, rivers, rain forests and valleys replete with every kind of tropical tree, foliage and vegetation imaginable."

Grenada experienced political turbulence in the 1980s. In October 1983, the prime minister, Maurice Bishop, was assassinated by the leftist People's Revolutionary Army (PRA). A joint U.S.-Caribbean force invaded the island to restore stability. An advisory council governed the country until a general election was held in

Avey took long walks on the beach as she processed her thoughts. (*Szymon Salwa / Shutterstock.com*)

December 1984, which restored democratic rule to the island.

CRITICAL OVERVIEW

Praisesong for the Widow was favorably received by reviewers. For Anne Tyler, in the *New York Times Book Review*, the novel "moves purposefully and knowledgeably toward its final realization." It is "a story that's both convincing and eerily dreamlike." In Tyler's opinion, the reader is carried along by Avey's story for two main reasons. First, "because of the subtle, intriguing aura of mystery, with scenes proceeding unexplained and strangers appearing to know and welcome her." The second reason is "because that true self of Avey's is described by means of breathtakingly vivid glimpses of her first years with her husband." Tyler concludes that Avey's "wistful journey to her younger self . . . is universal, and it is astonishingly moving."

In the *New York Times*, Christopher Lehmann-Haupt writes of some reservations about the novel's "ideology and didacticism," which suggest to him that Marshall's "major interest was not to captivate her readers but to educate them—to tell them a cautionary tale about the consequences of cultural alienation." However, Lehmann-Haupt offers a positive assessment in the conclusion of his review:

> By the sheer inventiveness of her detail, she calls our attention away from the message in the background and returns it to the characters on her page. In the long run those characters are interesting enough to lend their problems universal appeal. It's a close call, but art finally wins out over politics.

Jane Olmsted analyzed three of Marshall's novels, including *Praisesong for the Widow* in a 1997 article for *African American Review*. In that article, Olmsted quotes Velma Pollard, who wrote about cultural connections present in the book, as saying, "The novel celebrates a triumph in the removal of layer after layer of cultural overlay to expose a being that finds an important core which she had lost." Olmsted also quotes Barbara Christian, who notes that Marshall should receive praise for "insisting that 'New World black rituals are living and functional,' that they express the essential African truth 'that beyond rationality, the body and spirit must not be split.'"

CRITICISM

Bryan Aubrey

Aubrey holds a Ph.D. in English. In the following essay, he discusses some of the symbolic elements in Praisesong for the Widow.

Praisesong for the Widow is a novel of many journeys, both literal and metaphorical. It is also a carefully written novel that is rich in symbolism, with every incident large or small having its allotted place in the overall tapestry of meaning. At the beginning, the title of Part I, Runagate, is full of ironic meaning. Runagate means runaway, and the title is an allusion to the poem "Runagate, Runagate" by African American poet Robert Hayden, which describes African American slaves as they escape from the South to freedom in the North. Like them, Avey

> AVEY ONLY REALLY BEGINS TO MAKE PROGRESS ON THIS SPIRITUAL JOURNEY TO HER AUTHENTIC SELF WHEN SHE TAKES YET ANOTHER PHYSICAL JOURNEY, THE TURBULENT CROSSING OF THE NARROW CHANNEL OF WATER IN THE SCHOONER TO CARRIACOU. IT IS HERE THAT THE DEATH AND REBIRTH SYMBOLISM RECURS."

Johnson is also about to run away to find freedom, but the kind of slavery she will escape is very different from that experienced by her ancestors. She already has the freedom that they sought, only to find herself—although she does not yet realize it—a slave to a culture and a lifestyle that is alien to her own roots and the deepest springs of her own being. It is this that she must escape.

The problem for Jay and Avey Johnson—although because of Jay's early death it will only be Avey who discovers it—is that they are victims of their own success. In this novel of journeys, Jay's journey was to realize the American dream. He worked hard to better himself in a society where racism held him back. Unfortunately for Avey's later life, for every step he took on the ladder of success, he paid a price in authenticity. When he was young he loved African American music and danced with Avey in their living room and recited African American poetry. These activities connected him, and Avey too, to their cultural heritage. As she later realizes, "something in those small rites, an ethos they held in common, had reached back beyond her life and beyond Jay's to join them to the vast unknown lineage that had made their being possible."

However, when he became fixated on material and professional success, he turned his back on all that. Instead, he became a member of a long-established fraternal society, the Freemasons, that has its own set of rituals and membership requirements. Although there is a separate tradition of African American Freemasonry, the organization is not known for its ethnic diversity. The fact that Jay managed to join a Freemason

WHAT DO I READ NEXT?

- *Roots: The Saga of an American Family* (1976) is a famous novel by Alex Haley based on his own family's history. Haley traced his ancestry to The Gambia, in Africa, where a man named Kunta Kinte was kidnapped in 1767 and transported to Maryland. Haley believed he was the seventh-generation descendent of Kinte. The novel was hugely successful and was made into a television mini-series. Doubts have been expressed by many, however, about the historical veracity of the novel.

- Like *Praisesong for the Widow*, Toni Morrison's novel *Tar Baby* (1981) addresses the theme of cultural authenticity in the lives of black people. It is also set in the Caribbean as well as the United States. The main character is Janine, an African American fashion model who has been sponsored by a wealthy white family that lives in the Caribbean. The Europeanized Janine finds her life upturned when she meets and falls in love with an impoverished black American named Son, who embodies everything she has tried to leave behind.

- Marshall's *The Fisher King* (2000) is a novel about two African American families who, in the 1940s, live as neighbors in Brooklyn. However, a family feud develops when the families are joined by marriage and the young couple concerned moves to Europe. The novel begins forty years later when a new generation resolves to end the long-standing feud. Reviewers praised the novel for the skill with which Marshall presents family relationships and the issues that affect African Americans.

- Mildred B. Taylor is noted for her novels for young adults about African American families. *The Road to Memphis* (1990) is set in the South in the early 1940s against a background of U. S. involvement in World War II. The Logan family, which includes Cassie, in her last year of high school, and her older brother Stacey, has to deal with a series of crises that threaten to separate them. The novel won the Coretta Scott King Award in 1991.

- *In Search of our Mothers' Gardens* (1983) is a collection of thirty-six nonfiction pieces by African American author Alice Walker. Walker discusses her own work and that of other writers such as Flannery O'Connor and Zora Neale Hurston. She also writes about many other topics, including the civil rights movement and the antinuclear movement of the 1980s.

- *No-No Boy*, a novel by John Okada, was first published in 1957. Set in Seattle after World War II, it tells the story of a young Japanese American who refused to serve in the U. S. armed forces during the war, a decision he regrets. He now has to overcome his self-hatred and find a new sense of belonging. An edition of the novel published by the University of Washington in 1978 remains in print.

Lodge and become a Master Mason shows the extent to which he had embraced and been accepted by a form of culture and community far removed from that which he enjoyed as a young man. At some level of her being, Avey is aware of the price they both have paid, for this cultural shift. When she and Jay go with other Lodge members on a weekend tour of the Laurentian mountains in Canada, the sight of the snowy mountains and the Arctic sky almost make her cry, although she does not know why. For months afterwards, she thinks of how long ago the Eskimos used to send their old people out on the ice to die. She has a vision of the "bent figure of an old woman . . . left huddled on some snowy waste, while the sleds filled with the members of her tribe raced away toward warmer ground." This series of images suggests that Freemasonry, and Jay's embrace of it, is associated in Avey's mind with snow, ice, cold, and death. Even the town in New York they move to when he becomes successful, North White Plains, suggests the same cluster of images—the exact opposite of the heat of the Caribbean, where Avey will find her true self once more.

Indeed, the old Eskimo woman is not the only image of death in this novel, which is essentially a story of symbolic death and rebirth. At the beginning, when Avey is hurriedly packing her bags at night, desperate to leave the cruise ship, she carefully folds her elegant dresses and evening gowns and places them in a garment bag, which she then zips up "as if sealing a tomb." All those fashionable, expensive trappings of her status as a contented member of the African American middle class are being put, so to speak, to their final rest; they belong to a person who no longer really exists. Avey then recalls some of the events that took place in the couple of days she has spent on the cruise ship. When she was trying to find some solitude she passed the Lido, where there were many elderly people sunbathing. An old man stopped her and tried to get her to sit on the empty deck chair beside him. But she was horrified by his attentions and had a disturbing vision of him:

> In a swift, subliminal flash, all the man's wrinkled, sunbaked skin fell away, his thinned-out flesh disappeared, and the only thing to be seen on the deck chair was a skeleton in a pair of skimpy red-and-white striped trunks and a blue visored cap.

It is a vision of death and, although Avey does not fully understand this at the time, a revelation of her own spiritual state; she has adopted a lifestyle that is deadly for her ultimate well-being. Were she to sit down quietly beside the old man, as he has invited her to do, she would be accepting the death of her real self. Instead, she flees. She now has an instinctive sense, if not of what the right course for her might be, at least of what is the wrong one.

However, she still has a long way to go. She has strayed so far from her racial and cultural heritage that she continues to shy away from it. This becomes clear when she expresses such a lack of understanding of and even distaste for the crowds of people heading for Carriacou who swarm around her as she is waiting on the wharf for a taxi. The incident in which one of the Carriacou islanders mistakes her for someone he knows is full of symbolic significance. The man takes her by the elbow and starts to steer her out of the crowd, then realizes his mistake. As he apologizes, he explains that she closely resembles a woman he knows named Ida. "Is twins if I ever saw it. Don' ever let anybody tell you, my lady, that you ain' got a twin in this world!" Avey is indignant at the idea that she might look like a twin of some unknown woman. "What was the matter with these people?" she wonders. The point of course, is that racially and culturally, she has a great deal in common with "these people," but she has erected a wall around herself and cannot recognize it. She sees only differences instead of underlying similarities, separateness instead of a shared cultural heritage.

Avey only really begins to make progress on this spiritual journey to her authentic self when she takes yet another physical journey, the turbulent crossing of the narrow channel of water in the schooner to Carriacou. It is here that the death and rebirth symbolism recurs. The sea crossing is a painful experience for Avey, who suffers from horrible and prolonged sea sickness. It is as if her whole body is being purged and she has completely lost control of it. She is taken to Rosalie Parvay's house to recover, where eventually, near dawn, she manages to fall sleep. When she awakens hours later, she seems to exist in a kind of limbo; the old, manufactured self has died but a new, authentic self has yet to emerge. However, it is clear that some kind of rebirth is at hand:

> She lay gazing humbly around her. For the longest while when she first woke up she had lain there as if still asleep with her eyes open. Framed by the pillow her face had retained the inanimate cast of sleep. Her body under the sheet covering her had remained motionless. Flat, numb, emptied-out, it had been the same as her mind when she awoke yesterday morning unable to recognize anything and with the sense of a yawning hole where her life had been.

Empty in body and mind, Avey is like a newborn baby, and the sense of a profound rebirth is strengthened when she passively allows Rosalie to bathe and massage her. Refreshed, made clean, and accepting the kind touch of a stranger, Avey is now ready to grow into her new self, untainted by the old. When she takes part in the dancing at the Big Drum festival, she reconnects to her childhood self and to all other people of African descent, whether in the United States

She began her journey on a Caribbean cruise. (*R. Gino Santa Maria | Shutterstock.com*)

or the Caribbean. It is a rebirth that makes her whole as a person.

Source: Bryan Aubrey, Critical Essay on *Praisesong for the Widow*, in *Novels for Students*, Gale, Cengage Learning, 2011.

John Oliver Killens

In the following review, Killens uses the word "praise" to describe the story of a middle-aged, black, woman protagonist.

In a season in which the pickings have been sparse in the realm of literature about the black experience, it becomes an occasion for celebration, to come across a novel that one can almost unreservedly sing praises to and genuflect, a moment in literature that is both beautifully crafted and spiritually uplifting. Such a moment has arrived in Paule Marshall's latest novel, *Praisesong for the Widow*.

From her very first novel, *Brown Girl, Brownstones*, Ms. Marshall has demonstrated a capacity and a discipline to write some of the most elegant and sensitive prose currently being rendered in the English language. From her classical *Brown Girl, Brownstones* to *Soul Clap Hands and Sing* to *The Chosen Place, The Timeless People*, she has meticulously sustained the exquisiteness of her prose, a prose rich in imagery and metaphors, always with a rhythm that is both Caribbean and Afro-American.

Brown Girl is the story, sometimes painful, sometimes joyous, of the growing up in Bedford-Stuyvesant in Brooklyn, N.Y., of a young, first-generation Afro-Caribbean-American girl and her struggle for identity and self-realization. She is torn between loyalties to an old Britishly-influenced culture in the West Indies clashing sharply with that of the brave "New World" of the U.S.A., where "one can pick gold up from the very streets." One can make it here, if one only has the "get-up-and-go." Torn also between her father's romantic idealism and her mother's hard-working, hard-driving opportunism. The novel emphatically reminds us that the story of the Afro-Caribbean is as much a part of the American black experience as Richard Wright's *Black Boy* and Margaret Walker's *For My People*. The eternal search of the black man and woman for an elusive Promised Land. "How shall we sing the Lord's song in a strange land?"

Now comes the author with the poignant story of a widow, who has lost her husband along with some of the tenderest moments of her life, as she sought the ever elusive "better way of life," that will-o-the-wisp siren, that beguiles, lures and inveigles, always there just out of reach. The search for happiness and the "better way of life" from Bed-Stuy to suburban split-leveled Westchester is just as far distant and unattainable as Bed-Stuy was to Barbados in the first novel. *Praisesong for the Widow* is the story of a widow woman in the middle age of life attempting to establish a connection with her African roots via dreamily reminiscing on her visits as a young girl to the African-cultured Southland and as a middle-aged widow to Grenada in the Caribbean which is rich with African cultural myths, folkways, songs, dances, humanism.

If we have one quarrel with the novel, it is that it takes too long to get underway. We are made to spend too much time on the boat with the widow on her way to her Africa in the West Indies. The first 70 pages have a dream-like quality, exquisitely rendered in her poetic and inimitable prose that has become Paule Marshall's trademark, but after awhile one becomes impatient to get off the boat and get "the show on the road," so to speak. No matter, if the reader is patient, the reward that comes afterwards will be well worth the waiting for. Even so, in these reminiscent pages there are some beautiful black man-woman love scenes almost unheard of in modern American literature, all praises due to God or Allah and Paule Marshall. It is as if love scenes between black men and women are an embarrassment to black and white American writers, as if love has become a stranger to us black folk. But Ms. Marshall has rendered love for us as I remember love to be, for which I am deeply grateful.

Paule Marshall has done another rare and wonderful thing. She has given to our literature a black middle-aged woman protagonist, a gift heretofore unprecedented. But now that we are off the boat with the widow in her Caribbean Africa, things begin to happen.

Like Jason, she seeks, unknowingly, the golden fleece of her African roots. She had not intended to tarry for any length of time in Grenada. She would get off the boat, get into a taxi and head for the airport and catch the next plane back to New York. Through a series of mishaps, seemingly predestined, she misses the plane and becomes involved in an annual "Carriacou Excursion!" In a kind of fatalistic mood, she gives in and lays back and lets whatever happens happen.

And what happenings! She meets an elderly man in a rum shop who becomes a kind of African father image. Ms. Marshall's poetic imagery casts a hypnotic spell, as she weaves her Ulyssean tale of Avey Johnson's journey to her beginnings. *Praisesong* is on another level, a kind of celebration of the spirit, the very human African spirit. It is fascinating to see this highly sophisticated, middle-aged, middle-class woman from suburban New York become completely captivated by the "juba celebration," so much so that she merges into the crowd of the outdoor dancers.

It becomes almost impossible to tell where she leaves off and where the others of her tribe (or nation) begin. It becomes a nostalgic mood of deja vu. It is as if Avey Johnson has been on a long journey all the days of her empty though eventful life and she has come home at long last! And what a joyous self-fulfilling homecoming! Once we get off the boat with Avey, we are swept along. The superb writing at this point becomes irresistible:

> She should have been disappointed and she had felt a momentary twinge of disappointment when she first entered the yard and had seen what little was there. She should be silently accusing Lebert Joseph of having deceived her again. Had she risked her life on the decrepit boat, disgraced herself to her permanent shame for this?
>
> To her surprise though she felt neither disappointment nor anger. Rather she found herself as the time passed being drawn more and more to the scene in the yard. The restraint and understatement in the dancing, which was not even really dancing, the deflected emotion in the voices were somehow right. It was the essence of something rather than the thing itself she was witnessing. Those present—the old ones—understood this. All that was left were a few names of what they called nations which they could no longer even pronounce properly, the fragments of a dozen or so songs, the shadowy forms of long-ago dances and rum kegs for drums. The hare bones. The burnt-out ends. And they clung to them with a tenacity she suddenly loved in them and longed for in herself. Thoughts—new thoughts—vague and half-formed slowly beginning to fill the emptiness.

If one went in for nitpicking, one could make a case that, when the author takes us reminiscently on the Southern trip of her youth, one still hears beneath it all an Afro-Caribbean rather than an Afro-Southern voice. But what was important, at least for this reader, was the skillful connecting of the Southern experience with that of the Caribbean, both as an African experience, a connection that my friend, the historian, William Mackey, Jr., has insisted upon for as long as I can remember. So that on the whole, I would rather sing a song of praise and exultation for the widow and the author who wrote this beautifully lyrical song. Let us indeed sing, joyously, a *Praisesong for the Widow*.

Source: John Oliver Killens, Review of *Praisesong for the Widow*, in *Crisis*, Vol. 90, No. 7, August/September 1983, pp. 49–50.

SOURCES

Bureau of Western Hemisphere Affairs, "Background Note: Grenada," in *U.S. Department of State: Diplomacy in Action*, March 19, 2010, http://www.state.gov/r/pa/ei/bgn/2335.htm (accessed July 8, 2010).

Christian, Barbara T., "Paule Marshall," in *Dictionary of Literary Biography*, Vol. 33, *Afro-American Fiction Writers After 1955*, edited by Thadious M. Davis, The Gale Group, 1984, pp. 161–70.

"Grenada," in *CIA: World Fact Book*, https://www.cia.gov/library/publications/the-world-factbook/geos/gj.html (accessed July 8, 2010).

Lehmann-Haupt, Christopher, "Books of the Times," in *New York Times*, February 1, 1983.

Marshall, Paule, *Praisesong for the Widow*, G. P. Putnam's Sons, 1983.

———, *Triangular Road: A Memoir*, Basic Books, 2009, pp. 121, 126.

Olmsted, Jane, "The Pull to Memory and the Language of Place in Paule Marshall's *The Chosen Place, The Timeless People*, and *Praisesong for the Widow*, in *African American Review*, Vol. 31, No. 2, Summer 1997, pp. 249–67.

Patterson, Orlando, "For African-Americans, a Virtual Depression—Why?" in *Nation*, June 30, 2010, http://www.thenation.com/article/36882/african-americans-virtual-depression (accessed September 5, 2010).

Tyler, Anne, "A Widow's Tale," in *New York Times Book Review*, February 20, 1983.

FURTHER READING

Delamotte, Eugenia C., *Places of Silence, Journeys of Freedom: The Fiction of Paule Marshall*, University of Pennsylvania Press, 1998.

> Delamotte examines how Marshall shows the relationships of body and soul, material and spiritual, and the difference between American materialism and African American spirituality.

Denniston, Dorothy Hamer, *The Fiction of Paule Marshall: Reconstructions of History, Culture, and Gender*, University of Tennessee Press, 1995.

> Denniston's book as a whole takes the view that Marshall's fiction reclaims African culture for all people in the African diaspora. Denniston provides a very detailed and thorough reading of the novel.

Pettis, Joyce Owens, *Toward Wholeness in Paule Marshall's Fiction*, University Press of Virginia, 1995.

> Pettis traces the theme of spiritual regeneration in *Praisesong for the Widow*.

Taylor, Patrick, *Nation Dance: Religion, Identity and Cultural Difference in the Caribbean*, Indiana University Press, 2001.

> This book is a collection of essays that examine the diverse spiritual, religious, and cultural traditions in the Caribbean.

SUGGESTED SEARCH TERMS

Paule Marshall

Paule Marshall AND Praisesong for the Widow

Grenada

Carriacou

big drum nation dance

African American women authors

middle passage

slavery

ring shout

Freemasonry

The Red Tent

ANITA DIAMANT

1997

The Red Tent was published in 1997. Author Anita Diamant spent several years researching and writing this novel, which focuses on Dinah, the only daughter of Jacob and Leah, briefly mentioned in the book of Genesis. *The Red Tent* is not a religious text, and readers do not need knowledge of the biblical story on which it is based. In fact, many of the characters in *The Red Tent* differ significantly from their biblical descriptions and actions.

In the Jacob narration in Genesis, Dinah is barely mentioned. Diamant creates a history for Dinah and imagines what her life might have been like, filling in the gaps and adding information not supplied in the biblical narrative, in which men's stories dominate. Although set in the biblical past of the Jewish patriarchs between 1800 and 1500 BCE, the themes found in *The Red Tent* are topically relevant to modern readers. These themes include childbirth and motherhood, natural and lunar cycles, and the importance of dreams. *The Red Tent* became a *New York Times* best seller, largely through word-of-mouth recommendations and through promotions by Christian and Jewish groups.

AUTHOR BIOGRAPHY

Diamant was born June 27, 1951, in Newark, New Jersey, to Maurice and Helene Diamant. Diamant was raised in Denver, Colorado, and attended Washington University in St. Louis, Missouri, where she earned a bachelor of arts degree in comparative literature in 1973. Two years later, Diamant earned a master's degree in English at the State University of New York at Binghamton. For several years after finishing college, Diamant worked as a journalist and staff writer for several publications, including the *Boston Phoenix*, the *Boston Globe*, *Boston Magazine*, and *New England Monthly*, as well as several popular women's magazines, including *Self*, *Parenting*, and *McCalls*. Diamant married Jim Ball in 1983. The couple have one daughter.

Diamant's first several books were nonfiction texts that dealt with Jewish life-cycle events. These titles include *The New Jewish Wedding* (1985), *The Jewish Baby Book* (1988), *Living a Jewish Life* (1991), and *Choosing a Jewish Life: A Handbook for People Converting to Judaism and for their Family and Friends* (1997). In 1997, *The Red Tent* became Diamant's first novel to be published. Since then, however, she has published several other novels, including *Good Harbor: A Novel* (2001), *The Last Days of Dogtown: A Novel* (2006), and *Day After Night: A Novel* (2009). In summer 1999, *The Red Tent* was named a significant Jewish Book of the Year by *Reform Judaism* magazine. In 2001, Book Sense, the independent booksellers' alliance, named *The Red Tent* their book of the year.

PLOT SUMMARY

Prologue

In the prologue of *The Red Tent*, Dinah tells readers that her name is pronounced Dee-nah. She is the narrator and will tell her own story, since most people know her name only because of a violent episode in her life. She laments that there was so much more to tell of her life than the brief mention that appears in Genesis, where she is given no voice to tell her story. Dinah celebrates the importance of memory and claims that the stories of women should be told and remembered. She claims it is women and their daughters who will keep the stories of women alive.

Part 1: My Mothers' Stories

CHAPTERS 1–2

In chapter 1, Dinah begins her story with the arrival of Jacob in Laban's camp. Leah, Rachel,

MEDIA ADAPTATIONS

- *The Red Tent* is available as an audiobook (MacMillan 2002). The narrator is Carol Bilger, and the unabridged story is twelve hours long.

Zilpah, and Bilhah are the four daughters of Laban, a cruel, drunken father who treats his wives badly and cheats everyone who crosses his path. Jacob first meets Rachel and is captivated by her beauty. When Jacob tells Rachel he will marry her, she runs back to the camp to share the news. However, Rachel is not yet of marriageable age. The oldest sister, Leah, is also attracted to Jacob. After several months of work, Jacob is ready to bargain with Laban for Rachel to become his wife. Laban drives a hard bargain, but Jacob agrees and is willing to wait for Rachel to be old enough to wed. When Rachel reaches the age of menarche (the onset of menstruation), the wedding is arranged. Rachel is welcomed into the red tent with a special ceremony that recognizes that she is now a woman. The wedding to Jacob is scheduled for seven months later.

In chapter 2, Zilpah notices that Jacob and Leah are attracted to one another and decides that Leah should be married to Jacob. Zilpah tells Rachel of the terrors of the wedding night and, building on the young girl's fears, convinces Rachel that Leah should take her place under the wedding veil, which Leah agrees to do. After the wedding, Jacob is not unhappy to discover himself married to Leah, and the two celebrate their marriage for the seven days decreed by ancient custom. During their seven days of isolation, Leah and Jacob devise a plan to secure a dowry from Laban for Leah, as well as the dowry promised for Rachel, whom Jacob will also wed. Rachel is angry that she succumbed to wedding night fears and lost her position as first wife, but still agrees to wed Jacob in a month. Both Leah and Rachel are soon pregnant, but Rachel miscarries and Leah delivers a healthy son, Reuben. A rift between Leah and Rachel results and is fueled by Rachel's jealousy. According to custom, Jacob circumcises his new son. Leah soon gives birth to four more sons in quick succession—Simon, Levi, Judah, and Zebulun. Rachel suffers several more miscarriages and becomes an apprentice to the midwife, Inna.

CHAPTER 3

When Rachel continues to suffer miscarriages, her handmaiden Bilhah tells Rachel she will go to Jacob and bear a son for her. Bilhah's son by Jacob is named Dan. Leah tells her handmaiden, Zilpah, to go to Jacob and she too becomes pregnant. Although Zilpah dreams she will have a daughter, she gives Jacob two more sons, twins Gad and Asher. Leah also has twin sons, Naphtali and Issachar. While Jacob has been busy growing a family, Laban has been growing rich off Jacob's labors. Laban owns everything that Jacob has earned. Ruti, Laban's fifth wife, is again pregnant and cannot bear to give the husband, who beats her and treats her so badly, another child. Rachel gives Ruti a potion to drink that causes a miscarriage. Leah is again pregnant and feels she is not strong enough to go through another pregnancy, but Rachel believes this child will be a daughter, and she agrees to help Leah with her chores and ease the burden of another pregnancy. Leah gives birth to Dinah, and Rachel finally gives birth to her first child, a boy, Joseph.

Part 2: My Story

CHAPTERS 1–2

In chapter 1, Dinah is one of only a few girls in the camp. She plays with Joseph but is more closely tied to Jacob's four wives, all of whom become her mothers. Although only a child, Dinah is welcomed into the red tent and into the women's lives. Laban continues to gamble, and one day he gives Ruti to a trader as payment for a debt. When the trader arrives to claim his slave, Leah and Jacob trade spices and cloth for Ruti, and the trader leaves satisfied.

In chapter 2, Jacob dreams of returning to Canaan, the land of his father. Jacob also wishes to see his brother, Esau. Although he has spent years increasing his father-in-law's wealth, Jacob must negotiate with Laban to leave the camp and take his wives and children, his flocks, and his belongings. Laban is very greedy and not especially honest, and finally Jacob threatens

Laban that God will not look kindly upon him if he cheats Jacob, who is favored by God. Laban finally agrees to a price. Jacob's wives and children begin to pack up the camp and separate the flocks of animals in preparation for leaving. Ruti commits suicide rather than remain with Laban without the company of Jacob's wives, who have the been the only ones to care for her. When Laban leaves to gamble, he leaves his sons to watch Jacob's preparations and to guard against anything being taken that was not agreed upon in the negotiations. Rachel drugs Laban's son Kemuel and steals the teraphim (idols of household gods) from Laban's tent. The family leaves the following morning, with Jacob unaware that Rachel has stolen Laban's teraphim.

CHAPTERS 3–4

In chapter 3, the family journeys to Canaan. Along the way, they find the midwife, Inna, by the road. She has been cast out from the town and joins Jacob's family as they move to a new land. The journey is a pleasant one until an angry Laban appears, accusing Jacob of stealing his teraphim. Jacob does not know that Rachel stole the gods, and he encourages Laban to search the tents. Laban even enters the red tent, where no man is allowed. Rachel confesses that she stole her father's deities and that she sat on them during her menstrual cycle. The teraphim are worthless to Laban, because he believes them to be tainted, so he leaves without another word. As the group continues on their journey, Jacob begins to fear the meeting with Esau. When the family must cross a deep river, Jacob helps everyone else cross and waits to cross until the next day. When he does not appear the next morning, several of his sons cross the river and find Jacob beaten and injured. The family camps by the river for several months while Jacob heals.

In chapter 4, Esau's eldest son visits the camp and tells Jacob that Esau is on his way to greet Jacob and his family. Jacob is afraid of Esau, fearing he will want revenge because Jacob stole his birthright. When Esau arrives, Jacob walks to his brother and bows to him, but Esau embraces Jacob with love. After the two families are introduced to one another, Dinah meets a girl of her own age, Tabea. This is the first time Dinah has met a girl with whom she can play, since there were no girls in Laban's camp. Dinah and Tabea share stories about their families, and most importantly, Dinah learns that Esau's wives do not use a red tent. At dinner that evening, Jacob and Esau also tell stories and sing songs. Jacob decides that he will not live on his brother's land and instead settles his family on a parcel of land large enough to support his wives and many children. The family has barely settled on the new land when a messenger arrives to invite the family to visit Rebecca, Jacob's mother.

CHAPTERS 5–6

In chapter 5, Dinah's mothers prepare for the family's visit to see Rebecca, also known as the Oracle of Mamre. Rebecca is well known as a healer and is much honored in the land. At Mamre, Dinah once again sees Tabea and learns that her friend has reached the age of menarche. However, Tabea's mother does not adhere to the old customs of celebrating menarche, which results in an angry scene with Rebecca, who says that Tabea's mother has dishonored her daughter by not celebrating women's rituals. Both Tabea and her mother are banished. Leah tries to explain to an angry Dinah that Rebecca is defending the customs of women, which are in danger of being lost. When Jacob's family ends their visit and prepares to leave, Dinah is told she must stay with her grandmother for three months. Although she is initially angry with Rebecca, Dinah comes to admire the woman for her healing powers and her compassion for the sick.

Dinah returns to her father's camp in chapter 6. After the softness of the women's camp with Rebecca, Jacob's camp seems crude and loud. Jacob wants to move again to a larger piece of land, and after negotiations with Hamor, the king of Shechem, the family is promised a large piece of land, and once again Jacob's family moves. Dinah finally reaches the age of menarche and receives the ceremony of womanhood in the red tent. After Levi's wife witnesses Dinah's ceremony, she tells her husband, who complains to Jacob of the women's ceremonies. Jacob destroys the female teraphim but refuses to interfere with the red tent.

CHAPTERS 7–8

In the past Rachel learned to be a midwife by accompanying Inna when she delivered women's babies. Now, in chapter 7, Dinah learns the techniques of the midwife by accompanying Rachel as she delivers babies. One day the midwives are called to King Hamor's palace to deliver a baby. While there, Dinah meets the

king's son, Shalem. After the baby is delivered and Rachel and Dinah return to their camp, the king sends for Dinah, summoning her to the palace to visit with the young mother. Dinah again meets Shalem, who quickly claims Dinah as his wife, although they are not formally married. After several days, King Hamor journeys to Jacob's camp to arrange for the marriage. When Jacob is reluctant to accept the king's offers, Hamor reminds Jacob that Dinah is no longer a virgin. Two of Jacob's sons, Simon and Levi, are especially insulted and convince Jacob to demand that all of the men in Shechem must be circumcised for the wedding to take place. Hamor agrees. While the men are healing from the circumcision, Simon and Levi murder all of the men and boys of Shechem, including Dinah's love, Shalem. Dinah is taken screaming and covered in blood back to her father's camp.

In chapter 8, Dinah spits at Jacob and curses her father and brothers. She flees Jacob's camp in the middle of the night and returns to Shechem. With her departure, there is no female heir to the traditions of the red tent. Before this chapter ends, Dinah describes the fates of her family. Leah will awaken paralyzed and beg her daughters-in-law to poison her. Rachel dies in childbirth along the side of the road after Benjamin is born. Zilpah dies after Jacob destroys her goddesses, and Bilhah flees the camp after she is caught in her tent with Reuben. All four mothers die terrible deaths, as punishment for what the men of the family have done. Jacob changes his name to Isra'El so that no one will know that it was his sons who massacred the males of Shechem.

Part 3: Egypt

CHAPTERS 1–2

In chapter 1, Dinah takes refuge with Shalem's mother, Re-nefer. The two women flee Shechem with the help of a servant. They journey to Egypt and the home of Re-nefer's brother, Nakht-re. Dinah learns that she is pregnant with Shalem's son. In Egypt, Dinah is given sanctuary and treated well, but she must promise Re-nefer that she will never mention to anyone what happened in Shechem. A midwife named Meryt helps Dinah deliver her son. It is a difficult labor, and Dinah must tell Meryt what to do to deliver the baby safely. Dinah wants to name her son, Bar-Shalem, after his father. However, Re-nefer claims the baby as her own son and names him Re-mose. Dinah is forbidden to even speak

Shalem's name or to call her son by any name but Re-mose. Her son will be raised as a prince of Egypt, and Dinah will only be allowed to see him if she agrees to cooperate. Dinah becomes her son's wet nurse and cares for him when he is young, but at nine years old, he is sent to an academy in Memphis to study.

In chapter 2, it becomes clear how lonely Dinah has been since Re-mose left for school. She becomes friends with the midwife, Meryt. Dinah agrees to teach Meryt about herbs and all that she knows about midwifery, but she refuses to attend any births. Eventually, though, Dinah is convinced to leave the house and garden sanctuary where she has lived since fleeing her family many years earlier. Dinah attends some births, and when convinced by Meryt that she must purchase a box to store the gifts that she receives for attending births, Dinah finally goes to the market place. After discovering a beautifully carved box, Dinah meets Benia, a carpenter. They are attracted to one another, and he is told to deliver the box the following day. When she returns home, Dinah discovers that Re-mose has returned from school. He has been gone five years and returns a young man. At a banquet held in his honor, Dinah sees Rebecca's former messenger, Werenro, who was thought to have died many years earlier. Dinah tells Werenro about Shalem and her son and discovers that telling the story lifts a terrible burden.

CHAPTERS 3–4

The box that Dinah bought from Benia is delivered in chapter 3, but Dinah does not see Benia when he brings the box. For some time, things continue as they have with Dinah working as a midwife. When Re-nefer and her brother Nakht-re die, Dinah no longer has a home. Meryt will be moving to the Valley of the Kings to live with her son, and she invites Dinah to come and live with her. Dinah agrees and pays a scribe to write to Re-mose telling him where she has gone. After they arrive in the Valley of the Kings, Dinah and Meryt are soon busy delivering babies. Eventually Benia finds Dinah, and they find they love one another and happily share the home that Benia has established. Benia is gentle and loving, and Dinah learns of the deaths of his first wife and his children. She does not tell him about Shalem.

In chapter 4, Re-mose appears and asks Diana to accompany him back to Thebes, where she is needed to deliver his master's baby. For a couple of days after the delivery, Dinah is ill. As she is recovering, she listens to the servants talk about their master, a Canaanite called Zafenat Paneh-ah. After she learns that his brothers sold him as a slave, Dinah begins to believe that Re-mose's master is her brother Joseph. Re-mose asks his master if he knows a woman named Dinah, but Joseph replies that his sister, who was named Dinah, died long ago. Joseph tells Re-mose about his father's death, and Re-mose threatens to kill Joseph, who is brother to those who murdered his father. After he threatens Joseph, Re-mose is jailed. Dinah is summoned by Joseph, who promises that he will not hurt Re-mose if he leaves and promises never to return. Dinah tells Re-mose the story of his birth and the agreement she was forced to make with Re-nefer not to tell him the truth. She knows she will likely never see him again but begs Re-mose to leave and never return.

CHAPTER 5

When Dinah returns to the Valley of the Kings and Benia, she finally tells Meryt and Benia the truth about who she is and what happened to her. When Meryt dies, Dinah begins to dream of her mothers. First she dreams of the woman who became like a mother to her—Meryt. Then she dreams of Bilhah, Zilpah, and Rachel. After she reaches the age when she no longer menstruates, Dinah finally dreams of Leah, whom Dinah is at long last able to forgive. Several years later, Joseph visits to tell Dinah that Jacob is dying. Joseph begs Dinah to come with him to see Jacob. Although she is reluctant to do so, after Joseph begs all night, Dinah finally agrees to go with Benia accompanying her.

When they arrive at the camp, Dinah is surprised to see that her brothers are old men. Her three oldest brothers, Reuben, Simon, and Levi, have all died. Jacob does not initially recognize Joseph, but when he does, he begs Joseph for forgiveness and curses the memories of his three oldest sons. In speaking with a young girl at Jacob's camp, Dinah learns that her own story has become a legend. It is assumed that Dinah died of grief. Knowing that her story has been too terrible to be forgotten helps Dinah find peace in the camp. As they prepare to return home, Judah gives Dinah Leah's lapis ring and explains that Leah never forgot her. Dinah understands that her mother forgave her before she died. After she and Benia return to their home, Dinah no longer delivers babies. As she dies, Dinah sees the faces of her mothers and of the other women in her life, who welcome her.

CHARACTERS

Benia

Benia is Dinah's second husband. Benia was married previously, but his wife and children died. He is a carpenter and a good and gentle man who loves Dinah. After their initial meeting, he moves to the Valley of the Kings. When Dinah moves there with Meryt, Benia finds Dinah, and they marry. He completely accepts and loves her, in spite of her past.

Benjamin

Benjamin is the youngest of Jacob's sons. His mother, Rachel, dies giving birth to him.

Bilhah

Bilhah is Rachel's handmaiden and the fourth of Laban's daughters. She becomes one of Jacob's wives and is the mother of Dan. She is described as small and dark and is also known for her gentleness. Her love for Jacob's son, Reuben, results in her being banished from the camp.

Dinah

Dinah is the protagonist and first-person narrator in *The Red Tent*. She is Leah's daughter and the only daughter of Jacob. Because she is the only daughter, she is spoiled and nurtured as the daughter to all four of the mothers—Leah, Rachel, Zilpah, and Bilhah. From the time she is a small child, Dinah has free access to the red tent, even though she is not supposed to enter until she reaches the age of menarche. Dinah carefully watches and thinks about the activities in the camp and is intelligent enough to understand and draw conclusions based on what she observes. She is also a careful observer of human nature and of the relationships between the men and women who live within the camp. Dinah's narrations paint a detailed picture of her family because she includes many small details about their life. Her observations about Jacob are especially interesting, since they show him as both a strong leader and as a frightened brother, whose fear of Esau leads everyone in the camp to be afraid. After the murder of her husband, Dinah curses her father and her brothers. She tells the story of her life, beginning as a spoiled and beloved daughter and ending as a strong and loving woman.

Esau

Esau is Jacob's brother. Although Jacob has stolen Esau's birthright and the blessing of their father, Esau makes a success of his life and forgives Jacob when they meet. Jacob takes his family and leaves Laban to journey to Canaan because he wants to reconcile with Esau.

Hamor

Hamor is the king of Shechem and the father of Dinah's first husband, Shalem.

Inna

Inna is the midwife who delivers many of the children born to Jacob and his wives. She takes Rachel as her apprentice and trains her to be a midwife as well.

Isaac

Isaac is the father of Jacob and Esau. He is also the son of Abraham. Isaac has only a small role in the novel but is revered because he is one of the men to whom God has spoken.

Jacob

Jacob is Dinah's father. He is the son of Isaac and Rebecca and marries Leah and Rachel, as well as their handmaidens Bilhah and Zilpah. Jacob steals his brother Esau's birthright and then flees to live with his uncle Laban. Jacob is described as charming and attractive. He is also a talented herdsman and quickly increases Laban's flock and wealth. He insists that his sons be circumcised. Although he believes in one God, he tolerates the polytheistic beliefs (beliefs in multiple gods) of the women. Jacob teaches his sons how to manage the flocks and how to be successful in managing the land. At the beginning of the novel, Jacob is charismatic and always righteous in his dealings. By the end of the novel, however, his wisdom has declined, and he is controlled by his sons, Simon and Levi, who are greedy and belligerent. Jacob allows these two sons to slaughter the men and boys of Shechem, including Dinah's husband. As he is dying, Jacob names each of his twelve sons but does not mention Dinah, whom he appears to have forgotten.

Joseph

Joseph is Rachel's oldest son. He is the same age as Dinah. As a child he plays with Dinah until his brothers make fun of him for playing with a girl. Joseph is sold into slavery in Egypt, where he is called Zafenat Paneh-ah. Joseph reappears at the end of the novel, when Dinah journeys to Egypt to deliver his wife's baby. When Jacob is dying, Joseph demands that Dinah accompany him to see his father. Joseph is much like Jacob in personality and good looks, which he uses to achieve success in Egypt.

Judah

Judah is one of the most compassionate and caring of Jacob's sons. He is also wise and becomes the leader after Reuben, Simon, and Levi die. At the end of the book, Judah gives Dinah the lapis ring that belonged to their mother, Leah. The ring is a sign of Leah's forgiveness and her love for Dinah.

Kemuel

Kemuel is Laban's son. Rachel drugs him so that she can steal the teraphim.

Kiya

Kiya is one of Meryt's granddaughters. She becomes close to Dinah and is loved like a daughter. Kiya learns the art of midwifery from Meryt and Dinah and takes over as a midwife when Meryt dies and Dinah retires.

Laban

Laban is the father of Leah, Rachel, Zilpah, and Bilhah. He is a greedy man who drinks and gambles. He is also a poor camp leader and shepherd and is made wealthy only through Jacob's skills as a herder. Laban cheats Jacob whenever given a chance and beats his fifth wife, Ruti, who bears Laban two sons. Laban chases after Jacob's family when they leave because Rachel has stolen his teraphim, but he turns back because he fears Jacob's God.

Leah

Leah is Dinah's mother and the first of Jacob's wives. She loves Jacob and agrees to take Rachel's place at her wedding to Jacob. She has two different-colored eyes, which makes her self-conscious about her appearance, but her eyes are also a defining feature, since they are often noted for their strong vision. Leah is capable and wise and is the person who most clearly runs the camp efficiently. She is the matriarch of Jacob's tribe and is talented both in the domestic sphere, where her beer brewing is renowned, and in the male work sphere, where she reveals important and crucial knowledge about herding and breeding of animals. Leah knows and understands that her father Laban is cruel and a poor leader. She protects Ruti from Laban's abuse whenever she is able to do so. Leah gives Jacob eight of his twelve children. Although she is a strong woman, she is unable to protect her only daughter, Dinah, from the cruelty of Jacob and his sons.

Levi

Levi is one of the sons of Leah and Jacob. Like his brother Simon, Levi is known for his cruelty and jealousy. His desire is to be powerful. Like Simon, Levi is intolerant and judgmental, and together they are responsible for the massacre of Shechem.

Meryt

Meryt is an Egyptian midwife who delivers Dinah's baby. Meryt quickly understands that Dinah is also a talented midwife. Although Meryt is much older than Dinah, Meryt begins to study midwifery with Dinah, who teaches the older midwife about herbs that help with delivering babies. Meryt becomes Dinah's close friend and surrogate mother. Meryt also introduces Dinah to Benia, and when Meryt moves to the Valley of the Kings to live with her adopted son, she offers a home to Dinah. At the conclusion of the book, when Dinah dreams of all her mothers, Meryt is included.

Nakht-re

Nakht-re is the brother of Re-nefer. He gives sanctuary to Dinah and helps his sister raise Re-mose.

Rachel

Rachel is the second of Jacob's wives. As a young woman, she is selfish and arrogant. She is initially afraid to marry Jacob and so begs Leah to take her place under the veil. After Leah marries Jacob, Rachel is angry and petulant that she has given up the position of first wife. She knows that she is a beauty and that Jacob loves her best, but when she is unable to bear children as easily as her older sister, Leah, jealousy begins to consume Rachel's personality. Rachel becomes a midwife after studying with Inna and eventually trains Dinah to be a midwife. As she develops confidence in her abilities as a midwife, Rachel's jealousy of Leah begins to lessen, and she becomes more mature and caring. Rachel gives Jacob two sons and dies in child-birth with the second one.

Rebecca

Rebecca is Jacob's mother and the Oracle of Mamre. Mamre is said to be the place where Abraham camped, set up an altar to worship God, and was then visited by angels who told him that Sarah would give birth to a son, Isaac. Rebecca is a wise person who sees visions of the future. Her vision for Dinah predicts unhappiness. When Rebecca banishes Tabea, Dinah thinks that Rebecca is cruel and hates her, but Rebecca understands the importance of keeping alive the women's rituals, since these separate the women from the men and give the women status. Rebecca insists that Dinah spend three months with her, and while Dinah still does not like Rebecca at the end of the three months, she respects Rebecca because of her compassion for those in need.

Re-mose

Re-mose is Dinah's son by Shalem. Dinah names him Bar-Shalem, but is forbidden by Re-nefer to ever call him by that name. Instead, Re-nefer names the boy Re-mose. Re-mose knows that Dinah is his birth mother, but he considers Re-nefer his mother, because she raised him. He is intelligent and determined to succeed as a scribe. Eventually, Dinah tells him the truth about his father. After Re-mose threatens Joseph, who is a brother of the murderers, Dinah forces Re-mose to leave to save him from punishment. She never sees him again.

Re-nefer

Re-nefer is Hamor's queen and the mother of Shalem, Dinah's first husband. She blames herself for the massacre of all the males of Shechem because she arranged for Shalem and Dinah to be together. After the murder of Hamor and Shalem, Re-nefer helps Dinah to escape and takes her to Egypt and the home of Nakht-re, Re-nefer's brother. After Dinah bears Shalem's son, Re-nefer takes the child to raise as her own. She makes Dinah promise that she will never speak of the massacre perpetuated by her brothers and that she will never tell Re-mose about how or why his father was killed.

Reuben

Reuben is the son of Leah and Jacob. He is good and wise, but his affair with Bilhah results in his banishment from the camp and her banishment and death.

Ruti

Ruti is Laban's fifth wife. She is treated badly by him and, after giving birth to two sons, seeks an abortion when she discovers she is pregnant again. Laban gambles Ruti as a wager, and Jacob negotiates a payment of the debt so that she is not given as a slave. After Ruti learns that Jacob will be leaving with his wives, she chooses to die rather than be left with Laban and her own sons, who also treat her badly.

Shalem

Shalem is Dinah's first husband. He is the son of King Hamor, and when he takes Dinah without her father's permission, his willingness to marry Dinah and pay an expensive bride price for her is too little satisfaction for her family, who consider her dishonored. Although he loves Dinah and she loves him, Dinah's brothers murder him, while he sleeps in her arms.

Simon

Simon is one of the sons of Leah and Jacob. Like his brother Levi, Simon is cruel and jealous of the success of others and overly concerned with being powerful. Also like Levi, Simon is intolerant and judgmental, and together they are responsible for the massacre of Shechem.

Tabea

Tabea is Dinah's cousin and the first girl of her own age that Dinah has ever met. The two girls bond immediately when Jacob takes his family to meet the family of his brother, Esau. When Tabea enters the age of menarche, her mother refuses to help her daughter in the traditional ceremonies of the red tent. Tabea is important because her mother's failure to accept the traditional ceremonies for Tabea reveal the importance of women's rituals and how extreme the punishment is when they are violated. Although it was not her fault, Tabea is banished from the family and camp.

Werenro

Werenro is Rebecca's slave. Werenro is the messenger sent to Jacob's family when they are invited to Rebecca's camp. Werenro entertains the camp with her songs. She is attacked and thought to have been murdered, but she reappears later when Dinah is in Egypt. Werenro is the first person to whom Dinah tells the truth about what happened to her. Telling Werenro the story of her love for Shalem and of his murder and the birth of their son, helps Dinah to finally begin healing.

Zafenat Paneh-ah
See Joseph

Zilpah
Zilpah is one of Jacob's secondary wives and Laban's third daughter. She was Leah's handmaiden, and she manipulated Rachel into asking Leah to take her place at the wedding with Jacob. Zilpah does not like men and does not enjoy her duties as Jacob's wife, although she gives him twin sons. Zilpah worships her goddesses and dies after they are destroyed.

THEMES

Dreams
Dreams are important means of prophecy in Diamant's novel. In *The Red Tent*, many of the characters have prophetic dreams. Jacob's dreams of the land of his father pull him to leave Laban's camp and move to Canaan, where his future awaits him. Of course, not all dreams are truly prophetic. Jacob's guilt at taking Esau's birthright haunts him, but Jacob's fearful dreams of Esau do not come to pass. When she is pregnant, Zilpah dreams that she will give birth to a girl, but instead, she gives birth to twin boys. In her case, Zilpah's dream manifests her deep desire to have a girl, as well as her dislike of men. Dreams for Dinah are sometimes nightmares that recall horrific events, as after the murder of Shalem. By the end of the novel, however, Dinah's dreams bring her peace and solace. After the death of Meryt, Dinah dreams of Meryt and each of her mothers. These dreams bring laughter, tears, adventure, cleansing, and forgiveness and reconciliation.

Natural Cycles
The lunar cycle marks the natural cycle of menstruation among the women of the camp. The red tent is the visual representation of this cycle of nature. The importance of the red tent as an icon of the lunar cycles is made clear in part 2, chapter 5, when Leah explains to Dinah why her cousin Tabea has been banished from Rebecca's camp. Leah tells Dinah that women understand that the cleansing of the body that occurs each month with menstruation is a gift from the great mother goddess, which unifies the women with nature. Although men think that menstruation is unpleasant, the women know that entry and sanctity in the red tent is an opportunity for the women to restore themselves. Women understand the importance of the lunar cycle, which signals a readiness for pregnancy and childbirth and preparation for motherhood. This natural cycle represents the strength of womanhood, as well. Leah explains to Dinah that there is a danger that the rituals of the women are being forgotten. If forgotten, then the lunar cycle will be the same for women as it is for lower animals. As a result, it is essential that women continue to celebrate their natural cycles in the red tent. The red tent and the women's rituals are threatened by Simon and Levi, whose wives witness the ceremony that Dinah undertakes when she reaches menarche. Jacob orders the teraphim used in the rituals destroyed, because for the first time he begins to understand that the women of the camp worship nature and the lunar cycle, while he and the men worship one God.

Motherhood
Motherhood is the force that unifies all of the women of *The Red Tent*. Much of the first section of the book is devoted to childbirth and the desire for motherhood. Because Leah, Rachel, Zilpah, and Bilhah are all wives of Jacob, they all become mothers to each of his children. Dinah often says that she has four mothers, with each mother assuming a different role in teaching Dinah how to be a woman. Leah teaches Dinah how to cook, and Rachel teaches Dinah the art of healing, especially the work of the midwife. Zilpah teaches Dinah stories about the gods and goddesses and about her love for nature. Bilhah teaches Dinah to be loyal and kind. Later in life, Meryt helps Dinah find her way again, and in turn Dinah becomes a mother figure to Meryt's granddaughter Kiya. In the red tent, the women come together as mothers, sharing childbirth and stories of motherhood that sustain all of them. Dinah has minimal contact with her father and brothers. It is the women, especially the mothers in the story, who give her strength and the knowledge to survive. In turn, Dinah is made strong enough to withstand the tragedy of her life, even as she is forced to give up her own child to ensure his survival.

TOPICS FOR FURTHER STUDY

- Read *Lilith's Ark: Teenage Tales of Biblical Women* (2006) by Deborah Bodin Cohen, which contains stories about Rebecca, Leah, Rachel, and Dinah. After you have completed the book, write an essay in which you compare Cohen's characterizations of these women with those provided by Diamant in *The Red Tent*. In writing your essay, consider the choice of words that each author uses to create these women's personalities.

- Diamant looked to the Bible for inspiration to write a novel. She chose Dinah's story because the book of Genesis contained only a brief mention of Dinah and no details. This allowed Diamant to create details and her own story. If you were going to write a novel, what episode or character in the Bible would you choose? Write a detailed proposal letter to an editor in which you outline your topic and the direction you would take in writing a novel. You will turn in the letter for grading, but you will also present your proposal to your classmates in an oral presentation.

- Search in the library or online for illustrations of some of the paintings that depict ancient biblical Israel, especially focusing on the places that Dinah visits and the people that she knows. Use these illustrations to create a PowerPoint presentation for your classmates. Be sure that you thoroughly understand the historical context for each illustration so that you can provide background information when you link the art to Diamant's novel in your presentation.

- Dinah lives in many places during her lifetime. Locate the modern place names for these places: Haran, Succoth, Canaan, Mamre, Shachem, Thebes, and the Valley of the Kings. Create a poster presentation, using Glogster or another online poster creator. Include a map with Dinah's many journeys labeled. Also include photos of the areas as they appear today. When you present your poster to your classmates, provide a brief history of each location, mentioning the different names by which each area has been known.

- Women's life-cycle events are important in Diamant's novel. The red tent is the center of these events, but menarche tents and huts were common in other cultures. Research the use of women's tents and huts in at least one other culture, and in a carefully constructed essay, compare what you learn about these tents or huts with the red tent in Diamant's novel.

- Watch the 1994 film *Jacob*, which is about the relationship between Jacob and Rachel, and write an essay in which you discuss the differences and similarities between the film and Diamant's novel.

- Diamant's novel is a fictionalized retelling of a biblical story from the book of Genesis. With two or three classmates, create a group presentation in which you research ancient Israel prior to the time of Jesus. Choose three or four different events in the history of ancient Israel. You might consider the exodus from Egypt, the creation of Jerusalem as Israel's capital, the division of the kingdom into Judah and Israel, the Assyrian or Babylonian invasions, the Persian or Greek occupations, the Maccabean revolt, or the Roman occupation as possible topics. Divide the work by assigning different chores to each member of the group. Good group presentations are multimedia, so take the time to prepare a PowerPoint presentation that includes graphs, photos, timelines, and video clips. Be sure to prepare handouts for your classmates, which should include a bibliography of your sources.

Women gathered in the Red Tent during their cycles of birthing, menses, and illness. *(Olga Kolos / Shutterstock.com)*

STYLE

Analepsis and Prolepsis

In telling her story, Dinah makes liberal use of analepsis and prolepsis (commonly referred to as flashback and flash-forward). She uses analepsis to tell of the past. Analepsis is not simply a flashback, however; instead, it is as if a memory from the past becomes the reality of the present. For instance, when Dinah is a small child, she and Joseph exchange stories of the past. Dinah tells Joseph of the goddess Utta, who taught women to weave, and the great mother goddess of fertility, Innana. Joseph tells Dinah stories about Isaac's binding and Abraham's meetings with God. In telling these stories, the past becomes the reality of the present.

Prolepsis is the anticipating of an event before it happens. An example of this is when Dinah, in an early chapter of the book, describes Rachel as small and explains that even when she is pregnant, she is small-breasted. At this point in the novel, Rachel has not had a child, nor even

reached the age of menarche, but the reader learns that she will be a mother much later in the story. Another example occurs when Dinah tells of the jealousy between Leah and Rachel in part 1, chapter 2 and then admits that she is rushing her story. She knows what is to happen and must remind herself to tell the story in the proper order as it unfolds. This anticipation of the story to come is prolepsis.

Bildungsroman Novel

A *bildungsroman* novel is one that traces the growth and development of a young person from youth to adulthood. The growth of the protagonist is not only a physical growth from youth to adulthood; rather this genre is more focused on the emotional and psychological maturity of the protagonist. Bildungsroman novels can be autobiographical or, as in the case of Diamant's novel, biographical. Dinah's life is told beginning with her innocent and sheltered childhood and tracing her life through the tragedies that follow until she finds maturity and happiness as an adult. Dinah must return to her father's camp for complete healing to occur. There she learns that her story has not been forgotten, and from her brother, Judah, she learns that her mother has forgiven her.

Midrash

Midrash is a Hebrew word for the rabbinic commentary about the Hebrew Scriptures, collectively known as the Old Testament. These biblical stories leave many details out and thus are often confusing as to how an event occurs or why a person behaves in the way he behaves. To begin to fill in the gaps in the stories, ancient rabbinic scholars began writing possible explanations, which in turn were endlessly discussed, which led to subsequent commentary upon more commentary. This is midrash. What Diamant does in her novel *The Red Tent* is create a midrash about Dinah's life. Genesis 34 offers little information about Dinah and her tragedy. For instance, readers of Genesis do not know how she felt about Shalem or what happened to her after her brothers had their revenge on the men of Shechem. Diamant tells Dinah's story by filling in the missing information, just as the ancient rabbis did when they created midrash about other biblical texts.

Symbolism

Symbolism is the use of an object to represent a concept. In *The Red Tent*, Diamant includes several objects that are important symbols. The red tent symbolizes a place of healing and nurturing for the women of the camp. In essence, the red tent symbolizes the women's lives. They gather each moon to celebrate the cleansing of menstruation, and they gather in the tent for childbirth and the celebration of motherhood. The women tell stories and rest from the hard work of the camp, and thus the tent also represents rest and a place of relaxation. Diamant also includes several symbols of childbirth, such as the bricks. The midwives' bricks were used when a woman was ready to give birth. The midwife had the pregnant woman stand on the bricks as she began to push out the baby. The act of standing on the bricks symbolized strength and recalled the bravery that each woman needed as she began to give birth. Even with the midwife's assistance, many women died in childbirth. The midwife's bricks helped women face childbirth with more confidence.

HISTORICAL CONTEXT

Midwifery

In Diamant's novel, ancient midwives use reeds, bricks, and knives to help bring babies into the world. There is only brief information in the Old Testament about midwifery. In fact, the first mention of midwives in Hebrew scripture occurs in Genesis when Rachel dies giving birth to Benjamin. Another mention is made in Genesis 38 when Judah's daughter-in-law, Tamar, gives birth to twins. The last reference occurs in Exodus 1 when pharaoh orders the Hebrew midwives to kill the first born sons of the Hebrews. This order makes clear that there were many Hebrew midwives and that they were a common feature in Jewish life. The Egyptians were well trained in midwifery techniques, and it is likely that the Hebrews learned some techniques for delivering babies from the Egyptians. The Talmud (the central text of Jewish traditions) records that midwives were well trained and that doctors were used only in especially difficult cases.

As Diamant notes in *The Red Tent*, the use of bricks or stones was common for midwives, as were birthing stools. These tools served much the same purpose in encouraging the pregnant mother to crouch down from a standing position to give birth. Diamant also mentions the use of reeds by midwives. Reeds were commonly used by ancient midwives to blow air into the baby if the infant did not begin breathing immediately after birth. Bas-reliefs (shallow sculptural carvings) from this period describe and illustrate techniques for childbirth. These illustrations show midwives, and sometimes multiple midwives, assisting with births. These bas-reliefs confirm Egyptian papyri (texts written on scrolls of papyrus paper) claiming that women were well employed as midwives. Like the Hebrew midwives of *The Red Tent*, the midwives of Egypt were knowledgeable about herbs, especially herbs that alleviate pain and help labor progress. The midwives who practiced their art at the time in which Diamant has set her novel were skilled professionals who were much in demand.

Menstrual Tents

Although menstrual tents are not specifically mentioned in Hebrew scriptures, menstrual tents and huts were common to many cultures

COMPARE
&
CONTRAST

- **1600 BCE:** Judaism, begun five decades earlier by Abraham, becomes better established by his grandson, Jacob, and his twelve sons, who become leaders of the twelve tribes of Israel.

  Today: More than five million Jews live in Israel, about one-third of the Jews in the world.

- **1500 BCE:** Geometry helps the Egyptians survey the boundaries of their fields after yearly flooding by the Nile erases all geographic lines.

  Today: The annual flooding of the Nile ends in the 1960s with the completion of the Aswan High Dam. Water stored behind the dam provides irrigation water year-round in Egypt, allowing farmers to more accurately fill the needs of their crops.

- **1400 BCE:** A nine-year-old boy, Tutankhamun, becomes king of Egypt and restores the worship of the old Egyptian gods, which had been rejected by the previous ruler in favor of monotheism.

  Today: It is estimated that 80 to 90 percent of Egyptians are Sunni Muslims, with the remainder of Egyptians observing some type of Christian belief.

in antiquity, including the ancient Hebrews. In ancient times in the land of Israel, when a woman was *niddah* (thought to be ritually unclean because she was menstruating), it was customary that she be segregated from the rest of the community in a special hut or tent. The book of Leviticus sets forth laws governing the behavior of women during menstruation and after childbirth. According to Leviticus, men became impure if they touched anything a menstruating woman had touched. Women were considered unclean whenever blood was present and thus were required to keep themselves physically separated from the rest of the camp at these times. Leviticus 12 and 15 include laws governing isolation after childbirth and during menstruation. Other non-Jewish societies also had customs that required women to be isolated in a menstrual tent or hut for a set number of days.

Menstruating women were not allowed to cook or work in the fields or associate with any male in the village or camp and were forced to live excluded from the rest of the community. It is important to remember that in many cases, while it may be Leviticus that called for the separation of women, it was the women who desired this separation.

In Diamant's novel, the women cherish the time spent apart, resting and telling stories and singing in the red tent. The use of menstrual huts is not limited just to antiquity or to ancient Israel. Menstrual huts were also common to Jewish societies living outside of Israel during the Diaspora (when Jews were forced to leave their homelands). For instance, twentieth-century Ethiopian Jews had a long tradition of using menstrual huts, in which women would live during the time they were required by Jewish law to be separated from the rest of the camp. Depending on the size of the community, each family might have its own hut, or several families would share a hut. In all cases, the huts were separated from the rest of the village and on the margin or boundary of the camp. While in the huts, the women did not perform chores. Instead they talked and told stories and rested, just as the women of Diamant's novel do in the red tent. When the Ethiopian Jews immigrated to Israel late in the twentieth century, the use of menstrual huts ended. Ethnographic studies by anthropologists find that the use of menstrual huts remains common to many societies; they are often the last artifact to be discarded when societies make attempts to modernize.

She learned many crafts from her "mothers" in the tent. (*Pinosub / Shutterstock.com*)

CRITICAL OVERVIEW

Although the *The Red Tent* is set in a place and time thousands of years in the past, Diamant's novel appealed to contemporary readers, who turned the book into a best seller. An example of how perception of the book changed within a few years of publication can be found in two reviews that Sandee Brawarsky wrote for the *New York Jewish Week* newspaper. In January 1998, Brawarsky listed five books published during 1997 that she recommended to readers. *The Red Tent* earned a brief mention as an "imaginative" text that "conveys the texture of biblical life and provides a female perspective on the stories of Genesis." By 2000, Brawarsky decided that Diamant's novel deserved a longer individual review because readers kept asking her if she had read the book. Brawarsky observed that her family had read the book, as had several local book clubs. The publisher of the paperback edition sent copies to rabbis and to women ministers, as well as to

many book clubs. The resulting word-of-mouth discussions made *The Red Tent* a best seller.

In a review of *The Red Tent* for *Lilith* magazine, Natalie Blitt writes that *The Red Tent* is "a beautiful tale" that allows readers to "imagine the smells and sounds" of Jacob's camp. Readers are also able visualize the biblical story as a place "filled with cooking, laughing, weeping and, most importantly, storytelling." In a review for the *Jewish News of Greater Phoenix*, writer Vicki Cabot says of *The Red Tent* that "Diamant gives voice to the besmirched maiden and affecting poignancy to her story." Cabot also notes Diamant's careful research into the history and culture of the time, which in turn creates "an imaginative look at the feminist side of Biblical life." The biblical story of Dinah offers little of substance for readers, but as Cabot suggests, Diamant is able to fill in the empty spaces in the story and give voice to that which "remains silent in the original Biblical text."

As might be expected of any book that significantly rewrites biblical text, not all critics were happy with the way Diamant uses *The Red Tent* to re-envision Genesis 34. In an essay published in the *Women's League Outlook*, Benjamin Edidin Scolnic writes that *The Red Tent* is both anti-male and anti-Semitic. Scolnic cites especially the depiction of Jacob and Diamant's "virulent antipathy toward the essential early Hebrew ritual of circumcision." Scolnic reminds his readers that "fiction is a powerful tool"; he then wonders how Diamant could "depict the Israelite characters in such a horrible light while creating non-Israelites who are nothing short of perfect."

CRITICISM

Sheri Metzger Karmiol

Karmiol teaches literature and drama at the University of New Mexico, where she is a lecturer in the University Honors Program. In the following essay, she discusses Diamant's use of midrash *to tell the story of Dinah's physical and emotional journeys in* The Red Tent.

Anita Diamant's novel *The Red Tent* is a revisioning of Genesis 34, which takes the reader beyond the biblical text and into the story of Dinah's life. In her novel, Diamant weds the rabbinic midrash tradition, which is a completely male-dominated genre, to a feminist reading of

WHAT DO I READ NEXT?

- Michelle Moran's novel *Nefertiti* (2007) is a fictionalized account of the life of the Egyptian queen Nefertiti. This novel has many of the same themes as Diamant's novel, including love, ambition, and religious conflict.

- Diamant's novel *Day After Night: A Novel* (2009) takes place in Palestine just after the end of World War II. In this novel, Diamant explores the lives of Jewish women refugees from several different backgrounds, including several survivors of Nazi concentration camps. These women have survived the war and now must survive in Palestine, where the British Mandate seeks to blockade their arrival.

- *Pitching My Tent: On Marriage, Motherhood, Friendship, and Other Leaps of Faith* (2003), by Diamant, is a collection of essays about the different seasons of a woman's life—love, marriage, motherhood, middle age, and death.

- Fredrick Buechner's novel, *The Son of Laughter* (1993), is a reimagining of the story of Jacob, the father of Dinah.

- Ita Shere's book, *Dinah's Rebellion: A Biblical Parable for Our Time* (1990), provides a feminist analysis of Dinah's story, as well as the tales of the Jewish patriarchs.

- *Journeys With Elijah: Eight Tales of the Prophet* (1999), by Barbara Diamond Golden and Jerry Pinkney, is a book designed for young-adult readers. Elijah appears in a collection of stories set in several different regions, including Argentina, China, and the Middle East. This book also includes a selection of watercolor illustrations to accompany the text.

- *Rebekah* (2002) is one of several novels that Orson Scott Card has written about the women of Genesis. Other novels focus on Rachel, Leah, and Sarah.

biblical text. Instead of the biblical story, which focuses on male stories and exploits, Diamant privileges the female story, pulling Dinah's life

> HER JOURNEY IS BOTH PHYSICAL AND EMOTIONAL, BUT AT ITS ESSENCE, DINAH'S STORY IS A FORM OF LITERARY BIOGRAPHY IN WHICH THE READER JOURNEYS WITH DINAH FROM HER CHILDHOOD TO HER DEATH AND EVEN BEYOND."

from the male shadows that keep her hidden from view. Rather than focus on Jacob and his sons and the journey they undertake in their efforts to establish a monotheistic view of life, Diamant allows Dinah to narrate her story. Her journey is both physical and emotional, but at its essence, Dinah's story is a form of literary biography in which the reader journeys with Dinah from her childhood to her death and even beyond.

Midrash is intertextual writing, in which the writer reads, extrapolates, and rewrites the text. For example, in the early chapters of *The Red Tent*, Dinah lives on the fringes of the male world, just as she does in the biblical account. Her father Jacob barely notices that she exists, and her name is not mentioned. His whole focus is on his sons, and indeed, Dinah's birth is almost an afterthought among the births of so many sons. In a sense, Diamant rescues Dinah from biblical obscurity. She does this by using biblical *midrash* to bring Dinah from beyond the shadows of her brothers' lives.

In her essay, "The Redemption of Dinah in Anita Diamant's *The Red Tent*," Jessica Schantz argues that books that delve deeper into biblical texts are welcomed by readers. Schantz points out that Diamant is engaging "the mainstream readership's desires to hear the 'undertold' and misrepresented stories of biblical women," which in turn leads readers to a "discerning relationship with biblical storytelling." In Genesis, readers learn about Jacob's preparation to move his family to Canaan. Dinah is never mentioned. However, in *The Red Tent*, when Dinah tells the story of the move, she tells readers that as the family begins to prepare for their departure from Haran, there is one night when she brings Jacob his food. He thanks Dinah, and she says, "It was the first time I remember hearing my name in his mouth." She is still a child, but she is so taken back by his sudden use of her name that she cannot reply. Diamant's midrash gives readers that small detail in Dinah's world.

Unlike in biblical text, where the men are central to the story, in *The Red Tent*, the perspective is given to the women and specifically to Dinah. She tells the story of her journey, which is far more complex and detailed than in Genesis 34. Neither Jacob nor Joseph, nor any other male descendent, is given her story to tell. Indeed, at the conclusion of the book, when Dinah accompanies Joseph to Jacob's camp one final time, it is a female child who recounts the genealogy of Dinah's life, the stories of grandmothers, mothers, children, and grandchildren, in which Dinah and her story are remembered. In the women's lineage, Dinah is more than a story of rape and revenge.

In an interview with Faith L. Justice in *Copperfield Review*, Diamant says that the female narrator allows readers to see the female world and not the men's world. This is because, according to Diamant, "Dinah wouldn't have known what the men's world was like." In shifting the narration to Dinah, her story gains preeminence, as her memory recalls the details of her life, supplying the missing pieces of the biblical account and creating her own midrash in the process. Dinah complains in the prologue of *The Red Tent* that her life is little more than "a footnote" and her story "a brief detour between the well-known story of my father, Jacob, and the celebrated chronicle of Joseph, my brother." It is Diamant's use of midrash that takes Dinah beyond "the voiceless cypher in the text" and makes her a living memory.

Dinah's physical journey moves her around the Middle East, from present day Iraq and Syria to Israel, the West Bank, and finally to Egypt. In *The Red Tent*, Dinah is born in her grandfather's camp, not far from Haran. She lives in a women's world, where the women worship polytheistic goddesses associated with fertility and childbirth, while the men in the family are beginning to adopt the worship of a single God. Dinah has a privileged place in the women's world because she is the only daughter, but outside the women's tent, she is lonely and alone. Her father barely acknowledges her, and when her older brothers make fun of Joseph for playing with her, he no longer has anything to do with her. As the cherished daughter, Dinah stays in the red tent long after the sons are weaned and pushed out. She is safe and secure in the love

shown her by her four mothers. Even the family gods and goddesses seem to be part of the family that loves her, and in fact, Dinah describes these gods and goddesses as if they were relatives who are "interested in everything that happened to me." These small minutiae of daily life are essential in understanding Dinah's journey to adulthood, but in the men's story of these events, her life is of small significance, except as it directly affects their own lives.

Dinah remains in Haran until her father, Jacob, realizes that he cannot continue to work only to enrich Laban, while Jacob's own sons have no land they can claim as their own. Jacob also feels the call of his father's land, so the family begins a journey to Canaan. The journey to Canaan is noteworthy because of Dinah's experiences in crossing the Euphrates and Jabbok rivers. In both cases, she responds to the water, which she experiences as "an embrace." Dinah's personality is further defined when Inna pronounces Dinah "a child of water." Schantz suggests that "Dinah's experiences could be interpreted as a form of mikveh," a ritual of purification that also suggests a coming-of-age experience. For the men, the river is only work, since they must help animals and belongings cross the water, but for Dinah it is an important moment in her journey toward self-awareness. At the conclusion of the novel, she recognizes the pull the water had for her but also realizes that she was able to find great happiness far from the water.

After the family arrives in Succoth, they make a short journey to Mamre to visit Jacob's mother, Rebecca. For Dinah, however, the visit in Mamre is stretched to three months before she is allowed to return to her father's camp. In Mamre, she is lonely, miserable, and angry. It is with her grandmother Rebecca that Dinah first experiences acute hatred and anger, but it is also where she begins to understand the uniqueness of women's lives and the importance of maintaining women's rituals and their stories. Upon her return to Jacob's camp, the masculinity of that camp is an assault to her senses. Dinah complains of the men, who have "become impossibly crude and brutish." For the first time, she notices that they "grunted rather than spoke, scratched themselves and picked their noses, and even relieved themselves in plain sight of the women." They also "stink." Dinah had never noticed because she lived in a men's camp and had never before been exposed to a different world, as she was at Mamre, a women's camp. Dinah's brief sojourn to her grandmother's camp is a significant change in her emotional and physical journey toward adulthood.

After the family settles in Canaan, Dinah's next journey takes her to Shechem, where she meets Shalem. Of her time with Shalem, Dinah notes that the tears that she sheds when with him are "the first tears of happiness in my life." In Shechem, she experiences love and passion and, after Shalem's murder, rage and hatred for her family, whom she curses. Although she was often lonely and alone in Jacob's camp, when not with the mothers, she is isolated after Shalem's death. The next part of her physical journey takes Dinah to Thebes in Egypt, where she gives birth to Shalem's son. In Thebes, Dinah is a wet nurse to her own child, but she is even more of an outsider in this culture, where she is forbidden to even reveal her identity. In the past, she felt invisible to Jacob and her brothers, but in Thebes, she is truly invisible. After her son leaves to study at an academy, Dinah can find no purpose in the home that Renefer has provided for her. Dinah's decision to return to a career as a midwife gives her life value, although not peace. When she lived in Canaan, Dinah was an assistant to Rachel, who was regarded as the master midwife. In Egypt, Dinah is the experienced midwife, and Meryt, though older, takes on the role of assistant midwife.

When Dinah's journey takes her to the Valley of the Kings, she finally finds her own place and peace. She and Benia marry and establish a home, where she belongs. This is also where she completes her journey to adulthood in finding forgiveness and in being forgiven. After Dinah shares her story with Meryt and Benia, she feels cleansed of the past. Dinah briefly journeys back to Jacob's camp in Canaan, when she accompanies Joseph to Jacob's deathbed. Jacob can name each of his sons, but he never mentions Dinah's name. For her father, she is forgotten, as if she never existed. It is the women who will remember Dinah's name. In the prologue to *The Red Tent*, Dinah says that the "reason women wanted daughters was to keep their memories alive." In addressing the women, who will read her story, Dinah says that these readers "come hungry for the story that was lost."

At the end of *The Red Tent*, Dinah lives out her life in the Valley of the Kings, where she quietly passes the remainder of her years and is welcomed back into the world of her mothers when she dies. Although Diamant creates a fictional re-visioning

> IN THIS WAY, WRIGHT COMPELLINGLY ARGUES, DIAMANT, WHO IS STEEPED IN KNOWLEDGE OF RABBINIC MIDRASH, PROVIDES A COUNTER-NARRATIVE NOT ONLY TO THE REDACTED BIBLICAL STORY BUT ALSO TO THE MISOGYNIST MIDRASHIC NARRATIVES OF THE RABBIS."

of the biblical Dinah, Diamant's adoption of the rabbinic midrashic tradition adds a sense of authenticity to the story. Readers cannot know what really happened to Dinah. Because she was a woman, her story was unimportant to the authors of Hebrew scripture. It is only in *The Red Tent* that Dinah's journey is finally told.

Source: Sheri Metzger Karmiol, Critical Essay on *The Red Tent*, in *Novels for Students*, Gale, Cengage Learning, 2011.

Paul Eggers

In the following essay, Eggers explains the motivations that generated the rewriting and appropriation of the stories of Genesis in modern novels, including The Red Tent.

Terry Wright's excellent new book, *The Genesis of Fiction*, examines six renowned novelists—Mark Twain, John Steinbeck, Jeanette Winterson, Jenny Diski, Anita Diamant, and Thomas Mann—who have mused in print and sometimes in interviews over the ideologies, textual antecedents, and even, in some cases, the didactic motivations generating and informing their own rewriting and appropriation of the stories found in the Book of Genesis. The authors are examined in separate chapters, in order of the biblical story they have drawn from, beginning with Adam and Eve and ending with Joseph and his brothers. By charting the intertextual influence of the Bible and related, midrashic commentary on selected works from each author, Wright elucidates the principles governing each writer's reading and rewriting of Genesis, then discusses the ways these novelists help make the Bible speak to their own time.

Wright begins by providing a useful and very readable gloss on both the practice of rabbinic midrash and on Harold Bloom's influential *The Book of J* (1991). Midrash, Wright points out, is a slippery term that has come to mean different things to different people. At its most basic, rabbinic midrash confronts the white space in the spare, minimalist prose found in much of the Old Testament, posing questions and supplementing the existing text with oftentimes fanciful stories. Implicit in this project is the understanding that the stories found in the Bible are not reducible to abstract doctrines. The purpose of the supplements provided by midrashic material, says Wright, is to "tease out" the mysteries and ambiguities of the biblical stories—especially those purportedly written by J of the Documentary Hypothesis, a writer Bloom finds sublime, mysterious, and eccentric, much closer to Kafka than to the Torah. What is fundamental to midrash, however, and how it differs from the concepts of Derridean "supplement" and postmodern indeterminacy, is the retention of the biblical story as the authoritative text. Though the novelists discussed perform a midrashic function in contributing to our modern understanding and appreciation of the Book of Genesis, they do not, argues Wright, subordinate their imaginative engagement with their own work to the authority of the Bible.

The examination of the individual writers begins with Mark Twain, whose irritations with, and savagery toward, Old Testament narratives have been examined previously in Alison Ensor's *Mark Twain and the Bible* (1969) and Baetzhold and McCullough's *The Bible According to Mark Twain* (1995). Twain, Wright shows, was particularly interested in the biblical narrative of Adam and Eve's expulsion from the Garden of Eden, which in Twain's view exposes God's childish and monstrous nature. Returning in various narratives again and again to the Adam and Eve story—from Adam's perspective, from Eve's, from Satan's, even from other animals—Twain asks, incredulously and acidly, how God could respond so severely to the simple, childlike disobedience of His creations, who, after all, did not know right from wrong when first partaking of the apple. In this way, Twain, who Wright argues likely had some knowledge of rabbinic midrash, forces modern readers to confront the myriad questions arising from the terse biblical rendition of the story.

The Cain and Abel story, perhaps the most frequent Old Testament story to be echoed in modern novels, is of course the framework for Steinbeck's 1952 *East of Eden*. Steinbeck's record of the creation of his novel, *Journal of a Novel*, published in 1970, traces the intertextual influences behind the work, most notably through his friendships with Joseph Campbell, Eric Fromm, and, especially, Louis Ginzberg, whose massive seven-volume *The Legends of the Jews* (1909–25) examines the crucial Hebrew work timshol (thou mayest conquer sin, implying choice, not thou shalt), around which much of the moral weight of *East of Eden* rests. By focusing on individual words, providing commentary on biblical texts, and even reproducing biblical texts in the novel, Steinbeck's work provides a midrash-like "narrative augmentation" to the Bible story. However, as Wright cautions, the end product, the novel itself, is not proof that Steinbeck read *The Legends of the Jews*. Nonetheless, the parallels between Steinbeck's work and the work of the rabbis are undeniable, and, echoing the Book of Genesis, *East of Eden* provides for the modern reader a case study of the need for each generation to renew and refight the battle between good and evil.

Three novels by Jeanette Winterson, *Oranges are Not the Only Fruit* (1985), *Boating for Beginners* (also 1985), and *Lighthousekeeping* (2005), are the subject of Wright's discussion of The Flood and God's subsequent destruction of the Tower of Babel. The meanings Winterson's stories take on run counter to those imposed on the "original" stories redacted by P, or the Priestly Writer of the Documentary Hypothesis, which Winterson finds to serve the interest of an authoritarian male-dominated institution. In her own subversive prose, argues Wright, Winterson recalls the sly, evocative storytelling of J, whom Harold Bloom finds so appealing; and in letting J out of her institutional bottle, Winterson "reconstitutes" J's words in a way that makes the Bible story speak to modern, especially female, readers.

Jenny Diski's *Only Human* (2000) and *After These Things* (2004) offer, in Wright's words, "a bleak retelling of the biblical narrative" of Abraham's aborted sacrifice of Isaac, "a modern redaction which edits out the Priestly Writer's [P's] confident belief in a guiding, providential hand behind the events narrated in Genesis." As Diski herself acknowledges, she was heavily influenced by the work of biblical and midrashic scholars. Profoundly conflicted about religion, Diski focuses primarily on the human elements in the original story, examining actions and responses through the lens of contemporary psychoanalytic understanding of human behavior. In drawing creatively upon midrashic material about the Akedah (the binding of Isaac as he is about to be sacrificed), Diski's "supplement" Wright suggests, is perhaps best viewed in the Derridean sense of the term, in that it both adds onto and replaces the original text.

Perhaps the most overtly feminist writer—Anita Diamant, whose *The Red Tent* (2002) is examined in the next chapter—focuses on the rape of Dina. In the biblical narrative, Dinah is raped by Shechem, and the story is told from a male perspective, taking no account of the experience of Dinah herself. The main purpose of the biblical narrative, as Wright notes, is "clearly to celebrate the piety, courage, and ingenuity of the patriarchs." Diamant's novel reverses the tables, telling and retelling, from a variety of female perspectives, Dinah's story with the express purpose of foregrounding the piety, courage, and ingenuity of the women involved, reducing the patriarchs to sketchy, contentious figures, apparently incapable of solidarity or compassion—the role typically assigned to women in the final redacted form of Genesis and most certainly in the narratives composed in the midrash of the ancient rabbis. In this way, Wright compellingly argues, Diamant, who is steeped in knowledge of rabbinic midrash, provides a counter-narrative not only to the redacted biblical story but also to the misogynist midrashic narratives of the rabbis.

The final author considered by Wright is Thomas Mann, in his massive *Joseph and His Brothers* tetralogy (1942, in German). Spending much time usefully summarizing the influence of Schopenhauer, Nietzsche, and Freud on Mann's thinking, Wright lays out a convincing argument that Joseph performs the most staunchly midrashic function of any of the novels considered. In many places in *Joseph*, Mann advertises the fact that he is drawing upon "tradition," upon earlier Hebrew commentators. In places, the clear influence of midrashic material takes the form of events and characters found in midrashic material; in others, such material is directly lifted from midrashic writings, especially from the work of Micha bin Gorion. In all cases, the sometimes supernatural fables composed by the rabbis are replaced by modern psychological realism. In this way, midrashic material provides a mediating narrative framework between the spare verses of Genesis and Mann's elaborate, sprawling work; and, says Wright, it is through the strong midrashic element found in Joseph that Mann was able to find a sufficient counter to Nazi ideology.

Though Wright is enthusiastically welcoming of the way modern novelists have appropriated biblical and midrashic narrative, he reserves his highest praise for Mann's work. *Joseph*, Wright finds, "is the most impressive of all the novels considered in this book, I would argue, because it grapples seriously with the fundamental questions raised by the biblical stories it relates"; further, of all the novels considered, *Joseph* most closely follows the midrashic method by continually probing at the details of the text until answers begin to appear. In comparison, Diamant's subversive *Red Tent*, which certainly cannot be said to show deference to commonly held attitudes, "is no masterpiece," though we are given no reason for this conclusion; and Wright seems almost disapproving of Diski's reworking of the sacrifice of Isaac, which "goes well beyond the limits one would normally expect of midrash." Why one would expect Diski to follow midrashic practice and defer to the authority of the original text is a question not addressed.

Wright's criteria for novelistic worth, it would seem, stem largely from the degree to which the modern novelist remains faithful to the approach and constraints of midrashic writers. This is by no means a fault in Wright's framework, but it does suggest a bias worthy of identification, and it gives rise to an interesting question: to what extent, if any, should adherence to the authority of the original text be a measure of the worth of modern, biblically based novels? The question is obviously beyond the scope of what can be expected from Wright's engaging study, but the fact that such a question seems to linger in the white space of the text—much in the same way that questions about implication and contextualization seem to arise from the Bible itself—points toward its close intertextual ties with the works it examines. For literary and biblical scholars alike, Wright's book is a welcome addition to literature studies.

Source: Paul Eggers, "The Genesis of Fiction: Modern Novelists as Biblical Interpreters," in *Christianity and Literature*, Vol. 57, No. 4, Summer 2008, pp. 613–616.

Tracie Welser

In the following essay, Welser explains the world-wide response to this book that has emphasized the importance of creating women-only spaces in our societies.

When Anita Diamant's novel *The Red Tent* was first published in 1997, it didn't cause much of a stir. According to *Newsweek* reviewer Susannah Meadows, thousands of copies of the imaginative story of a minor biblical character named Dinah lingered in warehouses after a lackluster debut. In a surprising move, the author herself began a campaign to enhance the book's appeal: by word-of-mouth. Copies were sent to rabbis, female Christian ministers and independent booksellers. Within months, the book's popularity soared, and reviewers began to take notice. Recently, the book hit several bestseller lists and was optioned for a film version. But what makes this book remarkable, in spite of reviews that characterize the book as melodramatic and revisionist, is the response of women around the world to the premise referred to in the novel's title: the importance of creating women-only spaces.

The Red Tent is the retelling of events in the book of Genesis (chapter 34), of the family of Jacob and his wives, daughters and sons. As Jacob's only daughter, Dinah is barely mentioned in the Bible, the victim of a rape avenged by her brothers. In Diamant's retelling, Dinah is the narrator, allowing the reader to become acquainted with her as a central character rather than a secondary one. In a world of restrictive patriarchy, Dinah takes comfort and gains wisdom in the red tent, a refuge for women (and a required segregation from the company of men) during times of menses or childbirth.

Many Jewish and Christian women have embraced Diamant's book; interestingly, a great number of women who see themselves as neither have also been captivated by the idea. As one reviewer, Christine Schoefer of *New Moon Network* magazine, prophetically noted, "I expect that reading this book will awaken in women the longing for a red tent and the wisdom that women shared there." Although at least one rabbi has publicly stated that there is no proof this proto-feminist tradition ever existed in biblical times, and the author herself acknowledges that it is mostly her own creation, a number of Red Tent groups have formed based on the idea.

> EVEN IF YOU HAVE NOT READ ANITA DIAMANT'S *THE RED TENT*, IT IS PLAIN THAT THIS BOOK PUBLISHED IN 1997 HAS MADE A LASTING IMPACT ON WOMEN'S CULTURE IN THE UNITED STATES AND ELSEWHERE (IT HAS BEEN PUBLISHED IN TWENTY-FIVE COUNTRIES)."

For feminists, the creation of women-only spaces is nothing new. But with the advent of this novel, a revived, larger and more mainstream acceptance of woman-space has become apparent, in the form of permanent spaces and organized meet-ups, virtual Red Tent groups, and mobile spaces arranged at festivals. These groups have manifested with differing modes and purposes: to share menstrual and birthing information, for spiritual reasons, for the purpose of activism, to simply provide a safe haven for women's voices or a combination of these.

The Red Tent Women's Project of Brooklyn is one example of a permanent woman-space. Just over a year old, the Project is a center for women in the New York area, providing workshops, support groups and organizing space for activism. Most events and workshops are free and open to women of all backgrounds. According to the Project's website, the main goals of the organizers are educating and empowering women. They currently offer yoga and meditation classes, a women writers group, a support group for motherless daughters, empowerment workshops, a book club and more. The Project also has an ongoing Clothesline Project display that is continuously growing.

In the virtual world, numerous groups based on a Red Tent model exist, including blogs, myspace and Yahoo groups. A particularly noteworthy instance is www.theredtent.tribe.net, created in 2004. This is a forum-style site with overt interest in the biological aspects of women's knowledge and a Goddess-centered perspective. With over 600 members, the message board could be a bit more robust, but topics are up-to-date, and a strong sense of community is evident. Many touching testimonials to the power of women's spaces, as well as questions, recommendations and support, are posted there. After attending a Red Tent gathering at this year's Womongathering, one member remarked, "The Red Tent is alive and well. The message needs to be carried to every woman, everywhere." The Goddess, she says, "gives us this creative, divine spark, so that we can find our way out of the underworld and show the light for our sisters so that they can get out too." In this way, the virtual presence of Red Tent culture is a safe haven for women's voices and a link to face-to-face experiences.

At gatherings and festivals, Red Tent facilitators offer intimate spaces for women to meet and discuss issues such as body image, self-acceptance and the sacred feminine. Organizers and participants alike are passionate about the Red Tent and often form lasting friendships. One example is the Red Tent Tribe of Florida Pagan Gathering (FPG). FPG is a twice-annual event that takes place in Ocala, Florida. In 2004, women of FPG chose to dedicate a space as exclusively woman-space (FPG is not a women's festival, but a four-day gathering open to all people of pagan and Goddess faiths). Inspired by Diamant's book, the women worked to establish a presence at the event, or as they call it, "a festival womb space." Their stated purpose is "to honor and represent Women's traditional sense of solidarity." They welcome all women to participate in the Red Tent, which takes physical form as a lovely canopy draped with red curtains and festooned with Goddess prayer flags, wind chimes, and bits of lace and velvet. Inside, rugs, cushions, and perhaps even chocolates offer visitors a welcoming atmosphere. Enthusiasm for temporary spaces like this one attests to the appeal of the Red Tent as a specific type of woman-space.

Even if you have not read Anita Diamant's *The Red Tent*, it is plain that this book published in 1997 has made a lasting impact on women's culture in the United States and elsewhere (it has been published in twenty-five countries). The yearning that many women feel for women's spaces, and the creation of those spaces online, in permanent places and temporary spaces, demonstrates the strength and power of ideas to change women's lives for the better.

What follows is a portion of an interview by Tracie Welser with one the FPG Red Tent organizers, Melora Asherah Firepixie.

Who can I say was/is the founder of this Red Tent at FPG? I got the idea that it was mostly you, but I want to be accurate.

MAF: There are four key facilitators that have helped the Red Tent grow to what you see at FPG today: Ann Marie Augustino, Lynn Carol Henderson, Lady Skyefire, and myself.

How did the book The Red Tent *influence you?*

I read this book in 2004. The story became a bridge to the past for me. I immediately felt connected to these women in certain aspects—their relationships with each other, their relationships within their community, and their place in society as a whole. I saw this book as a tool to helping me reshape and reaffirm my personal female relationships in a very subtle and specific way. This book as a whole helped me better appreciate the relationships I had and long for the closeness the characters felt for each other. The book became the lead topic of Women's Circle at FPG October 2004, and from that meeting of thirty women grew the Red Tent, which made its debut in May 2005.

What advice would you give to women who want to start a tent in their area?

The first piece of advice I would give women is to draw on active support from their fellow sisters. A Red Tent should be created with the love and fellowship of our sisters. It is also created with actual assistance! Draw on strengths from everywhere and delegate responsibilities to make this truly a community effort. Assign everyone who wants to be a part of creating a women's space one or two tasks, and accept any/all donations. The first Red Tent was put together by just three of us, and we provided all the decorations, led every workshop. It was beautiful and successful—but hard work and loving effort. Now we have a multitude of physical volunteers to assist us and an additional facilitator to assume more responsibilities. This takes time, so share the responsibilities to make this happen and it will.

The second piece of advice is to start sharing ideas, talk to each other, ask questions about each other and really listen to each other. This conversation thread was the very first Red Tent meeting place and the true definition of a Red Tent. Set up a "Mission Statement" right away so that volunteers and coordinators can work towards a common known goal. The Red Tent is designed [to] forge a sacred women's space for sharing ideas and life stories. The Red Tent bridges the gap for women to communicate with each other because we share a common thread—we are women! Creating a space where age, race, life experience, family, sexual orientation and religion disappear—if only for a short while—is a place for us to share and listen to each other.

The third and final piece of advice is to lead with your heart. Listen to your inner voice and follow your instincts. Women may not even know that they are missing this sisterhood of friendship until you share it with them. *The Red Tent* stirs up a bond among women that they can take with them to other places. This happens when you share with your heart and soul. So follow your heart and a whole sisterhood will be waiting to embrace you with open arms.

Source: Tracie Welser, "The Red Tent: A Woman-Space Phenomenon," in *off our backs*, Vol. 37, Nos. 2–3, October 2007, pp. 41–43.

Judith Rosen

In the following review, Rosen shares how Diamant successfully marketed her own book, and why she chose to write about Dinah.

While others had given up on her biblical novel, the author revived it with a successful word-of-mouth campaign directed to Jewish synagogues

It was not an encouraging sign. After her first novel, *The Red Tent*, based on the biblical story of Dinah, was published in 1997, it was virtually ignored by the mainstream press—even though it received promising advance reviews in *Publishers Weekly* and *Kirkus Reviews*, calling it "cubits beyond most Woman-of-the-Bible sagas."

Despite this initial lack of attention, *The Red Tent* eventually became a publishing success story. Not only is it the bestselling book at Diamant's neighborhood bookstore in Newton, Mass., which has sold more than 500 copies, but the paperback edition was on the *Publishers Weekly* bestseller list. It remains on the *Book Sense* bestseller list (based on sales at over 350 independent booksellers) and in January was 12th on the *New York Times* bestselling paperback fiction list.

"This book continues to grow," says Diane Higgins, senior editor at St. Martin's Press. "Sales figures get stronger every month." After

> IN FACT, IT IS DIAMANT'S KEENLY IMAGINED SENSE OF WOMEN AND COMMUNITY IN ANCIENT TIMES, RATHER THAN LITERAL BIBLICAL TRUTH, THAT IS PART OF THE BOOK'S APPEAL."

disappointing hardcover sales of 11,000 copies, the paperback edition (by Picador USA, a division of St. Martin's) has gone to press 14 times. There are more than a half-million copies in print, and the book has been translated into 15 languages. Last July, it came out in large-print and unabridged audio editions.

The story of the novel's recovery and success is a testament to Diamant's faith and resourcefulness. During an interview at her home, she talks about her transition from writing nonfiction to fiction and the remarkable turnaround of her first novel. We sit at her kitchen table, the modern-day equivalent of the novel's "red tent," where women would gather and talk.

After growing up in Denver, Diamant moved to Boston in 1975 and began a 25-year career as a journalist. Her first job was at the now-defunct women's newspaper *Equal Times*. She then wrote for a succession of local publications: the *Boston Phoenix*, *Boston Magazine* and the *Boston Globe*. Her work also has appeared in national magazines, including *Parenting*, *McCall's* and *Self*.

Diamant says that while working as a journalist, she became interested in exploring her Jewish roots and began writing a series of guidebooks on Jewish life. She started with *The New Jewish Wedding* (1984), which, she notes, has never gone out of print, and will be reissued in a substantially revised edition this Spring. The final book in the series, *How to Be a Jewish Parent*, co-written with Karen Kushner, came out last September.

Now in her late 40s, Diamant turned to fiction writing as "a midlife correction. I wanted to do something different, and I needed a challenge. I'd been writing nonfiction for more than 20 years, and I didn't want to take a 9-to-5 job. I started out thinking I would write about [biblical figures] Rachel and Leah because of the conflict between them, but I kept getting drawn into the

Dinah story. There is violence, sex, greed and drama, all the stuff you need to carry a plot through," she says.

Loosely based on Genesis, the first book of the Bible, *The Red Tent* clearly has a strong religious appeal. Still, Diamant bristles at the idea raised by some critics that it's a midrash, or commentary. "It is not midrash; it's a novel," she says emphatically. Her story of Dinah fleeing to Egypt is entirely made up.

Diamant sees her novel as part of what she terms "a larger cultural shift in which women have reappropriated the Bible and other texts." For her, *The Red Tent* fits squarely into the tradition of Marion Zimmer Bradley's retelling of the Arthurian legend, *The Mists of Avalon*, or Sena Jeter Naslund's *Ahab's Wife: The Star-Gazer*, a re-imagining of Moby Dick.

Long used to writing fast for her journalism assignments, Diamant quickly completed the first 25 pages of *The Red Tent* so she could apply for a writing fellowship. She knew she couldn't expect an advance, because most publishers won't buy a first novel unless they can read the entire manuscript. The Arthur and Elizabeth Schlesinger Library at Radcliffe College in Cambridge, Mass., offered her a library fellowship on the strength of a sample chapter. In addition to providing her with a research assistant, she says the fellowship gave her "a sense of purpose that was hugely important."

But the Radcliffe seal of approval didn't put challah on the table. So Diamant wrote another guide, this one for those thinking of converting to Judaism—*Choosing a Jewish Life*—and accepted a variety of freelance writing assignments while she worked on the novel.

She found support for her fiction project in a writers' group. "No one was waiting for this book, but they were," she says. The group helped in more than artistic ways. She discussed questions about working with editors, publicity expectations, contracts and other business matters with the members.

Ultimately, Diamant had no trouble selling the finished book, although it wasn't easy to find an agent. "Even with several nonfiction books, I had a lot of rejections from agents. Finally, I went to somebody who was a friend of a friend, and she sold it on the first go-round."

From there, it seemed as if everything had finally fallen into place. Her editor suggested a new title but made few changes overall. "I had wanted to call it 'The Book of Dinah,' but with Jane Hamilton's *The Book of Ruth* recently selected for the Oprah reading group, he didn't think that was a good idea. He came up with *The Red Tent*." He also convinced her to use the King James Bible spelling for her character's names.

When the book initially didn't meet St. Martin's Press sales expectations, the company decided that rather than paying the high cost of warehousing unsold hardcover copies, it would shred them before publishing the paperback edition. During this time the first editor left and the project was taken on by Higgins. Diamant convinced her to try a word-of-mouth sales campaign in the Jewish community, where the author is well-known for her nonfiction books.

"A light bulb went off," says Higgins. "We all had faith that this book would take off, and I thought, 'a signed first edition will be valuable some day.'"

Following up on the suggestion, in the fall of 1998, St. Martin's mailed close to 1,500 copies of *The Red Tent* to Reform rabbis with a cover note. As a result, many of the rabbis mentioned it to their congregations, and the book got its first national coverage the following summer with a write-up in *Reform Judaism*, a publication sent to 350,000 households. The magazine recommended that its subscribers read four books a year and named *The Red Tent* as one of the best books in Jewish literature.

St. Martin's followed this push with an equally large second mailing to 1,500 female ministers, reading group leaders and community relations coordinators at Borders and Barnes & Noble. Soon, the book found its niche as a reading group selection. It was recommended by Mickey Perlman in her guide *What to Read: The Essential Guide for Reading Group Members and Other Book Lovers*, and St. Martin's made a special reading guide to accompany the novel (available at www.stmartins.com/RGG/Redtent.htm).

To boost sales even further, the publisher offered bookstores special discounts and promotional materials on orders of 10 or more copies in the fall of 1999. In January 2000, St. Martin's did its first national advertising for the book, a full-page ad in the *New York Times Book Review*, and sent Diamant on a tour to Chicago and cities throughout Florida.

The Red Tent's momentum keeps on going. Not only have all the mailings paid off many times over with increased sales, but the book is starting to reach readers well beyond the Jewish community. "I've gotten letters from men whose daughters gave them the book. I got a wonderful letter from a nun," says Diamant.

In fact, it is Diamant's keenly imagined sense of women and community in ancient times, rather than literal biblical truth, that is part of the book's appeal.

This ". . . sweeping piece of fiction offers an insider's look at the daily life of a biblical sorority of mothers and wives," wrote a reviewer for Amazon.com. A *Los Angeles Times* writer observed that by giving Dinah a voice, *The Red Tent* "struck a chord with women who may have felt left out of biblical history."

Higgins credits Diamant's research as being so thorough that when you read the book, "you can feel the dust." Even so, Diamant reminds readers at the very start that what they are about to read is fictional: "Maybe you guessed that there was more to me than the voiceless cipher in the text," says Dinah.

Not only has Diamant given Dinah a voice in *The Red Tent*, but with her three-year struggle to gain recognition for the book, she's also encouraged other writers not to give up hope in their own work. "If you can keep a book alive, and are willing to do your own work, it can happen. It's true," she says, speaking from experience. At the beginning, no book group or bookstore reading series within driving distance was too small for the author to attend. "You have to take advantage of every opportunity," Diamant advises, "and see who your core community is."

What's harder for her is finishing her second novel—which, she jokes, is about Gloucester, Mass., without the storm (referring to Sebastian Junger's bestseller *A Perfect Storm*). Set on Cape Ann, Mass., it focuses, like much of *The Red Tent*, on female friendship, but in a contemporary setting. To complete it, says Diamant, who prefers to edit her own writing, "I gave myself deadlines. They're not hard and fast, but if you know what the deadline is, it helps you build in the structure." Even so, she hasn't found a good strategy for meeting "expectations, not just from my readers, but from me."

While *The Red Tent*'s success enabled Diamant to spend a month writing and researching on Cape Ann last summer, it also means there are a lot more business details to attend to, a lot more letters to write. Still, she has no real complaints.

"For the first time in my life," she says, "I'm not worried about money, and I'm doing this—writing." What more could a writer ask for?

Source: Judith Rosen, "Anita Diamant's *Red Tent* Turns to Gold," in *Writer*, Vol. 114, No. 4, April 2001, p. 30.

Susannah Meadows

In the following review, Meadows provides a real-life example of the influence of Diamant's The Red Tent.

At 3202 Shalom Way in South Bend, Ind., there is a monument to Dinah. Her name is carved into the faux Western Wall stone across a towering window of the Jewish Community Center of St. Joseph Valley, though her story amounts to a few lines in Genesis. That, and a starring role in Anita Diamant's soapy Biblical novel, *The Red Tent*. The wife of the Jewish Federation president, Sandy Barton, suggested to her husband that Dinah be honored with her own window. "It absolutely would not have happened without *The Red Tent*," she says.

Recently the book appeared on that other megalith, the paperback best-seller list, reaching the *New York Times*'s in December and the *Los Angeles Times*'s No. 1 this month. There are 750,000 copies in print, rights have been sold to 15 countries and Hollywood has optioned the film rights. And, if that weren't enough, Julia Roberts told *Oprah* magazine that *Tent* is one of her favorite books ever. Says first-time novelist Diamant, "I'm going to be able to send my daughter to college!"

Dinah's story in the Bible is generally referred to as "the rape of Dinah." Diamant makes up a new, fleshier tale for her in which, instead of rape, there is a love story—and Dinah gets to narrate it. Jacob's only daughter also tells of her mother and three aunties—and all the sex they had with their shared husband. They were ruled by men, gods and curses, except during those sacred days of menstruation and giving birth, when, sequestered in the red tent, they were renewed by their private community of each other. Faithful to New Age principles, the book is achingly earnest: the line "a local oracle . . . foresaw love and riches for me in the steaming entrails of a goat" is not supposed to make you laugh.

With its trinity of woman empowerment, God and quivering thighs, the commercial appeal of the book seems obvious, but it took an unheard-of two and a half years to become a best seller. According to publisher St. Martin's, an approximate "not many" were sold when it was first published in 1997. It was ready to pulp the remaining hardcovers squatting in a warehouse when it heard from Diamant. She had address lists for more than 1,000 rabbis: "Let's send them out."

Books reached essentially every woman Reform rabbi in the United States with a letter from Rabbi Liza Stern, of the Women's Rabbinic Network. She suggested using it to teach women "to see themselves as central to the story, not as marginal two-bit players in a story about men." Also to embellish the Bible themselves. And the sex? "It made it a good read."

Independent booksellers were the next to enlist in the cause. The entire staff at Newtonville Books in Newton, Mass., was struck by the book, says owner Tim Huggins. "They were handselling it to everyone who came in," including a lot of book-club members.

Finally, in late 1998, *The Red Tent* took off. It had crossed over to the Christian community (another mailing went to women ministers) and on and exponentially on. Says Diamant, "It's become a real word-of-mouth book-group find."

Ellen Berliner Davis, whose group in Parkland, Fla., took Diamant to lunch, didn't mind that a rape was reimagined as a love story. "A lot of discussion had to do with the believability of the rape scene [in the Bible]." Amy Wisotsky, whose group in East North Fork, N.Y., is reading the novel now, shared the book with her 19-year-old daughter. "I keep thinking about the unity and bonds between the women." Also: "They go to the market, I go to the mall. You could relate." Says Diamant, "Reading groups are like the red tent. You get together once a month but [the books] are really not why you're there."

Sandy Barton, whose word led to the monument, likes to think of the book as a midrash, a Jewish oral tradition that fills in the holes in Biblical texts. "It's like 'The West Wing'—you wish these were the conversations they were having." Having read in the Bible that Jacob loved only his wife Rachel, Barton says, "It was nice to know Jacob loved Leah, too." Even though it's made up? "Even though it's made up!"

"Baloney!" says an Orthodox Jewish rabbi who did not wish to be associated by name with the book. He says it is a mockery and like an argument a rapist would use in court. "A woman was raped! It's disgusting to portray it as a love story." But he believes good can come from bad. "It's going to give me tremendous material for a sermon!" In that way, he is like all the other readers: he can't resist talking about *The Red Tent*.

Source: Susannah Meadows, "Meeting Under a Big 'Tent,'" in *Newsweek*, February 5, 2001, p. 61.

Jane Redmont

In the following review, Redmont argues that despite not intending to, Diamant participated in feminist midrash genre writing in The Red Tent.

The best fiction writers create a world and bathe us in it: its sounds and sights, its language and climate, the intricate relationships among its inhabitants. Anita Diamant has performed this wondrous craft: She has brought forth one of those books that appear effortless precisely because the writer has pondered even the length of the breath between each character's words. Reading *The Red Tent* one can almost hear the bleating of sheep and the beating of human hearts and smell the hot dust on the road.

The world of *The Red Tent* is the world of the biblical patriarchs, but not as the Bible has shown it to us. Rather it is what we have not read and heard: this world as seen and lived by the sole daughter and several wives of Jacob. In the red tent of the title, the women gather to menstruate and to give birth but also to rest and to talk, passing on wisdom and spinning collective memory. They love and delight in their sons, but it is daughters who carry the family stories. "Dinah, my last-born," Leah says when she finally names her "My daughter My memory."

Dinah (whose name, Diamant tells us on the first page, is pronounced Dee-nah) is the book's narrator, but the story begins before her birth, with the meeting between Jacob and Rebecca at Laban's well and soon after, the encounter of Jacob and Leah, the woman who would give birth to Dinah, youngest and only daughter among her many children.

Dinah grows up with four mothers—the women who are Jacob's two wives and two concubines—observing the dynamics among them, noting their relations with father, husband

and sons struggling with awkward fingers to learn the art of the spindle, smelling the brewing of beer and the cooking coriander-flavored stews, discovering love and sex. This is a woman's book but its men are well-drawn, and, like its women, by turn tenderhearted and crafty.

Fertility is central in *The Red Tent*'s world, that of fields and river banks, of sheep and goats, of women and men. Life is marked by the rhythm of seasons, the waxing and waning of the moon, the cycles of women and the births— and sometimes deaths—of children. The midwife's craft, which Dinah learns and which will help ensure her survival, is vital to the life of communities both rural and urban, one of the most transferable and honored skills in the ancient world. It will accompany Dinah when the tribe sets out on the road to a new land, and later, after horror and grief have taken possession of her life, when she emerges and revives.

In Dinah's world, what we call religion is as daily as the work of sheepherding and spinning, but here, too, men and women have their distinctive spheres. Occasionally these parallel cultures meet: In a community that is at its root an extended family, the boundaries between them are inevitably porous, though remarkably well-preserved. Early in the life of the ancestors of the people [of] Israel, the God of Abraham is present, but so, too, are other deities both competing and coexisting, especially those tied to the realities of fertility, birth and death. Sarah, Rebecca and their female descendants continue their relationship to the protective goddesses and gods even as their lives are shaped by their men's covenants and conversations with a faceless One who wants no rival. Women as well as men perform sacrifices, sing, question, give praise. Diamant depicts this complex dance skillfully and sympathetically.

A straightforward fictional narrative *The Red Tent* can also be read as midrash, the imaginative retelling of Torah, which Rabbi Lawrence Kushner (author of *Honey from the Rock* and other books on Jewish mysticism and spirituality and Diamant's teacher) calls the literature that sprouts up in the blank spaces between the words and letters of Hebrew scripture. Midrash answers the unasked but undeniable questions in the text, the ellipses, the contradictions. What did Cain say to Abel before he killed his brother? The answer is midrash. The words of Torah are like photographs, terse, without background or explanation. Midrash tells what happened before and after the picture was taken and explains the relationships between and among the people in the photograph.

Feminist midrash writes women into the Torah, but also imagines—and thus interprets— the stories of the women who are already there as Dinah is, briefly and without voice in the 34th chapter of Genesis. For the most part, Jewish feminists have used midrash in the classic, rabbinic way, in sermon or teaching form. Diamant, herself a Jewish feminist, did not set out to write midrash, though she is familiar with the form. She wrote *The Red Tent* as a work of fiction, not as a theological commentary. Still, she said in an interview, "simply invoking the names of the matriarchs—Rachel, Leah, Rebecca—and the lesser characters who are nonetheless biblical, means I'm participating]in[a 2,000-year-old conversation about what really happened and what it really means." Fictionalizing the Torah is part of the ancient tradition of midrash whose original meaning is "to search or "investigate."

Above all, *Tent* is a fine novel. This healthy, passionate tale, told also with great delicacy is, quite simply, a great read. That it participates in the genre feminist midrash will make it all the more compelling for NCR readers with interests in biblical studies, women's issues and feminist readings of ancient texts and times. Diamant, who until now was best known as an author of nonfiction books on contemporary Judaism (*The New Jewish Wedding*, *The New Jewish Baby Book*, *Living a Jewish Life* [with Howard Cooper] *Choosing a Jewish Life* and others), has made a smooth and shining transition to fiction. One can only hope she continues to write in both genres. Meanwhile, run, don't walk, to the nearest bookstore, and put *The Red Tent* on your spring or summer reading list—at the top.

Source: Jane Redmont, "Biblical Women Take Center Stage at Last," in *National Catholic Reporter*, Vol. 34, No. 29, May 22, 1998, pp. 28–30.

SOURCES

"Anita Diamant Biography," in *Anita Diamant Home Page*, http://www.anitadiamant.com/about.asp?page = about (accessed April 21, 2010).

Anteby, Lisa, "'There's Blood in the House': Negotiating Female Rituals of Purity Among Ethiopian Jews in Israel," in *Women and Water: Menstruation in Jewish Life and Law*, edited by Rahel Wasserfall, Brandeis, 1999, pp. 169–70.

Blitt, Natalie, Review of *The Red Tent*, in *Lilith*, Vol. 23, No. 1, March 31, 1998, p. 42.

Brawarsky, Sandee, "A Red-Hot Novel: Three Years After Its Publication, Anita Diamant's retelling of the Biblical Story of Dinah has Become a Publishing Phenomenon," Review of *The Red Tent*, in *New York Jewish Week*, Vol. 212, No. 36, February 4, 2000, p. 49.

———, "The Last Chapter of '97: Five Titles to Savor From a Year Gone By," Review of *The Red Tent*, in *New York Jewish Week*, Vol. 210, No. 35, January 2, 1998, p. 24.

Buckley, Thomas, and Alma Gottlieb, *Blood Magic: The Anthropology of Menstruation*, University of California Press, 1988, pp. 8–13.

Cabot, Vicki, "Speaking Volumes: Woman's Voice; 'Red Tent' Tells Other Side of Story," Review of *The Red Tent*, in *Jewish News of Greater Phoenix*, Vol. 52, No. 19, January 14, 2000, p. 34.

Delany, Janice, Mary Jane Lipton, and Emily Toth, "Women in the Closet: Taboos of Exclusion," in *The Curse: A Cultural History of Menstruation*, Dutton, 1976, pp. 8–10.

Diamant, Anita, *The Red Tent: A Novel*, Picador, 1997.

Feeney, Jon, "The Last Nile Flood," in *Saudi Aramco World*, May/June 2006, http://www.saudiaramcoworld. com/issue/200603/the.last.nile.flood.htm (accessed August 14, 2010).

Finding, Ann, *Anita Diamant's The Red Tent: A Reader's Guide*, Continuum, 2004, pp. 25–40.

Harmon, William, and Hugh Holman, *A Handbook to Literature*, 11th ed., Pearson Prentice Hall, 2009, pp. 24–25, 65, 345, 439, 540.

Hertz, J. H., *The Pentateuch and Haftorahs*, 2nd ed., Soncino Press, 1981, pp. 130–31, 147, 208.

Klein, Michelle, *A Time to be Born: Customs and Folklore of Jewish Birth*, Jewish Publication Society, 2000, p. 123.

Justice, Faith L., "An Interview With Anita Diamant," in *Copperfield Review*, http://www.copperfieldreview.com/ interviews/diamant.html (accessed April 21, 2010).

"Mapping the Global Muslim Population," in *Pew Research Center*, http://pewforum.org/newassets/images/ reports/Muslimpopulation/Muslimpopulation.pdf (accessed August 14, 2010).

Meacham, Tirzah, "An Abbreviated History of the Development of the Jewish Menstrual Laws," in *Women and Water: Menstruation in Jewish Life and Law*, edited by Rahel Wasserfall, Brandeis, 1999, pp. 23–28.

Rich, Tracy R., "The Land of Israel," in *Judaism 101*, http://www.jewfaq.org/israel.htm (accessed August 14, 2010).

Roth, Cecil, "Niddah," in *Encyclopaedia Judaica*, Vol. 12, Keter, 1972, pp. 1142–49.

Schantz, Jessica, "The Redemption of Dinah in *The Red Tent*," in *Women in Judaism: A Multidisciplinary Journal*, Vol. 5, No. 2, Spring 2008, http://wjudaism.library. utoronto.ca/index.php/wjudaism/article/view/3519/1562 (accessed April 21, 2010).

Scolnic, Benjamin Edidin, "When Does Feminist Interpretation Become Anti-Semitic?," Review of *The Red Tent*, in *Women's League Outlook*, Vol. 72, No. 2, December 31, 2001, p. 27.

Towler, Jean, and Joan Bramall, "Midwives in Early History," in *Midwives in History and Society*, Routledge, 1986, pp. 6–12.

Trager, James, *The People's Chronology*, Henry Holt, 1992, pp. 7–8.

FURTHER READING

Alter, Robert, ed., *Genesis: Translation and Commentary*, W. W. Norton, 1997.

> This translation of Genesis tries to capture the rhythm of the original Hebrew poetry. The commentaries on the text are extensive and especially useful for students hoping to learn more about the history and meaning of biblical text.

Armstrong, Carole, *Women of the Bible: With Paintings from the Great Art Museums of the World*, Simon & Schuster, 1998.

> This book for young adults is a collection of brief biographies of women from the Bible. Each biography is accompanied by colored illustrations of paintings. Leah and Rachel are two of the women included in this text.

Dershowitz, Alan, *The Genesis of Justice: Ten Stories of Biblical Injustice that led to the Ten Commandments and Modern Morality and Law*, Grand Central, 2000.

> Each chapter from this book focuses on an act of injustice as a way to understand contemporary thoughts about how people define justice and injustice. The stories of Jacob and of Dinah each receive a chapter.

Ebeling, Jennie R., *Women's Lives in Biblical Times*, T & T Clark International, 2010.

> This book uses archaeological, iconographic, and ethnographic research to examine the lives of women living in ancient Israel. The author focuses on how women lived during the twelfth and eleventh centuries BCE.

Frankel, Ellen, *The Five Books of Miriam: A Woman's Commentary on Torah*, HarperOne, 1997.

> In this biblical commentary, Frankel uses the voices of women from the Bible to comment upon and present the five books of Moses, providing a woman's view of the text. This is not a feminist book but is an opportunity to

hear feminine voices in place of the traditional male voices of biblical commentary.

Monaghan, Patricia, *The New Book of Goddesses and Heroines*, Llewellyn, 1997.
     The author of this book presents an encyclopedia about myth, goddesses, and the heroines of legends. The author also includes photographs of art, including statues and paintings that depict goddesses and heroines.

Sjoo, Monica, *The Great Cosmic Mother: Rediscovering the Religion of the Earth*, HarperOne, 1987.
     This young-adult book is a clearly organized reference text that is useful for students wanting to learn more about ancient ideas of religion and matriarchal religious beliefs.

SUGGESTED SEARCH TERMS

Diamant AND Red Tent

Red Tent AND biblical women

Dinah AND Genesis

Jacob AND Dinah

Dinah AND biblical justice

Red Tent AND Dinah story

Jacob AND Leah

Leah AND Rachel

Shane

JACK WARNER SCHAEFER
1949

Shane is a western novel that was first published in book form by Jack Warner Schaefer in 1949; a later edition, published in 1954, contains minor changes in language. Although the book never achieved best-seller status, it has remained popular with readers and is widely regarded as one of the finest examples of the Western genre. It tells the story of a homesteading family living in the Wyoming Territory in the late 1880s. It is told from the point of view of Bob Starrett, a young boy who becomes fascinated with a mysterious stranger, Shane, who appears from nowhere and who reverts to his earlier gunslinging ways to protect the Starretts from the local cattle baron, who wants to force the Starretts off their land. The novel embodies many features of the traditional Western, especially the sense that justice is meted out by the forces of right to those who would use their wealth and power to exploit other people.

Schaefer wrote a number of other western novels. In 1975, the Western Literature Association presented him its Distinguished Achievement award. When the Western Writers of America surveyed its members in 1985 to compile a list of the one hundred greatest westerns of all time, *Shane* received the highest number of votes.

AUTHOR BIOGRAPHY

Schaefer was born on November 19, 1907, in Cleveland, Ohio, far from the American West

that he celebrated in his novels and short stories. As a child he was an avid reader, absorbing adventure tales and the works of Charles Dickens and William Makepeace Thackeray. He pursued his interest in literature at Oberlin College in Ohio, where he studied the Greek and Roman classics and creative writing and completed a bachelor's degree in 1929. That year he enrolled in graduate school at Columbia University to study English, but he dropped out a year later when the university refused to give him permission to write his master's thesis about film.

Schaefer began his career as a journalist in 1930 and married his first wife, Eugenia Hammond Ives, with whom he had four children, in 1931. He worked as a reporter for United Press International, then as an editorial writer for the *Baltimore Sun*. He moved on to become an associate editor for the Norfolk *Virginia-Pilot* and the editor of the New Haven (Connecticut) *Journal Courier*. He also worked as the director of education at the Connecticut State Reformatory. While he was in Norfolk, Schaefer began writing fiction. He had long been a devoted reader of American history, and he began to write a tale about the conflict between cattle ranchers and homesteaders in the American West, specifically Wyoming. In time, the focus of his story became a mysterious loner with a Colt .45 pistol. The tale was originally intended as a short story, but it evolved and grew into the novel *Shane*.

Although 1949 is conventionally given as the date of publication of *Shane*, in fact Schaefer submitted it to *Argosy* magazine, which printed it in 1946 in three parts under the title *Rider from Nowhere*. Schaefer, though, wanted to be a writer, so in 1948 he abandoned journalism, which he later said was a poor training ground for real writers. He revised the novel and submitted it to book publishers, and in 1949, Houghton Mifflin published it in book form. The book became popular, although at the time Schaefer wrote it, he had never been west of Toledo, Ohio. During this period, he also was divorced from Eugenia, and in 1949, he married Louise Wilhide Deans.

Schaefer pursued a successful career as a writer. He finally had an opportunity to visit the West when he traveled there on assignment for *Holiday* magazine. He was so enamored with the West that he moved to Santa Fe, New Mexico, where he lived until his death from heart failure on January 24, 1991. From the 1950s until about

1967, he wrote numerous western novels and collections of short stories. Some of his better-known works include *The Canyon* (1953), *Old Ramon* (1960), *The Plainsmen* (1963), *Monte Walsh* (1963), and *Mavericks* (1967). After 1967 he abandoned the western in favor of books with environmental themes, including *An American Bestiary* (1975) and *Conversations with a Pocket Gopher* (1978).

PLOT SUMMARY

Chapters 1–2
The novel opens with Shane appearing on horseback at the Starrett farm. He is observed by the Starretts' son, Bob, who is struck immediately by the stranger's heroic magnificence. Shane asks Bob's father, Joe Starrett, whether he can have some water for himself and his horse. Joe readily agrees and persuades Shane to remain at the farm overnight to allow his horse to rest. Shane also meets Bob's mother, Marian Starrett, who serves him a home-cooked meal. During the meal, Joe and Marian ask Shane questions about himself, but Shane does not give very informative answers. Eventually, the conversation turns to the farm and Joe's plans for it. He explains to Shane that Fletcher, a local cattle rancher, is trying to take over all the farms in the area to use them for cattle grazing. The following morning, Marian, who is not entirely sure she trusts this mysterious man, serves him a breakfast of flapjacks. It begins to rain, and Joe persuades Shane to stay on at the farm because, even after the rain stops, the roads and trails will be muddy. Shane agrees, and after the storm passes, Joe shows him the farm, including a large stump that he has been trying unsuccessfully to get rid of.

A peddler named Ledyard appears and tries to sell Joe a new cultivator. When the peddler quotes an inflated price, Shane intervenes and tells Joe and the peddler that he has recently seen such a cultivator at half the price. The peddler grows angry with Shane, but he agrees to lower the price. Shane then gets an ax from the barn and starts to work on the stump, saying that he wants to repay his debt to the Starretts. Joe joins him with another ax, and the two men chop away at it.

Chapters 3–4
Bob continues to watch Shane and his father hack away at the stump. Marian appears

MEDIA ADAPTATIONS

- In 1953, *Shane* was made into an Academy Award–winning film starring Alan Ladd, Jean Arthur, Van Heflin, and Jack Palance. The film was directed by George Stevens. Paramount Home Video released the film on DVD in 2000.
- On February 22, 1955, the Lux Radio Theater broadcast a radio adaptation of *Shane* with Alan Ladd and Van Heflin.
- In 1966, the American Broadcasting Company created a television series based on *Shane*. Starring David Carradine, the series ran for seventeen episodes.
- A 2010 audiobook version of *Shane*, read by Grover Gardner, is available from Blackstone Audio. Running time is just over four hours.

wearing a hat that she has fashioned according to what Shane told her he has seen in the cities. She becomes frustrated that the men pay more attention to the stump than to her, so she returns to the house, where she remarks to Bob that there is something strange about the way the two men are attacking the stump. She also restores her hat to its former style, saying that she is proud to dress like a farmer's wife rather than a stylish city woman. She takes the men some biscuits, which they devour before attacking the stump again. After Joe has cut some of the roots, the men manage to get the stump to move a few inches. Marian suggests that they hitch the horses to the stump to finish the job, but the men insist they want to complete their task using manpower. As Marian watches in amazement, she forgets about an apple pie baking in the oven. The pie burns, and although Marian is angry at herself, she immediately makes a new one, refusing any help until the new pie is perfect.

The following morning, Bob wakes up distressed, thinking that Shane has already left. Shane assures Bob, though, that he would not leave without saying good-bye. Joe questions Shane about his past, but again Shane fails to provide any specific information. Joe then points out to Shane that the farm is too much work for one man and asks Shane to remain as a hired hand. Shane notes that he never thought of himself as a farmer, but he agrees to stay on. Shane adjusts well to farming life, though he seems always to be on the alert. He takes Joe's place at the dinner table, which troubles Bob and Marian until they realize that he wants to face the door and see anyone who approaches the house. Meanwhile, Bob begins to wonder why Shane does not carry a gun as all the other men do. He is reassured, though, when he sees a Colt .45 in Shane's room. He questions his father about why Shane hides the gun away. Joe says that he trusts Shane, so Shane must have a good reason for doing so. Joe cautions Bob not to become too attached to Shane because Shane is likely to leave at any time. Bob, though, suspects that there is a deeper reason why he should not become attached to Shane.

Chapters 5–6

Chapter 5 represents a transition. It is now the end of summer. Shane has continued to work on the farm and has cleared an alfalfa field in Joe's absence as an anniversary present for Joe and Marian. Bob thinks that this has been the happiest summer of his life, and Shane suggests that he has taken to the farming life and would like to stay. One day Shane sees Bob playing with a makeshift toy gun. He gives Bob pointers about how to handle and aim the gun, making clear that he knows his way around guns. Shane has become Bob's hero, taking the place of Fletcher, who has given indications during the summer that he is going to force the area's farmers off their land. With Joe as their leader, the farmers meet to decide how to counter this threat. Joe has no answers and believes that Fletcher will continue to apply pressure to force the farmers to leave. The farmers all predict that Fletcher will find a way to drive Shane away.

A few weeks pass, and a pitchfork breaks. Shane offers to take the pitchfork to a blacksmith for repairs. Joe offers to accompany him, but Shane insists on going alone. Bob, though, sneaks out of the house and joins Shane in the wagon. When they arrive in town, they encounter two of Fletcher's men, including a man named Chris. The other appears to recognize Shane and immediately flees, saying that he is leaving the town for good. Shane and Bob sit in the saloon, but Chris enters and does what he can to antagonize Shane. He gives Shane a drink of whiskey, then comments sarcastically that he thought that farmers drank only soda pop. He complains to the bartender about a smell, saying that the place smells like pigs, suggesting that Shane is a pig farmer. Shane grows angry at Chris's taunts, but he controls himself and lets them pass. Shane and Bob return home, where Bob tells Joe about the confrontation.

Chapters 7–8

The situation involving the farmers and Fletcher escalates. Fletcher and his men ride by Joe's farm and treat him rudely, making sarcastic comments about pigs. Joe is becoming increasingly irritated by the situation, and the other farmers are beginning to lose faith in Joe's ability to put a stop to Fletcher's harassment. During a meeting of the farmers, Shane rides away. Later, the men learn that Shane has ridden into town and confronted Chris in the saloon. The men got into a fistfight, which Shane won handily, leaving Chris with a broken arm. Marian expresses her fears to Joe, who assures her that Chris will recover. Marian says that it is not Chris she is worried about. She is worried that Fletcher will come after Shane for retribution.

Shane grows increasingly troubled. He spends more of his time alone, often wandering about the farm. Bob overhears a conversation between his mother and Shane. Marian wonders whether Shane expected that the situation with Fletcher would get as bad as it has. She speculates that Shane is planning on leaving, but she begs him to stay, saying that Joe and the other farmers cannot fight Fletcher alone. Shane reassures Marian that she and her family will not lose their farm.

Chapters 9–10

Shane and Joe always work together, watching each other's backs. One Saturday, Shane and the Starrett family go into town for supplies. Marian also wants to talk to Bob's teacher about her son's behavior problems; with so much happening, and with so many opportunities to go fishing and pursue other activities, Bob is having trouble in school. Shane goes into the saloon and is talking to the bartender, Sam Grafton, when a group of Fletcher's men, including Curly, Red Marlin, and Morgan, gather outside. A fight

breaks out, and for a while, Shane is able to hold his own against the group of men. Finally, though, they subdue Shane and are about to give him a beating when Joe appears and joins the fight. Shane kills Fletcher's right-hand man, Morgan, as Bob and Marian watch.

Shane is bloodied and injured. He and the Starretts return to the farm, where Marian tends to Shane's injuries and expresses her admiration for his bravery. In a subtle gesture, Shane runs his hand through Marian's hair when she begins crying. After Shane leaves, Joe confesses that he knows that Marian has fallen in love with Shane. Rather than being jealous or angry, though, he acknowledges that Shane is the better man and tells his wife not to worry herself.

Chapters 11–12

Although Fletcher appears to be lying low and not bothering Joe or Shane, the two men know that he is planning retaliation for the death of his hired hand, so the two are more watchful than ever. Shane, Joe, and Marian all agree that something will happen. Joe says that whatever happens, it is not likely to be another saloon fight but something more final. Shane is edgy because he does not like waiting. Their fears are realized the following night when Fletcher appears in town with Stark Wilson, a hired gunman. The bartender recognizes the gunman's name and says that Wilson is a dangerous killer. The following day, word reaches Joe and Shane that Fletcher and Wilson goaded a townsman, Ernie Wright, into a fight, during which Ernie was killed. Shane, though, knows that the fight with Ernie was a ruse. Fletcher will take over Ernie's farm, then decide what to do about Joe depending on how Joe reacts to the incident. Shane says that Fletcher will probably do something to provoke a confrontation between Wilson and Joe. Joe now feels remorse for having involved Shane in such a dangerous situation and says that he is considering selling out to Fletcher and moving away. Marian and Bob agree that if Joe did that, Shane would never forgive him.

Joe and Shane attend Ernie's funeral. Later, Fletcher, Wilson, and some of Fletcher's men ride up to the Starrett house. Fletcher says that he has a proposition: he claims that he thinks Joe and Shane are both good men and would like the two to come work for him, but the other homesteaders would have to leave. Joe and Shane refuse. Fletcher offers Joe a thousand dollars, but Joe still refuses. Fletcher says that he will wait in the saloon for Joe to make the right decision. As he leaves the yard, Fletcher makes an offensive comment to the effect that Joe would not like someone taking his place with Marian. Joe grows angry, but Shane holds him back. Shane then insults Wilson, saying that he is not much of a man without his guns. Now Wilson grows angry, but he restrains himself when he sees that Shane is not armed. After Fletcher and his men leave, Marian expresses her fears about the seemingly inevitable showdown that is coming.

Chapters 13–16

Bob concludes that his father is going to go into town and agree to Fletcher's terms or die trying. When Joe says that Marian will be in better hands (Shane's) than his own, Shane grows agitated and goes into the house, followed by Marian. Marian returns outside looking anguished and pale. Later, Bob finds Shane coming in from the pasture. He notices that Shane is wearing the clothes that he wore when he first arrived and that he is wearing his gun. Joe and Shane quarrel about which of the two is going to go into town and confront Fletcher. Joe insists that it is his business, but Shane says that a farmer is not equipped to take on Fletcher. To prevent Joe from putting himself in danger, Shane strikes him with the butt of his gun, knocking him unconscious.

In the climactic chapter, Bob sneaks away to follow Shane into town, noticing that he has his bed roll with him. Shane knows that Bob is following him but does not send him back. When Shane arrives at the saloon, Fletcher, Wilson, and Fletcher's men are there waiting for him. Shane and Wilson approach each other. Shane insists that he is there to deal with Fletcher, but Wilson insists that he wants to deal with Joe. Shane tells Wilson that his killing days are over. The two men stare each other down. Suddenly a shot rings out and Wilson is hit. As Wilson reaches for his gun, Shane shoots him again. Shane wheels around and shoots up into the saloon's balcony, hitting Fletcher, who is taking aim at him. Bob notices that blood is spreading on Shane's shirt. Shane leaves, telling Bob to go back home and that he is going to do for the Starretts the only thing he can.

Joe and Marian learn from someone in the bar what Shane did. Joe is glad that Shane is alive, but he is saddened that Shane has left. Chris reappears and offers to work for Joe,

who accepts Chris's offer. The following morning, Joe tells Marian that he wants to leave the farm. Marian, though, protests, saying that they have put down roots that cannot be pulled up and suggests that, instead, Joe try to pull up a post that Shane has sunk in the ground. The final chapter makes clear that Shane has become a local legend. For Bob, his spirit is still alive, and Shane will always remain his hero.

CHARACTERS

Chris

Chris is one of Fletcher's men. Early in the novel, Chris appears to be a bully, one of the "bad guys" in the story. He taunts Shane about being a pig farmer, which, in the Old West, would have been an insult. Chris, though, undergoes a change of heart and later offers to work for Joe, who accepts his offer. By changing his perspective on Joe and disassociating himself from Fletcher and his gang, the character of Chris suggests that at least some people can learn to distinguish right from wrong.

Curly

Curly is one of Fletcher's men. He takes part in the fistfight involving Shane and Joe Starrett.

Fletcher

Fletcher is the local cattle baron. Like many cattle barons in the Old West, he has no use for farmers because farming takes up land that could be used for grazing cattle. He gathers around him a gang of men, and he tries to intimidate the farmers, including Joe, into selling him their land, probably for a low price. Fletcher is in many ways a stereotypical antagonist. He serves as a foil, or contrast, to Shane and Joe, who behave honorably, unlike Fletcher. When he is shot at the end of the novel, the reader feels as though justice has been done and that Fletcher has gotten what he deserved.

Jane Grafton

Jane Grafton is Bob Starrett's schoolteacher and the daughter of Sam Grafton, the bar owner.

Sam Grafton

Sam Grafton is the bartender who owns the saloon where the final climactic shoot-out takes place. He is a minor character who, like saloon keepers throughout the Old West, served as a conduit for information in the community. He serves to identify Wilson, for example.

Ledyard

Ledyard is a peddler who appears briefly early in the novel. He tries to sell Joe a new cultivator, but at an inflated price. Shane intervenes and says that he has seen similar cultivators being sold for half the price. The peddler is angry at Shane, but he agrees to lower his price. The peddler is not a fully developed character. He is a plot device that shows a person failing to act honestly and with integrity.

Red Marlin

Red Marlin is one of Fletcher's men. He takes part in the fistfight involving Shane and Joe Starrett.

Morgan

Morgan is Fletcher's foreman. He takes part in the fistfight involving Shane and Joe Starrett.

Shane

Shane appears at the Starrett farm in Wyoming seemingly out of nowhere. He is a mysterious stranger, but as seen through Bob Starrett's eyes, he is also magnificent and heroic. Bob thinks that Shane "was the symbol of all the dim, formless imaginings of danger and terror in the untested realm of human potentialities beyond my understanding." He is a man of complete honesty and integrity. After the Starretts invite him to stay at the farm, he feels he needs to repay them, so he grabs an ax and starts hacking away at the large stump that has long been a source of annoyance to Joe. He and Joe work comfortably together, share the same values, and admire one another. Shane becomes a role model for Bob, teaching him not only how to aim and handle a gun but also, more importantly, how to become a man by doing the right thing. Shane is drawn into the dispute between Fletcher and the farmers. He knows that he cannot simply walk away from the dispute but has to do something.

Although he is reticent about talking about his past life, the reader soon begins to sense that Shane has been a gunslinger. He owns an impressive Colt .45, and when he encounters two of Fletcher's men in town, one of the men flees, suggesting that he knows Shane, either personally or by reputation, and is afraid of him. Shane confirms for the reader that he is an expert gunfighter during the final climactic scene when he shoots Wilson and Fletcher. Shane does not say very much. He is a man of action. Thus, the reader has to infer his feelings about the Starretts and his involvement in the conflict with Fletcher. He gives only the briefest of indications that he is attracted to Marian when he runs his hand through her hair. He is eager to protect her, but he has too much integrity to act on any feelings he might have for her. At the end of the novel, Shane is shot, and the reader is left to wonder whether his injury is serious, for Shane simply rides away and disappears, never to be heard from again.

Bob Starrett

The novel is narrated from Bob Starrett's point of view. Bob is in many respects a typical boy of the era. He enjoys the outdoors and is impatient with being in school. He is mystified as to why Shane does not carry a gun, as all the other men do. He becomes fascinated by the Colt .45 he finds in Shane's room, and later Shane shows him how to aim and handle a gun. He is inclined to hero worship. Before the novel begins, Bob admired Fletcher and his men. His allegiance, though, changes after the appearance of Shane, and he holds Shane in awe. Bob's perspective on events is limited by his age. For example, he does not understand that his mother has fallen in love with Shane, and he is uncertain about the future of the family and the farm. Through his association with Shane, though, Bob grows and learns some things about becoming a man. In particular, he learns that being a man is not a matter of carrying a gun and dominating other people. True manhood is shown by doing the right thing. Bob also gains new respect for his father through Shane. By watching Shane and his father work together and observing their close relationship, he realizes that his father, too, is a hero.

Joe Starrett

The novel has two heroes, Shane and Joe Starrett. Shane is the mysterious gunslinger who appears out of nowhere. Joe, though, is the more ordinary hero. He owns a farm, and he has a wife and son. He is content to go about his own business, but he is forced into a conflict by Fletcher. He tries to do the right thing, and the other farmers in the area look up to him as their leader in opposition to Fletcher. Joe knows that his wife is falling in love with Shane, but he does not exhibit jealousy or anger, for he knows that in some ways Shane is his superior. If Shane represents a sense of manliness and justice in the abstract, Joe represents these values in everyday life. He would rather avoid a fight, but if a fight comes to him, he will stand up for himself and for what is right.

Marian Starrett

In some ways, Marian, Joe's wife, is the most complex character in the novel. She typifies the frontier woman who is strong and self-sufficient. When she burns a pie early in the novel, she is frustrated with herself, but rather than complaining, she immediately bakes another pie, refusing help from anyone. As she begins to fall in love with Shane, she wants to protect him from danger, though she knows how much the conflict with Fletcher affects Shane. She is loyal and honest, and she never tries to hide her feelings or deceive anyone. Despite her feelings for Shane, she loves her husband and remains loyal to him.

Stark Wilson

Wilson, like his employer Fletcher, is a stock character, the bad gunslinger who can be hired. He appears on the scene to intimidate Joe, Shane, and the other farmers. Wilson, though, shows one moment of integrity when he restrains himself from gunplay when he observes that Shane is not armed; the code of the West would condemn shooting an unarmed man. In the end, Shane and Wilson, like two medieval knights, do battle. In the town's saloon, they attempt to stare each other down as the tension builds. Finally, Shane shoots Wilson.

Ernie Wright

Ernie Wright appears in the novel strictly as a plot device. Fletcher and Wilson are trying to provoke conflict in the community, so Fletcher antagonizes the hot-headed Wright to provoke a fight. Wright is shot to death in the fight.

THEMES

Coming of Age

Shane is in many respects what is referred to as a coming-of-age novel. This type of novel features a central character who is on the cusp of adulthood, like Bob Starrett. The character observes events and the interactions of surrounding adults and, in important ways, grows into adulthood. Although *Shane* is not strictly speaking a young-adult novel, this theme is one that is common to many such novels, for it explores the fundamental question that every young person faces: how to make the transition from childhood to adulthood.

The novel is narrated from the perspective of Bob Starrett. Bob behaves in many ways like a typical boy. He loves to go fishing. He enjoys the outdoors, so he is impatient when he is confined in the schoolroom. He is susceptible to hero worship, and it is made clear that before the novel opens, he regarded Fletcher and his cowboys as heroes. This changes, of course, when Shane appears on the scene. Shane becomes for Bob the model of what a man should be; of course, so is Joe, but Joe is Bob's father, and very often adolescent boys do not recognize the heroism and integrity of their fathers. The wisdom that Shane teaches Bob is not very complex, but it is important. It is apparent that Bob is absorbing the lesson, for even early on he reflects, "He was a man like father in whom a boy could believe in the simple knowing that what was beyond comprehension was still clean and solid and right." Thus, as a result of his encounter with Shane, Bob is able to evolve into young manhood.

Integrity

Throughout *Shane*, one of the characteristics that marks the good characters is their integrity and honesty. For example, after the Starretts take Shane in and persuade him to stay, Shane feels obligated to earn his keep by helping Joe remove the stump that has been frustrating him. When the peddler appears and tries to overcharge Joe for a new cultivator, Shane steps in and points out the peddler's dishonesty. Joe and Shane work well together on the farm, and each grows to respect the other. Fletcher, as the novel's antagonist, is a man without integrity. He tries to bully the farmers into selling their land to him. He gathers around him a gang that intimidates the other farmers, who look to Joe and Shane to stand up to the cattle baron. Ultimately, Fletcher hires Wilson, a gunslinger, to enforce his will by driving Shane and Joe away. Wilson and Chris, one of Fletcher's hired hands, rely on insults to antagonize Joe and Shane and provoke fights. When it becomes clear that Marian has fallen in love with

TOPICS FOR FURTHER STUDY

- Prepare a paper or interactive online timeline of the key events that would have had a direct or indirect effect on the Starrett family and the cattle barons of Wyoming during the time of the novel *Shane*. Events might include the development of the plow, the mapping of the West by the U.S. Army Corps of Engineers, the Civil War, the Homestead Act, the coming of the railroad, and the development of the Wyoming Territory. Share your timeline with your classmates and explain the importance of each item on the timeline.

- What nineteenth-century inventions and technological developments would have had an impact on the settlement of the western frontier and on life in Wyoming during this time? Examples might include the Colt Peacemaker gun, barbed wire, the railroad, and the plow. Prepare a chart of these inventions and developments, perhaps with illustrations, and explain how each in its own way changed the West.

- Investigate the life of cowboys on the western frontier and be prepared to comment on whether depictions of cowboys in movies and television programs are accurate. Pay particular attention to the role that African American and Hispanic cowboys played in settling the West. Summarize your findings in a multimedia presentation that you present to your class or post on your Web site or social networking site. Invite your classmates to comment.

- Investigate the role of women in settling the American frontier. Use print and Internet research to locate quotations from autobiographies, letters, and similar documents that illustrate how women responded to the harsh conditions of life on the frontier. Using the information you have found, write your own story about a woman, famous or otherwise, who appears in a community, changes it, then leaves.

- Imagine that you and a group of your classmates are given the opportunity to star in your own reality television show. The premise of the show is that the group, perhaps representing a family, will be taken to an isolated area in the West and live exactly as homesteaders would have lived in the 1880s, with no electricity, cars or trucks, grocery stores, radio or television, and the like. You would be given some farm and carpentry tools, basic clothing, a cow (for milk), horses (for transportation and perhaps plowing), chickens (for eggs), a plot of ground for growing food, and other basic necessities. Script the first episode of the show, and then record it. Show the episode to your class.

- Read T. T. Flynn's young-adult novel, *The Man from Laramie*, about a mysterious stranger who rides into town and becomes the center of conflict. Write a brief essay comparing the two works, placing emphasis on the differing tones of the works and the differing depictions of the stranger.

Shane, Shane never takes advantage of the situation. Through the heroic actions of Shane and his father, Bob Starrett learns what it means to be a man—acting with integrity. At one point Shane enforces the lesson to Bob: "'It's a lovely land, Bob. A good place to be a boy and grow straight inside as a man should.'"

Justice

The popular image of the Old West was that it was a lawless place, with gunslingers, shoot-outs on the street, cattle rustling, horse thieving, and the like. In fact, the people tended to be more law abiding than movies and television shows suggest. There was a strong sense of community, for

Alan Ladd as Shane in a scene from the 1953 film adaptation of the novel (Getty Images)

people realized that they had to rely on their neighbors to survive the harsh conditions.

Nevertheless, a common theme of Western novels has to do with justice and how it is achieved. The Old West was an era that had police forces, usually in the form of a town marshal and his deputies, as well as a court system. However, many settlers lived in small towns and isolated areas that were beyond the reach of the marshals and the courts. Communications and travel were difficult, so criminals were often able to get away with their crimes simply by moving on to a new area. Farmers and others often had to protect themselves from criminals, so most carried guns (which were also necessary for protection against predatory wildlife). *Shane* depicts a common situation in which people have to take matters into their own hands to achieve justice. It is unjust that Fletcher is trying to take over all the land in the area for his own purposes. It is unjust that he relies on a gang of bullies to intimidate people. It is unjust that he hires the gunslinger Wilson to bring matters with Joe and Shane to a head. It is

unjust that he provokes a fight with Ernie Wright that results in Wright's death. Shane, then, becomes a figure of frontier justice. He does not want to carry his gun or take part in gunplay. But he feels an obligation to protect the Starrett family, so he straps on his gun, goes into town, and sees that justice is done. At the end of the novel, the reader agrees that Fletcher and his men have gotten what was coming to them and that right has prevailed. Even a character such as Chris comes to realize the injustice of Fletcher and offers to go to work for Joe.

STYLE

Point of View

When writing a work of fiction, the author has an initial important choice to make: who is going to tell the story. Authors have two typical choices. One is to adopt the third-person point of view, narrating the story *about* the characters. Third person is a grammatical term that refers to the use of *he*, *she*, and *they*. The narrative voice, then, reports on the actions of the characters and can usually (but not always) enter into their minds and report what they are thinking. The other possibility is to adopt the first-person point of view. In a first-person narrative, one of the characters tells the story, using *I* and *me* to refer to his or her own actions and thoughts. This is the point of view Schaefer chose for *Shane*. The novel is narrated by Bob Starrett, who takes over the author's role of observing the action and reporting it to the reader. By having Bob tell the story from his own perspective, Schaefer is able to recreate the boyish wonder the character of Shane creates in those who encounter him. Shane is clearly a larger-than-life hero, but he is especially larger than life to a young boy.

Symbolism

Shane does not rely heavily on symbolism. The character of Shane could be regarded as a symbolic character, a representative of justice, integrity, and all that is good. Otherwise, the story relies on two primary symbols. One is the stump. The stump plays a prominent role early in the story. The stump has nagged at Joe, who has been unable to get rid of it, although he also says that he has developed a kind of affection for it and that he admires the stump's toughness. After Shane appears on the scene, he and Joe work doggedly at the stump with axes and are finally able to move it. The suggestion is that people can overcome obstacles through hard work and cooperation, and eventually those obstacles can be surmounted. Then, later in the novel, a post that Shane has sunk is referred to. Joe is having second thoughts about hanging on to the farm. The conflict with Fletcher is getting to be too much for him, and he begins to think that it would be easier to just move on. Marian, though, disputes this view by telling Joe that rather than leaving, he should try to pull up the post, which Joe cannot do. The post, sunk into the ground, is thus a parallel to the stump. The stump is a temporary obstacle. The post, though, is more permanent, suggesting that the Starretts are tied to the land and cannot leave—not because they are not free to do so but because leaving would be a betrayal of the values that Shane has brought to the valley.

Plot

Although the plot structure of *Shane* is conventional, Schaefer uses it to good effect. Plots are typically described as having a three-part structure. The first part is called rising action. This part introduces the characters and the situation in which they find themselves. It also introduces the conflict that stands at the heart of the novel, in this case the conflict between Joe Starrett and Fletcher. The action becomes more and more tense. In this novel, for example, a dispute breaks out between Shane and Chris, who tries to antagonize Shane and provoke a fight. The tension continues to escalate as it becomes more and more clear that Fletcher is planning to take action and Joe and Shane become more wary and watchful. The tension escalates until it reaches a climax, the shoot-out in the saloon in town. In turn, the climax leads to the denouement, or the resolution of the novel's conflicts: Shane leaves and Marian persuades Joe to remain on the farm. The falling action ties off the loose ends of the novel. In the case of *Shane*, the falling action consists primarily of Bob's reflections on the effect that Shane has had on the Wyoming valley.

Within this plot structure, two types of characters are needed. One is the protagonist, the "main" character about whom the story is told. Clearly, Shane is the principal protagonist in the novel, although Shane and Joe are so closely identified that they can be thought of as dual protagonists. Pitted against the protagonist is the antagonist. This is the character or set of characters who challenge the protagonist, block the protagonist's progress to a goal, or otherwise create obstacles for the protagonist. Clearly, Fletcher is the novel's antagonist. Often the antagonist is the "bad guy" in a novel, but not always. Sometimes the "bad guy" is the protagonist, and many contemporary westerns have focused more on the thoughts and actions of the character the audience sees as evil or deeply flawed. As a more conventional western, though, *Shane* casts the characters in conventional roles.

Sometimes, authors employ secondary conflicts, which make the book richer and more complex. One such secondary conflict in *Shane* has to do with Marian's feelings for Shane. It becomes clear that Marian is falling in love with Shane and that Shane might reciprocate her feelings. This introduces an element of conflict with Joe, who, of course, does not want to lose his wife. Interestingly, though, Schaefer chooses not to allow this potential conflict to erupt in action. Both Shane and Joe are men of too much integrity to let jealousy mar their relationship. The reader suspects that Shane takes action at the end of the novel primarily because he wants to protect Marian, but this motivation is never made explicit.

HISTORICAL CONTEXT

Homesteading

The historical context of *Shane* is the settlement of the American frontier, the Old West, which is part of the mythology of the United States. In 1838, the U.S. Army Corps of Engineers mapped the area west of the Mississippi River, and in 1845 New York City journalist John O'Sullivan coined the term "Manifest Destiny" to capture the idea that it was the destiny of America to stretch all the way from the Atlantic to the Pacific Ocean. A key event in the history of the settlement of the West was the passage of the Homestead Act in 1862. The act said that any man or woman who was the head of a family and a U.S. citizen could get 160 acres of land free. (The novel uses the phrase "staking out their hundred and eighties," referring to 180 acres, but this is a mistake.) The act required the settler to build a home on the property and make improvements within six months and then live there for five years. All this could be done for a fee of just eighteen dollars. Interestingly, even in modern life, homeowners in most states can take what is called a homestead exemption from their property taxes on a home in which they live (as opposed to renting out to others).

Wyoming was organized as a territory in 1868. It joined a number of other territories (Montana, Idaho, and Utah, for example) in becoming eligible for statehood. In 1890, Wyoming became the forty-fourth state of the Union. At the time in which the novel is set, the 1880s, Wyoming was still a sparsely populated territory, with only about 20,000 people. It is generally thought that Wyoming granted women the right to vote in all elections (and Wyoming elected the nation's first woman governor) as a way of attracting more women to the state. Most of these settlers pursued one of two occupations. Some, called homesteaders, or nesters, became farmers. They were called nesters because, in the absence of inexpensive fencing, they often surrounded their farmland with piles of brush, giving the appearance of a huge nest. These homesteaders grew crops on their land, some for sale and some for their personal use.

Cattle Ranching

The other chief occupation in the West was cattle ranching. Particularly after the Union Pacific Railroad was completed through the Wyoming Territory in 1869, it was lucrative for ranchers to graze cattle, which could then be sent to market by rail (or by cowboys who drove the herds to market towns, usually to the east). Considerable conflict quickly developed between homesteaders and ranchers. Homesteaders staked out pieces of land that were off limits to cattle. Ranchers, though, wanted to have as much land available as possible for grazing. The result was what are still called "open range" laws. In these states (Idaho is an example), ranchers are still allowed to graze their cattle on any open land, with some exceptions. If a farmer or other person wants to keep the cattle out, it is that person's obligation to fence them out, not the cattle rancher's obligation to fence them in. A key development was barbed wire, which was invented in 1874 and was widely used by farmers to fence off their land, as well as by ranchers who wanted to contain their cattle. Cattle ranching acquired an aura of glamour. Many cattle ranchers became wealthy and employed cowboys to protect their property and herds. Farmers came to see these wealthy and powerful ranchers as arrogant and greedy. Ranchers, for their part, often regarded "dirt farmers" as lesser beings, not worthy of respect. Water became a source of conflict as more and more homesteaders acquired water rights for irrigation. Ranchers saw homesteaders as a threat to their way of life. As more and more homesteaders settled land in Wyoming and other territories, conflict between farmers and ranchers became more frequent, and often violent.

The conflict between cattlemen and homesteaders reached a climax with the Johnson County War; although this conflict took place after the time setting of *Shane*, Schaefer probably based the conflict in his novel on the events surrounding those that occurred in Johnson County, Wyoming, in 1892. By this time, cattle rustling was becoming more commonplace. Farmers were resentful of bossy cattlemen and saw little harm in snatching an occasional steer for themselves. Juries were becoming more reluctant to convict men of cattle rustling. Cattlemen became exasperated

COMPARE & CONTRAST

- **1880s:** Settlers are attracted to the Wyoming Territory to engage in farming and cattle ranching.

  1940s: Wyoming is considered an isolated state. Agriculture and ranching are still major economic enterprises, but the oil business is beginning to boom. Trona, a mineral that is the chief source of sodium carbonate, is discovered, and its extraction becomes an important industry.

  Today: Although farming and cattle ranching are still important economic activities in Wyoming, the petroleum, mineral extraction, and tourism industries are the major drivers of the state's economy.

- **1880s:** Wyoming is a sparsely settled territory of about 20,000 people, with a large majority male population.

  1940s: The population of Wyoming is just under 300,000 people.

  Today: Wyoming is still sparsely populated. With just over a half million people, it is the smallest U.S. state by population and has

  the second lowest population density (just ahead of Alaska). The male population is only slightly larger than the female population.

- **1880s:** One of the first buildings constructed in a new western community is likely to be a one-room schoolhouse. Teachers, always women, begin teaching as young as sixteen. A typical salary is about twelve dollars a month. School is open only a few months of the year because children are needed on the farms.

  1940s: The first legislation to establish junior colleges in Wyoming is passed in 1945.

  Today: Students attend school in much larger, multi-use facilities. Teachers, men and women, need a teaching degree and certification. Salaries for Wyoming teachers average just over 40,000 dollars a year. In schools throughout the country, students still have summers off, a throwback to the days when children were needed to work on farms.

with this state of affairs and decided to take action against thieves and rustlers. Their first move was to hang a man named Jim Averill, whose store was regarded as a hangout for rustlers. They also hanged a nearby homesteader named Cattle Kate Watson, who acquired many stolen animals. In response, homesteaders formed their own loose association headed by a sheriff named Red Angus. The war erupted in 1892 when the Wyoming cattle ranchers imported a band of gunmen, the "Regulators," who attacked cattle-rustling strongholds in Johnson County. In retaliation, about a hundred homesteaders attacked and pinned down the ranchers' gunmen. Eventually, the federal government intervened and sent troops to quell the conflict—but not before considerable blood had been shed.

CRITICAL OVERVIEW

Shane met with immediate critical success. Two comments are representative of the esteem in which critics held the novel. In a review in *Library Journal*, J. E. Brown writes that the novel "captivates the reader's attention from beginning to end. [Schaefer's] skill in depicting a character, a situation, or a mood, with a minimum of words, gives the story a tightly-woven quality." Writing in the *Chicago Sunday Tribune*, reviewer Al Chase calls the novel "a tragic, taut little tale of a grim, unforgettable, mysterious and at times sinister figure of a man."

Later critics of *Shane* have tended to focus on the novel's place in western literature. These critics note that a considerable amount of

Shane helped put up some of the fence. *(Jesse Kunerth / Shutterstock.com)*

western fiction relies heavily on conventional elements: gunslingers, cattle ranchers, cowboys, a stampede, poker games and drinking in a saloon, and the like. While *Shane* employs many of these elements, critics tend to agree that Schaefer has transcended the conventions to write a novel that is deeper and more satisfying. Marc Simmons, in his forward to *Shane: The Critical Edition*, writes that "by any standard of measurement, Jack Schaefer's *Shane* rates as a classic in the literature of the American West." Gerald Haslam, in "Jack Schaefer," writes that the opening lines of *Shane* "illustrate the crispness of expression and the directness of syntax that enliven Schaefer's writing." He praises the novel further, saying that

> Jack Schaefer has found his material and has presented it honestly, illuminating the recesses of an otherwise dimly seen time and place, and of the people who inhabit that time and place. In doing so, he has raised himself above the horde of Western authors who have been satisfied with far less than this.

In a similar vein, in "The Western Writer: Jack Schaefer's Use of the Western Frontier,"

Robert Mikkelsen says that "Schaefer gives his work the two qualities which characterize it and distinguish it from run-of-the-mill popular fiction: use of the frontier to reveal men's true natures and fresh description of that frontier." He concludes his essay by saying that Schaefer's "achievement is a sensitive reconstruction of the western frontier."

CRITICISM

Michael J. O'Neal

O'Neal holds a Ph.D. in English literature. In the following essay, he examines Schaefer's handling of point of view in Shane.

That *Shane* is written from a first-person point of view is readily apparent. The story is narrated by Bob Starrett rather than by a third-person omniscient narrator. Thus, the actions and events recorded in the novel are those that Bob perceived himself; no outside narrator comments on the action. Bob refers to himself as "I" and "me" as he narrates the events of that summer.

WHAT DO I READ NEXT?

- Walter Van Tilburg Clark's *The Ox-Bow Incident* (1940) is a classic western novel suitable for young adults in which a posse captures three cowboys suspected of rustling cattle. The novel explores the meaning of frontier justice.

- *The Virginian: A Horseman of the Plains* (1902), by Owen Wister, is regarded by many readers as the quintessential western novel and has been popular among young-adult readers. Also set in Wyoming, it tells the tale of a nameless hero known only as the Virginian. He earns the enmity of the local bully, Trampas, leading to a decisive shoot-out.

- For a Native American perspective on the settlement of the West and farming in particular, read a short speech by a Nez Perce religious figure named Smohalla. The speech can be found under the title "Smohalla Speaks" in Margo Astrov's *The Winged Serpent: American Indian Prose and Poetry* (1992).

- For an African American perspective on the Old West, read Nathan ("Nat") Love's *The Life and Adventures of Nat Love*, written in 1907 but available in a 2008 edition and as a free e-book at http://www.gutenberg.org/etext/21634. Love was a former slave who headed west after the Civil War. His book is a blend of real-life adventures and tall tales.

- For a woman's perspective on the frontier, read *Pioneer Women: Voices from the Kansas Frontier* (1981) by Joanna L. Stratton.

- One of the most prominent names in American western literature is that of Louis L'Amour, the author of dozens of novels and hundreds of short stories. L'Amour's *Hondo* (1983) tells the tale of rugged Hondo Lane, who enforces justice on the dangerous Arizona frontier trail.

When Schaefer decided to put the words of the novel into the mouth of one of his characters, he created for himself a number of problems and opportunities, as does any author who decides on first-person narration rather than third-person narration. The first problem is that Bob is not really a major character. While he does take part in some of the action in the novel, as when he follows Shane to the saloon for the final shoot-out, he is not a major actor in the same sense that Shane, Joe Starrett, and even Fletcher are. In this way the novel contrasts with a novel such as Mark Twain's *Huckleberry Finn*. That novel, too, is narrated in the first person by one of the characters, but Huck is the central character. Bob, then, is more of an observer than an actor. In a way, then, Bob becomes Shaefer's "voice" in the novel. Much like an authorial voice, he watches and tries to understand the meaning of events. He serves as a reporter.

That said, one of the chief attractions of the novel is that Bob grows and matures as a result of the events that take place. At the beginning of the novel he is, in many respects, a typical boy who might be found on the frontier in the late nineteenth century. He enjoys spending time on the farm, going fishing, and doing the things that a "typical" boy living at that time and place might enjoy. His chief limitation is that he directs his need for hero worship not at his admirable father but at Fletcher and his men. Fletcher is the glamorous cattle baron and has power and influence. In his employ are cowboys who know how to handle a horse, shoot a gun, brand cattle, and live what, in Bob's mind, is probably an exciting life, in contrast to the unglamorous work of farming. Bob is on the cusp of manhood, in some respects still a boy, in others trying to figure out for himself how to become a real man. The events that take place in *Shane* show him how, for he learns that hard work, loyalty, and doing the right thing are more important than glamour.

The chief problem that any writer faces when he or she allows a youngster to narrate a novel is that the perceptions of the youngster are necessarily limited; a term often used to describe this kind of novel is "primitive consciousness." Bob does not always understand what is happening around him. He does not know what to make, for example, of the relationship between Shane and his mother. He is uncertain about his father's future course of action. He wonders why Shane does not carry a gun, particularly after he spots a beautiful Colt .45 in Shane's room. Schaefer wants these sorts of limited perceptions in the novel. They enable him to create more effectively the sense of mystery and heroism that surrounds Shane. When Shane appears on the scene, the reader can look at him in much the same way that the childish Bob does, as a force that will change the valley but that cannot be fully understood or evaluated by common means. But the author wants the reader to understand these matters. Thus, to incorporate into the novel a more mature, adult perspective, Schaefer combines the limited perceptions of the boy with the more refined perceptions of the adult Bob, who is narrating the book from a time later in his life. In this way, Schaefer has the best of both worlds. He can give the reader the perspective of the young Bob, trying to make sense out of events as they unfold. At the same time, he can give the reader the perspective of the older Bob, who has learned the meaning of the events through reflection. Indeed, this is a technique that many first-person novels employ. The narrator reports events, but by definition he or she is doing so after the passage of time. So the reader gets both the immediacy of the events as they happen and a later, more mature or considered perspective on the events.

Schaefer accomplishes the balancing act primarily through subtle yet effective hints at the more mature perspective. For example, at one point Bob makes this reflection: "[Shane] was dangerous as mother had said. But not to us as father too had said. And he was no longer a stranger. He was a man like father in whom a boy could believe in the simple knowing that what was beyond comprehension was still clean and solid and right." At another point Shane says, "'A man can keep his self-respect without having to cram it down another man's throat. Surely you can see that, Bob?'" In response, Bob reflects, "It was a long, long time before I did see it and then I was a man myself and Shane was not there for me to tell." After Shane comments on the beauty of the land, Bob remembers, "My gaze followed his, and I saw our valley as though for the first time and the emotion in me was more than I could stand." At the end of the novel, Bob says of Shane, "He was there. He was there in our place and in us. Whenever I need him, he was there. I could close my eyes and he would be with me and I would see him plain and hear again that gentle voice." Through passages such as these, the reader gets a double perspective: the wide-eyed wonder of the boy and the more insightful perspective of the man, a man looking back on

Thirsty from the trail, Shane let his horse drink first, and then he drank from the same bucket.
(*Lena Lir | Shutterstock.com*)

the events after a "long, long time." This double perspective enriches the novel and partially explains why *Shane* transcends the commonplaces of the Western novel and has remained popular with readers for more than half a century.

Source: Michael J. O'Neal, Critical Essay on *Shane*, in *Novels for Students*, Gale, Cengage Learning, 2011.

Michael Platt

In the following review, Platt describes Shane *as an American story that represents something necessary for our preservation in perilous times.*

Sometimes taught in middle schools, Jack Schaefer's 1949 Western novella *Shane* (which inspired the classic movie) deserves mature respect as well.

Jack Schaefer handles words as accurately, cleanly, and thoughtfully as Shane does an axe, his fists, or his gun: "The smooth invitation of it tempted your grasp. I took hold and pulled the gun out of the holster. It came so easily that I could hardly believe it was there in my hand. Heavy like father's, it was somehow much easier to handle. You held it up to aiming level and it seemed to balance itself into your hand."

That "into" in "into your hand" is choice. And there is not a bad sentence in the book. The power of good writing in it is enough to blow away whole armies of the mediocre authors imposed upon college freshmen today. There is also much to displease whiners: those who hate warriors, who think guns rather than criminals commit crimes, who wish for a world where virtue will be unnecessary. The story is clear that war is for the sake of peace, that warriors fight so that farmers may increase, and that disarming bad men is good.

The story is heroic, yet in *Shane* the hero doesn't win the girl, ride off into the sunset, and live happily ever after; his heroism means giving up the girl (who is married), and riding off into the night wounded, perhaps mortally. When I was a boy, seeing the movie, I found Jack Palance in black thrilling and Alan Ladd's killing him mighty satisfying. I did not realize there was a whole other drama in the storm. Shane could have let Starrett go into town to be killed by gunfighter Stark Wilson. Then he could have enjoyed the love of Starrett's wife Marion. But Shane doesn't do that; instead he saves the husband, forgoes the wife, and kills the fastgun.

The story, features a well-married couple and a good family, but instead of sonic vague approval of "family values," there is an exhibition of the self-restraint self-sacrifice, the saying no to pleasure, that marriage may require. Starrett sees that Shane is a superior man. He rejoices Marion will have a good husband and his son a good father if he should be killed. Respect, not envy, is what he feels. Marion, too. She admires Shane, she cares for him terribly, but there is not one kiss in which she betrays her vows. No one in Shane offers the excuses most people nowadays would try on Dr. Laura Schlessinger.

It turns out not to be easy for a boy to "honor your father and mother," even if you are a good boy of a good dad. What if the hired man is simply a naturally better human than your own father? Of course you will fall in love with him. But is that not disloyal? Thus Bob, the boy, is painfully divided to see Shane and his father fight it out for the honor of facing Wilson, the hired gun the big rancher Fletcher has brought in to scare off the small landholders.

Shane is an American story. In Joe Starrett we have the civil hero, the man whose decency

unto death serves his family. And in *Shane* we have the super-civil hero whose courage serves the good of all families, unto the sacrifice of family life, and even continued existence, for himself. Starrett and his virtues represent the civil best of America, but Shane and his virtues represent something that is necessary for our preservation in perilous times.

Source: Michael Platt, "*Shane*," in *American Enterprise*, Vol. 9, No. 3, May–June 1998, p. 84.

C. Phillip Jean

In the following essay, Jean suggests that the removal of the oak stump and later the posting of the corral fence are symbolic of the thesis of the story.

Two things that Shane does while staying with the Starrets are to help uproot the old burr oak stump and later to post a new section for a larger corral fence while Joe is away on business. Both the removal of the stump and the setting of the fence's corner post are done to please Marian. The thesis of this essay is that both actions symbolize the relegation of the masculine, individualistic, aggressive, destructive, unguided principle that Freud termed the id to the feminine, community-oriented, civilized, constructive, channeled principle analogous to what Freud termed the superego.

In *Civilization and Its Discontents*, which appeared in 1930, Freud came closer than anywhere else to positing a theory of history. Essentially, Freud sees history as an enduring conflict between man's instinctual needs and civilization, the desires of the individual versus the claims of society. States a biographer of Freud:

The individual is caught between the insatiable desires of the id, with its boundless impulse toward self-gratification, and the tyrannical claims of the superego imposed on him by his parents and by society. . . .

The idea that civilization is based upon instinctual renunciation had dominated [Freud] for many years. Incongruously enough, it had first struck him forcefully one evening when, as a young man of twenty-six, he had been watching a performance of the opera *Carmen* in Vienna. As he told his fiancee immediately afterwards: "The mob gives vent to its appetites, and we deprive ourselves. We deprive ourselves in order to maintain our integrity, we economize in our health, in our capacity for enjoyment, our emotions; we save ourselves for something, not knowing for what. And this habit of suppression of natural instincts gives us the quality of refinement."

Marian is the embodiment of of the second of Freud's principles, the superego. Joe had undertaken the building of the ranch for her, and Shane later promised Marian that *she* would not lose the place. Joe and Shane represent the first principle, the id.

The burr oak stump is first introduced by Bob Starret:

> That was the one bad spot on our place. It stuck out like an old scarred sore in the cleared space back of the barn—a big old stump, all jagged across the top, the legacy of some great tree that must have died long before we came into the valley and finally been snapped by a heavy windstorm. . . . The huge old roots humped out in every direction, some as big about as my waist, pushing and twisting down into the ground like they would hold there to eternity and past.

The stump is primitive, ancient, powerfully aggressive and—as a phallic symbol—masculine. It is the antithesis of the civilized cleared land. Joe alone has been unable to uproot the stump. In fact, his struggles against it serve as an outlet for similarly aggressive forces in his own nature or id:

> He went over to the stump now and kicked the nearest root, a smart kick, the way he did every time he passed it. "Yes," he said, "That's the millstone around my neck. That's the one fool thing about this place I haven't licked yet. But I will. There's no wood ever grew can stand up to a man that's got the strength and the will to keep hammering at it." . . . "You know, Shane, I've been feuding with this thing so long I've worked up a spot of affection for it. It's tough. I can admire toughness. The right kind."

The removal of the stump comes about when community effort on the part of Joe and Shane occurs as a result of an unwritten but civilized contract that is acknowledged by Shane: in return for the supper, lodging, and breakfast he has received, he attacks the stump, telling Joe, "A man has to pay his debts." Marian is the major cause of this contract because her cooking is what primarily attracts Shane, and her cooking represents the civilizing force:

> She was proud of her cooking. . . . That was one thing she learned back home . . . that was of some use out in this raw land. As long as she could still prepare a proper dinner, she would tell father when things were not going right, she knew she was still civilized and there was hope of getting ahead.

While the men labor together cutting stump roots, Marian serves them some of her biscuits on the stump. Her cooking is a parallel action to their clearing the land—both are constructive, channeled work. While the men finished the laborious task of uprooting the stump, Marian baked them an apple pie. In her excitement of viewing their finished chore, she let the pie burn. Undaunted, she launches into the preparation of a second pie with all the fervor the men had exhibited in clearing the land. The connection between the two chores is made explicit when Shane, upon tasting the second pie, tells Marian, "Yes. That's the best bit of stump I ever tasted."

Just as cooking is a sign of civilization in *Shane*, so too is the fencing in of land. Joe tells Shane,

> The open range can't last forever. The fence lines are closing in. Running cattle in big lots is good business only for the top ranchers and it's really a poor business at that. Poor in terms of the resources going into it. Too much space for too little results. It's certain to be crowded out.

Later on while Joe is gone to purchase cattle to extend his ranch holdings, Shane contributes to the ranch by refencing the corral to increase its size, as Bob reflects:

> We would have enough fodder to carry a few more young steers through the winter for fattening next summer, so father rode out of the valley and all the way to the ranch where he worked once and came back herding a half-dozen more. He was gone two days. He came back to find that Shane, while he was gone, had knocked out the end of the corral and posted a new section making it half again as big.

Shane did the posting, one learns, because Marian insisted: "She rode me like she had spurs to get it done by today. Kind of a present. It's your wedding anniversary," Shane tells Joe. The civilizing action is a continuation of the community spirit earlier exhibited in the removal of the stump. Shane sees the new corral as making possible more constructive action by him and Joe: "Now we can really get going next year. . . . We ought to get enough hay off that new field to help us carry forty head."

Shane cannot stay with the Starretts forever, and after he leaves, having accomplished his mission there, one learns that his influence will always be felt on the ranch. The corner post he set has replaced the stump he helped to remove. Marian impresses this fact upon Joe:

"He's not gone. He's here, in this place he gave us. He's all around us and in us, and he always will be."

She ran to the tall corner post, to the one Shane had set. She beat at it with her hands. "Here, Joe. Quick. Take hold. Pull it down."

Father stared at her in amazement. But he did as she said. No one could have denied her in that moment. He took hold of the post and pulled at it. He shook his head and braced his feet and strained at it with all his strength. The big muscles of his shoulders and back knotted and bulged till I thought this shirt, too, would shred. Creakings ran along the rails and the post moved ever so slightly and the ground at the base showed little cracks fanning out. But the rails held and the post stood.

It is indeed Marian's moment, for she has been the instrument of civilization's relegating of more primitive, violent forces to a secondary place. One is perhaps reminded of a similar role played by the bride in Crane's short story, "The Bride Comes to Yellow Sky." The roles of the Scratchy Wilsons and the Stark Wilsons will forever be of less importance.

Source: C. Phillip Jean, "Shaefer's *Shane*," in *Explicator*, March 1, 1989, pp. 49–52.

SOURCES

Brown, J. E., Review of *Shane*, in *Library Journal*, October 1, 1949, p. 74.

Chase, Al, Review of *Shane*, in *Chicago Sunday Tribune*, November 13, 1949, p. 22.

Haslam, Gerald, "Jack Schaefer," in *Shane: The Critical Edition*, edited by James C. Work, University of Nebraska Press, 1984, pp. 19, 55.

Mikkelsen, Robert, "The Western Writer: Jack Schaefer's Use of the Western Frontier," in *Shane: The Critical Edition*, edited by James C. Work, University of Nebraska Press, 1984, pp. 302, 306.

Schaefer, Jack, *Shane*, Houghton Mifflin, 1954, pp. 31, 114, 189, 190, 212–13.

"*Shane*," in *Latitudes: Resources to Integrate Language Arts and Social Studies*, Perfection Learning Corporation, 1993.

Simmons, Marc, "Foreword," in *Shane: The Critical Edition*, edited by James C. Work, University of Nebraska Press, 1984, p. vii.

FURTHER READING

Erdoes, Richard, *Saloons of the Old West*, Knopf, 1979.
  Students of the Old West can find in this book photographs, facts, legends, and anecdotes about the iconic saloons of the Old West.

Freedman, Russell, *Children of the Wild West*, Houghton Mifflin, 1983.
  Text and historical photographs give readers a picture of life in the American West from 1840 to the early 1900s from the viewpoint of young people.

Jeffrey, Julie Roy, *Frontier Women: "Civilizing" the West? 1840–1880*, rev. ed., Hill and Wang, 1998.
  This volume is an account of the diverse contributions made by American women, including women of color, to the settlement of the frontier and the American West.

Katz, William Loren, *Black People Who Made the Old West*, Africa World Press, 1992.
  This volume contains photos and text that tell the stories of African Americans who helped settle the American frontier.

Rosa, Joseph G., *The Gunfighter: Man or Myth?* University of Oklahoma Press, 1980.
  This volume, illustrated with contemporary photographs, examines the myths and realities of gunslingers on both sides of the law in the American West.

SUGGESTED SEARCH TERMS

American frontier

cowboys

homesteading

Jack Schaefer

Johnson County War

Old West

Shane

Wyoming Territory

Shane AND Jack Schaefer

Jack Schaefer AND western literature

Jack Schaefer AND cowboy literature

The Third Man

GRAHAM GREENE

1950

Graham Greene was one of the most prolific, popular, and acclaimed authors of the twentieth century, producing dozens of stage plays, screenplays, novels, and "entertainments"—his term for his less literary works of fiction, which were usually espionage thrillers. A British citizen born in 1904, Greene traveled widely, on his own, in the employ of his government, and as a journalist. He trekked across Liberia in 1935, worked as a secret agent in Sierra Leone during World War II, and witnessed uprisings against colonizing powers in Kenya, Malaysia, and Vietnam. Accordingly, much of his fiction is set in foreign locales, including Mexico and Cuba. *The Third Man* takes place in Vienna, Austria, which was occupied by the victorious Allied powers after World War II. Originally conceived as a screenplay and produced in 1949 as a film, which won the Grand Prix at the Cannes Film Festival, the treatment was subsequently published by Greene in condensed form in *American Magazine* in March 1949 and as a novella in 1950. In the novella, Colonel Calloway, a Scotland Yard detective stationed with the military police in Austria, narrates how Rollo Martins arrived in Vienna to find that his friend Harry Lime had just been killed in an accident—and was believed by the police to have been a ruthless racketeer. Following his conscience, Martins tries to clear his friend's name, but the truth proves more elusive, and fatal, than he expected.

Graham Greene (AP Images)

AUTHOR BIOGRAPHY

Greene was born Henry Graham Greene in Berk-hampsted, England, on October 2, 1904, the fourth of six children born to Charles and Marion Greene. In his upper-middle-class family, the young Greene experienced a sheltered childhood infused with rigid Victorian values, which he would later come to question. Greene's father was the headmaster at the Berkhampsted School, which proved such a burden socially and emotionally that in his adolescence Greene sought to escape his circumstances and even experimented with solitary Russian roulette. When he was sixteen, his parents decided to send him to London for six months of psychoanalysis, then a fairly new therapeutic approach, which he would recall as a very pleasant period of his life. Scholars note that this experience surely fueled his later development as an author with a great capacity for psychological insight and an intuitive understanding of people's motivations and the meanings of their dreams. He was a passionate reader, and early literary influences included H. Rider Haggard, Marjorie Bowen, Joseph Conrad, and Henry James. After finishing his secondary schooling in 1922, Greene studied history at Balliol College, Oxford University, where he led a carefree—that is, a fiscally irresponsible and often intoxicated—existence. After gaining a bachelor of arts degree in 1925, inspired by his future wife, Vivien Dayrell-Browning, he converted to Catholicism in 1926. He became a journalist, serving as a subeditor at the London *Times* by 1930.

Meanwhile Greene wrote *The Man Within* (1929), his first published novel and his third attempt at publication. After his next two novels proved failures, Greene finally gained critical attention in the 1930s through several novels, including *Brighton Rock* (1938), in which he began substantially exploring religious themes. Meanwhile, he gained greater popular attention through his "entertainments," including *The Confidential Agent* (1939), a thrilling melodrama. He also wrote travelogues about his journeys to Liberia and Mexico. In World War II, he joined MI6, Britain's counterintelligence agency, and was stationed in Sierra Leone from 1941 to 1943.

For the next three decades, he produced novels, plays, screenplays, and story collections almost on an annual basis—including *The Third Man* (1950) and *The Quiet American* (1955), one of his most famous novels—and from time to time he meandered around the globe, often for journalistic purposes. He visited such far-flung locales as Kenya, Malaysia, Vietnam, Poland, Russia, Congo, Haiti, the Dominican Republic, and the United States. He served as a director for the publishing firm Bodley Head for a decade, until 1968, when he retired to focus exclusively on writing. He lived in a villa in Antibes, France, until his death in Switzerland on April 3, 1991.

PLOT SUMMARY

I

The narrator, a police agent, introduces the reader to the "cheerful fool" Rollo Martins, whom he first met at the frigid February funeral of Harry Lime. Martins will be shocked by the events to be related, in the setting of the shelled city of Vienna, which, after World War II, was jointly occupied by the major victorious powers: Britain, the United States, Russia, and France.

MEDIA ADAPTATIONS

- *The Third Man* was originally produced in 1949 as a film, directed by Carol Reed and starring Joseph Cotten, Alida Valli, Trevor Howard, and Orson Welles as Harry Lime. The soundtrack of the film makes exclusive use of the zither, played by the Viennese musician Anton Karas. The film won the Grand Prix Award at the 1949 Cannes Film Festival and the British Academy Award for best film.

- *The Third Man* was produced on audiocasette by Audio Partners in 1998, read by Martin Jarvis, complete with the background zither music from the film.

II

Martins, who writes westerns as Buck Dexter, was invited to Austria by his friend Lime, who pledged to cover his expenses. During a layover in Frankfurt on the flight from London, Martins is recognized as "Mr. Dexter" by a journalist who boosts his ego by calling him a novelist. In Vienna, with Lime absent, Martins disregards a welcoming note from some man named Crabbin—seemingly a mistake—and takes a taxi to Lime's apartment. But no one answers at Lime's door; Martins rings the bell repeatedly, until a neighbor informs him Lime was recently run over by a car and killed "instantaneously."

At the funeral in the Central Cemetery, Rollins meets the narrator, Calloway, who afterward rides with him to a bar. While Martins drinks, Calloway asks questions about Lime and their friendship. When the questions grow pointed, Calloway reveals that he is a detective and that Lime was sure to be convicted of racketeering before his accidental death; perhaps Martins was to be involved. The tipsy Martins grows belligerent and defends Lime's honor; he intends to clear Lime's name and make Calloway "look the fool." He tries to assault Calloway, but the detective's burly driver subdues him and dispatches him to Sacher's, a hotel.

III

As related by Colonel Calloway—who concedes that he will indeed be proved a fool in this case—Martins is believed by the hotel's head porter to be a Mr. Dexter who has a room reserved for a week. Crabbin then welcomes him and states that Dexter's *The Curved Prow* is his favorite; Mr. Dexter will be given meal tickets and pocket money for a week. Martins accepts the arrangement and then mentions his antagonism toward the colonel and his friendship with Lime—prompting Crabbin to tell him about Lime's actress friend, Anna Schmidt. In his room, after an odd dream, Martins is called up by Kurtz, who was instructed to look after Martins by the dying Lime—implying that Lime did not die instantly. Martins agrees to meet Kurtz the next day and, puzzled, falls asleep.

IV

At a café, Kurtz, with his lame toupee and false compliments, strikes Martins as phony. He tells Martins about the accident and a failed cable (telegram) telling Martins not to come. Martins relates his intent to clear Lime's name, an effort that Kurtz considers unwise; Kurtz responds with deliberate indifference when Martins posits a conspiracy among the true racketeers.

V

At the Josefstadt Theater in the afternoon, Martins is welcomed into Anna Schmidt's austere dressing room. She relates that Cooler, an American who was present at Lime's accident and whom Kurtz mentioned, gave her some money as instructed by the dying Lime. As it turns out, all the men present at the accident—Kurtz, the driver of the car, Cooler, and the doctor—knew Lime personally. Martins sees Anna to her tram.

VI

Martins next visits Dr. Winkler at his home/office, where the waiting room is filled with religious antiques and curios. The immaculate Winkler reveals the barest details of Lime's death, which occurred before he arrived on the scene. Winkler professes to know nothing of any illegal racket and says he does not know Cooler by name.

VII

Calloway relates that Martins might have safely abandoned his quest at this point, or he might have next visited Cooler, which could have somehow saved two men's lives, but Martins proceeds back to Lime's flat, to interview the neighbor who first told him of Lime's death—a man named Koch. Koch and his wife are cautious, but since the inquest is over, Koch relates all he knew of the accident, which he did not see but only heard; he ran to the window and saw a dead man being carried inside by three men, while the driver of the car stayed on the street. Martins knows of Kurtz and Cooler, but the identity of the third man is a mystery. Koch shows Lime's flat to Martins, who reveals that he believes Lime was murdered; afraid of getting further involved, Koch ushers Martins out. Back at the hotel, Crabbin has left a note detailing a lecture schedule for Mr. Dexter.

VIII

At five o'clock the next afternoon, Martins visits the kindly Cooler, who relates the accident over drinks. Martins mentioned "the other man," who was seen by Lime's neighbor, but Cooler asserts that no one else was there and points out that accounts of accidents are notoriously unreliable. Cooler mentions that Anna Schmidt is indeed a Hungarian whose father was a Nazi and whose papers were fixed to make her appear Austrian. Cooler thinks Lime was too dutiful to be involved in a racket.

IX

That evening, Martins tipsily walks the long way to Anna's flat in the British zone. He deposits himself on the couch and begins talking, to find himself falling in love with her. But she has yet to forget Lime. They grow convinced that Cooler and Kurtz lied about the circumstances of Lime's death. They walk together to Koch's flat, but a crowd is lingering outside, which frightens Anna. Martins walks ahead and learns that Koch has been killed. A small boy, Hansel, who overheard the police talking with Koch's widow, Ilse, informs his father that they were talking about a suspicious "foreigner" who had visited; Hansel notes that Martins, too, is a foreigner. When Koch is carried out and Ilse surveys the crowd, Martin ducks—to be perceived again by Hansel. He walks back to Anna, and, now sure of a conspiracy, sends her home.

Distrustful of the police, Martins heads back to the hotel, where he declines to meet Calloway in the bar as requested, instead walking back outside—to be ushered into an official-looking British vehicle. He is driven quickly

through town to a large gathering, where Mr. Crabbin nervously greets Mr. Dexter, whose fans are eagerly awaiting him. Martins halfheartedly impersonates the literary Dexter, announcing that his chief influence was Zane Grey, an author of cheap Westerns, which leaves Crabbin flabbergasted. Martins is asked questions, but his mind is reeling over the murders. He eventually signs dozens of books, authored by one Benjamin Dexter, as "B. Dexter," which is not an untruth. When a policeman arrives, Martins tried to escape but sees Paine coming up the stairs; he ducks into a dark room, where an unseen presence rattles his nerves. He opens the door, giving himself up, only to realize he has been spooked by a parrot.

X

Calloway's men have been tailing Martins until he meanders to Anna's flat on foot, when they lose him. Now Calloway and Martins have their second interview. Martins's conclusion about Lime's murder surprises Calloway, who has not heard about the third man from Koch. Calloway, now believing that Martins is acting honestly, first relates the police knowledge of Cooler's inconsequential tire racket and then what is known about Lime's own racketeering. Lime was smuggling penicillin, which was sometimes diluted, with disabling and even fatal consequences, including at a children's hospital. The police determined Lime's guilt by getting Harbin, a middleman in the racket, to write a pointed letter to Kurtz, eliciting an incriminating written response from Lime. Martins is appalled at his friend's evident guilt.

XI

Martins next goes barhopping, to then drunkenly seek Anna at three in the morning, get invited in, and tell her of Lime's guilt. She still thinks Lime is "the man we knew," but Martins objects; he confesses his love for her, but she still loves Lime. A figure on the street may have been watching them through the curtainless window. When Martins leaves, he sees someone in the alley who appears to be the living Lime.

XII

Back talking with Calloway, Martins relates the harrowing encounter; Lime quickly disappeared behind a newspaper kiosk. After getting another drink, Martins returns to Anna's, to find she has been whisked away by the International Patrol at the behest of the Russian member, whose nation is for the time being in charge. Hungary at the time is effectively part of the Soviet bloc, making Anna "a Russian national." In that incident, Calloway stops the patrol at a roadblock, assures the Russian that Anna's papers are in order, and keeps her in the British zone.

XIII

Calloway relates that he had a man trying to locate Harbin, but the squealer is nowhere to be found. Lime's body will be dug up. Meanwhile, Martins shows Calloway the kiosk where Lime disappeared, which is actually an entrance to the sewer. Martins commits himself to seeking out Lime by first visiting Kurtz again in the Russian zone.

XIV

Martins surprises Kurtz, who is evidently expecting someone else; Dr. Winkler is in the kitchen. Martins tells Kurtz to send Lime to meet him at the Great Wheel. After an hour, the stocky, nonchalant Lime arrives, and they board one of the Ferris wheel cars alone together. Lime is convivial, but Martins asks about the victims of his scheme; Lime replies that he cares more about money than about the lives of unknown people. Lime notes that Harbin was the one who was killed in the car accident and buried. Martins thinks of shoving Lime out of the car to his death, but Lime has a gun. When Lime departs, Martins calls out that Lime should not trust him, but Lime does not hear him.

XV

After the Sunday matinée, Martins tells Anna about meeting Harry and asks for her help catching him, but she refuses. Planning with Calloway, Martins will tell Cooler that he should flee, as the police have identified Harbin's body—incriminating Cooler, Kurtz, and Winkler—and then Martins will send word to Lime that he is in hiding and needs help himself.

XVI

Martins warns Cooler, and after midnight, Martins waits for Lime in a café near a sewer entrance. Thinking Lime will not show up, Martins nervously calls Calloway—but Lime arrives just then, to see Martins chatting, suspects a trap, and promptly leaves. Martins does not identify Lime quickly enough for the undercover police to nab him before he reaches the sewer.

Underground, Bates, the policeman accompanying Martins, is shot in the hand by Lime, losing his torch (flashlight) in the water. Martins takes the lead with a second torch and calls after Lime, who emerges into the light—to fire and kill Bates. Surrounded, Lime jumps in the water and is swept past Martins, who fires uncertainly and wounds Lime. Martins follows Lime up a sidestream, to find him unarmed and whimpering; Martins fires once more and kills him.

XVII

Lime's true funeral is conducted during a thaw. Afterward, Martins walks off with Anna.

CHARACTERS

Mrs. Bannock

Mrs. Bannock is forthright with Mr. Dexter, whose books she disapproves of, regarding her preference for good narrative storytelling.

Bates

In the final chase, the policeman Bates accompanies Martins into the sewer and leads the way. When a shot from Lime grazes Bates's hand and his flashlight goes out, Martins takes the lead; but when Lime emerges, he fires and, missing Martins by a foot, kills Bates instead.

Colonel Calloway

A British military police detective, Calloway narrates the story of Martins's adventure in Vienna, as pieced together from Martins's own statements and the related police reports; the police began following Martins after he failed to return to England following Lime's first, fake funeral. As a seeker of truth, Calloway comes across as perfectly objective, duly noting his own failures as well as those of the police in general. When he realizes Martins is acting honestly, he persuades Martins to help catch Lime by appealing to his sense of humanity, showing him pictures of the afflicted children whose lives were marred by the diluted penicillin. Calloway has a prudent sense of his role as an officer of the law. Saying he is "not a good citizen," he does not concern himself with the American Cooler's tire racket, which is inconsequential compared to Lime's racket; when Martins effectively murders Lime, who could easily have been arrested and given medical attention, Calloway affirms that he will pretend the killing was legitimate in the context of the chase. Calloway narrates objectively but acts subjectively, not necessarily as his office dictates but as his conscience and sense of moral order dictate.

Carter

Calloway briefly mentions how his assistant, Carter, lost Harbin's trail but did recognize that the body presumed to be Lime ought to be dug up.

Cooler

An American who purports to have a strong sense of duty, Cooler is an accomplice in the faking of Lime's death. He was across the street at the time of the accident and helped to carry the body inside. But while he and Kurtz claim to have carried Lime's body inside, in actuality, Kurtz, Cooler, and Lime together carried Harbin's body inside. Cooler seems genuine, and Martins trusts him, but once Calloway reveals Cooler's involvement in a tire racket, Martins finds him as two-faced and despicable as Calloway does.

Crabbin

Representing the British Cultural Relations Society, Crabbin welcomes to Vienna the man whom he presumes to be the famous novelist Benjamin Dexter—understood to be modeled after the British novelist E. M. Forster—but who is actually Rollo Martins, whose pseudonym is Buck Dexter. Crabbin arranges a lecture schedule for Mr. Dexter and manages to secure his rushed transportation to the Institute. There, Crabbin is bamboozled by Mr. Dexter's irritability and very unliterary comments.

Buck Dexter

See Rollo Martins

The Driver

The driver of the car that killed the man believed to be Lime, referred to throughout simply as "the driver," was shaken up after the accident and did not help carry the body inside.

Frenchman

Part of the International Patrol that detains Anna Schmidt, an unconcerned Frenchman declines to participate in the matter.

Hansel

In eavesdropping on the police and Ilse after Koch's death, Hansel overhears that they are looking for a foreigner; in relaying the news to his father outside the building, Hansel unnerves Martins by identifying him as just such a foreigner.

Harbin

Harbin was part of the racket run by Harry Lime, but the police pressured him to cooperate with their investigation. He led them to Kurtz and allowed a letter to be dispatched by the police in his name. For his betrayal, Harbin was hit by the car, killed, and buried, with the police believing his body to be Lime's.

Head Porter

At Sacher's hotel, the head porter receives Martins and wonders aloud whether he might be a Mr. Dexter who has a room reserved for a week, allowing Martins to take advantage of the circumstances.

Journalist

During his layover in Frankfurt, Martins is approached by a journalist who—as the reader later understands—mistakes Martins for the literary novelist Benjamin Dexter.

Herr Koch

Residing in the apartment opposite Lime's, Koch happens to hear the accident on the street and rushes to the window in time to see three men carrying a dead body inside. But he does not provide a statement for the inquest, and so Kurtz and Cooler's claim that only they carried Lime's body inside goes unchallenged. Koch was wise to wish to remain uninvolved. Koch tells Martins his version of the story, and later that evening, Koch hears someone downstairs and descends, to have his throat slit. Martins must have been followed to Koch's flat.

Ilse Koch

Ilse is wary when Martins shows up at their flat the second time and her husband invites the foreigner in; her concern is validated when Koch is murdered. As she is led from her house by the police afterward, she scans the crowd, as if looking for the foreign visitor, but Martins evades her worried gaze.

Kurtz

Kurtz, a player in Lime's racket, was accompanying Lime at the time of the accident in front of his apartment building. He sometimes wears a toupee, which was possibly used in the staging of the accident. Martins finds him to be palpably phony. Kurtz's name is a prominent connection to Joseph Conrad's novella *Heart of Darkness*, which features a rogue ivory trader named Kurtz whose role prefigures that of Harry Lime.

Harry Lime

Lime is one of Greene's most famous villains, being portrayed as personally appealing to virtually everyone he meets and yet, at heart, profoundly and remorselessly evil. He was evidently uninterested in saving Martins from capture and punishment when they were carrying out his plans as boys; the reader gathers that Lime especially appreciated Martins's unflinching acceptance of the role of obedient, and expendable, right-hand man. Lime trained as a medical doctor and even has skill as a musical composer, but he has nonetheless descended into the world of drug trafficking, dealing in the antibiotic penicillin. As seen in the police file photograph, he is stocky, as he enjoys food too much, and has "a look of cheerful rascality"—as if his present misdeeds have no more consequence than somebody else's punishment, just as when he was a boy. Indeed, he has the morality of a self-centered child who has not yet learned to feel empathy; he shrugs off the disfigurements, derangements, and deaths he causes with chilling childish indifference. As Calloway remarks, "Evil was like Peter Pan—it carried with it the horrifying and horrible gift of eternal youth." This comparison suggests that in his youthful ignorance, Lime, like Peter Pan—who in J. M. Barrie's *Peter Pan* remarks, "To die will be an awfully big adventure"—lacks a sense of the meaning of death. The termination of any number of the "dots" moving around the planet, as caused by his actions, has no effect on Lime's conscience at all. Following his own conscience, Martins ends Lime's life to prevent the future suffering of others on Lime's account.

Rollo Martins

The protagonist of the novel, Rollo Martins by profession writes Westerns, considered "cheap novelettes," using the pen name of Buck Dexter. Upon entering school as a boy, he at once began worshipping Lime, who was "a year older and knew the ropes." He admired and was drawn into Lime's pranks and deviant plans—and as if Lime meant for as much to happen, the inept Martins "was always the one who got caught."

As an adult, he remains a "cheerful fool," in Calloway's words, or, in his own words, a "silly fool" and "buffoon." He is almost always open to suggestion, especially for any sort of "new excitement," whether a drink or a girl or anything else. Calloway perceives that Martins has never really grown up, explaining his persisting affection for Lime; it is this affection that motivates Martins to seek the truth about Lime's purported racketeering and apparent death.

Through his independent investigation and emotional trials—which culminate in his killing the man who was once his best friend—Martins experiences a sort of rebirth. When he arrives in Vienna, his identity is in a sense subsumed beneath that of Lime; having grown up in Lime's shadow, he accordingly defined himself in relation to Lime. His westerns might be partly drawn from his and Lime's childhood adventures, which entailed, for example, the illicit borrowing of a gun, which they shot at rabbits with. Martins surely identifies with his westerns' "imaginary cattle rustlers who couldn't even shoot a rabbit clean." In the end, Martins ends Lime's life, an act that leaves him to define himself independently of Lime's terminated existence.

Pat O'Brien

The American in the International Patrol finds the abduction of Anna and the complacency of the British officer to be indecent.

Paine

Paine is a policeman who does Calloway's bidding, roughing Martins up in the bar Calloway takes him to and fetching Martins from his appearance at the Institute as "Mr. Dexter."

Russian

The Russian member of the International Patrol believes that Anna Schmidt's papers have been falsified to make her appear Austrian when she is really Hungarian, in which case she would be a "Russian national." The Russian insists that the patrol detain Anna.

Anna Schmidt

Anna Schmidt is a Hungarian who is using false papers to pose as an Austrian so as to live in the British zone of Vienna, and work in the Josefstadt Theater. Her father is said to have been a Nazi, explaining her fear of the Russian authorities (as Hungary was now within the Soviet bloc). Harry Lime was the one who arranged her papers, and the two were also lovers before Lime's faked death. She willingly tells the curious Martins what she knows. Although he at first finds her homely, he soon confesses his feelings for her, but she admits that her heart still belongs to Harry. He tries to sway her by arguing that Lime has been proven evil, but she asserts that nonetheless "he was the man we knew," and she refuses to help the police capture him. Anna can be understood to have finally put Harry behind her when she leaves Lime's true funeral with Martins catching up to walk by her side.

Corporal Starling

The Briton in the International Patrol, Starling believes the Russian officer is entitled to address his nation's concerns about Anna Schmidt's papers.

Gräfin von Meyersdorf

The Gräfin (Countess) is a dignitary at the reception for Mr. Dexter.

Dr. Winkler

Extremely orderly and clean, Winkler stymies Martins, when he pays a visit to the doctor's office, by giving minimal responses to his questions. Among his religious memorabilia, the doctor has a Jansenist crucifix; the Jansenist sect believed that Christ died to save only the elect. Winkler was presumably participating in Lime's penicillin racket, and so his possibly being a Jansenist—and it seems from the description that he is—would explain his being complicit in the deaths caused by the diluted penicillin; those who died were, as a Jansenist might argue, simply not among the elect. The doctor proves to have been an accomplice in the falsification of the death certificate: he identified the deceased Harbin as Lime.

THEMES

Underworld

The setting and circumstances of *The Third Man* frame Martins's excursion to Vienna as a voyage through the underworld. Following World War II, the city remains in ruins, which are buried under snow drifts and frozen, signifying lifelessness. The trip to the frozen graveyard marks the beginning of Martins's journey, where deceit and death will abound. The men involved in Harry's racket are themselves part of society's underworld, that of criminals and the black market, and the hunt for Lime eventually leads underground, to the city's sewers. The underworld imagery can be understood to reflect the subconscious journey that Martins is embarking upon in seeking to come to terms with his relationship with Lime and to establish his own identity. Martins's dream is significant in that it is a reflection of his subconscious state of displacement—the turmoil in the depths of his mind. Martins is able to emerge from this underworld after he finally, at the peak of the Great Wheel, sees Lime for who he truly is: a threat to innocent people's lives, including Martins himself. After the frozen first funeral, Lime's true funeral occurs during a symbolic spring thaw, and Martins, striding after Anna Schmidt, has finished his journey.

Duality

As narrator, Calloway introduces the reader to the duplicity inherent in Rollo Martins's personality, identifying his dual selves with his "absurd" first name and "sturdy" Dutch last name: Rollo is his curious, spontaneous, visceral self, while Martins is his rational, cautious, grounded self. From time to time, Calloway, playing amateur psychologist—a natural role for a detective—pins the man's actions on either Rollo or Martins. For example, in the course of his investigation, Rollo is the one who "decided to toss a coin" over whether to visit Cooler or Koch first. Calloway implies that, had Martins made a more reasoned decision, he might have gone to Cooler first, "to complete his picture of those sinister birds who sat around Harry's body," instead of going to Koch first and then divulging Koch's secret role to the potentially suspicious Cooler. Another duplicitous character is Lime, who can convey congeniality and benevolence on the surface despite his sinister true self. This duality, too, is embodied in the character's name, as "Harry" evokes Rollo's schoolyard chum, while Greene once reported having chosen the name "Lime" to evoke the quicklime used in the decomposition of corpses. Greene seems to suggest through these characters that such dualities are common to all people, in part because life can be seen as framed by the either-or decisions that a person makes, where one side of the personality favors one option while the other side favors the opposing option.

TOPICS FOR FURTHER STUDY

- Read a western by Zane Grey—whom Rollo Martins, also known as the western author Buck Dexter, names as his biggest influence—and write a paper discussing its worth as literature. In your paper, compare its plot devices, dialogue, visceral appeal, and redeeming value for the reader with those aspects of *The Third Man*.

- Keep a dream diary for a week, recording in as much detail as possible the contents of whatever dreams you can remember upon waking up. At the end of the week, use one dream as the starting point for a book chapter about a fictional version of yourself: the chapter should include a description of the dream—elaborated upon or altered as you choose—and events before and/or after the dream that reflect its contents. (The chapter need not have a complete plot or resolution as would be expected with a short story.)

- Read the young-adult cold war mystery *Charity* (1996), by Len Deighton. Although set at the end of the cold war, the novel features a plot very similar to that of *The Third Man*. Read the novel and create a Venn diagram to show the plot and theme similarities and differences as the protagonists in both novels retrace the victims' last steps to try to solve the mystery.

- Watch the film versions of *The Third Man* (1949) and *The Fallen Idol* (1948), for which Greene also wrote the screenplay. Write an essay comparing and contrasting the qualities of the two films, discussing the writing, acting, cinematography, and pictures as a whole—citing lines and scenes from the films to support your contentions—and giving your assessment of which film is superior overall.

- Research the practice of criminology at the midpoint of the twentieth century, and write a paper or create a Web page discussing the tools and methods that would have been available to detectives like Colonel Calloway and also relating major innovations in criminology that have been made since 1950. Include appendices with graphics, visuals, or illustrations if appropriate.

- Create a questionnaire including at least ten statements related to moral issues in *The Third Man*, to which a person would respond by stating that they either strongly agree, agree, disagree, or strongly disagree. For example, one statement could be "Harry Lime deserved to die." Distribute the questionnaire to your classmates and collect the responses, which should be anonymous. Design and build an Excel spreadsheet to compile and graph the results. Write commentary relating what conclusions can be drawn about the ethics of your peers and post it to your Web page and invite classmates to comment on your conclusions.

Complementing the characters' internal duplicity are the story's various role reversals, which represent external duplicity. An overarching role reversal is that between Martins and Calloway, where the professional writer becomes an amateur detective, while the professional detective serves as an amateur writer. Working in concert, both their sleuthing and their narrating fuse, allowing them to catch the criminal and produce a comprehensive account of the experience. Another role reversal occurs when Martins is mistaken for Benjamin Dexter and trades his persona as author of cheap westerns for a literary novelist's persona; in a sense, Benjamin Dexter is the flip side of Buck Dexter, where genre authors—those working in the realms of fantasy, science fiction, and mystery—complement the supposedly more serious authors of literature. This

The story begins and ends at a Lime's funeral. *(nagib | Shutterstock.com)*

duplicity reflects Greene's own writing career, alternating as he did between serious "novels" and thrilling "entertainments." Perhaps the most significant role reversal in *The Third Man* occurs when Martins goes from being Lime's best friend to being his most dangerous enemy; only with Martins's help are the police able to corner Lime. Overall, then, Greene may be suggesting that duality, the coexistence of opposing sides, is an essential aspect of wholeness.

Morality

The various characters in *The Third Man* follow uniquely oriented moral compasses. Calloway seeks to solve his own nation's concerns and is willing to ignore those of others—such as Cooler's tire racket in the American zone, and the Russians' concern about Anna Schmidt—to prioritize Lime's more consequential penicillin racket. Anna, her love for Lime consummated, remains loyal to him even when the evidence of his criminality is clear; her morality is figured on interpersonal rather than societal terms. Cooler speaks of his refined sense of moral duty but nonetheless participates in illegal rackets for personal gains. The police generally experience moral duty as equivalent to their duty as officers of the law; Bates, assigned to protect Martins in the sewer chase, insists on shielding Martins from fire, yielding only after a shot has grazed his hand and Martins insists on going first in the interest of capturing Lime. Lime, of course, has virtually no sense of moral duty, acting exclusively for his material gain. Martins perhaps possesses the most refined sense of morality: he is driven at first by his loyalty to Lime, seeking to clear his friend's name and explain his suspicious death. When he is made aware of the cost in human lives of Lime's racket, he prioritizes the good of society and innocent people and is willing to sacrifice Lime's life in exchange. Though Calloway's duty, strictly speaking, might demand that he report Martins's murder of Lime, he does not seem to act immorally in choosing to "forget that bit." Rather, Calloway's personal sense of moral duty compels him to cause no trouble for Martins, who played an essential role in Lime's capture and, arguably, killed a man who, based on his actions and intents, no longer deserved to live freely within human society.

STYLE

An Entertainment

Among his many works of fiction, Greene labeled some as "novels" and some as "entertainments." As he remarked in a 1955 interview, cited by Marc Silverstein in "After the Fall: The World of Graham Greene's Thrillers," "In one's entertainments one is primarily interested in having an exciting story as in a physical action, with just enough character to give interest in the action." In the novels, conversely, "one is primarily interested in the character and the action takes a minor part." Furthermore, the novels more directly address weighty themes, especially in relation to religion, politics, and morality, and are more likely to end tragically. On the other hand, as Greene notes in the preface to *The Third Man*, an entertaining thriller may be "too light an affair to carry the weight of an unhappy ending."

The primary significance of Greene's classification of his own work as "entertainment" may be that he enters into a sort of contract with the reader, who accordingly expects the work to function within the formulaic boundaries of his favored spy thriller genre. In his escapist fantasies, the sensational action may not be entirely realistic, but the chaotic workings of the plot will inevitably be resolved to provide a sense of moral clarity. As Silverstein notes, the hero's completion of his mission "reaffirms our sense of justice and ethical coherence." The thinner characterization, in turn, allows the reader to more easily project his or her identity onto the protagonist and so vicariously participate in the experience of the story. Ultimately, each individual reader will determine the value of the Greene volume in his or her hands, whether "novel" or "entertainment."

Displaced Narration

The narrative style employed by Greene in this entertainment, with Calloway narrating Martins's experiences as related to him by Martins and as witnessed by the police, has provoked much critical commentary, both negative and positive. Some, leaning on Greene's own claim in the preface that the film version, the "finished state of the story," is superior to the novella, identify the displaced narration as problematic. The reader is distanced from Martins, the main character, and some of the tension inherent in the plot is defused through Calloway's occasional

comments anticipating the action to come. On the other hand, many such remarks only leave the reader guessing all the more, such as when Calloway states that "Martins wasn't wrong, not entirely wrong" when he sensed that the Lime he knew was dead and gone. Another issue is the difficulty in assigning authorship to interpretive or philosophical asides, such as when, parting ways with Martins after their first meeting, Anna is described as "a little dark question mark on the snow": the reader cannot be sure whether this image originated with Martins or with Calloway. While this uncertainty has overwhelmed some critics, others have recognized that it simply forces the reader to adopt a more open-minded perspective regarding the narration, which must be understood as a fusion of the narrative voices of Calloway, the detective with literary leanings, and Martins, the author of Westerns with an eye for details and a sharp memory.

Literary Allusion

Greene's allusions to other works of literature lend added depth to this thrilling entertainment. He nods toward the prolific Western author Zane Grey, and H. Rider Haggard, author of *Allan Quatermain*. Calloway refers to Henry James in lauding Benjamin Dexter, a veiled version of the real-life author E. M. Forster (whom Greene pokes fun at). The naming of one character as "Kurtz" evokes Joseph Conrad's famous novella *Heart of Darkness*, which *The Third Man* parallels in several respects. In Conrad's novella, a man named Marlow travels upriver in colonial Africa in search of a wayward trader named Kurtz who has forsaken engagement with civilization to live a sort of primitive life in the depths of the jungle. Marlow is analogous with Martins, as both men embark on quests to confront their corrupt counterparts, meanwhile gaining essential self-knowledge. And Conrad's Kurtz is analogous with Greene's Lime, as both men have submitted to their inherent evil nature and so are ultimately slain, their ambiguous dying words suggesting their consciousness of their moral darkness. Also significantly alluded to is the Bible, as the title of the work is understood to evoke the passage in Luke 24 where two men traveling to Emmaus are joined by an unknown third man who turns out to be the risen Christ. In Greene's novella, the third man carrying the body after the accident turns out to be Lime himself. But it is Martins who plays the role of

Jesus in the scene on the Great Wheel in which Lime urges Martins to join his racket, a refiguring of the devil's temptation of Christ. In turn, in betraying Lime, Martins's role shifts to echo that of the biblical Judas.

HISTORICAL CONTEXT

The Third Man is set in Vienna, the capital of Austria, in the late 1940s. The modern republic of Austria came into existence following World War I, when the expansive Austro-Hungarian Empire was broken up. When the Habsburg monarchy relinquished power to allow the birth of the republic, the nation was originally declared to be named "German Austria" and to be "part of the German Republic," but in the 1919 Treaty of Saint-Germain-en-Laye the Allies obliged the nation to exclude "German" from the name, and so it became the Republic of Austria. Nonetheless, with a significant portion of the population being ethnic German Austrians, a majority thought union with Socialist Germany, referred to as *Anschluss*, Austria's annexation, would be the best way to forestall any new form of imperialism, and this notion was supported by the first chancellor, Karl Renner. These feelings persisted through the 1920s, and by 1933, in conjunction with the rise of the National Socialist Party, or Nazis, in Germany, Austria's National Socialists were making large gains in local elections and were poised to win shares of parliamentary seats. To keep the Nazis from gaining power, Chancellor Engelbert Dollfuss disbanded the parliament and established an autocratic Fascist state. After civil war between the two major parties left Austria's Fascists still in power, Dollfuss was assassinated in a failed Nazi coup attempt. The succeeding chancellor, Kurt Schuschnigg sought to keep the nation independent of Germany, but by 1938 Nazi gains and political pressures were overwhelming, and in March, Adolf Hitler—who was born in Austria and lived in Vienna through his adolescence—was able to send in his Germany army to occupy the country, and the Anschluss was achieved. Austria effectively merged with Germany, becoming part of the Third Reich.

During the war, some 65,000 Austrian Jews and over 6,000 Romani were killed in the Holocaust, while nearly 250,000 Austrians lost their lives serving in the army of the Third Reich in April 1945, the German forces surrendered Vienna in April 1945 to the Soviet Red Army, with the American, French, and British forces subsequently sweeping in from the north, west, and south. With cold war demarcations already being drawn across Europe between the Communist Soviet bloc and the democratic West, Austria was considered critical central territory. Joseph Stalin clearly wanted as much of Austria as possible on the Soviet side of the descending Iron Curtain. The nation was carved into four occupied territories, with Vienna, situated in the Russian zone, likewise divided up internally. The Soviets helped bring to power the experienced Socialist and former chancellor Renner, who had already established a provisional government declaring Austria's independence from Germany. Through elections in 1945, Leopold Figl, heading the victorious Austrian People's Party, became the new chancellor, while Renner, heading the Socialists, was named to the subsidiary role of president. Those two parties captured around 50 and 44 percent of the vote, respectively, while the nation's Communists garnered less than 6 percent. Austria, for the present ruled by a coalition government, seemed destined to remain out of Stalin's reach.

Although Communists within Austria wielded only minor influence, the four-power occupation of Austria, and its internal cold war division, lasted for ten years. As the economy churned back toward prewar levels through the late 1940s, Figl's coalition focused on alleviating severe food shortages by distributing Allied food rations and de-Nazifying the Austrian government from top to bottom. The government also had to cope with the economic strain of the Soviet seizure in June 1946 of a great deal of Austrian industry within the Soviet zone deemed "German external assets," which they were able to claim based on the occupation agreement signed at the 1945 Potsdam Conference. The Soviet Union's seizure of profits from these assets—which included the grand Danube Shipping Company, oil fields outside Vienna, and 600,000 acres of farmland—would cost Austria an estimated billion dollars over the ten-year occupation, then an astounding sum.

Greene's *The Third Man* is understood to take place in the earliest phase of the four-power occupation of Austria, when much of Vienna remained in ruins. It was, in fact, the producer Sir Alexander Korda who specifically

COMPARE
&
CONTRAST

- **Late 1940s:** Immediately following World War II, food in Vienna is scarce and rationed out in meager portions of 600 calories per person per day; by 1948, rations equal 2,100 calories per day.

  Today: Throughout Austria, which has the twentieth-highest gross domestic product per capita in the world, food is plentiful and is not rationed.

- **Late 1940s:** With the Soviet Union occupying roughly a quarter of Austria and siphoning away profits from industry in that zone, the Austrian government recognizes that Communist Russia poses a significant threat to the nation's sovereignty and autonomy.

  Today: Since Austria's occupiers departed in 1955, leaving the nation to declare its political neutrality with respect to the cold war, and since the Soviet Union disintegrated in

1991, Austria has no concerns about Communism or losing its autonomy.

- **Late 1940s:** Many Austrians cooperated with the Third Reich during World War II, and the postwar Austrian government must address the lingering presence of Nazis. Over 500,000 Austrians are registered Nazis in 1946, but many had joined the party after the *Anschluss*, prompted by fear and mass hysteria. By 1948, over 100,000 government officials have been suspended or removed from their posts, while thousands of war criminals are to be convicted in courts of law and sentenced.

  Today: Far-right political ideologies—marked by nationalism and xenophobia—continue to appeal to a portion of the Austrian population. In 2010, the presidential candidate from the Freedom Party of Austria, which has been characterized as neo-Nazi, wins 15 percent of the vote.

---

requested that Greene pen a screenplay set during this occupation. Greene visited Vienna for three weeks in 1948 and, after being told about the diluted-penicillin racket and being shown the sewers by the British Legation, conceived the story for the film, which he later published as the novella. Although the ambience of the "smashed dreary city" is established in the opening chapter and acutely evoked throughout, Greene did not prioritize any discussion of Austrian political or historical matters in his entertainment. Nonetheless, the logistics of the divisive four-power occupation are essential to the plot, in that the various powers only had exclusive authority within their own zones. The Russians could only have controlled the destiny of Anna Schmidt, whose father is said to have been a Nazi, by first transporting her to the Russian zone via the International Patrol, and the British military police needed to lure Lime into the British zone in order to catch him.

CRITICAL OVERVIEW

Greene concedes in his introduction that the *The Third Man* was never intended to be read, only to be seen, and that the film—which was very popular—should be considered the superior version. Many critics have tended to agree, often faulting Calloway's secondary narration, which serves to dissipate much of the tension inherent in the film. The London *Times Literary Supplement* gave the novella little notice, stating, "The prime interest in this pre-script story is that it shows the way in which one creative mind goes to work on a film." In *Graham Greene*, A. A. DeVitis notes that *The Third Man* is "perhaps Greene's most popular entertainment," but he somewhat dismissively characterizes it as "simple, economical, austere." In *Graham Greene, the Entertainer*, Peter Wolfe ambivalently states, "Thin in inspiration, blurred in focus, and obvious in its emotions, *The Third Man* nevertheless has merit." He posits that in

Lime hides in the tunnels of the underground sewer system. (*Zolran | Shutterstock.com*)

comparison to the film, the novella "makes different points, and generates its own reality"; he concludes, "Although its subject matter clashes with its form, it embodies timeliness, formal learning, and sound seasoned craftsmanship. For these strengths and for its place in Greene's development, it is worth reading."

Other critics have found greater merit in the novella. In *Quadrant*, Neil McDonald affirms that it is a "considerable literary achievement." In *Understanding Graham Greene*, R. H. Miller asserts that "the mark of the skilled novelist is all too evident in the deft handling of the printed version," adding that "the texture of Greene's descriptions" compensate for "what it may lack in sophisticated use of point of view." In "Spies and God's Spies: Greene's Espionage Fiction," William Chace focuses on the unique characterization of Harry Lime, to conclude that the novella is interesting "because of the way it endorses the amoral character of romantically rapid flight in strange places, of perpetual youth apparently maintained against all odds and of conspiracies against the *status quo*."

In "'This Strange, Rather Sad Story': The Reflexive Design of Graham Greene's *The Third*

Man," Norman Macleod argues convincingly that Greene self-consciously structured this work in the established style of his other entertainments so as to comment on that style, and he also included characters—Martins and Calloway— who function as reflections of himself as an author, making the work a sort of postmodern prism. In Macleod's words, "Greene is arguing that he is the same novelist, whether he is being 'serious' or being an 'entertainer,' and that his complex literary voice and personality embrace elements that are only apparently discordant." Macleod concludes, "In all kinds of ways, *The Third Man* is a more interesting—and more significant—piece of fictional writing than it has (usually and tendentiously) been assumed to be."

CRITICISM

Michael Allen Holmes

Holmes is a writer and editor. In the following essay, he considers how Greene's female characters and narrative commentary on women in The

WHAT DO I READ NEXT?

- Greene relates the events of the majority of his adult life in *Ways of Escape* (1980), including his time as a secret agent in Sierra Leone during World War II and his experiences in the film industry.

- John le Carré, who formerly worked for Britain's intelligence agencies MI5 and MI6, may be the world's most famous author of espionage fiction. His best-known work is *The Spy Who Came In from the Cold* (1963).

- The Polish-born British novelist Joseph Conrad legitimized the espionage thriller as a work of literature with *The Secret Agent* (1907), which addresses anarchism and terrorism in London in the late 1880s.

- Vienna as depicted in *The Third Man* bears some resemblance to the unreal city of T. S. Eliot's 434-line poem *The Waste Land* (1922), a challenging modernist work with shifting style, themes, and settings.

- Evelyn Waugh, like Greene, has been classified as a Catholic novelist owing to his own religious identity and his treatment of Catholicism and religious concerns in his works. His novel *Brideshead Revisited* (1945) deals with the grace of God as perceived in the lives of an aristocratic family.

- In *Boy Kills Man* (2005), a young-adult novel by Matt Whyman, two thirteen-year-old best friends are drawn into the violent world of the streets in a city in Colombia.

Third Man *denote the functioning of a strictly masculine moral code in the underworld of Vienna.*

The few women who are present in *The Third Man* do not play especially significant roles. Anna Schmidt is a critical character in that she provides Rollo Martins with information about Harry Lime and also becomes Martins's romantic interest. But in this sense her role boils down to data source and motivating factor;

> ALTHOUGH THE 'CHEERFUL FOOL' WHOM THE READER MEETS AT THE NOVELLA'S OPENING MAY NOT HAVE BEEN ABLE TO PULL THE FINAL TRIGGER, MARTINS RECEIVES A BLESSING ALONG THE WAY—FROM NONE OTHER THAN ANNA."

she is not embroiled in the action and, aside from her acting, she performs very little herself. Otherwise, there is Ilse, Koch's wife, who has almost no lines and likewise serves primarily as a source of information, in this case for the police. The women at the lecture at the Institute serve as comic distractions. And the only other women are those occasional fleeting figures who Martins is inclined to regard with wistful uncertainty, who are given no names and are minimally described. Aside from being subjugated in terms of roles, women seem to be subjugated by the narrator, Calloway, who makes a few comments that can be interpreted as dismissive toward women. Whether Greene intended it or not, a compound effect of this work's treatment of women is the subtle designation of Vienna's criminal underworld as operating within a moral code that can be defined as strictly masculine.

Most of the women in the novella are expressly marginalized. In the scene in which Martins returns to Lime's flat to interview Koch, Ilse is pejoratively described as "a mountainous wife whom he obviously kept under very strict control." Through the remainder of the scene, "his wife" is mentioned just once by the narrator while being named twice by Koch; his comment "Ilse, the keys," does not even elicit a narrative description of her responsive action. When Martins returns again with Anna in tow, the stunned "Frau Koch"—*Frau* meaning "Mrs."—is heard crying and then paces dumbfounded through the crowd. Martins bends over to fumble with his shoelace, and she fails to recognize him. At this point, her role ceases to be relevant. The women at the lecture by "Mr. Dexter" at the Institute function as parodies of elitist upper-class connoisseurs of literature. Mrs. Bannock, "a large woman in black silk," is tactless and overbearing; the Gräfin von Meyersdorf seems to have not even read Dexter's work, nor can she spell "Zane"; and "a gentle kind-faced woman in a hand-knitted jumper" is oozing with overwrought appreciation for Virginia Woolf, significantly remarking, "No one has written about *feelings* so poetically." The only other female characters are those women Martins happens to notice from time to time. There is, as Calloway notes, "a girl—just like any other girl, I thought—hurrying by outside my office in the driving snow"; she is not described. There is also "one beautiful shrewd-looking French journalist who made one remark to her companion and fell contemptuously asleep"—perhaps a feminist unimpressed by the novella's overmasculine milieu.

The one major female character is Anna Schmidt, who, despite her limited appearances, plays a pivotal role, since she serves as an intermediary between the protagonist, Martins, and the antagonist, Lime, who used to be best friends. Although she is no longer in contact with Lime by the time Martins arrives, of all the characters, she had the most intimate relationship with Lime, and only through her does Martins get a sentimental sense for his lost friend. She is the interpersonal link between them. Interestingly, she is portrayed by Greene not as a classical femme fatale—which, being an actress, she plausibly could have been—but as a very average woman. As Martins told Calloway, her face "wasn't beautiful," with a mouth that "didn't try to charm," and he felt no innate physical attraction toward her. According to both Martins and Crabbin, she is a fairly bad actress. On the surface, then, Anna is representative not of attractive women as a motive force (though she will indeed become a motive force for Martins) but of ordinary women generally. Indeed, her assumed name, Schmidt being the German form of "Smith," is an everywoman's name—though one historically based, typically, on the occupation not of a woman but of a man as a blacksmith.

Beyond marginalizing women in terms of roles, Greene has Calloway utter telling comments about women that might be interpreted as stereotypical or even misogynistic. When he sees Martins shed tears at Lime's funeral, he is surprised because Lime was not "the kind of man whom I thought likely to have mourners—genuine mourners with genuine tears. There was the girl of course, but one excepts women

from all such generalizations." This comment is ambiguous because the reason for excluding women as such is unclear: is it because none of their actions can be understood as "genuine," or is it because women are deemed so consistently peculiar that generalizations simply cannot be made about them? What this comment does surely reveal is that Calloway, being a Scotland Yard detective, is more inclined to characterize and assign types to men than women, since dangerous criminals in mid-twentieth-century Europe were surely, as they are in America today, most often men. And if men are more likely to be criminals, Calloway's occupation demands that he devote more attention to men's personalities, motivations, and actions.

Calloway next offers gendered commentary when describing Martins's "great contemporary, Benjamin Dexter," who is understood to be modeled after the British literary giant E. M. Forster. Dexter is said to have "a wider feminine streak" than the novelist Henry James, such that "his enemies have sometimes described his subtle, complex, wavering style as old-maidish." In turn, Dexter's "passionate interest in embroidery" and his habitual tatting, or making intricate patterns with lace, seem "a little affected." With Crabbin imagining Mr. Dexter to be such a character, Martins's claim that he was hit by a soldier when trying to "punch his bloody colonel in the eye" leaves Crabbin speechless. Martins then relates his intent to hunt the colonel down to exact revenge by citing the plot of one of his own westerns—a genre that exemplifies masculine morals and codes of honor. This is, of course, the opposite of what Crabbin has expected from Mr. Dexter.

Two educational theorists who have developed frameworks for moral codes are Lawrence Kohlberg and Carol Gilligan. Kohlberg devised a theory of moral development involving six stages through which a person may progress. A child begins with a basic understanding of right and wrong as defined by what will be punished and what will not; fear is a motivating factor. In the second stage, a child will recognize that morality depends on people's needs. In the third stage, the child becomes aware of social expectations, as exemplified by the golden rule, and the need for other people's approval. Not all people progress through all six stages. The fourth stage is reached when law, social duty, and authority are considered supreme; breaking the law or failing in a social duty produces guilt. At the fifth stage, universal principles of justice are understood as superior to specific societies' laws; laws are intended to uphold these principles, but they do not always do so, in which case they must be changed. A person at the fifth stage will be close to bringing their moral beliefs and their everyday actions into accord. The sixth stage—effectively defining the perfectly moral person—places the highest priority on human life and equality; unethical rules must not only be changed but should also be broken, even if a penalty is incurred. Carol Gilligan, who at first worked alongside Kohlberg, eventually engaged in alternative research and responded to Kohlberg's framework in her own publications—such as *In a Different Voice* (1982)—by demonstrating that girls tend not to follow this specific path of moral development. Instead of basing morality on rules and abstract concepts of justice, girls tend to prioritize interpersonal relationships and the need to care for and love others. Kohlberg's moral code, to the contrary, makes no mention of love and assigns no moral relevance to it—so that an analysis of a woman's moral decisions using Kohlberg's code might lead one to disparage a feminine ethical approach as "subtle, complex, wavering," in Greene's words.

The moral issues in *The Third Man* are, by and large, straightforward. Although Martins is only made aware of his old friend's true character midway through the story, Lime is unconditionally evil; in Kohlberg's scheme, he is perhaps mired in the first stage, content with his murderous behavior as long as he can escape punishment for it. Martins proves exemplary in his morals, foremost in honoring his friendship and seeking to clear Lime's name. He is not seeking to defy authority, but, as in Kohlberg's fifth stage, he is questioning the conclusions drawn by those in authority. Ultimately, reflecting the sixth stage, he selflessly puts his own life at risk for the sake of the many lives being destroyed by Harry's racket. The moral gray area of the story, then, seems to be embodied in Anna, the everywoman. Martins, operating under a masculine moral code, believes that Anna should assist in Lime's capture; Lime's one dishonest life is worth less than the life of even one of the children whose death or derangement he has caused. But Anna withstands his overtures about helping the police, citing her persisting love for Lime as her reason. When he accuses her of loving "a cheat, a murderer"—implying that affection should be withdrawn from such a person—

she responds by declaring that "a man doesn't alter because you find out more about him. He's still the same man." That is, he is still a person who deserves the care of the people with whom he is emotionally interdependent; his breaking moral rules does not justify the refusal of love. Anna's character demonstrates precisely the breach in Kohlberg's code identified by Gilligan; his code does not account for love. Greene may be revealing his opinion of the feminine, care-oriented perspective in these circumstances when he has Anna, at the Josefstadt Theater, playing the wishy-washy role of "an understanding—a terribly understanding—wife" (unlesss she is "an infatuated girl," which seems less likely given her offstage persona).

Anna's moral clarity is indeed disputable. Some might argue that it truly is her civic duty to offer assistance in the capture of a wanted criminal with whom she has a special relationship, as long as her life would not be jeopardized. Others might agree that it is not fair to force her any further into the role of betrayer, since the emotional repercussions of such a malign betrayal of a loved one could persist for years. Different societies have different rules related to when a person becomes legally responsible for failing to assist the police in catching a criminal. Communist and Fascist societies have been notorious for inspiring people to betray their own family members if they merely happen to deliver antigovernment rhetoric within the confines of their own homes, as this alone may make a person an enemy of the state. In *The Third Man*, Anna has at least told the police everything she knows; she could only be expected—or forced—to do more to assist in Lime's capture if the police were to happen to use her counterfeit papers as leverage. But Calloway attempts no such scheme, to the contrary acting aggressively to prevent the Russians from detaining and deporting her. This course of action might be read as Greene's acknowledgment that Anna's ethical stance, as Gilligan would argue, is legitimate and must be respected.

The moral crux of the novella, then, may instead lie in the definitive action that effectively concludes the story: Martins's killing of Lime. Calloway communicates his unofficial ethical viewpoint when he suggests to Martins in the telling afterwards, "We'll forget that bit." Regardless of the military police's actual rules of engagement, and regardless of the fact that Lime has not yet been convicted in a court of

Martin and Lime meet again and ride the ferris wheel as they talk. (zanks22 | Shutterstock.com)

law, Calloway is certain of Lime's guilt, and so, content to ensure that Lime will destroy no more lives, he condones Martins's assassination. In effect, Calloway is—calling to mind Kohlberg's sixth stage—acting to prioritize human life, in particular the child victims, with disregard for the confines of the law. Martins's final comment—"I never shall"—has been read as connoting Martins's tragic awareness of his own capacity to kill, which he has in a sense inherited from the departed Lime; Martins will never be the same. But it seems more likely that Martins is declaring his pride in the act. When hunting rabbits as a boy, he perhaps even wanted to let the poor defenseless animals get away, even if Lime would disparage his aim, but here he has acted decisively out of his own belief in the most ethical course of action, despite the hesitation he must have felt. Although the "cheerful fool" whom the reader meets at the novella's opening may not have been able to pull the final trigger, Martins receives a blessing along the way—from none other than Anna. In their final meeting before the police set the

dominoes toppling, upon hearing that Lime is still alive, she laments, "I wish he was dead." Martins agrees that "he deserves to be," but Anna replies, "I mean he would be safe then—from everybody." Even here she reveals her predominantly care-oriented moral perspective: she wants to protect him from the punishment he clearly deserves, and as she soon asserts, she "won't do a thing to harm him." She does not wish for him to be killed but for him to simply be dead, as if this might be achieved in some nonviolent or nonpunitive way. But Martins does not seem to absorb the subtlety and complexity of her reasoning; she may seem to waver, but she is resolutely retaining her feminine, care-oriented perspective in the face of Martins's overtures about acceding to the masculine moral consequence of capture and punishment. Martins, nonetheless, refuses to allow Lime even a vestige of safety; he focuses only on her stated wish that Harry be dead, and he makes that wish come true. Despite Anna's attempts to take refuge in a cocoon of care-oriented morality, her words are coopted by the agents of retribution,

Calloway and Martins, so that her feminine ethics are subsumed beneath the exclusively masculine ethics of the Viennese underworld.

Source: Michael Allen Holmes, Critical Essay on *The Third Man*, in *Novels for Students*, Gale, Cengage Learning, 2011.

Jim Gribble

In the following essay, Gribble compares the book to the film of the same name, detailing how some of the author's intricate literary subtleties were transferred to the screen.

Since Graham Greene wrote the story *The Third Man* as a first step towards the preparation of the film script one would expect the film to closely reflect the story. The major difference between the two is the figure of Colonel Calloway. The film presents him, from the outside, as a rather humorless, very British, very military man of principle whose only show of feelings is a mild protest to the Russian officer about taking Anna's passport. (Even his concern for the children who are the victims of the penicillin racket is something which he uses to persuade Martins to cooperate). Whereas the story presents him from the inside, as someone who has a keen personal interest in Martins and Anna and who is an intimate acquaintance of the reader. From the first page Calloway, the narrator, adopts a chatty familiarity with the reader:

> Rollo Martins believed in friendship, and that was why what happened later was a worse shock for him than it would have been for you or me (because you would have put it down to an illusion and me because at once a rational explanation—however wrongly—would have come to my mind). If only he had come to tell me then, what a lot of trouble would have been saved.

Calloway's narration continues throughout the story and it is largely through his eyes and words that we see and hear the events and characters. He also makes frequent observations to the reader about what is occurring.

The film firmly abjures such an approach. Although there is an introductory voice-over, which sets the scene in Vienna and introduces us to Martins as he enters Vienna, this is not Calloway's voice but that of an anonymous storyteller and there is no more voice-over narration in the film. Reed and Greene clearly decided to make a film which allows the characters and events to speak for themselves, without mediation.

> THE NIHILISTIC VIEW OF LIFE WHICH HARRY LIME EXPOUNDS ON THE GREAT WHEEL IS PARTLY SOPHISTICAL, PARTLY DESIGNED TO RATIONALIZE HARRY'S GREED AND RUTHLESSNESS, BUT IT HAS AN AFFINITY WITH ANNA'S SENSE OF POINTLESSNESS."

The reason for this change is that the camera is able to take over Calloway's role as omniscient narrator. It would be impossible to convincingly portray on film an army officer whose interest in the characters gives him access to Martins's and Anna's most intimate thoughts, feelings, and conversations. In fact, it is Graham Greene's remarkable technical achievement in the story that manipulates subtle shifts of point of view and time-shifts in order to enable the reader's suspension of disbelief in Calloway's omniscience. As an illustration of Greene's skill, consider what follows after Martins is finally convinced by Calloway of Harry Lime's participation in the penicillin racket. Chapter 11 begins, "After he left me, Martins went straight off to drink himself silly." Ostensibly, the narration continues in Calloway's voice but gradually we are given access to details to which Calloway could hardly be privy, such as the details of Martins's drunken thought processes. The point of view shifts subtly into Martins's consciousness and prepares us for direct access to the discussion between Martins and Anna on the night Martins first sees Harry Lime:

> By this time the spots were swimming in front of Martins's eyes, and he was oppressed by a sense of loneliness. His mind reverted to the girl in Dublin, and the one in Amsterdam. That was the thing that didn't fool you—the straight drink, the simple physical act: one didn't expect fidelity from a woman.

The reader is even able to accept en passant judgments about human nature which could be those of Calloway or of an omniscient narrator: "If you are in love yourself it never occurs to you that the girl doesn't know: you believe you have told it plainly in a tone of voice, the touch of a hand."

The film does not need to suspend the viewer's disbelief about having detailed access to Anna's and Martins's intimate conversations because in the cinema the camera always has omniscient access. And while we could be given access to Martins's drunken thoughts by means of voice-over, this would clearly be intrusive in a film which has abstained from narrative voice-over.

The film virtually reproduces the words of the story in Anna's and Martins's conversation, adding only some delicate visual cues and touches—Martins's flowers and the introduction of the cat. Reed's use of the cat matches Greene's verbal subtlety. Martins says of the cat, "Not very sociable, is she" and Anna replies, "No, she only likes Harry." A little later we see the cat rubbing itself against the shoes of the figure in the darkened doorway and the zither strikes some tense notes. The impossibility of the figure in the darkened doorway being Harry Lime is questioned at an almost subliminal level and Harry's capacity to inspire devotion is also underlined. At the same time the shadowed figure is menacing. The complexity of tone here matches the complexity of tone of the story but does not duplicate it—the film uses its own distinctive means of capturing the essence of the story. Martins taunts him—"Cat got your tongue"—and Harry's amused, cherubic face appears in the limelight. This intensely visual climax shows most clearly that Greene's story was written with the film in mind. Carol Reed takes full advantage of the opportunity Greene offered him and he brings to this memorable moment some visual touches which precisely echo the tones of Greene's story—an intricate blend of lightness, irony, and menace, which focuses on the ambiguous figure of Harry Lime, who exerts such influence over those who have become devoted to him—even the cat.

There is desolation in both story and film—not just the desolation of the mined city but the desolate lives of the characters who inhabit a world of cynicism and disillusionment. Love seems illusory and hopeless in face of such nihilism. And yet there is a comic imaginative exuberance in both the story and the film, which prevents either from becoming merely depressing. Greene's use in the story of the amused observations of Colonel Calloway also enables a degree of detachment from the characters and events which the film does not attempt. And Calloway's mediation of the story works against the reader's immersion in the events, while the film invites the more passive immersion, characteristic of films.

However, Greene does not allow the reader to accept Calloway's judgement entirely. Martins's blundering ineptness and Calloway's amused story-telling contrast strongly with the only genuinely powerful emotion expressed by a character in the story—Anna's heartbroken grief for Harry. Since Calloway presents his story to entertain the reader he is unresponsive to Anna's despair and Greene intends the reader to react to her grief with more naked, unmediated impact:

> She said, "When I got your card, I couldn't say no. But there's nothing really for us to talk about, is there?—nothing."
>
> "I wanted to hear. . ."
>
> "He's dead. That's the end. Everything's over, finished. What's the good of talking?"
>
> "We both loved him."
>
> "I don't know. You can't know a thing like that—afterwards. I don't know anything anymore except—"
>
> "Except?"
>
> "That I want to be dead too."

While these words are spoken in the film they have a much deeper resonance in the story because Calloway and Martins are shown to be insensitive to Anna's intense desolation. Her despair, her sense of the futility of life is redolent of the bleakness of vision in some of Graham Greene's other works. It undermines the 'entertainment' Calloway offers and puts into deeper perspective the events of the story.

In the film, the viewer is caught up in the 'action'—we have no access to Martins's or Calloway's inner life. But Martins's persistence with his reflex response to women shows him to be insensitive to Anna's grief ("You might get my name right") and the martinet Calloway of the film shows little evidence of feelings.

If Greene wants the reader to respond strongly to Anna's despair this would help to explain why Anna is given a much more substantial role in the film than in the story. This is partly because the narrator in the story can only claim access to Martins's account of their intimate conversations—she exists at a remove from the narrator and thus, to some extent, from the reader as well—we have no access to her thoughts and feelings (though, as I have suggested, she does speak from her heart). The camera's omniscient presence inevitably foregrounds Anna in a way that the story does not.

But quite apart from this foregrounding, Reed deliberately gives Anna a more prominent role in the film, from the early moment when we see her walking up the avenue of trees from the cemetery—the shot which prefigures the final shot in the film. She refuses to acknowledge Martins's existence as he waits for her outside the cemetery while the dead leaves fall from the avenue of trees. Graham Greene was surprised that this grim conclusion works so well (perhaps the only time an optimistic conclusion was changed by a film into a pessimistic one). Reed prepared the ground carefully, with touches like the photograph of her laughing face, which she finds in Harry's flat and which she puts in the waste-bin; and with her comment later that Harry said that sometimes she laughed too much (cf. the later exchange between Martins and Anna in both stories and film which concludes with her saying, "There's not enough for two laughs"). The camera examines the signs of inner strain as she tries to be amusing in the mannered costume comedy in which she performs. And, of course, in the film Martins decides to betray Harry in order to save Anna and this she bitterly rejects. This is followed, in the film, by her attempt to save Harry from the police. Reed's preparations give the closing shot of the film a powerful and somber inevitability, perfectly in keeping with the film's starker presentation of events, unmediated as it is by Calloway's story-telling.

The fundamental pessimism of the story is something the reader grasps more fully than the narrator, with his lame conclusion—"Poor Crabbin. Poor all of us, when you come to think of it." The nihilistic view of life which Harry Lime expounds on the Great Wheel is partly sophistical, partly designed to rationalize Harry's greed and ruthlessness, but it has an affinity with Anna's sense of pointlessness. Though of course Anna's sense of futility is due to her capacity to love and thus to be hurt deeply, while Harry's is related to his incapacity for human feeling of a non-exploitative kind—"In these days, old man, nobody thinks in terms of human beings. Governments don't, why should we?"

In the context of post-war Vienna, where national rapacity and greed is controlled only by expediency, Greene allows the question to stand, even though we are aware that Harry's slightly pitying disregard for other people, except as instruments for his purposes is one that comes quite naturally to him. When Orson Welles develops Harry's argument (in the speech which concludes with the reference to Switzerland's centuries of peace leading to the cuckoo clock) Harry's persuasive, self-promoting sophistry is made more vividly apparent. But although we do see it as sophistry in Harry's mouth, Greene is genuinely asking, in both book and film, what are the foundations for moral behavior in a world where personal and social values have been so eroded.

The film encourages a more hostile view of Harry than does the story. He seems more likely to have been capable of killing Martins in the film—his decision not to seems to be governed by the knowledge that Harbin's body has already been disinterred and that Martins has no revelation to make to the police. Whereas in the story it is Martins who has the murderous impulses on the Great Wheel. And Harry's death in the sewer is made more appropriate after his bullet kills Paine. Paine's character is well established in both book and film—the reader and the viewer warm to his amusing, loyal, salt-of-the-earth personality. Harry's death seems more thoroughly deserved after we see Paine shot. (In the story it is another soldier, Bates, who is shot). But Reed allows sympathy for the rat caught in the trap, lost in the echoing labyrinth of the sewers, fingers hopelessly straining through the grille towards the night sky.

The enigmatic figure of Harry Lime explicitly raises questions about the foundations of moral behavior. But his capacity to attract devotion from those who know him, his engaging insouciance, his personal charisma, brings to the fore an implicit dilemma for the reader and the viewer—the conflict between what S.L. Goldberg calls "conduct morality" and "life morality." Harry's participation in the penicillin racket is profoundly immoral conduct. But this does not affect Anna's devotion to Harry as a person. Martins accuses Anna:

> "But you still love him. You love a cheat, a murderer."

> "I loved a man," she said. "I told you—a man doesn't alter because you find out more about him. He's still the same man."

Anna's response reflects what Goldberg calls "The life-moral importance of loving, founded as it is in the particularity, indeed the uniqueness of human beings."

Although Martins is convinced of Harry's guilt, he remains torn in his feelings—appalled by Harry's actions but unable to stop his affections for the man. For the reader and the viewer the test is our first direct encounter with Harry on the Great Wheel. We know what Harry has done and we also know that even this is insufficient to destroy Anna's and Martins's devotion to him. What we make of him when we meet him will reveal to us whether or not we will be torn in our judgement of him. The reader of the story meets a different Harry Lime than does the viewer of the film, partly because the reader's encounter with Harry is mediated through Martins's narration while the film shows us Harry directly.

The reader hears Harry's distinctive whistle through Martins's ears, with all the powerful and emotional resonances for him:

> Somewhere behind the cake stall a man was whistling and Martins knew the tune. Was it fear or excitement that made his heart beat—or just the memories that tune ushered in, for life had always quickened when Harry came, came just as he came now, as though nothing much had happened, nobody had been lowered into a grave or found with cut throat in a basement, came with amusement, deprecating take-it-or-leave-it manner—and of course one always took it.

Harry's whistle had been heard before in the story and Anna's reaction then adds a further resonance for the reader. After meeting Anna, Martins tells Calloway,

> . . . I wanted to say, "Damn Harry. He's dead. We both loved him but he's dead. The dead are made to be forgotten." Instead, of course, all I said was, "What do you think? He just whistled his old tune as if nothing was the matter," and I whistled it to her as well as I could. I heard her catch her breath. . .

To Anna and Martins Harry's signature tune is powerfully evocative of the man, the unique individual to whom they were devoted. The reader's response to Harry is powerfully affected by their devotion to him ("She's a good little thing") but childishly incapable of seeing beyond his own self-interest when he relates that he betrayed her to the police. His immaturity, his boyishness, his incapacity to grasp his own cruelty is what the story emphasizes.

Although Orson Welles is as affable as the Harry Lime of the story, he is made more menacing in the film. In both story and film, Lime asks Martins what his response would be if he were offered twenty thousand pounds if one of the dots "moving like black flies at the base of the Wheel stopped moving forever," but this is followed in the film by the sophistical (and sophisticated) eloquence about the history of violence in relation to creativity. In the story he merely gives "his boyish conspiratorial smile." (cf. Shakespeare's "As flies to wanton boys are we to the gods;/They kill us for their sport").

The film audience has to be presented with a potent, charismatic figure if they are to believe that Harry could have earned the devotion of Anna and Martins, and Orson Welles's powerful voice, confident eloquence, probing eyes, and ambivalent menace combine to give him that kind of credibility. In the story his magnetism is something the reader feels through Anna and Martins rather than in direct response to Harry Lime. But neither the book nor the film allows us to conclude that Anna's devotion to Harry should be overridden by her knowledge of his criminal conduct. In fact the film is even more strongly in her support as she indignantly rejects Martins's help, and walks past Martins at the end. We are meant to feel she is right in all this and in this way the ending of the film is more profound than the ending of the story, revealing the way "life moral" considerations may transcend "conduct morality."

I have discussed what I believe to be the major concerns of the story and of the film and the intricate interaction between Graham Greene and Carol Reed is readily apparent. I will conclude by noting a few revealing details which suggest how subtle this interplay between their imaginations can be.

Readers of the story will notice that Cooler is replaced in the film by Mr. Pepisco, the Romanian, who appears at Martins's lecture for Crabbin and asks if he is writing a new book. Martins replies that it is a murder story called *The Third Man* and that it is based on fact. Pepisco comments that it is dangerous to mix fact and fiction and asks him if he has ever scrapped a book. Pepisco and two dangerous looking villains pursue Martins up a circular staircase. The parrot bites him as he escapes through the window and runs across the waste land. The next shot shows Calloway interviewing Martins, asking, "What happened to your hand?," to which Martins replies, "A parrot bit it." Calloway says impatiently, "Oh do stop it Martins." In the story Martins tries to escape the police at the lecture and while the parrot frightens him into revealing himself to Paine, it does not bite him.

The main reason for these changes is probably to replace most of the literary interchanges of the story with more visual dramatic action. But the irony concerning the parrot echoes a more understated irony in the story, When Martins opens the door to escape the parrot,

> Paine said respectfully, "We were looking for you, sir. Colonel Calloway wants a word with you."
>
> "I lost my way," Martins said.
>
> "Yes sir. We thought that was what happened."

These delicate echoes of the story in the film extend even to the most "literary" subtleties. In the story Calloway speculates on Crabbin's introduction to the lecture: "He would have touched lightly on various problems of technique—the point of view, the passage of time." Greene is knowingly referring to the technical problems he has dealt with so adroitly in his own story, *The Third Man*. In the film an echo of this kind of self-reflexiveness appears in the sequence I referred to above, when Martins replies to Pepisco that his next book is to be called *The Third Man*. These are details, of course, but very satisfying ones for both reader and viewer. They show how Greene's and Reed's imaginations transmute elements of even the most apparently literary subtleties into a form which is accessible to film.

Source: Jim Gribble, "*The Third Man*: Graham Green and Carol Reed," in *Literature Film Quarterly*, Vol. 26, No. 3, 1998, pp. 235–239.

Steve Vineberg

In the following excerpt, Vineberg describes Greene's screenplay for The Third Man *as a "small marvel of novelistic technique."*

> If this book of mine fails to take a straight course, it is because I am lost in a strange region; I have no map. I sometimes wonder whether anything that I am putting down here is true.

Perhaps no other contemporary novelist of worth has had as great an association with movies as Graham Greene. More than a dozen and a half films have been derived from his novels and stories, and he himself worked on the adaptations of four of them (*Brighton Rock*, 1947; *The Fallen Idol*, 1948; *Our Man in Havana*, 1959; and

GREENE HAS CHOSEN THIS SKEWED, BLOCKADED WORLD AS HIS SETTING BECAUSE THE CHARACTER AROUND WHOM THE PLOT SWINGS, HARRY LIME, IS PRESENTED ON SOME LEVEL AS THE RESULT OF THE MORAL CONFUSION THAT PERVADES THE EUROPE OF THE LATE FORTIES."

The Comedians, 1967); he reviewed films for *The Spectator* and *Night and Day* between 1935 and 1940; and he has written a handful of original screenplays as well, the most celebrated of which is *The Third Man*, directed by Carol Reed in 1949. Greene's script of *The Third Man* seems to me worthy of close analysis because it is a small marvel of novelistic technique. Three themes are carefully crosshatched: (1) the social and moral disintegration of post-war Europe; (2) the discrepancy between the real world and the world as fiction orders it; and (3) the nature of personal and social responsibility. Structurally, *The Third Man* is a spy thriller; psychologically, it is the chronicle of the coming of age of a naive Canadian writer, Rollo Martins. Through the employment of literary controls—irony, shift in consciousness, manipulation of the central character by juxtaposing his behavior and the behavior of others towards him, and by examining him in a hostile context—Greene illustrates a novelistic concern with the limitations of fiction in unearthing the truth.

Greene sets *The Third Man* in Vienna just after the Second World War—a burnt-out Vienna that appalls Martins when he first glimpses it, on a bus ride from the airport. Its citizens live in a state of constant deprivation. A "ratty little man" begs a cigarette from Rollo and he appeases Anna's landlady by offering her a handful of them; electricity is rationed; at the Josefstadt Theatre, where Anna performs, foreigners in the audience indicate their appreciation of the performance by throwing bouquets of coveted merchandise—tea from the British and whiskey from Americans. Martins, whose consciousness the film embraces at the outset, experiences Vienna as a post-Apocalyptic Babel: the

Allies have divided the city into four zones—British, American, French and Russian—each with its own landmarks and its own set of restrictions. His first instructions come from the Vice Consul at the airport: "Remember, Vienna is an occupied city. You must be extremely careful to observe all official regulations," but the complex of rules only reveals itself to him when he sets out to investigate the mystery of his friend Harry Lime's allegedly accidental death. Baron Kurtz, the first of Lime's companions whom Rollo encounters, cannot meet him in Sacher's Hotel, where Rollo is staying, because Kurtz is an Austrian and Sacher's is off limits to Austrians. The only bar that will accept Martins' American cash is a dive that Greene describes as follows: "The same semi-nude photographs on the stairs, the same half-drunk Americans at the bar, the same bad wine and extraordinary gins—you might be in any third-rate haunt in any other shabby capital of a shappy Europe." Lime hides out in the Russian zone, where he is safe from the British police (and where he can stay as long as he remains "useful" to the Russians).

The world of *The Third Man* is ruled by boundaries, geography, international politics. They touch the lives of the four major characters—Lime, who survives by manipulating them to his advantage; Colonel Calloway, whose job as police inspector requires him to strike bargains with them; Anna, whom the Russians claim when Calloway learns that Tyler (on Lime's behalf) forged her passport; and Martins, who falls in love with Anna and is thus affected by her difficulties. Furthermore, all the citizens of Vienna (a group not represented by any of the four above-mentioned characters) live under the shadow of international politics and must, like Kurtz, be careful not to antagonize the police by breaking geographical rules. Greene captures the farcical quality of this complicated, precarious political structure in the bizarre scene in which four military policemen, one from each of the foreign powers in residence in the city, arrive at Anna's apartment to transport her to headquarters. The most sympathetic of the quartet, the British M.P., tells her gently, "It's the law, Miss. We can't go against the protocol." Anna protests, "I don't even know what protocol means." "I don't either, Miss," the British M.P. replies.

Greene has chosen this skewed, blockaded world as his setting because the character around whom the plot swings, Harry Lime, is presented on some level as the result of the moral confusion that pervades the Europe of the late forties. On another level he is a modern vice figure whose personality is simply unleashed by an opportune political situation—sick people in need of drugs, poor people in need of money and not averse to obtaining it in morally repugnant ways, like Kurtz and Joseph Harbin. But whatever one's perception of Lime may be, his supremely cynical speech to Martins as they ride on the "Great Wheel" represents the culmination of the political thinking Greene has bared for us in the earlier scenes of the movie: "In these days, old man, nobody thinks in terms of human beings. Governments don't, so why should we?"

The feelings the name "Vienna" invariably evoke for the reader are ironically undercut throughout the film by this bleak vision; Greene emphasizes what Vienna has descended to by reminding us of her cultivated past. After Rollo receives admission to "the military zone of Vienna," we hear a Strauss waltz. En route to Harry's supposed grave, the camera shows us photographs of the dead on other gravestones in the cemetery: one is a dancing master, and others have, Greene suggests, "respectable faces with waxed moustaches and morning coats." Anna's cheap apartment was once a reception room, and her aging landlady strives to retain some scrap of dignity while she accepts Martins' appeasement bribe of four cigarettes. Baron Kurtz, who arranges to meet Rollo at the Mozart Café and who carries an ivory-handled cane and "an elegant little 18th century snuffbox," cuts a jarringly banal figure: "He wears a toupée, flat and yellow with the hair out straight at the back and not fitting close." We learn later that the "Baron" is in truth the son of a butcher and a cloakroom attendant, "a slatternly woman with a malevolent sour face" who blows her nose with her fingers; and that he himself holds down a job as a violinist at the Casanova Club.

As said, *The Third Man* is a spy thriller. Greene establishes this very early, when Rollo arrives at Lime's residence, 15 Stiftgasse, and examines the spy holes in the apartment doors. At the funeral, one of the mourners (Winkel) "carries a wreath that he has obviously forgotten to lay on the coffin"—a suspicious detail—and he and Kurtz watch Rollo, "uneasy and puzzled" at the presence of this stranger. Calloway is described as "more like an observer than a participant in the scene"—another spy—and Paine watches him in conversation with Martins. In order to pump information from Martins, Calloway proceeds to get him drunk, indicating to the waiter by a glance that he should leave the two men alone. Greene insists that Kurtz's "English accent is really too good. A man ought not to speak a foreign language so well"—another suspicious detail. The porter's wife interrupts his dialogue with Martins and Kurtz and gives them an angry look; clearly she has been listening in and does not approve of Rollo's attempts to involve her husband in the business of Lime's death.

In order to penetrate Greene's purpose in writing *The Third Man* as a thriller, it would be useful to examine the structure of the screenplay. The following list covers all the major plot developments in the script, though it is not a precise list of scenes. (Cinematic scenes are mostly very short; *The Third Man* contains one hundred and forty-two of them.) These developments are arranged in two movements that divide the film approximately in half:

FIRST MOVEMENT

1—Martins' arrival in Vienna (airport scene)
2—Martins' bus ride through Vienna
3—Martins' arrival at 15 Stiftgasse; he learns of Lime's death
4—Central Cemetery: Lime's first funeral; introduction of Calloway and Anna
5—Bar scene: Martins and Calloway; Calloway introduces the notion of Lime as racketeer
6—Martins meets Carter and Tombs at Sacher's Hotel and finds a means of staying in Vienna while he investigates Lime's death
7—Mozart Café: Martins meets Kurtz
8—Kurtz takes Martins to the scene of the accident: first interview with the porter
9—Martins refuses the plane ticket and gets a ticket for the Josefstadt Theatre instead
10—Martin's and Anna meet backstage: new light is thrown on Lime's death
11—Second interview with porter: introduction of the idea of "the third man"
12—Anna's papers are confiscated
13—Martins meets Winkel
14—Calloway interrogates Anna (first time); entrance of Brodsky (Russian officer); introduction of Joseph Harbin's photograph
15—Martins and Anna run into Kurtz at the Casanova Club; appearance of Tyler
16—Dawn montage: International Police car; Tyler finishing phone call and leaving home; Winkel leaving home; Kurtz leaving home and walking down street; man with his back to the camera joined by Kurtz, Tyler and Winkel
17—Porter agrees to talk to Martins
18—Anna and Martins reminisce about Lime

19—Discovery of the porter's body
20—Martins' "speech"; entrance of Tyler; Martins runs from Tyler and his men.

SECOND MOVEMENT

1—Calloway tells Martins about Lime
2—Martins tells Anna about Lime
3—Appearance of Lime; first chase through the sewers
4—Revelation: Harbin's body found in Lime's coffin
5—Anna is arrested by Russian M.P.
6—Calloway interrogates Anna (second time); she learns that Lime is alive; Calloway asks Martins' assistance
7—Interview with Frau Kurtz
8—Martins tells Kurtz and Winkel he wants to see Lime
9—Lime and Martins talk on the "Great Wheel"
10—Martins works with Calloway in exchange for Anna's release
11—Martins meets Anna at the train station; she discovers his collusion with Calloway
12—Martins tries to remove himself from Calloway's plan; Calloway takes him to the Children's Hospital
13—Martins as "dumb decoy duck"; Anna enters; second chase through the sewers, resulting in Lime's death
14—Lime's second funeral.

A cursory glance at this list reveals Greene's cleverness as a plot craftsman. The film has almost a perfect circular structure determined by the two funerals of Harry Lime; Lime himself does not appear until two-thirds of the way through the picture (in what must be the most elaborately prepared entrance in movie history); and the first half, which is pure thriller (the serious content—the nature of Lime's activities, Martins' dilemma, etc.—surfaces only in the second half), ends with a send-up of itself when Martins, who thinks he is being kidnaped, finds himself at the Cultural Centre addressing a group of culture-hungry transplanted Londoners. These strategies have thematic significance, too, however. Lime's first funeral is a fiction, so a second funeral is necessary. So much conflicting information is given to us about Lime's life and death that Greene must resurrect him, though perhaps Lime fails, in the final analysis, to set the record straight. And in parodying itself, Greene's pleasant fiction deconstructs itself, revealing a layer of serious drama that the viewer must address. *The Third Man* concerns the creation of fictions.

Film, as writers and directors have demonstrated many times, is ideally suited to handle the theme of the conflict between fact and fiction. The camera moves back, and we realize that we have been looking at a mirror image, or that someone else, someone unexpected, was in the scene all along and we could not have known it. However, the collaboration of Carol Reed and Graham Greene on *The Third Man* is unusual in that Greene, a novelist who normally employs the mode of literary fiction in his exploration of this theme, is linked with an artist whose professional explorative instrument is the camera. Thus the movie works in both ways at once—cinematically and novelistically.

> TYLER (his voice breaking clearly through the twitters): Mr. Martins, I'd like a word with you about your new novel.
> MARTINS: "The Third Man"?
> TYLER: Yes.
> (The meeting slowly quiets to hear them.)
> MARTINS: It's a murder story. I've just started it.
> TYLER: Are you a slow writer, Mr. Martins?
> MARTINS: Pretty quick when I get interested.
> TYLER: I'd say you were doing something pretty dangerous this time.
> MARTINS: Yes?
> TYLER: Mixing fact and fiction, like oil and water.
> MARTINS: Should I write it as straight fact?
> TYLER: Why no, Mr. Martins. I'd say stick to fiction, straight fiction.

The initial debate—the hinge of the spy story—is over the facts of Harry Lime's death. Martins learns from the porter at 15 Stiftgasse that Lime died accidentally and instantaneously, on his own doorstep, "bowled down like a rabbit" by a passing car. The porter claims to have been an eyewitness. Kurtz's version expands on the porter's: Tyler called to Lime from across the road, Lime began to cross, and after he had been hit, Tyler and Kurtz carried him to the far side of the road, where he died. Kurtz contradicts two details in the porter's story—he says that the vehicle was a truck, not a car, and that Lime died only after mentioning Martins' name and arranging for his safe trip home. Kurtz adds that the accident was clearly Harry's fault and that the driver has been officially exonerated. Anna's version, compiled from information given her by Kurtz and Winkel, is comically at odds with what Martins has already heard. She was told that Harry spoke of *her* at the last moment (prompting Martins to remark, "He must have been very clear in his head at the end: he remembered about me too"; that Winkel, Harry's physician, happened to be passing by a few moments after the accident occurred. This story contains too many coincidences for Rollo's satisfaction, and Anna, too, wonders if Harry's death was truly accidental. When Martins and Anna return to 15 Stiftgasse to interview the porter, he insists once again that Harry died at once ("He couldn't have been alive, not with his head in the state it was") and introduces the "third man"—the man who helped Tyler and Kurtz to carry the body across the street. Martins' further investigation sheds no more light on the incident, until the "third man" himself appears and turns out to be Harry Lime.

But this mystery is superficial—merely a dry run for the real mystery of identity at the root of Greene's screenplay, which he fills with alternative views of Harry Lime. Lime's name seems to have a mystical aura about it—it is practically the only name we hear for the first few scenes, it causes Anna to stop and stare at Martins and gains him access to Winkel's home. But who *is* Harry Lime? Rollo makes a drunken slip to Calloway that hints at the confusion of perspectives that the movie will unpack—"I guess there's nobody knew Harry like he did . . . (Corrects himself) . . . like I did"—because rather than fitting together in a jigsaw puzzle picture, like the reminiscences in *Citizen Kane*, the memories the characters offer of Lime cancel each other out. To Rollo he was a childhood hero who befriended and instructed a lonely boy starting at a new school; they drank together and indulged in adolescent tricks (Rollo was always clumsier and got caught); and just before his death, Harry invited Rollo, who he must have known was broke, out to Vienna to work for him in "some sort of charity organization which helped to get medical supplies." To Calloway, "He was about the worst racketeer who ever made a dirty living in this city," a murderer whose death is a blessing. Martins receives confirmation from Kurtz and Anna, but each unwittingly suggests a darker side of Harry—Kurtz says that everyone in Vienna is somehow involved in the black market, and Anna admits that Harry arranged to forge papers for her, though her interpretation of that action is colored by her love for him and by the benefit she has gained from this illegal act. "Harry never did anything," she insists when Calloway confiscates her letters. "Only a small thing, once, out of kindness." And who in the audience would champion the Russian bureaucrats (claiming Anna's "body" once they learn her Estonian origins) over a petty black marketeer who gallantly broke the law for the woman he loved? Who could resist the photograph on Anna's bureau of "a man grinning with great gaiety and vitality at the camera"?

As the film proceeds, however, Rollo's and Anna's efforts to keep their images of Harry alive become a desperate struggle, and even their portrait of the kind Harry, the charitable Harry, begins to seem oddly tainted. Presented with Joseph Harbin's photo, Anna tells Calloway, "You are wrong about Harry. You are wrong about everything . . . . What can I tell you but . . . You've got everything upside down." But this time Calloway has made no accusations; Anna appears to be fighting her instincts—she protests too much. And though in the remarkable scene in which Anna begs Martins to share his memories of Harry with her, he may think he is eulogizing his dead friend, all his recollections, particularly when seen in the context established by Calloway's insinuations, strike us as blatant instances of dishonesty. Harry taught Rollo how to put up his temperature before an exam, how to cheat, how to avoid things, how to perform the three-card trick. "He fixed my papers," Anna adds—and suddenly our perspective on that charitable act shifts. Rollo's summary of Harry was that "he just made it all seem such fun"; now Anna phrases the same sentiment more romantically: "He never grew up. The world grew up round him, that's all—and buried him."

Source: Steve Vineberg, "The Harry Lime Mystery: Greene's *Third Man* Screenplay," in *College Literature*, Vol. 12, No. 1, 1985, pp. 33–44.

SOURCES

Barrie, J. M., *Peter Pan*, Wordsworth Editions, 1993, p. 96.

Brook-Shepherd, Gordon, *The Austrians: A Thousand-Year Odyssey*, Carroll & Graf, 1997, pp. 377–95.

Chace, William M., "Spies and God's Spies: Greene's Espionage Fiction," in *Graham Greene: A Revaluation; New Essays*, edited by Jeffrey Meyers, St. Martin's Press, 1990, pp. 156–80.

Chatman, Seymour, "Who Is the Best Narrator? The Case of *The Third Man*," in *Style*, Vol. 23, No. 2, Summer 1989, pp. 183–96.

Cornwell, John, "The Confessions of Graham Greene," in *Observer*, September 24, 1989, pp. 33–34.

DeVitis, A. A., *Graham Greene*, rev. ed., Twayne Publishers, 1986, pp. 27, 42–45.

Donaghy, Henry J., *Conversations with Graham Greene*, University Press of Mississippi, 1992, p. 72.

Gale, Robert L., *Characters and Plots in the Fiction of Graham Greene*, McFarland, 2006, pp. 299–301.

Greene, Graham, *The Third Man*, Penguin Books, 1999.

Kellogg, Gene, "Graham Greene," in *The Vital Tradition: The Catholic Novel in a Period of Convergence*, Loyola University Press, 1970, pp. 111–36.

Kelly, Richard, *Graham Greene*, Frederick Ungar, 1984, pp. 133–37.

Kunkel, Francis L., *The Labyrinthine Ways of Graham Greene*, rev. ed., Paul P. Appel, 1973, pp. 57–63.

Macdonald, Andrew, "Graham Greene," in *Dictionary of Literary Biography*, Vol. 77, *British Mystery Writers, 1920–1939*, edited by Bernard Benstock and Thomas F. Staley, The Gale Group, 1989, pp. 134–52.

Macleod, Norman, "'This Strange, Rather Sad Story': The Reflexive Design of Graham Greene's *The Third Man*," in *Dalhousie Review*, Vol. 63, No. 2, Summer 1983, pp. 217–41.

McCay, Mary, Review of *The Third Man*, audiobook version, in *Booklist*, Vol. 95, No. 16, April 15, 1999, p. 1542.

McDonald, Neil, "The Return of Harry Lime," in *Quadrant*, January 2000, p. 92.

Miller, R. H., *Understanding Graham Greene*, University of South Carolina Press, 1990, pp. 2–6, 104–106.

Miyano, Shoko, *Innocence in Graham Greene's Novels*, Peter Lang, 2006, pp. 35–42.

Muuss, Rolf E., *Theories of Adolescence*, 6th ed., McGraw-Hill, 1996, pp. 176–208.

Review of *The Third Man* and *The Fallen Idol*, in *Times Literary Supplement* (London, England), August 4, 1950.

Silverstein, Marc, "After the Fall: The World of Graham Greene's Thrillers," in *Novel: A Forum on Fiction*, Vol. 22, No. 1, Fall 1988, pp. 24–44.

Thomas, Brian, *An Underground Fate: The Idiom of Romance in the Later Novels of Graham Greene*, University of Georgia Press, 1988, pp. 1–12.

Wolfe, Peter, *Graham Greene, the Entertainer*, Southern Illinois University Press, 1972, pp. 122–32.

Woodcock, George, "Graham Greene: Overview," in *St. James Guide to Crime and Mystery Writers*, 4th ed., edited by Jay P. Pederson, St. James Press, 1996.

FURTHER READING

Delillo, Don, *Underworld*, Scribner, 1997.
    In this novel, considered one of the best of the late twentieth century, Delillo considers various sorts of underworlds, especially the subconscious of the individual and of modern American society.

Dorril, Stephen, *MI6: Inside the Covert World of Her Majesty's Secret Intelligence Service*, Touchstone, 2002.
This comprehensive study is intended to appease exacting history buffs as well as casually curious readers.

Freud, Sigmund, *The Interpretation of Dreams*, translated by A. A. Brill, Macmillan, 1913.
Greene was made aware of Freudian understanding of the significance of dreams during his psychoanalysis; Freud lived and worked in Vienna but escaped after the *Anschluss* in 1938.

Keyserlingk, Robert H., *Austria in World War II: An Anglo-American Dilemma*, McGill–Queen's University Press, 1988.
In this historical study, Keyserlingk focuses on the Allies' approach and response to Austria's ambiguous participation in World War II.

SUGGESTED SEARCH TERMS

Graham Greene

The Third Man AND Graham Greene

Graham Greene AND entertainment

Graham Greene AND spy

The Third Man AND literature AND film AND adaptation

The Third Man AND film noir

World War II AND Vienna

Vienna AND Austria AND occupation

Vienna AND occupation AND penicillin

Villette

CHARLOTTE BRONTË

1853

While best known for her novel *Jane Eyre*, Charlotte Brontë was also the author of three other novels as well as a small number of poems. Her 1853 novel *Villette* was not particularly well received by Brontë's contemporaries but is regarded among more recent critics and readers as an intense psychological portrait of a young woman tormented by her isolation, sense of loss, and unfulfilled longing. The protagonist of *Villette*, Lucy Snowe, is flung from one set of unpromising circumstances to another, until she resolves to make her way in the (fictional) French-speaking city of Villette. (Brontë herself studied and taught at a girls' school in French-speaking Brussels, Belgium.) There, Lucy is hired first as a governess and soon after as a teacher of English at a girls' school. The novel, based on some of Brontë's own experiences, traces Lucy's emotional journey, her struggle to find connection and personal fulfillment in a world in which single, young women who must provide for themselves are not looked upon with much favor or regarded as having much potential. Throughout the novel, Lucy's emotional battles take their toll on her mental and physical health. In addition to exploring the course of Lucy's personal fortunes, the novel also serves, to some degree, as a commentary on Brontë's society, as it touches on issues of class and religion. The status of women in this society, as well as Brontë's facility in drawing realistic psychological portraits of her characters, have resulted in a sustained interest in this and other Brontë novels.

Charlotte Brontë (The Library of Congress)

First published by the firm Smith, Elder, in London in 1853, *Villette* is available in a modern edition published in 2001 by The Modern Library. This edition includes a section of notes, written by Deborah Lutz, in which most of the French passages of the novel are translated.

AUTHOR BIOGRAPHY

Born in Yorkshire, England, on April 21, 1816, Brontë was the daughter of Patrick Brontë and Maria Branwell Brontë. Brontë's father was an ordained priest in the Church of England, and he raised Brontë and her siblings (four sisters and a brother) with the help of Brontë's aunt following Maria's death in 1821. In 1820, the Brontës moved from Yorkshire to the town of Haworth, where Patrick Brontë's had been appointed curate. With her sisters Maria and Elizabeth, Brontë attended the Clergy Daughters' School at Cowan Bridge in Lancashire in 1824. Along with many other students, Brontë's sisters Maria and Elizabeth contracted tuberculosis, and both died in 1825.

Brontë returned home to study under her father's tutelage. In 1831, with the help of financial support from her godparents, Brontë was able to attend a small private school, Roe Head, run by Margaret Wooler and her sisters. Brontë then taught at the Wooler school from 1835 to 1838. She also worked as a governess. In 1842, Brontë and her sister Emily traveled to Brussels to attend school at the Pensionnat Heger. They remained for a year, returning home after their aunt's death. Brontë returned to Brussels alone to work for a year as a teacher. After returning to England, Brontë and her sisters Emily and Anne sought publication for their poetry, which was published using pseudonyms. *Poems by Currer, Ellis, and Acton Bell* was published in 1846. In 1847, Brontë published the novel that was to secure her fame, *Jane Eyre*, under her pseudonym Currer Bell. It was well received by critics and readers alike.

Brontë soon suffered a number of personal blows. Her brother Branwell and her sister Emily died in 1848, followed by her sister Anne in 1849. Brontë published two more novels: *Shirley* in 1849 and *Villette* in 1853. The following year, she married a man in her father's employ, Arthur Bell Nicholls. Brontë died on March 31, 1855, possibly due to complications from a pregnancy. Following Brontë's death, her friend and biographer Elizabeth Gaskell solicited Brontë's unpublished manuscripts from Nicholls and saw to the publication of Brontë's novel *The Professor* in 1857.

PLOT SUMMARY

Volume One

CHAPTER 1: BRETTON

In the opening chapter of Volume One, the reader is introduced to the first-person narrator of the story, Lucy Snowe. As the story proceeds, the narrator will eventually reveal that she is a much older Lucy, writing the novel later in life than when the events occurred. The young Lucy, the reader is told, often visited her godmother, Mrs. Bretton, in the town of Bretton, in England. Lucy reveals nothing about her own parents or family. She describes the situation in her godmother's home, which Louisa Bretton shares with her teenage son, John Graham Bretton, as a peaceful one that is interrupted by the arrival of a young child, Polly Home.

MEDIA ADAPTATIONS

- In 1970, Charlotte Brontë's *Villette* was adapted as a British television series directed by Moira Armstrong and produced by the British Broadcasting Corporation (BBC).
- A DVD book version of Brontë's *Villette* was released by MiMar Publishing in 2010.
- BBC Audiobooks published an audiocassette recording of their Radio 4 dramatization of *Villette* in 1999. This dramatization is an abridged, adapted version of the story.
- An unabridged audiobook recording of *Villette* on CD was published in 2007 by Naxos Audiobooks. The novel is read by Mandy Weston.

CHAPTER 2: PAULINA

Polly, whose given name is Paulina, begins to form a strong attachment to Graham. With Lucy, Polly is more reserved, but she does seek Lucy's confidence and comfort on occasion.

CHAPTER 3: THE PLAYMATES

The development of a playful relationship between Graham and Polly is depicted. Lucy observes this in a detached manner but listens to and councils Polly when she entrusts her with the secret of her affection for Graham. Polly is told that her father is coming to take her to the Continent (this term refers to continental Europe, as opposed to the British Isles).

CHAPTER 4: MISS MARCHMONT

Lucy returns to her home after six months. Eight years pass. Seeking employment, she secures a position as a caretaker and companion to an ailing elderly woman, Miss Marchmont. The chapter closes with Miss Marchmont's death.

CHAPTER 5: TURNING A NEW LEAF

Lucy resolves to travel to London to decide her next course of action.

CHAPTER 6: LONDON

After only a brief stay in England, Lucy has set her mind on a journey to the Continent. She immediately secures passage on board a ship set to cross the English Channel that night. Lucy meets the young, talkative Ginerva Fanshawe. Lucy arrives in a small port town and seeks lodging.

CHAPTER 7: VILLETTE

Lucy decides to move on to the city of Villette, which Ginerva has mentioned. Seeking lodging, she happens upon the *Pensionnat de Demoiselles* (a school for girls), which takes on both day students and boarders. The school is run by the widow Madame Modeste Beck. Lucy asks Madame Beck for a job and is hired as the governess for Madame Beck's three daughters.

CHAPTER 8: MADAME BECK

Learning that Madame Beck is prone to spying as a means of controlling her school, Lucy remains unperturbed by Madame Beck's methods. After the hasty departure of the school's English teacher, Lucy is asked to immediately take over the class.

CHAPTER 9: ISIDORE

Using her own powers of emotional manipulation, in addition to physically thrusting a girl into a closet and locking her in for the duration of the class, Lucy gains quick control of a decidedly unruly classroom. Lucy also learns that Ginerva Fanshawe is a pupil at the school. Ginerva confides in Lucy that a young man she calls Isidore is romantically pursuing her.

CHAPTER 10: DR. JOHN

When one of Madame Beck's daughters falls ill, Dr. John is summoned. Lucy alludes to the fact that he seems familiar to her.

CHAPTER 11: THE PORTRESS'S CABINET

Dr. John, Lucy suspects, is the object of desire of at least two women in the house: Madame Beck, who Lucy decides handles her futile longing with dignity, and the portress, Rosine, who apparently makes an unwanted advance toward Dr. John.

CHAPTER 12: THE CASKET

In the garden where Lucy takes to walking, the better to enjoy her solitude, she finds a casket, or a box, containing a love letter. Both the author and the intended recipient are unknown.

CHAPTER 13: A SNEEZE OUT OF SEASON

Madame Beck spies on Lucy in an attempt to discover more about the letter. Georgette Beck is out of sorts, and Madame Beck unnecessarily, in Lucy's opinion, summons Dr. John. Another letter is found; Dr. John tears it up, knowing who it is from and suspecting Lucy knows as well.

CHAPTER 14: THE FÊTE

After a student falls ill, Lucy is asked to play the role of a man in the production the school is performing. Reluctantly she agrees but then warms to the task during the performance. At the party afterwards, Lucy realizes that Dr. John is Ginerva's Isidore, but that he is not the suitor she prefers.

CHAPTER 15: THE LONG VACATION

During an eight-week break at the school, Lucy is left alone with a disabled child for whom she must care until the girl's family takes her. Subsequently left alone, she succumbs to a fever, but her ailment seems as much a mental disturbance as a physical one. Her state becomes one of near hysteria, and she leaves the school and finds herself seeking absolution from a Catholic priest, Père Silas. She faints on her way home.

Volume Two
CHAPTER 16: AULD LANG SYNE

Lucy wakes in surroundings that appear to be her godmother's home in England. She discovers that Mrs. Bretton has moved to Villette and brought many of her furnishings with her. Lucy was found and delivered to the Bretton home by the priest to whom she confessed. Although surprised to find herself with Mrs. Bretton, Lucy reveals to the reader that she already knew that Dr. John was Graham Bretton; she simply opted not to share this information either with Graham or with the reader.

CHAPTER 17: LA TERRASSE

Lucy spends the rest of the school vacation, along with an extra two weeks, recuperating in the Bretton home.

CHAPTER 18: WE QUARREL

As Graham and Lucy renew their friendship, she scolds him for thinking so highly of the fickle, shallow Ginerva.

CHAPTER 19: THE CLEOPATRA

At a museum, Lucy encounters Paul Emanuel. He is dismayed by her independence and her frank appraisal of a painting he finds vulgar.

CHAPTER 20: THE CONCERT

Lucy attends a concert with Graham Bretton and his mother. Ginerva Fanshawe, sitting in another section of the theater, regards Mrs. Bretton, whispers a comment to her companion, and laughs at Mrs. Bretton's expense. Graham sees this exchange and immediately dismisses any feelings he once had for Ginerva.

CHAPTER 21: REACTION

Returning to the school, Lucy grieves her return to loneliness. Paul Emanuel attempts to comfort her. She cherishes the prospect of receiving a letter from Graham.

CHAPTER 22: THE LETTER

Having received the letter from Graham, Lucy delays her gratification and does not read it immediately. She tucks it away until she has time to read it alone. When she finally reads it in an isolated garret, she believes she sees the ghost of the nun who is rumored to haunt the school.

CHAPTER 23: VASHTI

As this chapter opens, Lucy confesses, "A new creed became mine—a belief in happiness." She even speaks of the possibility of love, a flame of hope fanned by Graham's invitation to see a theatrical performance. During the show, someone calls out that there is a fire, and a mad rush for the exits ensues. A young woman is hurt, and Graham rushes to help.

CHAPTER 24: M. DE BASSOMPIERRE

Seven weeks pass in which Lucy hears nothing from Graham. She learns from Ginerva that the injured girl from the theater is in fact Ginerva's cousin, the daughter of Ginerva's wealthy uncle, Monsieur de Bassompierre, and that Graham has been spending time with the de Bassompierre family. Mrs. Bretton, via letter, invites Lucy back to the Bretton's home for a visit. The girl, Lucy discovers, is none other than Paulina Home; Monsieur de Bassompierre is Mr. Home.

CHAPTER 25: THE LITTLE COUNTESS

With the Brettons, the Homes, and Lucy reunited, the group enjoys getting reacquainted. Lucy observes the ways in which Paulina has changed and notices Graham making the same observation.

CHAPTER 26: A BURIAL

Lucy realizes that Graham's attentions have turned elsewhere. She buries the letters she has received from him. Paulina becomes increasingly devoted to Lucy, and Lucy is asked to live with the de Bassompierres as Paulina's companion. Valuing her independence, Lucy turns down the offer. Paulina seeks Lucy's reassurance that Graham favors her over Ginerva. Paulina agrees to Lucy's plan to bring Ginerva to a party to which Graham and Paulina both have been invited in order to determine which of them—Ginerva or Paulina—Graham truly favors.

CHAPTER 27: THE HÔTEL CRÉCY

Ginerva questions Lucy, wondering how a person with no money, titles, or connections to speak of manages to obtain an invitation to a party such as Paulina's. At the party, Lucy inwardly considers the differences between Paulina and Ginerva and watches the gentlemen at the party, noting the way they are all drawn to Paulina, despite Ginerva's unquestionable beauty. Paul Emanuel asks forgiveness from Lucy for any way he might have offended her in the past.

Volume Three

CHAPTER 28: THE WATCHGUARD

Lucy recounts her now frequent conversations and quarrels with Paul Emanuel.

CHAPTER 29: MONSIEUR'S FÊTE

On the occasion of Paul's birthday celebration, a misunderstanding prevents Lucy from giving Paul the gift she has made for him. He is angered and hurt, and Lucy later finds him sitting at her desk, exploring its contents. He does not apologize when she discovers him. She gives him her gift, a handmade chain for a pocket watch. Their rift is mended.

CHAPTER 30: M. PAUL

Paul foists upon Lucy lessons in arithmetic. Lucy is amazed at how much academic knowledge Paul wrongfully supposes she possesses. They argue over intellectual matters.

CHAPTER 31: THE DRYAD

Lucy considers her future and ponders the notion of starting her own school. She suspects her feelings for Graham are as effectively buried as his letters to her. As she whispers goodbye to Graham, saying, "You are not mine," Paul overhears her last words, her "Good night, and God bless you!" Another lengthy, philosophical

conversation ensues, at the close of which both Paul and Lucy see the ghostly figure of the nun.

CHAPTER 32: THE FIRST LETTER

Paulina reveals to Lucy that she has received a letter from Graham. She wishes to simultaneously encourage his attention, convey the reciprocity of her feelings, and spare her father the pain of accepting the fact that his daughter is old enough to be in love.

CHAPTER 33: M. PAUL KEEPS HIS PROMISE

Paul takes Lucy and some of the girls from school on an outing to the countryside. Lucy warmly acknowledges how happy Paul becomes when he is able to make others happy. Paul confides in Lucy that he might have to leave the country for a period of several years.

CHAPTER 34: MALEVOLA

Lucy is asked by Madame Beck to take a basket of gifts to the elderly Madame Walravens. There she learns from Père Silas, the same priest to whom she confessed earlier in the novel, that Madame Walravens is Paul's benefactor.

CHAPTER 35: FRATERNITY

Lucy questions Paul about the stories the priest and Madame Walravens told her about his past, including his relationship with the long dead Justine Marie.

CHAPTER 36: THE APPLE OF DISCORD

Lucy, a Protestant, and Paul, a Catholic, argue over the topic of religion.

CHAPTER 37: SUNSHINE

Lucy and Mr. Home discuss Paulina's relationship with Graham. He somewhat reluctantly allows the courting to continue. Lucy divulges the future fate of the couple: Paulina and Graham wed and have children, and Mr. Home lives well into old age.

CHAPTER 38: CLOUD

Lucy learns, after noting Paul's prolonged absence from the school, that he is to sail for the West Indies. Tormented by his impending departure and by the fact that he has not divulged to her the details regarding his trip, Lucy is shocked by Madame Beck's attempts to prevent a final meeting between Paul and Lucy. Madame Beck has Lucy sedated in order to keep her on the school grounds. Lucy somehow overcomes the effects of the sedative and escapes. She happens upon a celebration in town and spies Madame Beck and her family, along with Paul's brother Josef and Père Silas.

CHAPTER 39: OLD AND NEW ACQUAINTANCE

Overhearing the group discussing a wedding and seeing Paul arrive, Lucy assumes the worst. Returning to the school in an overwrought state, Lucy spies the figure of the nun lying in her bed. Approaching it, she finds a bolster of fabric dressed like the nun, and a note attached, addressed to her, allegedly from the nun, bequeathing to Lucy her garments.

CHAPTER 40: THE HAPPY PAIR

Lucy receives a letter from Ginerva in which she explains that she eloped with the Colonel de Hamal and that he, in fact, was the nun. He disguised himself to secretly enter and pass through the dormitories in order to be with Ginerva. As a joke, Ginerva left the figure of the nun for Lucy to find.

CHAPTER 41: FAUBOURG CLOTILDE

Paul arrives at the school, determined to speak to Lucy despite Madame Beck's strenuous objections. In her desperation to speak with him, Lucy admits to loving him. He explains that the marriage she overheard talk of was the impending nuptials of his goddaughter, Justine Marie, to a young German man. Paul then takes Lucy to a small home he has rented for her and explains that he hopes she will live there and begin her own school. They profess their love, and Paul promises to return to her.

CHAPTER 42: FINIS

The novel ends with Lucy explaining how the subsequent years were joyous to her as she opened her own school and waited for Paul's return. She recounts that his ship was destroyed in a storm on his return voyage and encourages the reader to assume Paul safely returned to Villette and to Lucy.

CHARACTERS

Monsieur de Bassompierre
See Mr. Home

Desiree Beck
Desiree is Madame Beck's eldest daughter. Desiree feigns illness in order to be visited by the handsome Dr. John (Graham Bretton).

Fifine Beck
Fifine Beck is Madame Beck's second daughter. Lucy develops an affectionate relationship with Georgette and Fifine.

Georgette Beck
Georgette Beck is Madam Beck's youngest daughter, for whom Lucy displays a genuine affection.

Madame Modeste Beck
Madame Beck runs the *Pensionnat de Demoiselles*, the school for girls that Lucy happens upon when she is in search of an inn in Villette. Madame Beck, whom Lucy states is forty years old, first hires Lucy as a governess for her own children and, not long after, as an English teacher at the school. Throughout the course of the novel, Madame Beck is shown to be shrewd and manipulative. She shamelessly spies on her pupils and instructors and uses the information gathered to her advantage. Lucy admires Madame Beck's intelligence and independence and does not appear to even take issue with Madame Beck's secretive and invasive habits. Her undemonstrative, unsentimental, practical nature also draws respect from Lucy. Suspecting that Madame Beck is interested in pursuing a romantic relationship with Graham Bretton, Lucy becomes frustrated when Madam Beck tampers with Lucy's letters from Graham. Lucy's respect for Madam Beck is further diminished when it becomes clear that Madam Beck is attempting to keep Paul Emanuel from developing a more intimate relationship with Lucy.

John Graham Bretton
John Graham Bretton first appears in the novel as a teenage schoolboy (of sixteen, as Lucy later recalls) whom Lucy knows as Graham. He is the son of her godmother, Louisa Bretton. When Lucy next encounters Graham, ten years later, he is known to her as Dr. John, the doctor who treats the children of Madame Beck at the school in Villette. Graham, or John, becomes the object of Lucy's affection throughout much of the novel, yet Graham, who is also referred to by his first love interest in the novel, Ginerva Fanshawe, as Isidore, has little interest in Lucy beyond friendship. He casually writes her letters that she prizes above all other treasures. Initially Graham is obsessed with the fickle Ginerva, who does not think very highly of him. When Ginerva scorns Graham's mother, Graham becomes quickly

enamored with Paulina Home, whom he treats after an injury. He does not at first recognize Paulina, but before long, recognition is transformed into reminiscing about their shared past at the Bretton home in England. Soon, a romance flourishes. Graham is shown to be kind and sweet but somewhat shallow and occasionally imperceptive.

Louisa Bretton

Mrs. Louisa Bretton, a widow, is the mother of Graham Bretton and the godmother of Lucy. As a child, Lucy visits Mrs. Bretton and confides to the reader how peaceful and enjoyable her stays with her godmother are. Mrs. Bretton is portrayed as kind, motherly, and very close to her son Graham, as well as to Lucy. Like many of the characters Lucy first encounters in England, Mrs. Bretton finds her way to Villette as well. It is to Mrs. Bretton's home in Villette that Lucy is brought after she faints on her way home from confessing to Père Silas. Lucy informs the reader that her godmother lives well into old age.

Mrs. Cholmondeley

Mrs. Cholmondeley is Ginerva Fanshawe's acquaintance and chaperone in Villette.

Colonel de Hamal

Colonel de Hamal is one of Ginerva Fanshawe's love interests. He is depicted as vain, petty, and wealthy, and Ginerva chooses him over Dr. John Graham Bretton.

Josef Emanuel

Josef Emanuel is Paul Emanuel's half-brother. He appears sporadically in the story when he visits Paul.

Paul Emanuel

Monsieur Paul Emanuel is a teacher at Madame Beck's school. Lucy initially finds him to be controlling, overly frank, and at times annoying. Where others fail to notice Lucy at all or think her shy and reserved, Paul sees her as vibrant and somewhat bold. While his interest in her quickly becomes apparent, Lucy, for much of the novel, is embroiled in a battle with herself over her feelings for Graham. After Graham's preference for Paulina becomes clear and finding that she approves of this match, at least more so than she did of his attachment to Ginerva, Lucy denies herself any more emotional indulgences where Graham is concerned. She gradually comes to see that love with Paul is possible and more realistic than anything else she could have imagined.

Lucy's change in feeling toward Paul is often criticized as a fault in the novel, in that the reader is unprepared to believe the likelihood of such a shift in Lucy's feelings, yet as Lucy's attachment for Paul grows, her reflections on her past opinions are colored in a new light, as Lucy attempts to emphasize how Paul's faults can just as easily be embraced as his virtues. She now regards Paul's previously annoying frankness as a refreshing honesty, for example. Before leaving to attend to the Walravens estate in the West Indies, Paul professes his love for Lucy. Although Lucy suggests the possibility that Paul survives the wreck of the ship that was to bring him home, she implies that he never returns.

Ginerva Fanshawe

Ginerva Fanshawe is the young English girl Lucy meets on board the ship bound for Europe. Lucy's descriptions of Ginerva are unrelentingly negative. The girl has an utter disregard for anyone else's feelings and is shown to be selfish, greedy, manipulative, and cruel to those who care about her. Unable to bear the ordinary, good-natured appeal of Graham (known to her as Dr. John), she refers to him as Isidore, in an effort to make him seem more interesting or exotic. Ginerva cruelly allows him to lavish gifts upon her and encourages his courtship, although she feels nothing but repulsion for him. Eventually she elopes with Colonel de Hamal. Lucy informs the reader that, throughout Ginerva's married life, she continues to correspond with Lucy, and describes the trials and sufferings of motherhood.

Goton

Goton is the chef at Madame Beck's school. She occasionally prepares special meals for a grateful Lucy but is also complicit in Madame Beck's desire to control Lucy; she prepares the sedative that Lucy drinks.

Mr. Home

Later known as Monsieur de Bassompierre, Mr. Home is Paulina's father and Ginerva Fanshawe's uncle. The wealthy Mr. Home is known in Villette by his French title, Monsieur de Bassompierre. Lucy becomes reacquainted with Mr. Home when he and Lucy attend the same theatrical production in Villette and Paulina is injured. Mr. Home is extremely protective of his daughter Paulina and is resistant to the idea of her having grown into a young woman, old enough to be pursued by suitors. Paulina initially attempts to shield her father from her romance with Graham, but Mr. Home gradually accepts the idea.

Paulina Mary Home

When the young Lucy first meets Polly at the Brettons' home in England, Polly is a child of six. Although Polly confides in Lucy, and even snuggles with her in bed for comfort, she is in some ways disdainful and dismissive of Lucy, even as a young girl. When they meet again ten years later in Villette, Polly, who now goes by her more adult-sounding given name, Paulina, is somewhat warmer toward Lucy. She is well-liked, charismatic, and intelligent and soon wins the heart of Graham. Lucy fades gradually from Graham's life and watches his romance with Paulina blossom.

Isidore

See John Graham Bretton

Dr. John

See John Graham Bretton

Justine Marie

Although Lucy does not understand at first, and therefore neither does the reader, there are in fact two Justine Maries in the novel. We hear of the first as the young woman to whom Paul Emanuel was betrothed before her death, some twenty years before. The niece of that Justine Marie is a schoolgirl who was given the same name, and Paul Emanuel serves as her guardian. She is related to the Beck family and to the Walravens family. When Lucy spies them together after Paul was to have already departed by ship, she wrongly suspects that the two of them are to marry.

Madame Kint

Madame Kint is the mother of Madame Beck. She appears sporadically in the story to visit her daughter.

Victor Kint

Victor Kint is the brother of Madame Beck. He appears in the story, along with his mother, on random visits to see his sister.

Miss Marchmont

Miss Marchmont is the elderly, ailing woman for whom Lucy works as a caretaker and companion for some time before she leaves for Villette. Miss Marchmont reveals to Lucy that her lover was killed when she was a young woman, and that she has been alone ever since. She is sometimes regarded as an example of what Lucy's possible future self will endure.

Rosine Matou

Rosine is the portress at Madame Beck's school. She answers the door and generally does Madame Beck's bidding.

Henrich Mühler

Henrich Mühler is the suitor of the young Justine Marie.

The Nun

The nun is a figure of legend at Madame Beck's school. As the story goes, a young nun was buried alive for some unknown transgression against her Catholic vows. At several points in the story, Lucy is certain she sees the ghost of the nun. Once, both Lucy and Paul see her. In fact, the nun is later revealed to be Ginerva's suitor, the Colonel de Hamal, disguised in order to pay his lover secret visits.

Madame Panache

Madame Panache is temporarily hired by Madame Beck to teach history at the school.

Polly

See Paulina Mary Home

Père Silas

Père Silas, or Father Silas, is the Catholic priest to whom the Protestant Lucy, in a fit of delirium, fever, or insanity, confesses. He appears to admire Lucy's self-recrimination and suggests that her ability to be critical of herself and of her emotions and motivations would make her a good Catholic. The priest also has connections to the Walraven family and is later encountered by Lucy in the Walravens' home, when he tells Lucy about the first Justine Marie and her fate.

Lucy Snowe

Lucy is the protagonist (main character) of *Villette* and the first-person narrator of the story. From the beginning of the novel, Lucy reveals herself to be extremely reserved and often judgmental of others. From an early age she was left to fend for herself; she makes general references to her relations but not to parents. After a six-month stay with her godmother, Louisa Bretton, the young Lucy (her age is not given) returns to an undisclosed home and allows the reader to assume that she was happy to return to her "kindred." Eight years pass during which Lucy undergoes some amount of turmoil that she does not describe in specific terms. For a time, she is employed as caretaker to the elderly, ailing Miss Marchmont.

During her time in Villette, Lucy tentatively allows herself moments of transformation. Generally reserved, Lucy indulges briefly in her enjoyment of Graham Bretton's company, cherishing the letters he sends her. When his affections shift from Ginerva Fanshawe to Paulina Home, however, Lucy once again buries her emotions, symbolically entombing Graham's letters in the garden. Her turmoil and sense of isolation manifest themselves physically and emotionally when Lucy falls ill and on more than one occasion wanders through Villette in a state of mental distress. Lucy eventually comes to terms with a notion of love devoid of romance and instead based on intellectual compatibility and affection. Paul Emanuel becomes the object of Lucy's love, and she waits eagerly, and in vain, for his return at the end of the novel.

Zélie St. Pierre

Mademoiselle St. Pierre is a teacher at Madame Beck's school. Paul Emanuel informs Lucy that Mademoiselle St. Pierre was once interested in his romantic attentions. However, he never returned that interest. Mademoiselle St. Pierre's disdain for Lucy may at least in part be attributed to her witnessing Paul's attachment to Lucy.

Madame Walravens

Madame Walravens is the elderly old woman to whom Lucy is instructed by Madame Beck to deliver a basket of fruit. She later learns that Madame Walravens is Paul Emanuel's benefactor. It is she who sends Paul to oversee her estate in the West Indies. Lucy later informs the reader that the old woman died at age ninety.

THEMES

Love

In *Villette*, the notion of love is given a complex treatment. Lucy is often a detached observer, as cold as her name, Snowe. In this mode, she regards the displays of love and affection in others almost with disdain and often with disapproval. Early in the novel, when a young Polly cries at being left with strangers and with longing for her father's love, Lucy interrupts the display of emotion before it can go any further. Because Lucy does not share with the reader her own family background, it is unclear why Lucy has so little sympathy for little Polly, yet it is easy to imagine a number of scenarios that would have left Lucy without the experience of being loved by or having love for a parent.

As the novel progresses, Lucy's rigidity about suppressing her own emotions becomes apparent. She internalizes the assumptions of her society that, as she ages, it becomes less likely that she will find love and seems to find herself an undeserving or unwilling host for such emotions. Lucy sees the way others, such as Ginerva Fanshawe, play with the idea of love and toy with the feelings men have for her. Lucy judges Ginerva harshly for this behavior. As Lucy herself grows closer to Graham Bretton, she grows protective of him and more condemning of Ginerva. Lucy even chastises Graham for his ridiculous infatuation with a girl as shallow as Ginerva. Graham is disappointed that Lucy feels this way, and knowing this, Lucy tortures herself for having caused him any grief. She begs for his forgiveness and holds her tongue about Ginerva thereafter. Lucy states, "I grew most selfish, and quite powerless to deny myself the delight of indulging his mood, and being pliant to his will." Her love takes the form of bending herself to the whims and will of another. Although she recognizes Graham's "masculine self-love," Lucy nevertheless thwarts her own inclinations in order to allow Graham to gratify his own needs. "Graham's desire," Lucy insists, "must take precedence of my own."

After Graham has rejected the vapid Ginerva Fanshawe and promises to write to Lucy, she has a very schizophrenic argument with the voice in her head she names Reason. "But if I feel, may I *never* express?" she asks Reason, seeking permission from herself to engage in correspondence with Graham. Reason answers, "*Never!*" Lucy

TOPICS FOR FURTHER STUDY

- In her novel, Brontë repeatedly makes reference to issues related to class and wealth. Lucy is clearly a middle-class woman, having to work for her money, but in an intellectual, professional capacity rather than as a laborer (which would place her in the working class). Graham Bretton is described as bourgeois by the wealthy Ginerva Fanshawe, affirming his own middle-class status. Using print and electronic sources, research the issue of class in nineteenth-century England. How did one's social class status affect educational or economic opportunities? How commonly did members of different classes socialize with one another? What prejudices existed pertaining to social class? Write a report in which you discuss your findings. Be sure to cite all of your sources.

- The mysterious figure of the nun in *Villette* is commonly cited as an element reflective of the gothic romance genre. To investigate this genre further, briefly research the topic of the nineteenth-century gothic romance, and read a novel exemplifying this genre. Ann Radcliffe, a nineteenth-century author who published a number of gothic romances at the end of the 1700s and the beginning of the 1800s, published a highly popular gothic romance, *The Mysteries of Udolpho*, in 1794. Another gothic romance is Maria Edgeworth's *Castle Rackrent* (1800). Write an essay in which you explore the way the novel you have chosen employs the elements of gothic fiction, such as the combination of suspense and mystery with the supernatural or irrational and the incorporation of such elements with an unlikely romance.

- Brontë's novel takes place in the fictional town of Villette. Because Brontë herself spent time at a boarding school in Brussels, first as a student and then as a teacher, it has been speculated that she had French-speaking Belgium in mind as the location of Villette, although Villette could have just as easily been a town in France. Research either Belgium or France, and create a video or photo travelogue in which you discuss its culture, its people, and, briefly, its history. Create a presentation that includes a map of the country and its flag. Consider bringing examples of typical foods. Alternatively, create a Web page in which you present your information, and include links to other related sources.

- Much of Brontë's novel *Villette* takes place in a setting foreign to the protagonist, Lucy. While Lucy is in Villette to teach, rather than to learn, her observations about the differences between her own English Protestant background and the French Catholic people who surround her contribute to her own personal transformation. Similarly, Korean-born Young Ju in An Na's 2003 award-winning young-adult novel, *A Step from Heaven*, must face obstacles similar to Lucy's. She must learn a new language and must find her own place, her own role in a new world that is culturally very different from her homeland. Read *A Step from Heaven* with a book group and seek out the similarities between these two novels that may, on the surface, seem very different. How do Young Ju and Lucy Snowe deal with the difficulties of starting a new life in a new country? Does Lucy cope better, because she is older, or do you think that because her emotional development has been somewhat delayed until her arrival in Villette, she struggles as much as Young Ju? Create either a presentation for your class or an online blog in which members of your group discuss the books' themes, plot, and characters.

regards her true self in this exchange as a being capable of love and emotion and sees Reason, or reality, as the entity trying to destroy this ability to love. She fears that Reason refuses to let her be happy or hopeful, that Reason "could not rest unless I were altogether crushed, cowed, broken-in, and broken-down." Lucy battles with herself for the indulgence of loving and hoping to be loved in return. She acknowledges that perhaps she has no reasonable right to expect anything but a life of work and despondence. Nevertheless, she seeks to disobey Reason, whom she conceives of, interestingly, as "a step-mother" obeyed out of fear, not love. Lucy embraces hope, cherishes the letter from Graham, and then buries her feelings, and the letters, when Graham's love for Paulina becomes apparent.

Lucy's understanding of love evolves further in the third volume of the novel, when she begins to recognize Paul Emanuel's affection for and romantic interest in her. While they argue about intellectual and spiritual matters, they are deeply engaged with one another in a manner that Lucy and Graham never were. When Lucy believes that Paul is engaged to Justine Marie, Lucy is overcome with an unexpected jealousy. Now she begins to understand that her love for Paul is different than the "love born of beauty" that Graham and Paulina share. It was a "Love that laughed at Passion" but was based on "long acquaintance," marked by "constancy," and rooted in intellect. It is a love of which Reason might actually approve. She now regards Paul as her "king." For his part, Paul asks Lucy to receive his love, to "one day share my life. Be my dearest, first on earth." While Brontë is sometimes criticized for shifting Lucy's affections so, as a couple Lucy and Paul are well-suited, and they both acknowledge each other's faults within their love. Lucy does not have to suppress herself in any way with Paul, nor does she desire to, as she did with Graham. This love is mutual and enriching rather than one-sided and diminishing, yet it is almost immediately taken away from Lucy. Paul sails the next day, and Lucy intimates that he dies on his return trip, three years later.

Isolation

In *Villette*, Brontë sketches a psychological portrait of a woman transformed in many ways by her emotional isolation from the world around her. While Lucy mentions kinsfolk, presumably extended family members with whom she lives

when she is not staying with her godmother, Louisa Bretton, the reader is told nothing else about Lucy's family. She is, quite literally, alone in the world. After the death of her employer, Miss Marchmont, Lucy departs for London and then to the Continent, eventually ending up in Villette. Bound to none, her decisions are her own. She seeks solitude in the garden to escape the bustle of the school at times, yet Lucy is almost perpetually alone with her thoughts.

When left completely alone at the school while everyone is away on vacation, Lucy is overcome with loneliness. She develops a fever and wanders constantly in a state of anxiety and despair, unable to rest, stating "a want of companionship maintained in my soul the cravings of a most deadly famine." Lucy confesses to a strange desire, oddly reminiscent of the fate of the legendary nun, who was allegedly entombed alive. Considering the "autumn suns" and "harvest moons," Lucy feels that she "almost wished to be covered in with earth and turf, deep out of their influence; for I could not live in their light." Her isolation has tormented her to the point of suicidal thoughts. One night she arises, claiming to feel sane but utterly hopeless, and goes to the Catholic church to offer a confession. Lucy does not reveal what she tells the priest but states that she possessed a "pressure of affliction" whose weight could no longer be borne.

When Lucy leaves the church, she faints and recovers in the home of the Brettons. For some time, she fears she is hallucinating, not knowing that the Brettons have taken a house in Villette and brought with them many of their furnishings from the house Lucy remembers in England. Graham's (Dr. John's) professional opinion regarding Lucy's mental state is that "cheerful society would be of use; you should be as little alone as possible; should take plenty of exercise." Isolation breeds in Lucy what Graham describes as "hypochondria." It might be regarded by modern readers as a deep depression and is held at bay by the company Lucy shares in the ensuing chapters. Lucy suspects herself of slipping into that former state periodically during other portions of the novel, but through social contact with the Brettons and the Homes, by acknowledging her need to mourn the loss of Graham and take hold of her life once again, and finally through her newfound love for Paul, Lucy is able to remain free of the devastating consequences of the deep emotional isolation she suffers in the earlier part of the novel.

She was a reluctant school teacher, but it led to her power and freedom. (*Noam Armonn | Shutterstock.com*)

STYLE

Unreliable Narrator

An unreliable narrator is a storyteller whose ability to see and tell the truth is questionable. In *Villette*, Brontë employs Lucy Snowe as her first-person narrator. To narrate in the first person is to tell the story from the point of view of a character who refers to himself or herself as "I" throughout the work. It is from Lucy's personal perspective that the events of *Villette* are related to the reader.

Lucy, however, proves herself to be a narrator whose point of view cannot entirely be trusted as objective or, in some cases, even accurate. Her observations are colored by her intense belief in the superiority of the English, Protestant perspective over anything European or Catholic. Furthermore, as a narrator, she knowingly withholds information from the reader. Having introduced the reader to the character who has come to be known as Dr. John, Lucy much later reveals that Dr. John is, in fact, the Graham Bretton who has been introduced much earlier. Lucy further explains to the reader that she knew of his true identity long before she revealed this knowledge either to Dr. John or to the reader. As the novel progresses, Lucy begins to have intense episodes of nervous fevers and apparent hallucinations. Once she establishes her own temporary loss of her grasp of reality, the reader is forced to wonder about the reliability of her subsequent observations. Brontë's use of an unreliable narrator is an effective tool for establishing the psychological tension *Villette* exhibits and also creates an air of mystery that serves the novel's elements of gothic romance.

Gothic Romance

Although *Villette* cannot be strictly characterized as a gothic romance novel, the work does incorporate some elements of this popular nineteenth-century genre. This type of novel incorporates mystery, horror, and supernatural—or apparently supernatural—elements and dovetails such components with a realistic story that often focuses on the domestic cares and romantic prospects of its young female protagonist. Brontë uses Lucy's visions of the nun in a way that recalls the gothic romance genre. Her visions of the nun are so disturbing to her and go so long unexplained that this unexpectedly supernatural element is easily dismissed by the reader as a fiction created by Lucy's disturbed subconscious mind. At the same time, Paul Emanuel seems to lend credence to Lucy's visions, further complicating the reader's understanding of the nun. Eventually, the visions of the nun are explained by Ginerva Fanshawe, who tells Lucy that her lover dressed as a nun in order to infiltrate the school. Lucy's extreme emotional fluctuations, inspired by her vivid imagination and sentimental idealization of Graham Bretton, also contribute to the gothic nature of the novel. Brontë used similar gothic elements in her novel *Jane Eyre*.

HISTORICAL CONTEXT

Religion in Mid-nineteenth-Century England

In *Villette*, Brontë refers often to Protestantism and Catholicism, Protestantism being the dominant religion in England at the time. The two religions have a long-standing history of conflict in England and its neighbor states Scotland, Wales, and Ireland. (England annexed Wales with the 1536 Act of Union. In 1707, the Act of Union incorporated Scotland into the entity that was now known as Great Britain. In 1800, Northern Ireland joined what became known as the United Kingdom of Great Britain and Northern Ireland, although the designation "Britain" was and is still used to designated the entire United Kingdom.) Since 1689, the Church of England, or the Anglican Church, has been the established national faith. While it is a Protestant faith, some elements of Roman Catholicism were incorporated over the years, as the Catholic Church also fought for prominence in England.

By the nineteenth century, while Catholicism still thrived to some degree in Britain (Northern Ireland remained largely Catholic), Catholicism was regarded with some degree of suspicion by Protestants; anti-Catholic attitudes were prevalent. The patriarchal power of the Church, headed by the Pope in Rome and represented by bishops and priests in England in Britain, was regarded as dangerous to English national identity and to the power of the Church of England. As Susan David Bernstein explores in the 1997 *Confessional Subjects: Revelations of Gender and Power in Victorian Literature and Culture*, the 1850s marked a period of increased anti-Catholic sentiment, as

the Pope had recently revived its practice of hierarchical order of bishops and cardinals in England. Bernstein describes the reaction against this legitimization of Catholic procedure as a fear of aggressive action by the Pope in England. Focusing largely on Lucy's confession to the Catholic priest, Père Silas, Bernstein further explores the ways in which Brontë treats Catholicism in *Villette*, demonstrating that while anti-Catholicism exists as a strong element in her work, Brontë additionally links it with English practices that were equally as oppressive to women as the Catholic Church's doctrines were to its believers.

Gender Roles in Mid-nineteenth-Century England

Brontë uses Lucy—an unmarried Englishwoman no longer considered young by the standards of her time and in no way wealthy or connected with the upper classes—to explore the gender limitations in England during the nineteenth century. Lucy must work to support herself, as she has no family to rely on and no marriage prospects. Brontë's depiction reflects an ambiguous attitude toward Lucy's status. While her longing for love and companionship leaves her feeling isolated and depressed, she nevertheless is shown to value her independence. She takes pride in introducing herself as a teacher, in being able to rely on herself and her own abilities. Bernstein describes Lucy as having transgressed against societal norms in that "she voices a discontent rather than accept her meager lot and stifle her affliction, the proper path according to Victorian gender ideology." In Brontë's time, marriage was, for most middle-class women like Lucy, the only path toward economic security, and many women fought for greater economic independence.

The discontent of Victorian women with their limited lot in their world may have been overstated, some scholars maintain. The term Victorian refers to the time period in which Queen Victoria ruled England, from 1837 to 1901. Shani D'Cruze, in an essay in the 2004 *A Companion to Nineteenth-Century Britain*, states, "Certainly some articulate women found Victorian domesticity constraining and longed for the professional, political, or entrepreneurial opportunities and challenges open to their menfolk," and also argues that a good number were content with their family and household obligations as well as with their opportunities for meaningful action within the realms of religion and philanthropy. Other

COMPARE
&
CONTRAST

- **1850s:** The gothic novel, including romances and tales of suspense, is a popular type of fiction. Prominent authors in this genre include Charlotte Brontë, Emily Brontë, Edward Bulwer-Lytton, and Wilkie Collins. Included in this genre are stories with supernatural creatures. Mary Shelley's 1817 *Frankenstein* spawns other creature-based gothic novels, and the genre continues to be popular throughout the nineteenth century, as evidenced by the publication of Bram Stoker's *Dracula* in 1897.

  Today: The contemporary horror genre is a modern outgrowth of the nineteenth-century gothic novel, and a popular series emphasizes the particular fascination with the combination of gothic/horror elements and stories of romance. Stephanie Meyer's *Twilight* series becomes immensely popular with the publication in 2005 of its first volume. The protagonist of the series is particularly fond of nineteenth-century gothic romances, including Emily Brontë's *Wuthering Heights*.

- **1850s:** The Protestant-based Church of England is the national religion and the most widely practiced in England at this time.

  Anti-Catholic sentiment is prevalent during this time.

  Today: The number of Catholics is growing and is in position to become the most widely practiced religion in the United Kingdom, according to a 2007 article in the London *Times*. Immigration of large Catholic populations is cited as a contributing factor in this shift.

- **1850s:** While marriage rate statistics are not kept at this time, in 1857 the British government passes an act, the Matrimonial Causes Act, that revises marriage laws and makes divorce available. Although it is expensive, it becomes possible for individuals of any class to obtain a divorce. Some protest groups suggest a ban on marriage, believing the institution to be damaging and unpopular.

  Today: Britain's divorce rate is among the highest in the world, and marriage rates in England and Wales are cited as being the lowest since 1862, when such statistics began to be gathered.

---

historical scholars, such as John Perkin in *Women and Marriage in Nineteenth-Century England*, disagree, finding,

> Anti-marriage sentiment in nineteenth-century England was so strong that it provoked calls not only for change in the legal relations between husband [sic] and wives but even for a boycott of the institution and a crusade against marriage.

CRITICAL OVERVIEW

Before it was even published, *Villette* was criticized by Brontë's publisher, George Smith, for Lucy's shift in affection from Graham Bretton to Paul Emanuel. According to

Herbert J. Rosengarten in the *Dictionary of Literary Biography*, Brontë was able to convince Smith to publish the novel without revising this element. Many critics, including Rosengarten, have commented not only on the connection between the novel and Brontë's time studying and teaching in Brussels but on the work's relation to an earlier work of Brontë's, *The Professor*, which was published posthumously. Rosengarten emphasizes, however, the ways in which *Villette* is more accomplished than the early works and analyzes the way Brontë "distances herself from her narrator." Surveying the contemporary reaction to the novel, Rosengarten conveys the general sense of disapproval of Lucy's prolonged discontent.

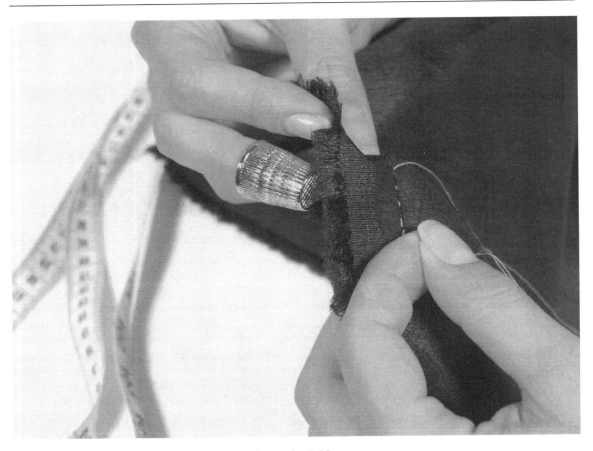

Lucy spend time sewing and looking after the Beck children. (Stephen Coburn | Shutterstock.com)

Modern critics, too, often focus on Lucy's suffering. Beverly Forsyth, in a 1997 essay for *Studies in the Novel*, maintains that in *Villette*, Brontë "explores human motivation in its bleakest and most frightening form. Lucy Snowe is to the outside world an independent, confident teacher, yet to the reader she embodies pain in the form of woman." Forsyth traces the development of Lucy's self-torment, along with her gradually unfolding relationship with Paul Emanuel.

Taking another approach in analyzing Lucy's pain, Tang Soo Ping, in a 1983 essay for the *Explicator*, focuses on the intensification of Lucy's sense of alienation from the world. Ping asserts that Lucy is "closed into herself, cloistered within the world of her feelings and imagination and so separated from the external world." Lucy's struggles, however, are not the sole critical approach to the work. Robyn Warhol, in a 1996 article for *Studies in English Literature, 1500–1900*, investigates the ways in which

Brontë employs the notion of doubleness in her work, and in so doing becomes "actively engaged in rewriting [gender codes]." The doubling to which Warhol refers includes "double perspectives," such as masculinity and femininity, as well as the "doubling of genres," such as the realist and the romantic novel.

Beginning her analysis from the starting point of genre, Toni Wein, in a 1999 essay for *Studies in English Literature, 1500–1900*, points out that Brontë employs elements of the gothic romance, such as the mysterious, ghostly nun, yet Brontë, argues Wein, subverts the reader's gothic expectations by building suspense in a slow and repeated manner, volume by volume, rather than in the more typical pattern of sustaining the reader's "arousal of attention until the narrative climax is reached." Wein further regards Brontë's *Villette* as a "new gothic" novel in its legitimization of female substitution of male objects of desire (such as Lucy transferring

WHAT DO I READ NEXT?

- Brontë's novel *Jane Eyre* is more well known and often more highly regarded than *Villette*. Originally published in 1847, the novel combines elements of the gothic romance with insightful prose that, as in *Villette*, contemplates the role of the single female in nineteenth-century English society. The novel is available from W. W. Norton in an edition published in 2000.

- Charlotte Brontë's sister Emily was a popular novelist of her day. Her *Wuthering Heights* employs gothic elements and tells of the disturbing romance between an orphan boy and the daughter of the man who found and raised him. Originally published in 1847, the novel is available from W. W. Norton in an edition published in 2002.

- First published in 1795, Matthew George Lewis's novel *The Monk* was among the first gothic romance novels to appear in England and was among the few such novels written by a man; the genre was later monopolized by female writers. A modern version was published by Oxford University Press in 2008.

- In the short stories collected in *Dreams and Realities: Selected Fiction of Juana Manuella Gorriti*, the nineteenth-century Argentine author Gorriti explores the lives of women in the turbulent world of nineteenth-century Latin America. The volume was published by Oxford University Press in 2003 and was translated by Sergio Waisman and edited by Francine Masiello.

- John Tosh's *Manliness and Masculinities in Nineteenth-Century Britain: Essays on Gender, Family and Empire*, published in 2004 by Longman, focuses on attitudes about masculinity during the nineteenth century and how these ideas shaped men's relationships with the women in their lives and with their families. Tosh additionally explores the way the concept of imperialism influenced men's perceptions about their own roles in various spheres.

- The 2006 young-adult novel *If You Come Softly* by Newbery Honor author Jacqueline Woodson is set, like Brontë's novel, in a private boarding school. A young couple must struggle to overcome racial prejudices in Woodson's novel. It was published by Perfection Learning and is available in a 2010 paperback edition by Speak.

---

her affections from Graham to Paul), contrasting the work with gothic novels written by men in which the interchangeable nature of their female objects of desire is routine.

CRITICISM

Catherine Dominic

Dominic is a novelist and a freelance writer and editor. In the following essay, she explores the way the characters in the love triangle of Madame Beck, Lucy, and Paul Emanuel employ means of secrecy, surveillance, and manipulation in order to consolidate and assert power in their various relationships in Villette.

Villette is a tale filled with a number of overlapping love triangles, so many, in fact, that the pattern that emerges is more of a complex web than a series of triangular relationships. Graham, Ginerva, and the Colonel de Hamal form one group; Graham, Ginerva, and Paulina form another. Although Lucy's own viability as a romantic contender in a love triangle would be disputed by Lucy herself, she may be regarded as a rival to both Ginerva and Paulina in the battle for Graham's affections. Lucy suspects that even

> IN ALL THE NOVEL'S LOVE TRIANGLES, LOVE IS ONLY ONE MOTIVE FOR ACTION. IN EACH GROUPING, AT LEAST ONE INDIVIDUAL ENGAGES IN MANIPULATION, SUBTERFUGE, OR VOYEURISM AS A MEANS OF CONSOLIDATING POWER, EITHER TO ADVANCE A ROMANTIC AGENDA OR SIMPLY FOR THE SAKE OF FEELING POWERFUL."

Madame Beck views her as a competitor for Graham's love. However, one additional trio, that of Lucy, Madame Beck, and Paul Emanuel, emerges late in the novel and deserves the attention of any student of *Villette*.

In all the novel's love triangles, love is only one motive for action. In each grouping, at least one individual engages in manipulation, subterfuge, or voyeurism as a means of consolidating power, either to advance a romantic agenda or simply for the sake of feeling powerful. (Voyeurism is the secretive observation of others. In terms of clinical psychology, the term is used specifically in relation to the voyeur gaining sexual pleasure from watching others engaged in private or sexual acts. In popular usage, it is more generally understood to refer to the act of watching a person without his or her knowledge.) In particular, Madame Beck, Paul Emanuel, and Lucy are guilty of being drawn to these methods, more so than the other characters in the book. Graham and Paulina are almost completely guileless. Ginerva and the Colonel do engage in the practices of manipulation for their own ends, as when they devise the trick of dressing the Colonel like the legendary nun in order to sneak him into the school to visit Ginerva. Furthermore, Ginerva herself, while typically straightforwardly cruel and too thoughtless to actually be cunning, does manage to sneak away through trickery in order to elope.

However, Madame Beck, Paul, and Lucy are unique in their attraction to power and their use of voyeuristic techniques to gain advantages over others. They unabashedly spy and lie and seem to admire these characteristics in each other. Their use of such methods can be charted through the course of the novel, thereby making

the three-way battle between these characters at the conclusion of the novel seem to be an almost inevitable outcome. In *Villette*, love is rarely free from the interference of those individuals who wish to manipulate, maneuver, and control.

Volume One

As the first volume begins, Lucy's voyeuristic tendencies are already apparent, despite the fact that she is only a girl herself, somewhere in age between six-year-old Polly and sixteen-year-old Graham. Always watching, observing, and often judging the behavior of those around her, Lucy, who shares a room with Polly, overhears little Polly missing her father and crying. Having feigned sleep, Lucy rouses herself loudly enough "to check this scene while it was yet within bounds." Already she has used deception and voyeurism—she has spied by listening while pretending to be asleep—in order to control a situation, in this case to avoid having to listen to Polly cry about her father any longer. Other instances occur during her time at Bretton, but Lucy's tendencies become more pronounced after she begins working in Villette.

During Lucy's first night at the school, two accomplished voyeurs spy on one another. Lucy feigns sleep as Madame Beck enters her room and stares at her apparently sleeping form. Lucy then, through a half-opened eye, watches Madame Beck rummage through all of her belongings. When Madame Beck finds the keys to the locked compartments of Lucy's trunks, she leaves the room with them. Lucy secretly follows, and sees Madame Beck making wax molds of the keys, in order to have copies produced. It is not the last time Lucy witnesses Madame Beck's surveillance techniques. Lucy regards this as "a very pretty system" for running the school; she later states that "Madame Beck ruled by espionage" and then describes her as both "great" and "capable."

The spying and counter-spying in which Madame Beck and Lucy engage continue as they attempt to discern the details concerning the mysterious love letters that are finding their way into the garden. As Madame Beck searches Lucy's belongings for a purloined letter and is once again secretly observed by Lucy, Lucy admires Madame Beck's stealthy, efficient technique. She even contemplates the attraction to Madame Beck she might feel if she were a man. In voyeuristically observing Madame Beck in her own act of espionage, Lucy is able to feel as though she has the upper hand over her employer. Her knowledge lends her the ability to feel as though the situation is under her own control rather than Madame Beck's.

In an exchange with Paul Emanuel just prior to her isolation-bred fever during the school holidays, Lucy admits to a perversity in her character that rivals her delight in secretive observations. Sensing Paul's competitive nature regarding their skill as instructors and how such abilities might compare in the upcoming school examinations, Lucy reveals how she enjoyed making Paul jealous, for "it lit up his nature, and woke his spirit." She delighted in making him angry. This skill is an example of Lucy's emotional manipulations designed to place herself in the position of power in any relationship. For his part, Paul expresses his need to try and control Lucy, stating that she is "one of those beings who must be *kept down*." He sees in Lucy "a passionate ardour for triumph."

Volume Two

Early in the second volume of *Villette*, Lucy informs the reader of one of her deceptions. She reveals that she has known for some time that Dr. John is Graham Bretton, a fact of which she informs the reader long after she first meets Dr. John at the school. She tells the reader she could not even leave a hint, for it "had not suited my habits of thought." That is, she controlled the reader's emotions and reactions by withholding and then divulging information in order to emphasize her position of power. Graham is surprised that she did not approach him with this knowledge or introduce herself; he confesses to feeling discomfort when he found her watching him closely. She had been studying him, presumably, to confirm his identity and perhaps to see whether he suspected hers.

Just as Graham has been the subject of Lucy's gaze, so she becomes the object of Paul's attention once again. In fact, she is watched and scolded for being unchaperoned in a museum and for regarding a particular painting of Cleopatra. Later, at a concert, Lucy once again becomes the watcher, spying Paul from her seat, as he takes charge of a group of young ladies. They trade places again when Paul studies Lucy after she has returned to the school and is crying with loneliness at being separated from Graham. Paul accurately assesses her feelings and offers unwanted advice; he still seeks to control her with his words, to control what he

deems wildness, to implore her to accept the bitterness of life rather than reaching toward a sweetness she cannot possess. While Paul speaks in metaphor, it is clear that he thinks poorly of Lucy for indulging her infatuation with Graham, and he does not withhold his judgment.

Lucy is not immune from her own manipulations. She tantalizes herself with Graham's letter, letting the anticipation of reading it build all day, until she is nearly frantic with the desire to read it. She alternately indulges in her desire to write Graham a letter filled with the warmth of her feelings and forces herself to tear it up and pen a more reasonable reply. When Graham's interest in Paulina becomes something Lucy can no longer ignore, she forces herself to bury his letters, but not before Madame Beck and, Lucy suspects, Paul have stolen the letters to read. Not long after, Lucy again manipulates a situation in order to establish a more powerful position. She suggests to Paulina, who feels threatened by Ginerva, that she ask Ginerva to attend a party with her and Graham so that Graham may be allowed to demonstrate his preference (between Ginerva and Lucy). In this instance, Lucy exercises her manipulative abilities to exert control in a situation in which she is otherwise powerless.

Volume Three

In the third volume, Paul's interest in Lucy intensifies after gradually building throughout the novel. It is only after Graham's feelings for Paulina are made clear that Lucy begins to view Paul as a possible romantic partner. The transformation is gradual in Lucy. She bristles at the way he attempts to control her self-expression, her appearance. She seems to him to be brazen and wild, deserving of his lectures on propriety. After Lucy unintentionally slights Paul, she finds him rummaging through her desk and knows that he has done it before. She finds that she does not mind; she sees in his secret explorations something appealing. When he realizes he has been discovered, he asks, "Do you think I care for being caught? Not I. I often visit your desk." This relationship continues to build, in part, based on the clandestine observations and suspicions that are tested and either disregarded or clung to. Lucy observes Paul's "love of power." Paul, who appears to follow Lucy closely based upon the frequency with which he appears at her side, approaches her as she questions her burial of her feelings for Graham. As she audibly bids Graham farewell, Paul approaches. In fact, Paul

Lucy set sail from England to teach at a girls' boarding school in France. (David Kocherhans | Shutterstock.com)

reveals how closely he watches much of the occurrences in the garden at the school, pointing to a nearby window in a college boarding house and explaining that he uses it as "a post for observation" of "female human nature." He confesses to spying on Lucy, Mademoiselle St. Pierre, and Madame Beck. Ironically, Lucy states that such activities are "dishonourable," despite her own voyeurism.

The ever-vigilant Madame Beck grows suspicious of Lucy and Paul and arranges for Lucy to take a gift basket to the elderly Madame Walravens. This sets into motion a series of schemes designed by Madame Beck to thwart any development of a relationship between Paul and Lucy. Lucy gradually discovers, through Madame Beck's machinations, Paul's history with a young woman twenty years prior. Between Madame Walravens and Père Silas, Lucy is also informed of Paul's long-standing grief, his (Catholic) devotion to God, and his duty to Madame Walravens as his benefactor. Unaware that this carefully

divulged information is designed to thwart her, Lucy continues to grow more interested in and attached to Paul. Eventually she begins to connect the apparently random elements and suspect that her burgeoning interest in Paul is being discouraged. Madame Beck claims that Madame Walravens despises her, and Lucy believes that Madame Beck herself is in love with Paul. Madame Beck then advises Lucy to forget the whole affair. Believing Père Silas and Madame Beck to be conspiring against her, Lucy finds her fears confirmed by Paul, when he tells her that his friends believe her to be dangerous, due to her Protestantism.

As Lucy and Paul simultaneously develop ever stronger feelings for one another, the conspiracy to keep them apart intensifies. Paul is to be sent away by Madame Walravens to mind her estate in the West Indies, and Madame Beck attempts to keep Lucy from him until he sets sail. Madame Beck insists that Lucy cannot marry Paul, and Lucy's suspicions about

Madame Beck's feelings for Paul are confirmed. Madame Beck has Lucy sedated to keep her in bed and away from a possible rendezvous with Paul, but the medication proves ineffective. Lucy's secret surveillance, however, yields faulty information. She spies on Paul at a celebration and comes to believe he is to be married to another. Paul, too, has more secrets. When he finally is able to see Lucy, he first must divert Madame Beck, who threatens to send for Père Silas and who cries out to Paul, "What you do is wrong." Paul is eventually able to reveal to Lucy the depth of his love, and the house he has rented for her to use as a school.

It seems, by this point in the novel, the power struggles, the secretiveness, the voyeurism, and the manipulations can finally end, yet Lucy is not done. On *Villette*'s final page, Lucy continues to exert control over the reader by withholding a final piece of information. Having described the storm that wrecked the ship by which Paul was to return to her, she states that the mourners waiting on the shore "listened for that voice, but it was not uttered." The voice, presumably, was Paul's. Despite the completeness of the devastation Lucy has described, she states that she has chosen to allow her readers hope: "Let them picture union and a happy succeeding life." In complete control over the information she divulges, Lucy first describes what is apparently Paul's death, then tells her readers that they may be allowed to imagine that he lived. She leaves the reader at her mercy, relishing once again the power she has over others.

Source: Catherine Dominic, Critical Essay on *Villette*, in *Novels for Students*, Gale, Cengage Learning, 2011.

Beverly Forsyth

In the following essay, Forsyth reveals the darker side of Lucy Snowe's character, transcending the sadomasochistic traits that have arisen from a life of anger and loneliness.

> Who are you, Miss Snowe? . . .
> Who am I indeed? Perhaps a
> personage in disguise.

Lucy's flip answer doesn't begin to untangle the mystery of who is Lucy Snowe. Is *Villete* a quaint nineteenth-century Gothic novel of lost love or a "terrifying account of female deprivation"? Hidden within the layers of subtext, Charlotte Bronte explores human motivation in its bleakest and most frightening form. Lucy Snowe is to the outside world an independent, confident teacher, yet to the reader she embodies pain in the form of woman. Instead of asking who is Lucy Snowe, perhaps it is more important to ask how did Lucy become the woman she is? Since Lucy refuses to speak of her childhood, the reader can only speculate about Lucy's formative years. Michelle A. Masse, who explores the topic of female pain in *In the Name of Love: Women, Masochism, and the Gothic*, states, "When a woman is hurt, as she is throughout the Gothic, the damage is not originally self-imposed: we must acknowledge that someone else strikes the first blow." Who struck the first blow? Was it an individual or society? A traditional reading dramatically limits the novel's scope. *Villette* is a revealing glimpse into social and sexual deviancies subtly interwoman throughout the text that create a subtext of repressed sexuality, voyeurism, and sadomasochistic behavior. These deviant tendencies give the modern reader a peek into the darker nature of female Gothic. By examining motivation at the subliminal level, the reader can gain an insight into the characters, their world, and perhaps even into the self. Masse states, "Feminism, which insists that we cannot look away from the body or face of a woman in pain, demands its own reconsideration of the narratives psychoanalysis and fiction offer." Unless the reader is willing to look into the face of pain, there is no way to know the real Lucy Snowe. And by taking time to know the woman behind the mask, we just may learn something about ourselves. Lucy's fiery heart lies imprisoned beneath years of frozen pain. Bronte's own words echo with haunting familiarity: The prisoner in solitary confinement—the toad in the block of marble—all in time shape themselves to their lot." Both Lucy and M. Paul have been confined and repressed by their environment. Although M. Paul and Lucy have serious problems, the unfolding relationship between the two lays a solid foundation for their love; because M. Paul accepts Lucy for the woman she is, Lucy finds the love she so desperately craves, which ultimately leads to her own self-acceptance. It would be easy to view Lucy Snowe as a quiet, submissive woman in search of an identity; however, I believe Lucy is a sadomasochistic personality with strong tendencies toward voyeurism and exhibitionism.

As a result of repression, a pattern of sadomasochistic behavior is established consistently throughout Lucy's life. Lucy's repression of information indicates sadistic tendencies. Lucy has already established herself as an unreliable

VILLETTE IS MANY THINGS TO MANY

PEOPLE. LUCY SNOWE IS UGLY, UNLOVED, AND

ALONE. WHAT WOMAN AT SOME POINT IN HER LIFE

COULD NOT UNDERSTAND THIS?"

narrator by suppressing information she should have readily—not grudgingly—shared with the reader. Although she recognizes Dr. John as Graham, she doesn't tell the reader until she is ready. Since Lucy tells this story as an old woman, she plays with the reader's emotions. Did M. Paul drown, or did he return to fulfill his marriage vow? Lucy knows, but the reader can only guess. She leaves the reader dangling in sadistic suspense. By repressing this information she exerts power over the reader. Lucy represses her memory, feelings, and actions as a "powerful aggressive weapon" to control herself; thus, it is only reasonable she would use this weapon to control the reader. Repression also disguises Lucy's sexual desires: "[T]he rebellious and the passionate reemerge as powerful subversive forces, warring against the . . . official surface of acquiescence . . . Passion becomes a kind of caged animal." Lucy's self-inflicted martyrdom produces a type of painful euphoria—an acceptable outlet for Lucy's frustrated desires: the lightning storm "woke the being I was always lulling, and stirred up a craving cry I could not satisfy." Her repression takes on an euphoric tone when she imagines herself like Jael who extends hospitality to the Canaanite army chief Sisera and then kills the slumbering chieftain by driving a tent pin through his temples and into the ground (Judges 4:18–21). According to Judges 4:9, Jael fulfilled Jehovah's prophecy that the Israelite oppressor would be delivered into the hands of a woman. Lucy identifies with both Jael, the slayer, and Sisera, the slain. Emotions rush through her: "the brain thrills to its core." By repressing herself, she receives pleasure from inflicting as well as receiving mental anguish.

The inward voices that torment, tease, and direct Lucy fill a masochistic need. Since there is no healthy outlet for her feelings, Lucy's voices produce a borderline schizophrenia. The voices do not begin until Lucy does not have another individual whose pain she can live through. Masse states, "Women's schooling in masochism, the turning inward of active drives, seems to naturalize that denial and makes it appear to spring from within rather than without." It is because Lucy has so repressed her desires that she must wage a war within herself. Although the voices do become less pronounced as she begins to verbally express her anger, she never completely relinquishes her tormentors.

Initially when Lucy accepts new challenges she exhibits a masochistic need for pain. She does not want to teach an English class or act in the play—both events will cause her pain. Then why does she? Because to accept the challenge will assure her attention even though she believes she will fail in the attempt. Even negative attention is attention. This perverse reasoning would have appalled Lucy, yet psychoanalysis often reveals that "the most powerful motivations of our psyche often turn out to be those we have most deeply repressed." Applying Masse's principle, Lucy's own abuse may allow her to feel she can abuse others. To subdue the rowdy students, Lucy inflicts emotional abuse. Lucy admits she used "sarcasm, flavoured with contemptuous bitterness for the ringleaders." To gain control Lucy administers humiliation by deliberately tearing up a girl's composition in front of the class and locking another girl in the closet. In the play, Lucy inflicts emotional abuse on Dr. John by making love to Ginerva. No doubt Lucy does grow from the new challenges that confront her; however, she initially accepts these challenges for the pain they cause.

The lure of the garden appeals to Lucy's deep-rooted need for pain. When she was with Miss Marchmont, Lucy deliberately forgot the outdoor beauty, so why does the garden attract her now? Even Lucy admits that the "alley was seldom entered even during day, and after dusk was carefully shunned." Lucy's nature responds to the garden—the site of the nun's grave: "imprisoning deep beneath that ground, on whose surface grass grew and flowers bloomed, the bones of a girl whom a monkish conclave of the drear middle ages had here buried alive for some sin against her vow." Once again Lucy is responding to another's pain by seeking out the burial site; however, others shun it for fear of seeing the ghostly embodiment of suffering.

Books are one way masochistic behavior is stressed upon Lucy's impressionable nature.

Masse states, "[T]he intertwining of love and pain is not natural and does not originate in the self: women are taught masochism through fiction and culture." The reader has no way of knowing the kind of books Lucy reads. Yet, the frequent references Lucy makes to books indicate a love for the written word. Many of these books may have a subliminal masochistic strain that Lucy is subconsciously detecting. Observing Polly's pain, Lucy asks: "How will she get through this world, or battle with this life? How will she bear the shocks and repulses, the humiliations and desolations, which books, and my own reason, tell me are prepared for all flesh?" No doubt these books do not openly advocate masochism, but Lucy makes a vivid mental link between women and pain.

Lucy learns masochistic behavior from direct observation. Kate Millett states, "Masochism is female; femininity is masochistic." This theory is extreme, yet it is one that Lucy seems to believe. Polly's sewing is analogous to the child's initiation into womanhood, minute drops of blood on the virginal cambric cloth suggesting the child's loss of innocence. According to Masse, the masochist's "principles never let her stop another woman's suffering, even when given the opportunity." Lucy sees the child willingly hurting herself in an attempt to please her father. Lucy observes the self-inflicted injuries for love as culturally acceptable. Although the child's actions are a clumsy attempt—not consciously masochistic—Lucy views the scene differently: "[S]he bored perseveringly with a needle, that in her fingers seemed almost a skewer, pricking herself ever and anon, marking the cambric with a track of minute red dots; occasionally starting when the perverse weapon—swerving from her control—inflicted a deeper stab than usual; but still silent, diligent, absorbed, womanly." Lucy views the needle as a perverse weapon that the child repeatedly stabs herself with to secure the love of her father. Lucy also takes note that the child endures the pain in womanly silence—suggesting this is proper conduct. It is possible that the father doesn't notice his daughter's self-inflicted injuries, but Lucy does, yet fails to say anything to the child The sewing incident does not in itself suggest that Lucy is sadomasochistic; it is only one in a series of incidents. When the young girl cries in the night, Lucy says: "I suffered her to do as she pleased. Listening awhile in the darkness, I was aware that she still wept—wept under restraint,

quietly and cautiously." Since Polly is not misbehaving, Lucy is not just having to endure a spoilt roommate. The unusual phrasing suggests a distorted view. Polly is in pain; Lucy suffers Polly. Once again Lucy subtly suggests repression of pain is an appropriate womanly action. Lucy doesn't console a grief-stricken child, but breathes in the pain. Lucy also feeds on Polly's pain when Lucy watches Polly quietly praying like a "precocious fanatic" for her Papa. Although Polly and Lucy are close, it is not Lucy, but Mrs. Bretton who attempts to coax the child out of her constant fretting by suggesting she count the ladies who pass the window. Lucy's eye is fixed on Polly as she sits "listlessly, hardly looking, and not counting." There is no indication that Lucy attempts to draw the child into conversation or a game, or divert her unhappiness. A single incident does not indicate masochistic behavior; it is only by examining a series of scenes that a subtle masochistic pattern becomes evident in Lucy's behavior.

Lucy absorbs Miss Marchmont's masochistic behavior, accepting it as her own. Lucy is an orphan with no past; she has no family, no friends, no roots. Lucy lives through Miss Marchmont: "Two hot, close rooms thus became my world; and a crippled old woman, my mistress, my friend, my all Her service was my duty—her pain, my suffering—her relief, my hope—her anger, my punishment—her regard, my reward." Even if given the opportunity, Lucy would never consider rebelling against her oppressor. Lucy has internalized the "strictures that bind" her to her employer. Lucy readily admits she does not go for walks or make friends while living with Miss Marchmont: "I forgot that there were fields, woods, rivers, seas, an ever-changing sky outside the steam-dimmed lattice of this sick chamber, I was almost content to forget it." Miss Marchmont forgets these pleasures as a way to punish herself for being deprived of Frank for 30 years; Lucy denies herself these simple pleasures to gain love and acceptance: "For these things I would have crawled on with her for twenty years, if for twenty years longer her life of endurance had been protracted." Lucy's self-repression is not masochistic self-destruction, but a masochistic need for attention. Early in the novel, Lucy's personality traits bear a strong resemblance to the female masochists in the novels of the Marquis de Sade:

> She is a nameless, faceless unit, not a personality with several names and an over-powering

sexual appeal. She has never had access to the only life-instilling forms of education, those of varied experiences which strengthen individuality, of energy-generating struggles. Nor does she. . . reach a higher level of existence through the verbalization of her beliefs. And she hasn't the slightest trace of imagination.

If someone were to ask Lucy who she was at this point in the novel, it is doubtful she could give an answer apart from Miss Marchmont. It is not even until chapter four that the reader knows for sure that the book is not about Polly and Graham, but rather Miss Snowe. We have no face or qualities to ascribe to the narrator, because this non-being has no life. The reader must learn about other characters before being privileged to receive tidbits of information about the narrator. This frozen woman has no hope, no tomorrow, no life other than what she experiences through others. Miss Marchmont's acceptance brings Lucy more pleasure than her internalized imprisonment. Lucy, who has already demonstrated a tendency for masochism, becomes a fully initiated masochist.

Lucy's sexuality is revealed in her subtle forms of exhibitionism. Many "exhibitionists turn out to be simply shy, submissive" people who have "uncommonly puritanical attitudes about sex." John Berger discusses how the visual observation shapes the physical relationship: "Men look at women. Women watch themselves being looked at. This determines not only most relations between men and women but also the relation of women to themselves. The surveyor of woman in herself is male: the surveyed female. Thus she turns herself into an object—and most particularly an object of vision: a sight." Lucy knows that M. Paul visits her desk and watches her. Lucy is a passionate woman who represses her sexual nature partly to avoid conflict with her Puritan ethics and partly as a "libidinal form of self-negation." Since there is no outlet for her desires, this form of exhibitionism is socially acceptable and an appropriate forum to express her sexuality—in essence she experiences "psychic relief." To know one is being watched is "a sign of one's erotic value." For Lucy to know that she is being observed by M. Paul charges the relationship with a sexual chemistry. Romance "revitalize[s] daily routines by insisting that a woman . . . doing what women do all day, is in a constant state of potential sexuality. You never can tell when you may be seen and being seen is a precious opportunity." For a plain, ugly woman

such as Lucy, exhibitionism is a socially appropriate means to affirm her sexuality. Dr. John views Lucy as an "inoffensive shadow" with a tendency toward drabness, whereas M. Paul sees a sensual, coquettish woman in a scarlet dress. An indirect form of voyeur-exhibitionism is when Lucy catches M. Paul at her desk:

> Do you think I care for being caught? Not I. I often visit your desk. Monsieur, I know it.

No accusations are made, no apology given. The desk scene is a subtle scene of dominance and submission. M. Paul touches, caresses, and rearranges items; when Lucy doesn't object it becomes a voluntarily submissive act. In effect, the desk activity becomes a release of sexual energy—a kind of foreplay that both religious people find acceptable. When M. Paul reveals to Lucy that he is a connoisseur of feminine nature, the conversation takes on an intimate tone: "I watch you and others pretty closely, pretty constantly, nearer and oftener than you or they think . . . There [his observation room] I sit and read for hours together; it is my way—my taste. My book is this garden; its contents are human nature—female human nature." Although Lucy remarks that such conduct is not right, she does not walk away. By revealing this secret about himself, M. Paul's conversation flows with an undercurrent of acknowledged sexuality. M. Paul's gaze is an overt sexual act: "The male gaze eroticizes, represents, and empowers the phallus. The body of a woman being gazed at is a fetish for the gazer, who asserts his own position as subject, hers as spec(tac)ular object." Although Dr. John and Lucy do not have the same kind of relationship as she does with M. Paul, there is also a chemistry that Lucy recognizes in Dr. John's gaze: "[W]hy then did he concentrate all on me—oppressing me with the whole force of that full, blue, steadfast orb? Why, if he would look, did not one glance satisfy him? why did he turn on his chair, rest his elbow on its back, and study me leisurely?" Lucy recognizes the erotic quality of the male gaze when she reveals to the reader that Dr. John's thoughts of her "were not entirely those of a frozen indifference, after all." Dr. John does not merely glance at Lucy, but his look takes on sexual dominance. Since Lucy does not look away from a prolonged stare, she acknowledges the attraction. This is a subtle form of exhibitionism since the proper conduct for a woman at that time would have been to modestly look away.

Lucy is a voyeur. She constantly watches people and she is aware that others watch her. Lucy is not appalled at Madame Beck's surveillance, because Lucy spies on her employer. By telling her story, Lucy invites the reader to gaze upon her. The reader in effect becomes a voyeur: "[I]f writing takes gazing as its metaphor, reading becomes viewing as well." Lucy exposes herself; even if the reader does not like what s/he sees, at least s/he is not looking away. Lucy encourages others to participate in her own deviance.

Lucy and M. Paul are attracted to each other because of their deviancies. Lucy is not an individual pattern of sadomasochism, but her attraction to M. Paul reflects a dual pattern in which "a sadist and a masochist pair up in a relationship to satisfy their complementary tastes." M. Paul tells Lucy: "I was conscious of rapport between you and myself." A surface reading may only indicate physical similarities, yet M. Paul is actually seeing similar mannerisms when he asks, "Do you know that you have many of my looks? I perceive all this, and believe that you were born under my star." Although M. Paul concentrates on their physical similarities, he is actually perceiving that they exhibit the same mannerisms. Lucy wonders if the "morbid fancies" that M. Paul warns her about are "wrought in his own brain." By observing Lucy, M. Paul perceives they are very much like in personality.

Villette is many things to many people. Lucy Snowe is ugly, unloved, and alone. What woman at some point in her life could not understand this? Although M. Paul and Lucy have serious deviancies, they are both in the process of transcending their stagnant, repressive lives. M. Paul softens his tyrannical attitude and Lucy doesn't have to converse with inward voices. She is learning to share her feelings. Anger and loneliness shaped their worlds. When these two people look at each other, they don't look away. They like what they see. Although M. Paul and Lucy possess these perversities, they are not perverted. Their behavior allows them to function as best they can in their oppressive environment. M. Paul would not have repressed Lucy. On the contrary, he is the catalyst that helps her to find herself. Although M. Paul is a devout Catholic, he encourages Lucy to remain a Protestant. Lucy says, "[H]e freely left me my pure faith. He did not tease nor tempt." During M. Paul's three year absence, he regularly writes to Lucy: "By every vessel he wrote; he wrote as he gave and as he loved, in full-handed, full-hearted plenitude."

Because M. Paul loves and accepts the woman Lucy, Lucy learns to accept herself. Through M. Paul's love and her own self-acceptance, Lucy's school thrives, and she gains a new found confidence: "Few things shook me now; few things had importance to vex, intimidate, or depress me: most things pleased—mere trifles had a charm." If Lucy and M. Paul had married, Lucy would not have been just a wife and mother. M. Paul appreciates her intellect, and together they would have operated a school. Her roles as wife and mother would have merely opened up new experiences and growth. If Lucy had married M. Paul, she would have transcended into Elaine Showalter's "Female phase." However, Lucy stays in the "Feminist phase" since she desires this denied opportunity of marriage. Since feminism does not look away from a woman in pain, by openly acknowledging these deviancies the reader is a step closer to understanding the dark need that calls to Gothic women of yesteryear and today. Once the Gothic woman understands that she does not need to embrace pain to exist, "then the Gothic [tragedy] will come to an end." Until that day, Gothic novels should not merely be read as quaint literature, but as a soul-wrenching cry for love.

Source: Beverly Forsyth, "The Two Faces of Lucy Snowe: A Study in Deviant Behavior," in *Studies in the Novel*, Vol. 29, No. 1, Spring 1997, pp. 17–25.

W. Robertson Nicoll

In the following excerpt, Nicoll presents a review of Villette *and a response by Brontë in which she protests the reviewer's judgments of her character.*

The *Christian Remembrancer*, a Church of England quarterly, contained in its number for April, 1853, an article entitled "New Novels by Lady G. Fullerton and Currer Bell." The Currer Bell novel, it is needless to say, was *Villette*. The reviewer began his notice of *Villette* with the following paragraph:

> After threading the maze of harrowing perplexities thus set forth by Lady Georgiana, having followed her characters through their course of fatal mistakes and hairbreadth perils, witnessed their bursts of tragic passion, listened to their turgid sentiments, and felt the whole to be the offspring of a lively imagination, confined within too narrow a sphere of observation—a society removed so high above many of the real troubles of life that they must needs allow idleness and luxury to coin some for them—it is, we own, a relief to turn to the work-day world of *Villette*. The rough winds of

> WHO MY REVIEWER MAY BE I KNOW NOT, BUT I
> AM CONVINCED HE IS NO NARROW-MINDED OR
> NATURALLY UNJUST THINKER."

common life make a better atmosphere for fiction than the stove heat of the "higher circles." Currer Bell, by hardly *earning* her experience, has, at least, won her knowledge in a field of action where more can sympathise; though we cannot speak of sympathy, or of ourselves as in any sense sharing in it, without a protest against the outrages on decorum, the moral perversity, the toleration of, nay, indifference to vice which deform her first powerful picture of a desolate woman's trials and sufferings—faults which make *Jane Eyre* a dangerous book, and which must leave a permanent mistrust of the author on all thoughtful and scrupulous minds. But however alloyed with blame this sympathy has necessarily been, there are indications of its having cheered her and done her good. Perhaps, as it was argued of Gertrude, she has been the better for a little happiness and success, for in many important moral points *Villette* is an improvement on its predecessors. The author has gained both in amiability and propriety since she first presented herself to the world—soured, coarse and grumbling; an alien, it might seem, from society, and amenable to none of its laws.

In the *Christian Remembrancer* for October, 1853, under the heading "Notices," the following paragraph appears:

A letter from the author of *Villette*, which claims at once our respect and sympathy, complains of a passage in our recent review of that work (April, 1853), which she says has been interpreted by some persons—not by herself, for this was not her own unbiassed impression—in a sense the remotest possible from our thoughts. We wrote in entire ignorance of the author's private history, and with no wish to pry into it. But her keen and vivid style, and her original and somewhat warped mode of viewing things, must excite speculation in her readers as to the circumstances of education and position which have formed both mind and style. Some grave faults in her earliest work we thought most easily accounted for by the supposition of a mind of remarkable power and great capabilities for happiness exposed to early and long trial of some kind, and in some degree embittered by the want of congenial employment. We refer our readers to the article in question, where not only is there no insinuation of "a disadvantageous occult motive for a retired life," but such a supposition is at variance with the whole line of suggestion, which tends to attribute what we must differ from in her writings to adverse circumstances, not to conduct. We will, however, distinctly state that we had no idea in our mind, and therefore could not desire to express any suspicion, of an unfavourable cause for a life of seclusion. We now learn with pleasure, but not with surprise, that the main motive for this seclusion is devotion to the purest and most sacred of domestic ties.

It is some time since I made note of this, but I had little hope of being able to recover the actual letter. However, in the *Christian Remembrancer* for July, 1857, there is printed a long and very able article on the life of Charlotte Brontë. In that article the letter in question is given in full as follows:

TO THE EDITOR OF THE *Christian Remembrancer.*
HAWORTH, NEAR KEIGHLEY, YORKSHIRE,
July 18, 1853.
SIR: I think I cannot be doing wrong in addressing you a few remarks respecting an article which appeared in the *Christian Remembrancer* for last April. I mean an article noticing *Villette.*
When first I read that article I thought only of its ability, which seemed to me considerable, of its acumen, which I felt to be penetrating; an occasional misconception passed scarce noticed, and I smiled at certain passages from which evils have since risen so heavy as to oblige me to revert seriously to their origin. Conscious myself that the import of these insinuations was far indeed from truth, I forgot to calculate how they might appear to that great public which personally did not know me.
The passage to which I particularly allude characterises me by a strong expression. I am spoken of as *an alien—it might seem from society, and amenable to none of its laws.*
The *G*—newspaper gave a notice in the same spirit. The *E*—culled isolated extracts from your review, and presented them in a concentrated form as one paragraph of unqualified condemnation.
The result of these combined attacks, all to one effect—all insinuating some disadvantageous occult motive for a retired life—has been such that at length I feel it advisable to speak a few words of temperate explanation in the quarter that seems to me most worthy to be thus addressed, and the most likely to understand rightly my intention. Who my reviewer may be I know not, but I am convinced he is no narrow-minded or naturally unjust thinker.

To him I would say no cause of seclusion such as he would imply has ever come near my thoughts, deeds or life. It has not entered my experience. It has not crossed my observation.

Providence so regulated my destiny that I was born and have been reared in the seclusion of a country parsonage. I have never been rich enough to go out into the world as a participator in its gaieties, though it early became my duty to leave home in order partly to diminish the many calls on a limited income. That income is lightened of claims in another sense now, for of a family of six I am the only survivor.

My father is now in his seventy-seventh year; his mind is clear as it ever was, and he is not infirm, but he suffers from partial privation and threatened loss of sight; and his general health is also delicate, he cannot be left often or long: my place consequently is at home. These are reasons which make retirement a plain duty; but were no such reasons in existence, were I bound by no such ties, it is very possible that seclusion might still appear to me, on the whole, more congenial than publicity; the brief and rare glimpses I have had of the world do not incline me to think I should seek its circles with very keen zest—nor can I consider such disinclination a just subject for reproach.

This is the truth. The careless, rather than malevolent insinuations of reviewers have, it seems, widely spread another impression. It would be weak to complain, but I feel that it is only right to place the real in opposition to the unreal.

Will you kindly show this note to my reviewer? Perhaps he cannot now find an antidote for the poison into which he dipped that shaft he shot at "Currer Bell," but when again tempted to take aim at other prey—let him refrain his hand a moment till he has considered consequences to the wounded, and recalled the "golden rule."

I am, Sir, yours respectfully,
C. BRONTE.

The critic goes on to say:

Though criticism was never more needed than in the case of Currer Bell, yet this is inevitably a sad book for critics. We do not blame ourselves for what has been said in our pages of the author of *Jane Eyre*. We could not do otherwise than censure what was censurable. Where would books get their deserts, how could judgment be given, if private considerations had weight to restrain independent public opinion? Critics would then be no better than partial friends. But such revelations as this book gives us are a lesson to weigh words. We should never forget that the unknown author has a known side; that he is not an abstraction. And here we are taught that the private side of a character may be in strong contrast to its public manifestation; that it needs rare discernment to form a true estimate of a writer from his works; and that the boldest, most fearless style, may emanate from a nature which has its sensitive, shrinking, timid side. We believe that all the critics thought they had a tolerably tough nature to deal with, that there was no need to sugar the bitter draught in this instance; and when a woman assumed a masculine tone, wrote as well or better than any man among them, and showed herself afraid of nothing, that gallantry and patronising tenderness which is commonly bestowed upon women was changed to gall. And now the administrators of the potion have to reflect on the private most feminine sorrows of this Amazon; of a patient life of monotonous duty; of the passionate hold the purest domestic affections had on her character; and which among them, if he could rewrite his criticism, would not now and then erase an epithet, spare a sarcasm, modify a sweeping condemnation? We own it wounds our tenderest feelings to know her sensitiveness to such attacks; and when she sheds tears over the *Times* critique—of all things in the world to weep over—our heart bleeds indeed.

I am not aware that Charlotte Brontë on any other occasion wrote to an editor about any review of her books.

Source: W. Robertson Nicoll, "Charlotte Brontë and One of Her Critics," in *Bookman*, Vol. 10, January 1900, pp. 441–43.

W. R. Greg

In the following review, Greg praises the power of the narrative, the individuality of the characters, and the graphic descriptions in Villette.

'*Villette*,' by the author of '*Jane Eyre*,' is a most remarkable work—a production altogether *sui generis*. Fulness and vigour of thought mark almost every sentence, and there is a sort of easy power pervading the whole narrative, such as we have rarely met. There is little of plot or incident in the story; nearly the whole of it is confined to the four walls of a *Pensionnat* at Brussels; but the characters introduced are sketched with a bold and free pencil, and their individuality is sustained with a degree of consistency, which marks a master's hand. The descriptions, too, whether the subjects of them be solemn, ludicrous, or pathetic, are wonderfully graphic and pictorial. It is clear at a glance that the groundwork and many of the details of the story are autobiographic; and we never read a literary production which so betrays at every line the individual character of the writer. Her life has evidently been irradiated by but scanty sunshine, and she is besides disposed to look rather pertinaciously on the shady side of every landscape. With an almost painful and unceasing consciousness of possessing few personal or circumstantial advantages; with spirits naturally the reverse of buoyant; with feelings the reverse of demonstrative; with affections strong rather than warm, and injured by too habitual repression; a keen, shrewd, sagacious, sarcastic, observer of life, rather than a genial partaker in its interests; gifted with intuitive insight into character, and reading it often with too cold and critical an eye; full of sympathy where love and admiration call it forth, but able by long discipline to dispense with it herself; always somewhat too rigidly strung up for the hard struggle of life, but fighting sternly and gallantly its gloomy battle,—the character which Lucy Snowe has here drawn of herself presents rather an interesting study than an attraction or a charm.

Source: W. R. Greg, "Recent Novels: *Villette*," in *Edinburgh Review*, Vol. 97, No. 198, April 1853, pp. 387–90.

Athenaeum

In the following review, the critic suggests that this story is in some places tedious, sometimes trivial, but the heart of its distinct protagonist keeps it alive.

So curious a novel as '*Villette*' seldom comes before us,—and rarely one offering so much matter for remark. Its very outset exhibits an indifference to certain precepts of Art, singular in one who by artistic management alone interests us in an unpromising subject. . . . During a considerable portion of the story we are led to expect that the old well-thumbed case of conscience is going to be tried again,—and that, having dealt with a Calvinistic missionary in '*Jane Eyre*,' Currer Bell is about to draw a full-length picture of a disciple of Loyola in '*Villette*.' But the idea is suggested—not fulfilled. Our authoress is superior to the nonsense and narrowness that call themselves religious controversy. She allows the peril of the position to be felt,—without entering on the covert rancour, the imperfect logic, and the inconclusive catastrophe which distinguish such polemics when they are made the theme of fiction.—We fancied, again, from certain indications, that something

of supernatural awe and terror were to be evoked:—but as a sequel to these, Currer Bell has fairly turned round upon herself with a mockery little short of sarcasm.—The tale is merely one of the affections. It may be found in some places tedious, in some of its incidents trivial,—but it is remarkable as a picture of manners. A burning heart glows throughout it, and one brilliantly distinct character keeps it alive.

'*Villette*' is a book which will please much those whom it pleases at all. Allowing for some superfluity of rhetoric used in a manner which reminds us of the elder Miss Jewsbury—and for one or two rhapsodies, which might have been "toned down" with advantage,—this tale is much better written than '*Shirley*,' the preceding one by its authoress.

Source: "A Review of *Villette*," in *Athenaeum*, No. 1320, February 12, 1853, pp. 186–88.

SOURCES

Bernstein, Susan David, "Histories and Fictions of Victorian Confession: Anti-Catholic Rhetoric and *Villette*," in *The Confessional Subjects: Revelations of Gender and Power in Victorian Literature and Culture*, University of North Carolina Press, 1997, pp. 41–72.

"Biographical Note," in *Villette*, The Modern Library, 2001, pp. v–vii.

Brontë, Charlotte, *Villette*, The Modern Library, 2001.

D'Cruze, Shani, "The Family," in *A Companion to Nineteenth-Century Britain*, edited by Chris Williams, Blackwell Publishing, 2004, pp. 253–72.

Dolin, Tim, Introduction to *Villette*, by Charlotte Brontë, Oxford University Press, 2000, pp. ix–xxv.

Forsyth, Beverly, "The Two Faces of Lucy Snowe: A Study in Deviant Behavior," in *Studies in the Novel*, Vol. 29, No. 1, 1997, pp. 17–25.

Gledhill, Ruth, "Catholics Set to Pass Anglicans as Leading UK Church," in *Times* (London, England), February 15, 2007, http://www.timesonline.co.uk/tol/news/article1386939.ece (accessed July 16, 2010).

Macinnes, Allan I., "Acts of Union: The Creation of the United Kingdom," in *BBC: British History In-Depth*, http://www.bbc.co.uk./history/british/empire_seapower/acts_of_union_01.shtml#4 (accessed July 16, 2010).

"Marriages," in *Office for National Statistics*, http://www.statistics.gov.uk/cci/nugget.asp?id = 322 (accessed July 16, 2010).

Merrett, Andy, "UK Divorce Rate Could Rise 2% in 2010," in *Family Relationships Magazine*, January 4,

2010, http://familyrelationships.org.uk/uk-divorce-rate-could-rise-2-in-2010 (accessed July 16, 2010).

Perkin, John, "Introduction," in *Women and Marriage in Nineteenth-Century England*, Routledge, 1999, pp. 1–9.

Ping, Tang Soo, "C. Brontë's *Villette*," in *Explicator*, Vol. 42, No. 1, 1983, pp. 25–26.

Rosengarten, Herbert J., "Charlotte Brontë," in *Dictionary of Literary Biography*, Vol. 21, *Victorian Novelists Before 1885*, Gale Research, 1983, pp. 25–54.

Warhol, Robyn, "Double Gender, Double Genre in *Jane Eyre* and *Villette*," in *Studies in English Literature, 1500–1900*, Vol. 36, No. 4, 1996, pp. 857–75.

Wein, Toni, "Gothic Desire in Charlotte Brontë's *Villette*," in *Studies in English Literature, 1500–1900*, Vol. 39, No. 4, 1999, pp. 733–46.

FURTHER READING

Byatt, A. S., and Ignês Sodré, Introduction to *Villette*, by Charlotte Brontë, The Modern Library, 2001, pp. xiii–lv.
> Byatt, a novelist, and Sodré, a psychoanalyst, introduce Brontë's *Villette* through a discussion of the novel's characters and their psychological and emotional motivations.

Gaskell, Elizabeth, *Gothic Tales*, edited by Laura Kranzler, Penguin, 2001.
> Gaskell was a nineteenth-century writer of gothic fiction and a friend of Charlotte Brontë. Gaskell additionally wrote a biography about Brontë, which was published in 1857. In this volume of stories, editor Kranzler gathers Gaskell's short gothic fiction, much of which was published anonymously by Gaskell in the mid-nineteenth century.

Gilbert, Sandra M., and Susan Gubar, *The Madwoman in the Attic: The Woman Writer and the Nineteenth-Century Literary Imagination*, 2nd ed., Yale, 2000.
> Originally published in 1979, Gilbert and Gubar's work is considered a groundbreaking work in the area of feminist criticism. The critics examine the literary and cultural context of the works of many nineteenth-century female authors, including novelists Jane Austen, Emily and Charlotte Brontë, and George Eliot, as well as a number of poets.

Grinnell, George, "Introduction: Interpreting Romantic Hypochondria," in *The Age of Hypochondria: Interpreting Romantic Health and Illness*, Palgrave Macmillan, 2010, pp. 1–27.
> In *Villette*, Dr. John Graham Bretton suggests that Lucy Snowe is suffering from hypochondria. In this introduction, Grinnell explores the prevalence of such a diagnosis in the nineteenth century and discusses the cultural and literary context of hypochondria.

Rogers, Rebecca, *From the Salon to the Schoolroom: Educating Bourgeois Girls in Nineteenth-Century France*, Pennsylvania State University Press, 2005.
> Rogers explores the social, cultural, and political aspects of the education of girls in mid-nineteenth century France. Students of *Villette* will benefit from this work by gaining historical insights into the realities of a French education during this time period, as Brontë's protagonist became immersed in this world.

SUGGESTED SEARCH TERMS

Charlotte Brontë

Charlotte Brontë AND Villette

Charlotte Brontë AND feminist criticism

Charlotte Brontë AND Emily Brontë

Charlotte Brontë AND Elizabeth Gaskell

Charlotte Brontë AND religion

Charlotte Brontë AND gothic romance

Charlotte Brontë AND Lucy Snowe

Charlotte Brontë AND Villette AND madness

Charlotte Brontë AND French education

Glossary of Literary Terms

A

Abstract: As an adjective applied to writing or literary works, abstract refers to words or phrases that name things not knowable through the five senses.

Aestheticism: A literary and artistic movement of the nineteenth century. Followers of the movement believed that art should not be mixed with social, political, or moral teaching. The statement "art for art's sake" is a good summary of aestheticism. The movement had its roots in France, but it gained widespread importance in England in the last half of the nineteenth century, where it helped change the Victorian practice of including moral lessons in literature.

Allegory: A narrative technique in which characters representing things or abstract ideas are used to convey a message or teach a lesson. Allegory is typically used to teach moral, ethical, or religious lessons but is sometimes used for satiric or political purposes.

Allusion: A reference to a familiar literary or historical person or event, used to make an idea more easily understood.

Analogy: A comparison of two things made to explain something unfamiliar through its similarities to something familiar, or to prove one point based on the acceptedness of another. Similes and metaphors are types of analogies.

Antagonist: The major character in a narrative or drama who works against the hero or protagonist.

Anthropomorphism: The presentation of animals or objects in human shape or with human characteristics. The term is derived from the Greek word for "human form."

Anti-hero: A central character in a work of literature who lacks traditional heroic qualities such as courage, physical prowess, and fortitude. Anti-heroes typically distrust conventional values and are unable to commit themselves to any ideals. They generally feel helpless in a world over which they have no control. Anti-heroes usually accept, and often celebrate, their positions as social outcasts.

Apprenticeship Novel: See *Bildungsroman*

Archetype: The word archetype is commonly used to describe an original pattern or model from which all other things of the same kind are made. This term was introduced to literary criticism from the psychology of Carl Jung. It expresses Jung's theory that behind every person's "unconscious," or repressed memories of the past, lies the "collective unconscious" of the human race: memories of the countless typical experiences of our ancestors. These memories are said to prompt illogical associations that trigger powerful emotions in the reader. Often, the emotional process is primitive, even primordial. Archetypes are the literary images that grow out of the "collective unconscious." They appear in literature as incidents and plots that repeat basic patterns of life. They may also appear as stereotyped characters.

Avant-garde: French term meaning "vanguard." It is used in literary criticism to describe new writing that rejects traditional approaches to literature in favor of innovations in style or content.

B

Beat Movement: A period featuring a group of American poets and novelists of the 1950s and 1960s—including Jack Kerouac, Allen Ginsberg, Gregory Corso, William S. Burroughs, and Lawrence Ferlinghetti—who rejected established social and literary values. Using such techniques as stream of consciousness writing and jazz-influenced free verse and focusing on unusual or abnormal states of mind—generated by religious ecstasy or the use of drugs—the Beat writers aimed to create works that were unconventional in both form and subject matter.

Bildungsroman: A German word meaning "novel of development." The *bildungsroman* is a study of the maturation of a youthful character, typically brought about through a series of social or sexual encounters that lead to self-awareness. *Bildungsroman* is used interchangeably with *erziehungsroman*, a novel of initiation and education. When a *bildungsroman* is concerned with the development of an artist (as in James Joyce's *A Portrait of the Artist as a Young Man*), it is often termed a *kunstlerroman*.

Black Aesthetic Movement: A period of artistic and literary development among African Americans in the 1960s and early 1970s. This was the first major African-American artistic movement since the Harlem Renaissance and was closely paralleled by the civil rights and black power movements. The black aesthetic writers attempted to produce works of art that would be meaningful to the black masses. Key figures in black aesthetics included one of its founders, poet and playwright Amiri Baraka, formerly known as LeRoi Jones; poet and essayist Haki R. Madhubuti, formerly Don L. Lee; poet and playwright Sonia Sanchez; and dramatist Ed Bullins.

Black Humor: Writing that places grotesque elements side by side with humorous ones in an attempt to shock the reader, forcing him or her to laugh at the horrifying reality of a disordered world.

Burlesque: Any literary work that uses exaggeration to make its subject appear ridiculous, either by treating a trivial subject with profound seriousness or by treating a dignified subject frivolously. The word "burlesque" may also be used as an adjective, as in "burlesque show," to mean "striptease act."

C

Character: Broadly speaking, a person in a literary work. The actions of characters are what constitute the plot of a story, novel, or poem. There are numerous types of characters, ranging from simple, stereotypical figures to intricate, multifaceted ones. In the techniques of anthropomorphism and personification, animals—and even places or things—can assume aspects of character. "Characterization" is the process by which an author creates vivid, believable characters in a work of art. This may be done in a variety of ways, including (1) direct description of the character by the narrator; (2) the direct presentation of the speech, thoughts, or actions of the character; and (3) the responses of other characters to the character. The term "character" also refers to a form originated by the ancient Greek writer Theophrastus that later became popular in the seventeenth and eighteenth centuries. It is a short essay or sketch of a person who prominently displays a specific attribute or quality, such as miserliness or ambition.

Climax: The turning point in a narrative, the moment when the conflict is at its most intense. Typically, the structure of stories, novels, and plays is one of rising action, in which tension builds to the climax, followed by falling action, in which tension lessens as the story moves to its conclusion.

Colloquialism: A word, phrase, or form of pronunciation that is acceptable in casual conversation but not in formal, written communication. It is considered more acceptable than slang.

Coming of Age Novel: See *Bildungsroman*

Concrete: Concrete is the opposite of abstract, and refers to a thing that actually exists or a description that allows the reader to experience an object or concept with the senses.

Connotation: The impression that a word gives beyond its defined meaning. Connotations may be universally understood or may be significant only to a certain group.

Convention: Any widely accepted literary device, style, or form.

D

Denotation: The definition of a word, apart from the impressions or feelings it creates (connotations) in the reader.

Denouement: A French word meaning "the unknotting." In literary criticism, it denotes the resolution of conflict in fiction or drama. The *denouement* follows the climax and provides an outcome to the primary plot situation as well as an explanation of secondary plot complications. The *denouement* often involves a character's recognition of his or her state of mind or moral condition.

Description: Descriptive writing is intended to allow a reader to picture the scene or setting in which the action of a story takes place. The form this description takes often evokes an intended emotional response—a dark, spooky graveyard will evoke fear, and a peaceful, sunny meadow will evoke calmness.

Dialogue: In its widest sense, dialogue is simply conversation between people in a literary work; in its most restricted sense, it refers specifically to the speech of characters in a drama. As a specific literary genre, a "dialogue" is a composition in which characters debate an issue or idea.

Diction: The selection and arrangement of words in a literary work. Either or both may vary depending on the desired effect. There are four general types of diction: "formal," used in scholarly or lofty writing; "informal," used in relaxed but educated conversation; "colloquial," used in everyday speech; and "slang," containing newly coined words and other terms not accepted in formal usage.

Didactic: A term used to describe works of literature that aim to teach some moral, religious, political, or practical lesson. Although didactic elements are often found in artistically pleasing works, the term "didactic" usually refers to literature in which the message is more important than the form. The term may also be used to criticize a work that the critic finds "overly didactic," that is, heavy-handed in its delivery of a lesson.

Doppelganger: A literary technique by which a character is duplicated (usually in the form of an alter ego, though sometimes as a ghostly counterpart) or divided into two distinct, usually opposite personalities. The use of this character device is widespread in nineteenth- and twentieth-century literature, and indicates a growing awareness among authors that the "self" is really a composite of many "selves."

Double Entendre: A corruption of a French phrase meaning "double meaning." The term is used to indicate a word or phrase that is deliberately ambiguous, especially when one of the meanings is risqué or improper.

Dramatic Irony: Occurs when the audience of a play or the reader of a work of literature knows something that a character in the work itself does not know. The irony is in the contrast between the intended meaning of the statements or actions of a character and the additional information understood by the audience.

Dystopia: An imaginary place in a work of fiction where the characters lead dehumanized, fearful lives.

E

Edwardian: Describes cultural conventions identified with the period of the reign of Edward VII of England (1901-1910). Writers of the Edwardian Age typically displayed a strong reaction against the propriety and conservatism of the Victorian Age. Their work often exhibits distrust of authority in religion, politics, and art and expresses strong doubts about the soundness of conventional values.

Empathy: A sense of shared experience, including emotional and physical feelings, with someone or something other than oneself. Empathy is often used to describe the response of a reader to a literary character.

Enlightenment, The: An eighteenth-century philosophical movement. It began in France but had a wide impact throughout Europe and America. Thinkers of the Enlightenment valued reason and believed that both the individual and society could achieve a state of perfection. Corresponding to this essentially humanist vision was a resistance to religious authority.

Epigram: A saying that makes the speaker's point quickly and concisely. Often used to preface a novel.

Epilogue: A concluding statement or section of a literary work. In dramas, particularly those of the seventeenth and eighteenth centuries, the epilogue is a closing speech, often in verse, delivered by an actor at the end of a play and spoken directly to the audience.

Epiphany: A sudden revelation of truth inspired by a seemingly trivial incident.

Episode: An incident that forms part of a story and is significantly related to it. Episodes may be either self-contained narratives or events that depend on a larger context for their sense and importance.

Epistolary Novel: A novel in the form of letters. The form was particularly popular in the eighteenth century.

Epithet: A word or phrase, often disparaging or abusive, that expresses a character trait of someone or something.

Existentialism: A predominantly twentieth-century philosophy concerned with the nature and perception of human existence. There are two major strains of existentialist thought: atheistic and Christian. Followers of atheistic existentialism believe that the individual is alone in a godless universe and that the basic human condition is one of suffering and loneliness. Nevertheless, because there are no fixed values, individuals can create their own characters— indeed, they can shape themselves—through the exercise of free will. The atheistic strain culminates in and is popularly associated with the works of Jean-Paul Sartre. The Christian existentialists, on the other hand, believe that only in God may people find freedom from life's anguish. The two strains hold certain beliefs in common: that existence cannot be fully understood or described through empirical effort; that anguish is a universal element of life; that individuals must bear responsibility for their actions; and that there is no common standard of behavior or perception for religious and ethical matters.

Expatriates: See *Expatriatism*

Expatriatism: The practice of leaving one's country to live for an extended period in another country.

Exposition: Writing intended to explain the nature of an idea, thing, or theme. Expository writing is often combined with description, narration, or argument. In dramatic writing, the exposition is the introductory material which presents the characters, setting, and tone of the play.

Expressionism: An indistinct literary term, originally used to describe an early twentieth-century school of German painting. The term applies to almost any mode of unconventional, highly subjective writing that distorts reality in some way.

F

Fable: A prose or verse narrative intended to convey a moral. Animals or inanimate objects with human characteristics often serve as characters in fables.

Falling Action: See *Denouement*

Fantasy: A literary form related to mythology and folklore. Fantasy literature is typically set in non-existent realms and features supernatural beings.

Farce: A type of comedy characterized by broad humor, outlandish incidents, and often vulgar subject matter.

Femme fatale: A French phrase with the literal translation "fatal woman." A *femme fatale* is a sensuous, alluring woman who often leads men into danger or trouble.

Fiction: Any story that is the product of imagination rather than a documentation of fact. characters and events in such narratives may be based in real life but their ultimate form and configuration is a creation of the author.

Figurative Language: A technique in writing in which the author temporarily interrupts the order, construction, or meaning of the writing for a particular effect. This interruption takes the form of one or more figures of speech such as hyperbole, irony, or simile. Figurative language is the opposite of literal language, in which every word is truthful, accurate, and free of exaggeration or embellishment.

Figures of Speech: Writing that differs from customary conventions for construction, meaning, order, or significance for the purpose of a special meaning or effect. There are two major types of figures of speech: rhetorical figures, which do not make changes in the meaning of the words, and tropes, which do.

Fin de siecle: A French term meaning "end of the century." The term is used to denote the last decade of the nineteenth century, a transition period when writers and other artists abandoned old conventions and looked for new techniques and objectives.

First Person: See *Point of View*

Flashback: A device used in literature to present action that occurred before the beginning of the story. Flashbacks are often introduced as the dreams or recollections of one or more characters.

Foil: A character in a work of literature whose physical or psychological qualities contrast strongly with, and therefore highlight, the corresponding qualities of another character.

Folklore: Traditions and myths preserved in a culture or group of people. Typically, these are passed on by word of mouth in various forms—such as legends, songs, and proverbs—or preserved in customs and ceremonies. This term was first used by W. J. Thoms in 1846.

Folktale: A story originating in oral tradition. Folktales fall into a variety of categories, including legends, ghost stories, fairy tales, fables, and anecdotes based on historical figures and events.

Foreshadowing: A device used in literature to create expectation or to set up an explanation of later developments.

Form: The pattern or construction of a work which identifies its genre and distinguishes it from other genres.

G

Genre: A category of literary work. In critical theory, genre may refer to both the content of a given work—tragedy, comedy, pastoral—and to its form, such as poetry, novel, or drama.

Gilded Age: A period in American history during the 1870s characterized by political corruption and materialism. A number of important novels of social and political criticism were written during this time.

Gothicism: In literary criticism, works characterized by a taste for the medieval or morbidly attractive. A gothic novel prominently features elements of horror, the supernatural, gloom, and violence: clanking chains, terror, charnel houses, ghosts, medieval castles, and mysteriously slamming doors. The term "gothic novel" is also applied to novels that lack elements of the traditional Gothic setting but that create a similar atmosphere of terror or dread.

Grotesque: In literary criticism, the subject matter of a work or a style of expression characterized by exaggeration, deformity, freakishness, and disorder. The grotesque often includes an element of comic absurdity.

H

Harlem Renaissance: The Harlem Renaissance of the 1920s is generally considered the first significant movement of black writers and artists in the United States. During this period, new and established black writers published more fiction and poetry than ever before, the first influential black literary journals were established, and black authors and artists received their first widespread recognition and serious critical appraisal. Among the major writers associated with this period are Claude McKay, Jean Toomer, Countee Cullen, Langston Hughes, Arna Bontemps, Nella Larsen, and Zora Neale Hurston.

Hero/Heroine: The principal sympathetic character (male or female) in a literary work. Heroes and heroines typically exhibit admirable traits: idealism, courage, and integrity, for example.

Holocaust Literature: Literature influenced by or written about the Holocaust of World War II. Such literature includes true stories of survival in concentration camps, escape, and life after the war, as well as fictional works and poetry.

Humanism: A philosophy that places faith in the dignity of humankind and rejects the medieval perception of the individual as a weak, fallen creature. "Humanists" typically believe in the perfectibility of human nature and view reason and education as the means to that end.

Hyperbole: In literary criticism, deliberate exaggeration used to achieve an effect.

I

Idiom: A word construction or verbal expression closely associated with a given language.

Image: A concrete representation of an object or sensory experience. Typically, such a representation helps evoke the feelings associated with the object or experience itself. Images are either "literal" or "figurative." Literal images are especially concrete and involve little or no extension of the obvious meaning of the words used to express them. Figurative images do not follow the literal meaning of the words exactly. Images in literature are usually visual, but the term "image" can also refer to the representation of any sensory experience.

Imagery: The array of images in a literary work. Also, figurative language.

In medias res: A Latin term meaning "in the middle of things." It refers to the technique of beginning a story at its midpoint and then using various flashback devices to reveal previous action.

Interior Monologue: A narrative technique in which characters' thoughts are revealed in a way that appears to be uncontrolled by the author. The interior monologue typically aims to reveal the inner self of a character. It portrays emotional experiences as they occur at both a conscious and unconscious level. images are often used to represent sensations or emotions.

Irony: In literary criticism, the effect of language in which the intended meaning is the opposite of what is stated.

J

Jargon: Language that is used or understood only by a select group of people. Jargon may refer to terminology used in a certain profession, such as computer jargon, or it may refer to any nonsensical language that is not understood by most people.

L

Leitmotiv: See *Motif*

Literal Language: An author uses literal language when he or she writes without exaggerating or embellishing the subject matter and without any tools of figurative language.

Lost Generation: A term first used by Gertrude Stein to describe the post-World War I generation of American writers: men and women haunted by a sense of betrayal and emptiness brought about by the destructiveness of the war.

M

Mannerism: Exaggerated, artificial adherence to a literary manner or style. Also, a popular style of the visual arts of late sixteenth-century Europe that was marked by elongation of the human form and by intentional spatial distortion. Literary works that are self-consciously high-toned and artistic are often said to be "mannered."

Metaphor: A figure of speech that expresses an idea through the image of another object. Metaphors suggest the essence of the first object by identifying it with certain qualities of the second object.

Modernism: Modern literary practices. Also, the principles of a literary school that lasted from roughly the beginning of the twentieth century until the end of World War II. Modernism is defined by its rejection of the literary conventions of the nineteenth century and by its opposition to conventional morality, taste, traditions, and economic values.

Mood: The prevailing emotions of a work or of the author in his or her creation of the work. The mood of a work is not always what might be expected based on its subject matter.

Motif: A theme, character type, image, metaphor, or other verbal element that recurs throughout a single work of literature or occurs in a number of different works over a period of time.

Myth: An anonymous tale emerging from the traditional beliefs of a culture or social unit. Myths use supernatural explanations for natural phenomena. They may also explain cosmic issues like creation and death. Collections of myths, known as mythologies, are common to all cultures and nations, but the best-known myths belong to the Norse, Roman, and Greek mythologies.

N

Narration: The telling of a series of events, real or invented. A narration may be either a simple narrative, in which the events are recounted chronologically, or a narrative with a plot, in which the account is given in a style reflecting the author's artistic concept of the story. Narration is sometimes used as a synonym for "storyline."

Narrative: A verse or prose accounting of an event or sequence of events, real or invented. The term is also used as an adjective in the sense "method of narration." For example, in literary criticism, the expression "narrative technique" usually refers to the way the author structures and presents his or her story.

Narrator: The teller of a story. The narrator may be the author or a character in the story through whom the author speaks.

Naturalism: A literary movement of the late nineteenth and early twentieth centuries. The movement's major theorist, French novelist Emile Zola, envisioned a type of fiction that would examine human life with the objectivity of scientific inquiry. The Naturalists typically viewed human beings as either the products of "biological determinism," ruled by hereditary instincts and engaged in an endless struggle for survival, or as the products of "socioeconomic determinism," ruled by social and economic forces beyond their control. In their works, the Naturalists generally ignored the highest levels of society and focused on degradation: poverty, alcoholism, prostitution, insanity, and disease.

Noble Savage: The idea that primitive man is noble and good but becomes evil and corrupted as he becomes civilized. The concept of the noble savage originated in the Renaissance period but is more closely identified with such later writers as Jean-Jacques Rousseau and Aphra Behn.

Novel: A long fictional narrative written in prose, which developed from the novella and other early forms of narrative. A novel is usually organized under a plot or theme with a focus on character development and action.

Novel of Ideas: A novel in which the examination of intellectual issues and concepts takes precedence over characterization or a traditional storyline.

Novel of Manners: A novel that examines the customs and mores of a cultural group.

Novella: An Italian term meaning "story." This term has been especially used to describe fourteenth-century Italian tales, but it also refers to modern short novels.

O

Objective Correlative: An outward set of objects, a situation, or a chain of events corresponding to an inward experience and evoking this experience in the reader. The term frequently appears in modern criticism in discussions of authors' intended effects on the emotional responses of readers.

Objectivity: A quality in writing characterized by the absence of the author's opinion or feeling about the subject matter. Objectivity is an important factor in criticism.

Oedipus Complex: A son's amorous obsession with his mother. The phrase is derived from the story of the ancient Theban hero Oedipus, who unknowingly killed his father and married his mother.

Omniscience: See *Point of View*

Onomatopoeia: The use of words whose sounds express or suggest their meaning. In its simplest sense, onomatopoeia may be represented by words that mimic the sounds they denote such as "hiss" or "meow." At a more subtle level, the pattern and rhythm of sounds and rhymes of a line or poem may be onomatopoeic.

Oxymoron: A phrase combining two contradictory terms. Oxymorons may be intentional or unintentional.

P

Parable: A story intended to teach a moral lesson or answer an ethical question.

Paradox: A statement that appears illogical or contradictory at first, but may actually point to an underlying truth.

Parallelism: A method of comparison of two ideas in which each is developed in the same grammatical structure.

Parody: In literary criticism, this term refers to an imitation of a serious literary work or the signature style of a particular author in a ridiculous manner. A typical parody adopts the style of the original and applies it to an inappropriate subject for humorous effect. Parody is a form of satire and could be considered the literary equivalent of a caricature or cartoon.

Pastoral: A term derived from the Latin word "pastor," meaning shepherd. A pastoral is a literary composition on a rural theme. The conventions of the pastoral were originated by the third-century Greek poet Theocritus, who wrote about the experiences, love affairs, and pastimes of Sicilian shepherds. In a pastoral, characters and language of a courtly nature are often placed in a simple setting. The term pastoral is also used to classify dramas, elegies, and lyrics that exhibit the use of country settings and shepherd characters.

Pen Name: See *Pseudonym*

Persona: A Latin term meaning "mask." *Personae* are the characters in a fictional work of literature. The *persona* generally functions as a mask through which the author tells a story in a voice other than his or her own. A *persona* is usually either a character in a story who acts as a narrator or an "implied author," a voice created by the author to act as the narrator for himself or herself.

Personification: A figure of speech that gives human qualities to abstract ideas, animals, and inanimate objects.

Picaresque Novel: Episodic fiction depicting the adventures of a roguish central character ("pic-aro" is Spanish for "rogue"). The picaresque hero is commonly a low-born but clever individual who wanders into and out of various affairs of love, danger, and farcical intrigue. These involvements may take place at all social levels and typically present a humorous and wide-ranging satire of a given society.

Plagiarism: Claiming another person's written material as one's own. Plagiarism can take the form of direct, word-for-word copying or the theft of the substance or idea of the work.

Plot: In literary criticism, this term refers to the pattern of events in a narrative or drama. In its simplest sense, the plot guides the author in composing the work and helps the reader follow the work. Typically, plots exhibit causality and unity and have a beginning, a middle, and an end. Sometimes, however, a plot may consist of a series of disconnected events, in which case it is known as an "episodic plot."

Poetic Justice: An outcome in a literary work, not necessarily a poem, in which the good are rewarded and the evil are punished, especially in ways that particularly fit their virtues or crimes.

Poetic License: Distortions of fact and literary convention made by a writer—not always a poet—for the sake of the effect gained. Poetic license is closely related to the concept of "artistic freedom."

Poetics: This term has two closely related meanings. It denotes (1) an aesthetic theory in literary criticism about the essence of poetry or (2) rules prescribing the proper methods, content, style, or diction of poetry. The term poetics may also refer to theories about literature in general, not just poetry.

Point of View: The narrative perspective from which a literary work is presented to the reader. There are four traditional points of view. The "third person omniscient" gives the reader a "godlike" perspective, unrestricted by time or place, from which to see actions and look into the minds of characters. This allows the author to comment openly on characters and events in the work. The "third person" point of view presents the events of the story from outside of any single character's perception, much like the omniscient point of view, but the reader must understand the action as it takes place and without any special insight into characters' minds or motivations. The "first person" or "personal" point of view relates events as they are perceived by a single character. The main character "tells" the story and may offer opinions about the action and characters which differ from those of the author. Much less common than omniscient, third person, and first person is the "second person" point of view, wherein the author tells the story as if it is happening to the reader.

Polemic: A work in which the author takes a stand on a controversial subject, such as abortion or religion. Such works are often extremely argumentative or provocative.

Pornography: Writing intended to provoke feelings of lust in the reader. Such works are often condemned by critics and teachers, but those which can be shown to have literary value are viewed less harshly.

Post-Aesthetic Movement: An artistic response made by African Americans to the black aesthetic movement of the 1960s and early '70s. Writers since that time have adopted a somewhat different tone in their work, with less emphasis placed on the disparity between black and white in the United States. In the words of post-aesthetic authors such as Toni Morrison, John Edgar Wideman, and Kristin Hunter, African Americans are portrayed as looking inward for answers to their own questions, rather than always looking to the outside world.

Postmodernism: Writing from the 1960s forward characterized by experimentation and continuing to apply some of the fundamentals of modernism, which included existentialism and alienation. Postmodernists have gone a step further in the rejection of tradition begun with the modernists by also rejecting traditional forms, preferring the anti-novel over the novel and the anti-hero over the hero.

Primitivism: The belief that primitive peoples were nobler and less flawed than civilized peoples because they had not been subjected to the tainting influence of society.

Prologue: An introductory section of a literary work. It often contains information establishing the situation of the characters or presents information about the setting, time period, or action. In drama, the prologue is spoken by a chorus or by one of the principal characters.

Prose: A literary medium that attempts to mirror the language of everyday speech. It is distinguished from poetry by its use of unmetered, unrhymed language consisting of logically related sentences. Prose is usually grouped into paragraphs that form a cohesive whole such as an essay or a novel.

Prosopopoeia: See *Personification*

Protagonist: The central character of a story who serves as a focus for its themes and incidents and as the principal rationale for its development. The protagonist is sometimes referred to in discussions of modern literature as the hero or anti-hero.

Protest Fiction: Protest fiction has as its primary purpose the protesting of some social injustice, such as racism or discrimination.

Proverb: A brief, sage saying that expresses a truth about life in a striking manner.

Pseudonym: A name assumed by a writer, most often intended to prevent his or her identification as the author of a work. Two or more authors may work together under one pseudonym, or an author may use a different name for each genre he or she publishes in. Some publishing companies maintain "house pseudonyms," under which any number of authors may write installations in a series. Some authors also choose a pseudonym over their real names the way an actor may use a stage name.

Pun: A play on words that have similar sounds but different meanings.

R

Realism: A nineteenth-century European literary movement that sought to portray familiar characters, situations, and settings in a realistic manner. This was done primarily by using an objective narrative point of view and through the buildup of accurate detail. The standard for success of any realistic work depends on how faithfully it transfers common experience into fictional forms. The realistic method may be altered or extended, as in stream of consciousness writing, to record highly subjective experience.

Repartee: Conversation featuring snappy retorts and witticisms.

Resolution: The portion of a story following the climax, in which the conflict is resolved.

Rhetoric: In literary criticism, this term denotes the art of ethical persuasion. In its strictest sense, rhetoric adheres to various principles developed since classical times for arranging facts and ideas in a clear, persuasive, appealing manner. The term is also used to refer to effective prose in general and theories of or methods for composing effective prose.

Rhetorical Question: A question intended to provoke thought, but not an expressed answer, in the reader. It is most commonly used in oratory and other persuasive genres.

Rising Action: The part of a drama where the plot becomes increasingly complicated. Rising action leads up to the climax, or turning point, of a drama.

Roman à clef: A French phrase meaning "novel with a key." It refers to a narrative in which real persons are portrayed under fictitious names.

Romance: A broad term, usually denoting a narrative with exotic, exaggerated, often idealized characters, scenes, and themes.

Romanticism: This term has two widely accepted meanings. In historical criticism, it refers to a European intellectual and artistic movement of the late eighteenth and early nineteenth centuries that sought greater freedom of personal expression than that allowed by the strict rules of literary form and logic of the eighteenth-century neoclassicists. The Romantics preferred emotional and imaginative expression to rational analysis. They considered the individual to be at the center of all experience and so placed him or her at the center of their art. The Romantics believed that the creative imagination reveals nobler truths—unique feelings and attitudes—than those that could be discovered by logic or by scientific examination. Both the natural world and the state of childhood were important sources for revelations of "eternal truths." "Romanticism" is also used as a general term to refer to a type of sensibility found in all periods of literary history and usually considered to be in opposition to the principles of classicism. In this sense, Romanticism signifies any work or philosophy in which the exotic or dreamlike figure strongly, or that is devoted to individualistic expression, self-analysis, or a pursuit of a higher realm of knowledge than can be discovered by human reason.

Romantics: See *Romanticism*

S

Satire: A work that uses ridicule, humor, and wit to criticize and provoke change in human nature and institutions. There are two major types of satire: "formal" or "direct" satire speaks directly to the reader or to a character in the work; "indirect" satire relies upon the ridiculous behavior of its characters to make its point. Formal satire is further divided into two manners: the "Horatian," which ridicules gently, and the "Juvenalian," which derides its subjects harshly and bitterly.

Science Fiction: A type of narrative about or based upon real or imagined scientific theories and technology. Science fiction is often peopled with alien creatures and set on other planets or in different dimensions.

Second Person: See *Point of View*

Setting: The time, place, and culture in which the action of a narrative takes place. The elements of setting may include geographic location, characters' physical and mental environments, prevailing cultural attitudes, or the historical time in which the action takes place.

Simile: A comparison, usually using "like" or "as," of two essentially dissimilar things, as in "coffee as cold as ice" or "He sounded like a broken record."

Slang: A type of informal verbal communication that is generally unacceptable for formal writing. Slang words and phrases are often colorful exaggerations used to emphasize the speaker's point; they may also be shortened versions of an often-used word or phrase.

Slave Narrative: Autobiographical accounts of American slave life as told by escaped slaves. These works first appeared during the abolition movement of the 1830s through the 1850s.

Socialist Realism: The Socialist Realism school of literary theory was proposed by Maxim Gorky and established as a dogma by the first Soviet Congress of Writers. It demanded

adherence to a communist worldview in works of literature. Its doctrines required an objective viewpoint comprehensible to the working classes and themes of social struggle featuring strong proletarian heroes.

Stereotype: A stereotype was originally the name for a duplication made during the printing process; this led to its modern definition as a person or thing that is (or is assumed to be) the same as all others of its type.

Stream of Consciousness: A narrative technique for rendering the inward experience of a character. This technique is designed to give the impression of an ever-changing series of thoughts, emotions, images, and memories in the spontaneous and seemingly illogical order that they occur in life.

Structure: The form taken by a piece of literature. The structure may be made obvious for ease of understanding, as in nonfiction works, or may obscured for artistic purposes, as in some poetry or seemingly "unstructured" prose.

Sturm und Drang: A German term meaning "storm and stress." It refers to a German literary movement of the 1770s and 1780s that reacted against the order and rationalism of the enlightenment, focusing instead on the intense experience of extraordinary individuals.

Style: A writer's distinctive manner of arranging words to suit his or her ideas and purpose in writing. The unique imprint of the author's personality upon his or her writing, style is the product of an author's way of arranging ideas and his or her use of diction, different sentence structures, rhythm, figures of speech, rhetorical principles, and other elements of composition.

Subjectivity: Writing that expresses the author's personal feelings about his subject, and which may or may not include factual information about the subject.

Subplot: A secondary story in a narrative. A subplot may serve as a motivating or complicating force for the main plot of the work, or it may provide emphasis for, or relief from, the main plot.

Surrealism: A term introduced to criticism by Guillaume Apollinaire and later adopted by Andre Breton. It refers to a French literary and artistic movement founded in the 1920s. The Surrealists sought to express unconscious thoughts and feelings in their works.

The best-known technique used for achieving this aim was automatic writing—transcriptions of spontaneous outpourings from the unconscious. The Surrealists proposed to unify the contrary levels of conscious and unconscious, dream and reality, objectivity and subjectivity into a new level of "super-realism."

Suspense: A literary device in which the author maintains the audience's attention through the buildup of events, the outcome of which will soon be revealed.

Symbol: Something that suggests or stands for something else without losing its original identity. In literature, symbols combine their literal meaning with the suggestion of an abstract concept. Literary symbols are of two types: those that carry complex associations of meaning no matter what their contexts, and those that derive their suggestive meaning from their functions in specific literary works.

Symbolism: This term has two widely accepted meanings. In historical criticism, it denotes an early modernist literary movement initiated in France during the nineteenth century that reacted against the prevailing standards of realism. Writers in this movement aimed to evoke, indirectly and symbolically, an order of being beyond the material world of the five senses. Poetic expression of personal emotion figured strongly in the movement, typically by means of a private set of symbols uniquely identifiable with the individual poet. The principal aim of the Symbolists was to express in words the highly complex feelings that grew out of everyday contact with the world. In a broader sense, the term "symbolism" refers to the use of one object to represent another.

T

Tall Tale: A humorous tale told in a straightforward, credible tone but relating absolutely impossible events or feats of the characters. Such tales were commonly told of frontier adventures during the settlement of the west in the United States.

Theme: The main point of a work of literature. The term is used interchangeably with thesis.

Thesis: A thesis is both an essay and the point argued in the essay. Thesis novels and thesis plays share the quality of containing a thesis which is supported through the action of the story.

Third Person: See *Point of View*

Tone: The author's attitude toward his or her audience may be deduced from the tone of the work. A formal tone may create distance or convey politeness, while an informal tone may encourage a friendly, intimate, or intrusive feeling in the reader. The author's attitude toward his or her subject matter may also be deduced from the tone of the words he or she uses in discussing it.

Transcendentalism: An American philosophical and religious movement, based in New England from around 1835 until the Civil War. Transcendentalism was a form of American romanticism that had its roots abroad in the works of Thomas Carlyle, Samuel Coleridge, and Johann Wolfgang von Goethe. The Transcendentalists stressed the importance of intuition and subjective experience in communication with God. They rejected religious dogma and texts in favor of mysticism and scientific naturalism. They pursued truths that lie beyond the "colorless" realms perceived by reason and the senses and were active social reformers in public education, women's rights, and the abolition of slavery.

U

Urban Realism: A branch of realist writing that attempts to accurately reflect the often harsh facts of modern urban existence.

Utopia: A fictional perfect place, such as "paradise" or "heaven."

V

Verisimilitude: Literally, the appearance of truth. In literary criticism, the term refers to aspects of a work of literature that seem true to the reader.

Victorian: Refers broadly to the reign of Queen Victoria of England (1837-1901) and to anything with qualities typical of that era. For example, the qualities of smug narrowmindedness, bourgeois materialism, faith in social progress, and priggish morality are often considered Victorian. This stereotype is contradicted by such dramatic intellectual developments as the theories of Charles Darwin, Karl Marx, and Sigmund Freud (which stirred strong debates in England) and the critical attitudes of serious Victorian writers like Charles Dickens and

George Eliot. In literature, the Victorian Period was the great age of the English novel, and the latter part of the era saw the rise of movements such as decadence and symbolism.

W

Weltanschauung: A German term referring to a person's worldview or philosophy.

Weltschmerz: A German term meaning "world pain." It describes a sense of anguish about the nature of existence, usually associated with a melancholy, pessimistic attitude.

Z

Zeitgeist: A German term meaning "spirit of the time." It refers to the moral and intellectual trends of a given era.

Cumulative Author/Title Index

Cumulative Nationality/Ethnicity Index

Swiss

Hesse, Hermann
  Demian: V15
  Siddhartha: V6
  Steppenwolf: V24

Turkish

Pamuk, Orhan
  My Name is Red: V27

Uruguayan

Bridal, Tessa
  The Tree of Red Stars: V17

Vietnamese

Duong Thu Huong
  Paradise of the Blind: V23

West Indian

Kincaid, Jamaica
  Annie John: V3

Zimbabwean

Dangarembga, Tsitsi
  Nervous Conditions: V28

Subject/Theme Index

Language and languages
  All the Pretty Horses: 38, 40
  The Brief Wondrous Life of
    Oscar Wao: 56–57, 61, 66–70,
    72, 73
  Herland: 126
  The Island of Dr. Moreau: 175
  Platero and I: 205
  Shane: 278–279
Latin American culture
  The Brief Wondrous Life of Oscar
    Wao: 68–69
Latin American history
  The Brief Wondrous Life of Oscar
    Wao: 58–60, 67, 68, 73
Loneliness
  The Brief Wondrous Life of Oscar
    Wao: 45, 53, 55
  Villette: 320, 333
Longing
  Villette: 310
Loss (Psychology)
  All Quiet on the Western Front: 1
  All the Pretty Horses: 28
  Extremely Loud & Incredibly
    Close: 108, 117
  Villette: 310
Love
  All the Pretty Horses: 24, 36
  The Brief Wondrous Life of Oscar
    Wao: 45, 47, 51, 52, 55–56, 67,
    69–70, 72
  Extremely Loud & Incredibly
    Close: 108
  Herland: 147, 149
  Platero and I: 200, 203, 207, 217
  Praisesong for the Widow: 234
  The Red Tent: 241, 242, 251, 259, 260
  Shane: 270–271, 273
  The Third Man: 298, 300, 302, 307
  Villette: 315, 318, 320, 328–329,
    331, 333
Loyalty
  All the Pretty Horses: 25, 26
  The Brief Wondrous Life of Oscar
    Wao: 72
  The Island of Dr. Moreau: 161, 170
  Lord of the Flies: 183
  Shane: 270, 277
  The Third Man: 291

M

Magic
  The Brief Wondrous Life of Oscar
    Wao: 57–58
Manipulation
  Villette: 312
  Villette: 315, 325–329
Marginalization
  Platero and I: 213
  The Third Man: 296–297

Marriage
  Extremely Loud & Incredibly
    Close: 107
  Herland: 129
  Praisesong for the Widow: 221,
    223
  The Red Tent: 237, 241, 242, 244,
    252
  Shane: 270, 279
  Villette: 323
Martyrdom
  Villette: 330
Masculinity
  The Brief Wondrous Life of Oscar
    Wao: 67
  Herland: 141
  Platero and I: 209
  The Red Tent: 251
  Shane: 279–281
  The Third Man: 296–300
Masochism
  Villette: 329–333
Materialism
  Praisesong for the Widow: 227,
    230
Melancholy
  The Brief Wondrous Life of Oscar
    Wao: 72
  Platero and I: 202, 209
Memory
  Extremely Loud & Incredibly
    Close: 108–109
  The Red Tent: 260
Menace. *See* Danger
Mental disorders
  The Island of Dr. Moreau: 160
  Villette: 313, 330
Metafiction
  The Crying of Lot 49: 96
Metaphors
  The Brief Wondrous Life of Oscar
    Wao: 61
  The Crying of Lot 49: 84, 92–99
  Herland: 146
  Platero and I: 197
  Villette: 333
Mexican history
  All the Pretty Horses: 29–30
Middle class
  Praisesong for the Widow: 227
Midwifery
  The Red Tent: 247
Military life
  All Quiet on the Western Front:
    5, 9
Misery
  All Quiet on the Western Front: 1
Misfortunes
  All the Pretty Horses: 27
Misogyny
  Herland: 144
  The Third Man: 297

Morality
  Herland: 149, 150
  The Third Man: 291, 297–300,
    302, 303
Mother-child relationships
  The Brief Wondrous Life of Oscar
    Wao: 45–46, 51
  Extremely Loud & Incredibly
    Close: 108
Motherhood
  Herland: 127, 128, 133, 146–151
  The Red Tent: 236, 241, 242, 244,
    247, 251
Motif
  All the Pretty Horses: 28
Motivation
  Villette: 329
Mourning. *See* Grief
Murder
  The Red Tent: 243
Music
  The Crying of Lot 49: 92–93
Mystery
  All the Pretty Horses: 39
  The Crying of Lot 49: 89–92
  The Third Man: 307
Mysticism
  All the Pretty Horses: 40
  Platero and I: 215–216
Mythology
  All the Pretty Horses: 34
  Praisesong for the Widow: 228

N

Narrators
  Villette: 321
Natural cycles
  The Red Tent: 236, 244, 261
Nature
  All the Pretty Horses: 34, 35
  Platero and I: 197, 199, 201, 203,
    204, 209, 213–215
  The Red Tent: 244
Nihilism
  The Third Man: 301, 302
Nostalgia
  Praisesong for the Widow: 234

O

Obedience
  The Island of Dr. Moreau: 159
Objectification
  Herland: 139, 141
Observation
  Villette: 331, 332
Obsession
  The Brief Wondrous Life of Oscar
    Wao: 72
Obstacles
  Shane: 273
Opposites
  Herland: 146